BATMAN

UNDER THE RED HOOD

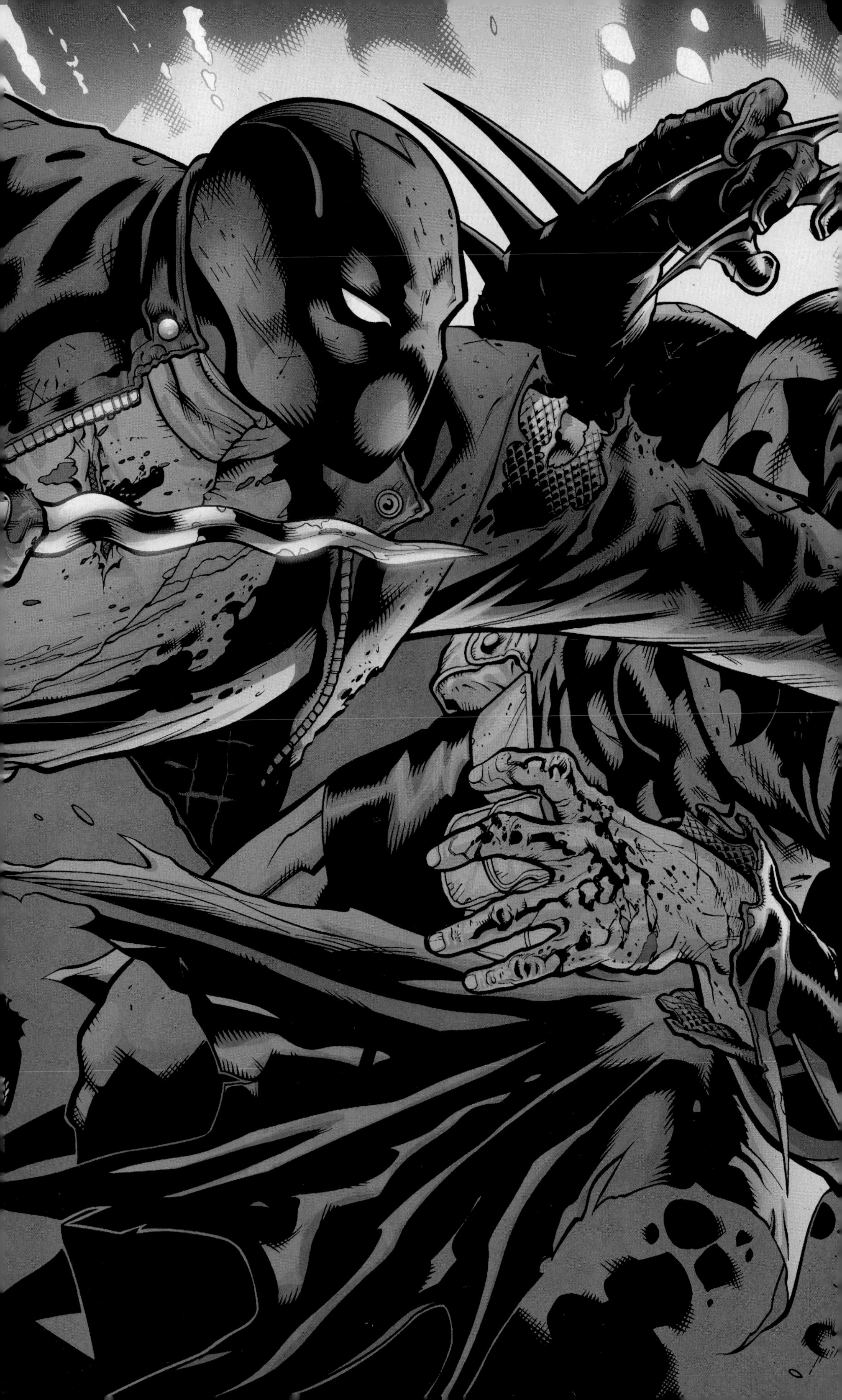

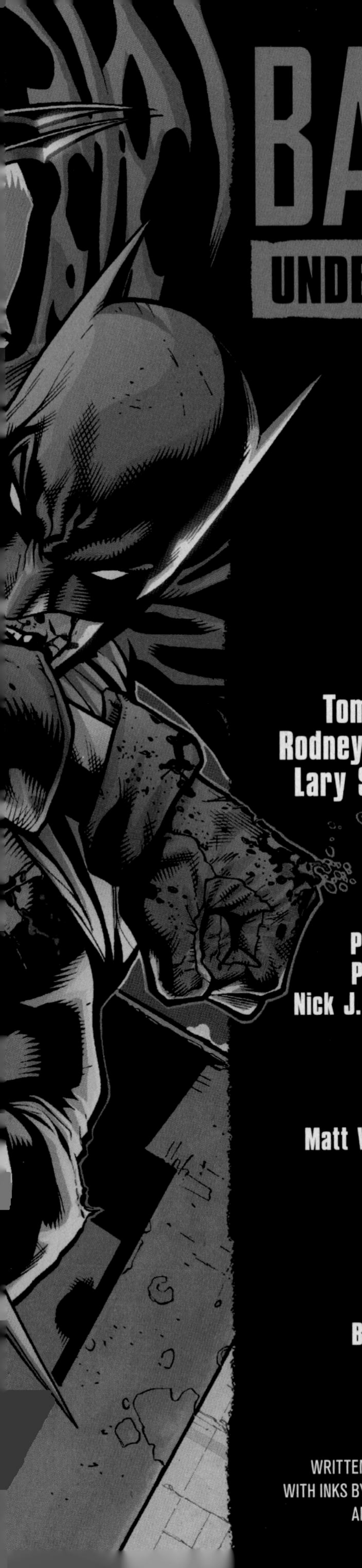

BATMAN
UNDER THE RED HOOD

Judd Winick
WRITER

Doug Mahnke
Paul Lee
Shane Davis
Eric Battle
PENCILLERS

Tom Nguyen   **Cam Smith**
Rodney Ramos   **Wayne Faucher**
Lary Stucker   **Mark Morales**
INKERS

Alex Sinclair
COLORIST

Pat Brosseau   **Rob Leigh**
Phil Balsman   **Ken Lopez**
Nick J.Napolitano   **Jared K.Fletcher**
Travis Lanham
LETTERERS

Matt Wagner   **Jock**   **Shane Davis**
ORIGINAL COVERS

PUBLICATION DESIGN BY
Curtis King Jr.

BATMAN CREATED BY
Bob Kane with Bill Finger

PAGES FROM
BATMAN: HUSH
WRITTEN BY **JEPH LOEB** AND PENCILLED BY **JIM LEE**
WITH INKS BY **SCOTT WILLIAMS**, COLORS BY **ALEX SINCLAIR**
AND LETTERS BY **RICHARD STARKINGS**

Bob Schreck Editor - Original Series
Michael Wright Associate Editor - Original Series
Brandon Montclare   Morgan Dontanville Assistant Editors - Original Series
Jeb Woodard Group Editor – Collected Editions
Steve Cook Design Director – Books

Bob Harras Senior VP – Editor-in-Chief, DC Comics

Diane Nelson President
Dan DiDio Publisher   **Jim Lee** Publisher   **Geoff Johns** President & Chief Creative Officer
Amit Desai Executive VP – Business & Marketing Strategy, Direct to Consumer & Global
Franchise Management
Sam Ades Senior VP – Direct to Consumer   **Bobbie Chase** VP – Talent Development
Mark Chiarello Senior VP – Art, Design & Collected Editions
John Cunningham Senior VP – Sales & Trade Marketing
Anne DePies Senior VP – Business Strategy, Finance & Administration
Don Falletti VP – Manufacturing Operations
Lawrence Ganem VP – Editorial Administration & Talent Relations
Alison Gill Senior VP – Manufacturing & Operations
Hank Kanalz Senior VP – Editorial Strategy & Administration
Jay Kogan VP – Legal Affairs   **Thomas Loftus** VP – Business Affairs
Jack Mahan VP – Business Affairs   **Nick J. Napolitano** VP – Manufacturing Administration
Eddie Scannell VP – Consumer Marketing
Courtney Simmons Senior VP – Publicity & Communications
Jim (Ski) Sokolowski VP – Comic Book Specialty & Trade Marketing
Nancy Spears VP – Mass, Book, Digital Sales & Trade Marketing

BATMAN: UNDER THE RED HOOD

Published by DC Comics. Cover and compilation Copyright © 2011. All Rights Reserved.
Originally published in single magazine form in BATMAN 617–618, 635–641, 645–650;
BATMAN ANNUAL 25 © 2003, 2005, 2006. All Rights Reserved. All characters, their distinctive
likenesses and related elements are trademarks of DC Comics. The stories, characters and
incidents featured in this publication are entirely fictional. DC Comics does not read
or accept unsolicited submissions of ideas, stories or artwork.

DC Comics, 2900 W. Alameda Ave., Burbank, CA 91505.
Printed by Transcontinental Interglobe, Beauceville, QC, Canada. 12/2/16. Seventh Printing.
ISBN: 978-1-4012-3145-3

Library of Congress Cataloging-in-Publication Data

Winick, Judd, author.
Batman : Under the Red Hood / Judd Winick, Doug Mahnke, Shane Davis,
Eric Battle, Paul Lee.
pages cm
"Originally published in single magazine form as Batman 617-18, 635-
641, 645-650; Batman Annual 25."
ISBN 978-1-4012-3145-3
1. Graphic novels. I. Mahnke, Doug, illustrator. II. Davis, Shane, illustrator. III. Battle, Eric, illustrator. IV. Lee, Paul, illustrator. V. Title.
PN6728.B36W584 2013
741.5'973–dc23
2012046010

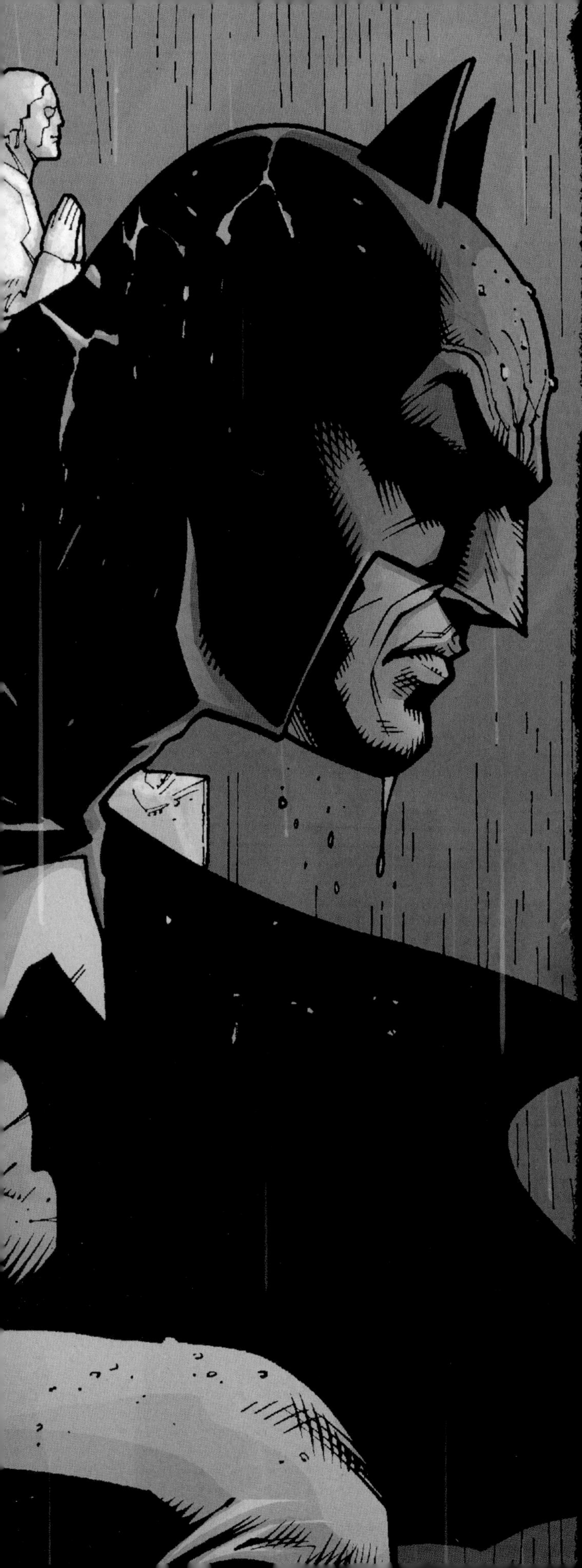

CAST OF CHARACTERS

BATMAN

Dedicated to ridding the world of crime since the callous murder of his parents, billionaire Bruce Wayne dons the cape and cowl of the Dark Knight to battle evil from the shadows of Gotham City. Over the years, Batman has suffered the loss of two crime-fighting partners: Jason Todd, the second person to take up the mantle of Robin; and Stephanie Brown, formerly the Spoiler and for a brief period of time the fourth Robin, who died from injuries inflicted by the Black Mask.

NIGHTWING

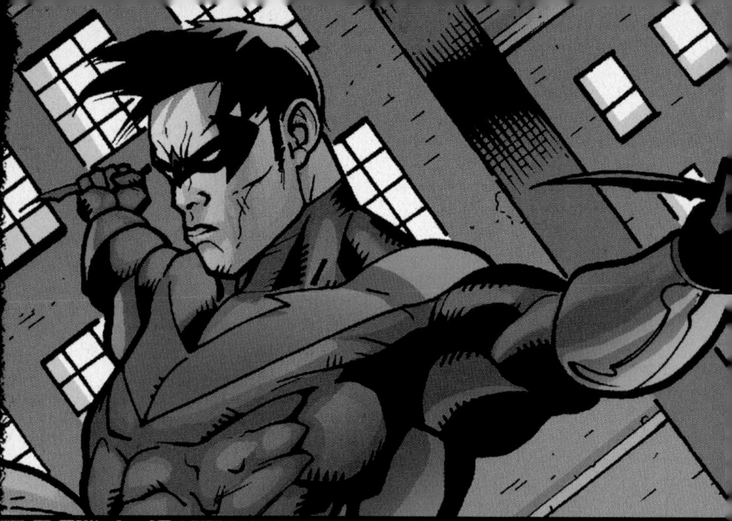

Dick Grayson's life changed forever when he witnessed his aerialist parents fall to their deaths, the victims of an extortion scheme. Knowing the pain of such a loss, the wealthy Bruce Wayne took in the youth, and in a short time Dick was being trained to work alongside Gotham City's famed crimefighter, Batman. Befitting his circus heritage, Dick chose a more colorful outfit than that of his new partner, and became Robin, the Boy Wonder. Batman and Robin proved to be a perfect crime-fighting team, but, as he grew to manhood, Dick began to separate himself from his mentor, unwilling to become a doppelganger of the obsessed Bruce Wayne. Asserting his independence, he changed his persona from Robin to Nightwing.

ONYX

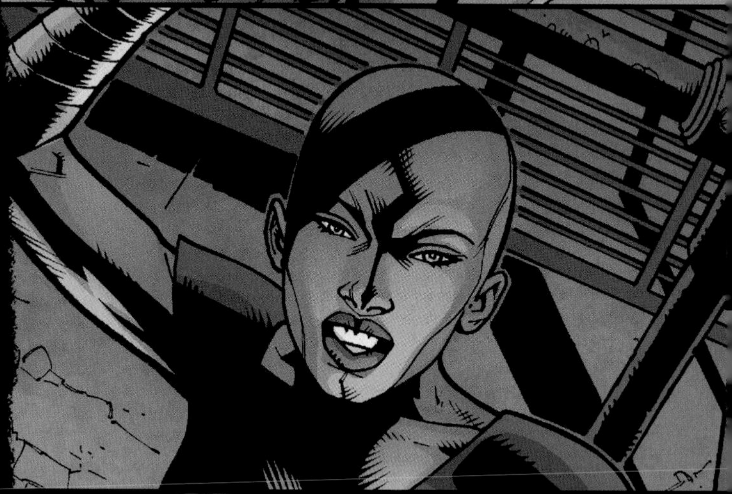

Onyx was schooled in the Sanctuary, a monastery outside Star City. Pursued by an unknown agent who wanted to kill her, Onyx was admitted to the all-male Sanctuary by the Master, who trained her in martial arts and gave her a new identity. Upon the Master's death, Onyx sought out Green Arrow, another student of the Sanctuary, to protect the monastery from a takeover by one of the Master's more ambitious protégés, a man named Lars. Onyx stayed at the Sanctuary, guarding the key to the Master's mysterious Book of Ages. She has yet to discover the identity of the man, or woman, who pursued her to the doors of the Sanctuary.

BLACK MASK

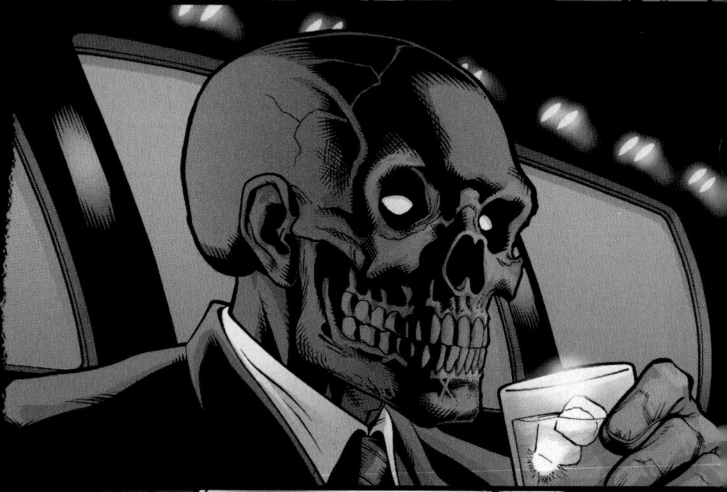

Roman Sionis's face was horribly burned in a fire during a fight with the Batman. As the Black Mask, Roman has become one of the most feared and psychotic crime bosses in Gotham's underworld. His preferred form of execution is slow, methodical torture, usually focusing on the face. During Gotham's recent Gang War, Black Mask has managed to take control over all crime in the city. All criminals must pledge their allegiance to him, or die.

MR. FREEZE

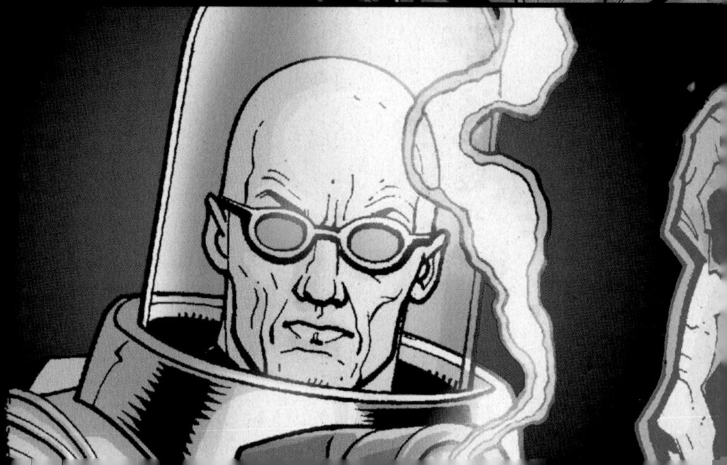

In an effort to make himself a more formidable criminal in Gotham City, the man who would become Mr. Freeze experimented with a cold-generating gun that would help him with his crimes. But his lab work resulted in a dangerous accident that bathed his body in a super-coolant solution. As a result, he must now wear a refrigerated containment suit at all times in order to continue living. His fractured psyche has made him one of Batman's most ruthless foes.

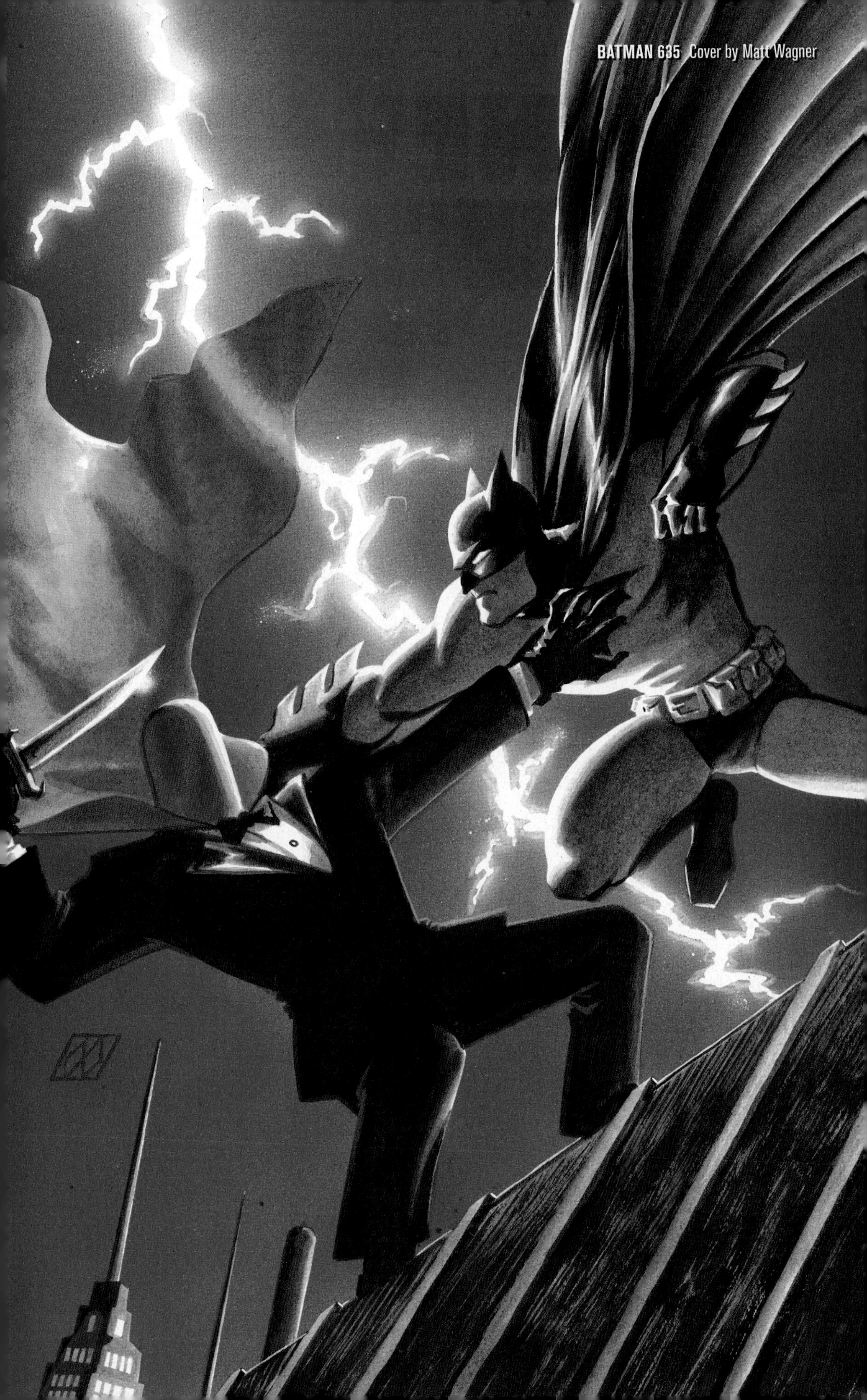

BATMAN 635 Cover by Matt Wagner

CHAPTER 1

NEW BUSINESS

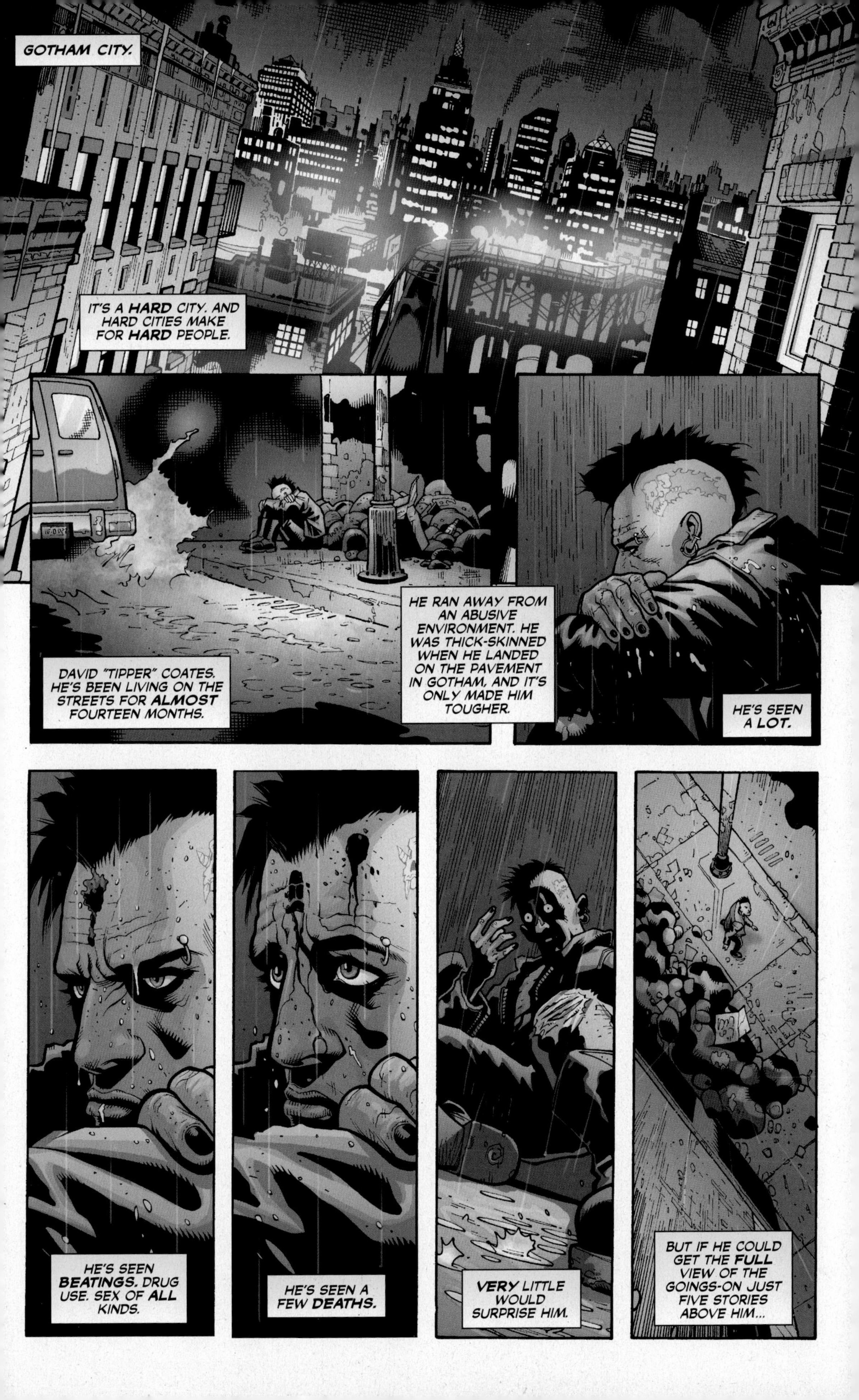
GOTHAM CITY.
IT'S A HARD CITY. AND HARD CITIES MAKE FOR HARD PEOPLE.
DAVID "TIPPER" COATES. HE'S BEEN LIVING ON THE STREETS FOR ALMOST FOURTEEN MONTHS.
HE RAN AWAY FROM AN ABUSIVE ENVIRONMENT. HE WAS THICK-SKINNED WHEN HE LANDED ON THE PAVEMENT IN GOTHAM, AND IT'S ONLY MADE HIM TOUGHER.
HE'S SEEN A LOT.
HE'S SEEN BEATINGS. DRUG USE. SEX OF ALL KINDS.
HE'S SEEN A FEW DEATHS.
VERY LITTLE WOULD SURPRISE HIM.
BUT IF HE COULD GET THE FULL VIEW OF THE GOINGS-ON JUST FIVE STORIES ABOVE HIM...

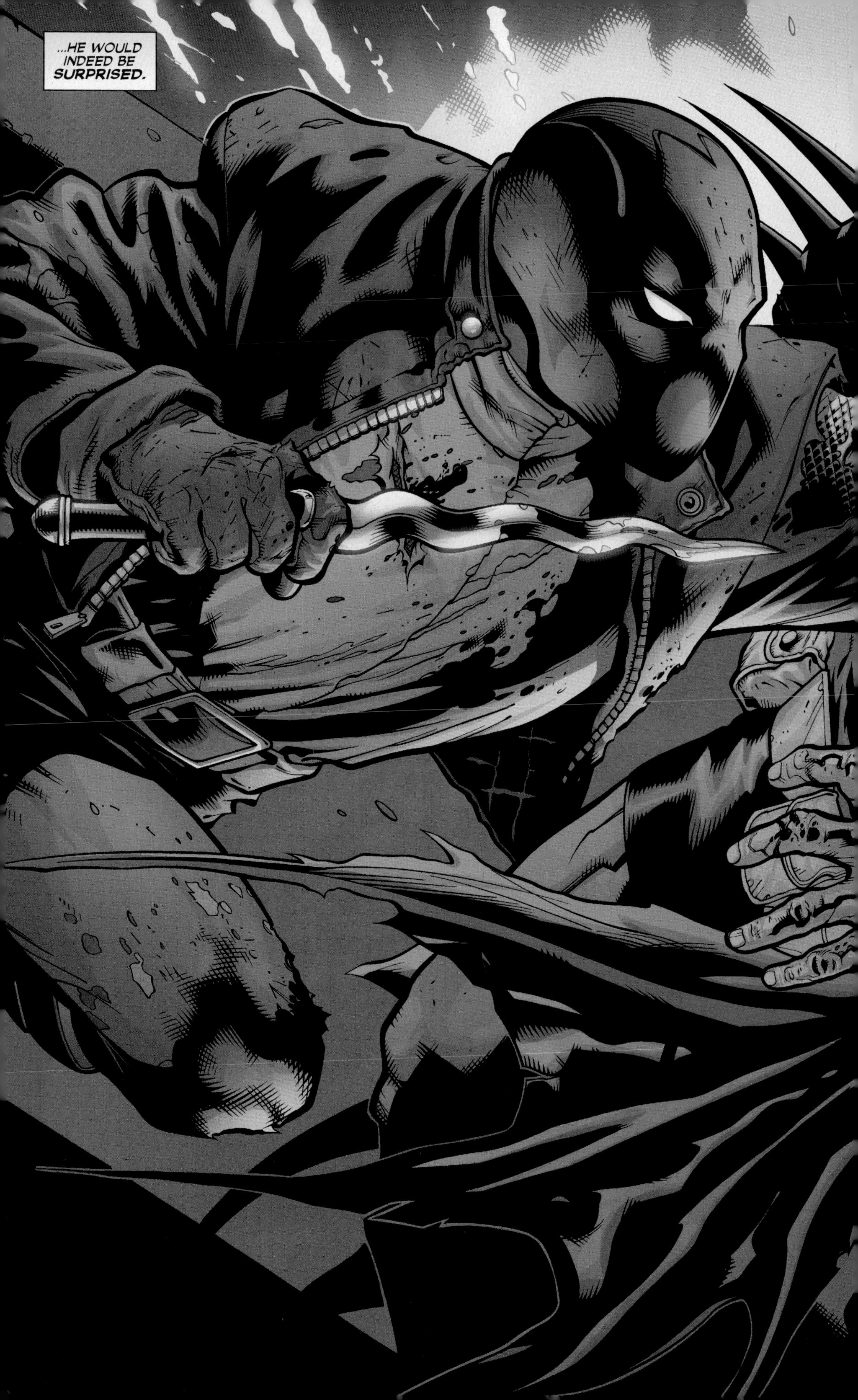
...HE WOULD INDEED BE SURPRISED.

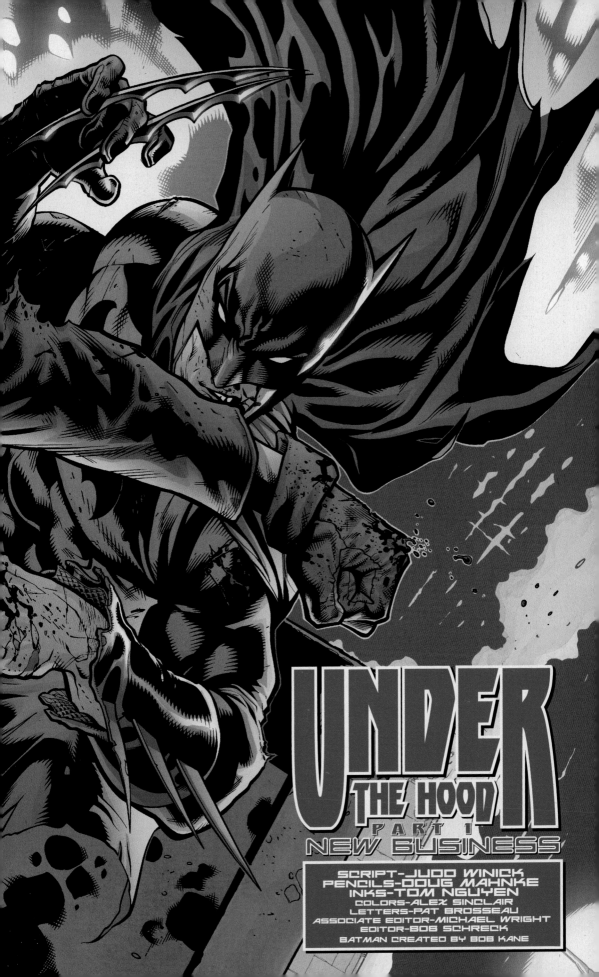

UNDER THE HOOD

PART 1
NEW BUSINESS

SCRIPT–JUDD WINICK
PENCILS–DOUG MAHNKE
INKS–TOM NGUYEN
COLORS–ALEX SINCLAIR
LETTERS–PAT BROSSEAU
ASSOCIATE EDITOR–MICHAEL WRIGHT
EDITOR–BOB SCHRECK
BATMAN CREATED BY BOB KANE

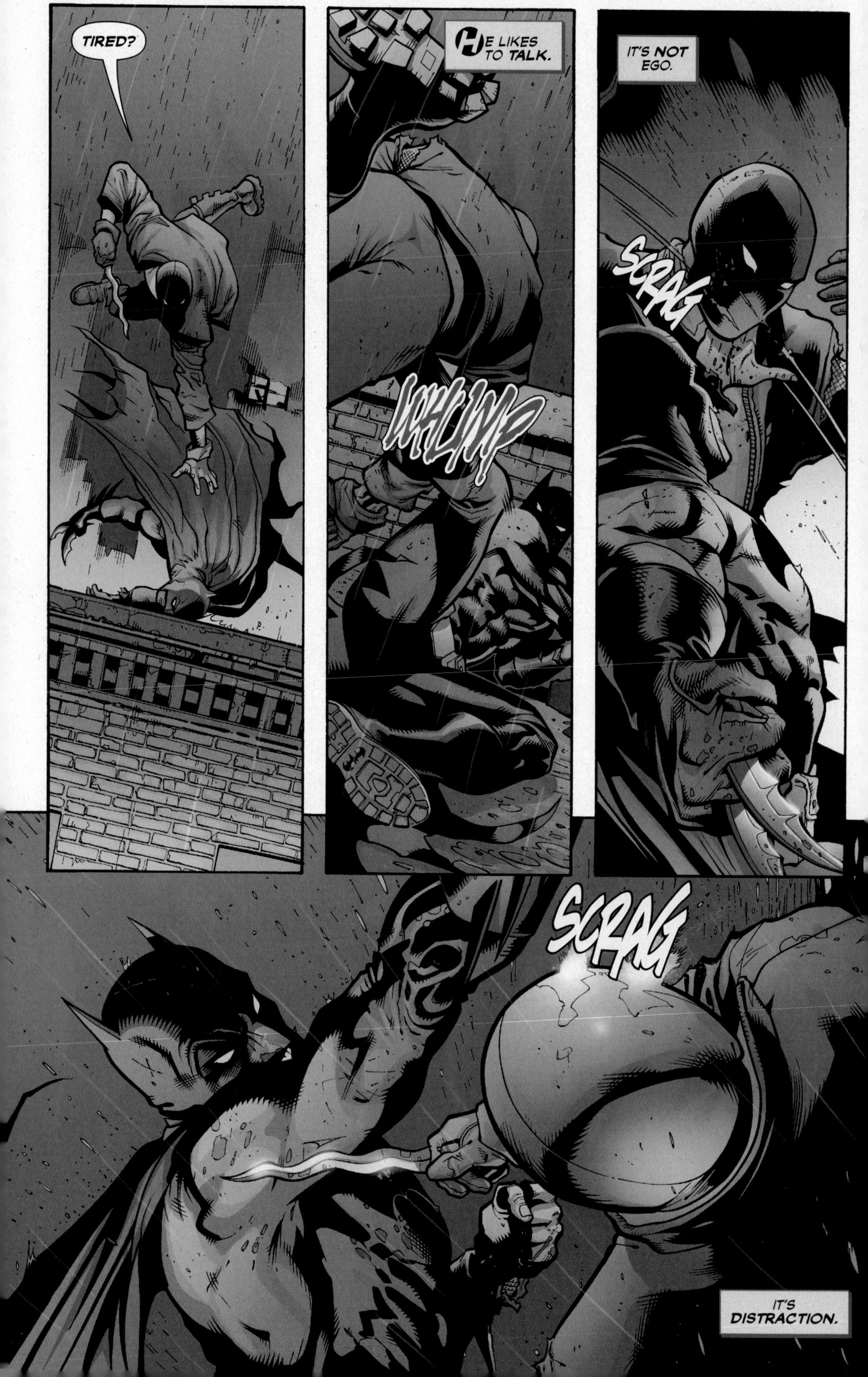
TIRED?
HE LIKES TO TALK.
WHUMP
IT'S NOT EGO.
SCRAG
SCRAG
IT'S DISTRACTION.

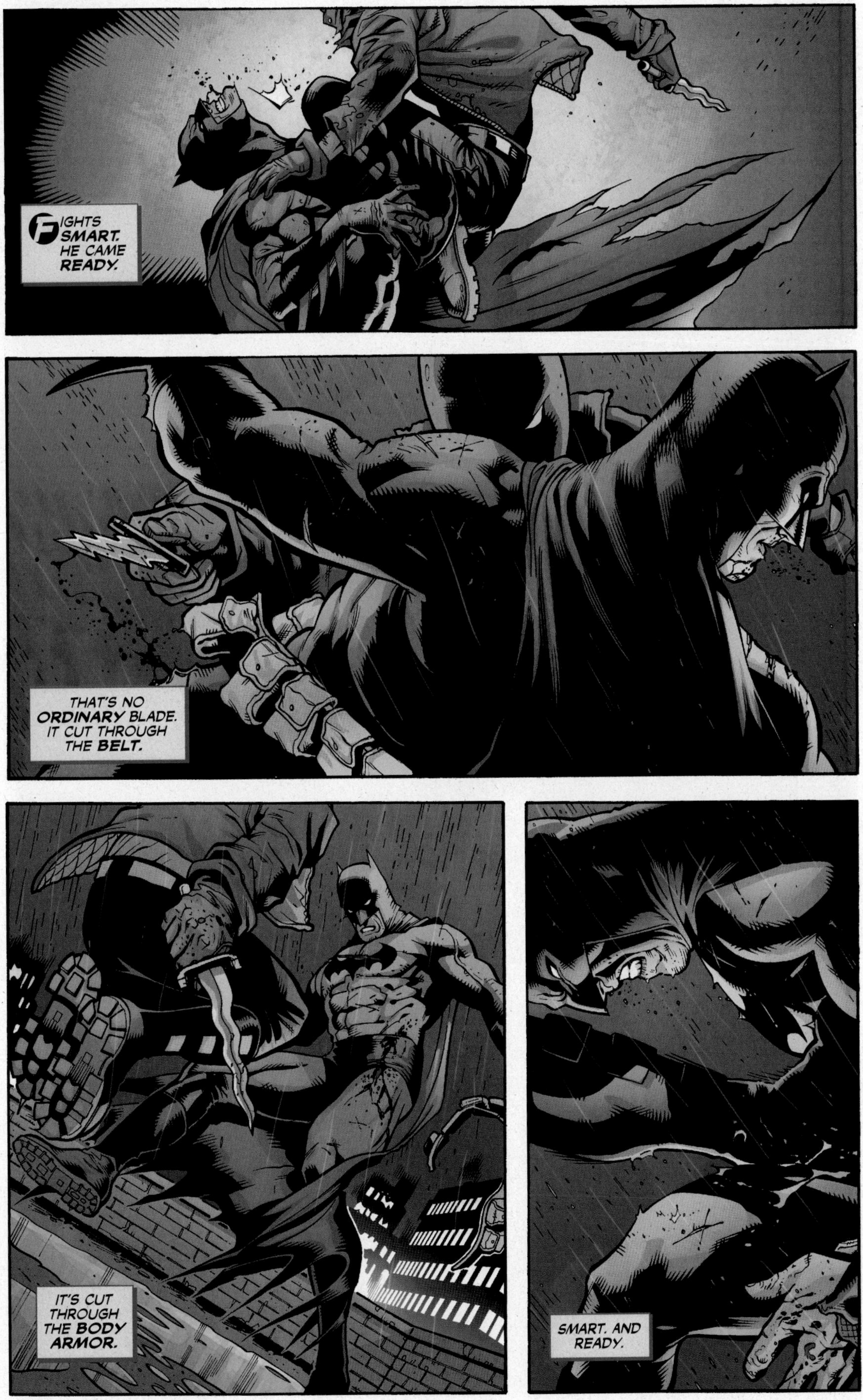
FIGHTS SMART. HE CAME READY.
THAT'S NO ORDINARY BLADE. IT CUT THROUGH THE BELT.
IT'S CUT THROUGH THE BODY ARMOR.
SMART. AND READY.

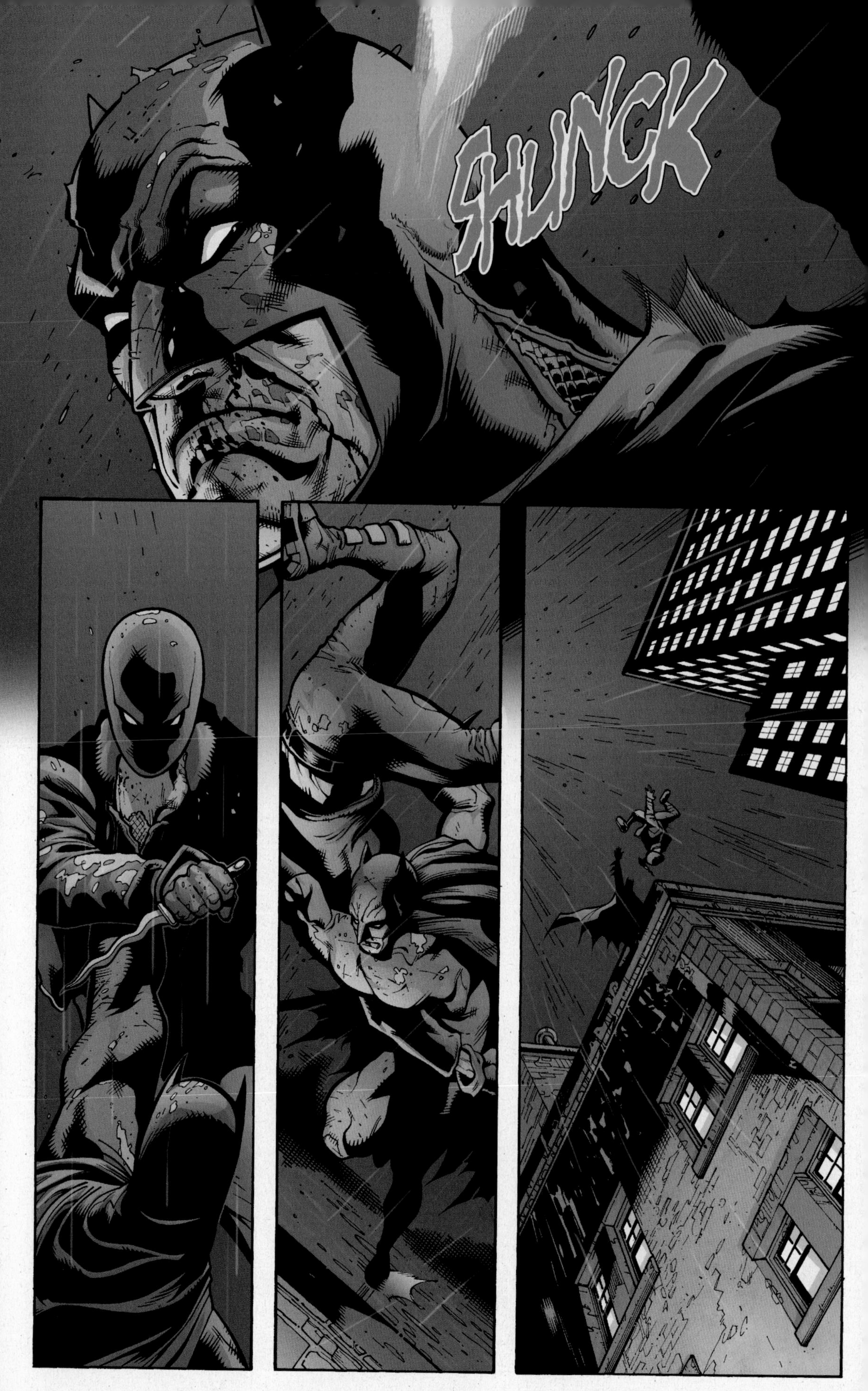
SHUNCK

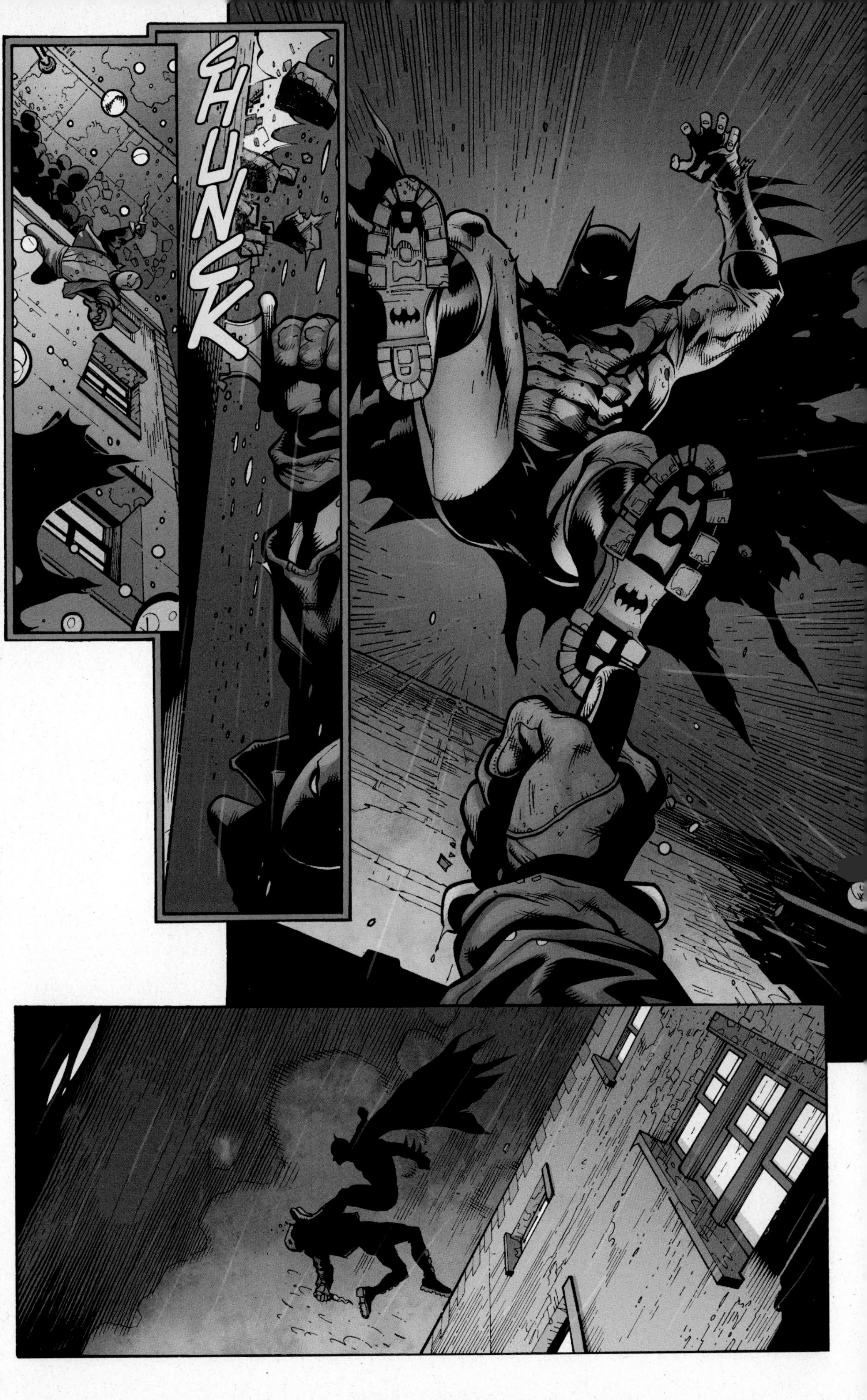
CHUNK

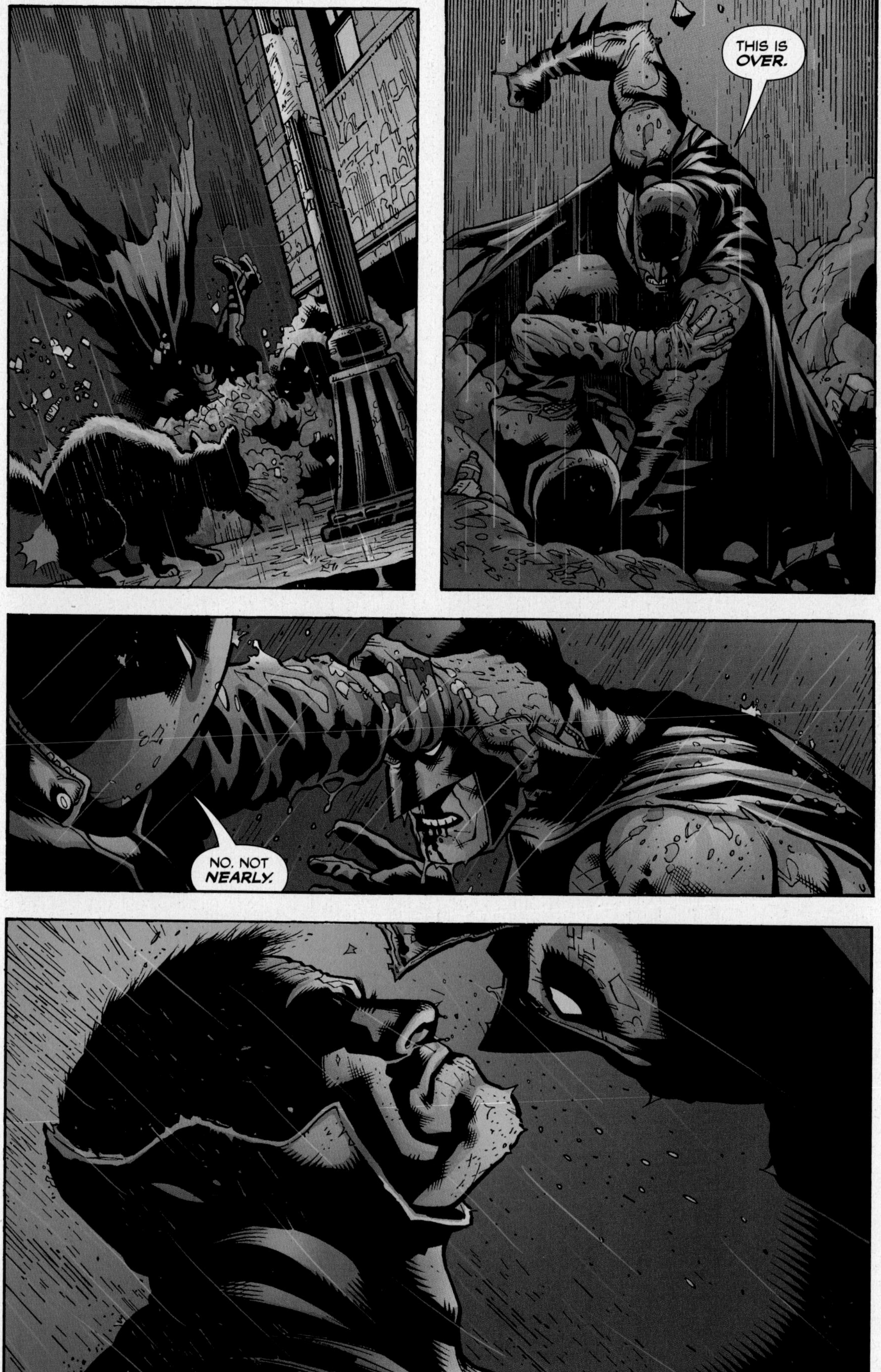
THIS IS OVER.
NO. NOT NEARLY.

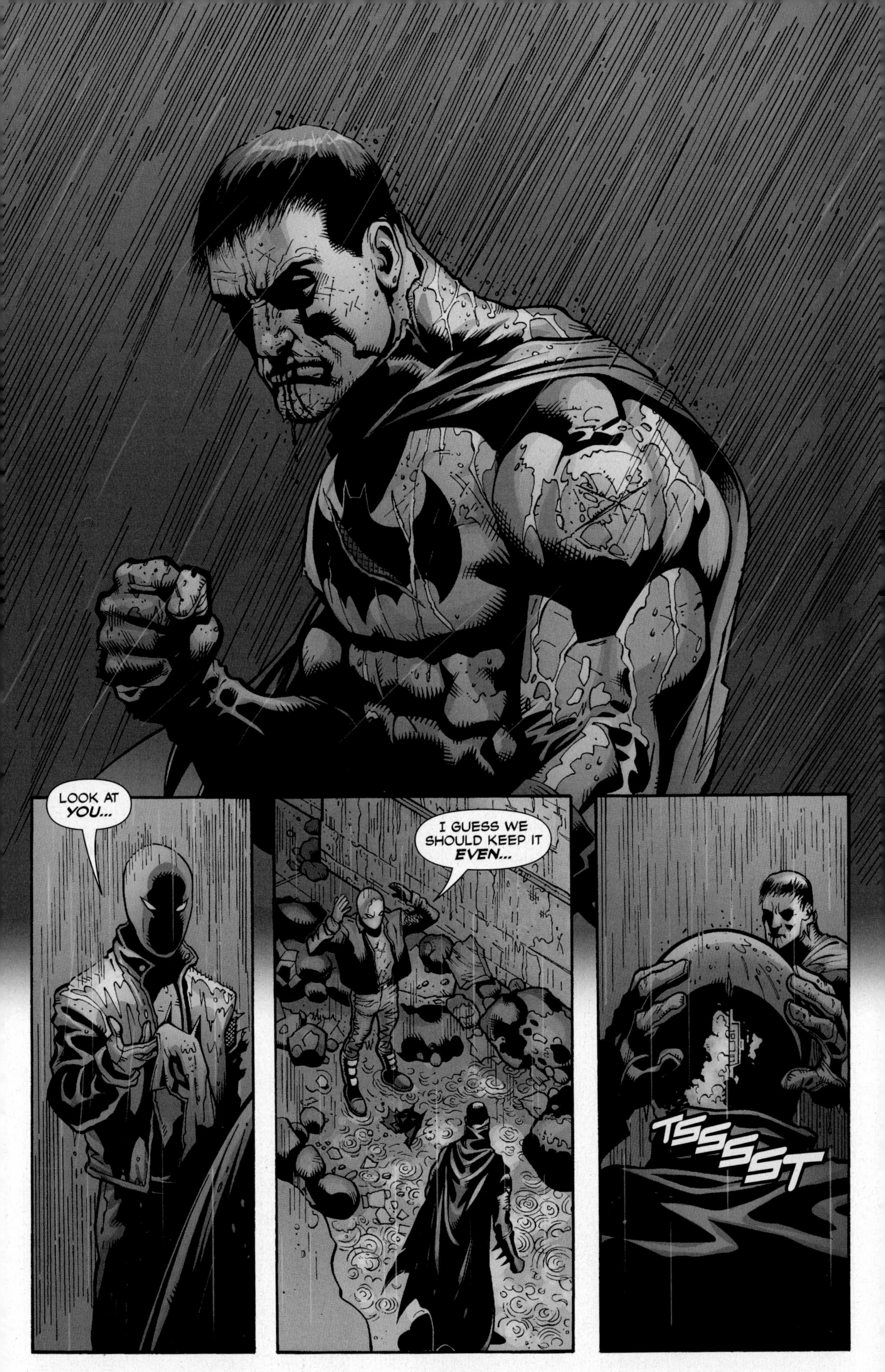
LOOK AT YOU...
I GUESS WE SHOULD KEEP IT EVEN...
TSSSSST

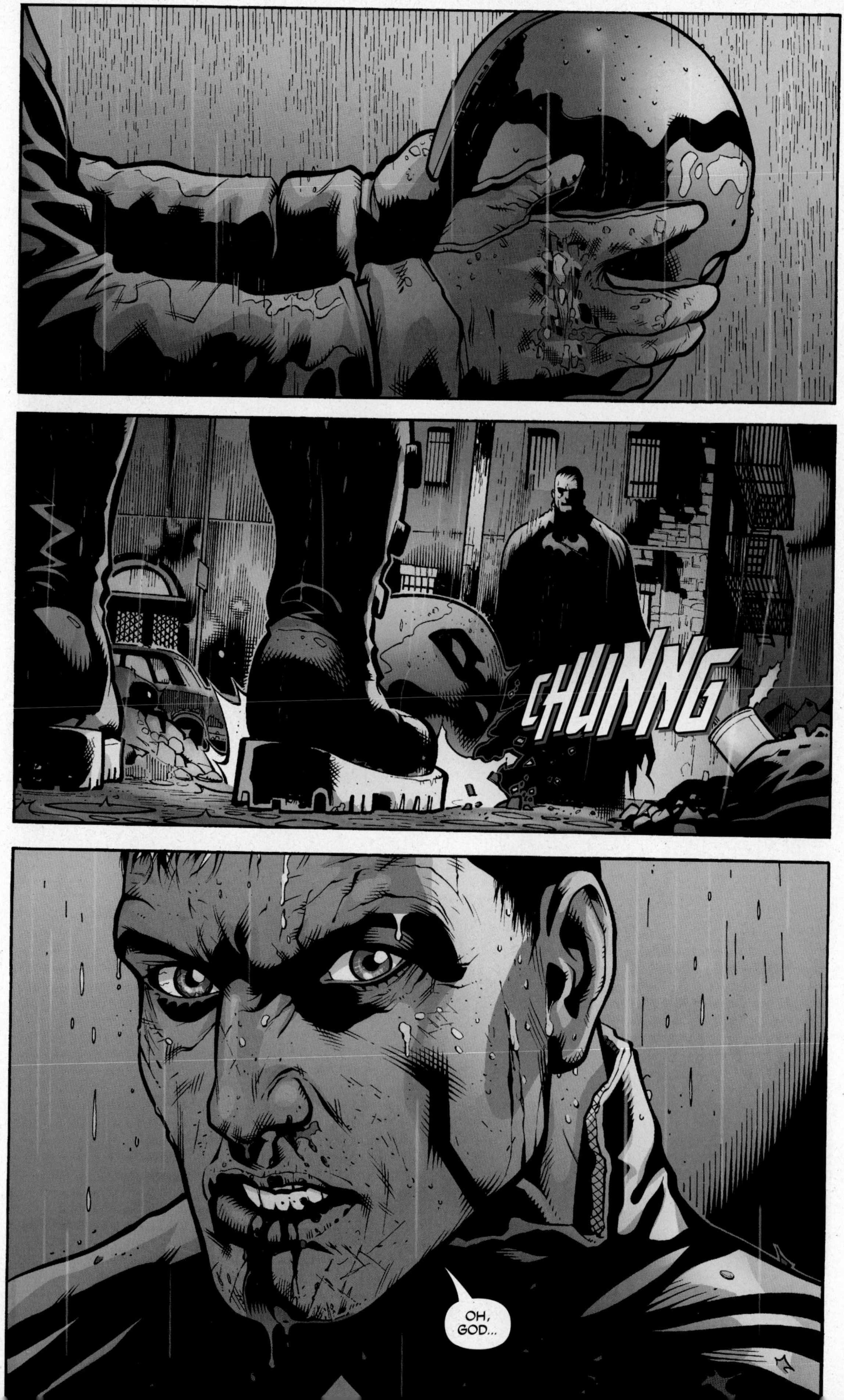

CHUNNG
OH, GOD...

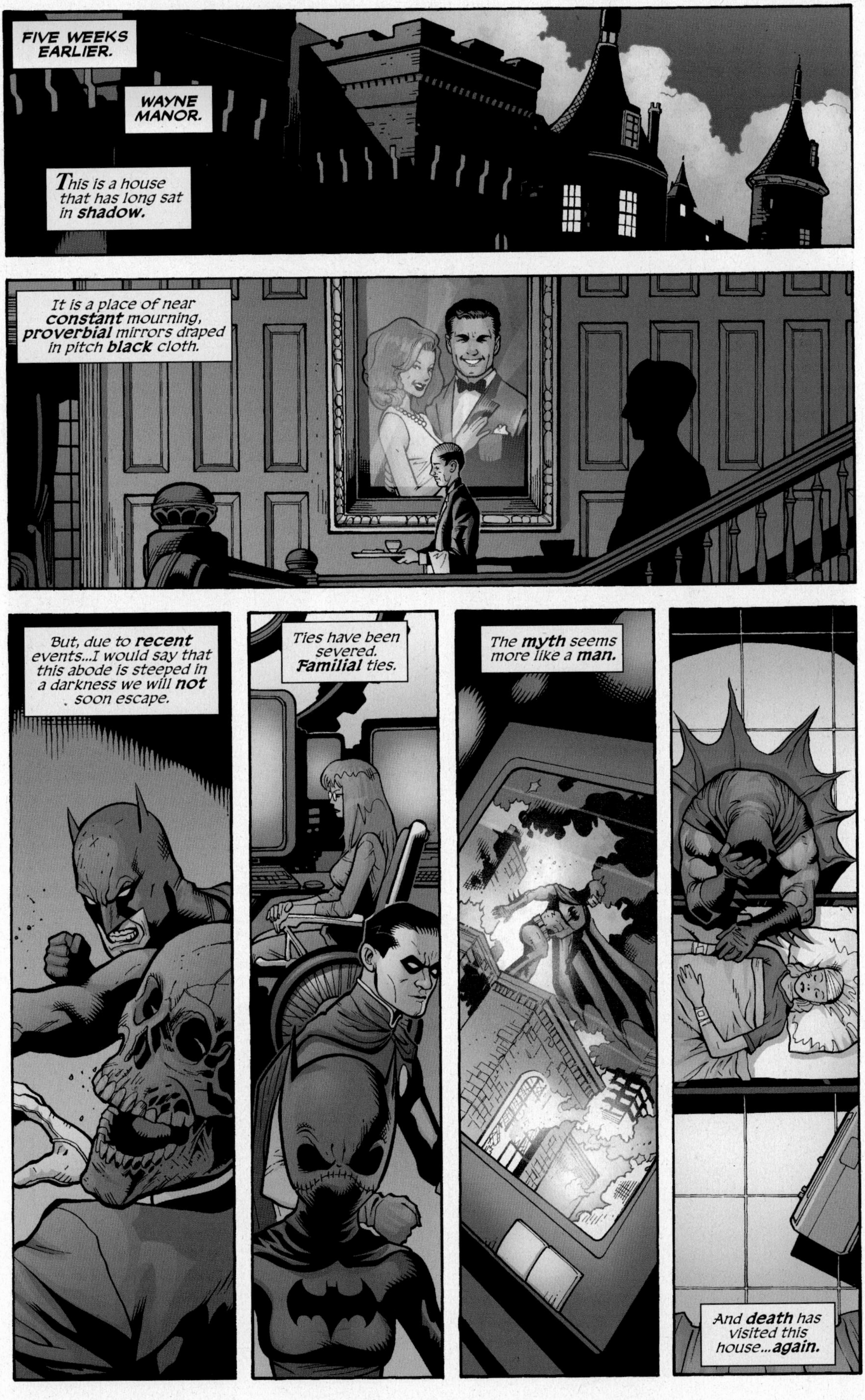
FIVE WEEKS EARLIER.
WAYNE MANOR.
This is a house that has long sat in shadow.
It is a place of near constant mourning, proverbial mirrors draped in pitch black cloth.
But, due to recent events...I would say that this abode is steeped in a darkness we will not soon escape.
Ties have been severed. Familial ties.
The myth seems more like a man.
And death has visited this house...again.

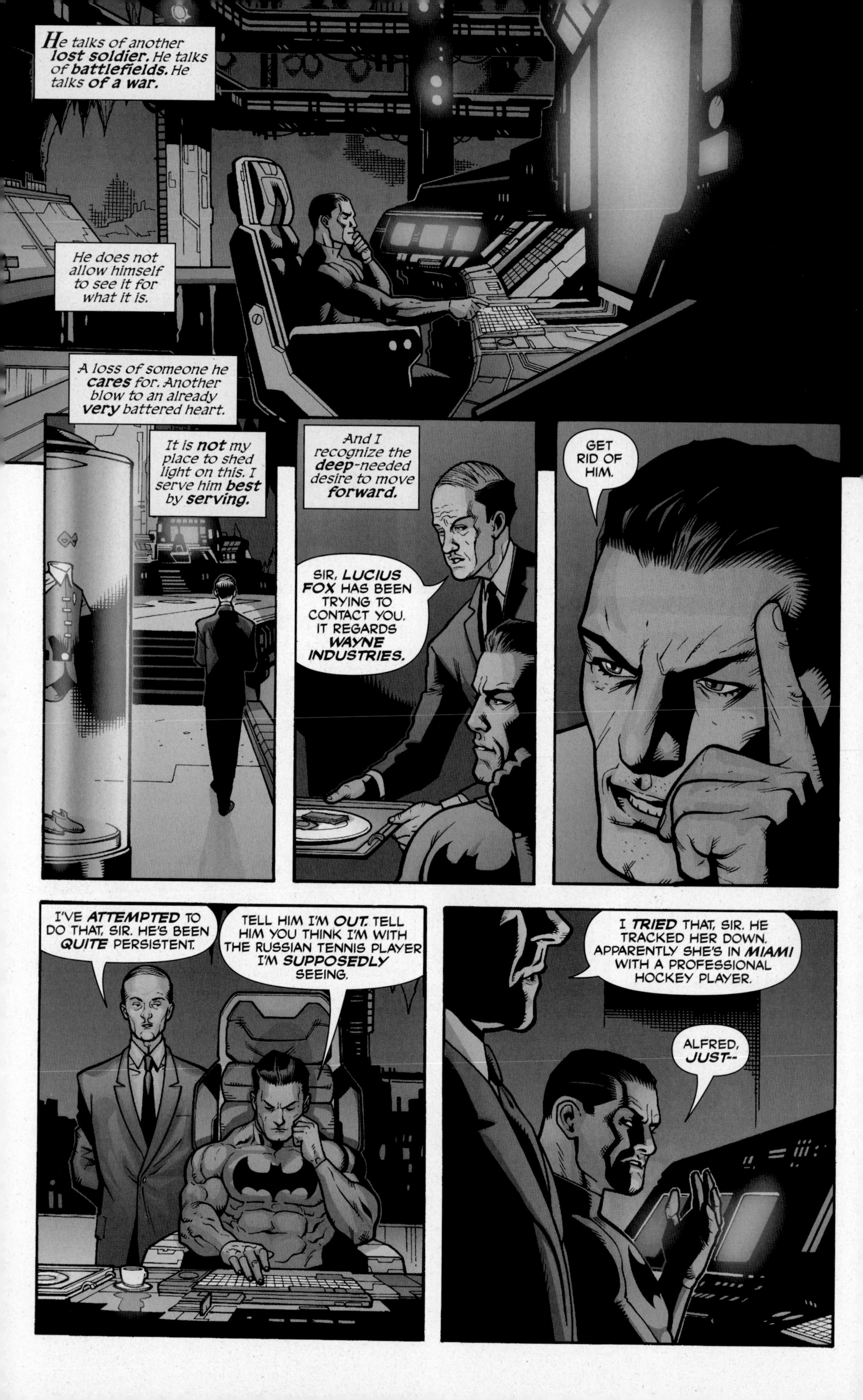
He talks of another lost soldier. He talks of battlefields. He talks of a war.
He does not allow himself to see it for what it is.
A loss of someone he cares for. Another blow to an already very battered heart.
It is not my place to shed light on this. I serve him best by serving.
And I recognize the deep-needed desire to move forward.
SIR, LUCIUS FOX HAS BEEN TRYING TO CONTACT YOU. IT REGARDS WAYNE INDUSTRIES.
GET RID OF HIM.
I'VE ATTEMPTED TO DO THAT, SIR. HE'S BEEN QUITE PERSISTENT.
TELL HIM I'M OUT. TELL HIM YOU THINK I'M WITH THE RUSSIAN TENNIS PLAYER I'M SUPPOSEDLY SEEING.
I TRIED THAT, SIR. HE TRACKED HER DOWN. APPARENTLY SHE'S IN MIAMI WITH A PROFESSIONAL HOCKEY PLAYER.
ALFRED, JUST--

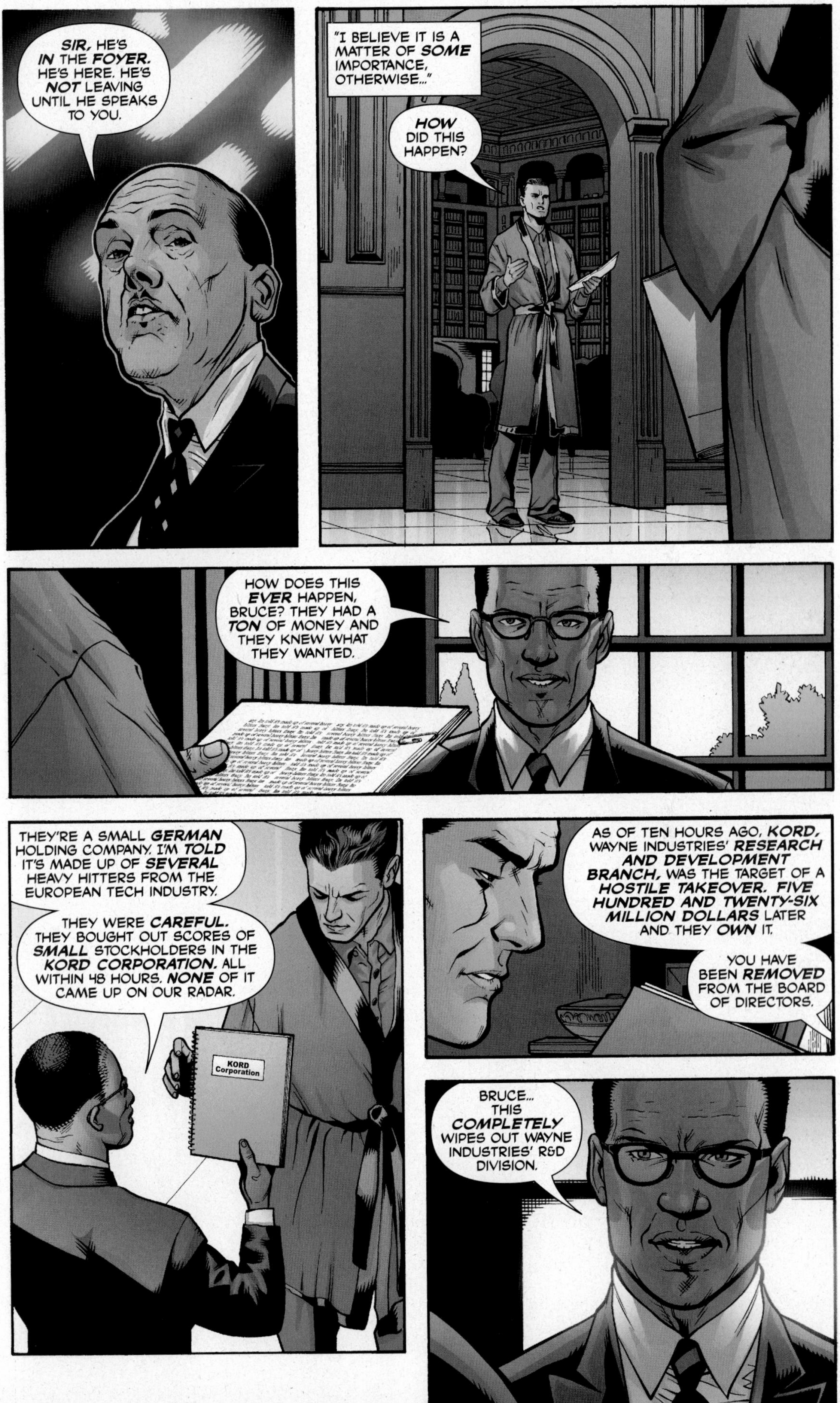
SIR, HE'S IN THE FOYER. HE'S HERE. HE'S NOT LEAVING UNTIL HE SPEAKS TO YOU.
"I BELIEVE IT IS A MATTER OF SOME IMPORTANCE, OTHERWISE..."
HOW DID THIS HAPPEN?
HOW DOES THIS EVER HAPPEN, BRUCE? THEY HAD A TON OF MONEY AND THEY KNEW WHAT THEY WANTED.
THEY'RE A SMALL GERMAN HOLDING COMPANY. I'M TOLD IT'S MADE UP OF SEVERAL HEAVY HITTERS FROM THE EUROPEAN TECH INDUSTRY.
THEY WERE CAREFUL. THEY BOUGHT OUT SCORES OF SMALL STOCKHOLDERS IN THE KORD CORPORATION. ALL WITHIN 48 HOURS. NONE OF IT CAME UP ON OUR RADAR.
KORD Corporation
AS OF TEN HOURS AGO, KORD, WAYNE INDUSTRIES' RESEARCH AND DEVELOPMENT BRANCH, WAS THE TARGET OF A HOSTILE TAKEOVER. FIVE HUNDRED AND TWENTY-SIX MILLION DOLLARS LATER AND THEY OWN IT.
YOU HAVE BEEN REMOVED FROM THE BOARD OF DIRECTORS.
BRUCE... THIS COMPLETELY WIPES OUT WAYNE INDUSTRIES' R&D DIVISION.

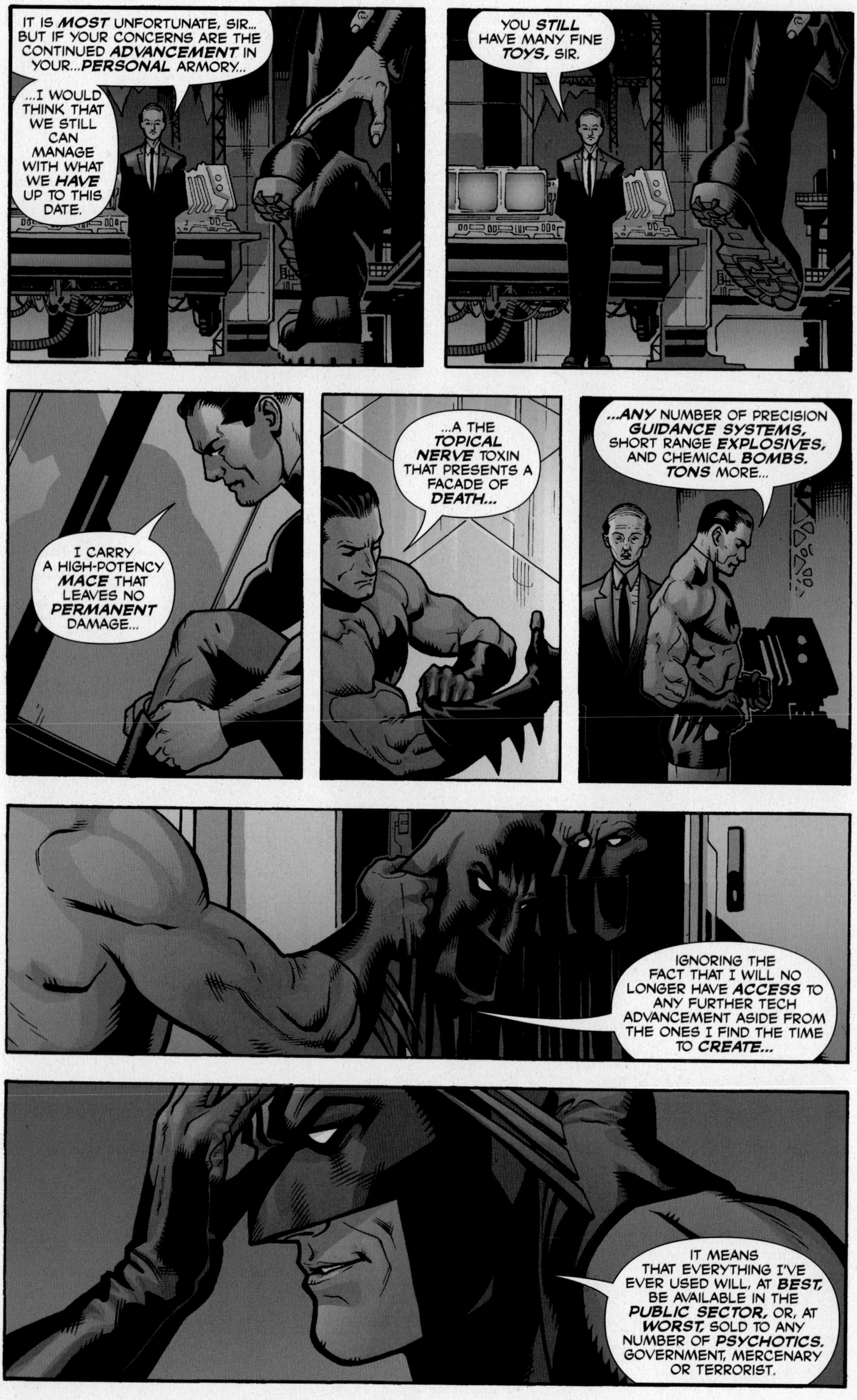
IT IS MOST UNFORTUNATE, SIR... BUT IF YOUR CONCERNS ARE THE CONTINUED ADVANCEMENT IN YOUR...PERSONAL ARMORY...
...I WOULD THINK THAT WE STILL CAN MANAGE WITH WHAT WE HAVE UP TO THIS DATE.
YOU STILL HAVE MANY FINE TOYS, SIR.
I CARRY A HIGH-POTENCY MACE THAT LEAVES NO PERMANENT DAMAGE...
...A THE TOPICAL NERVE TOXIN THAT PRESENTS A FACADE OF DEATH...
...ANY NUMBER OF PRECISION GUIDANCE SYSTEMS, SHORT RANGE EXPLOSIVES, AND CHEMICAL BOMBS. TONS MORE...
IGNORING THE FACT THAT I WILL NO LONGER HAVE ACCESS TO ANY FURTHER TECH ADVANCEMENT ASIDE FROM THE ONES I FIND THE TIME TO CREATE...
IT MEANS THAT EVERYTHING I'VE EVER USED WILL, AT BEST, BE AVAILABLE IN THE PUBLIC SECTOR, OR, AT WORST, SOLD TO ANY NUMBER OF PSYCHOTICS. GOVERNMENT, MERCENARY OR TERRORIST.

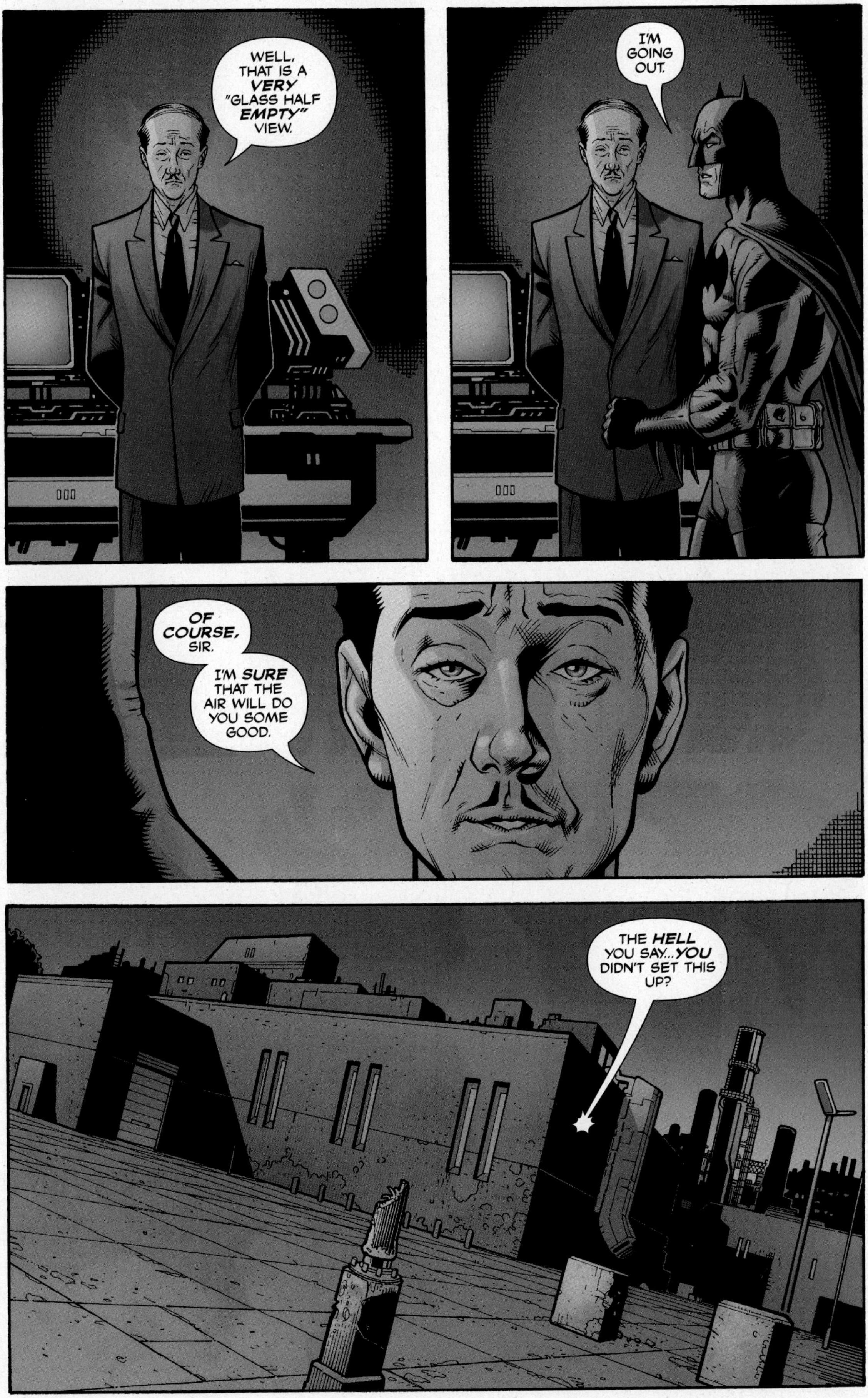
WELL, THAT IS A VERY "GLASS HALF EMPTY" VIEW.
I'M GOING OUT.
OF COURSE, SIR.
I'M SURE THAT THE AIR WILL DO YOU SOME GOOD.
THE HELL YOU SAY... YOU DIDN'T SET THIS UP?

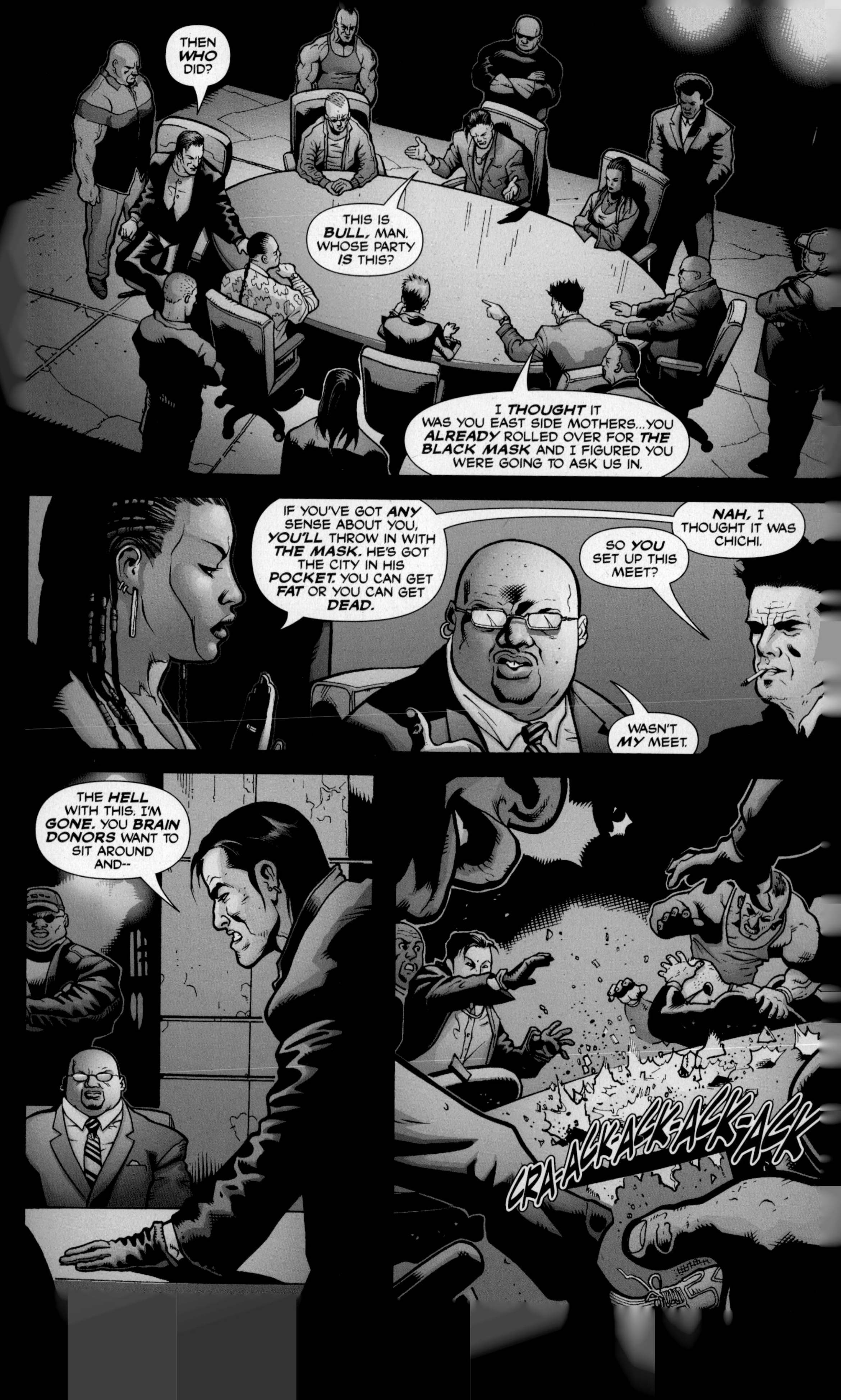
THEN WHO DID?
THIS IS BULL, MAN. WHOSE PARTY IS THIS?
I THOUGHT IT WAS YOU EAST SIDE MOTHERS...YOU ALREADY ROLLED OVER FOR THE BLACK MASK AND I FIGURED YOU WERE GOING TO ASK US IN.
NAH, I THOUGHT IT WAS CHICHI.
SO YOU SET UP THIS MEET?
WASN'T MY MEET.
IF YOU'VE GOT ANY SENSE ABOUT YOU, YOU'LL THROW IN WITH THE MASK. HE'S GOT THE CITY IN HIS POCKET. YOU CAN GET FAT OR YOU CAN GET DEAD.
THE HELL WITH THIS. I'M GONE. YOU BRAIN DONORS WANT TO SIT AROUND AND--
CRA-ACK-ACK-ACK-ACK

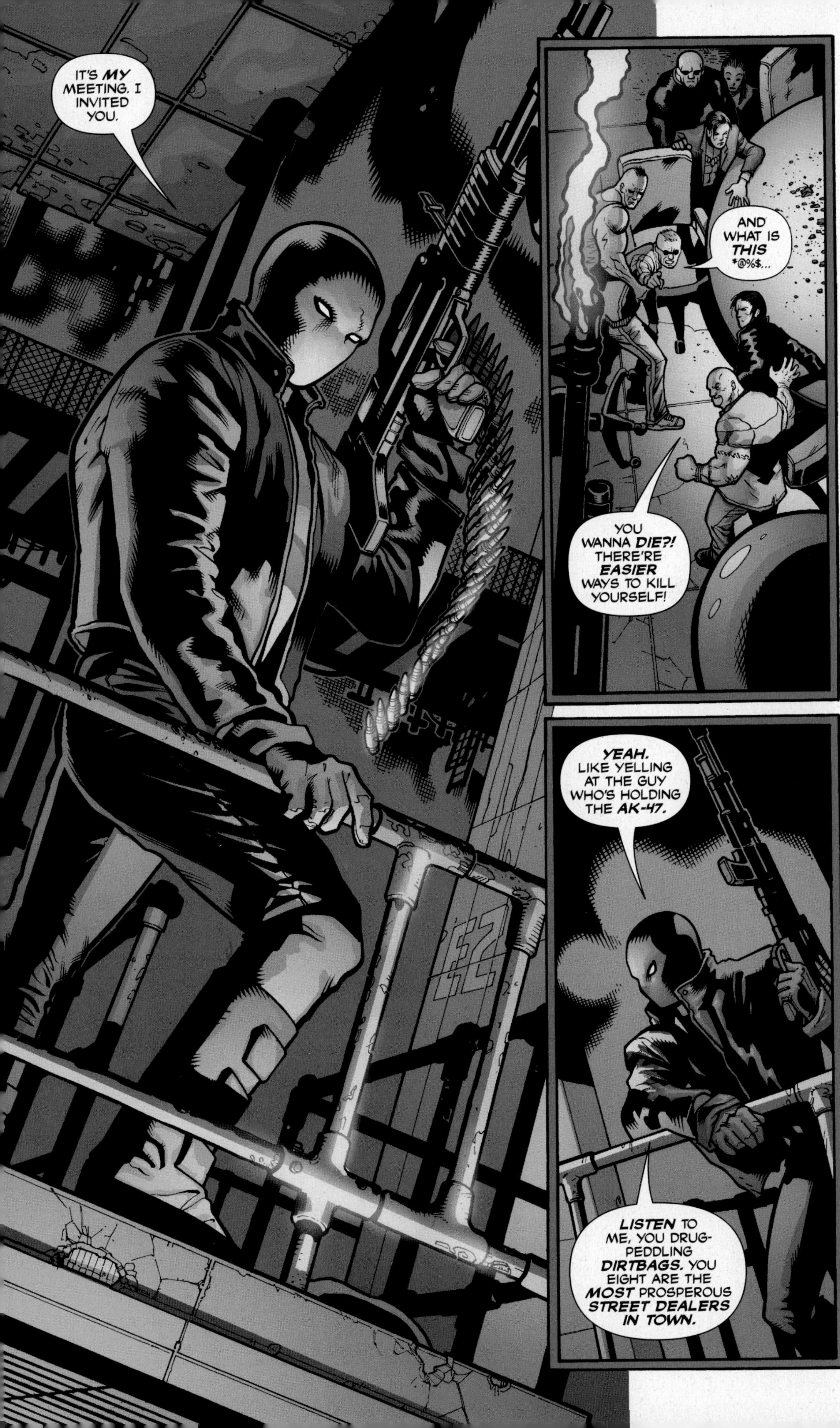
IT'S MY MEETING. I INVITED YOU.
AND WHAT IS THIS *@%$...
YOU WANNA DIE?! THERE'RE EASIER WAYS TO KILL YOURSELF!
YEAH. LIKE YELLING AT THE GUY WHO'S HOLDING THE AK-47.
LISTEN TO ME, YOU DRUG-PEDDLING DIRTBAGS. YOU EIGHT ARE THE MOST PROSPEROUS STREET DEALERS IN TOWN.

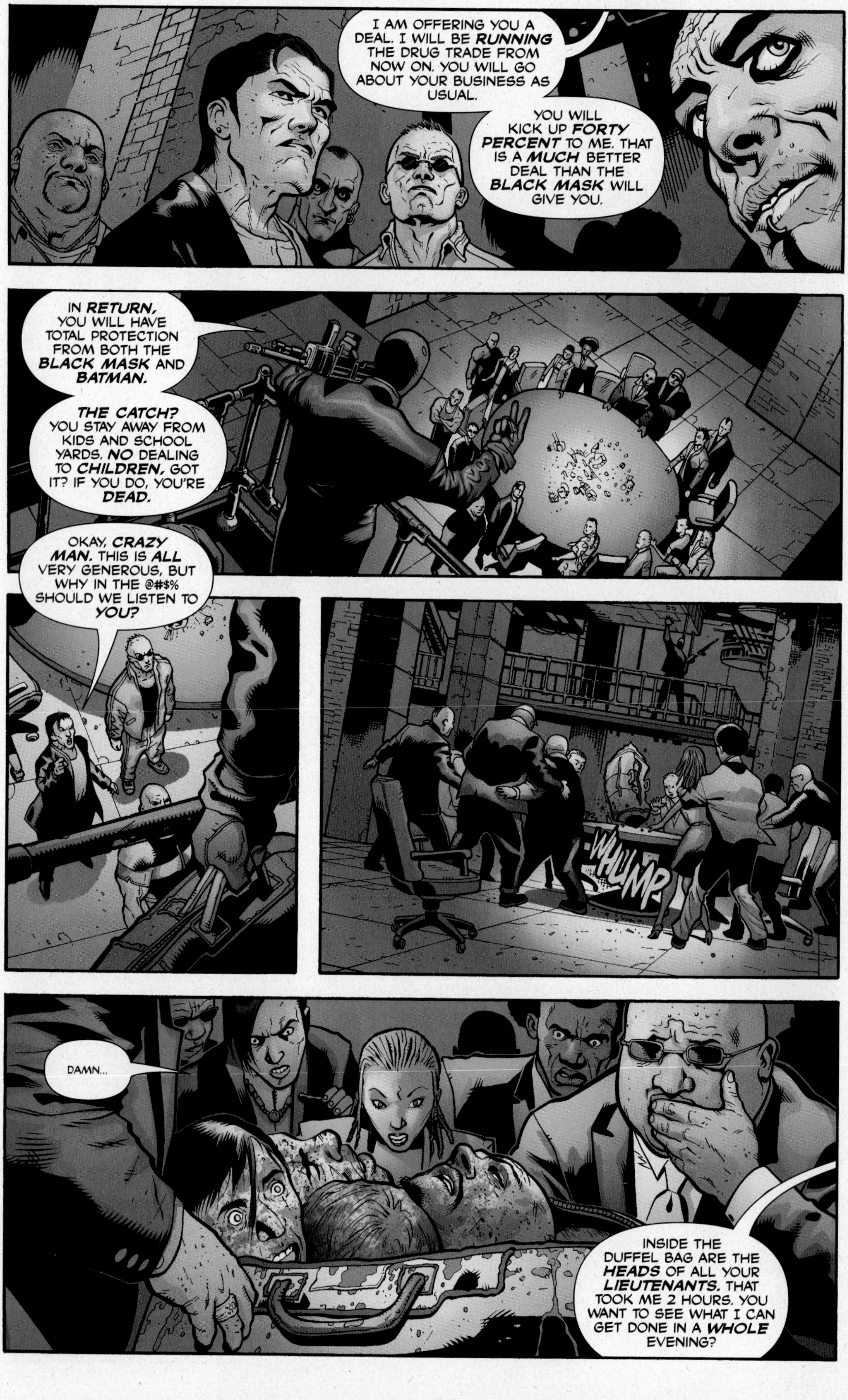
I AM OFFERING YOU A DEAL. I WILL BE RUNNING THE DRUG TRADE FROM NOW ON. YOU WILL GO ABOUT YOUR BUSINESS AS USUAL.
YOU WILL KICK UP FORTY PERCENT TO ME. THAT IS A MUCH BETTER DEAL THAN THE BLACK MASK WILL GIVE YOU.
IN RETURN, YOU WILL HAVE TOTAL PROTECTION FROM BOTH THE BLACK MASK AND BATMAN.
THE CATCH? YOU STAY AWAY FROM KIDS AND SCHOOL YARDS. NO DEALING TO CHILDREN, GOT IT? IF YOU DO, YOU'RE DEAD.
OKAY, CRAZY MAN. THIS IS ALL VERY GENEROUS, BUT WHY IN THE @#$% SHOULD WE LISTEN TO YOU?
WHUMP
DAMN...
INSIDE THE DUFFEL BAG ARE THE HEADS OF ALL YOUR LIEUTENANTS. THAT TOOK ME 2 HOURS. YOU WANT TO SEE WHAT I CAN GET DONE IN A WHOLE EVENING?

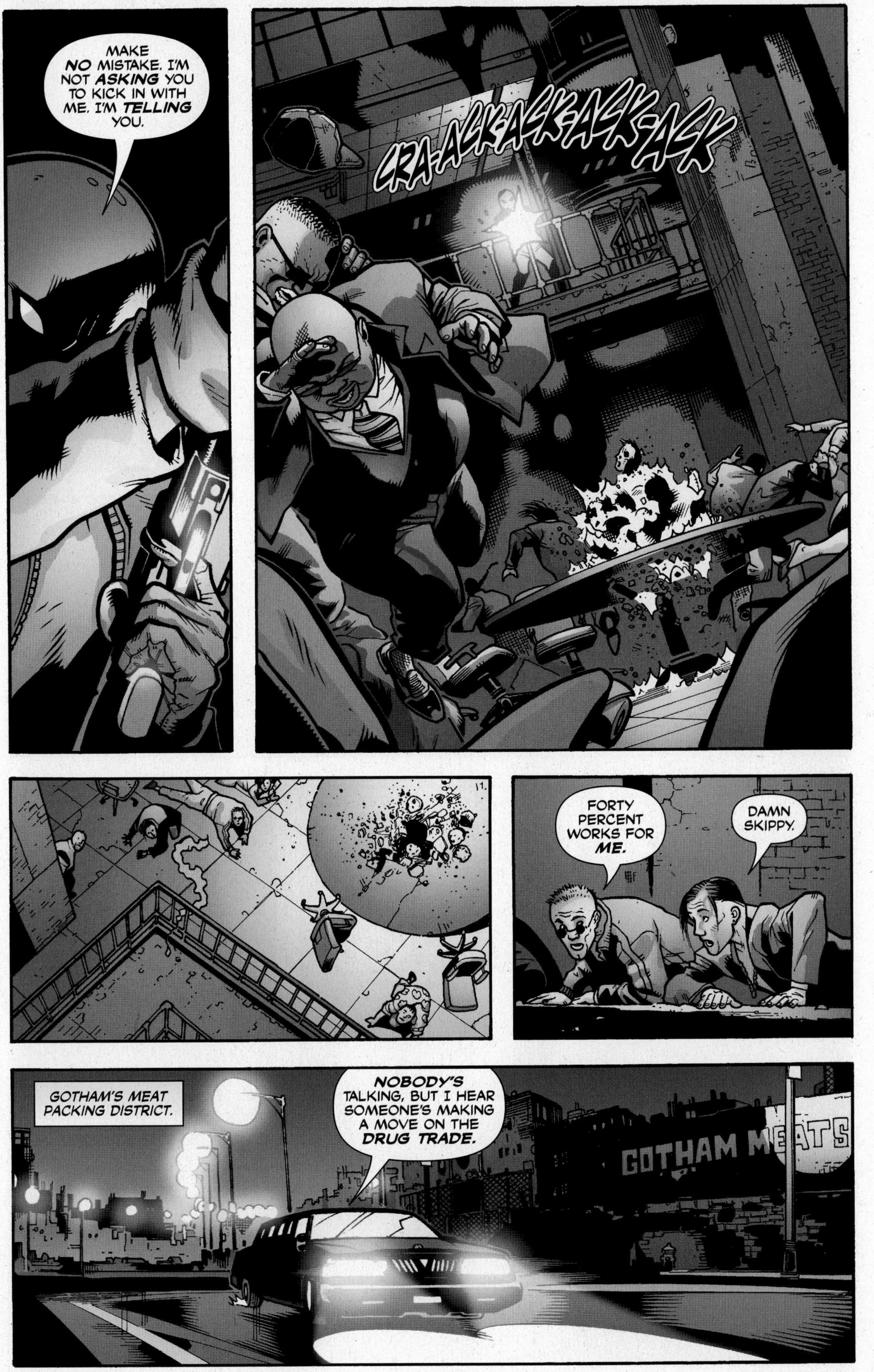
MAKE NO MISTAKE. I'M NOT ASKING YOU TO KICK IN WITH ME. I'M TELLING YOU.
CRA-ACK-ACK-ACK-ACK-ACK
FORTY PERCENT WORKS FOR ME.
DAMN SKIPPY.
GOTHAM'S MEAT PACKING DISTRICT.
NOBODY'S TALKING, BUT I HEAR SOMEONE'S MAKING A MOVE ON THE DRUG TRADE.
GOTHAM MEATS

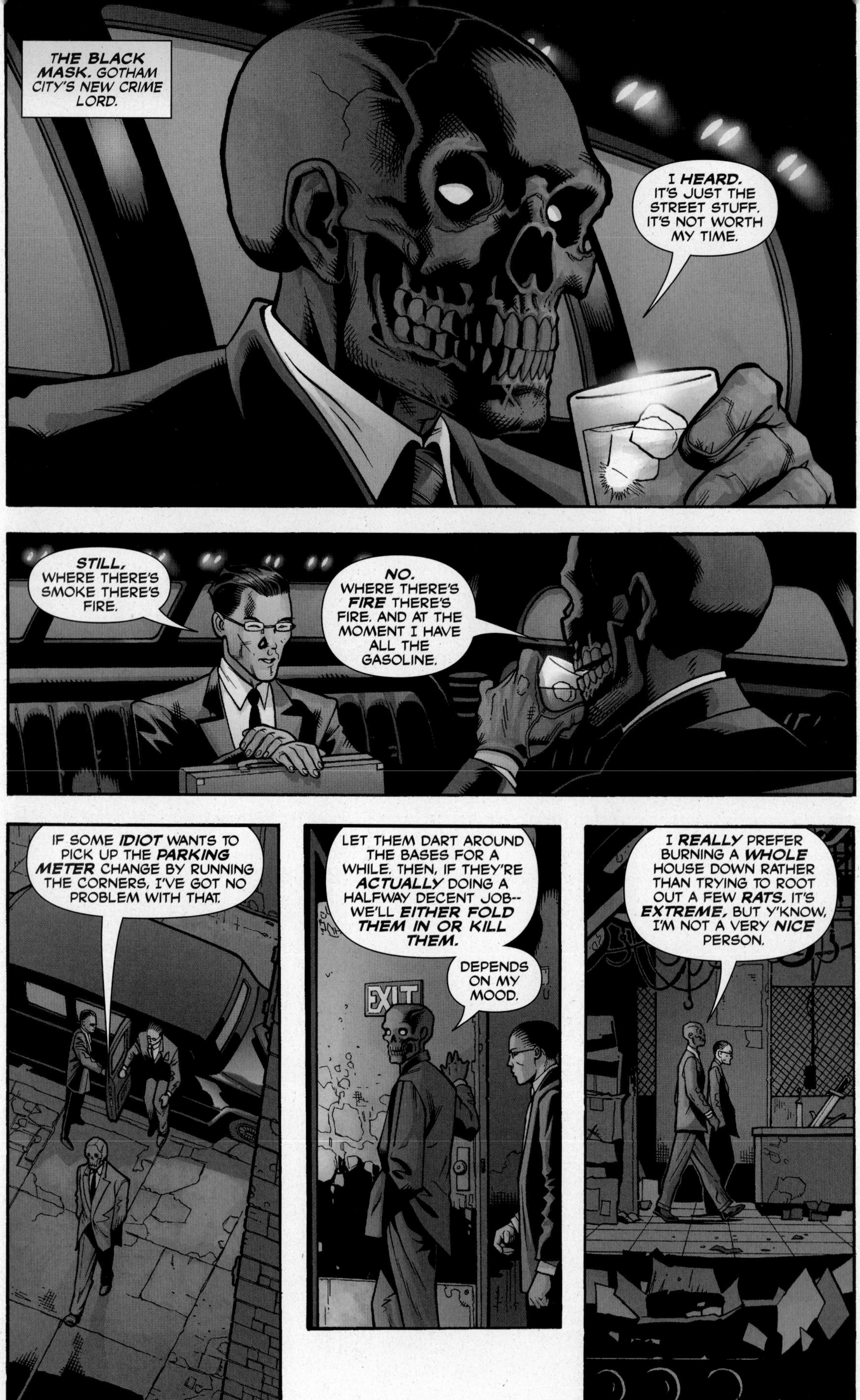
THE BLACK MASK. GOTHAM CITY'S NEW CRIME LORD.
I HEARD. IT'S JUST THE STREET STUFF. IT'S NOT WORTH MY TIME.
STILL, WHERE THERE'S SMOKE THERE'S FIRE.
NO. WHERE THERE'S FIRE THERE'S FIRE. AND AT THE MOMENT I HAVE ALL THE GASOLINE.
IF SOME IDIOT WANTS TO PICK UP THE PARKING METER CHANGE BY RUNNING THE CORNERS, I'VE GOT NO PROBLEM WITH THAT.
LET THEM DART AROUND THE BASES FOR A WHILE. THEN, IF THEY'RE ACTUALLY DOING A HALFWAY DECENT JOB-- WE'LL EITHER FOLD THEM IN OR KILL THEM.
DEPENDS ON MY MOOD.
EXIT
I REALLY PREFER BURNING A WHOLE HOUSE DOWN RATHER THAN TRYING TO ROOT OUT A FEW RATS. IT'S EXTREME, BUT Y'KNOW, I'M NOT A VERY NICE PERSON.

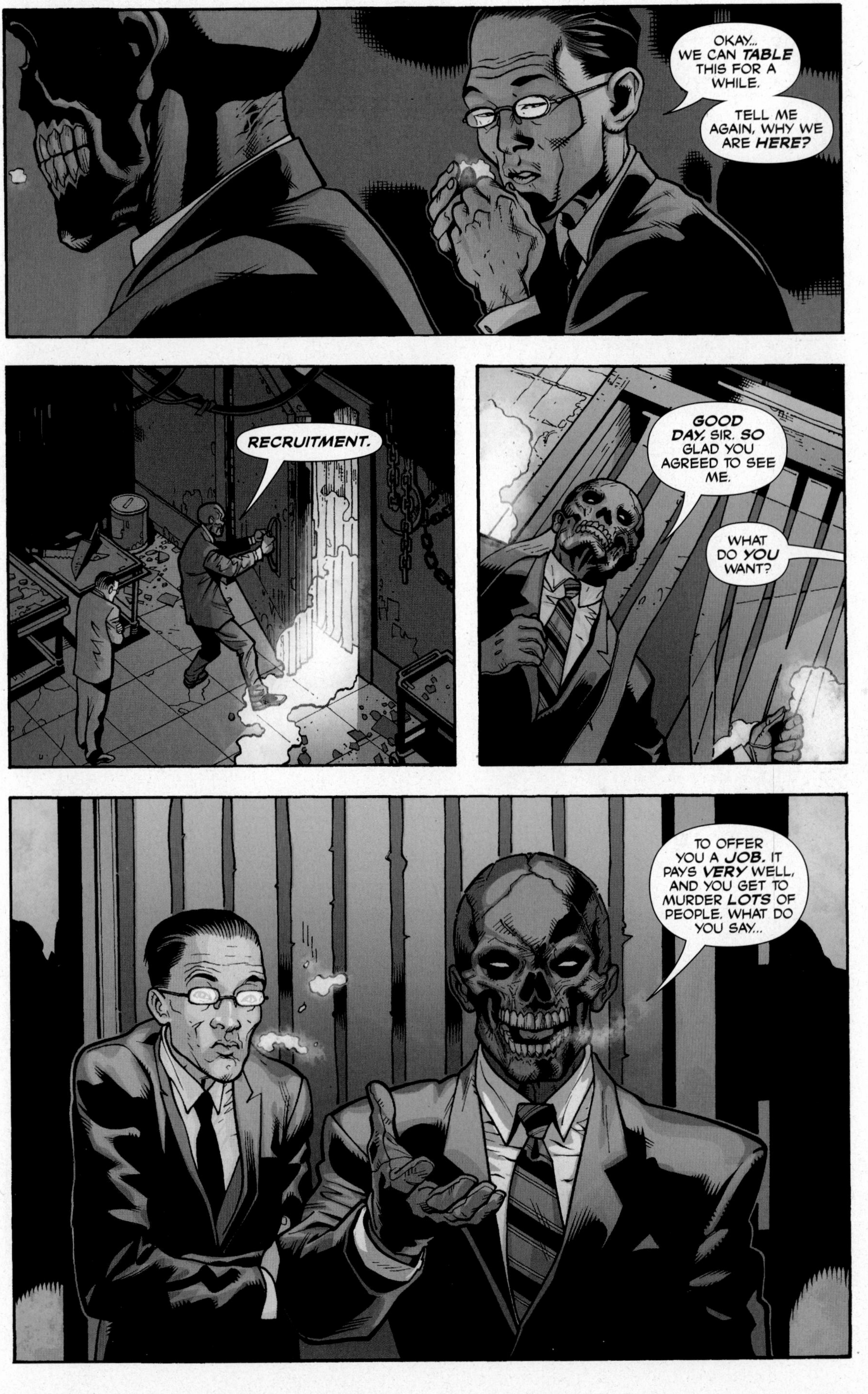
OKAY... WE CAN TABLE THIS FOR A WHILE.
TELL ME AGAIN, WHY WE ARE HERE?
RECRUITMENT.
GOOD DAY, SIR. SO GLAD YOU AGREED TO SEE ME.
WHAT DO YOU WANT?
TO OFFER YOU A JOB. IT PAYS VERY WELL, AND YOU GET TO MURDER LOTS OF PEOPLE. WHAT DO YOU SAY...

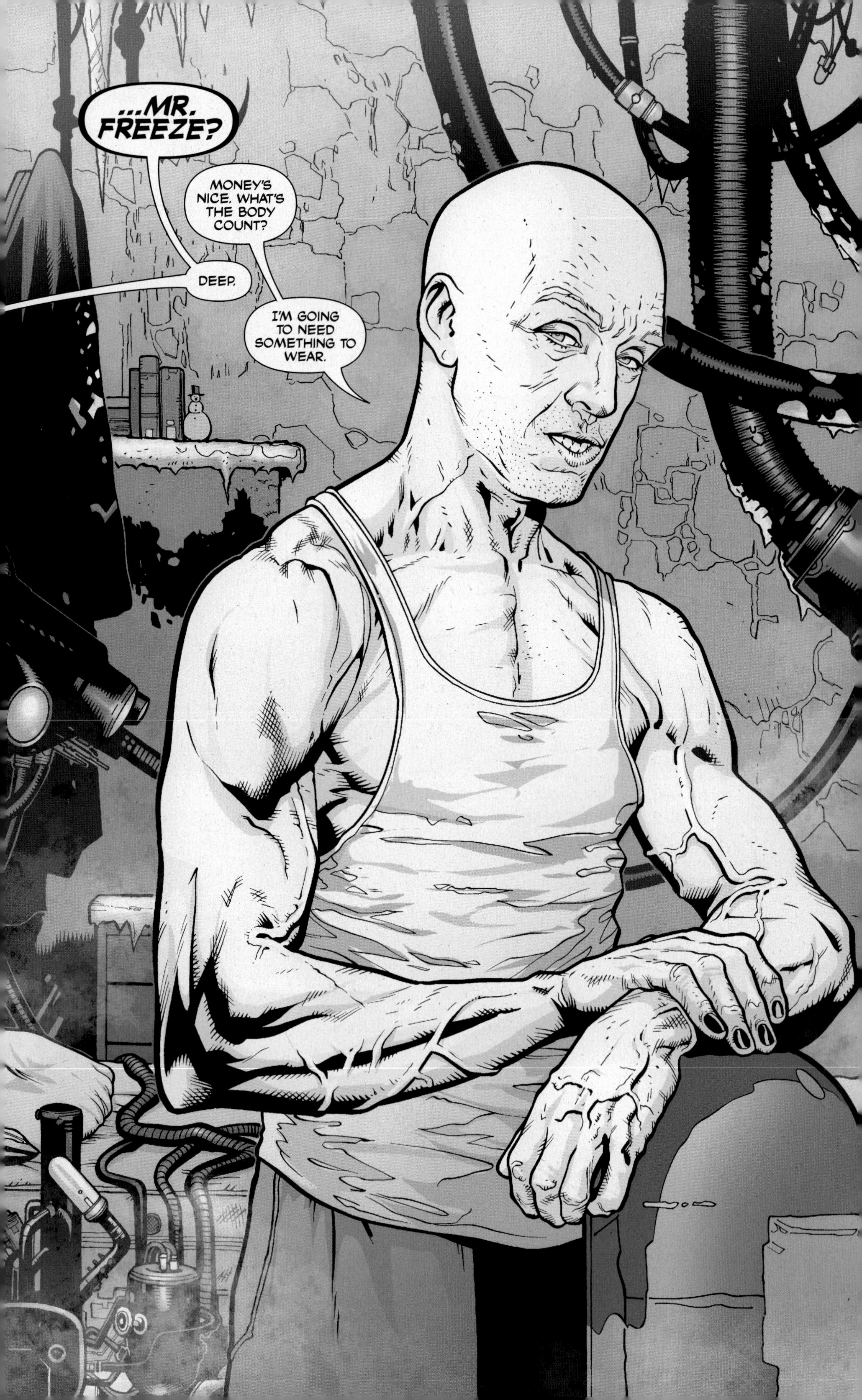
...MR. FREEZE?
MONEY'S NICE. WHAT'S THE BODY COUNT?
DEEP.
I'M GOING TO NEED SOMETHING TO WEAR.

BATMAN 636 Cover by Matt Wagner

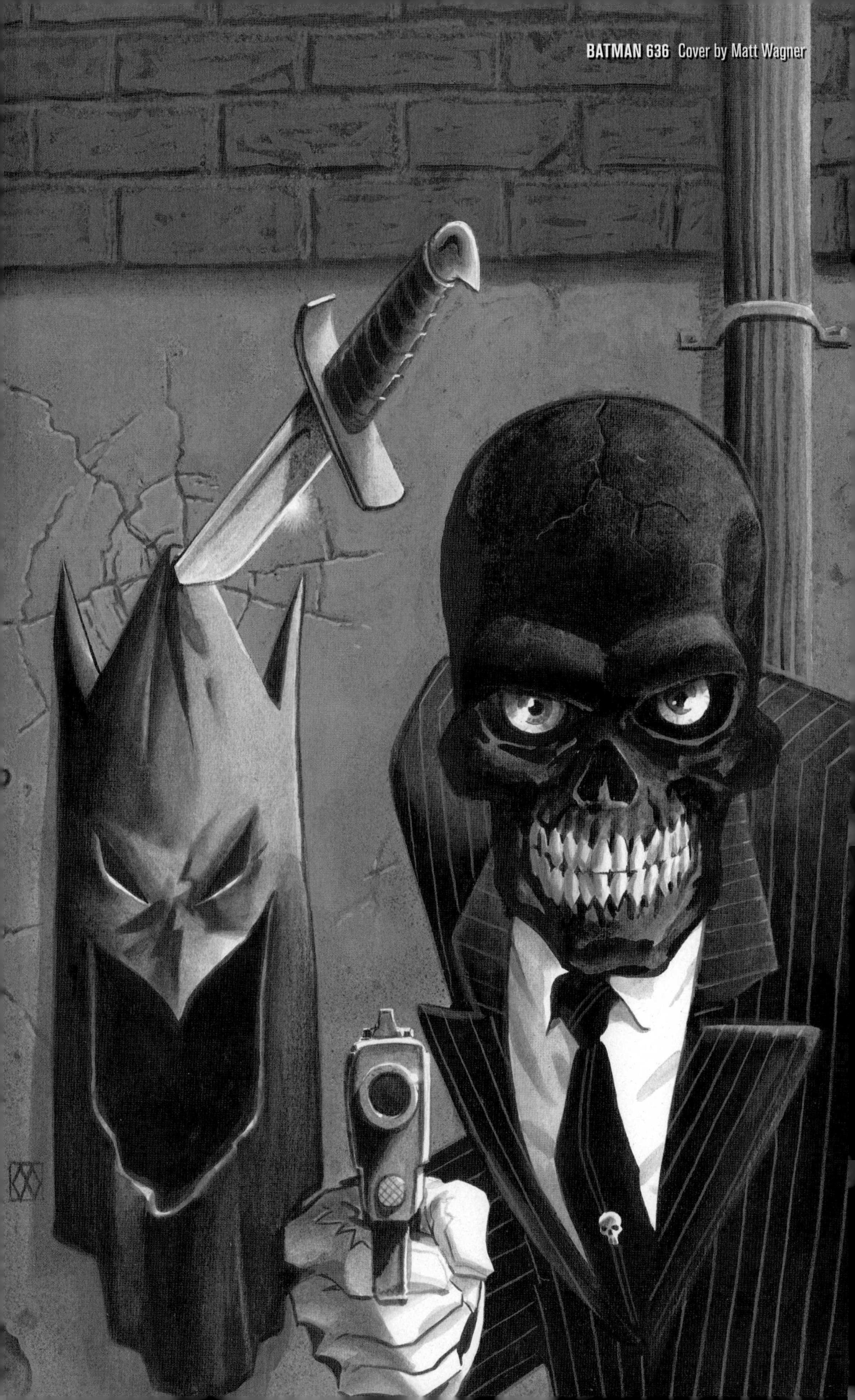

CHAPTER 2

FIRST STRIKE

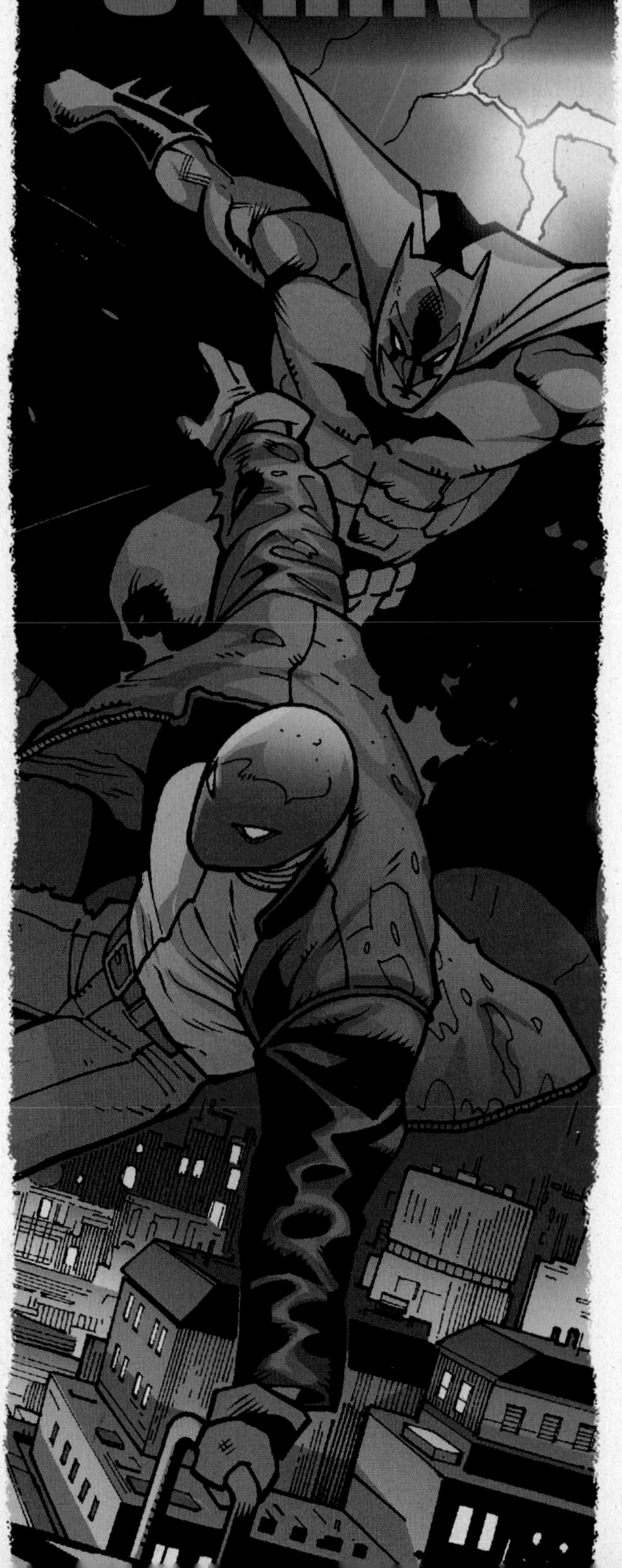

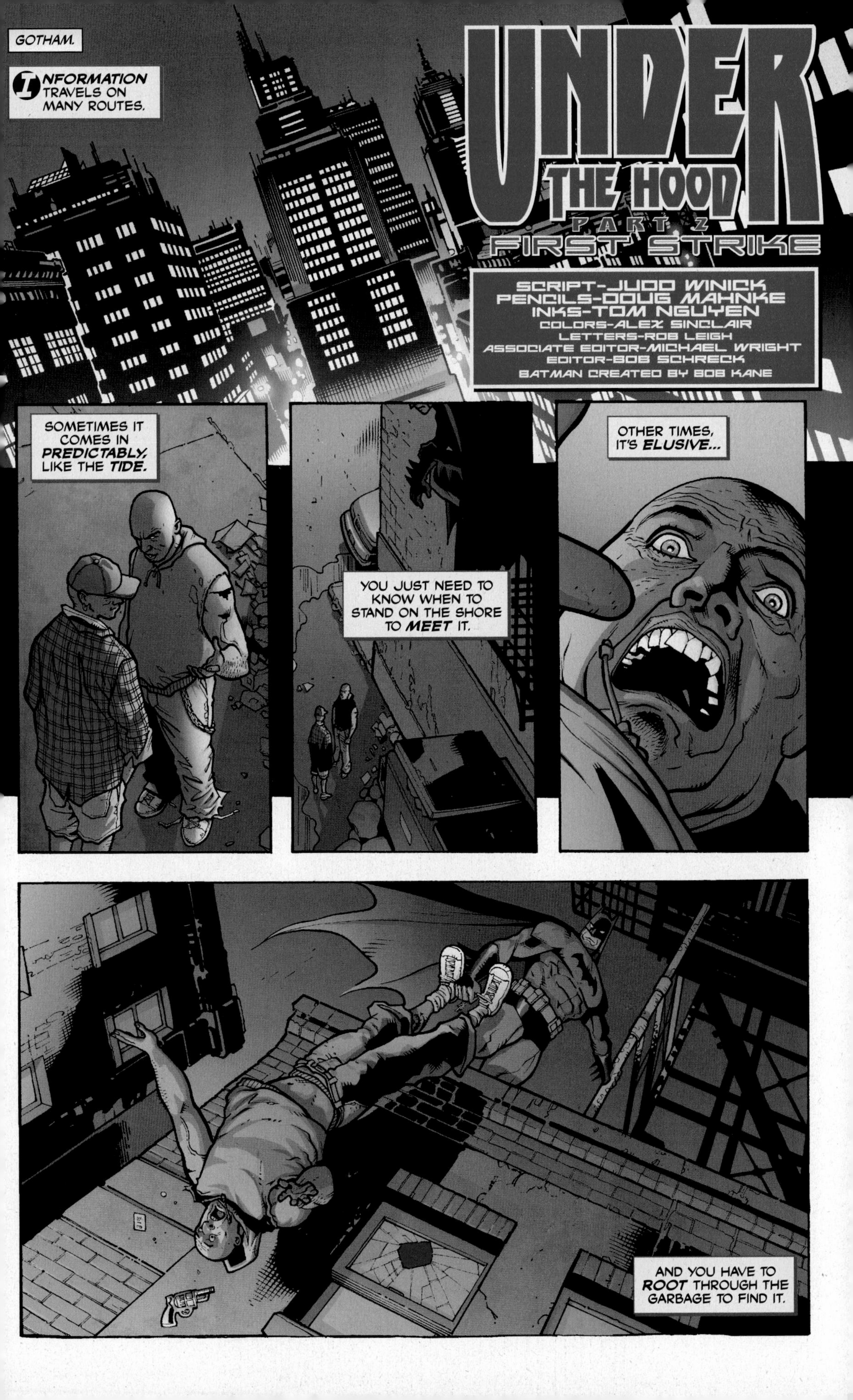
GOTHAM.
INFORMATION TRAVELS ON MANY ROUTES.
UNDER THE HOOD
PART 2
FIRST STRIKE
SCRIPT-JUDD WINICK
PENCILS-DOUG MAHNKE
INKS-TOM NGUYEN
COLORS-ALEX SINCLAIR
LETTERS-ROB LEIGH
ASSOCIATE EDITOR-MICHAEL WRIGHT
EDITOR-BOB SCHRECK
BATMAN CREATED BY BOB KANE
SOMETIMES IT COMES IN PREDICTABLY, LIKE THE TIDE.
YOU JUST NEED TO KNOW WHEN TO STAND ON THE SHORE TO MEET IT.
OTHER TIMES, IT'S ELUSIVE...
AND YOU HAVE TO ROOT THROUGH THE GARBAGE TO FIND IT.

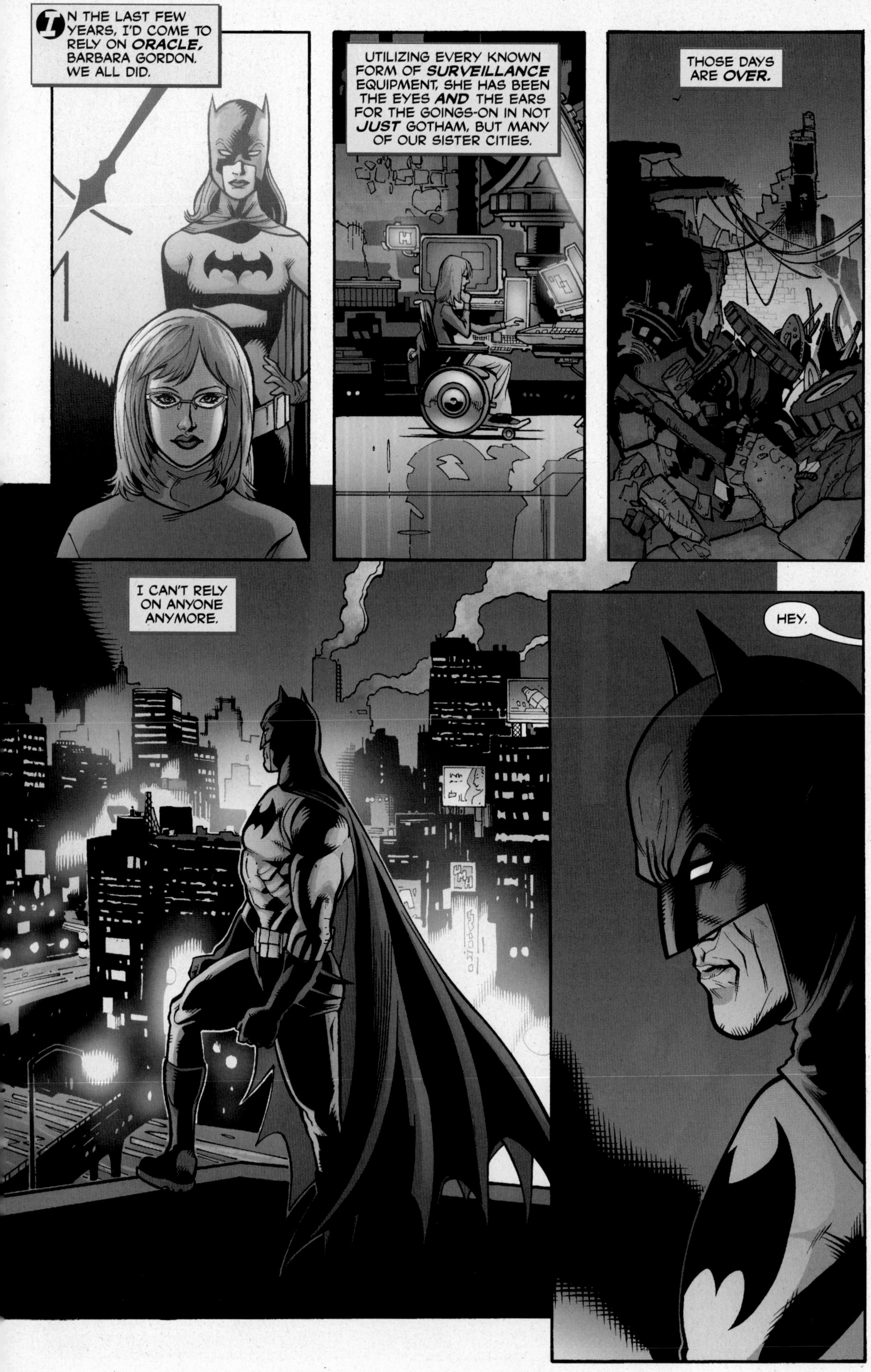

IN THE LAST FEW YEARS, I'D COME TO RELY ON ORACLE, BARBARA GORDON. WE ALL DID.
UTILIZING EVERY KNOWN FORM OF SURVEILLANCE EQUIPMENT, SHE HAS BEEN THE EYES AND THE EARS FOR THE GOINGS-ON IN NOT JUST GOTHAM, BUT MANY OF OUR SISTER CITIES.
THOSE DAYS ARE OVER.
I CAN'T RELY ON ANYONE ANYMORE.
HEY.

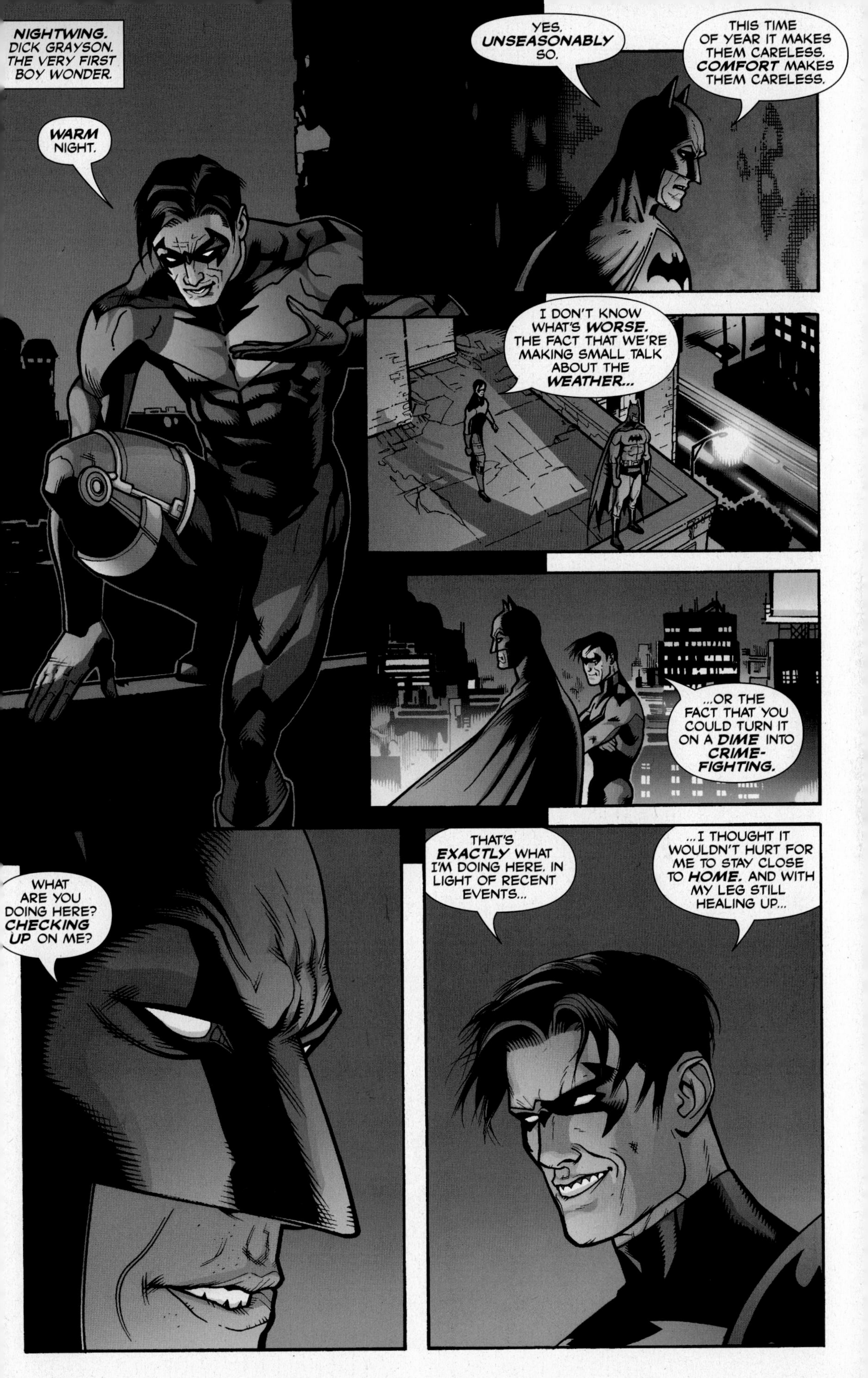
NIGHTWING. DICK GRAYSON. THE VERY FIRST BOY WONDER.
WARM NIGHT.
YES. UNSEASONABLY SO.
THIS TIME OF YEAR IT MAKES THEM CARELESS. COMFORT MAKES THEM CARELESS.
I DON'T KNOW WHAT'S WORSE. THE FACT THAT WE'RE MAKING SMALL TALK ABOUT THE WEATHER...
...OR THE FACT THAT YOU COULD TURN IT ON A DIME INTO CRIME-FIGHTING.
WHAT ARE YOU DOING HERE? CHECKING UP ON ME?
THAT'S EXACTLY WHAT I'M DOING HERE. IN LIGHT OF RECENT EVENTS...
...I THOUGHT IT WOULDN'T HURT FOR ME TO STAY CLOSE TO HOME. AND WITH MY LEG STILL HEALING UP...

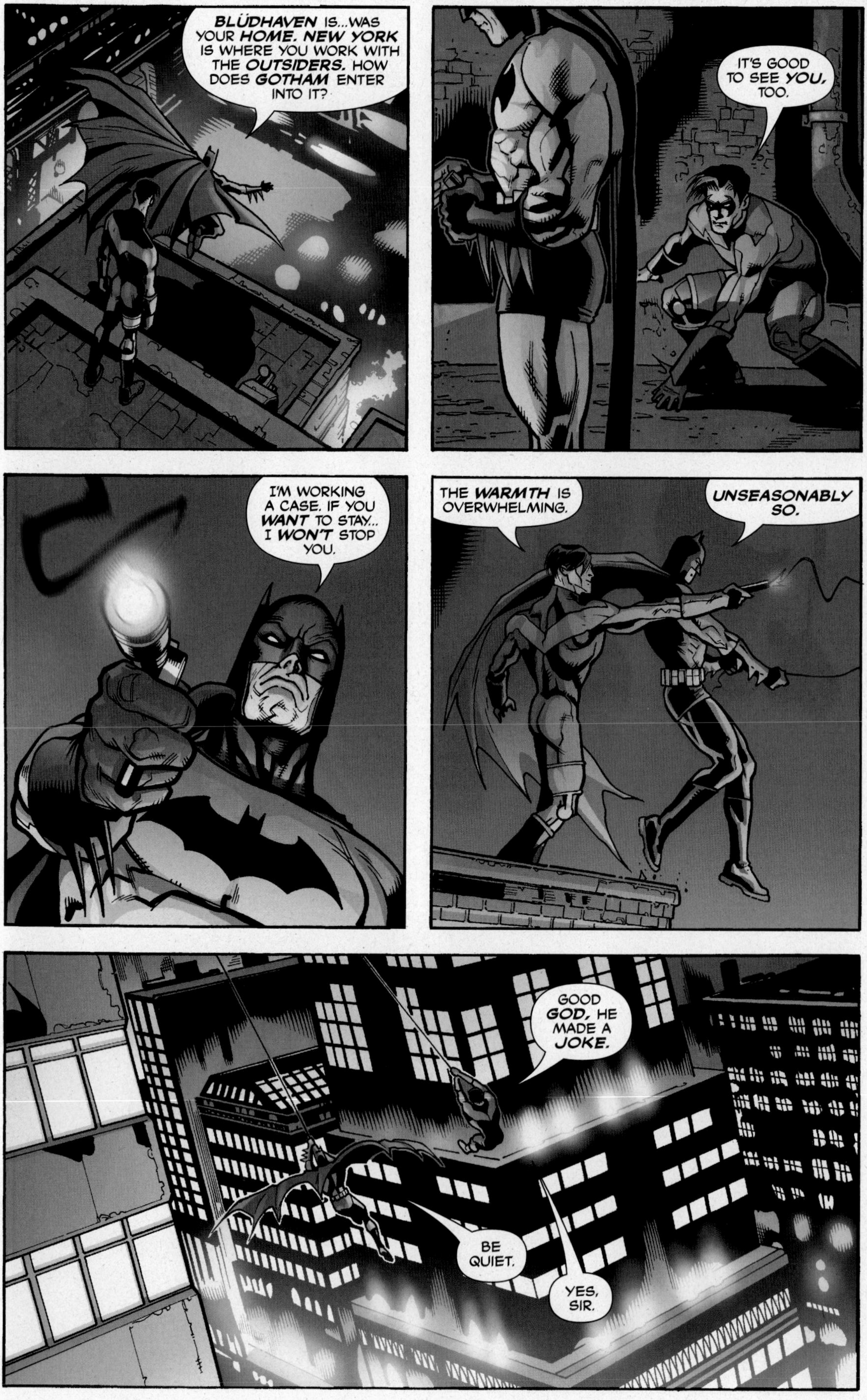
BLÜDHAVEN IS...WAS YOUR HOME. NEW YORK IS WHERE YOU WORK WITH THE OUTSIDERS. HOW DOES GOTHAM ENTER INTO IT?
IT'S GOOD TO SEE YOU, TOO.
I'M WORKING A CASE. IF YOU WANT TO STAY... I WON'T STOP YOU.
THE WARMTH IS OVERWHELMING.
UNSEASONABLY SO.
GOOD GOD, HE MADE A JOKE.
BE QUIET.
YES, SIR.

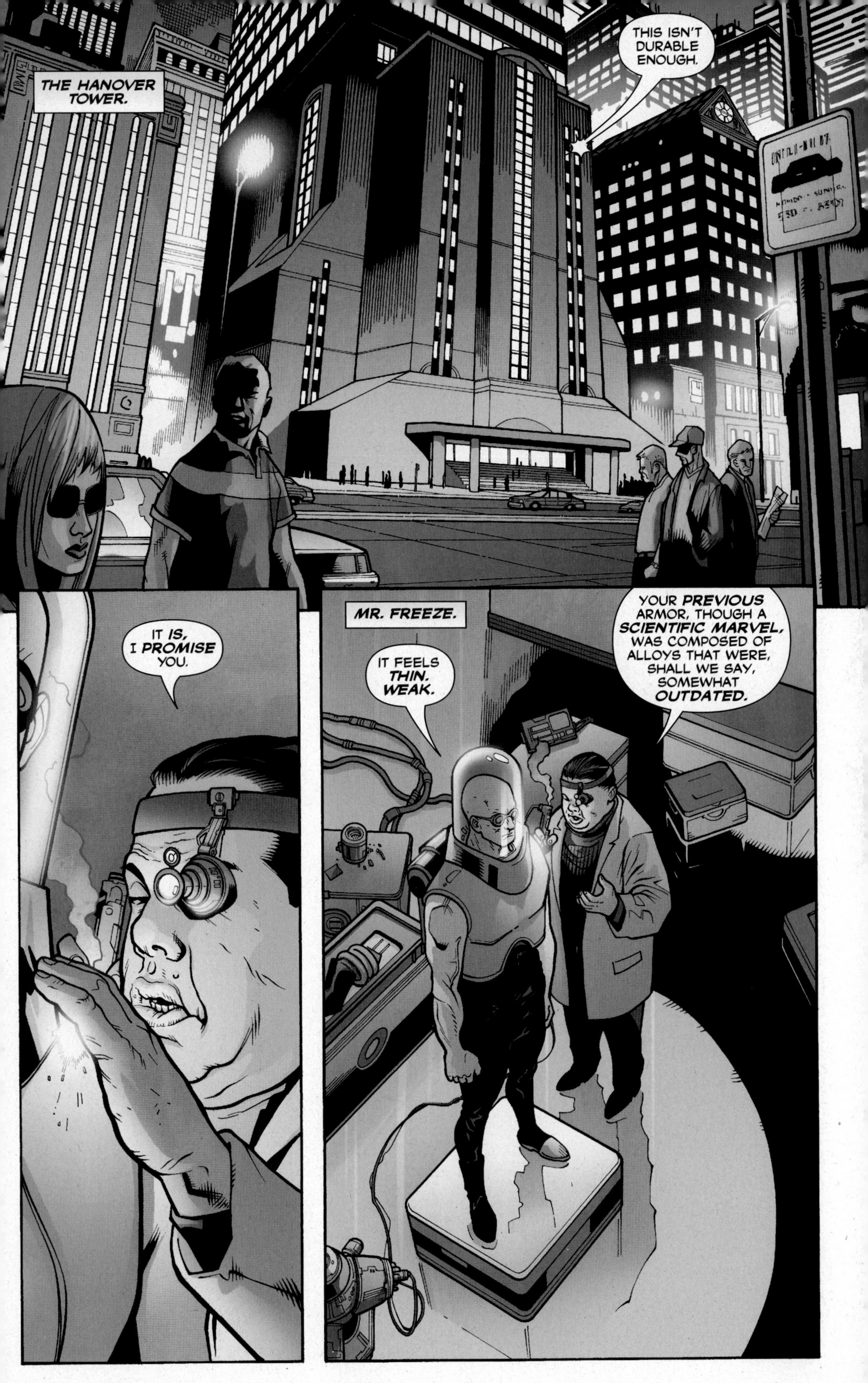
THE HANOVER TOWER.
THIS ISN'T DURABLE ENOUGH.
IT IS, I PROMISE YOU.
MR. FREEZE.
IT FEELS THIN. WEAK.
YOUR PREVIOUS ARMOR, THOUGH A SCIENTIFIC MARVEL, WAS COMPOSED OF ALLOYS THAT WERE, SHALL WE SAY, SOMEWHAT OUTDATED.

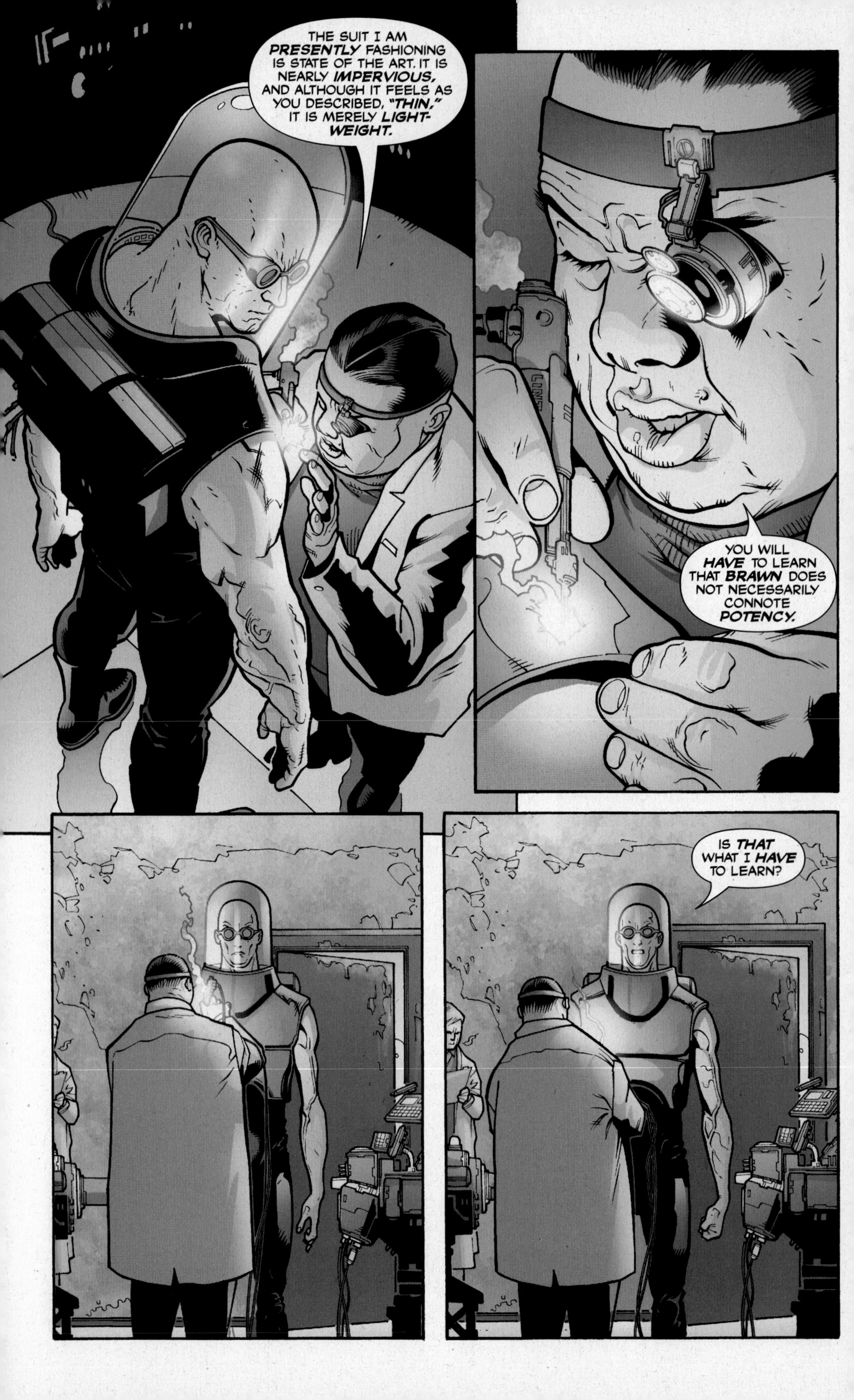
THE SUIT I AM PRESENTLY FASHIONING IS STATE OF THE ART. IT IS NEARLY IMPERVIOUS, AND ALTHOUGH IT FEELS AS YOU DESCRIBED, "THIN," IT IS MERELY LIGHT-WEIGHT.
YOU WILL HAVE TO LEARN THAT BRAWN DOES NOT NECESSARILY CONNOTE POTENCY.
IS THAT WHAT I HAVE TO LEARN?

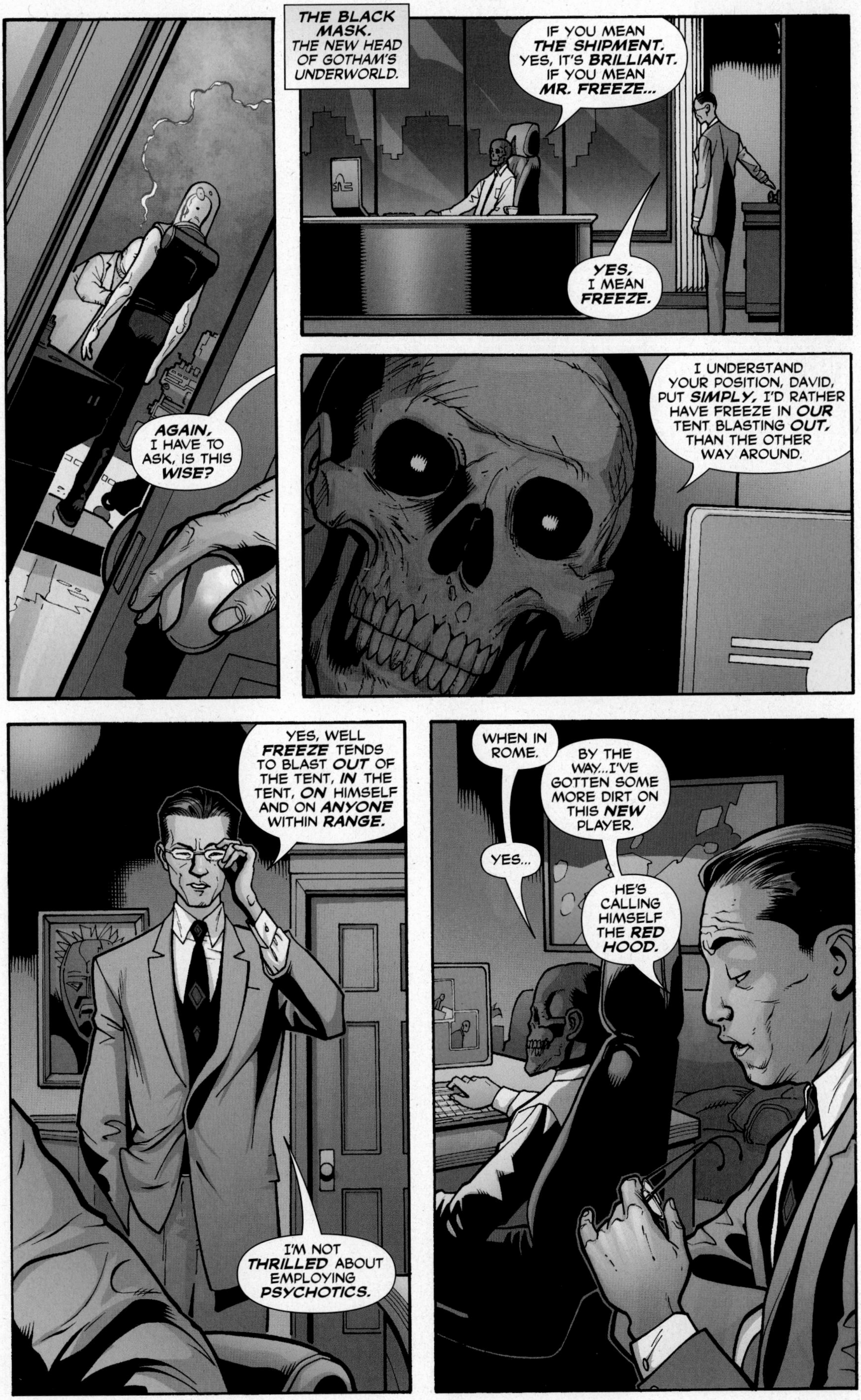
THE BLACK MASK. THE NEW HEAD OF GOTHAM'S UNDERWORLD.
IF YOU MEAN THE SHIPMENT. YES, IT'S BRILLIANT. IF YOU MEAN MR. FREEZE...
YES, I MEAN FREEZE.
AGAIN, I HAVE TO ASK, IS THIS WISE?
I UNDERSTAND YOUR POSITION, DAVID, PUT SIMPLY, I'D RATHER HAVE FREEZE IN OUR TENT BLASTING OUT, THAN THE OTHER WAY AROUND.
YES, WELL FREEZE TENDS TO BLAST OUT OF THE TENT, IN THE TENT, ON HIMSELF AND ON ANYONE WITHIN RANGE.
I'M NOT THRILLED ABOUT EMPLOYING PSYCHOTICS.
WHEN IN ROME.
BY THE WAY...I'VE GOTTEN SOME MORE DIRT ON THIS NEW PLAYER.
YES...
HE'S CALLING HIMSELF THE RED HOOD.

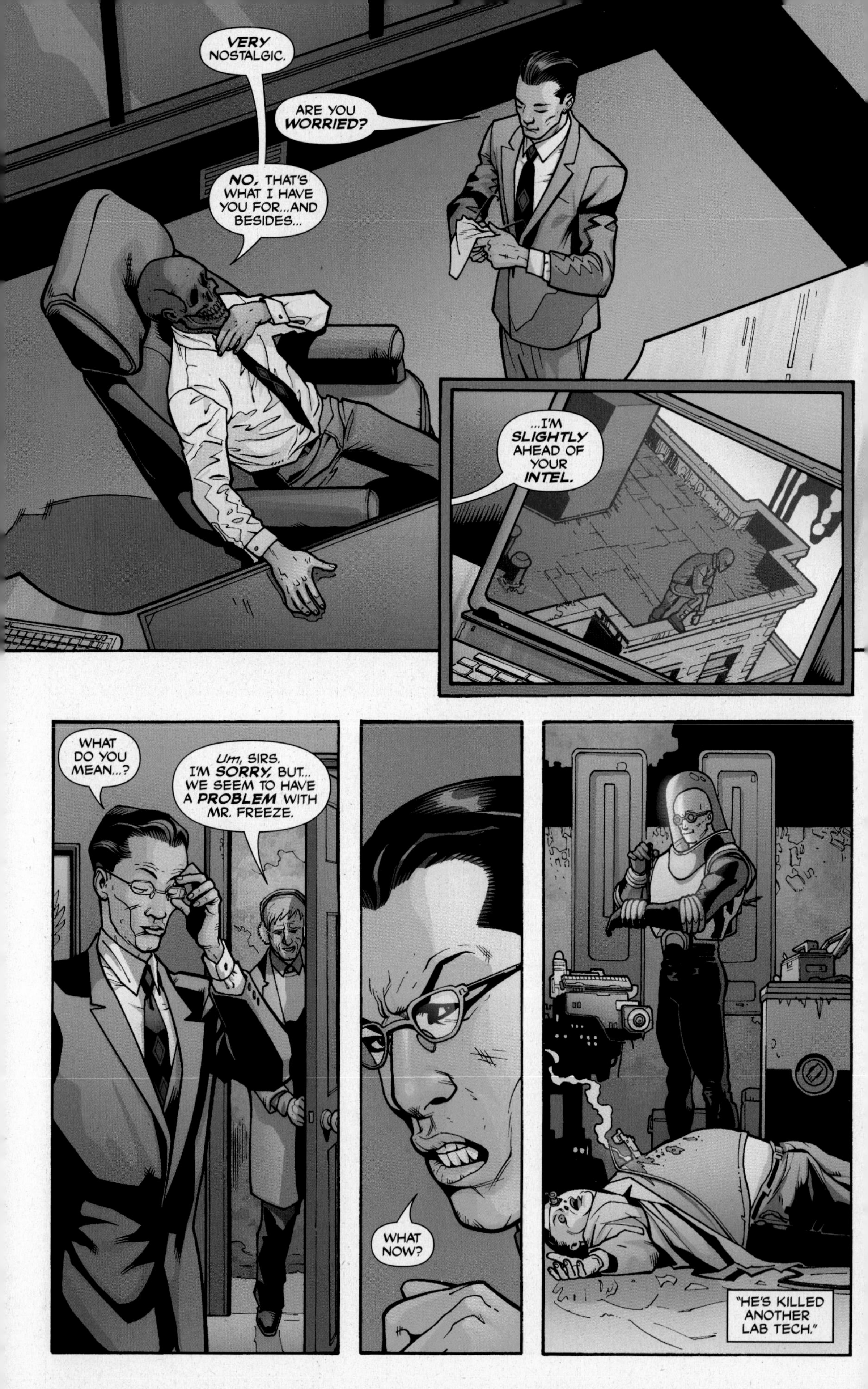
VERY NOSTALGIC.
ARE YOU WORRIED?
NO, THAT'S WHAT I HAVE YOU FOR...AND BESIDES...
...I'M SLIGHTLY AHEAD OF YOUR INTEL.
WHAT DO YOU MEAN...?
Um, SIRS. I'M SORRY, BUT... WE SEEM TO HAVE A PROBLEM WITH MR. FREEZE.
WHAT NOW?
"HE'S KILLED ANOTHER LAB TECH."

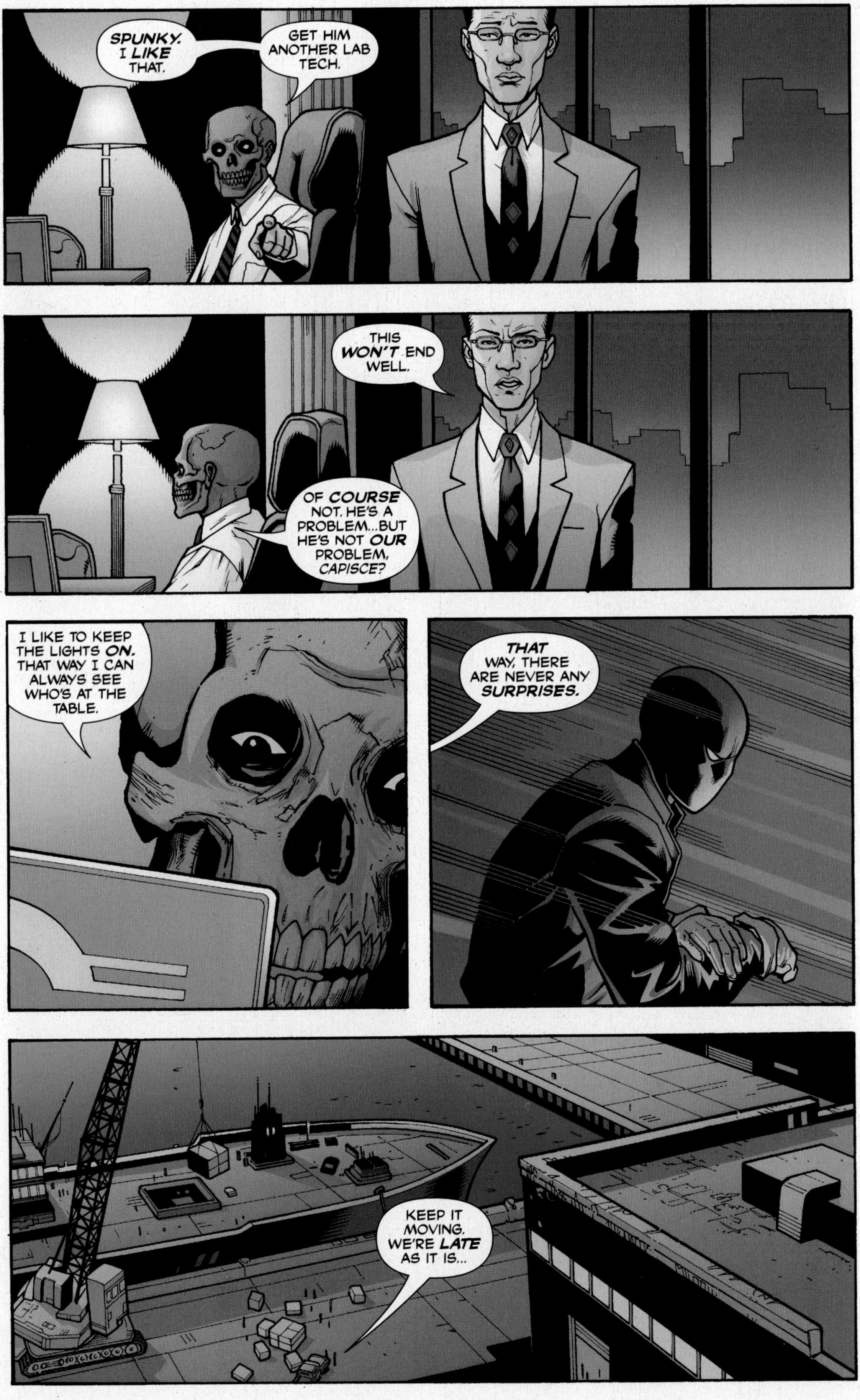
SPUNKY. I LIKE THAT.
GET HIM ANOTHER LAB TECH.
THIS WON'T END WELL.
OF COURSE NOT. HE'S A PROBLEM...BUT HE'S NOT OUR PROBLEM, CAPISCE?
I LIKE TO KEEP THE LIGHTS ON. THAT WAY I CAN ALWAYS SEE WHO'S AT THE TABLE.
THAT WAY, THERE ARE NEVER ANY SURPRISES.
KEEP IT MOVING. WE'RE LATE AS IT IS...

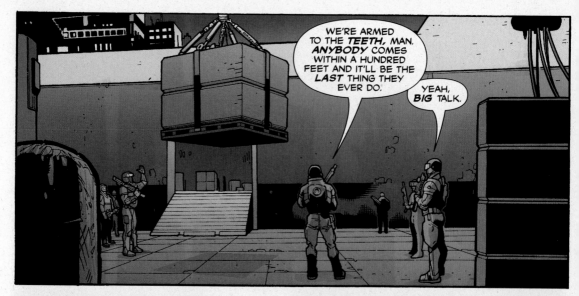

WE'RE ARMED TO THE *TEETH,* MAN. *ANYBODY* COMES WITHIN A HUNDRED FEET AND IT'LL BE THE *LAST* THING THEY EVER DO.

YEAH, *BIG* TALK.

HELL, YES. *BIG* TALK, *BIG* GUN, BIG BA--

HEY--!

YOU'RE *ALL* TOO *LOUD* AND TOO *STUPID.*

THE WORD WAS SOMETHING **BIG** WAS COMING IN.

TZOT TZOT TZOT

THAT'S **ALL** WE COULD GET. IT WAS **BIG**.

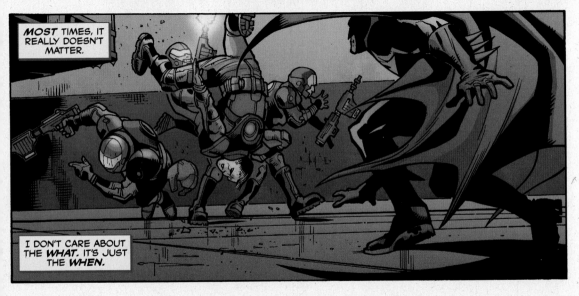

MOST TIMES, IT REALLY DOESN'T MATTER.

I DON'T CARE ABOUT THE *WHAT.* IT'S JUST THE *WHEN.*

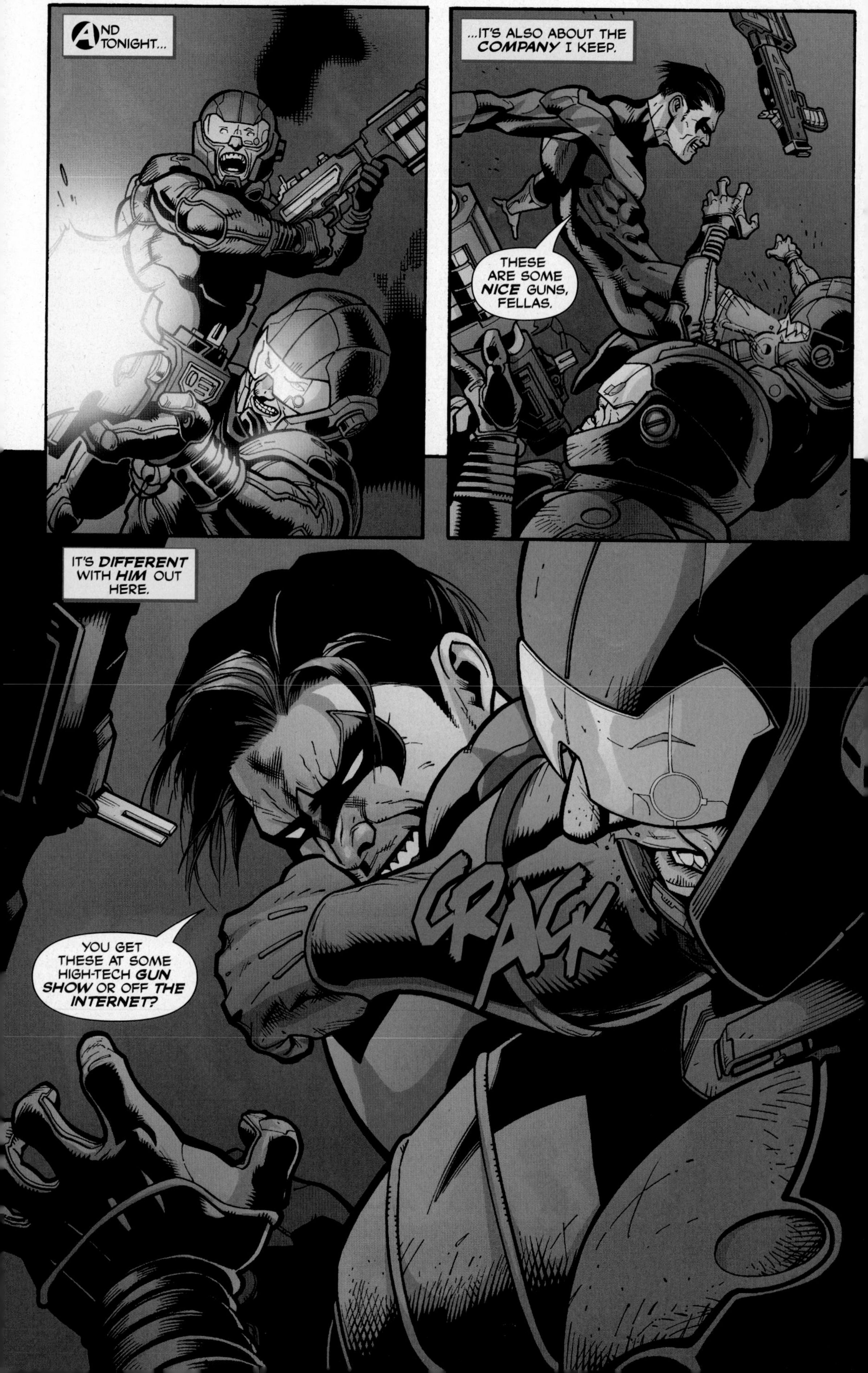

AND TONIGHT...
...IT'S ALSO ABOUT THE COMPANY I KEEP.
THESE ARE SOME NICE GUNS, FELLAS.
IT'S DIFFERENT WITH HIM OUT HERE.
YOU GET THESE AT SOME HIGH-TECH GUN SHOW OR OFF THE INTERNET?
CRACK

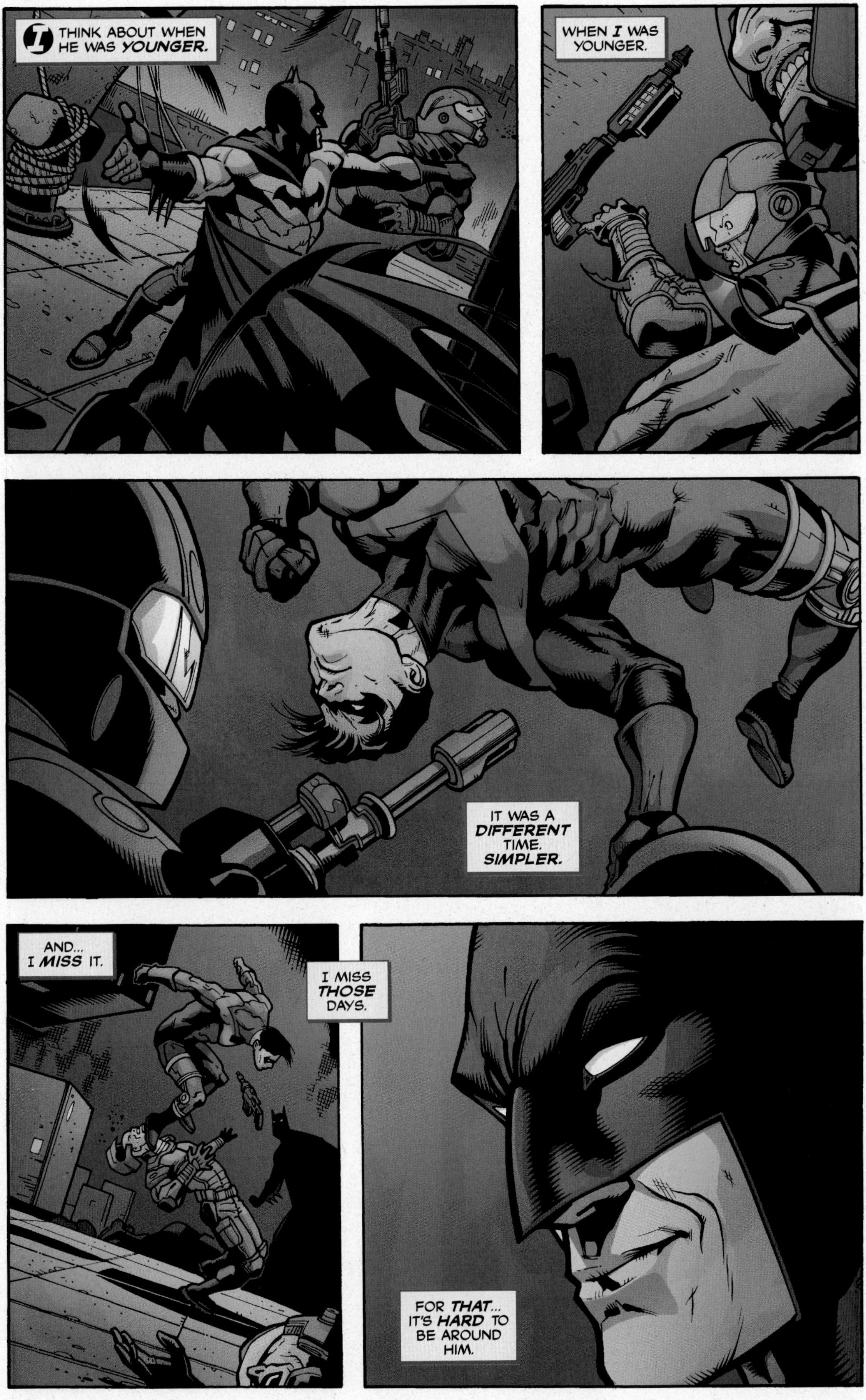
I THINK ABOUT WHEN HE WAS YOUNGER.
WHEN I WAS YOUNGER.
IT WAS A DIFFERENT TIME. SIMPLER.
AND... I MISS IT.
I MISS THOSE DAYS.
FOR THAT... IT'S HARD TO BE AROUND HIM.

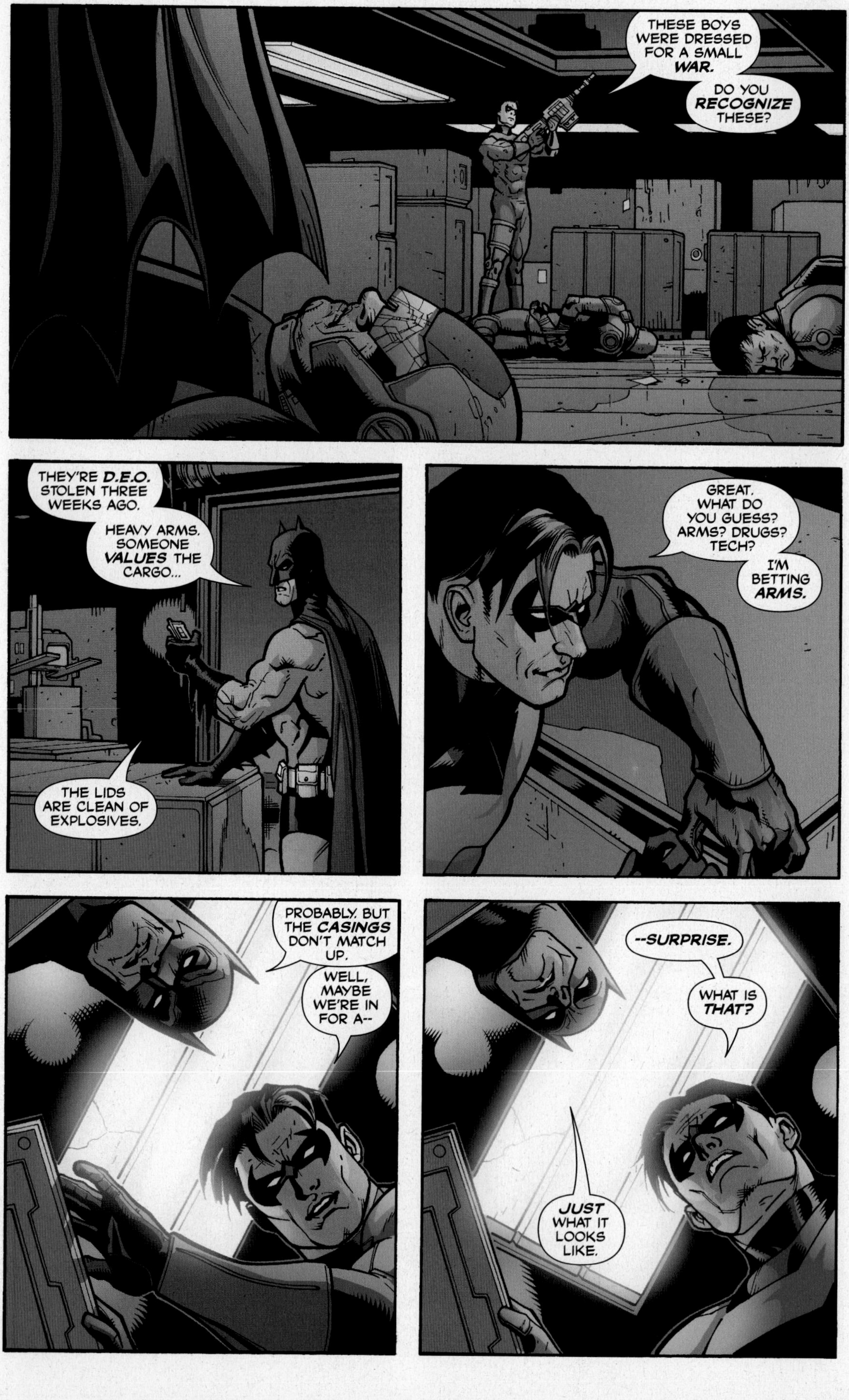
THESE BOYS WERE DRESSED FOR A SMALL WAR.
DO YOU RECOGNIZE THESE?
THEY'RE D.E.O. STOLEN THREE WEEKS AGO.
HEAVY ARMS. SOMEONE VALUES THE CARGO...
THE LIDS ARE CLEAN OF EXPLOSIVES.
GREAT. WHAT DO YOU GUESS? ARMS? DRUGS? TECH?
I'M BETTING ARMS.
PROBABLY. BUT THE CASINGS DON'T MATCH UP.
WELL, MAYBE WE'RE IN FOR A--
--SURPRISE.
WHAT IS THAT?
JUST WHAT IT LOOKS LIKE.

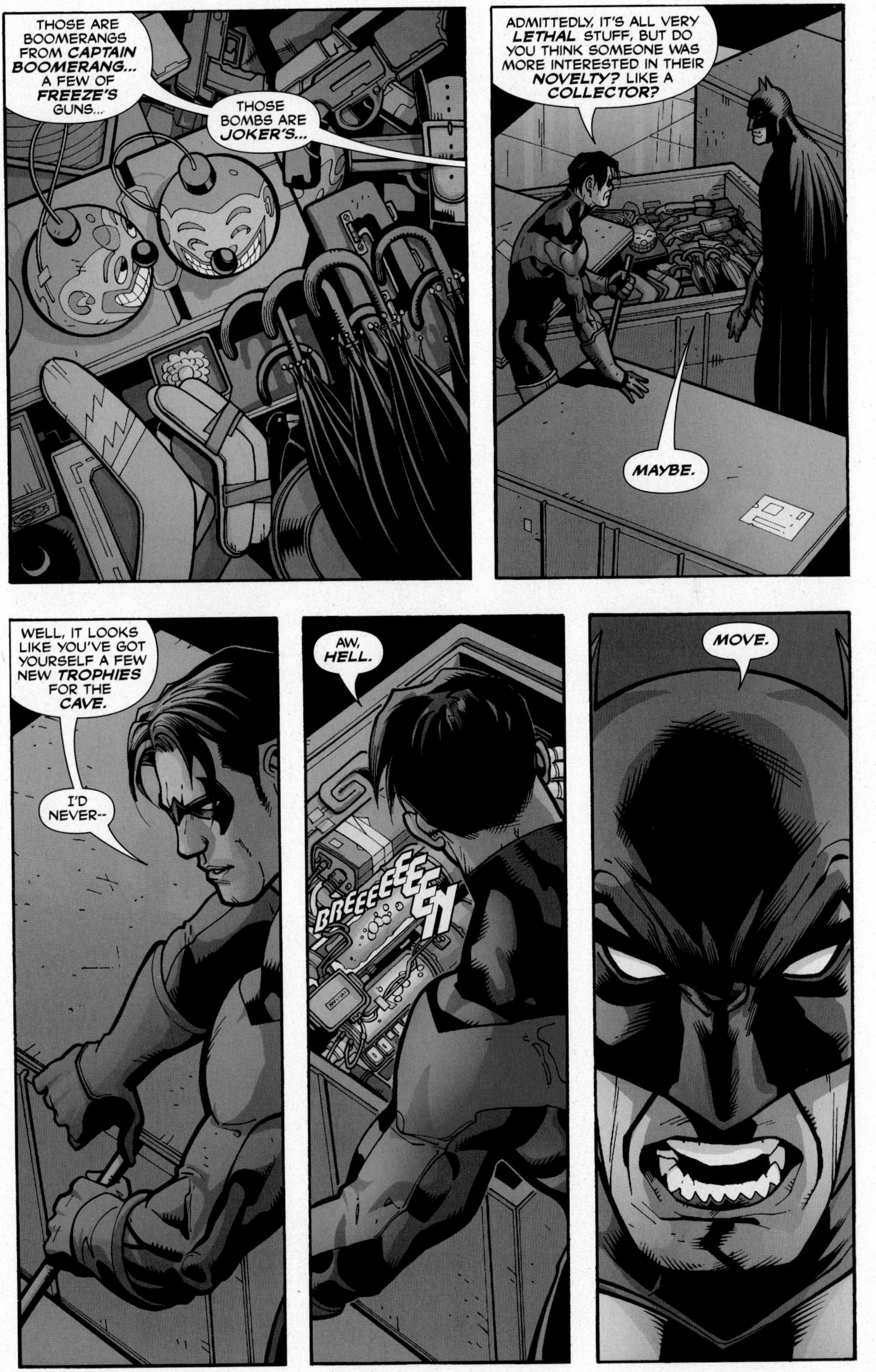
THOSE ARE BOOMERANGS FROM CAPTAIN BOOMERANG... A FEW OF FREEZE'S GUNS...
THOSE BOMBS ARE JOKER'S...
ADMITTEDLY, IT'S ALL VERY LETHAL STUFF, BUT DO YOU THINK SOMEONE WAS MORE INTERESTED IN THEIR NOVELTY? LIKE A COLLECTOR?
MAYBE.
WELL, IT LOOKS LIKE YOU'VE GOT YOURSELF A FEW NEW TROPHIES FOR THE CAVE.
I'D NEVER--
AW, HELL.
BREEEEEEEEN
MOVE.

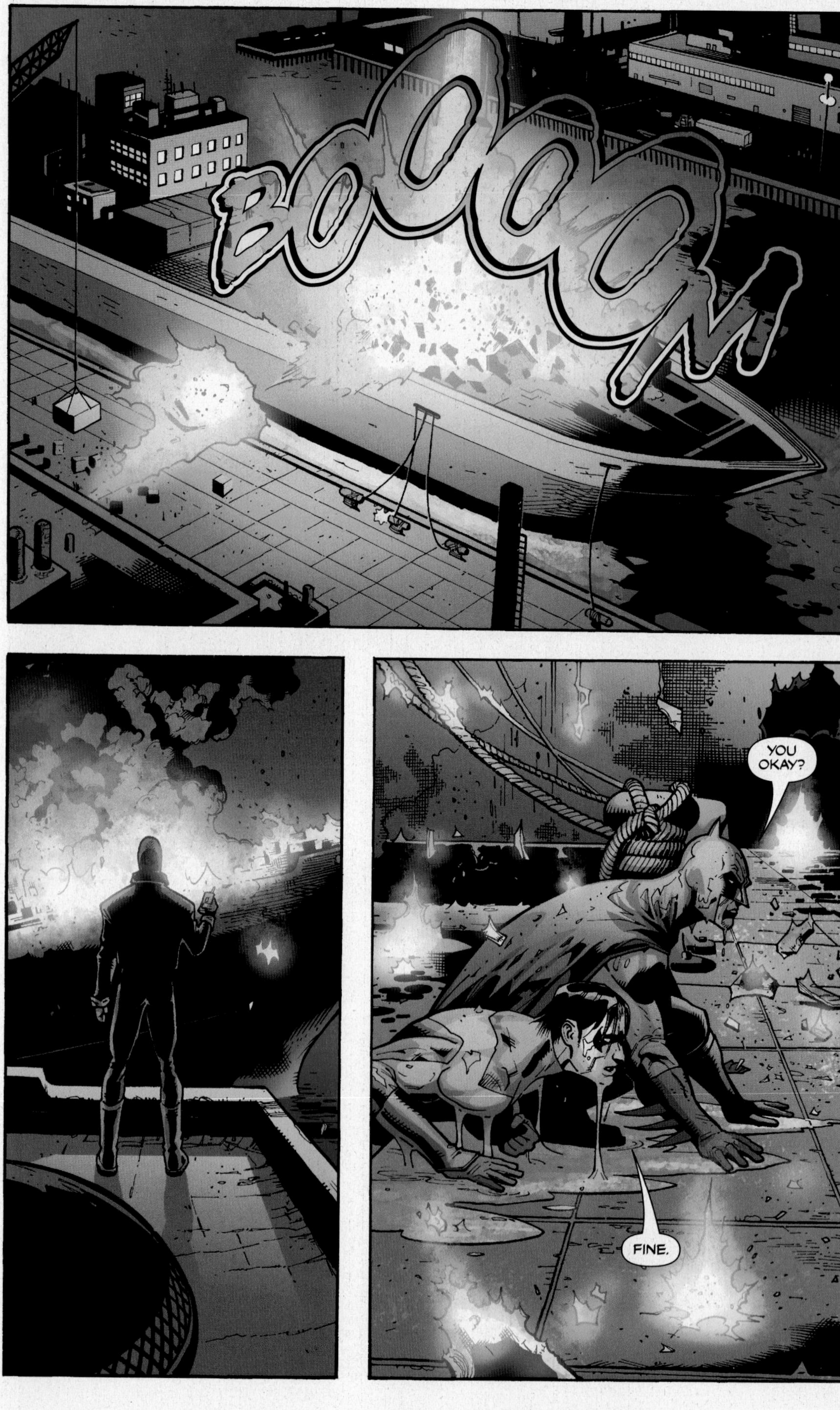
BOOOOOM
YOU OKAY?
FINE.

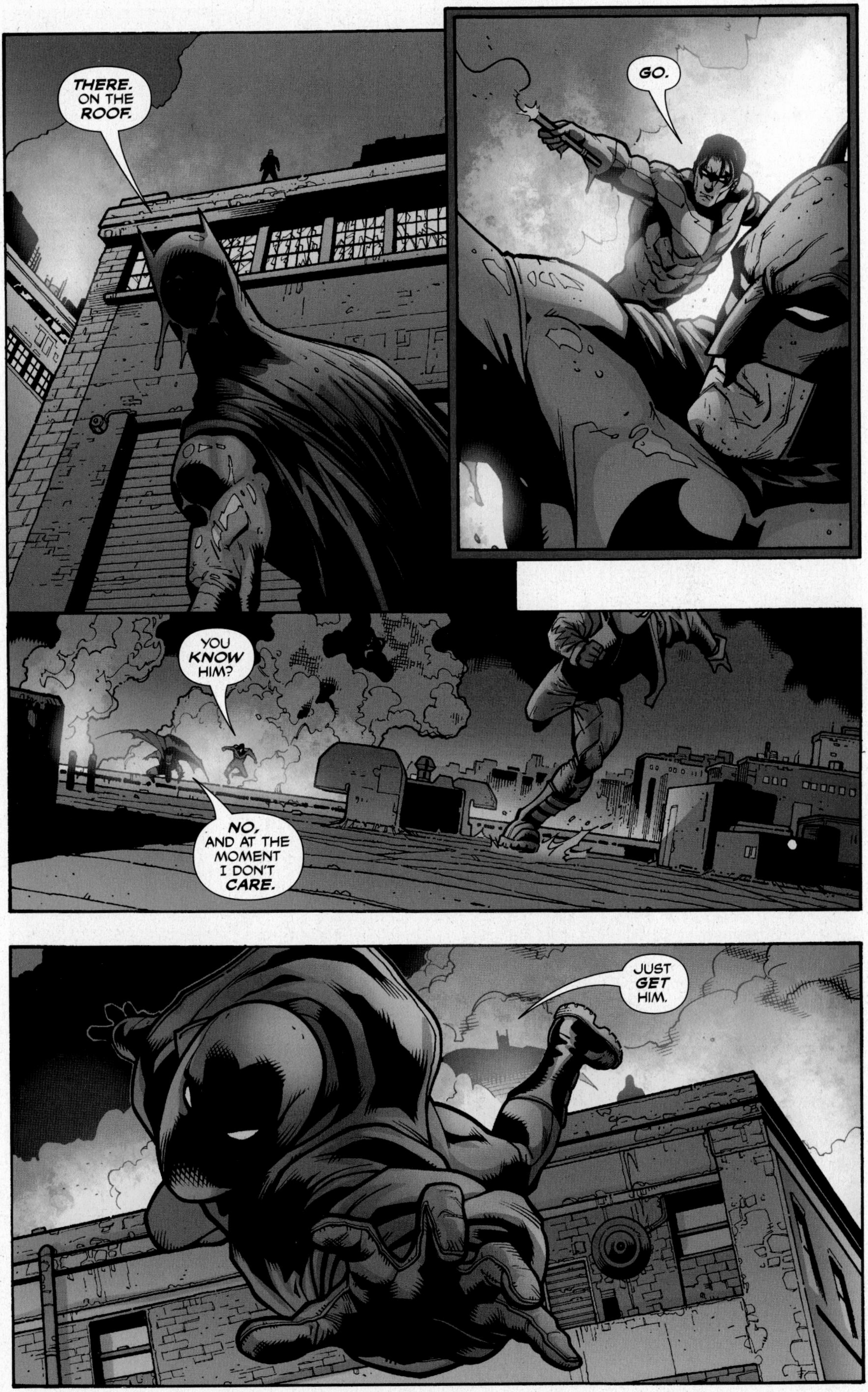
THERE. ON THE ROOF.
GO.
YOU KNOW HIM?
NO, AND AT THE MOMENT I DON'T CARE.
JUST GET HIM.

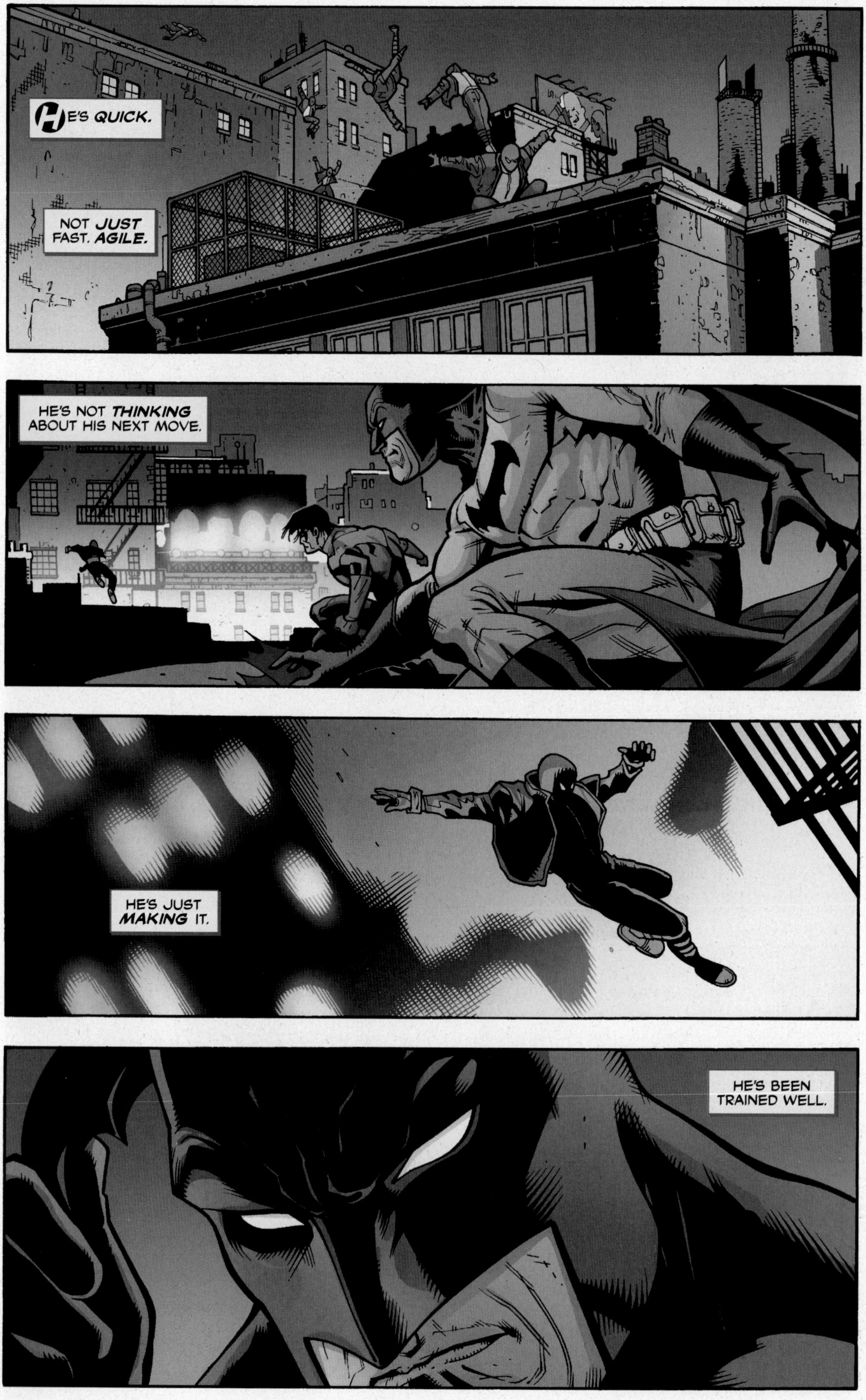
HE'S QUICK.
NOT JUST FAST. AGILE.
HE'S NOT THINKING ABOUT HIS NEXT MOVE.
HE'S JUST MAKING IT.
HE'S BEEN TRAINED WELL.

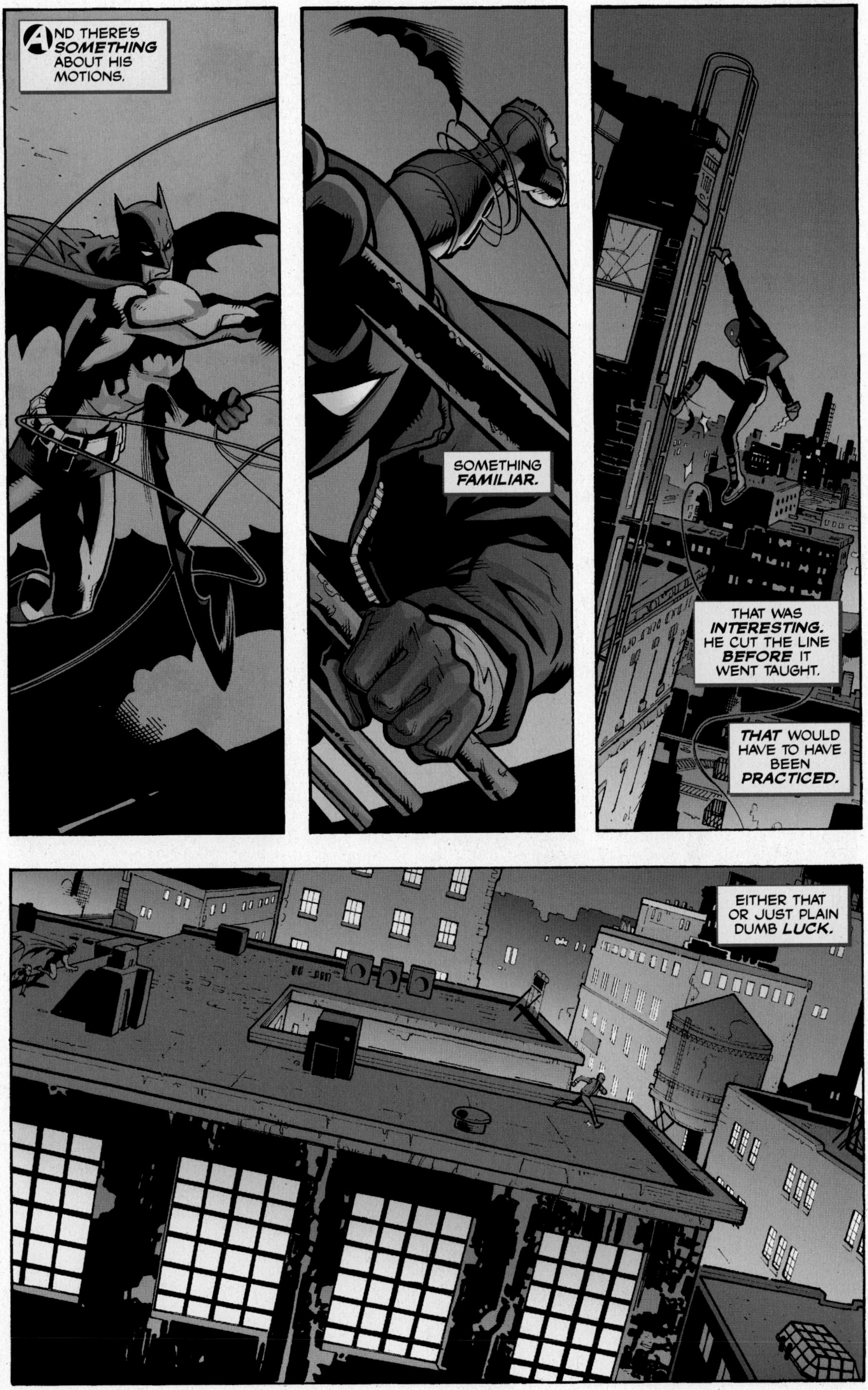
AND THERE'S SOMETHING ABOUT HIS MOTIONS.
SOMETHING FAMILIAR.
THAT WAS INTERESTING. HE CUT THE LINE BEFORE IT WENT TAUGHT.
THAT WOULD HAVE TO HAVE BEEN PRACTICED.
EITHER THAT OR JUST PLAIN DUMB LUCK.

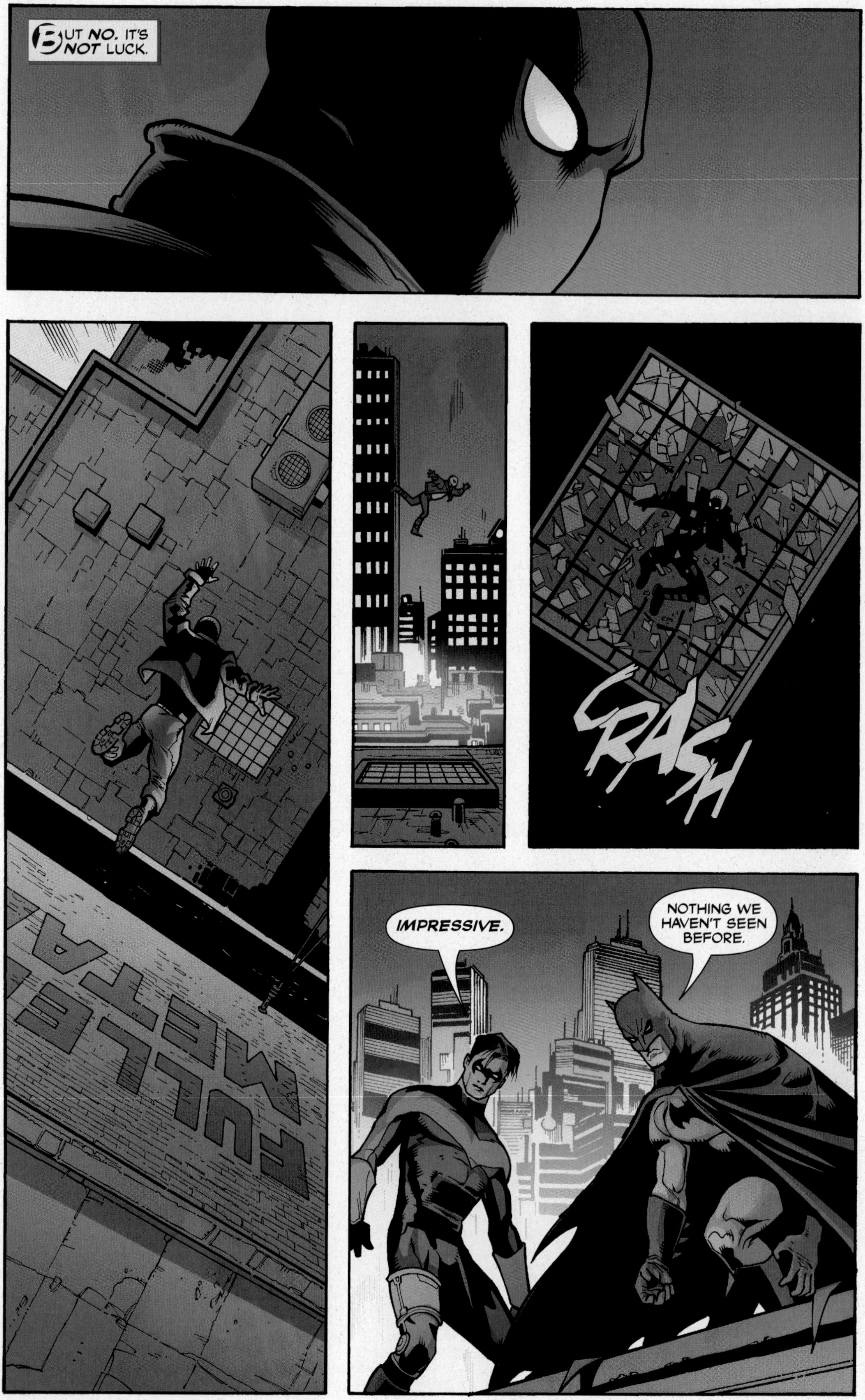
BUT NO. IT'S NOT LUCK.
CRASH
IMPRESSIVE.
NOTHING WE HAVEN'T SEEN BEFORE.

OR *DONE* BEFORE.

GOT THAT RIGHT.

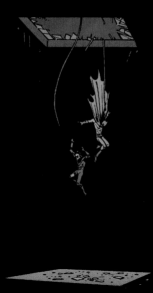

THAT HURT...

WHUMP

STAY SHARP.

OH, BOY.

STAY... *SHARP...*

W E HEARD THE SHIPMENT COMING WAS DELIVERING SOMETHING *BIG.*

I DIDN'T THINK *WEAPONS* FROM *ROGUE VILLAINS* WOULD BE CONSIDERED AS SUCH...

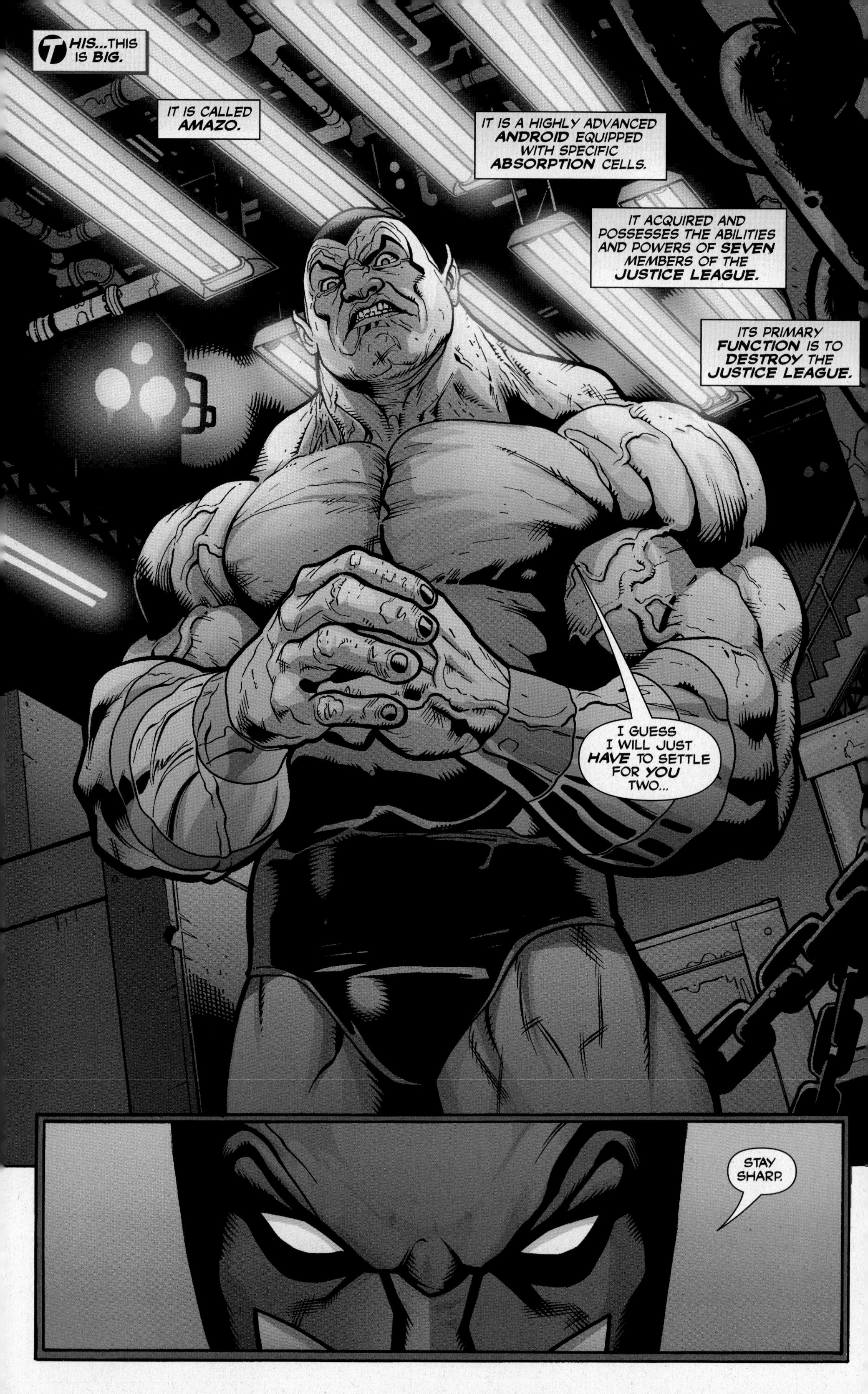
THIS...THIS IS BIG.
IT IS CALLED AMAZO.
IT IS A HIGHLY ADVANCED ANDROID EQUIPPED WITH SPECIFIC ABSORPTION CELLS.
IT ACQUIRED AND POSSESSES THE ABILITIES AND POWERS OF SEVEN MEMBERS OF THE JUSTICE LEAGUE.
ITS PRIMARY FUNCTION IS TO DESTROY THE JUSTICE LEAGUE.
I GUESS I WILL JUST HAVE TO SETTLE FOR YOU TWO...
STAY SHARP.

BATMAN 637 Cover by Matt Wagner

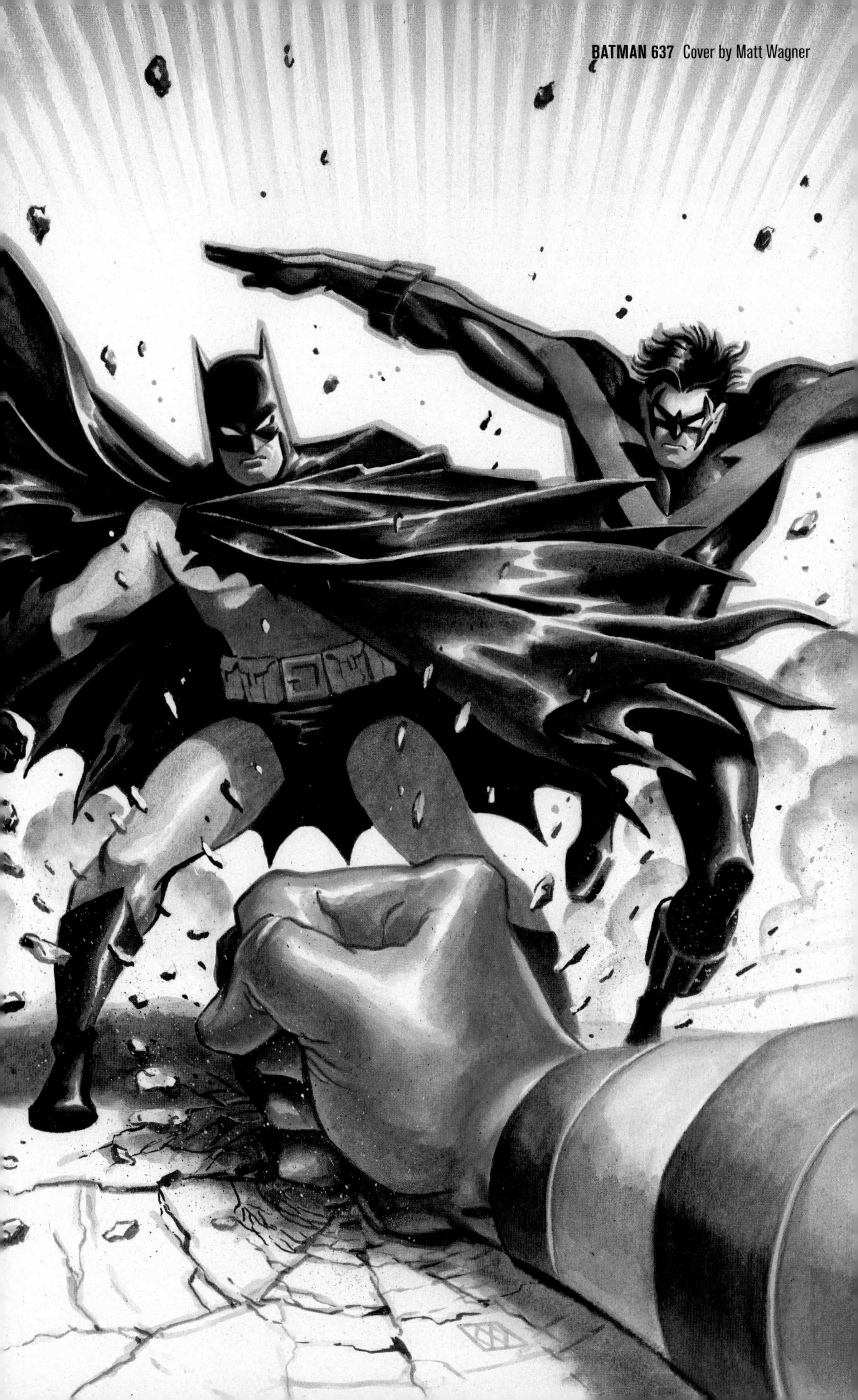

CHAPTER 3

OVER-NIGHT DELIVERIES

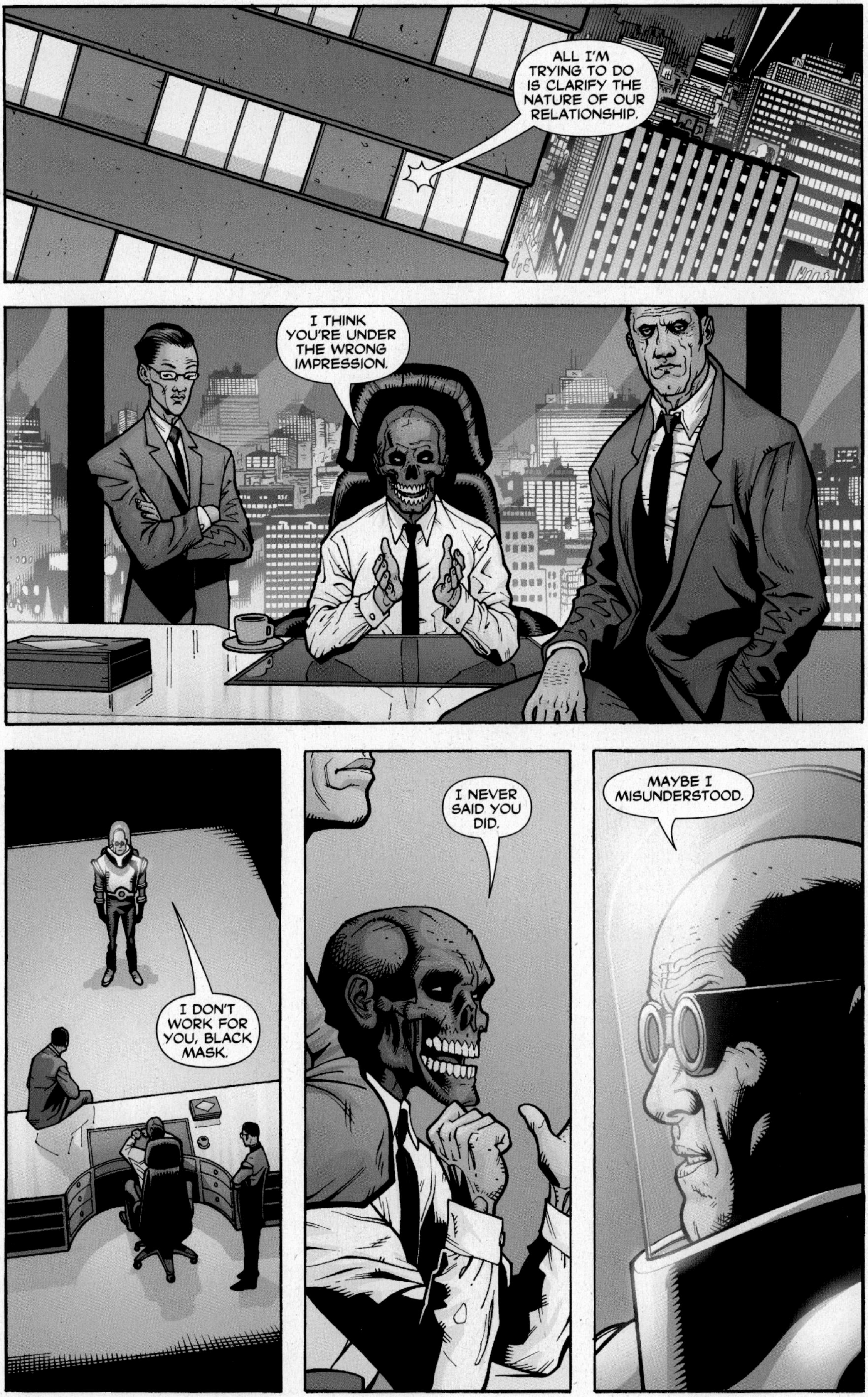
ALL I'M TRYING TO DO IS CLARIFY THE NATURE OF OUR RELATIONSHIP.
I THINK YOU'RE UNDER THE WRONG IMPRESSION.
I DON'T WORK FOR YOU, BLACK MASK.
I NEVER SAID YOU DID.
MAYBE I MISUNDERSTOOD.

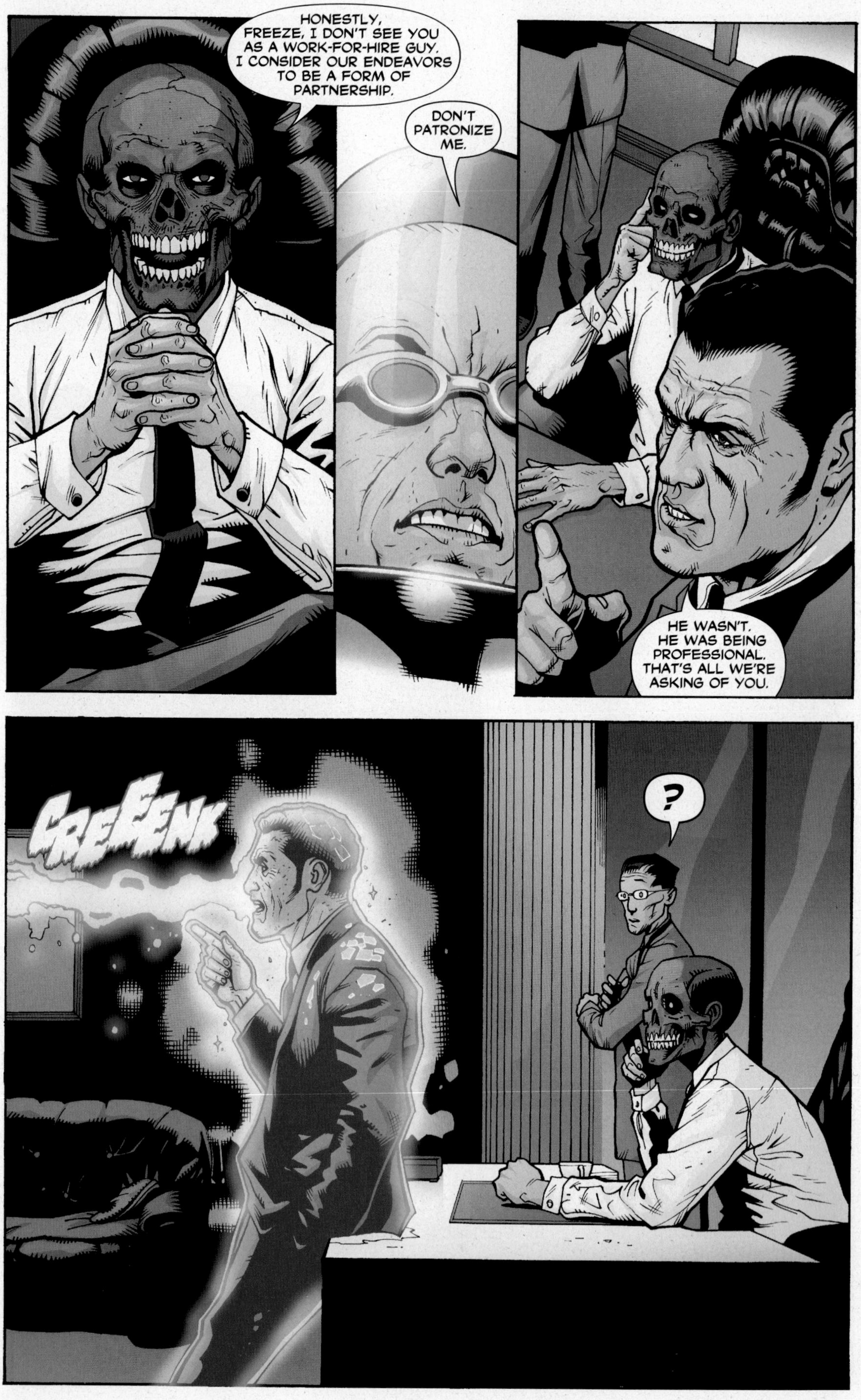
HONESTLY, FREEZE, I DON'T SEE YOU AS A WORK-FOR-HIRE GUY. I CONSIDER OUR ENDEAVORS TO BE A FORM OF PARTNERSHIP.
DON'T PATRONIZE ME.
HE WASN'T. HE WAS BEING PROFESSIONAL. THAT'S ALL WE'RE ASKING OF YOU.
CREEENK
?

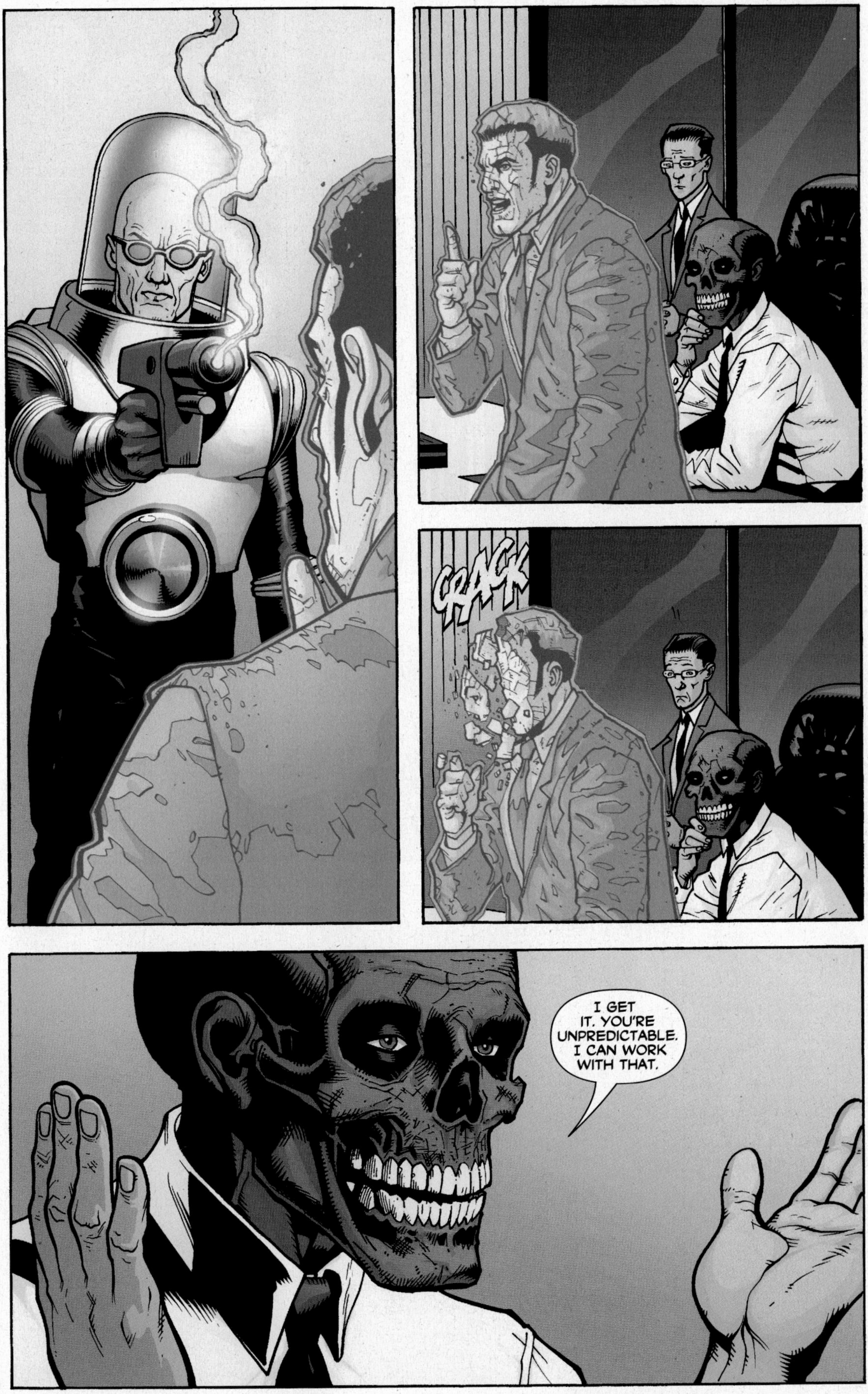
CRACK
I GET IT. YOU'RE UNPREDICTABLE. I CAN WORK WITH THAT.

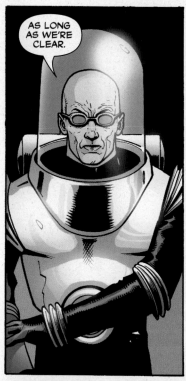

AS LONG AS WE'RE CLEAR.

AS CRYSTAL.

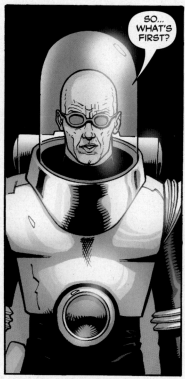

SO... WHAT'S FIRST?

WE HAD A PARTICULAR SHIPMENT COME IN. I WANT TO MAKE SURE THAT IT GETS TO US IN A TIMELY FASHION.

I WAS JUST COMING TO TELL YOU ABOUT THAT...

...NO ONE'S CALLED IN TO CONFIRM THE ARRIVAL. I THINK WE MAY ALREADY HAVE A PROBLEM...

DAMN IT... THERE'S SOME AWFULLY IMPORTANT CARGO THAT I WOULD PREFER NOT GO MISSING.

LIKE WHAT?

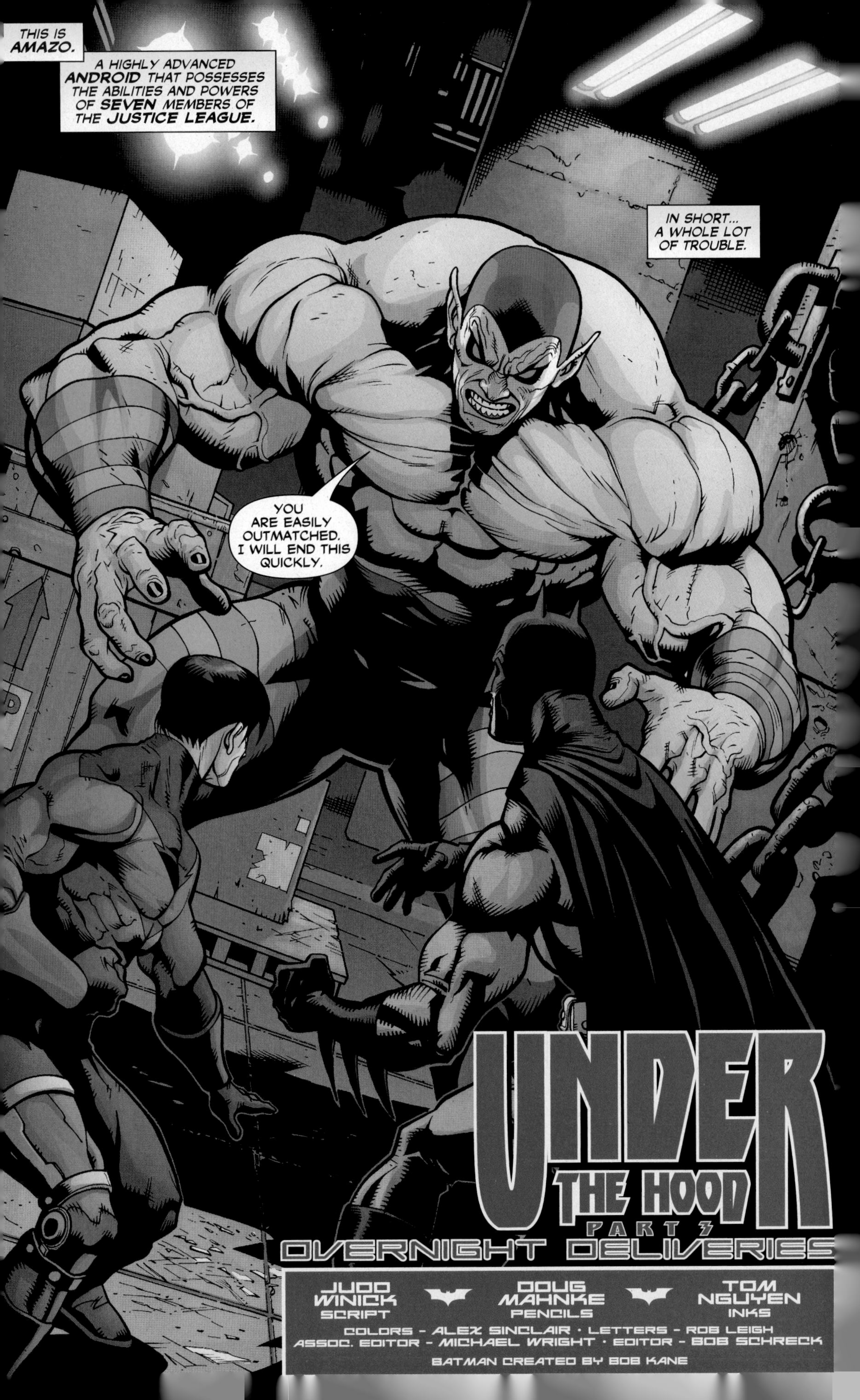
THIS IS AMAZO.
A HIGHLY ADVANCED ANDROID THAT POSSESSES THE ABILITIES AND POWERS OF SEVEN MEMBERS OF THE JUSTICE LEAGUE.
IN SHORT... A WHOLE LOT OF TROUBLE.
YOU ARE EASILY OUTMATCHED. I WILL END THIS QUICKLY.
UNDER THE HOOD
PART 3
OVERNIGHT DELIVERIES
JUDD WINICK SCRIPT
DOUG MAHNKE PENCILS
TOM NGUYEN INKS
COLORS - ALEX SINCLAIR · LETTERS - ROB LEIGH
ASSOC. EDITOR - MICHAEL WRIGHT · EDITOR - BOB SCHRECK
BATMAN CREATED BY BOB KANE

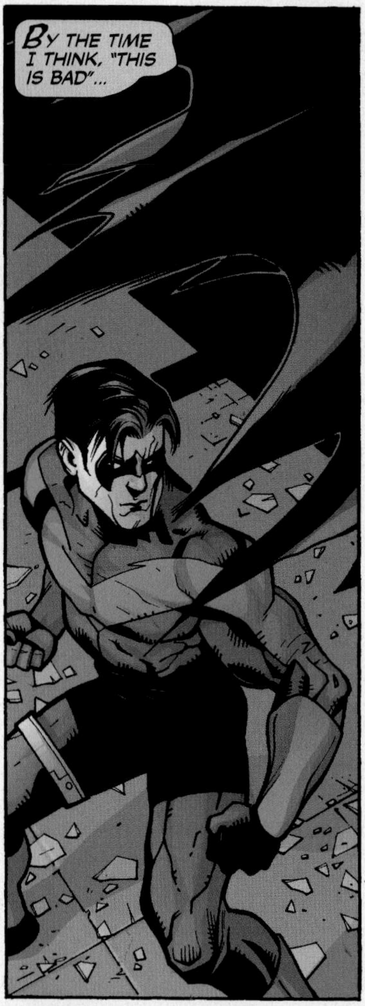
BY THE TIME I THINK, "THIS IS BAD"...
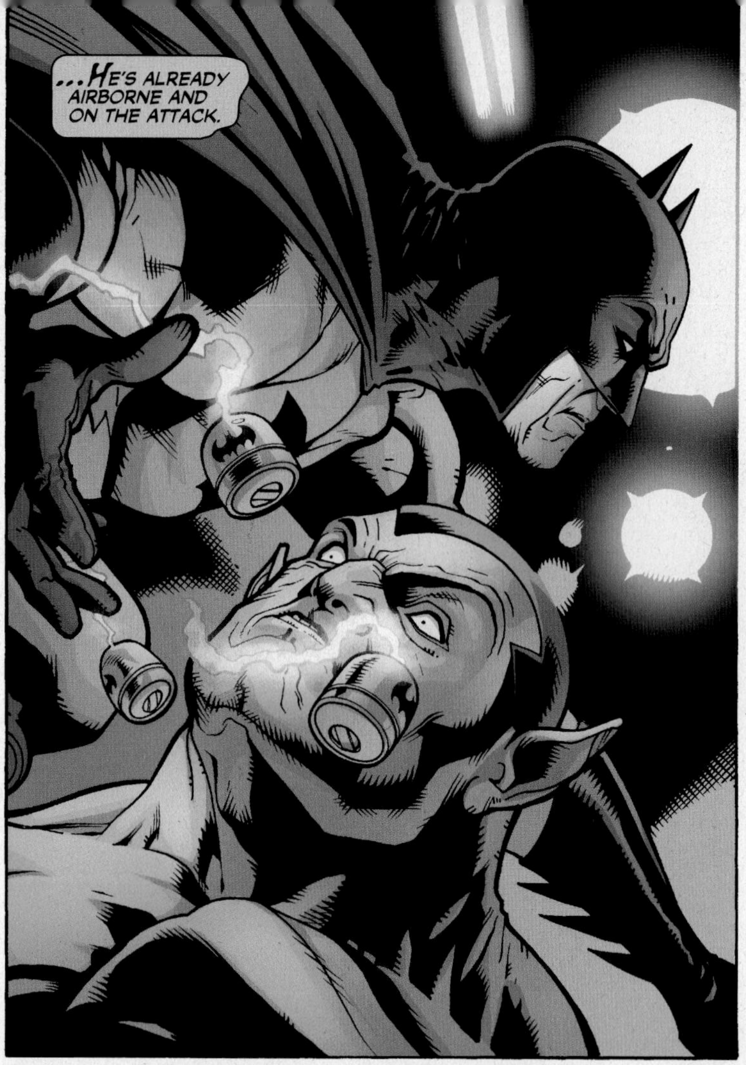
...HE'S ALREADY AIRBORNE AND ON THE ATTACK.
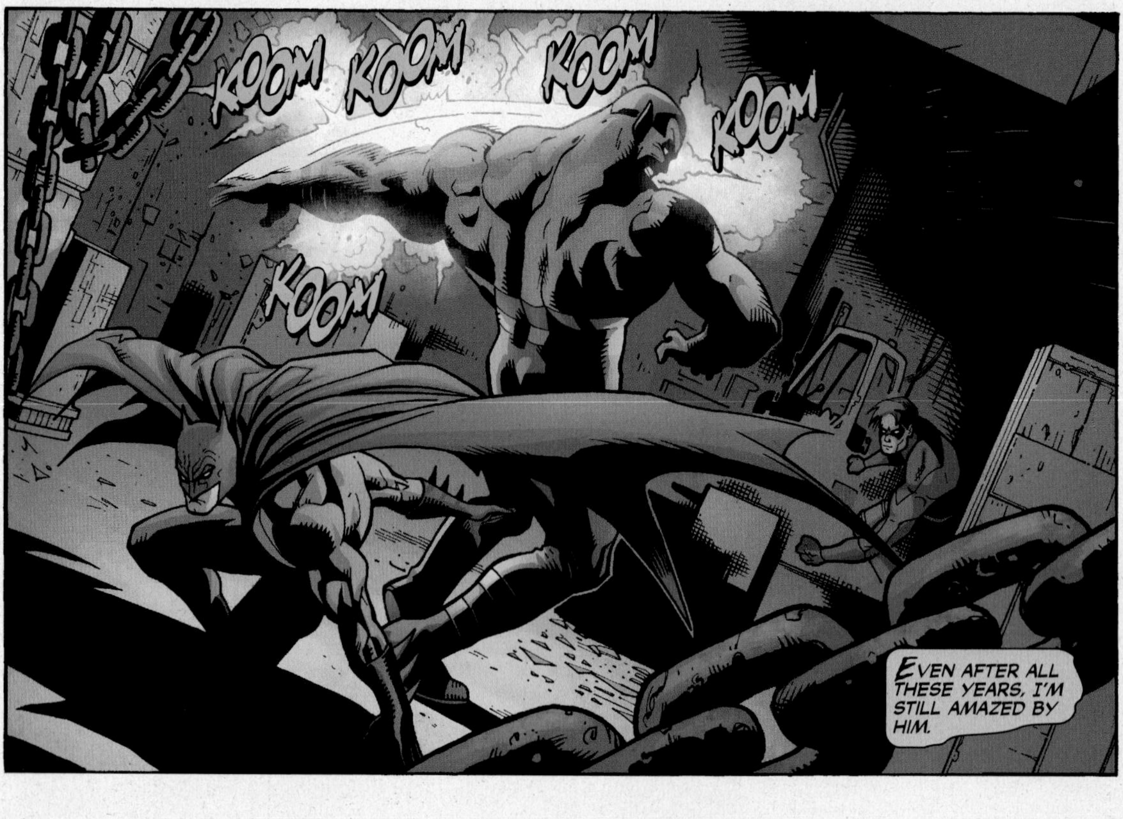
KOOM
KOOM
KOOM
KOOM
KOOM
EVEN AFTER ALL THESE YEARS, I'M STILL AMAZED BY HIM.

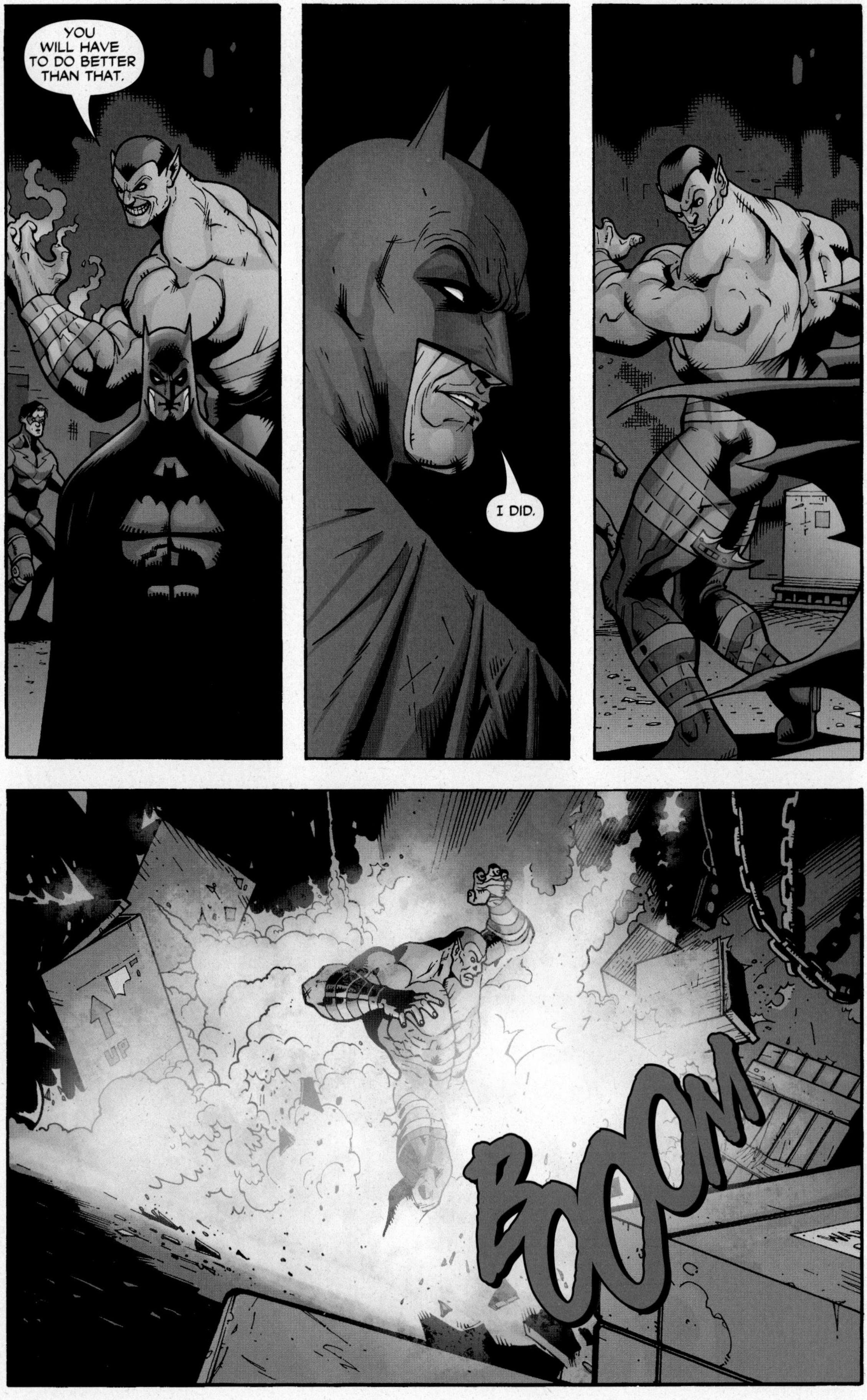
YOU WILL HAVE TO DO BETTER THAN THAT.
I DID.
UP
BOOOM

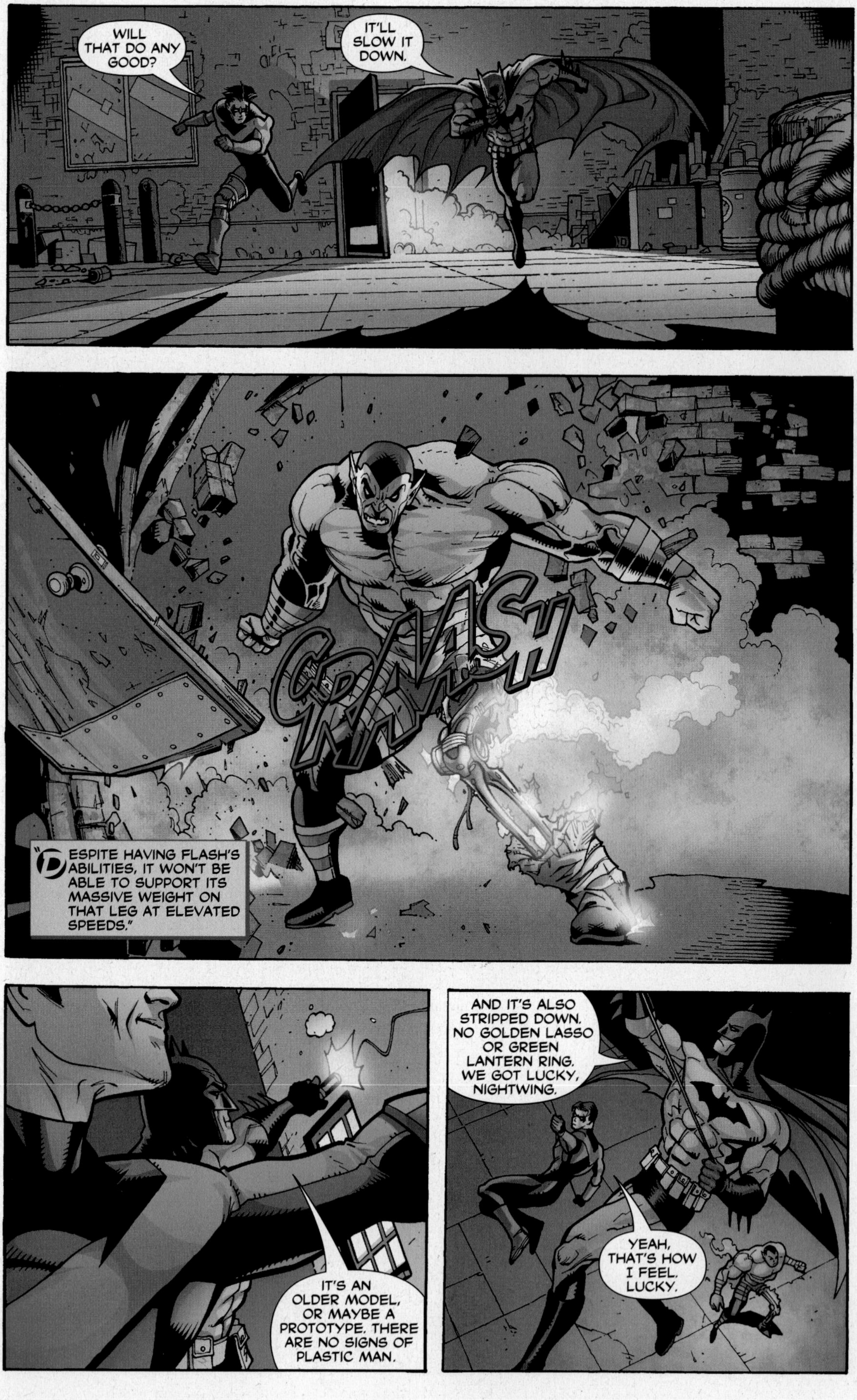
WILL THAT DO ANY GOOD?
IT'LL SLOW IT DOWN.
CRASH
"DESPITE HAVING FLASH'S ABILITIES, IT WON'T BE ABLE TO SUPPORT ITS MASSIVE WEIGHT ON THAT LEG AT ELEVATED SPEEDS."
IT'S AN OLDER MODEL, OR MAYBE A PROTOTYPE. THERE ARE NO SIGNS OF PLASTIC MAN.
AND IT'S ALSO STRIPPED DOWN. NO GOLDEN LASSO OR GREEN LANTERN RING. WE GOT LUCKY, NIGHTWING.
YEAH, THAT'S HOW I FEEL. LUCKY.

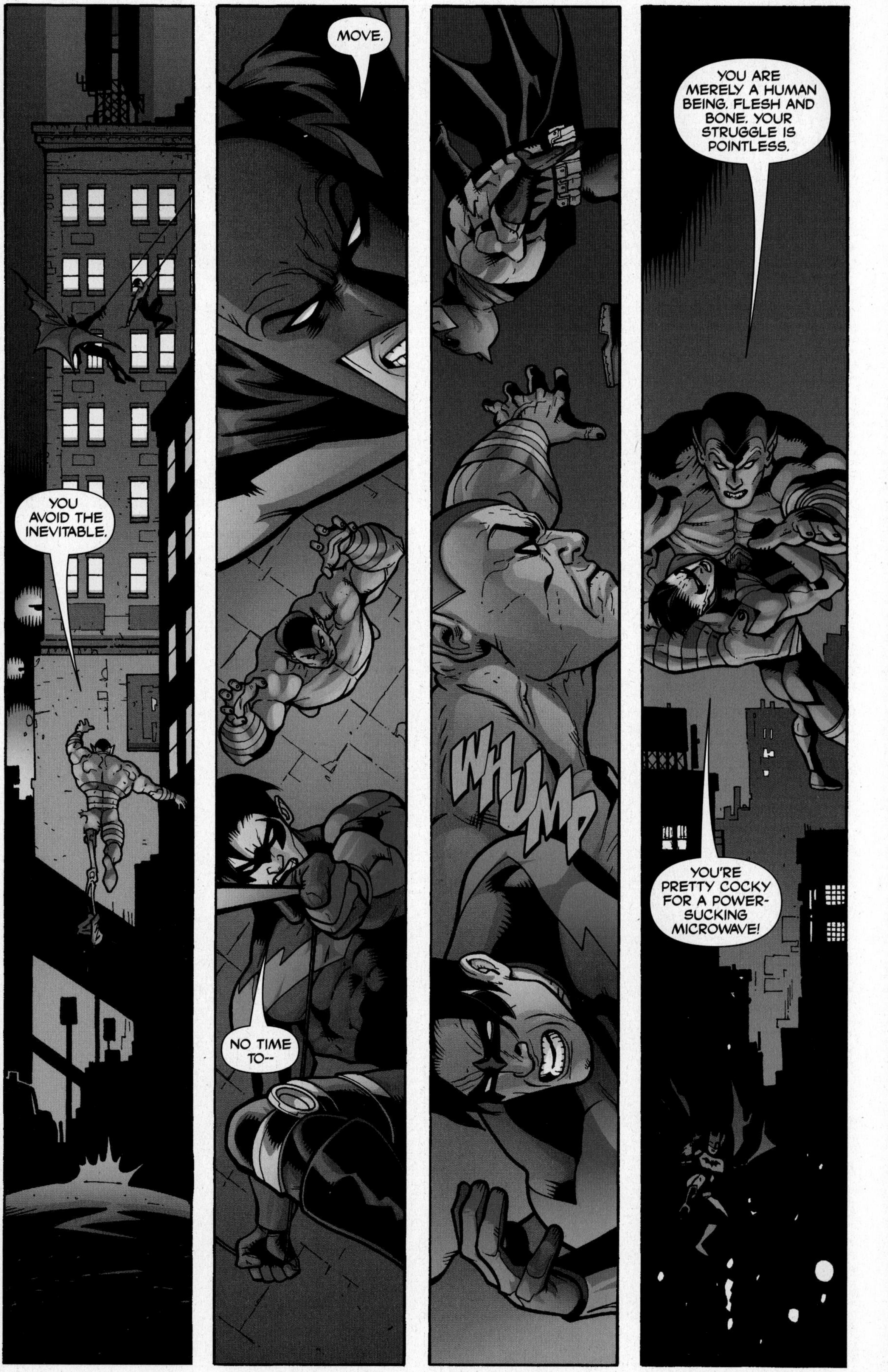
YOU AVOID THE INEVITABLE.
MOVE.
NO TIME TO--
WHUMP
YOU ARE MERELY A HUMAN BEING. FLESH AND BONE. YOUR STRUGGLE IS POINTLESS.
YOU'RE PRETTY COCKY FOR A POWER-SUCKING MICROWAVE!

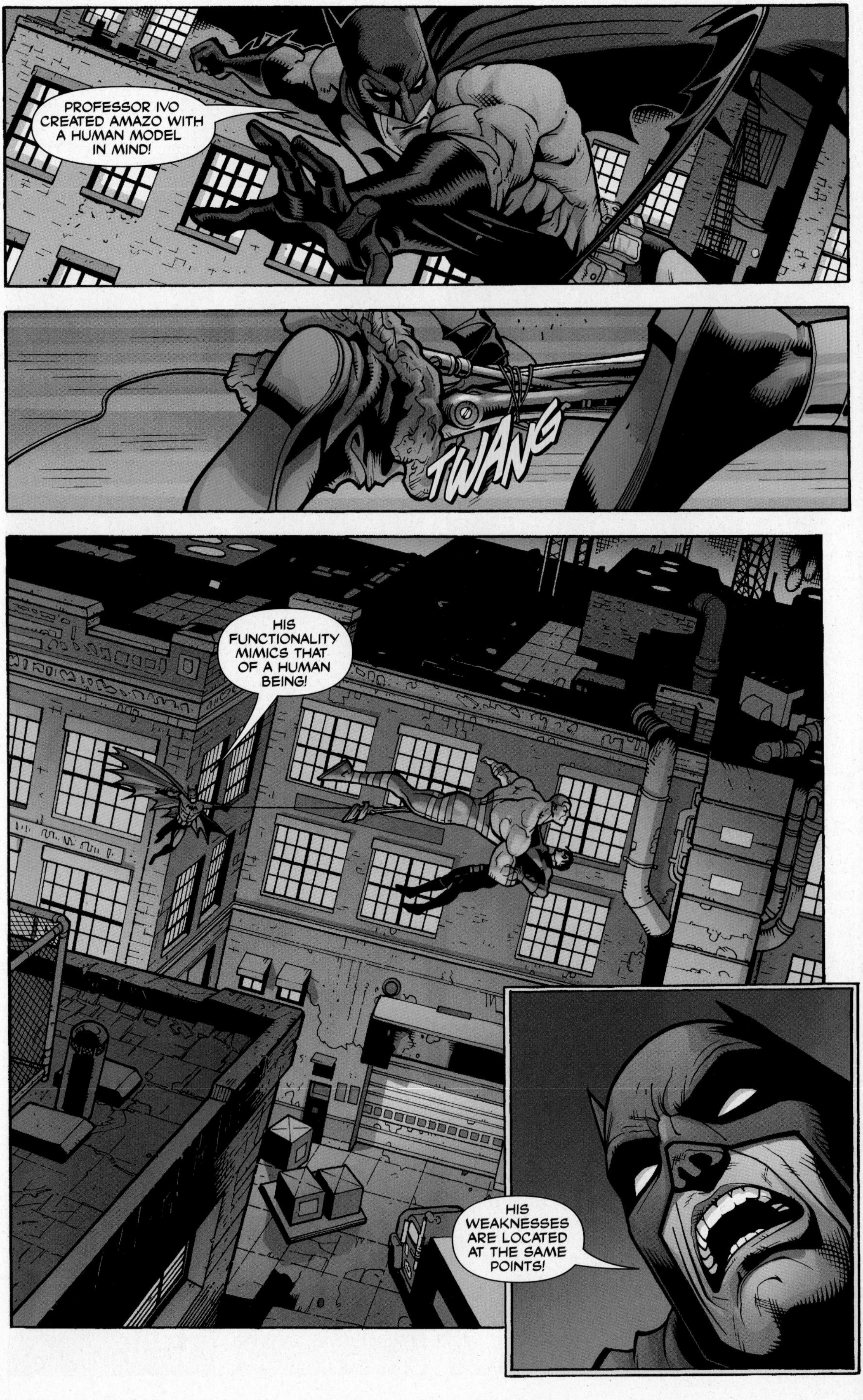
PROFESSOR IVO CREATED AMAZO WITH A HUMAN MODEL IN MIND!
TWANG
HIS FUNCTIONALITY MIMICS THAT OF A HUMAN BEING!
HIS WEAKNESSES ARE LOCATED AT THE SAME POINTS!

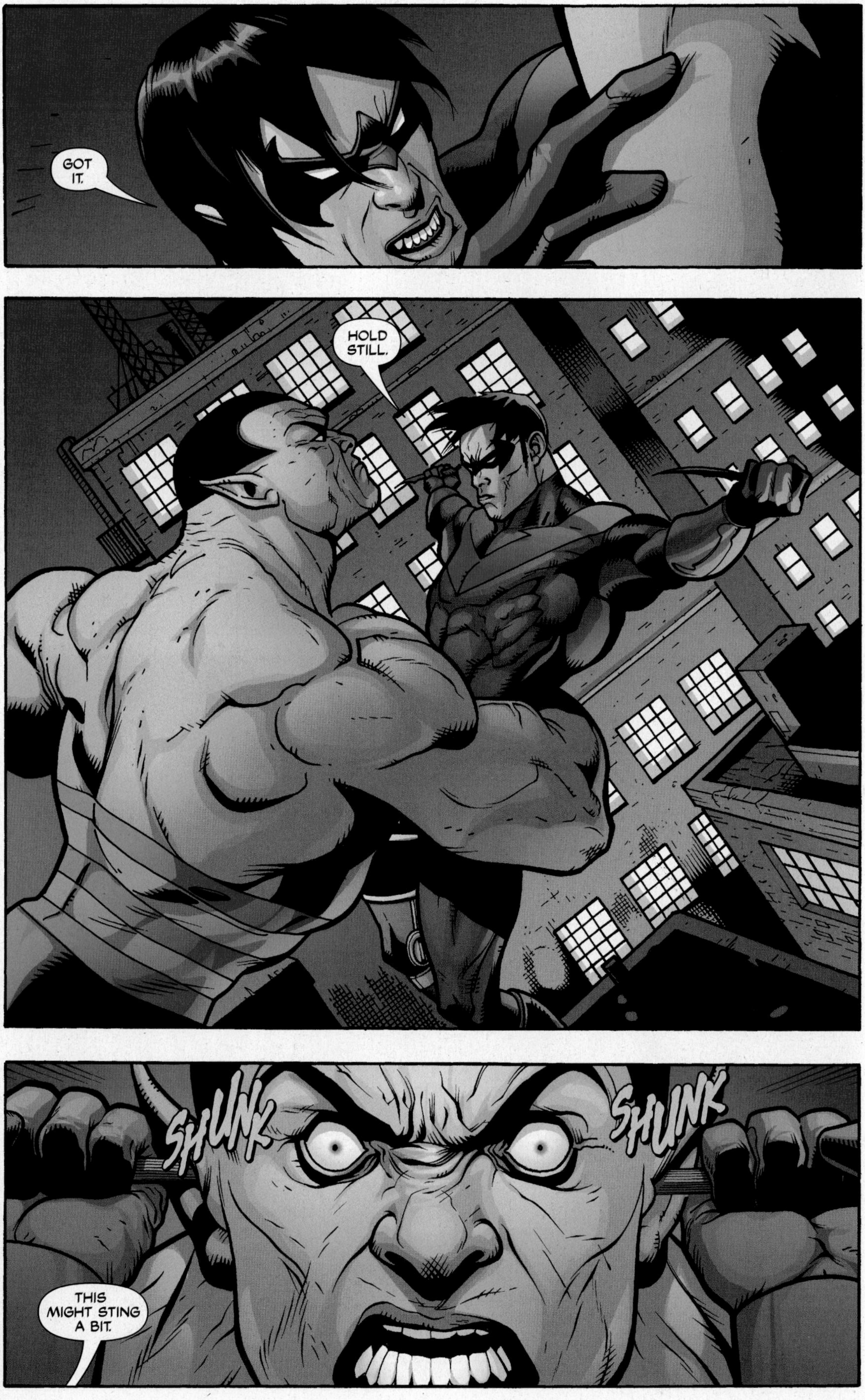
GOT IT.
HOLD STILL.
SHUNK
SHUNK
THIS MIGHT STING A BIT.

I DIDN'T GET DEEP ENOUGH TO NAIL HIS BRAIN PAN.

BUT IT SEEMS TO HAVE AFFECTED WHATEVER GYROS ARE IMPLANTED IN HIS "INNER EARS."

THAT'LL KEEP HIM OUT OF THE AIR.

IT'S A START. WE CAN'T--

GREEE-UUUNK

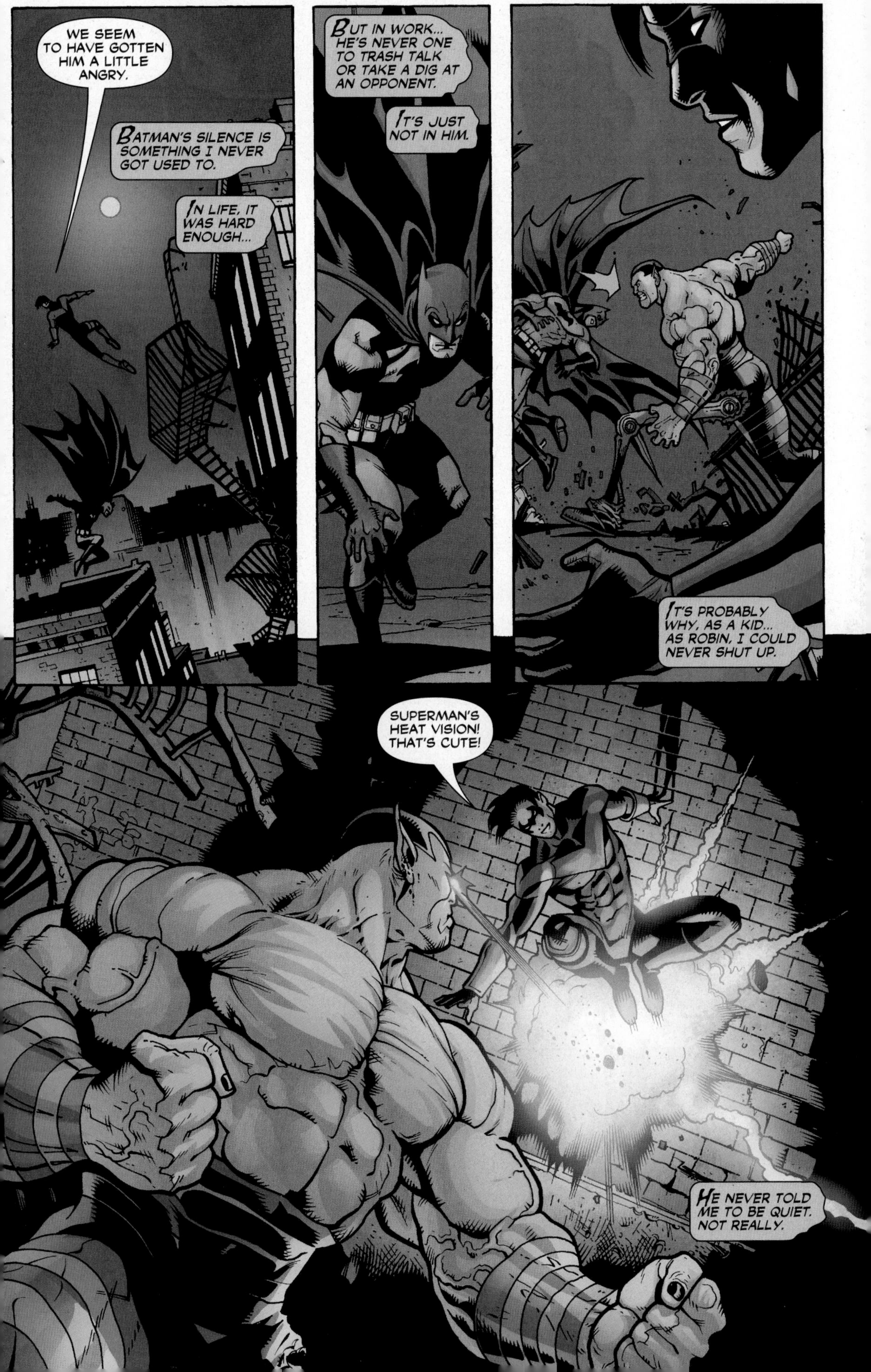
WE SEEM TO HAVE GOTTEN HIM A LITTLE ANGRY.
BATMAN'S SILENCE IS SOMETHING I NEVER GOT USED TO.
IN LIFE, IT WAS HARD ENOUGH...
BUT IN WORK... HE'S NEVER ONE TO TRASH TALK OR TAKE A DIG AT AN OPPONENT.
IT'S JUST NOT IN HIM.
IT'S PROBABLY WHY, AS A KID... AS ROBIN, I COULD NEVER SHUT UP.
SUPERMAN'S HEAT VISION! THAT'S CUTE!
HE NEVER TOLD ME TO BE QUIET. NOT REALLY.

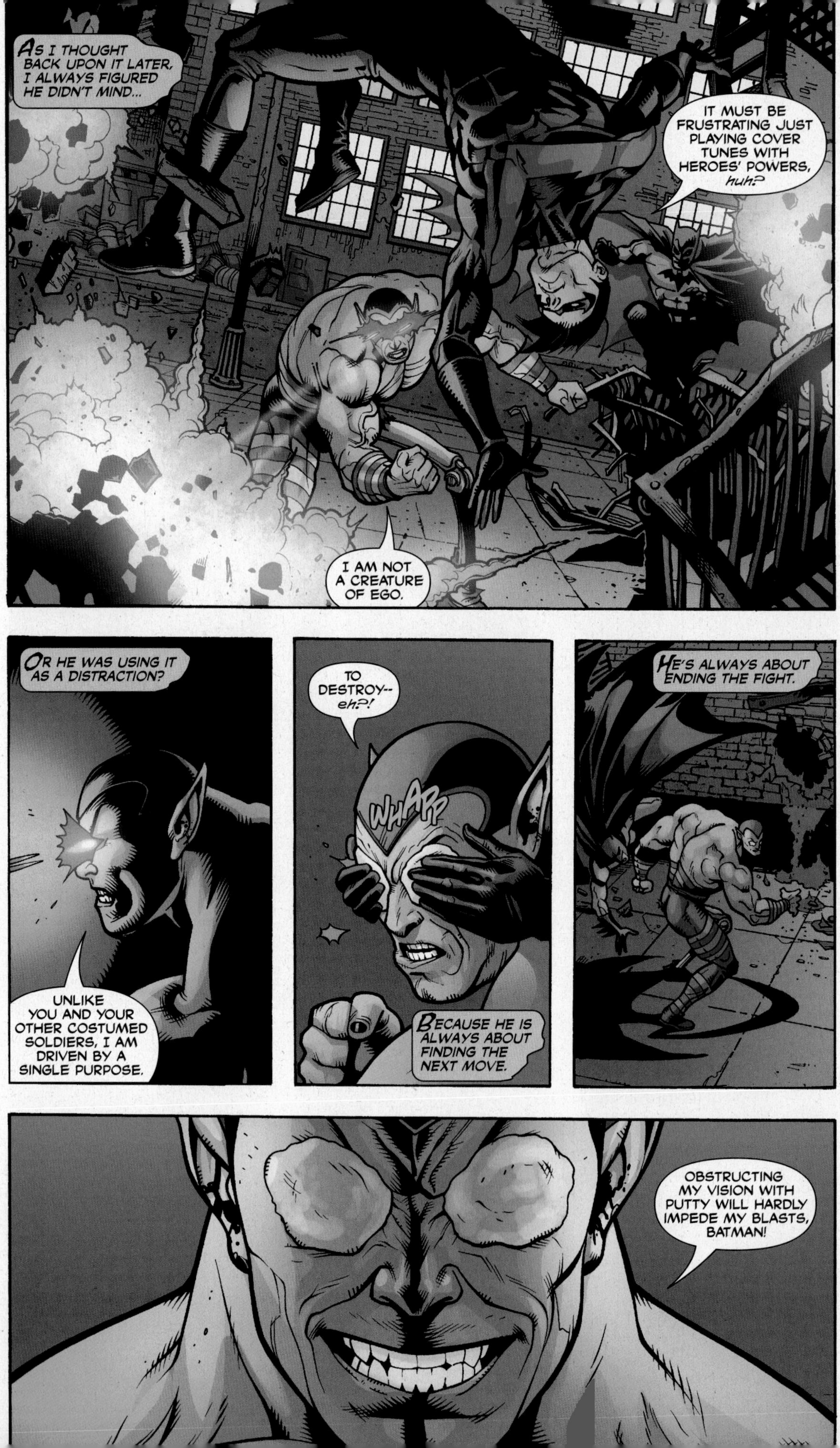
AS I THOUGHT BACK UPON IT LATER, I ALWAYS FIGURED HE DIDN'T MIND...
IT MUST BE FRUSTRATING JUST PLAYING COVER TUNES WITH HEROES' POWERS, huh?
I AM NOT A CREATURE OF EGO.
OR HE WAS USING IT AS A DISTRACTION?
UNLIKE YOU AND YOUR OTHER COSTUMED SOLDIERS, I AM DRIVEN BY A SINGLE PURPOSE.
TO DESTROY-- eh?!
WHAPP
BECAUSE HE IS ALWAYS ABOUT FINDING THE NEXT MOVE.
HE'S ALWAYS ABOUT ENDING THE FIGHT.
OBSTRUCTING MY VISION WITH PUTTY WILL HARDLY IMPEDE MY BLASTS, BATMAN!

BOOOM

NO, BUT FIRING HEAT VISION THROUGH PLASTIQUE EXPLOSIVES WILL.

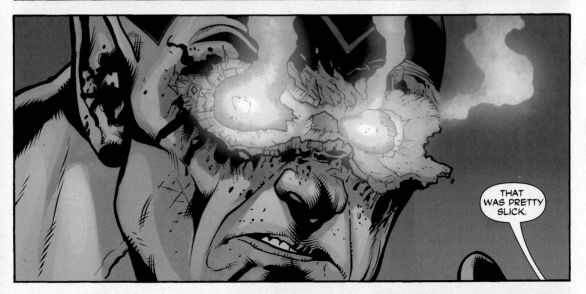

THAT WAS PRETTY SLICK.

WE SEEM TO HAVE SLOWED HIM UP A BIT.

A BIT. BUT WE'VE CERTAINLY EVENED THE ODDS.

GET READY.

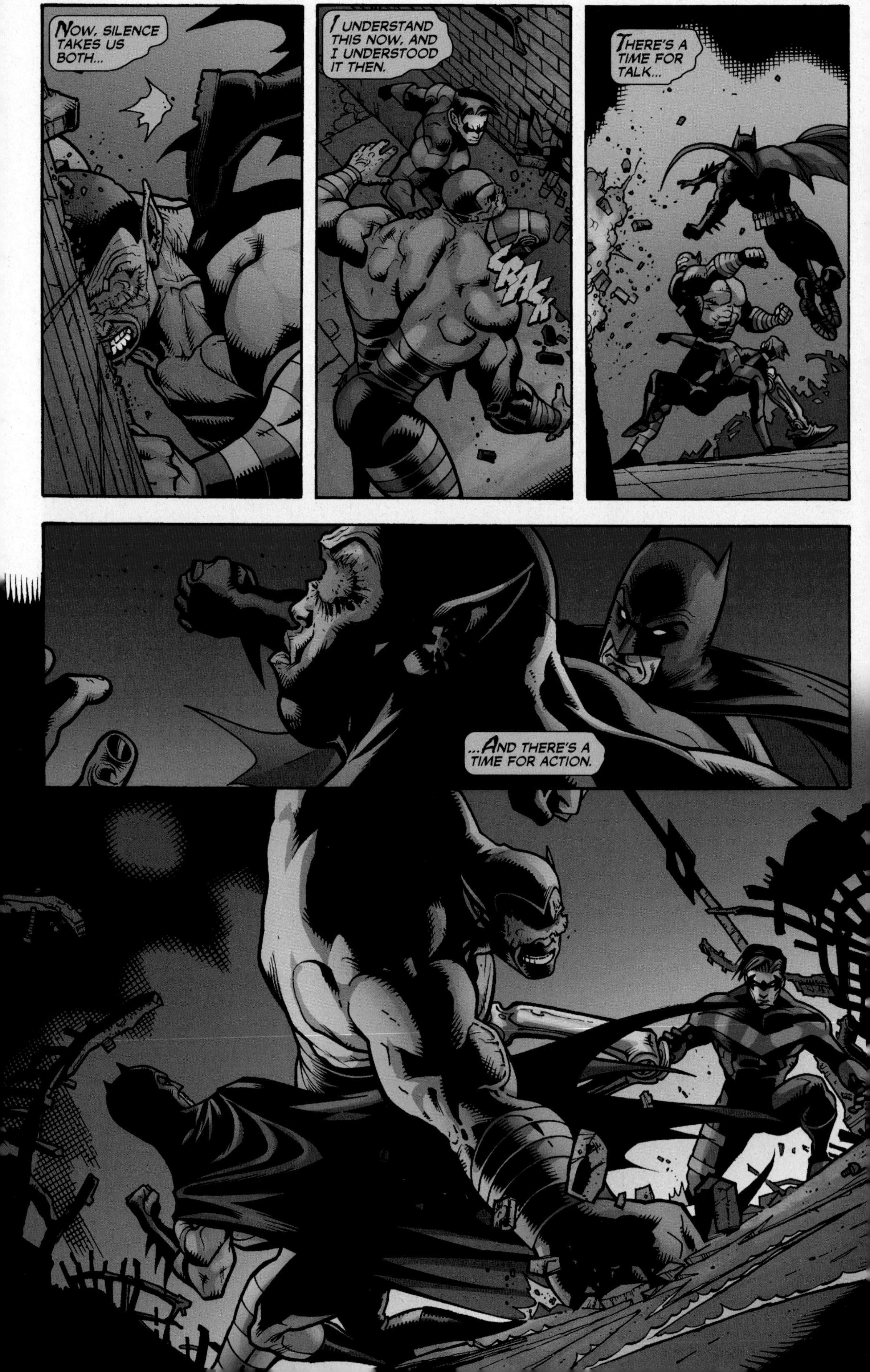

NOW, SILENCE TAKES US BOTH...
I UNDERSTAND THIS NOW. AND I UNDERSTOOD IT THEN.
CRACK
THERE'S A TIME FOR TALK...
...AND THERE'S A TIME FOR ACTION.

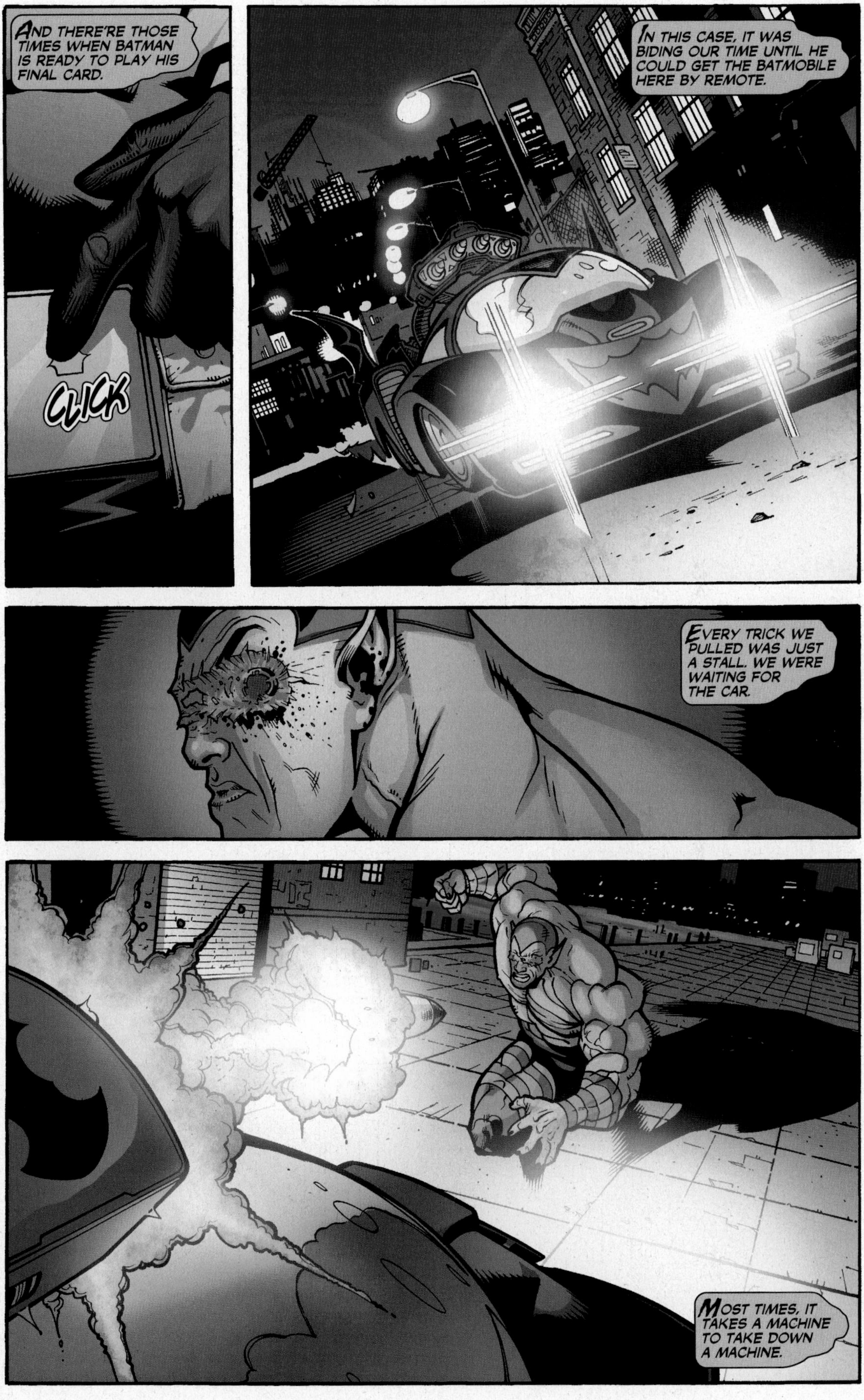
AND THERE'RE THOSE TIMES WHEN BATMAN IS READY TO PLAY HIS FINAL CARD.
CLICK
IN THIS CASE, IT WAS BIDING OUR TIME UNTIL HE COULD GET THE BATMOBILE HERE BY REMOTE.
EVERY TRICK WE PULLED WAS JUST A STALL. WE WERE WAITING FOR THE CAR.
MOST TIMES, IT TAKES A MACHINE TO TAKE DOWN A MACHINE.

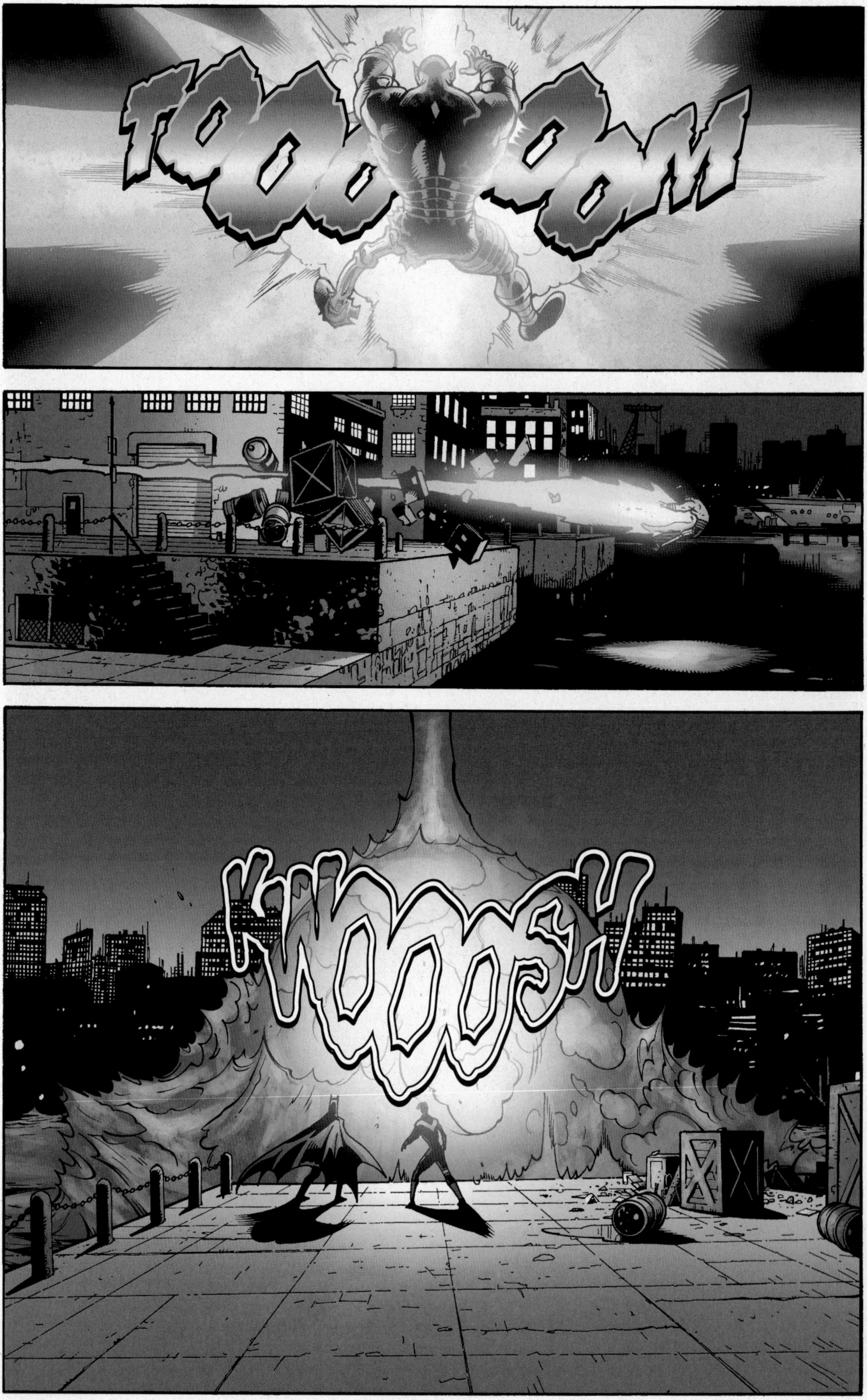
TOOOOOM
KWOOOSH

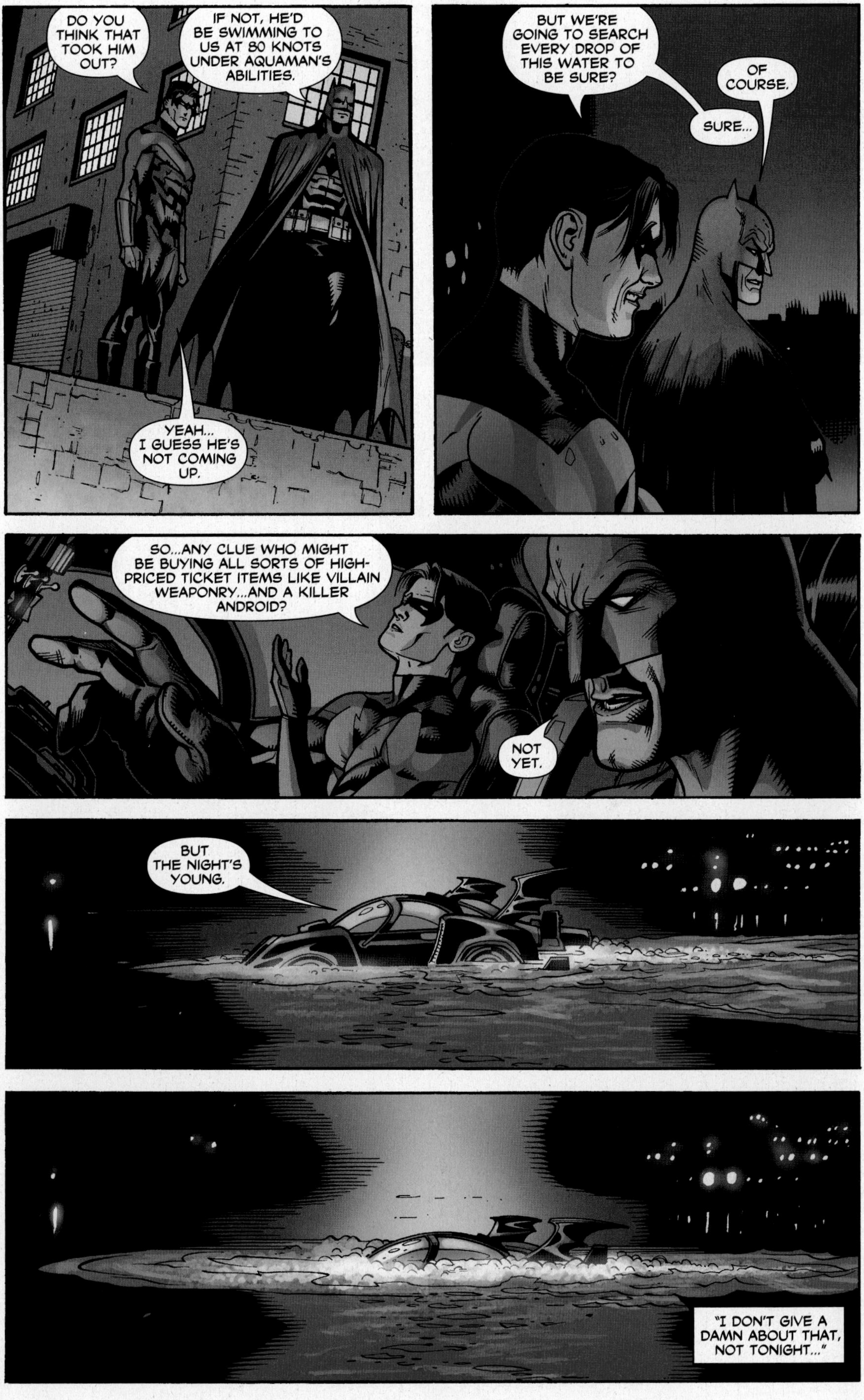
DO YOU THINK THAT TOOK HIM OUT?
IF NOT, HE'D BE SWIMMING TO US AT 80 KNOTS UNDER AQUAMAN'S ABILITIES.
YEAH... I GUESS HE'S NOT COMING UP.
BUT WE'RE GOING TO SEARCH EVERY DROP OF THIS WATER TO BE SURE?
OF COURSE.
SURE...
SO...ANY CLUE WHO MIGHT BE BUYING ALL SORTS OF HIGH-PRICED TICKET ITEMS LIKE VILLAIN WEAPONRY...AND A KILLER ANDROID?
NOT YET.
BUT THE NIGHT'S YOUNG.
"I DON'T GIVE A DAMN ABOUT THAT, NOT TONIGHT..."

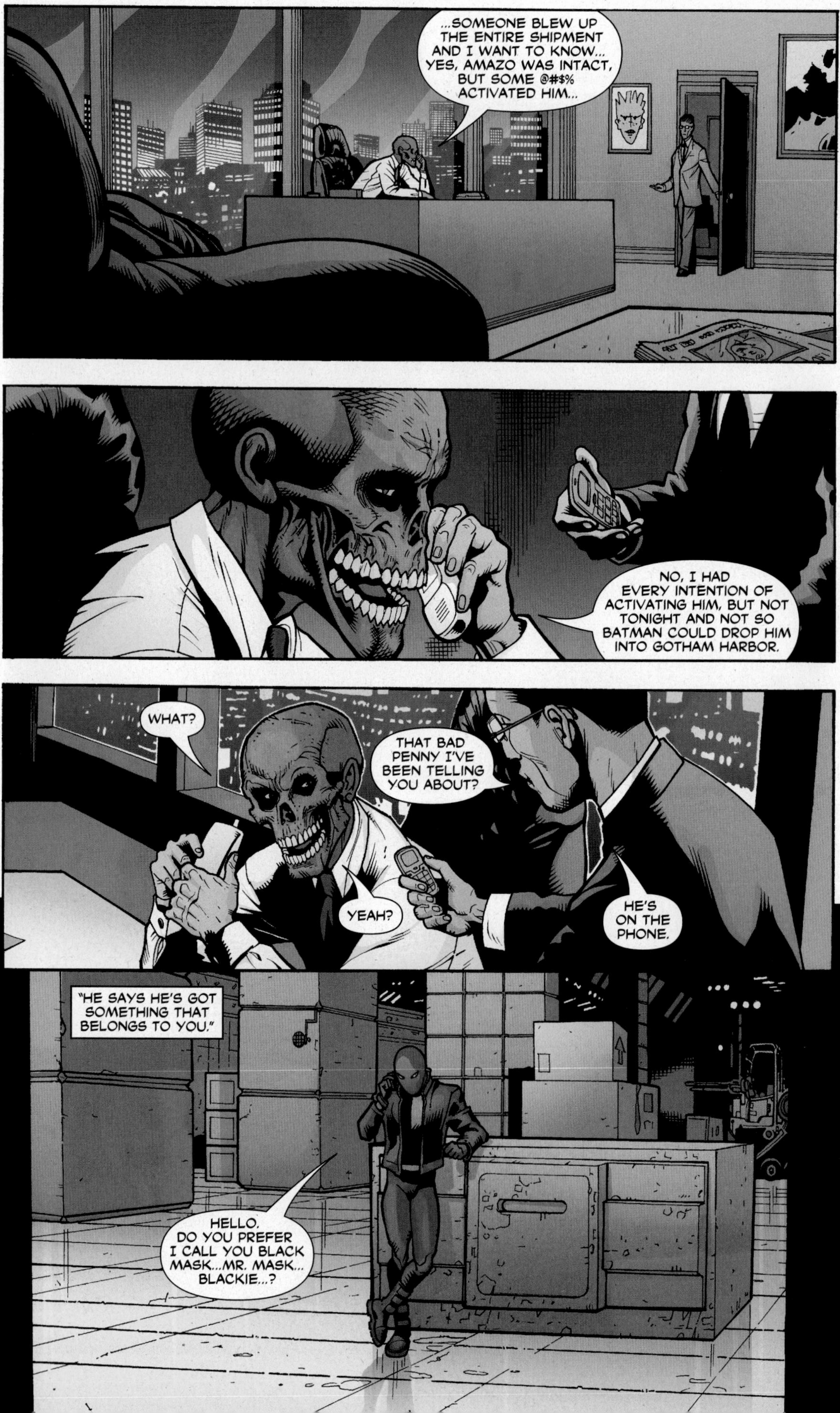
...SOMEONE BLEW UP THE ENTIRE SHIPMENT AND I WANT TO KNOW... YES, AMAZO WAS INTACT, BUT SOME @#$% ACTIVATED HIM...
NO, I HAD EVERY INTENTION OF ACTIVATING HIM, BUT NOT TONIGHT AND NOT SO BATMAN COULD DROP HIM INTO GOTHAM HARBOR.
WHAT?
THAT BAD PENNY I'VE BEEN TELLING YOU ABOUT?
YEAH?
HE'S ON THE PHONE.
"HE SAYS HE'S GOT SOMETHING THAT BELONGS TO YOU."
HELLO. DO YOU PREFER I CALL YOU BLACK MASK...MR. MASK... BLACKIE...?

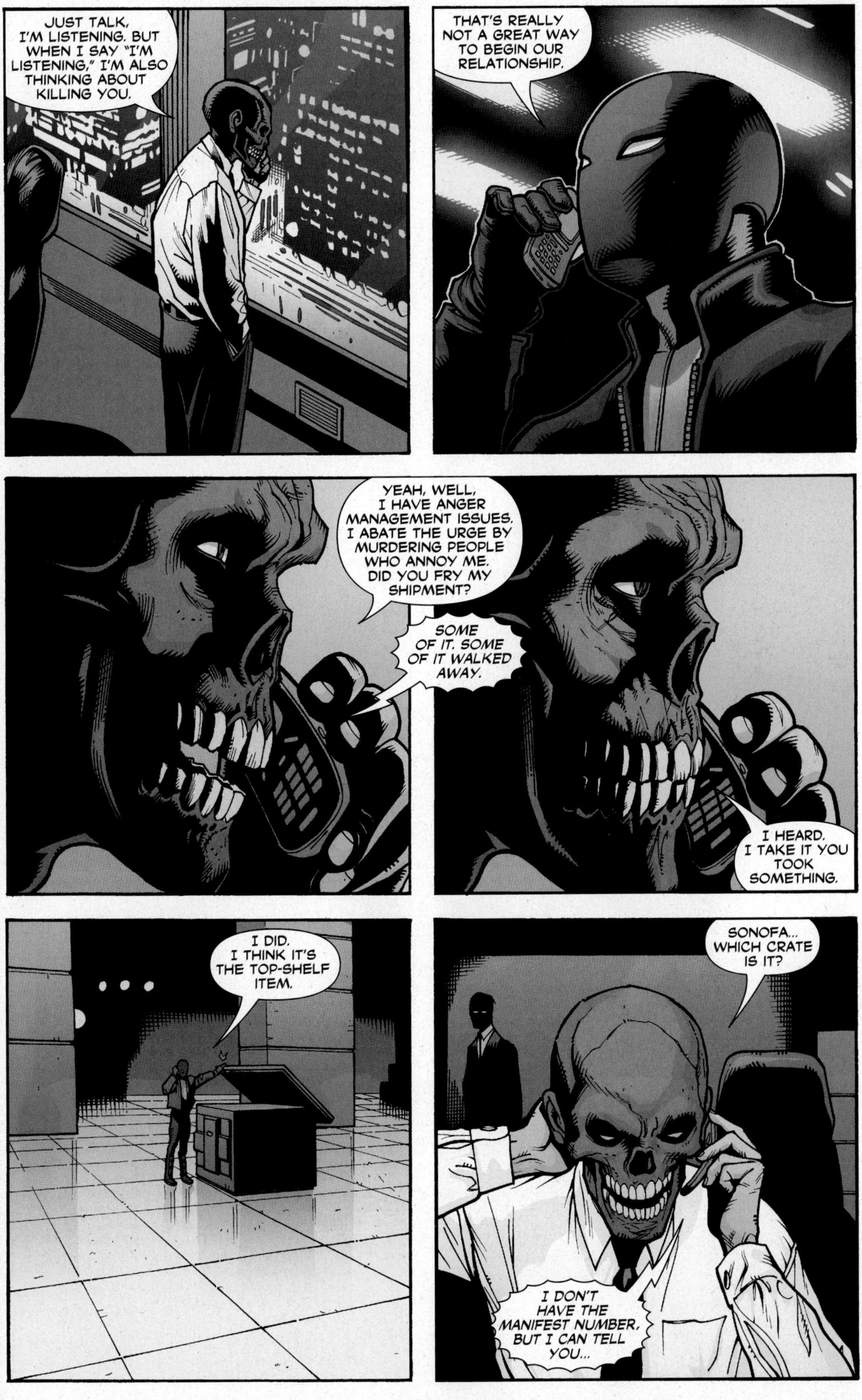
JUST TALK, I'M LISTENING. BUT WHEN I SAY "I'M LISTENING," I'M ALSO THINKING ABOUT KILLING YOU.
THAT'S REALLY NOT A GREAT WAY TO BEGIN OUR RELATIONSHIP.
YEAH, WELL, I HAVE ANGER MANAGEMENT ISSUES. I ABATE THE URGE BY MURDERING PEOPLE WHO ANNOY ME. DID YOU FRY MY SHIPMENT?
SOME OF IT. SOME OF IT WALKED AWAY.
I HEARD. I TAKE IT YOU TOOK SOMETHING.
I DID. I THINK IT'S THE TOP-SHELF ITEM.
SONOFA... WHICH CRATE IS IT?
I DON'T HAVE THE MANIFEST NUMBER, BUT I CAN TELL YOU...

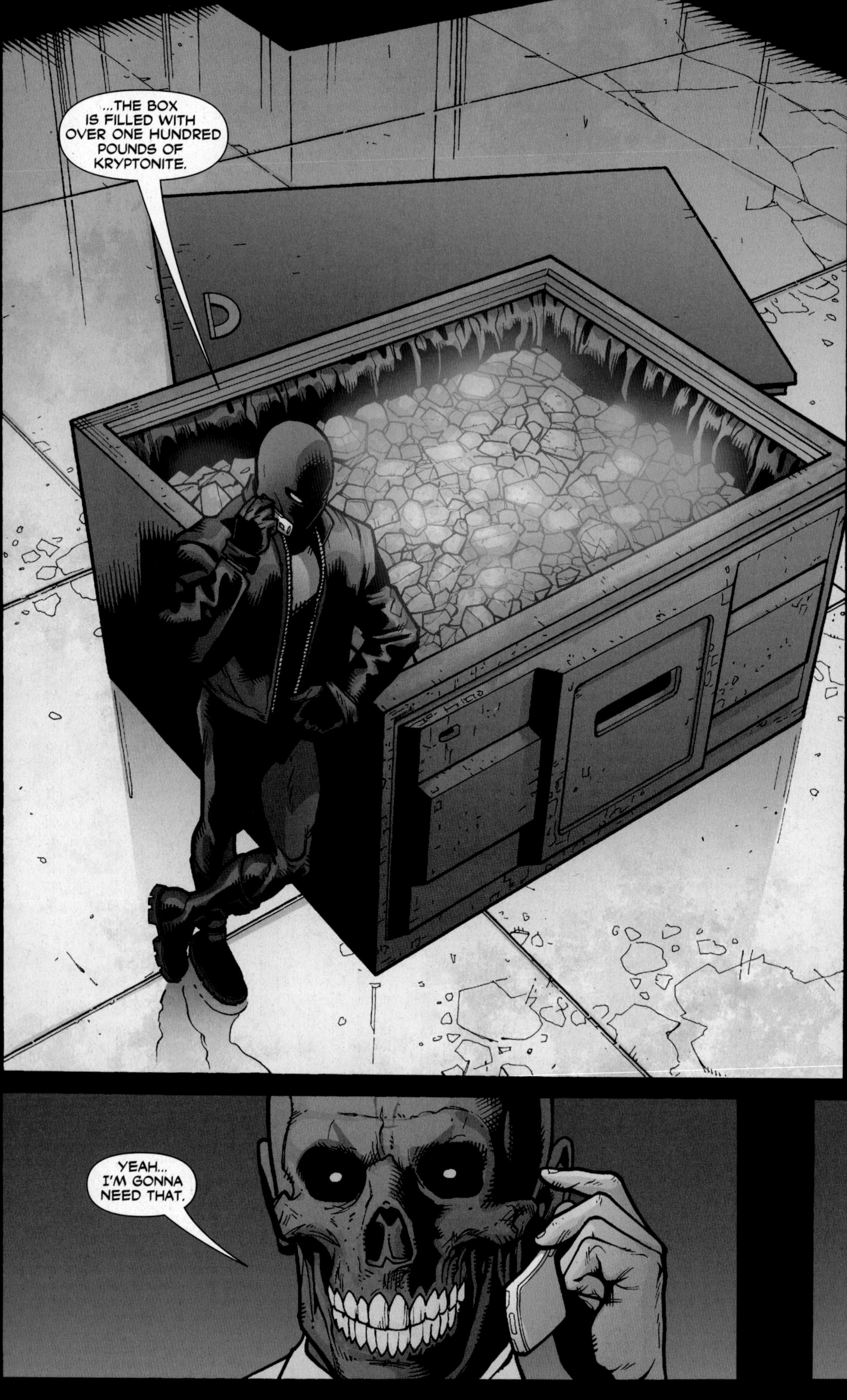
...THE BOX IS FILLED WITH OVER ONE HUNDRED POUNDS OF KRYPTONITE.
YEAH... I'M GONNA NEED THAT.

BATMAN 638 Cover by Matt Wagner

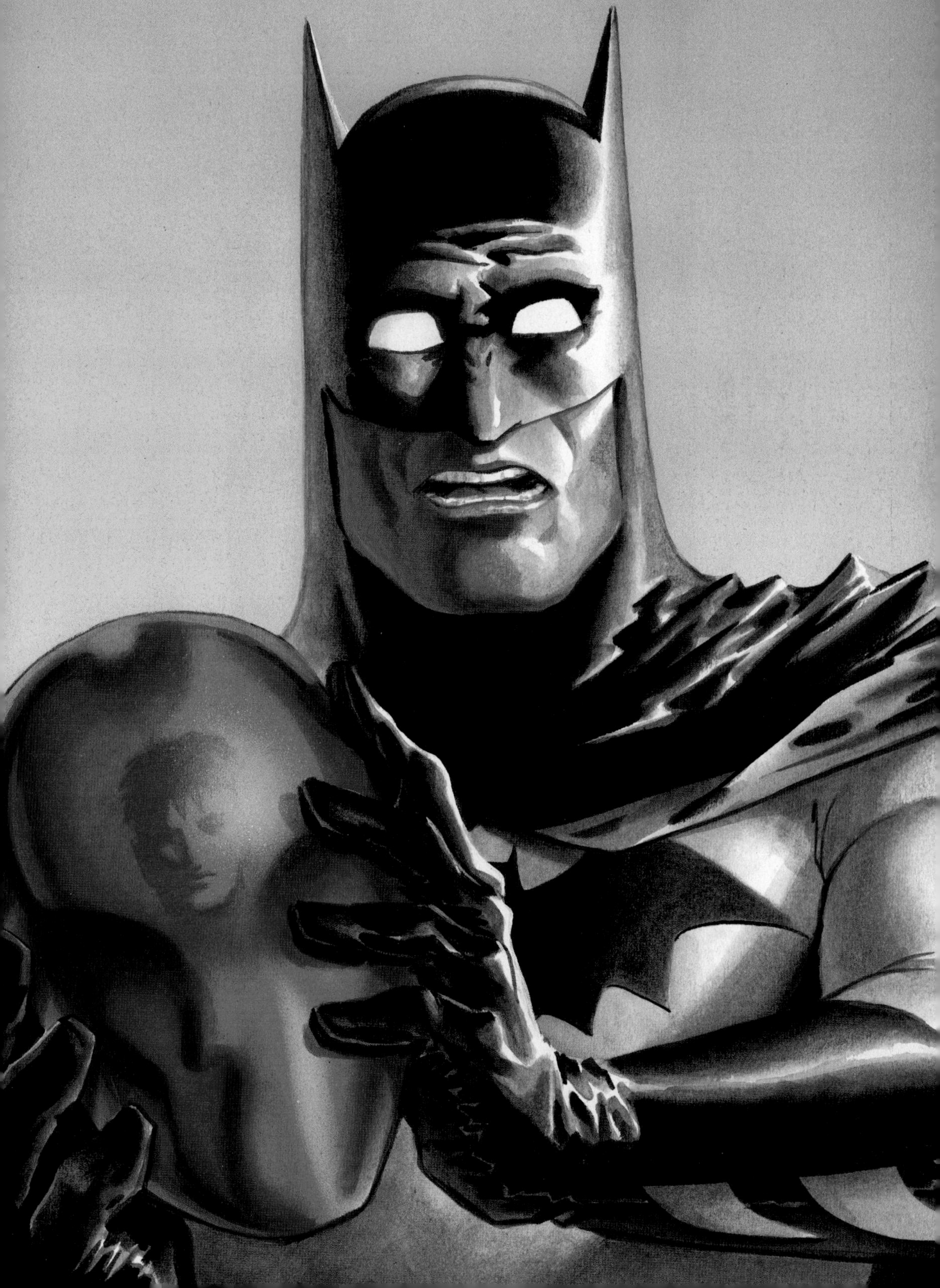

CHAPTER 4

BIDDING WAR

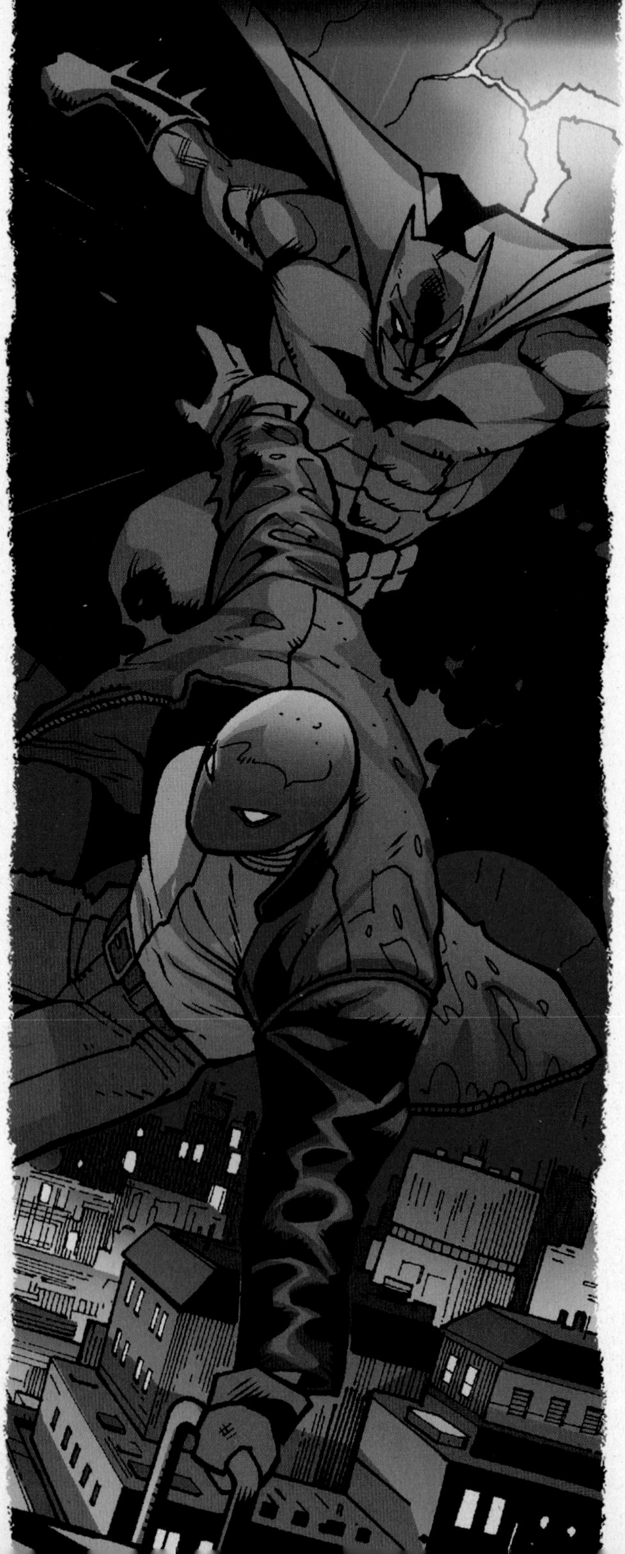

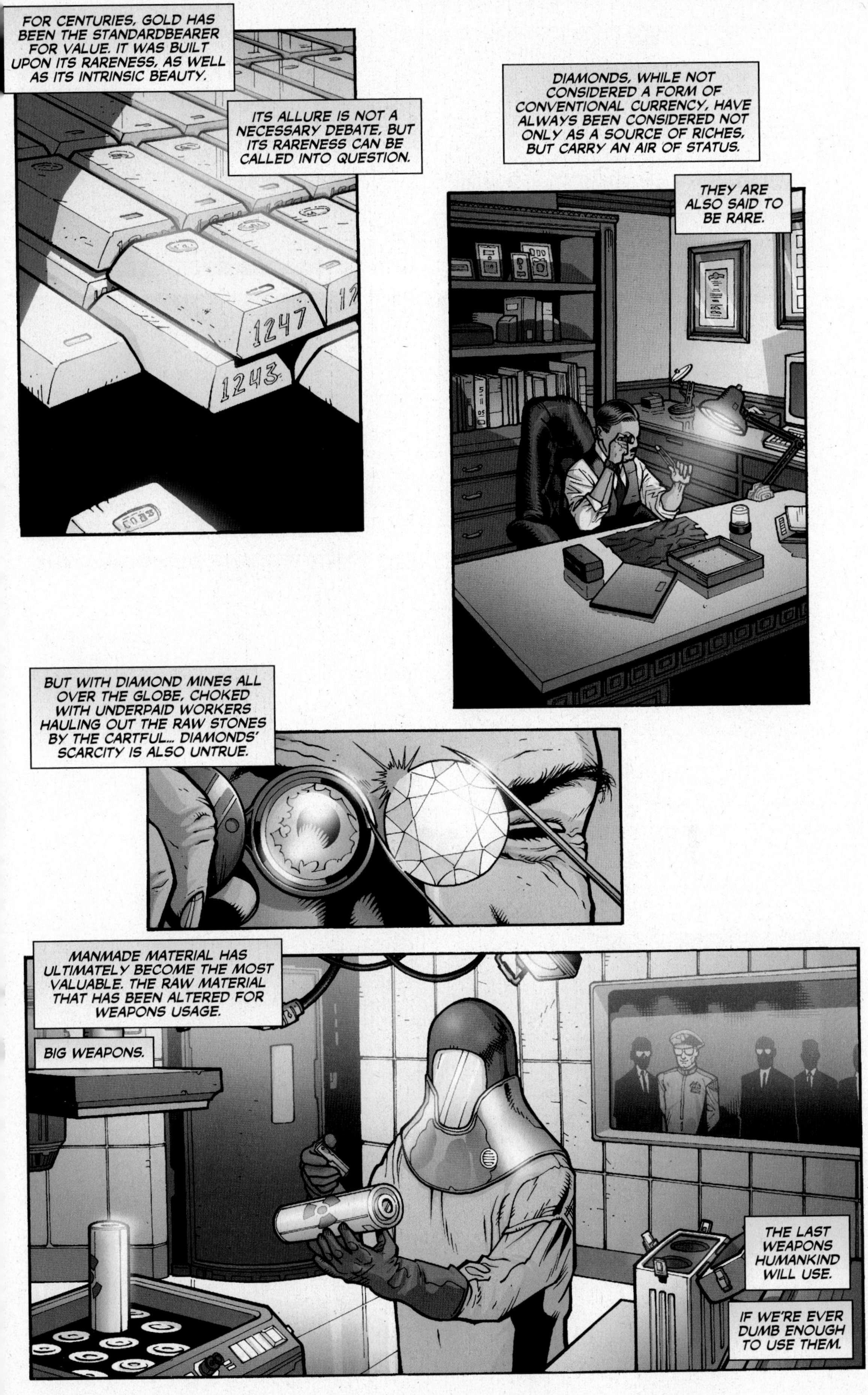
FOR CENTURIES, GOLD HAS BEEN THE STANDARDBEARER FOR VALUE. IT WAS BUILT UPON ITS RARENESS, AS WELL AS ITS INTRINSIC BEAUTY.
ITS ALLURE IS NOT A NECESSARY DEBATE, BUT ITS RARENESS CAN BE CALLED INTO QUESTION.
1247
1243
DIAMONDS, WHILE NOT CONSIDERED A FORM OF CONVENTIONAL CURRENCY, HAVE ALWAYS BEEN CONSIDERED NOT ONLY AS A SOURCE OF RICHES, BUT CARRY AN AIR OF STATUS.
THEY ARE ALSO SAID TO BE RARE.
BUT WITH DIAMOND MINES ALL OVER THE GLOBE, CHOKED WITH UNDERPAID WORKERS HAULING OUT THE RAW STONES BY THE CARTFUL... DIAMONDS' SCARCITY IS ALSO UNTRUE.
MANMADE MATERIAL HAS ULTIMATELY BECOME THE MOST VALUABLE. THE RAW MATERIAL THAT HAS BEEN ALTERED FOR WEAPONS USAGE.
BIG WEAPONS.
THE LAST WEAPONS HUMANKIND WILL USE.
IF WE'RE EVER DUMB ENOUGH TO USE THEM.

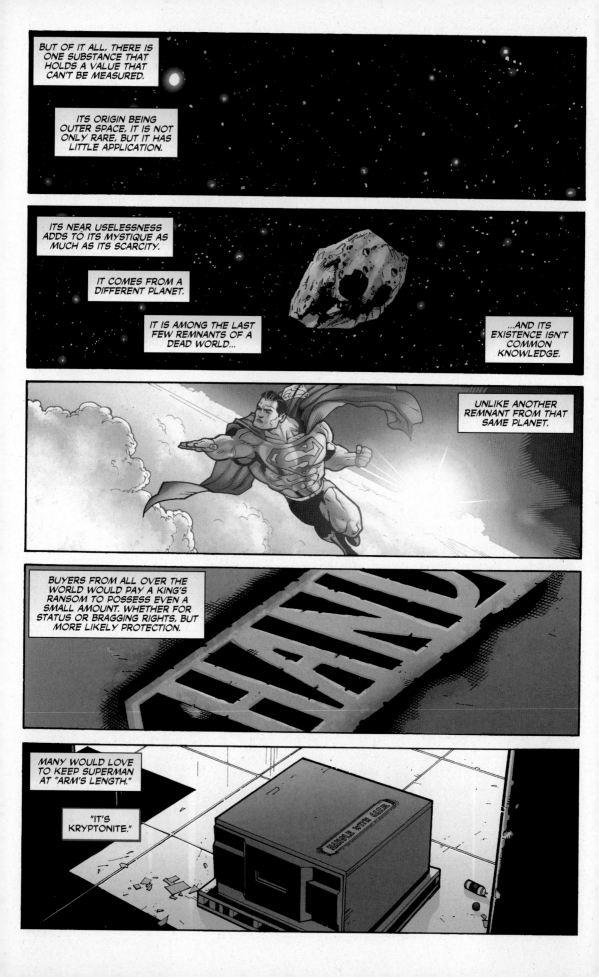

BUT OF IT ALL, THERE IS ONE SUBSTANCE THAT HOLDS A VALUE THAT CAN'T BE MEASURED.

ITS ORIGIN BEING OUTER SPACE, IT IS NOT ONLY RARE, BUT IT HAS LITTLE APPLICATION.

ITS NEAR USELESSNESS ADDS TO ITS MYSTIQUE AS MUCH AS ITS SCARCITY.

IT COMES FROM A DIFFERENT PLANET.

IT IS AMONG THE LAST FEW REMNANTS OF A DEAD WORLD...

...AND ITS EXISTENCE ISN'T COMMON KNOWLEDGE.

UNLIKE ANOTHER REMNANT FROM THAT SAME PLANET.

BUYERS FROM ALL OVER THE WORLD WOULD PAY A KING'S RANSOM TO POSSESS EVEN A SMALL AMOUNT. WHETHER FOR STATUS OR BRAGGING RIGHTS, BUT MORE LIKELY PROTECTION.

MANY WOULD LOVE TO KEEP SUPERMAN AT "ARM'S LENGTH."

"IT'S KRYPTONITE."

WHERE?

HERE.

YOU SURE? THERE USUALLY ISN'T A LOT OF THAT LYING AROUND.

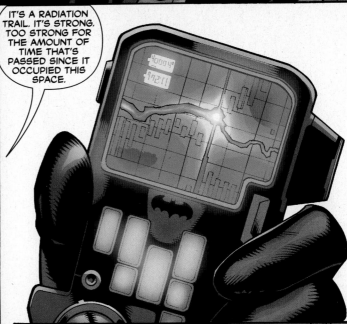

IT'S A RADIATION TRAIL. IT'S STRONG, TOO STRONG FOR THE AMOUNT OF TIME THAT'S PASSED SINCE IT OCCUPIED THIS SPACE.

SO...I GUESS THAT MEANS THERE WAS A GOOD AMOUNT OF IT SITTING HERE.

NO...IT MEANS THAT THERE WAS OVER A HUNDRED POUNDS.

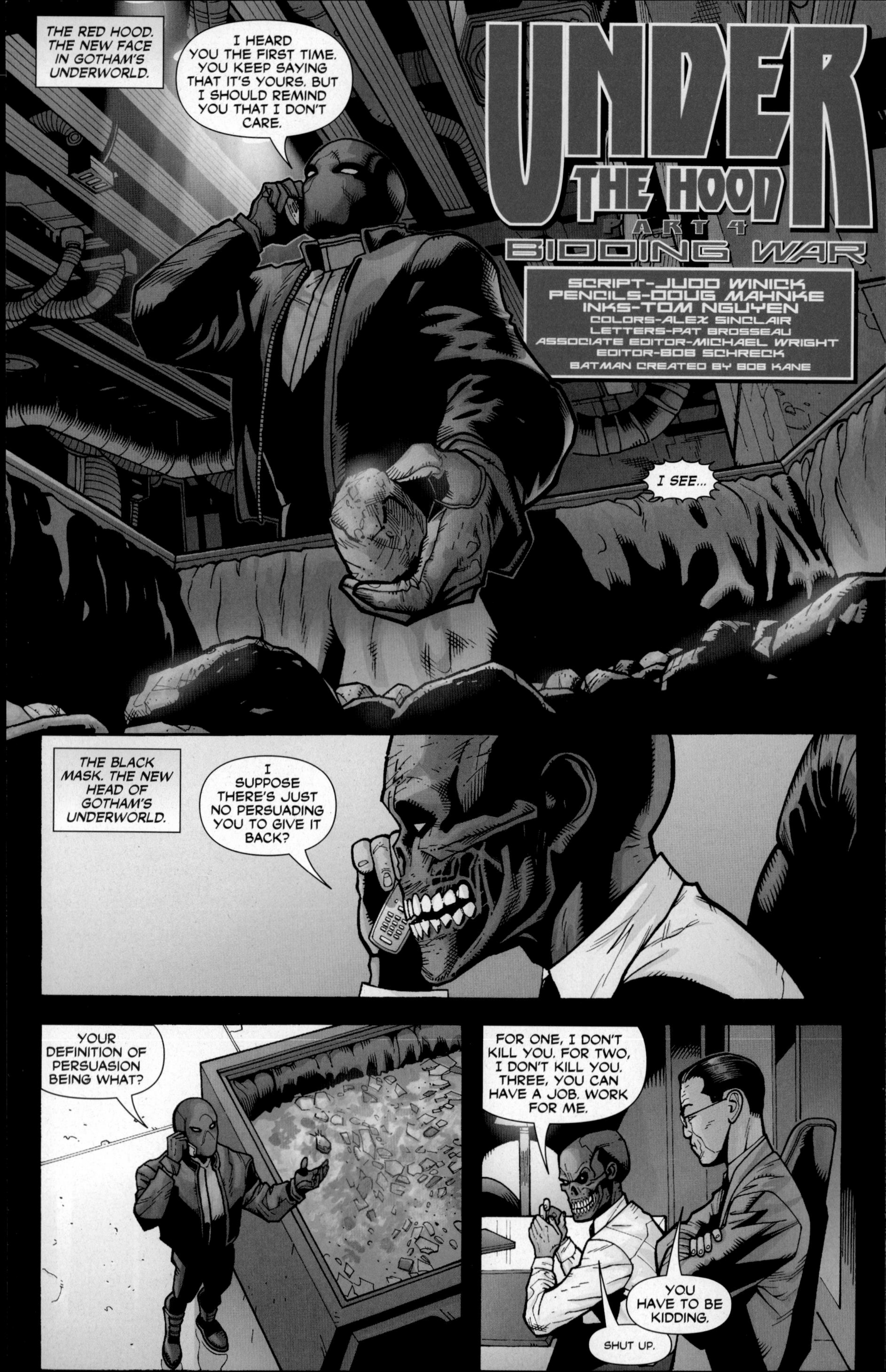
THE RED HOOD. THE NEW FACE IN GOTHAM'S UNDERWORLD.
I HEARD YOU THE FIRST TIME. YOU KEEP SAYING THAT IT'S YOURS. BUT I SHOULD REMIND YOU THAT I DON'T CARE.
UNDER THE HOOD
PART 4
BIDDING WAR
SCRIPT-JUDD WINICK
PENCILS-DOUG MAHNKE
INKS-TOM NGUYEN
COLORS-ALEX SINCLAIR
LETTERS-PAT BROSSEAU
ASSOCIATE EDITOR-MICHAEL WRIGHT
EDITOR-BOB SCHRECK
BATMAN CREATED BY BOB KANE
I SEE...
THE BLACK MASK. THE NEW HEAD OF GOTHAM'S UNDERWORLD.
I SUPPOSE THERE'S JUST NO PERSUADING YOU TO GIVE IT BACK?
YOUR DEFINITION OF PERSUASION BEING WHAT?
FOR ONE, I DON'T KILL YOU. FOR TWO, I DON'T KILL YOU. THREE, YOU CAN HAVE A JOB. WORK FOR ME.
YOU HAVE TO BE KIDDING.
SHUT UP.

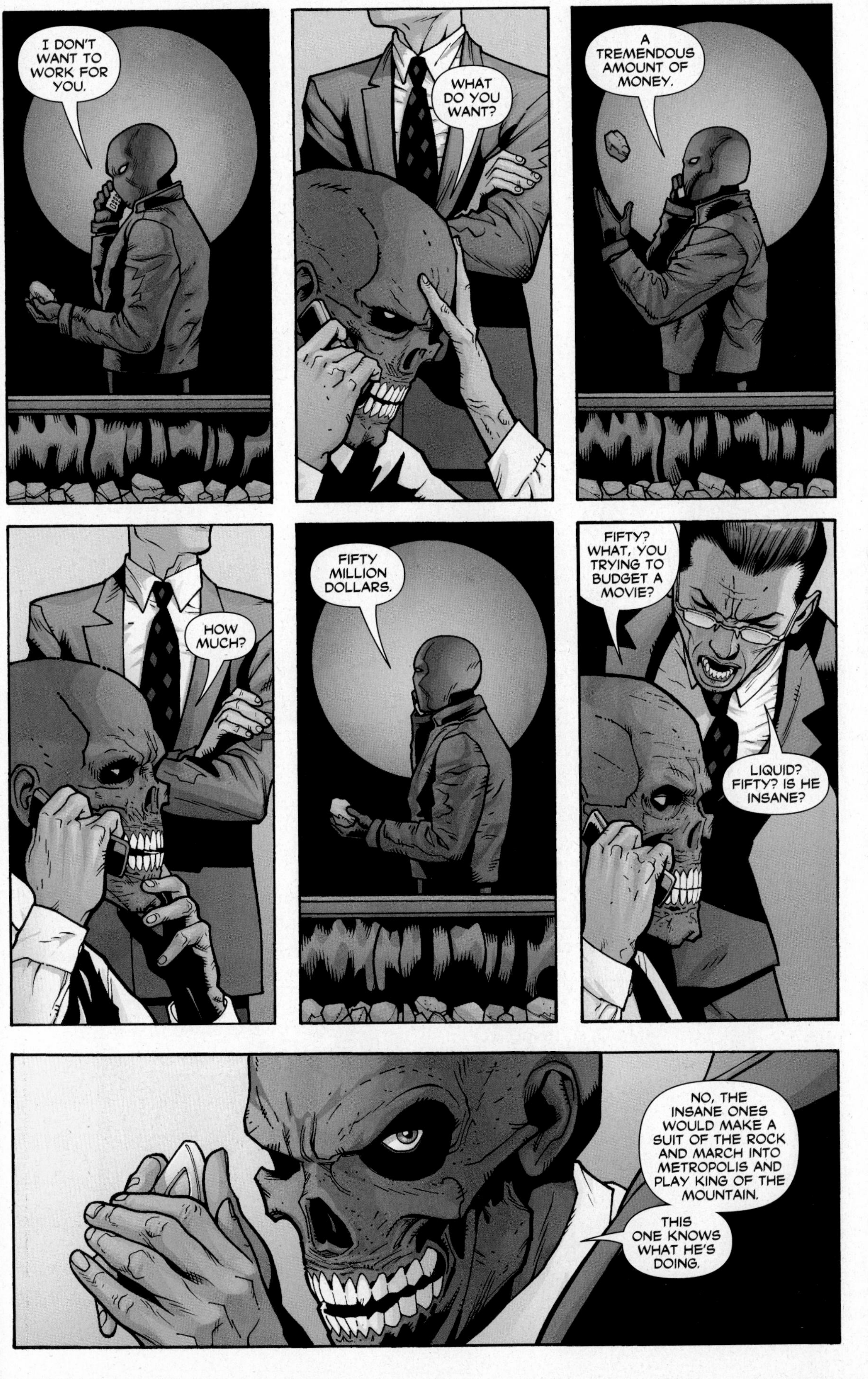
I DON'T WANT TO WORK FOR YOU.
WHAT DO YOU WANT?
A TREMENDOUS AMOUNT OF MONEY.
HOW MUCH?
FIFTY MILLION DOLLARS.
FIFTY? WHAT, YOU TRYING TO BUDGET A MOVIE?
LIQUID? FIFTY? IS HE INSANE?
NO, THE INSANE ONES WOULD MAKE A SUIT OF THE ROCK AND MARCH INTO METROPOLIS AND PLAY KING OF THE MOUNTAIN.
THIS ONE KNOWS WHAT HE'S DOING.

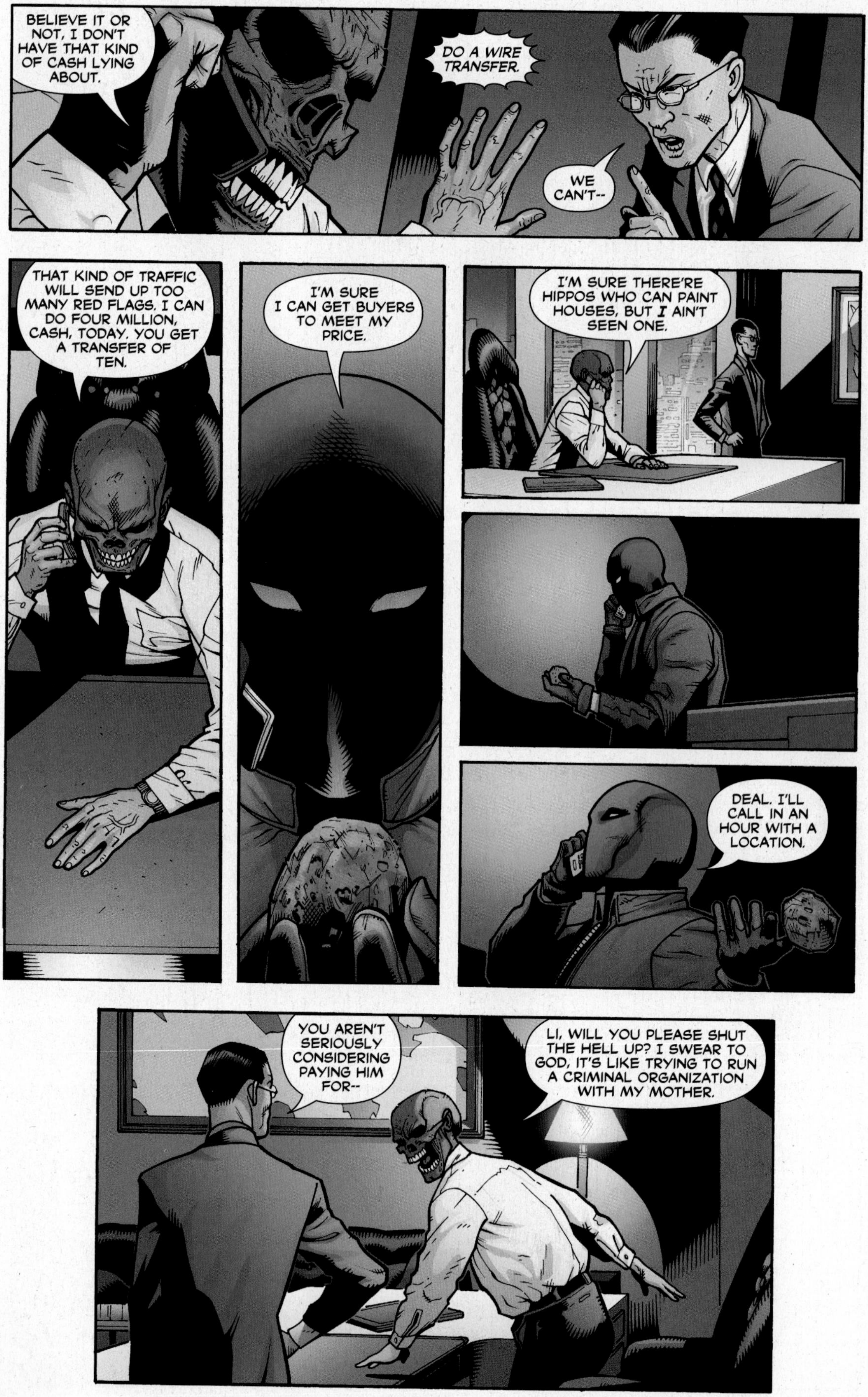
BELIEVE IT OR NOT, I DON'T HAVE THAT KIND OF CASH LYING ABOUT.
DO A WIRE TRANSFER.
WE CAN'T--
THAT KIND OF TRAFFIC WILL SEND UP TOO MANY RED FLAGS. I CAN DO FOUR MILLION, CASH, TODAY. YOU GET A TRANSFER OF TEN.
I'M SURE I CAN GET BUYERS TO MEET MY PRICE.
I'M SURE THERE'RE HIPPOS WHO CAN PAINT HOUSES, BUT I AIN'T SEEN ONE.
DEAL. I'LL CALL IN AN HOUR WITH A LOCATION.
YOU AREN'T SERIOUSLY CONSIDERING PAYING HIM FOR--
LI, WILL YOU PLEASE SHUT THE HELL UP? I SWEAR TO GOD, IT'S LIKE TRYING TO RUN A CRIMINAL ORGANIZATION WITH MY MOTHER.

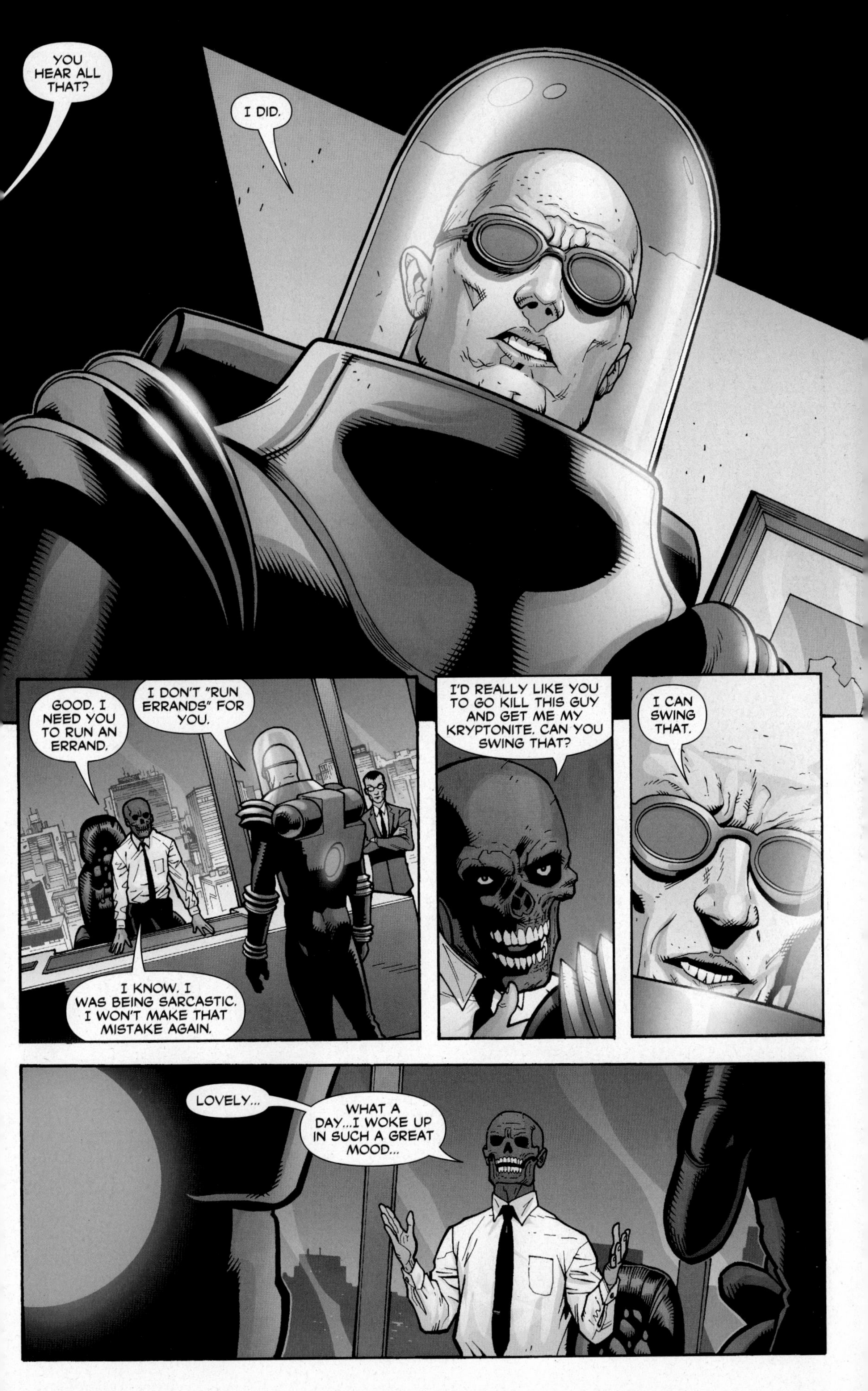
YOU HEAR ALL THAT?
I DID.
GOOD. I NEED YOU TO RUN AN ERRAND.
I DON'T "RUN ERRANDS" FOR YOU.
I KNOW. I WAS BEING SARCASTIC. I WON'T MAKE THAT MISTAKE AGAIN.
I'D REALLY LIKE YOU TO GO KILL THIS GUY AND GET ME MY KRYPTONITE. CAN YOU SWING THAT?
I CAN SWING THAT.
LOVELY...
WHAT A DAY...I WOKE UP IN SUCH A GREAT MOOD...

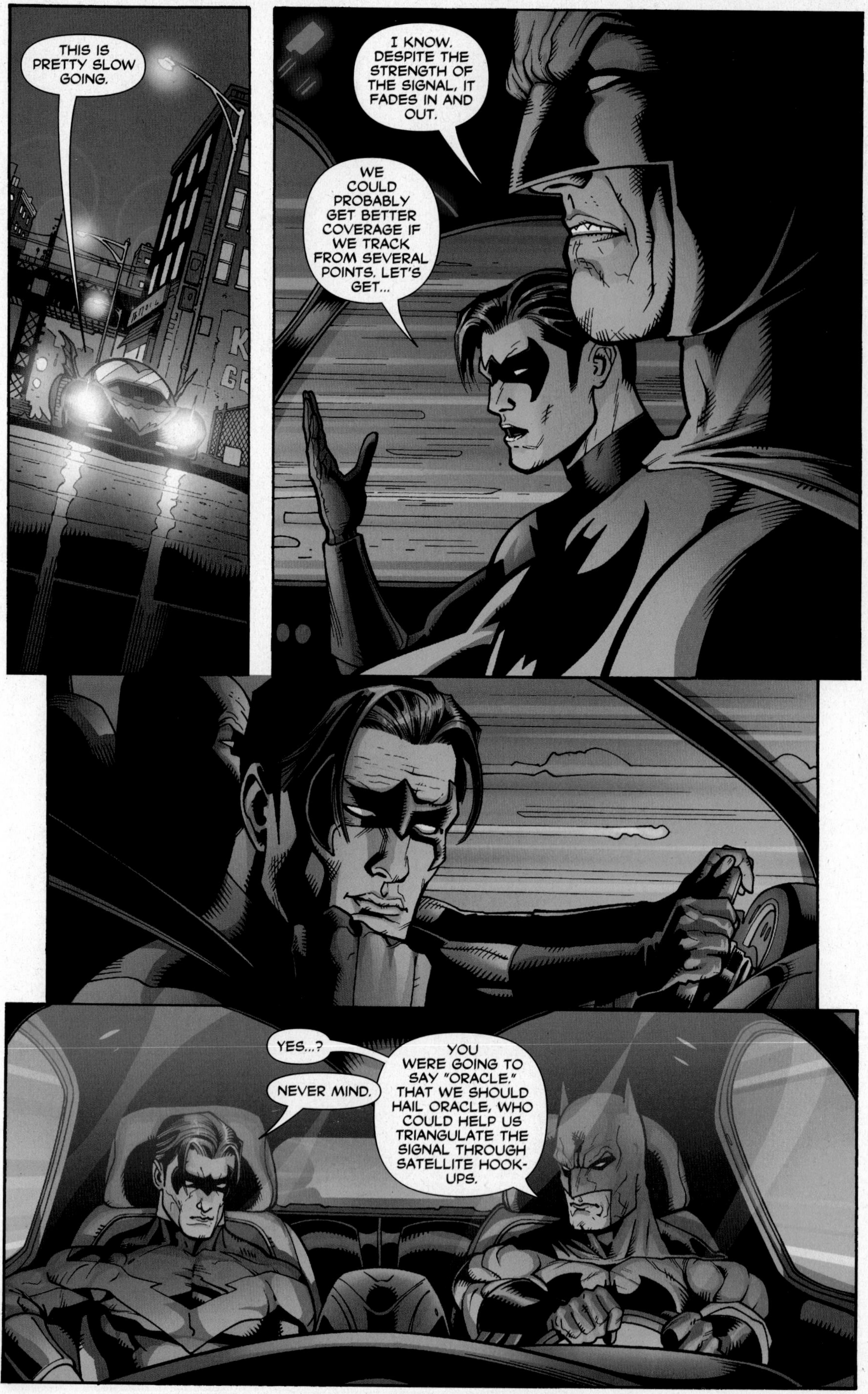
THIS IS PRETTY SLOW GOING.
I KNOW. DESPITE THE STRENGTH OF THE SIGNAL, IT FADES IN AND OUT.
WE COULD PROBABLY GET BETTER COVERAGE IF WE TRACK FROM SEVERAL POINTS. LET'S GET...
YES...?
NEVER MIND.
YOU WERE GOING TO SAY "ORACLE." THAT WE SHOULD HAIL ORACLE, WHO COULD HELP US TRIANGULATE THE SIGNAL THROUGH SATELLITE HOOK-UPS.

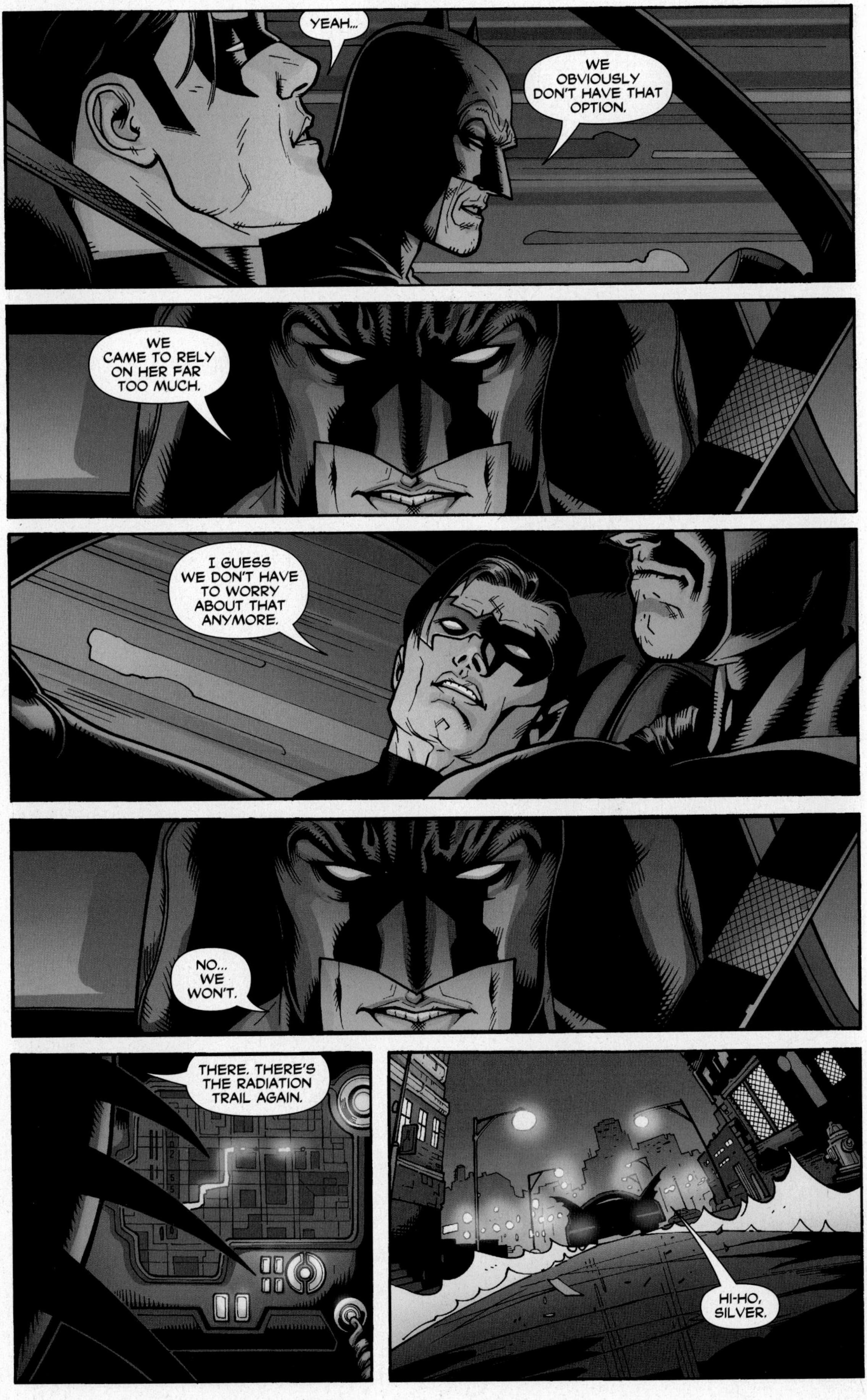
YEAH...
WE OBVIOUSLY DON'T HAVE THAT OPTION.
WE CAME TO RELY ON HER FAR TOO MUCH.
I GUESS WE DON'T HAVE TO WORRY ABOUT THAT ANYMORE.
NO... WE WON'T.
THERE. THERE'S THE RADIATION TRAIL AGAIN.
HI-HO, SILVER.

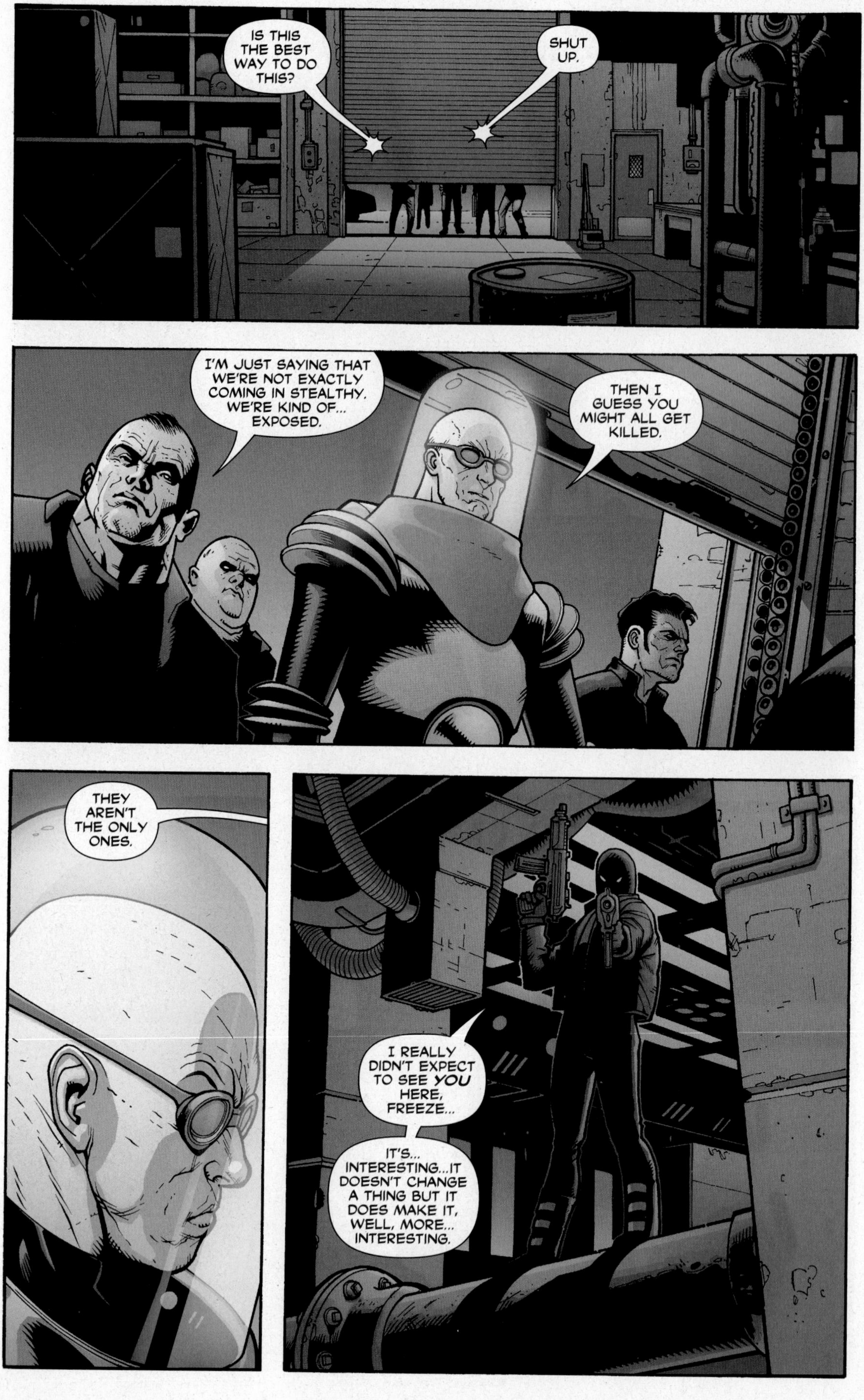
IS THIS THE BEST WAY TO DO THIS?
SHUT UP.
I'M JUST SAYING THAT WE'RE NOT EXACTLY COMING IN STEALTHY. WE'RE KIND OF... EXPOSED.
THEN I GUESS YOU MIGHT ALL GET KILLED.
THEY AREN'T THE ONLY ONES.
I REALLY DIDN'T EXPECT TO SEE *YOU* HERE, FREEZE...
IT'S... INTERESTING...IT DOESN'T CHANGE A THING BUT IT DOES MAKE IT, WELL, MORE... INTERESTING.

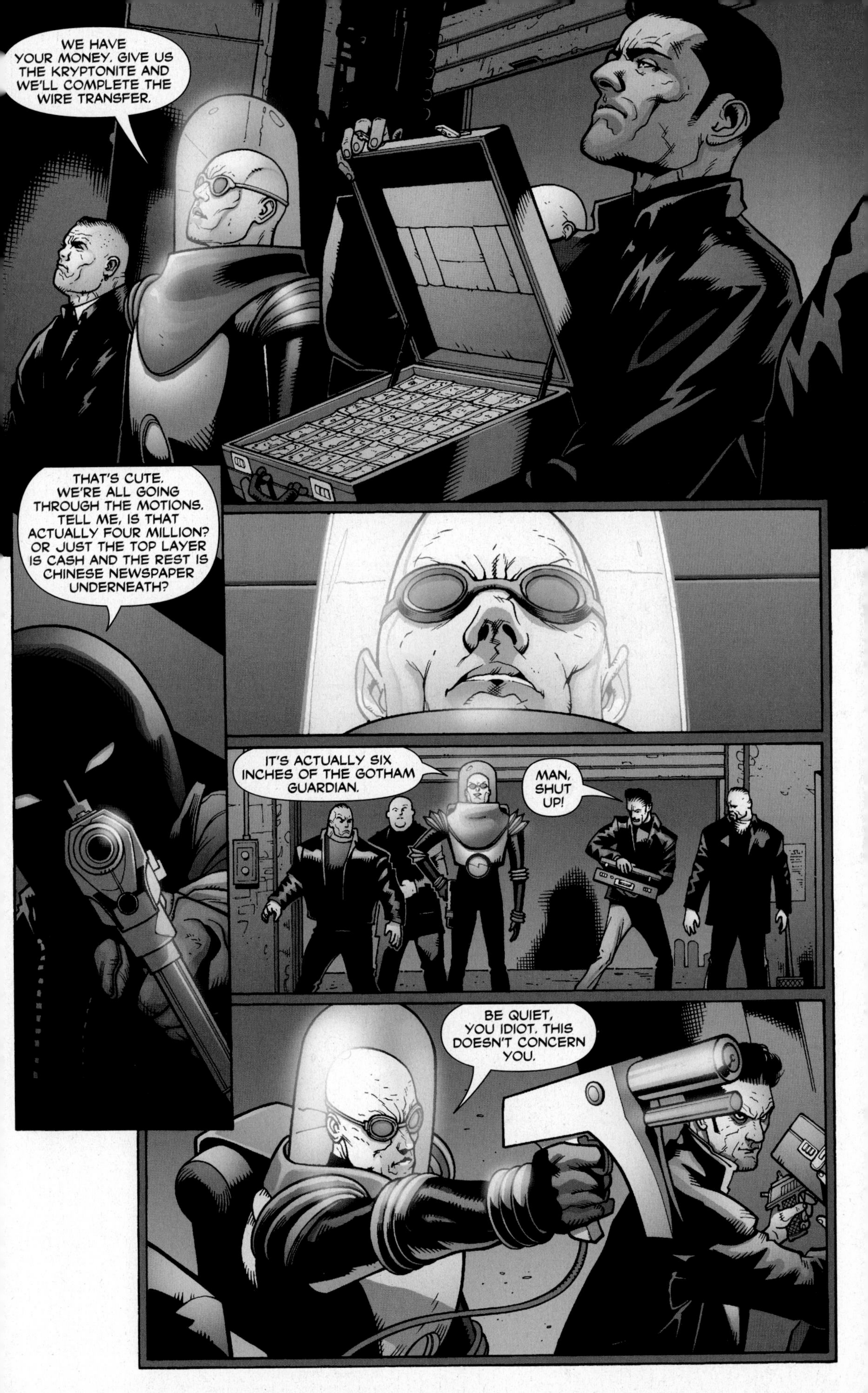
WE HAVE YOUR MONEY. GIVE US THE KRYPTONITE AND WE'LL COMPLETE THE WIRE TRANSFER.
THAT'S CUTE. WE'RE ALL GOING THROUGH THE MOTIONS. TELL ME, IS THAT ACTUALLY FOUR MILLION? OR JUST THE TOP LAYER IS CASH AND THE REST IS CHINESE NEWSPAPER UNDERNEATH?
IT'S ACTUALLY SIX INCHES OF THE GOTHAM GUARDIAN.
MAN, SHUT UP!
BE QUIET, YOU IDIOT. THIS DOESN'T CONCERN YOU.

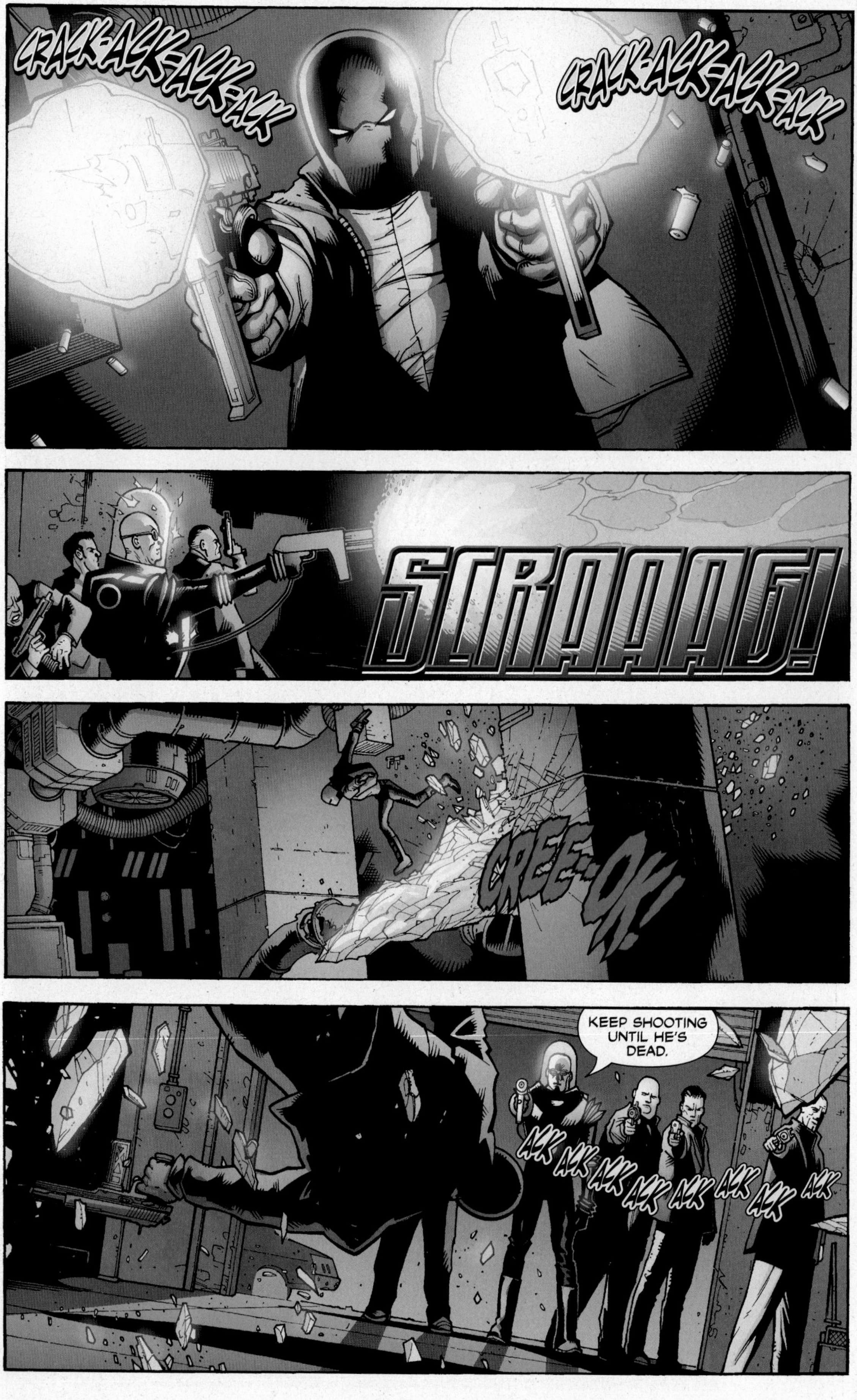
CRACK-ACK-ACK-ACK
CRACK-ACK-ACK-ACK
SCRAAAAG!
CREE-OK!
KEEP SHOOTING UNTIL HE'S DEAD.
ACK ACK ACK ACK ACK ACK ACK ACK

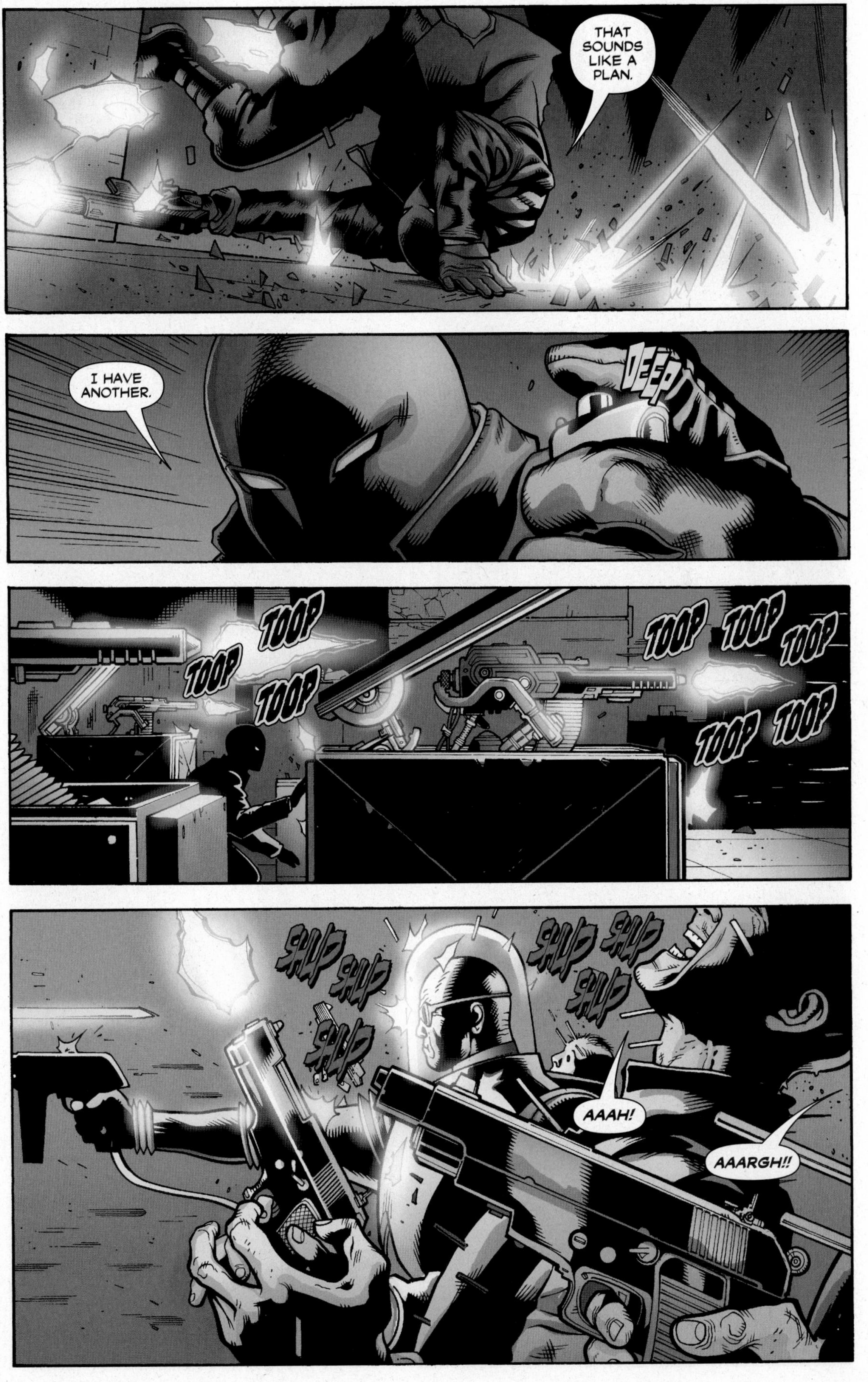
THAT SOUNDS LIKE A PLAN.
I HAVE ANOTHER.
DEEP
TOOP
TOOP
TOOP
TOOP
TOOP
TOOP
TOOP
TOOP
TOOP
SHUP
SHUP
SHUP
SHUP
SHUP
SHUP
AAAH!
AAARGH!!

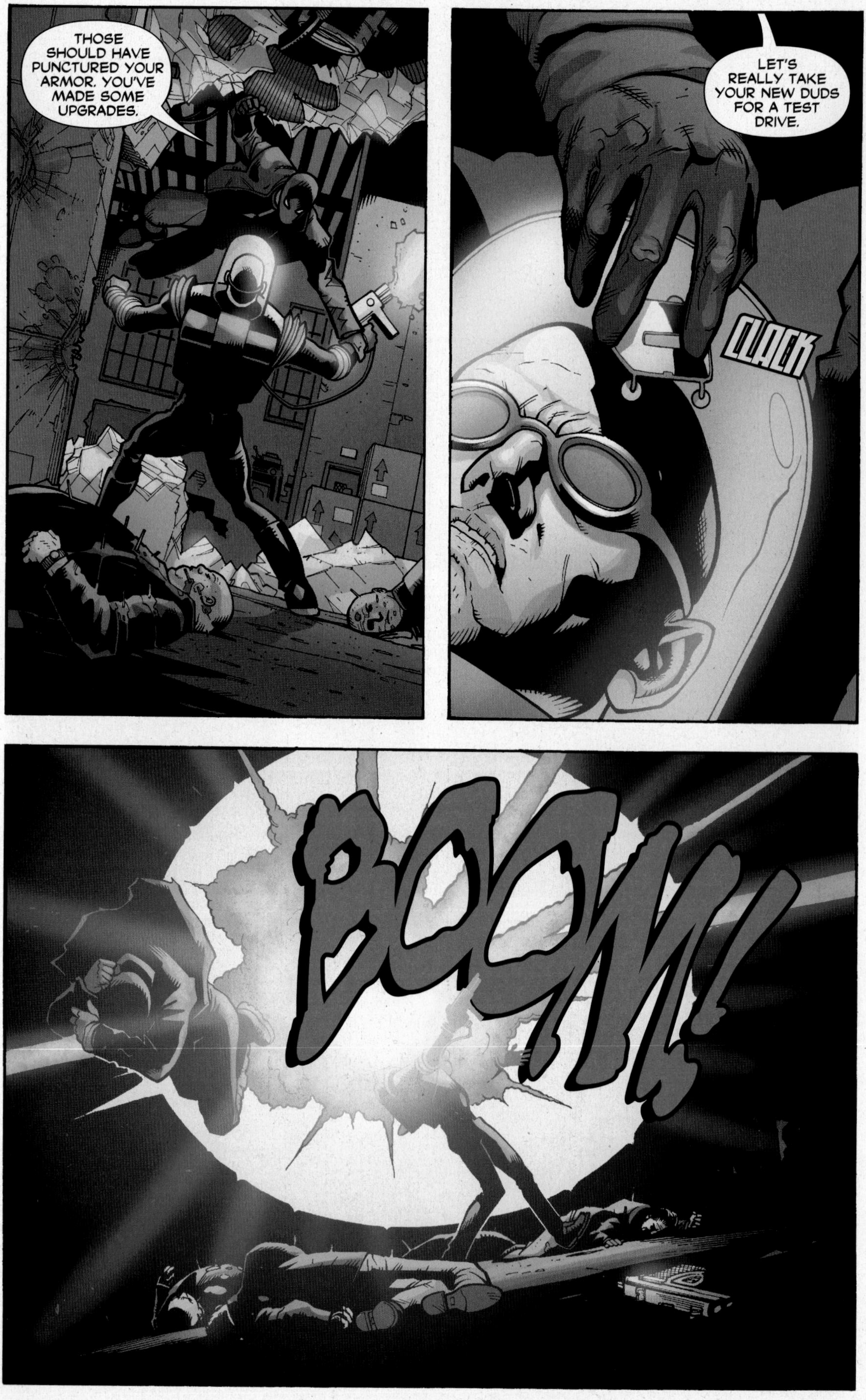
THOSE SHOULD HAVE PUNCTURED YOUR ARMOR. YOU'VE MADE SOME UPGRADES.
LET'S REALLY TAKE YOUR NEW DUDS FOR A TEST DRIVE.
CLACK
BOOM!

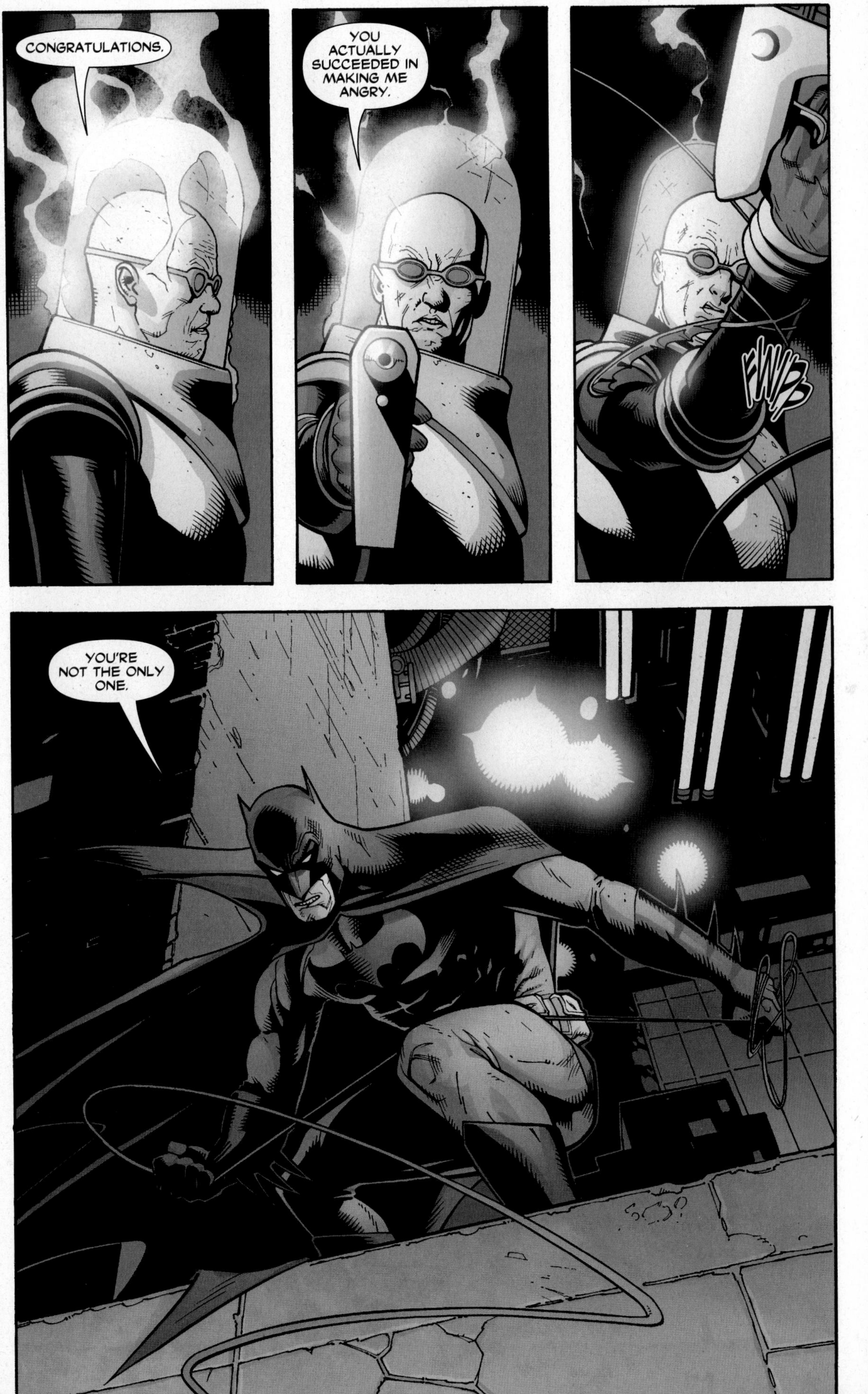
CONGRATULATIONS.
YOU ACTUALLY SUCCEEDED IN MAKING ME ANGRY.
FWIP
YOU'RE NOT THE ONLY ONE.

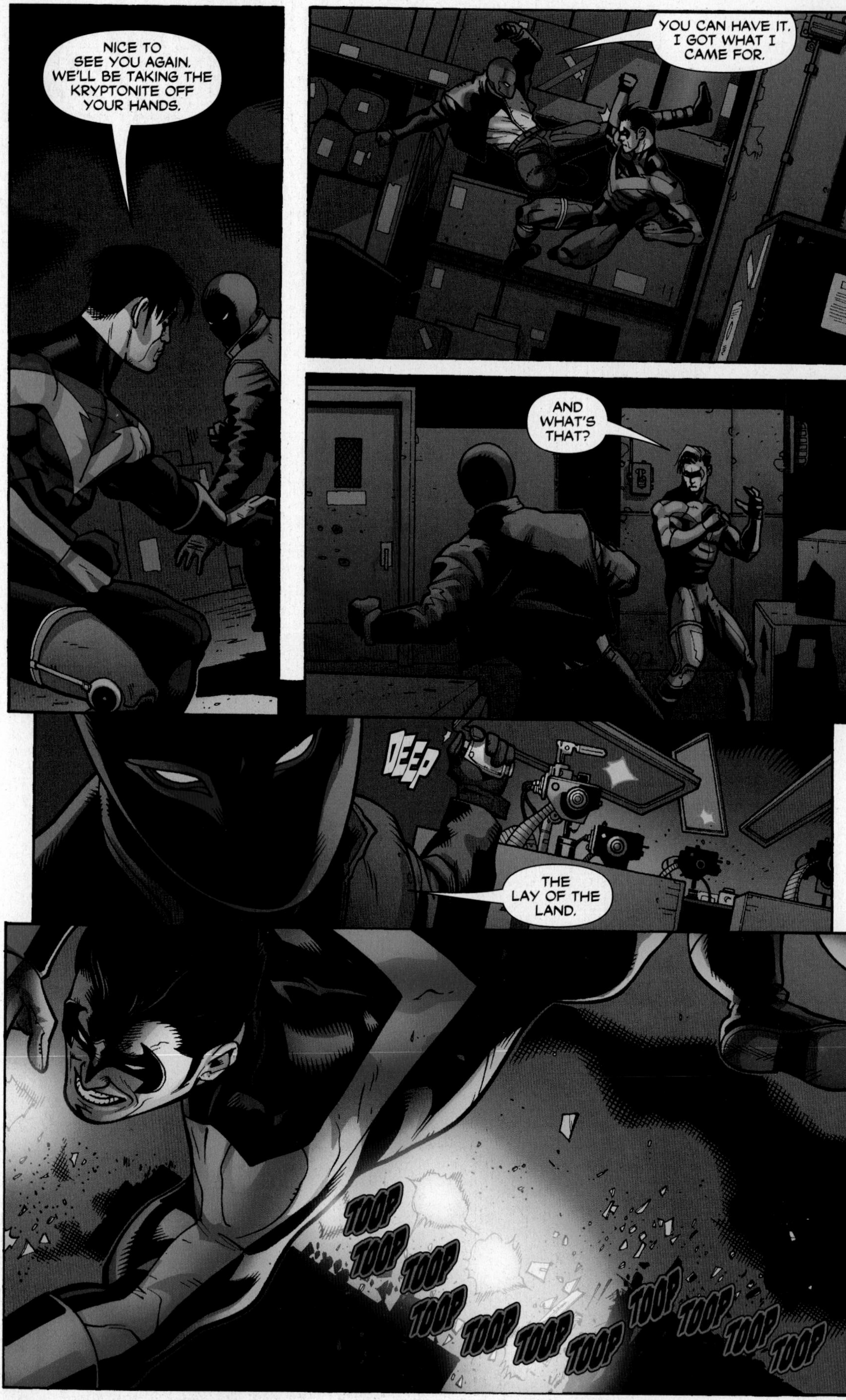
NICE TO SEE YOU AGAIN. WE'LL BE TAKING THE KRYPTONITE OFF YOUR HANDS.
YOU CAN HAVE IT. I GOT WHAT I CAME FOR.
AND WHAT'S THAT?
DEEP
THE LAY OF THE LAND.
TOOP TOOP TOOP TOOP TOOP TOOP TOOP TOOP TOOP TOOP TOOP

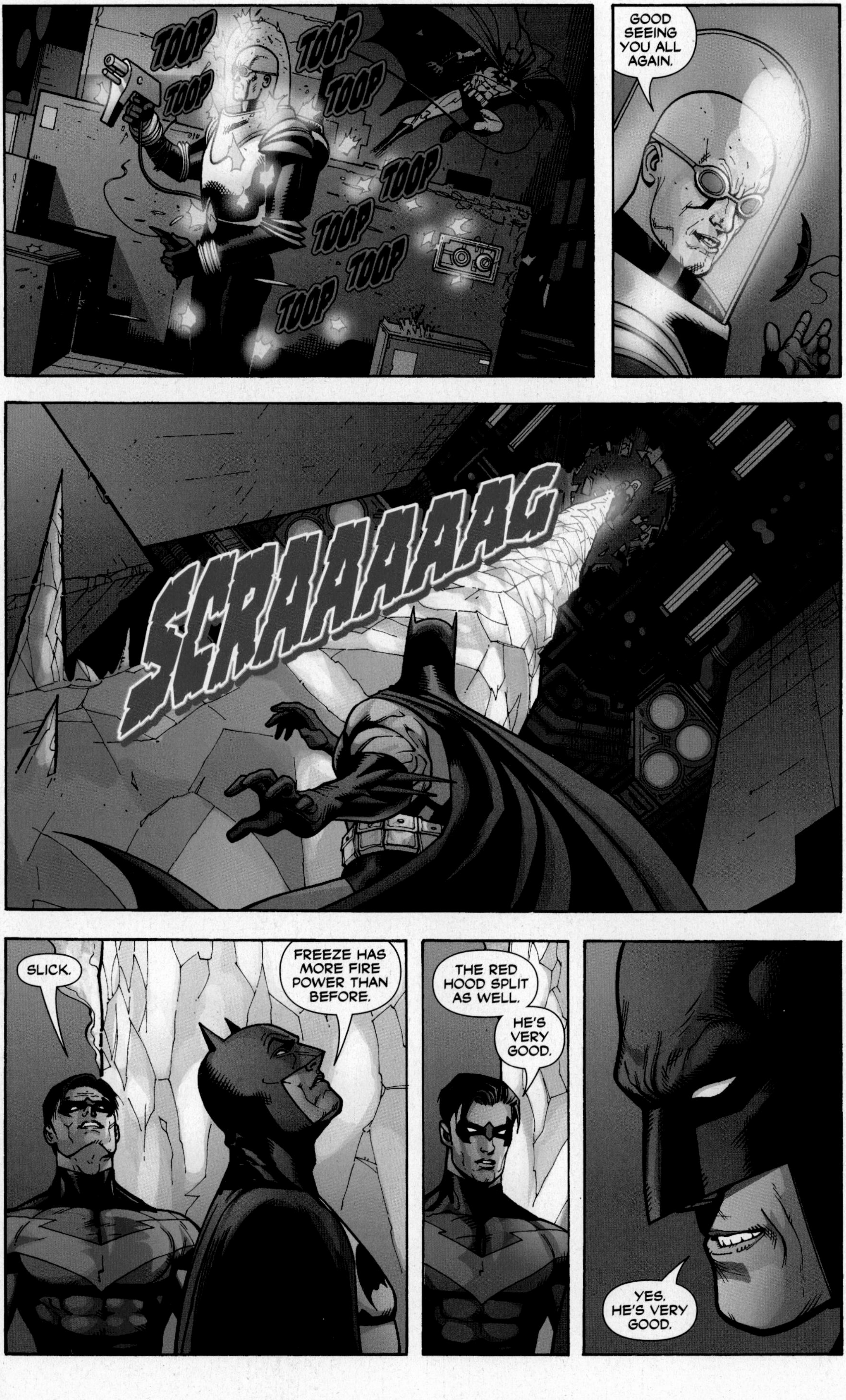
TOOP
TOOP
TOOP
TOOP
TOOP
TOOP
TOOP
TOOP
GOOD SEEING YOU ALL AGAIN.
SCRAAAAAAG
SLICK.
FREEZE HAS MORE FIRE POWER THAN BEFORE.
THE RED HOOD SPLIT AS WELL.
HE'S VERY GOOD.
YES. HE'S VERY GOOD.

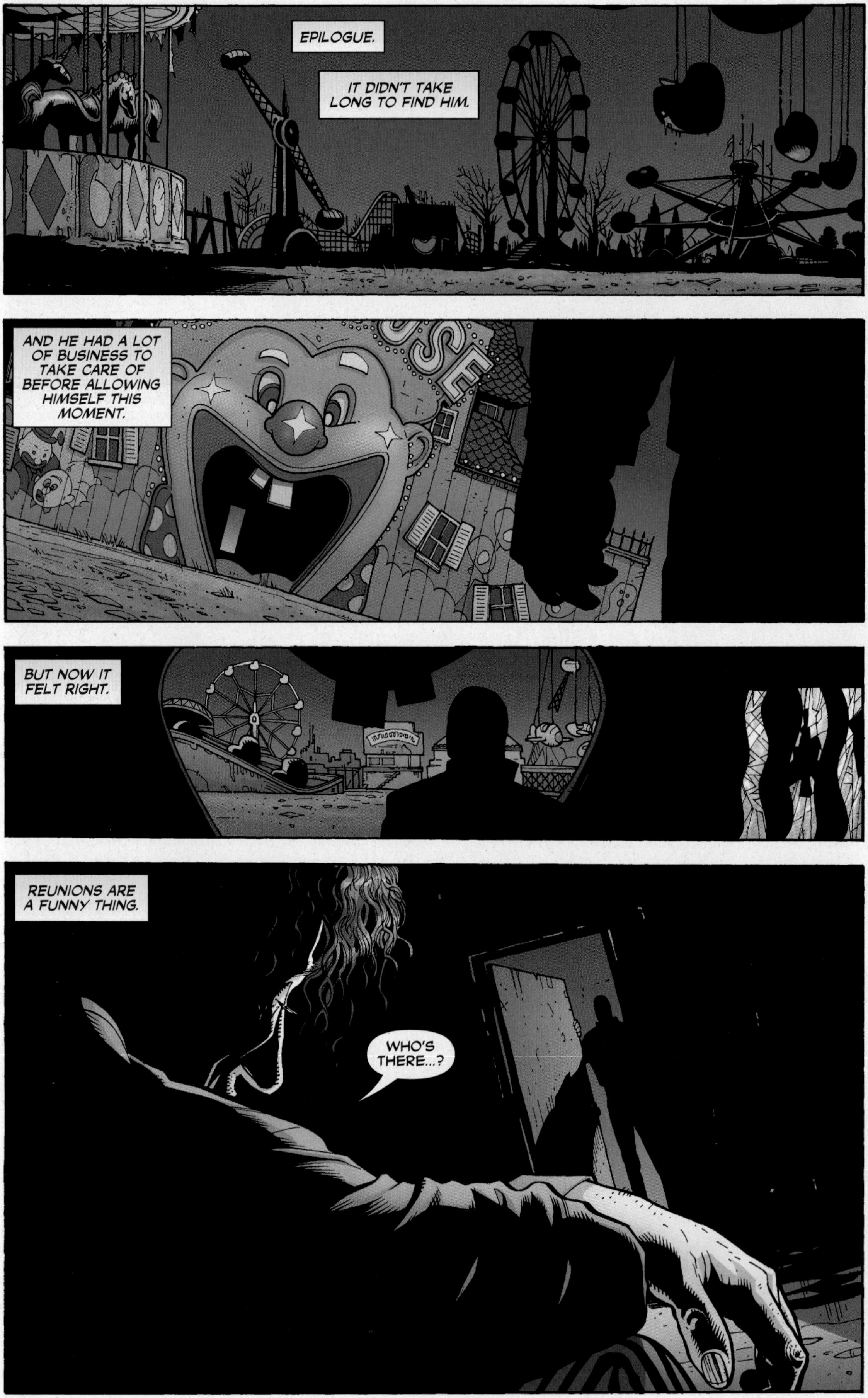
EPILOGUE.
IT DIDN'T TAKE LONG TO FIND HIM.
AND HE HAD A LOT OF BUSINESS TO TAKE CARE OF BEFORE ALLOWING HIMSELF THIS MOMENT.
BUT NOW IT FELT RIGHT.
REUNIONS ARE A FUNNY THING.
WHO'S THERE...?

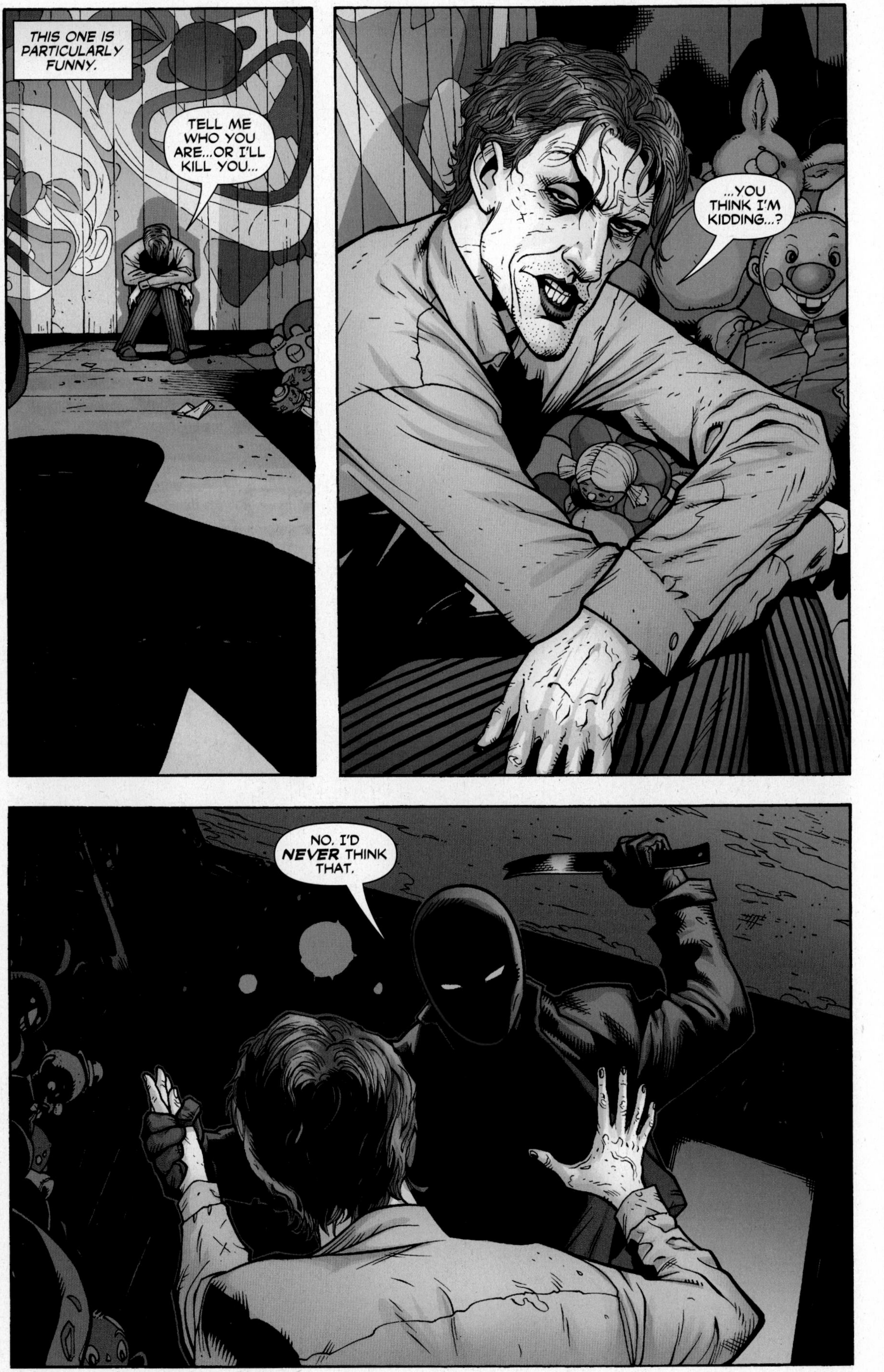
THIS ONE IS PARTICULARLY FUNNY.
TELL ME WHO YOU ARE...OR I'LL KILL YOU...
...YOU THINK I'M KIDDING...?
NO. I'D **NEVER** THINK THAT.

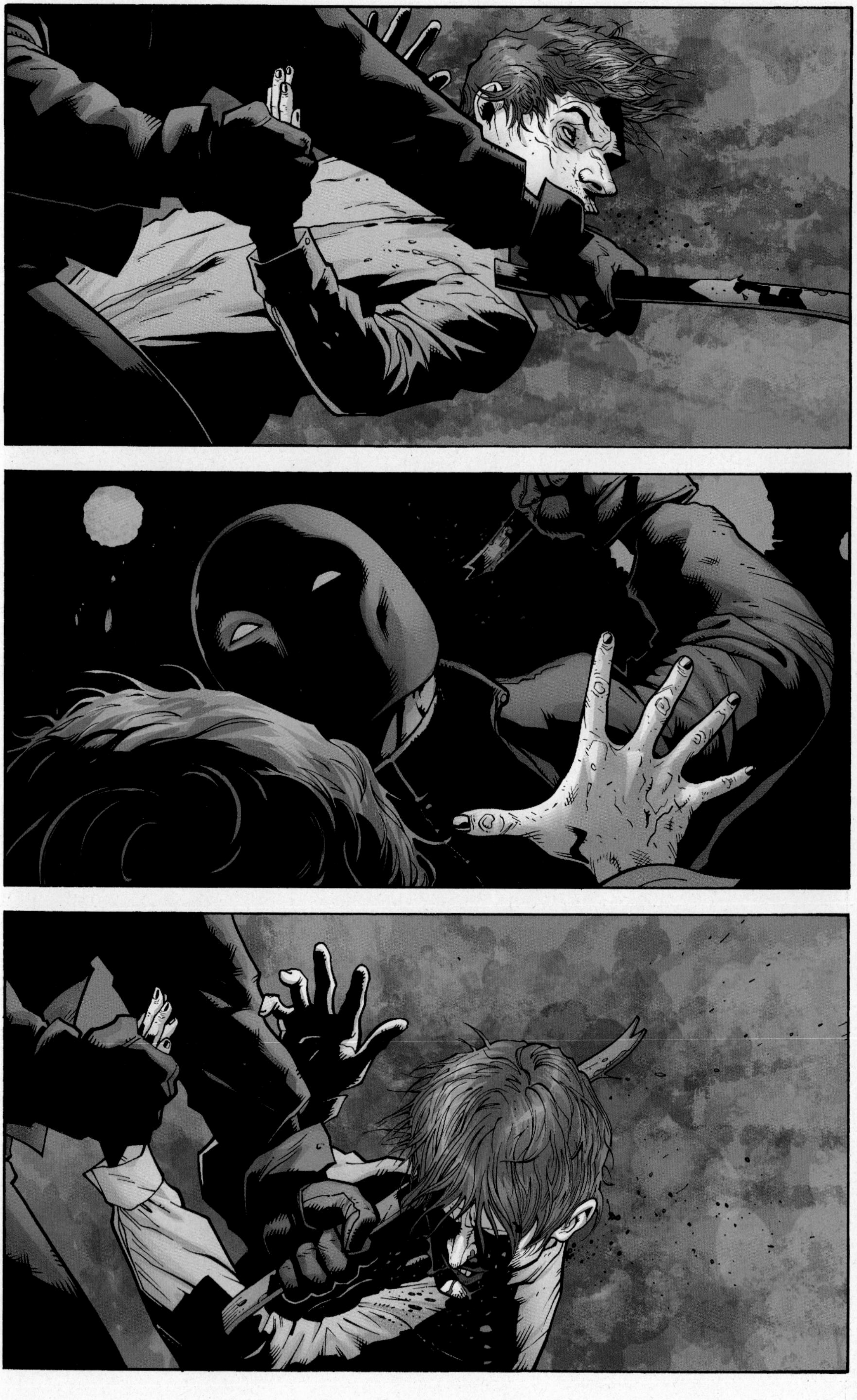

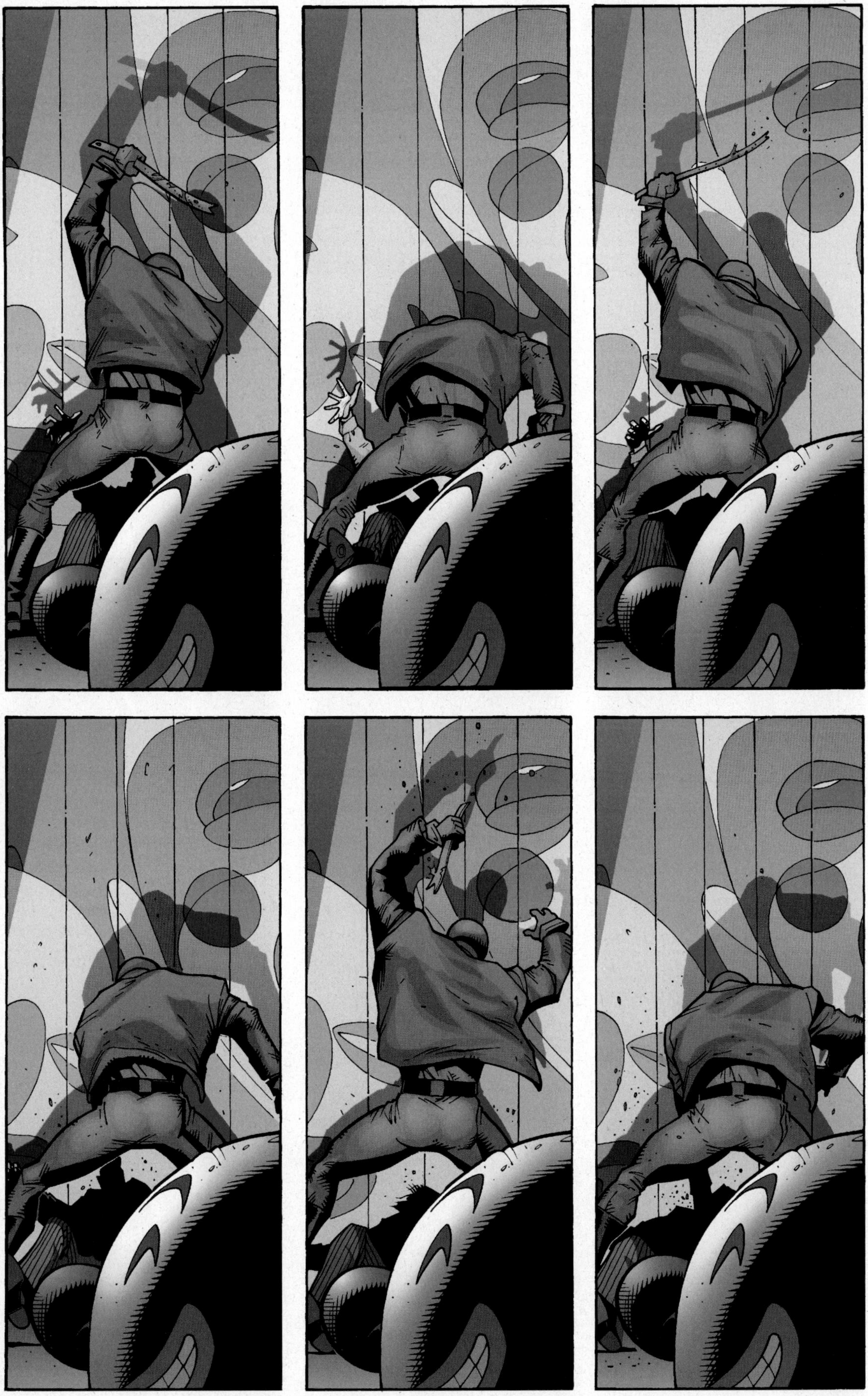

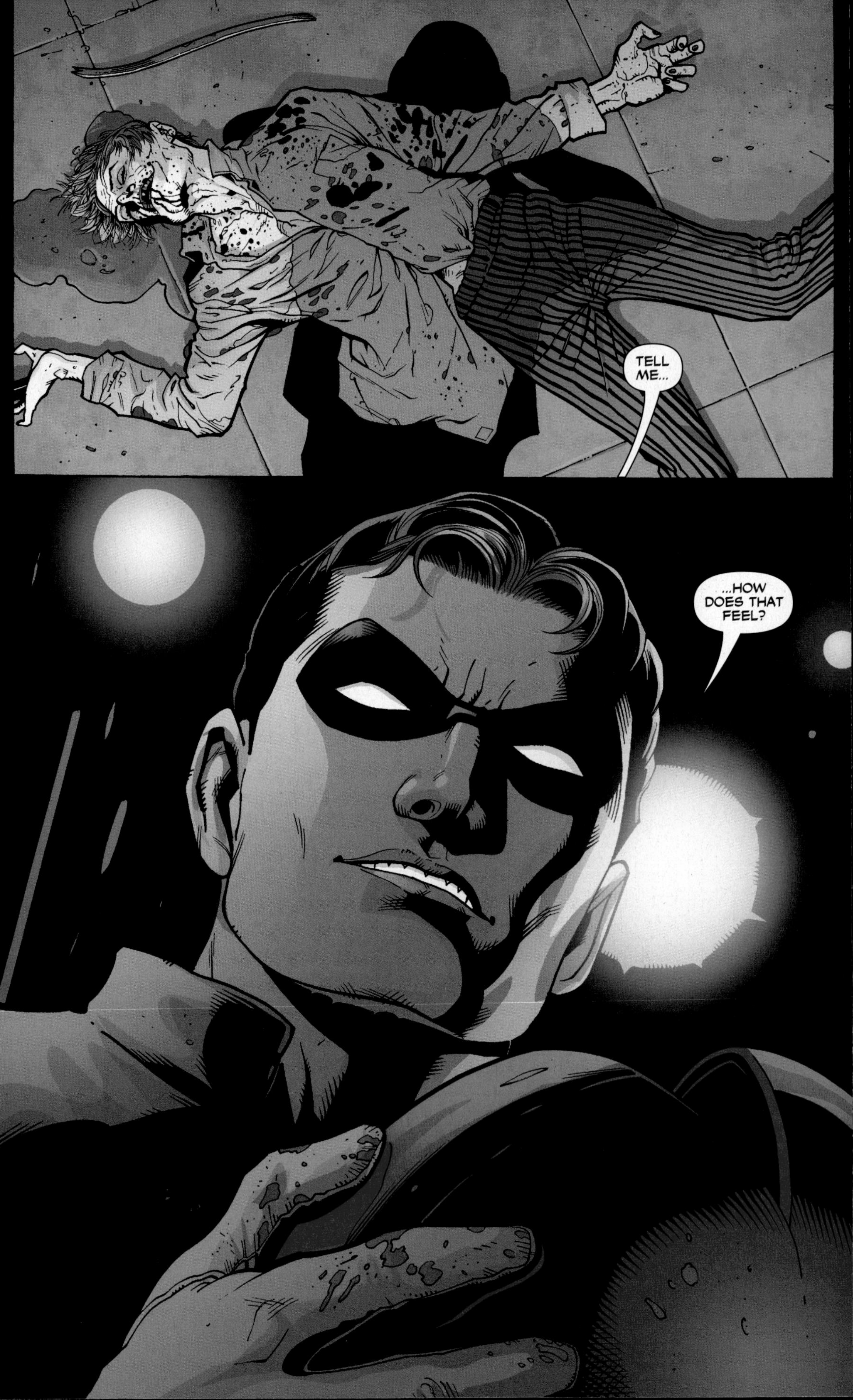
TELL ME...
...HOW DOES THAT FEEL?

BATMAN 639 Cover by Matt Wagner

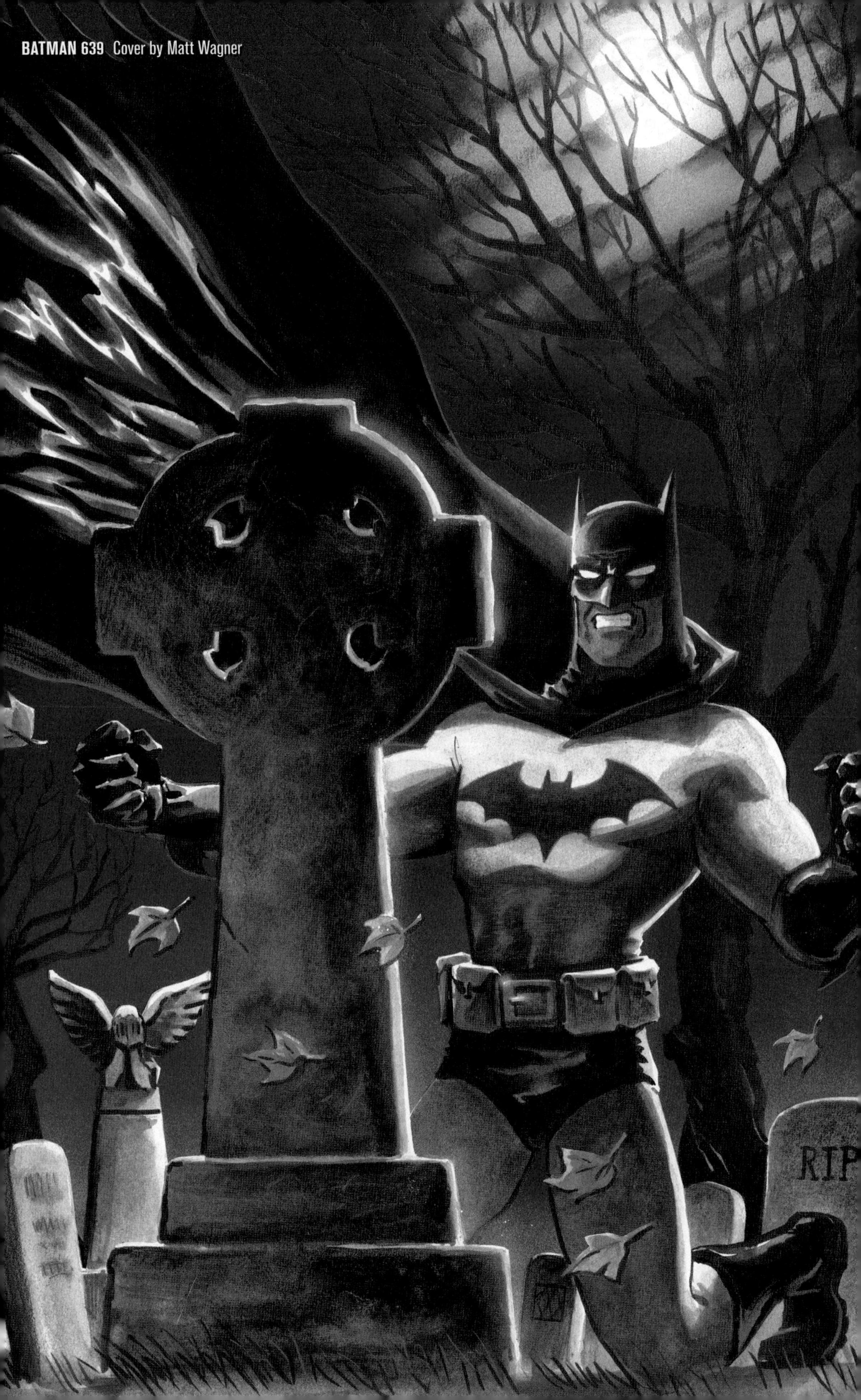
RIP

CHAPTER 5

THE WORD ON THE STREET

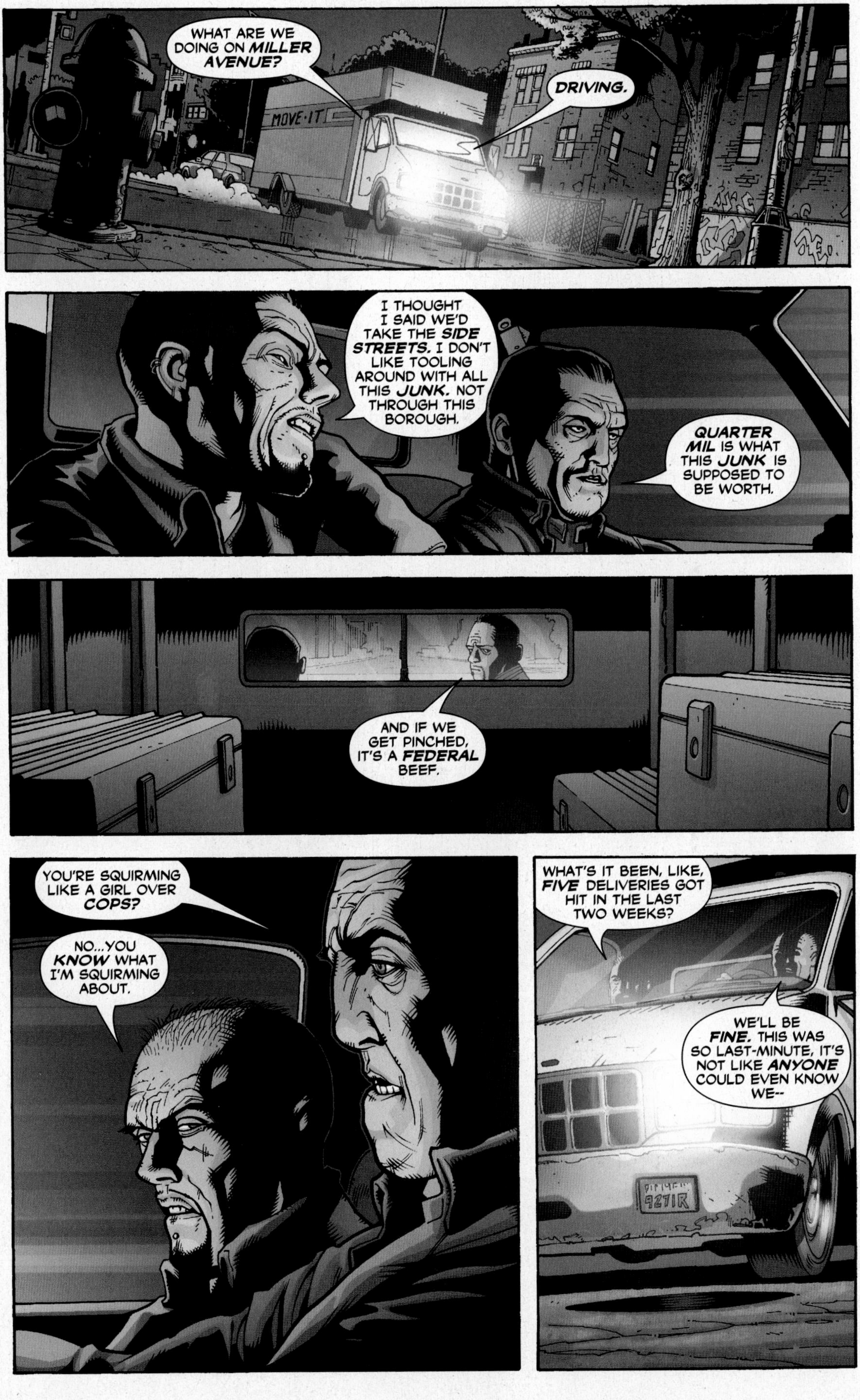
WHAT ARE WE DOING ON MILLER AVENUE?
DRIVING.
MOVE-IT
I THOUGHT I SAID WE'D TAKE THE SIDE STREETS. I DON'T LIKE TOOLING AROUND WITH ALL THIS JUNK. NOT THROUGH THIS BOROUGH.
QUARTER MIL IS WHAT THIS JUNK IS SUPPOSED TO BE WORTH.
AND IF WE GET PINCHED, IT'S A FEDERAL BEEF.
YOU'RE SQUIRMING LIKE A GIRL OVER COPS?
NO...YOU KNOW WHAT I'M SQUIRMING ABOUT.
WHAT'S IT BEEN, LIKE, FIVE DELIVERIES GOT HIT IN THE LAST TWO WEEKS?
WE'LL BE FINE. THIS WAS SO LAST-MINUTE, IT'S NOT LIKE ANYONE COULD EVEN KNOW WE--

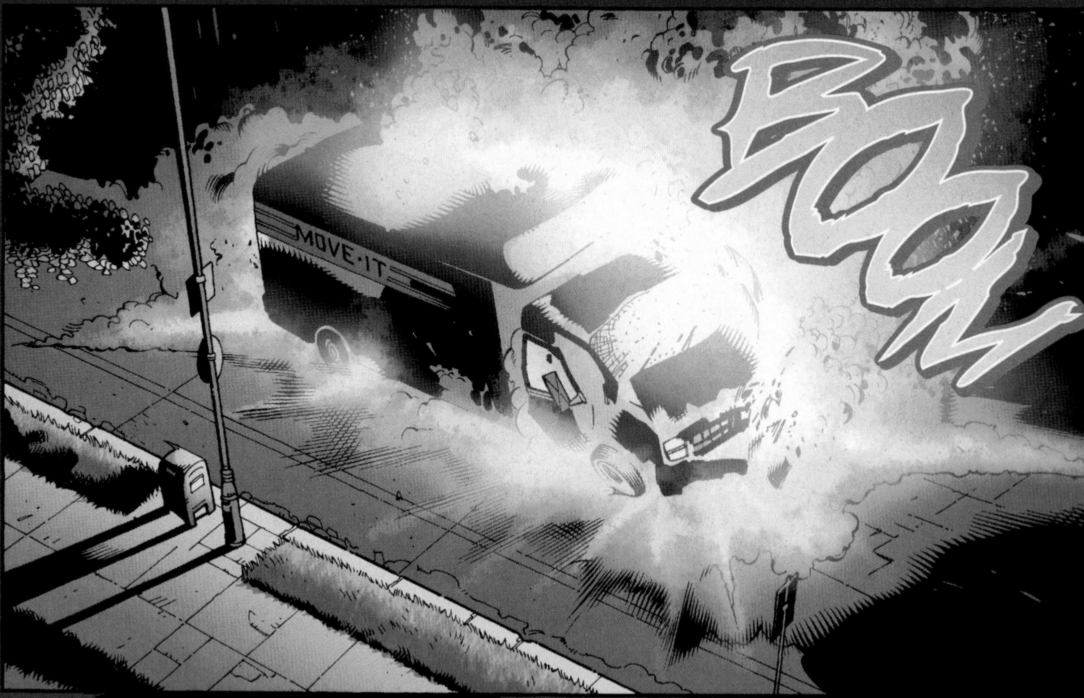
MOVE-IT
BOOM

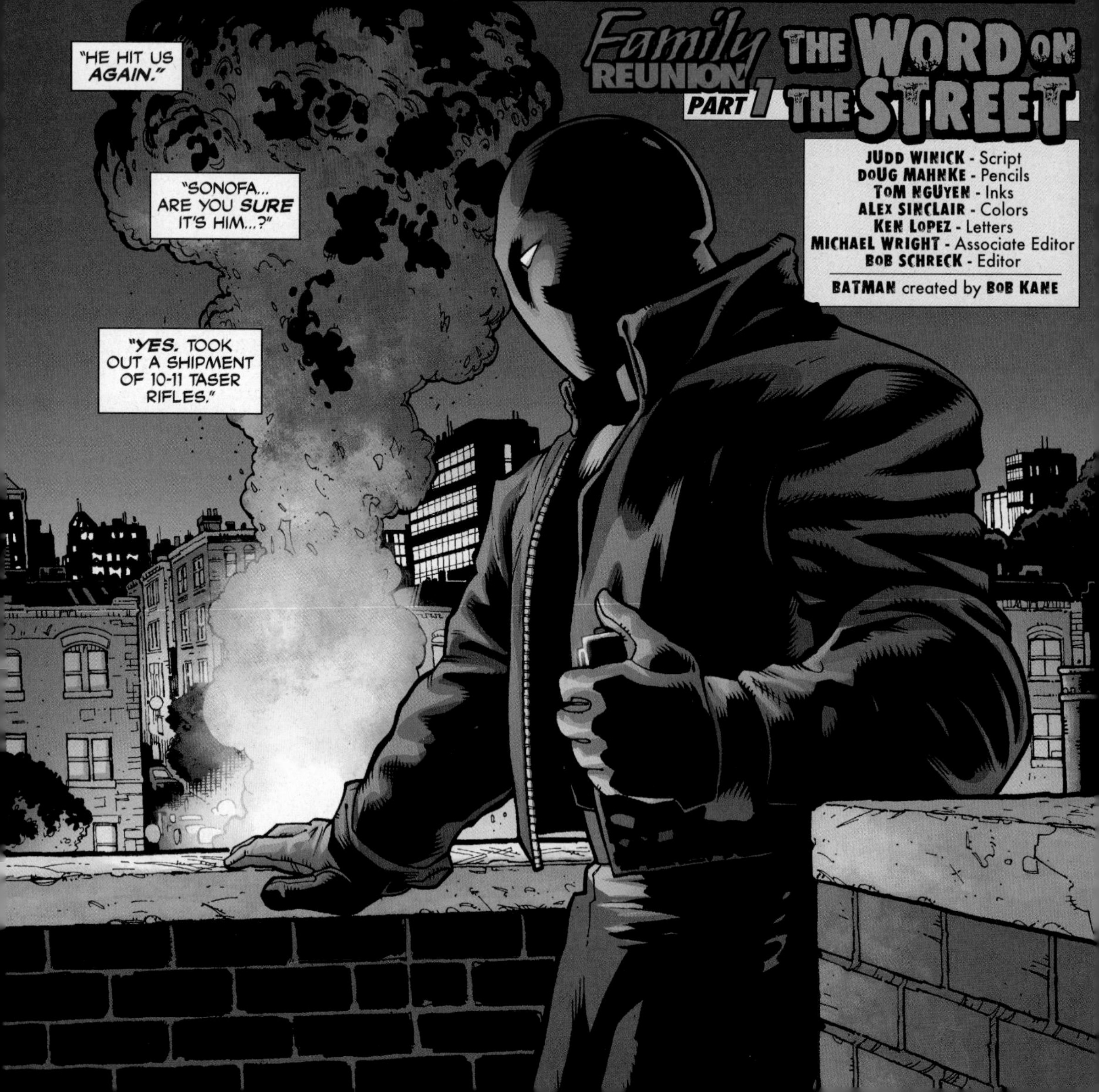
"HE HIT US AGAIN."
"SONOFA... ARE YOU SURE IT'S HIM...?"
"YES. TOOK OUT A SHIPMENT OF 10-11 TASER RIFLES."
Family Reunion Part 1
THE WORD ON THE STREET
JUDD WINICK - Script
DOUG MAHNKE - Pencils
TOM NGUYEN - Inks
ALEX SINCLAIR - Colors
KEN LOPEZ - Letters
MICHAEL WRIGHT - Associate Editor
BOB SCHRECK - Editor
BATMAN created by BOB KANE

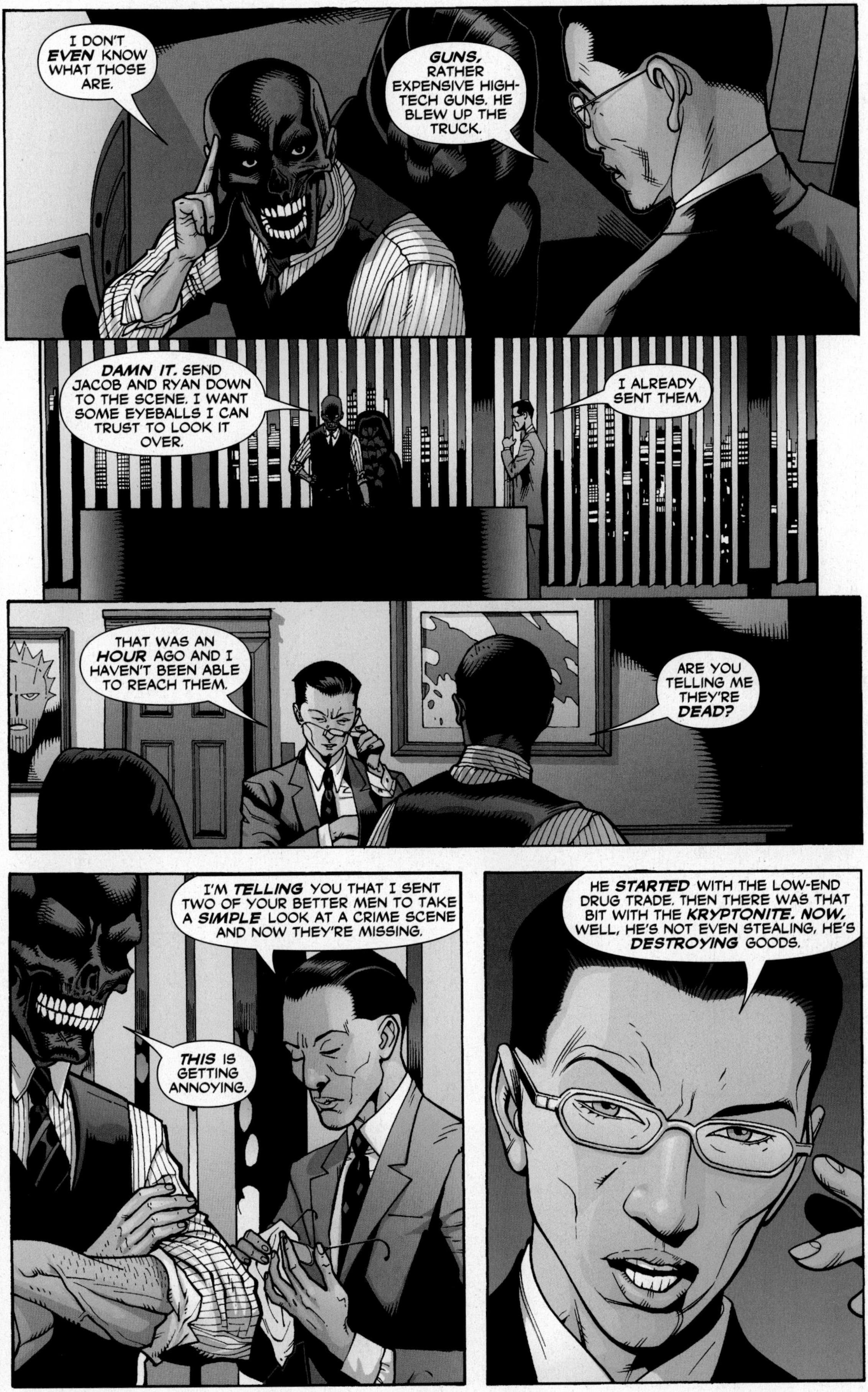
I DON'T EVEN KNOW WHAT THOSE ARE.
GUNS, RATHER EXPENSIVE HIGH-TECH GUNS. HE BLEW UP THE TRUCK.
DAMN IT. SEND JACOB AND RYAN DOWN TO THE SCENE. I WANT SOME EYEBALLS I CAN TRUST TO LOOK IT OVER.
I ALREADY SENT THEM.
THAT WAS AN HOUR AGO AND I HAVEN'T BEEN ABLE TO REACH THEM.
ARE YOU TELLING ME THEY'RE DEAD?
I'M TELLING YOU THAT I SENT TWO OF YOUR BETTER MEN TO TAKE A SIMPLE LOOK AT A CRIME SCENE AND NOW THEY'RE MISSING.
THIS IS GETTING ANNOYING.
HE STARTED WITH THE LOW-END DRUG TRADE. THEN THERE WAS THAT BIT WITH THE KRYPTONITE. NOW, WELL, HE'S NOT EVEN STEALING, HE'S DESTROYING GOODS.

YEAH... SENDS *QUITE* THE MESSAGE.

WHAT DO YOU WANT TO DO?

I WANT TO *SCORCH* THE EARTH, DIG UP HIS *ASHES* AND SEND THEM INTO *OUTER SPACE*...BUT THAT WOULD BE *STUPID.*

WHY'S THAT?

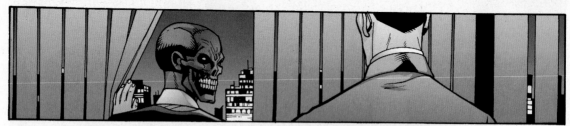

BECAUSE HE'S NOT JUST *MY* PROBLEM.

AND I'D RATHER HAVE SOMEONE *ELSE* THROW OUT OUR GARBAGE.

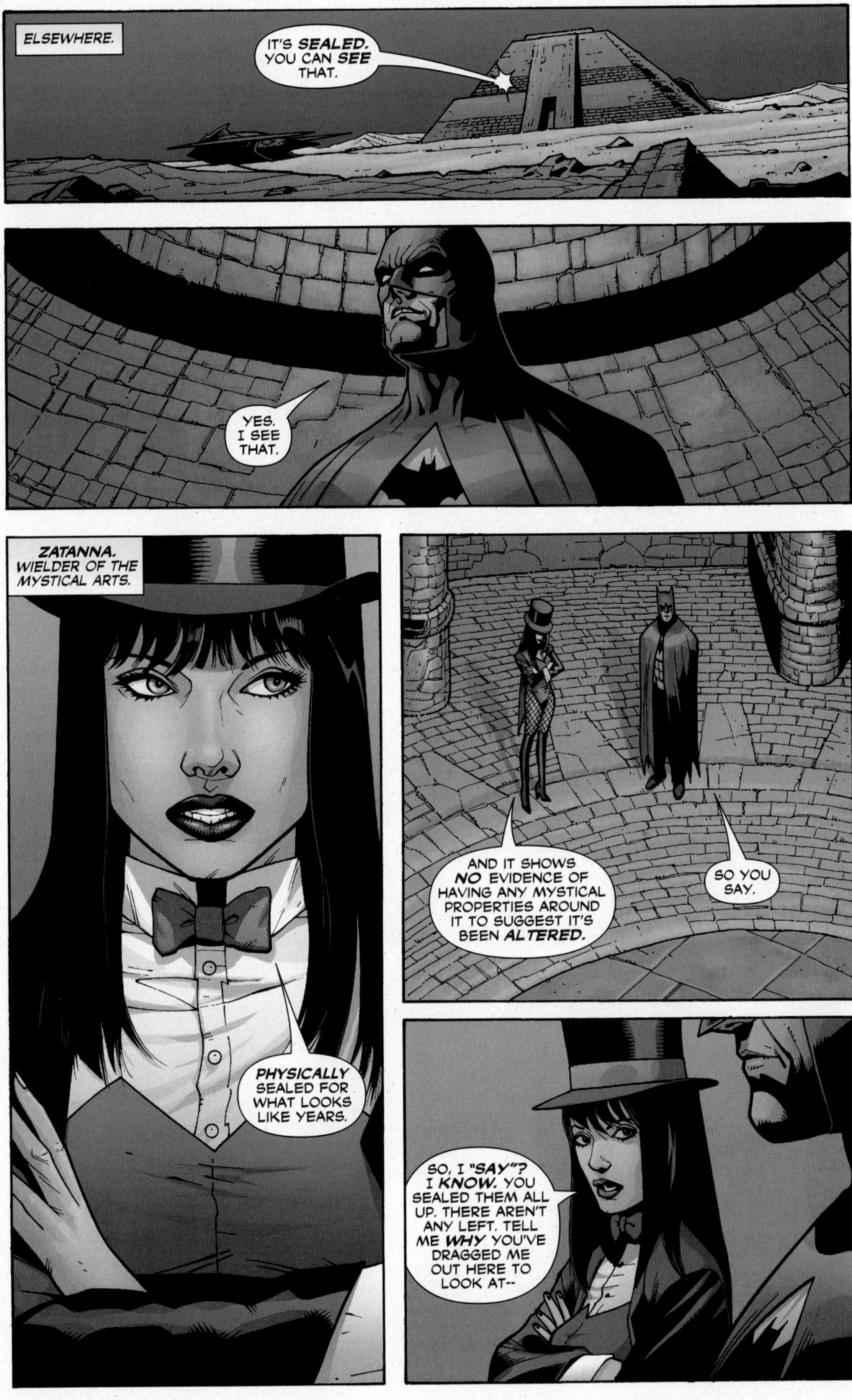
ELSEWHERE.
IT'S SEALED. YOU CAN SEE THAT.
YES. I SEE THAT.
ZATANNA. WIELDER OF THE MYSTICAL ARTS.
PHYSICALLY SEALED FOR WHAT LOOKS LIKE YEARS.
AND IT SHOWS NO EVIDENCE OF HAVING ANY MYSTICAL PROPERTIES AROUND IT TO SUGGEST IT'S BEEN ALTERED.
SO YOU SAY.
SO, I "SAY"? I KNOW. YOU SEALED THEM ALL UP. THERE AREN'T ANY LEFT. TELL ME WHY YOU'VE DRAGGED ME OUT HERE TO LOOK AT--

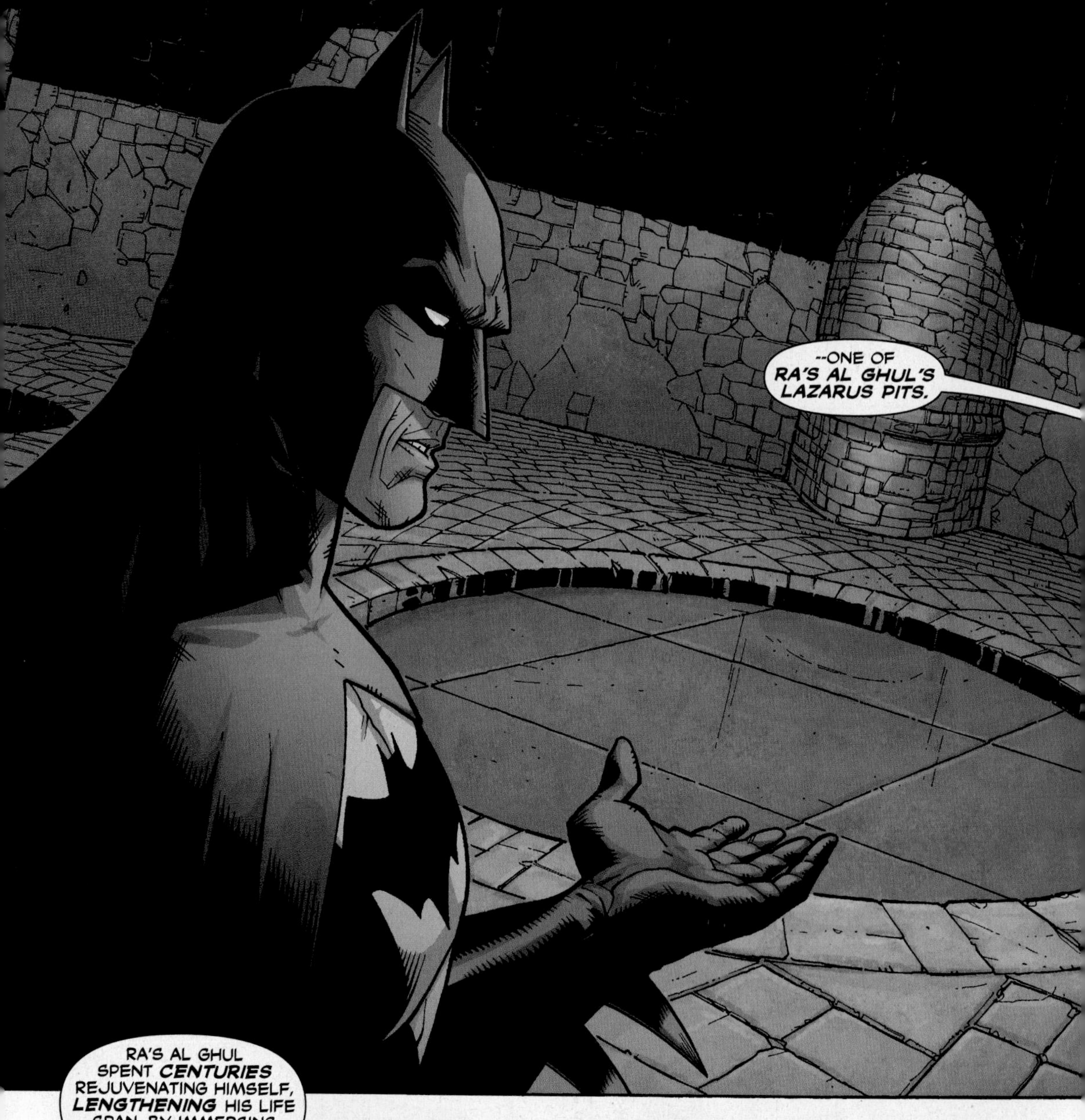
--ONE OF RA'S AL GHUL'S LAZARUS PITS.
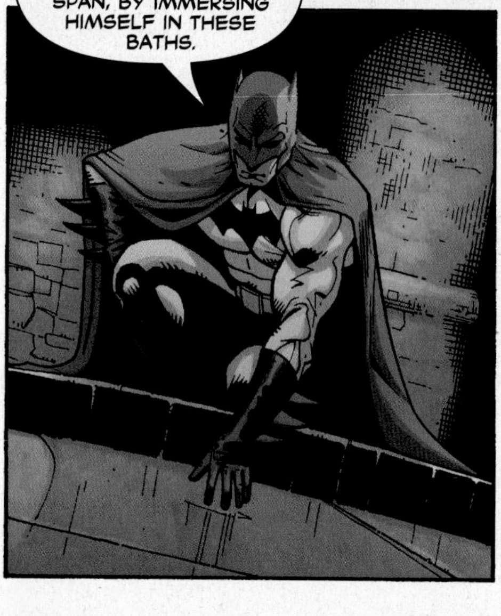
RA'S AL GHUL SPENT CENTURIES REJUVENATING HIMSELF, LENGTHENING HIS LIFE SPAN, BY IMMERSING HIMSELF IN THESE BATHS.
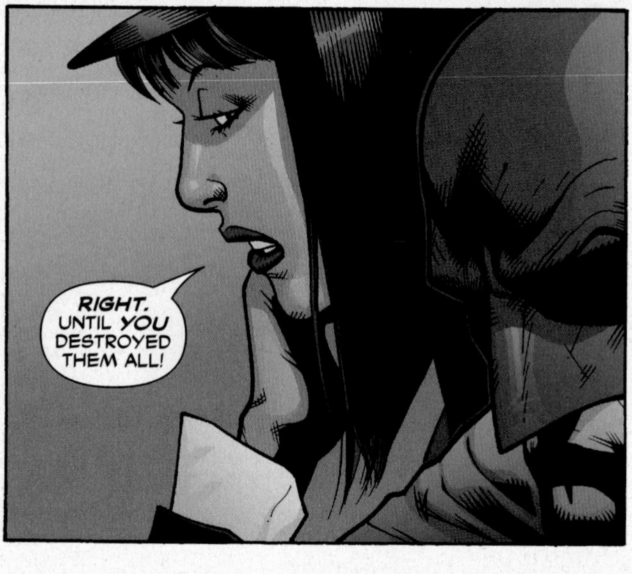
RIGHT. UNTIL YOU DESTROYED THEM ALL!

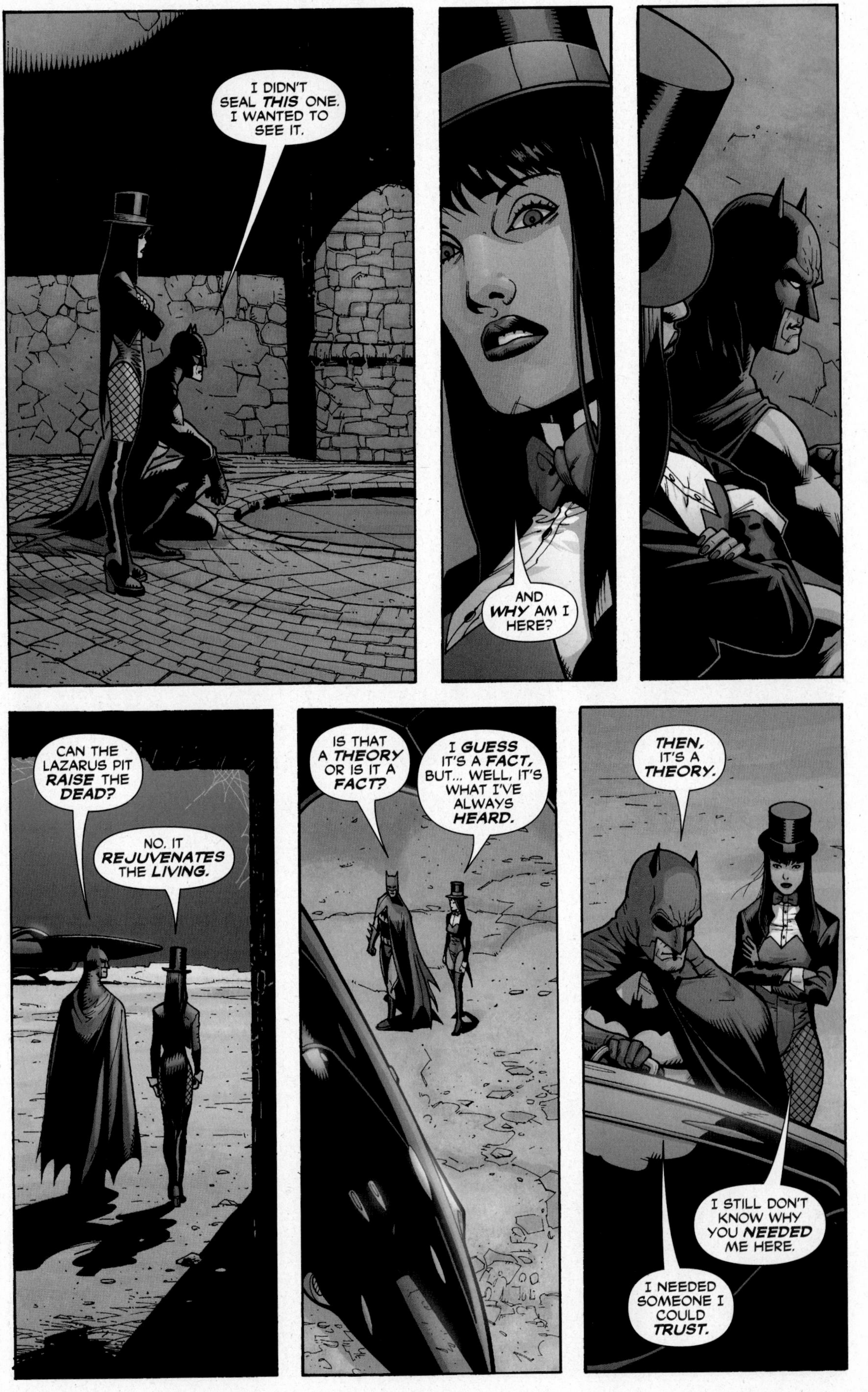
I DIDN'T SEAL THIS ONE. I WANTED TO SEE IT.
AND WHY AM I HERE?
CAN THE LAZARUS PIT RAISE THE DEAD?
NO. IT REJUVENATES THE LIVING.
IS THAT A THEORY OR IS IT A FACT?
I GUESS IT'S A FACT, BUT... WELL, IT'S WHAT I'VE ALWAYS HEARD.
THEN, IT'S A THEORY.
I STILL DON'T KNOW WHY YOU NEEDED ME HERE.
I NEEDED SOMEONE I COULD TRUST.

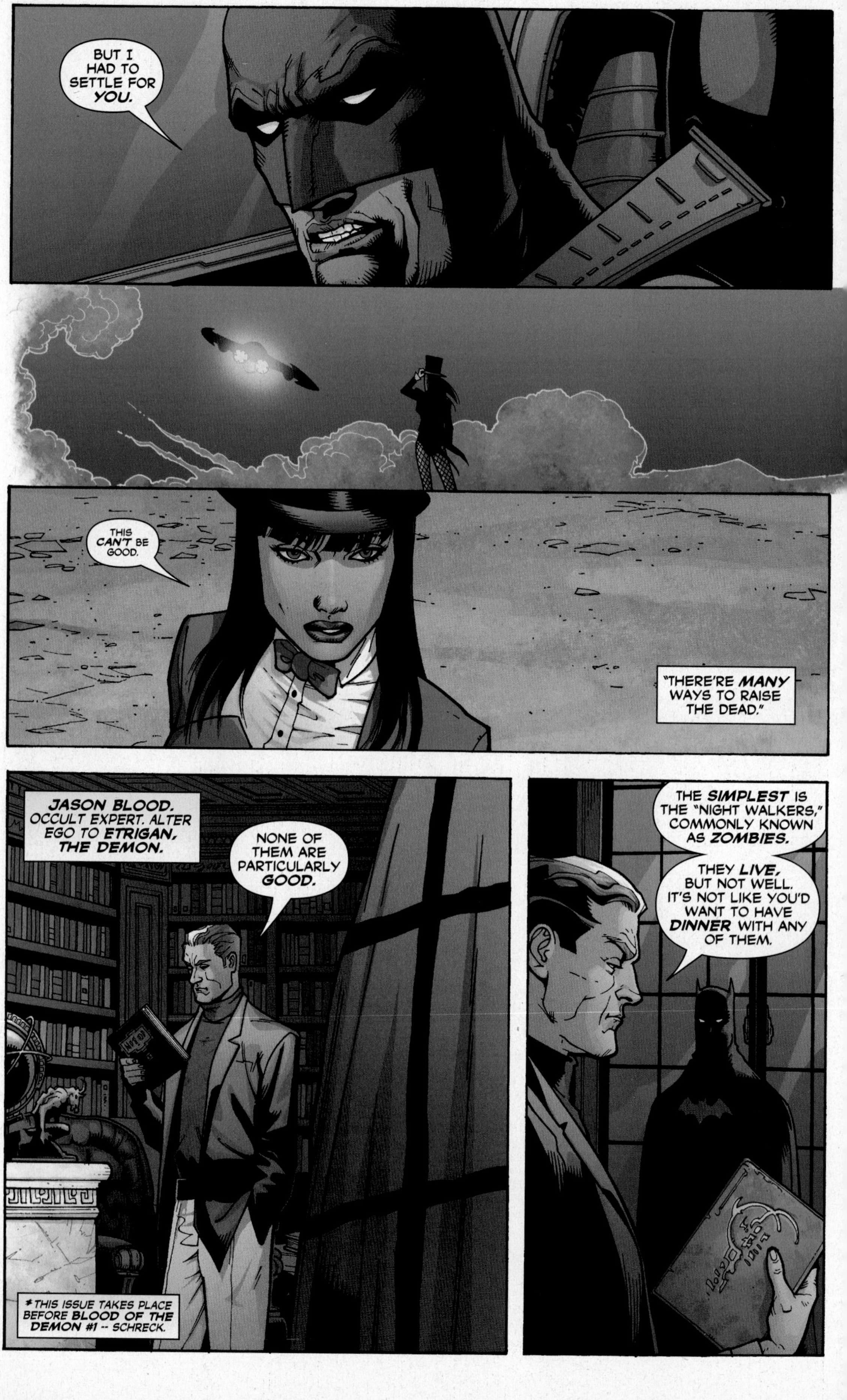
BUT I HAD TO SETTLE FOR YOU.
THIS CAN'T BE GOOD.
"THERE'RE MANY WAYS TO RAISE THE DEAD."
JASON BLOOD. OCCULT EXPERT. ALTER EGO TO ETRIGAN, THE DEMON.
NONE OF THEM ARE PARTICULARLY GOOD.
*THIS ISSUE TAKES PLACE BEFORE BLOOD OF THE DEMON #1 -- SCHRECK.
THE SIMPLEST IS THE "NIGHT WALKERS," COMMONLY KNOWN AS ZOMBIES.
THEY LIVE, BUT NOT WELL. IT'S NOT LIKE YOU'D WANT TO HAVE DINNER WITH ANY OF THEM.

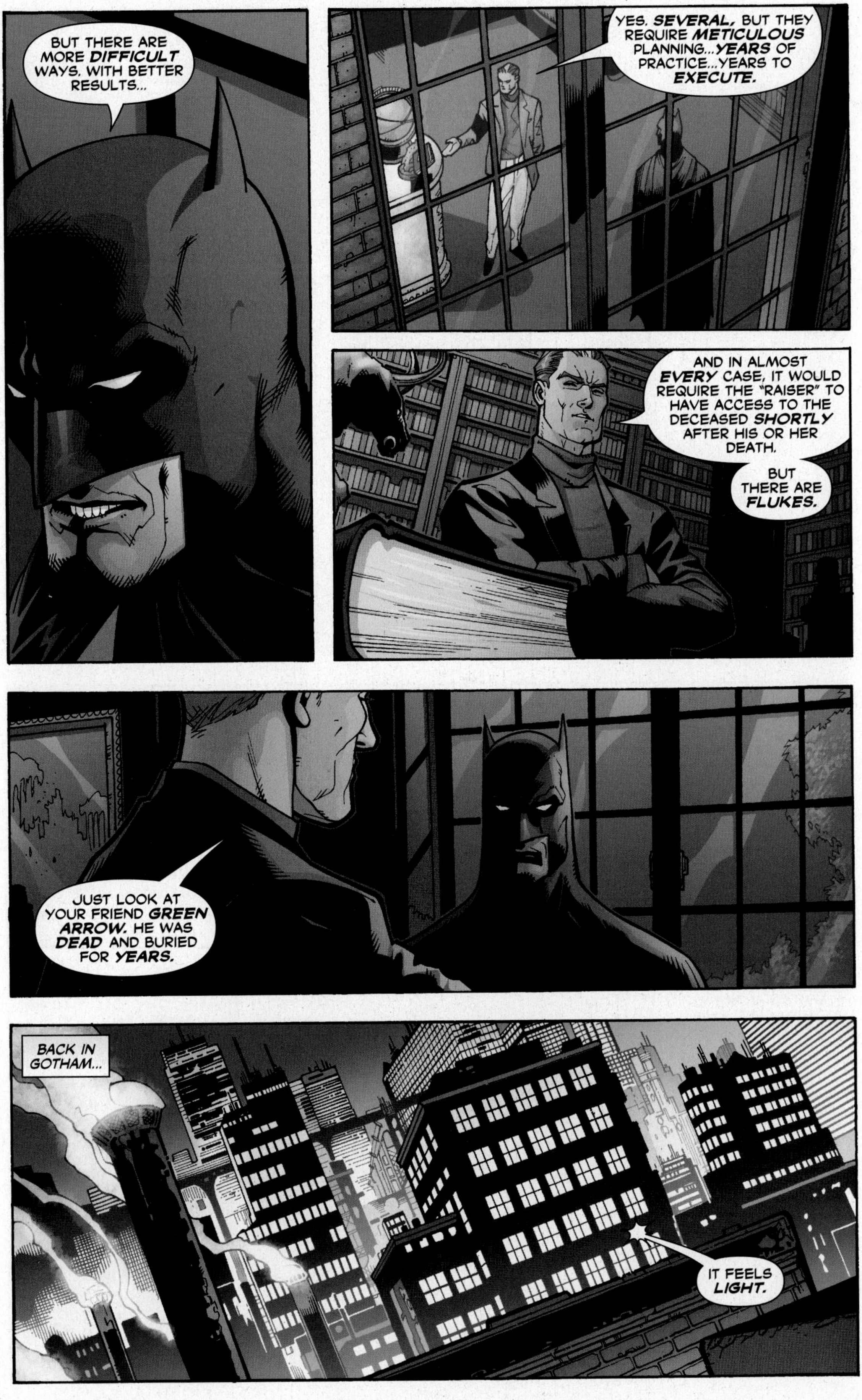
BUT THERE ARE MORE DIFFICULT WAYS, WITH BETTER RESULTS...
YES. SEVERAL, BUT THEY REQUIRE METICULOUS PLANNING...YEARS OF PRACTICE...YEARS TO EXECUTE.
AND IN ALMOST EVERY CASE, IT WOULD REQUIRE THE "RAISER" TO HAVE ACCESS TO THE DECEASED SHORTLY AFTER HIS OR HER DEATH.
BUT THERE ARE FLUKES.
JUST LOOK AT YOUR FRIEND GREEN ARROW. HE WAS DEAD AND BURIED FOR YEARS.
BACK IN GOTHAM...
IT FEELS LIGHT.

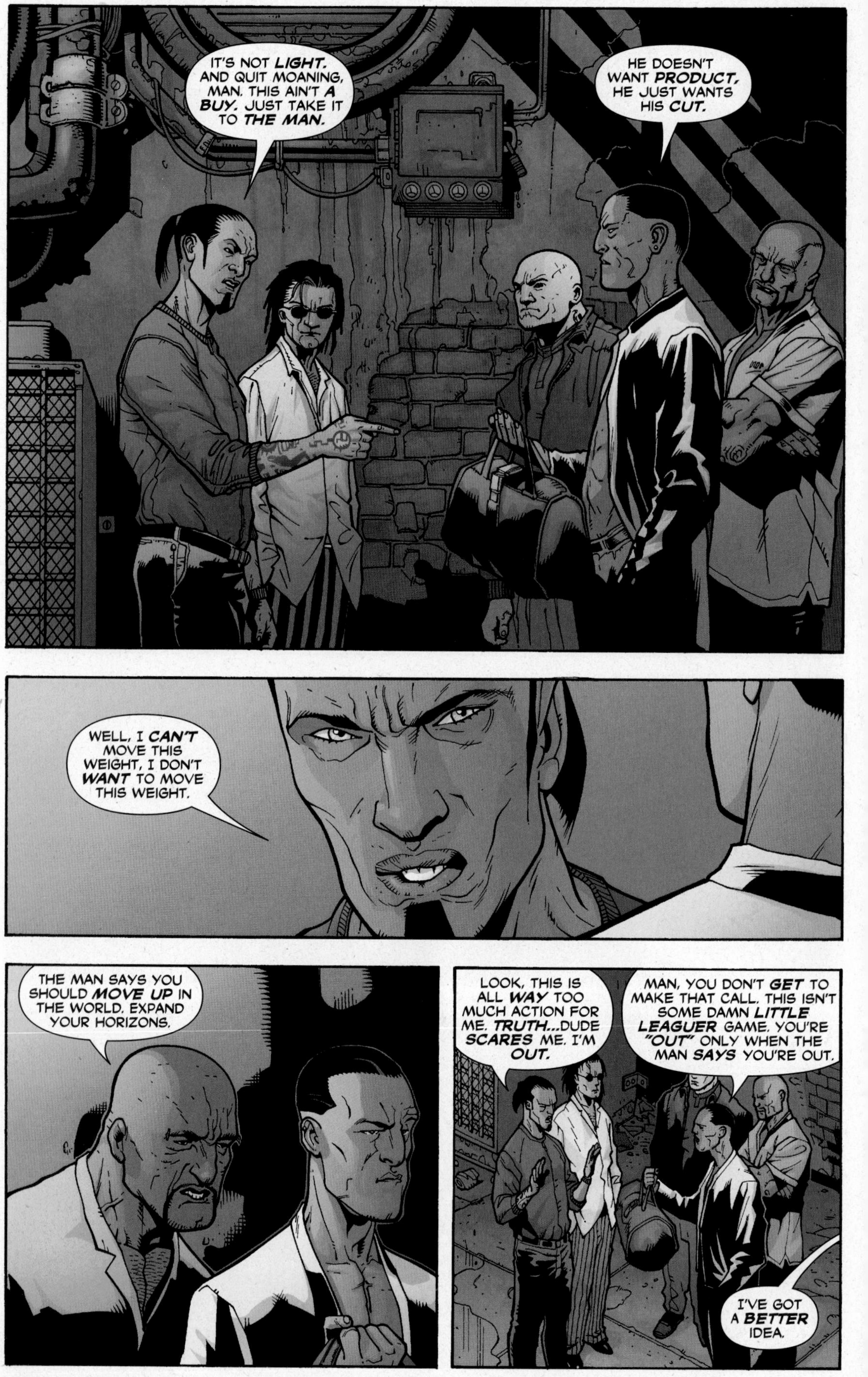
IT'S NOT LIGHT. AND QUIT MOANING, MAN. THIS AIN'T A BUY. JUST TAKE IT TO THE MAN.
HE DOESN'T WANT PRODUCT, HE JUST WANTS HIS CUT.
WELL, I CAN'T MOVE THIS WEIGHT, I DON'T WANT TO MOVE THIS WEIGHT.
THE MAN SAYS YOU SHOULD MOVE UP IN THE WORLD. EXPAND YOUR HORIZONS.
LOOK, THIS IS ALL WAY TOO MUCH ACTION FOR ME. TRUTH...DUDE SCARES ME. I'M OUT.
MAN, YOU DON'T GET TO MAKE THAT CALL. THIS ISN'T SOME DAMN LITTLE LEAGUER GAME. YOU'RE "OUT" ONLY WHEN THE MAN SAYS YOU'RE OUT.
I'VE GOT A BETTER IDEA.

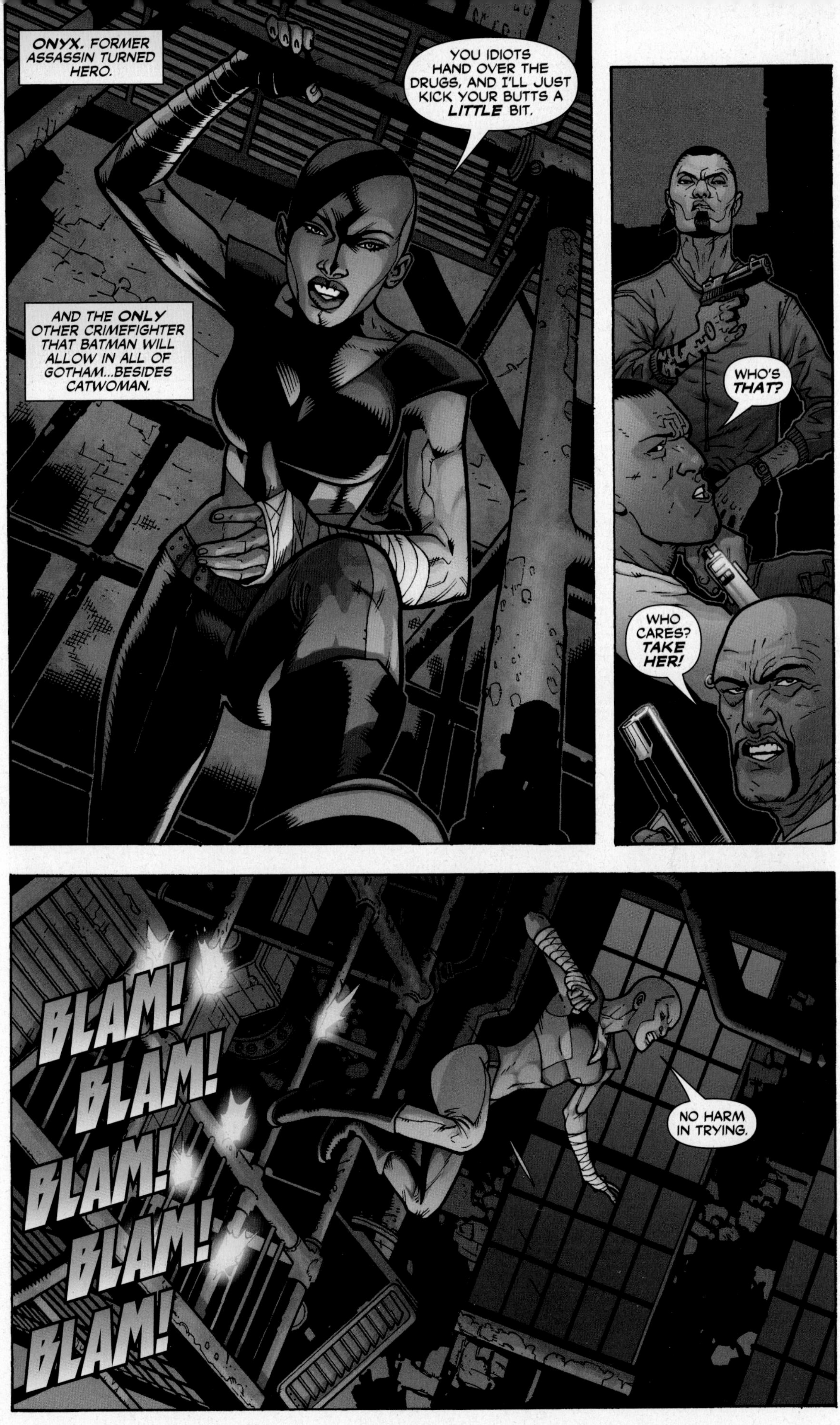
ONYX. FORMER ASSASSIN TURNED HERO.
YOU IDIOTS HAND OVER THE DRUGS, AND I'LL JUST KICK YOUR BUTTS A LITTLE BIT.
AND THE ONLY OTHER CRIMEFIGHTER THAT BATMAN WILL ALLOW IN ALL OF GOTHAM...BESIDES CATWOMAN.
WHO'S THAT?
WHO CARES? TAKE HER!
BLAM! BLAM! BLAM! BLAM! BLAM!
NO HARM IN TRYING.

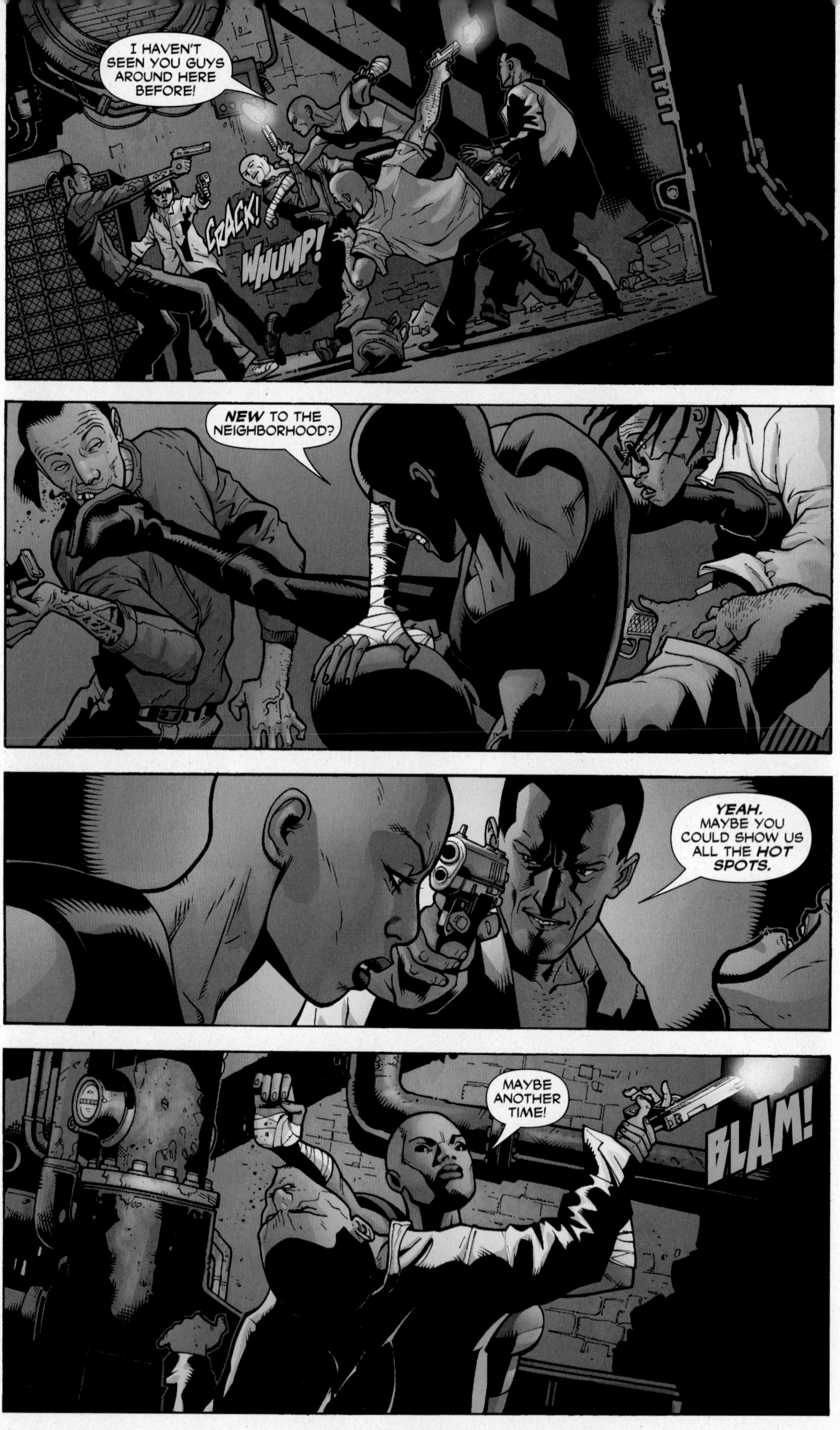
I HAVEN'T SEEN YOU GUYS AROUND HERE BEFORE!
CRACK!
WHUMP!
NEW TO THE NEIGHBORHOOD?
YEAH. MAYBE YOU COULD SHOW US ALL THE HOT SPOTS.
MAYBE ANOTHER TIME!
BLAM!

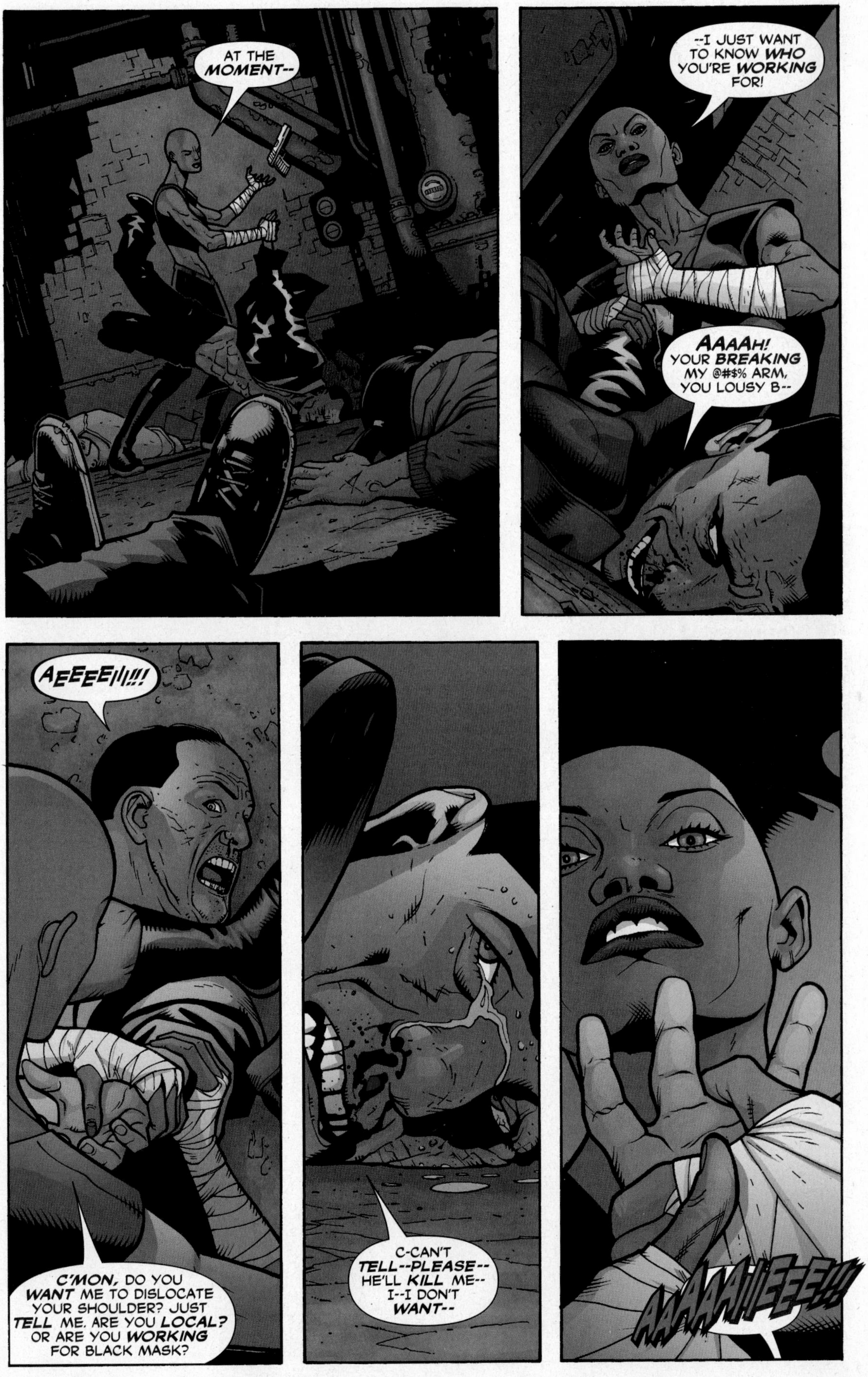
AT THE MOMENT--
--I JUST WANT TO KNOW WHO YOU'RE WORKING FOR!
AAAAH! YOUR BREAKING MY @#$% ARM, YOU LOUSY B--
AEEEEIII!!!
C'MON, DO YOU WANT ME TO DISLOCATE YOUR SHOULDER? JUST TELL ME. ARE YOU LOCAL? OR ARE YOU WORKING FOR BLACK MASK?
C-CAN'T TELL--PLEASE--HE'LL KILL ME--I--I DON'T WANT--
AAAAIIEEE!!!

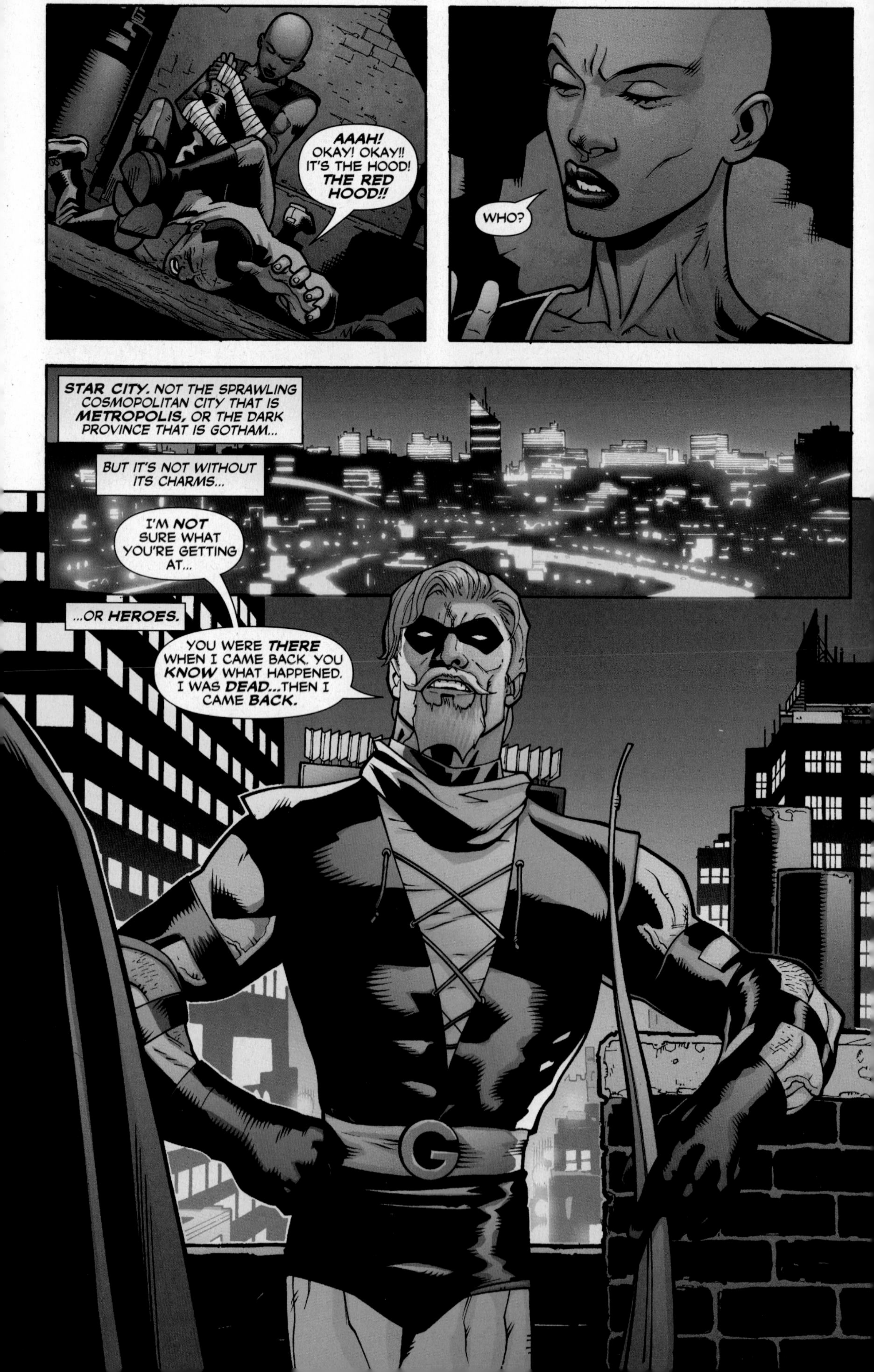
AAAH! OKAY! OKAY!! IT'S THE HOOD! THE RED HOOD!!
WHO?
STAR CITY. NOT THE SPRAWLING COSMOPOLITAN CITY THAT IS METROPOLIS, OR THE DARK PROVINCE THAT IS GOTHAM...
BUT IT'S NOT WITHOUT ITS CHARMS...
I'M NOT SURE WHAT YOU'RE GETTING AT...
...OR HEROES.
YOU WERE THERE WHEN I CAME BACK. YOU KNOW WHAT HAPPENED. I WAS DEAD...THEN I CAME BACK.

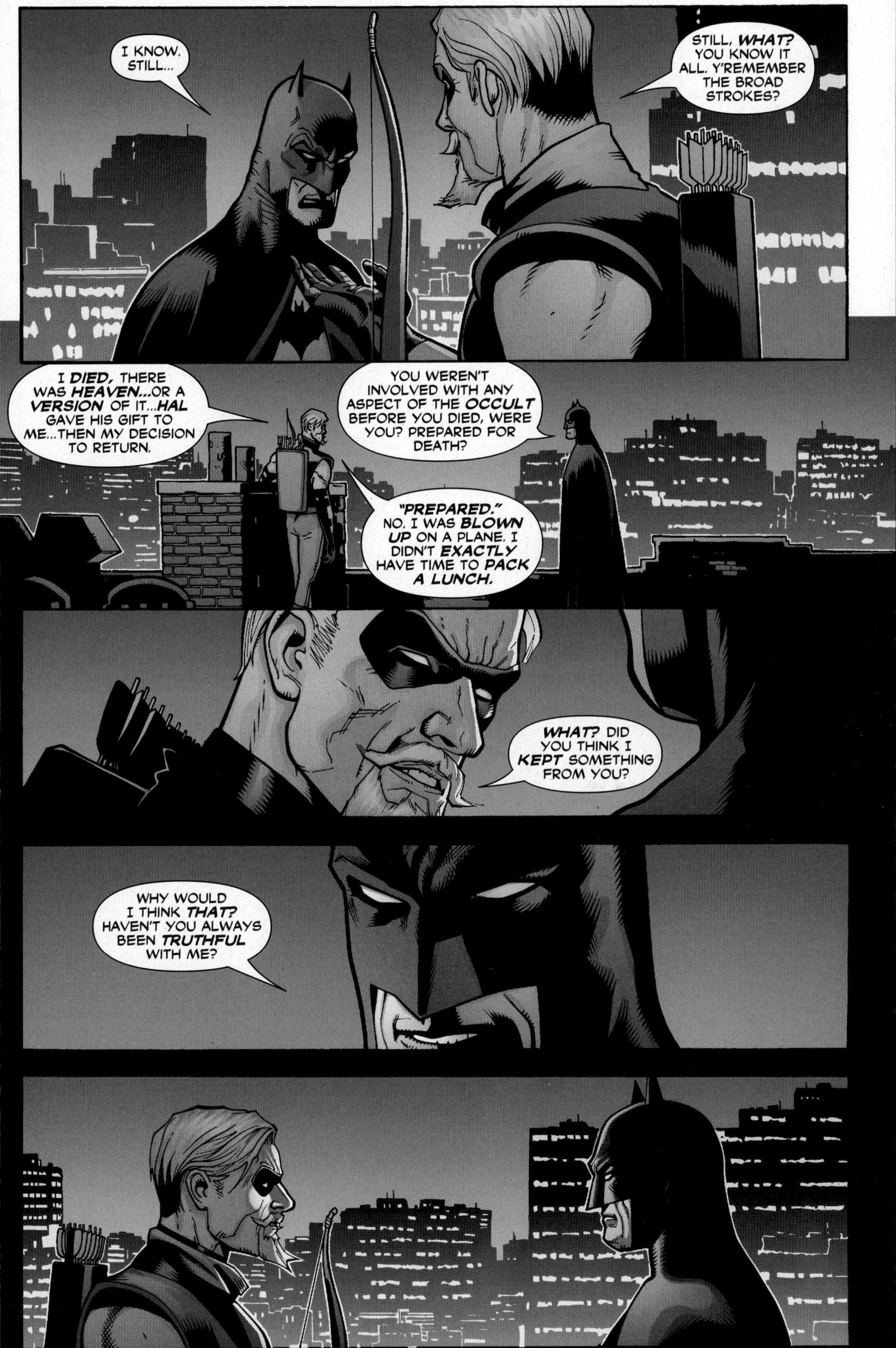
I KNOW. STILL...
STILL, WHAT? YOU KNOW IT ALL. Y'REMEMBER THE BROAD STROKES?
I DIED, THERE WAS HEAVEN...OR A VERSION OF IT...HAL GAVE HIS GIFT TO ME...THEN MY DECISION TO RETURN.
YOU WEREN'T INVOLVED WITH ANY ASPECT OF THE OCCULT BEFORE YOU DIED, WERE YOU? PREPARED FOR DEATH?
"PREPARED." NO. I WAS BLOWN UP ON A PLANE. I DIDN'T EXACTLY HAVE TIME TO PACK A LUNCH.
WHAT? DID YOU THINK I KEPT SOMETHING FROM YOU?
WHY WOULD I THINK THAT? HAVEN'T YOU ALWAYS BEEN TRUTHFUL WITH ME?

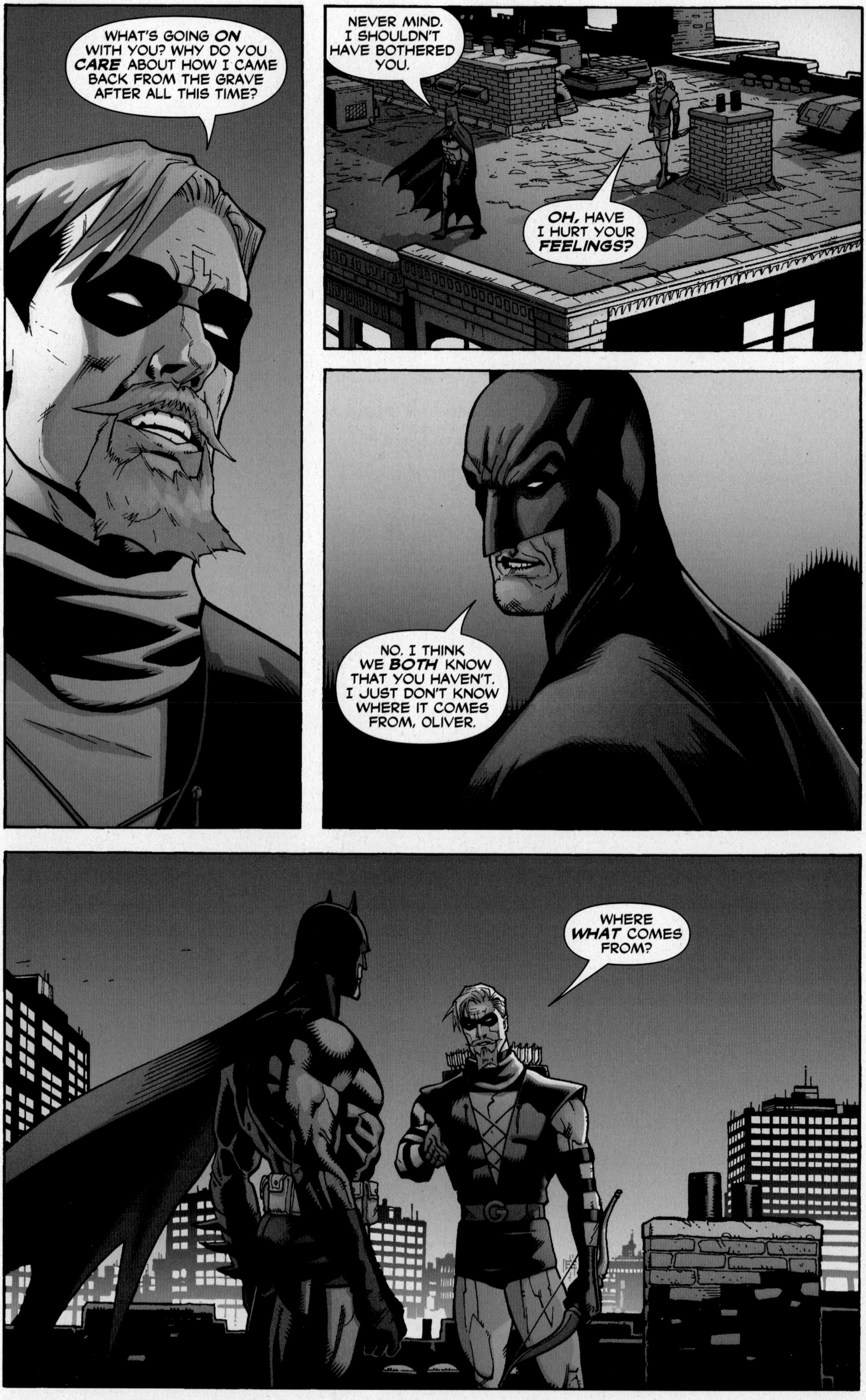
WHAT'S GOING ON WITH YOU? WHY DO YOU CARE ABOUT HOW I CAME BACK FROM THE GRAVE AFTER ALL THIS TIME?
NEVER MIND. I SHOULDN'T HAVE BOTHERED YOU.
OH, HAVE I HURT YOUR FEELINGS?
NO, I THINK WE BOTH KNOW THAT YOU HAVEN'T. I JUST DON'T KNOW WHERE IT COMES FROM, OLIVER.
WHERE WHAT COMES FROM?

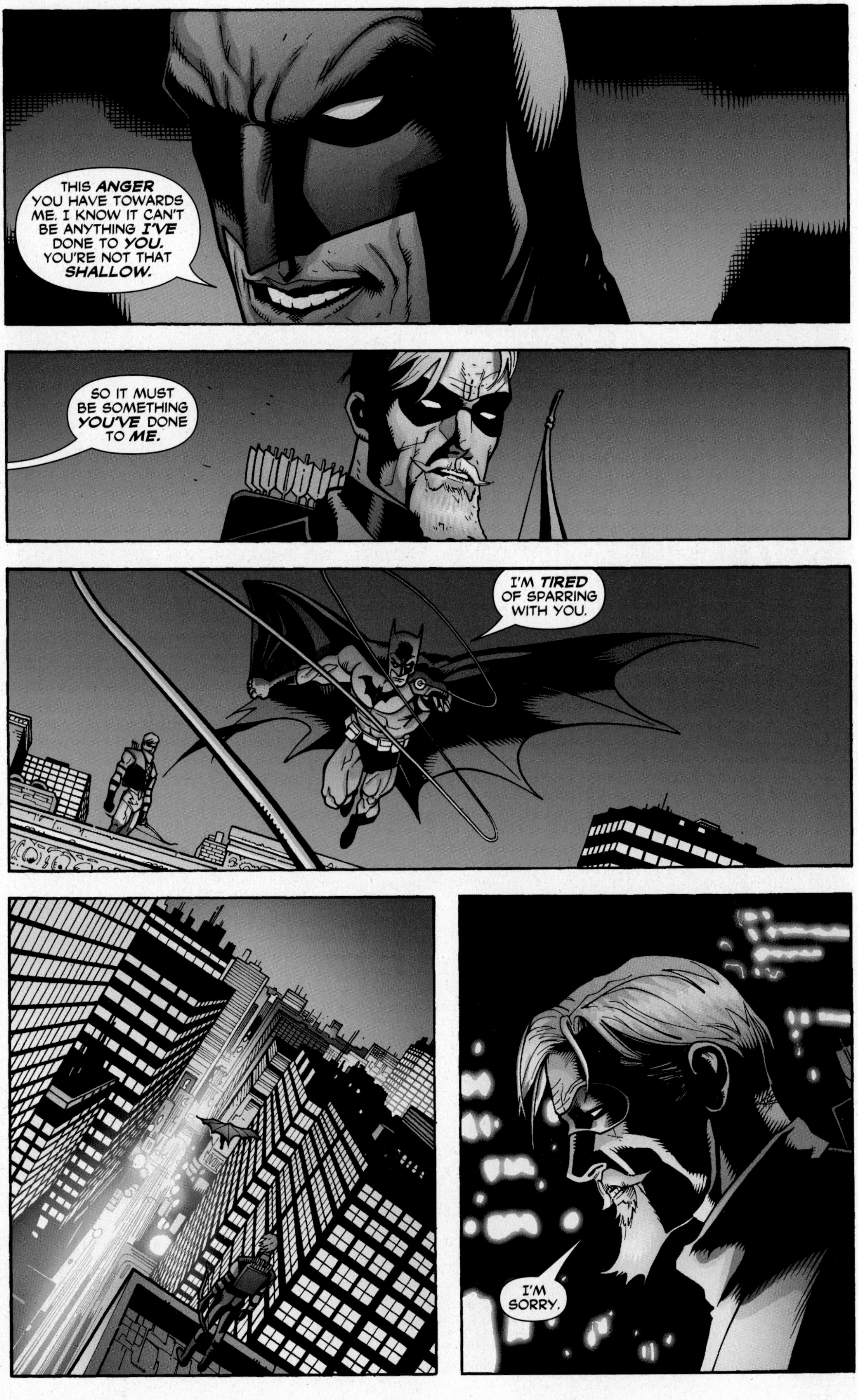
THIS ANGER YOU HAVE TOWARDS ME, I KNOW IT CAN'T BE ANYTHING I'VE DONE TO YOU. YOU'RE NOT THAT SHALLOW.
SO IT MUST BE SOMETHING YOU'VE DONE TO ME.
I'M TIRED OF SPARRING WITH YOU.
I'M SORRY.

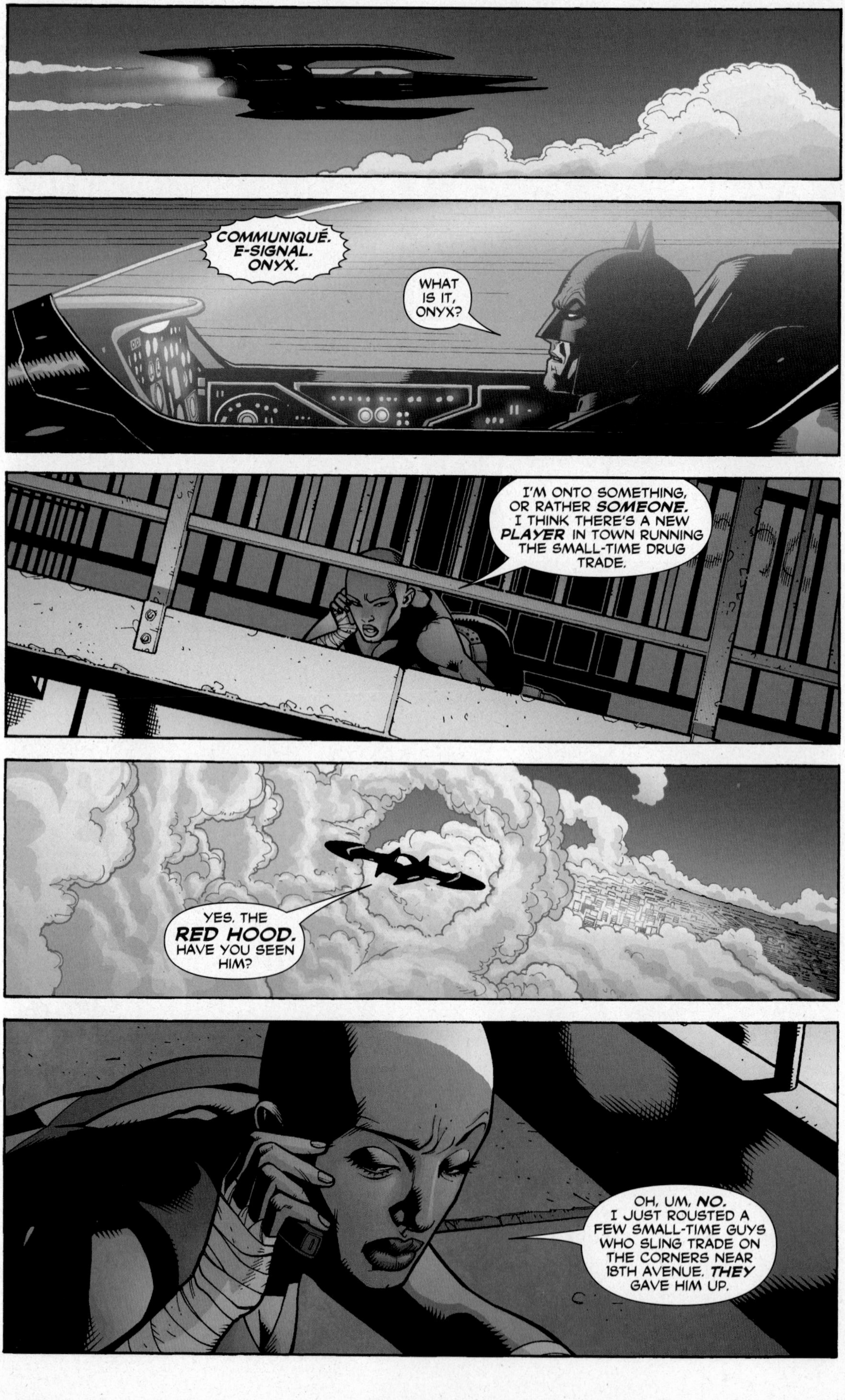
COMMUNIQUÉ. E-SIGNAL. ONYX.
WHAT IS IT, ONYX?
I'M ONTO SOMETHING, OR RATHER SOMEONE. I THINK THERE'S A NEW PLAYER IN TOWN RUNNING THE SMALL-TIME DRUG TRADE.
YES. THE RED HOOD. HAVE YOU SEEN HIM?
OH, UM, NO. I JUST ROUSTED A FEW SMALL-TIME GUYS WHO SLING TRADE ON THE CORNERS NEAR 18TH AVENUE. THEY GAVE HIM UP.

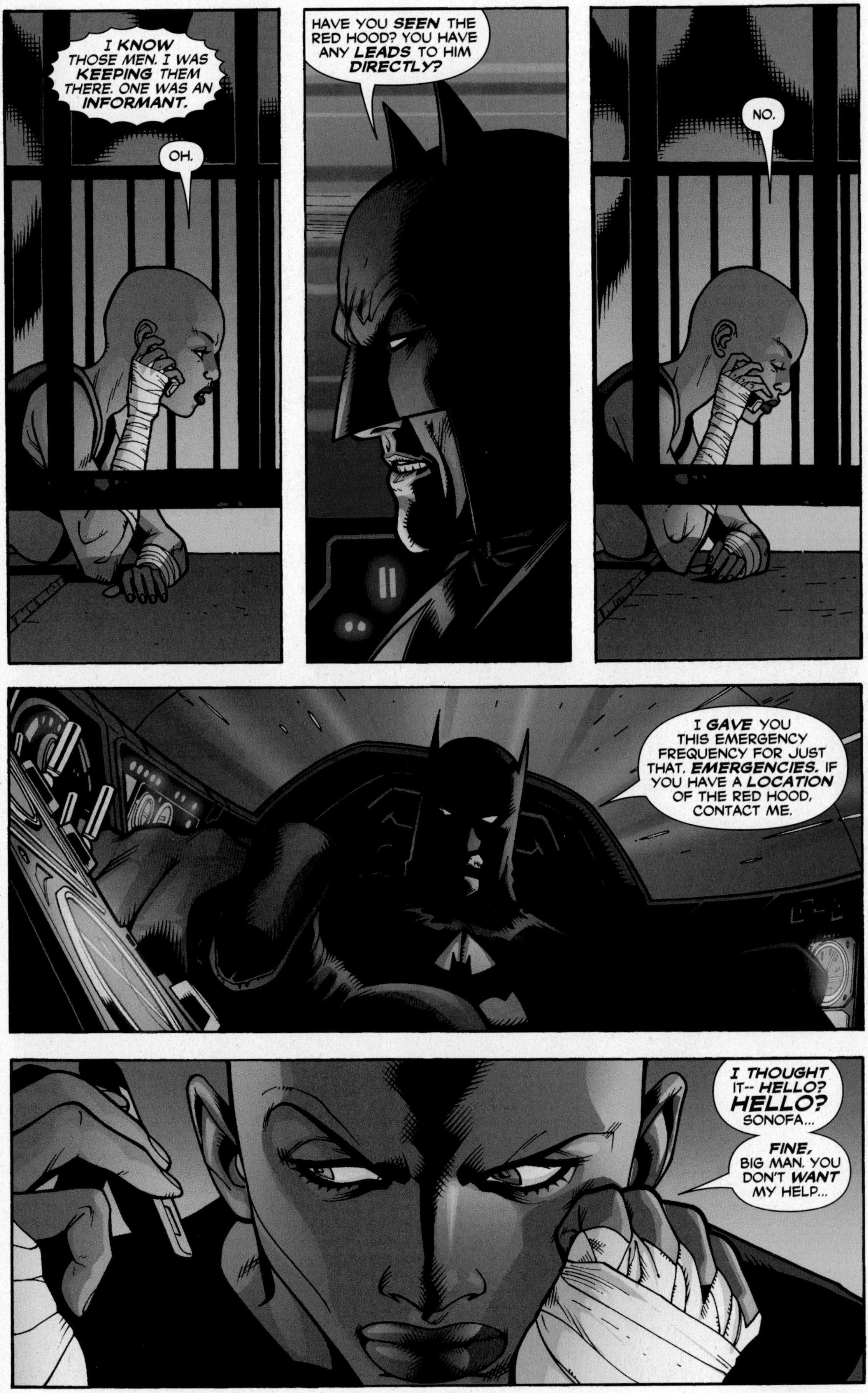

I KNOW THOSE MEN. I WAS KEEPING THEM THERE. ONE WAS AN INFORMANT.
OH.
HAVE YOU SEEN THE RED HOOD? YOU HAVE ANY LEADS TO HIM DIRECTLY?
NO.
I GAVE YOU THIS EMERGENCY FREQUENCY FOR JUST THAT. EMERGENCIES. IF YOU HAVE A LOCATION OF THE RED HOOD, CONTACT ME.
I THOUGHT IT-- HELLO? HELLO? SONOFA...
FINE, BIG MAN. YOU DON'T WANT MY HELP...

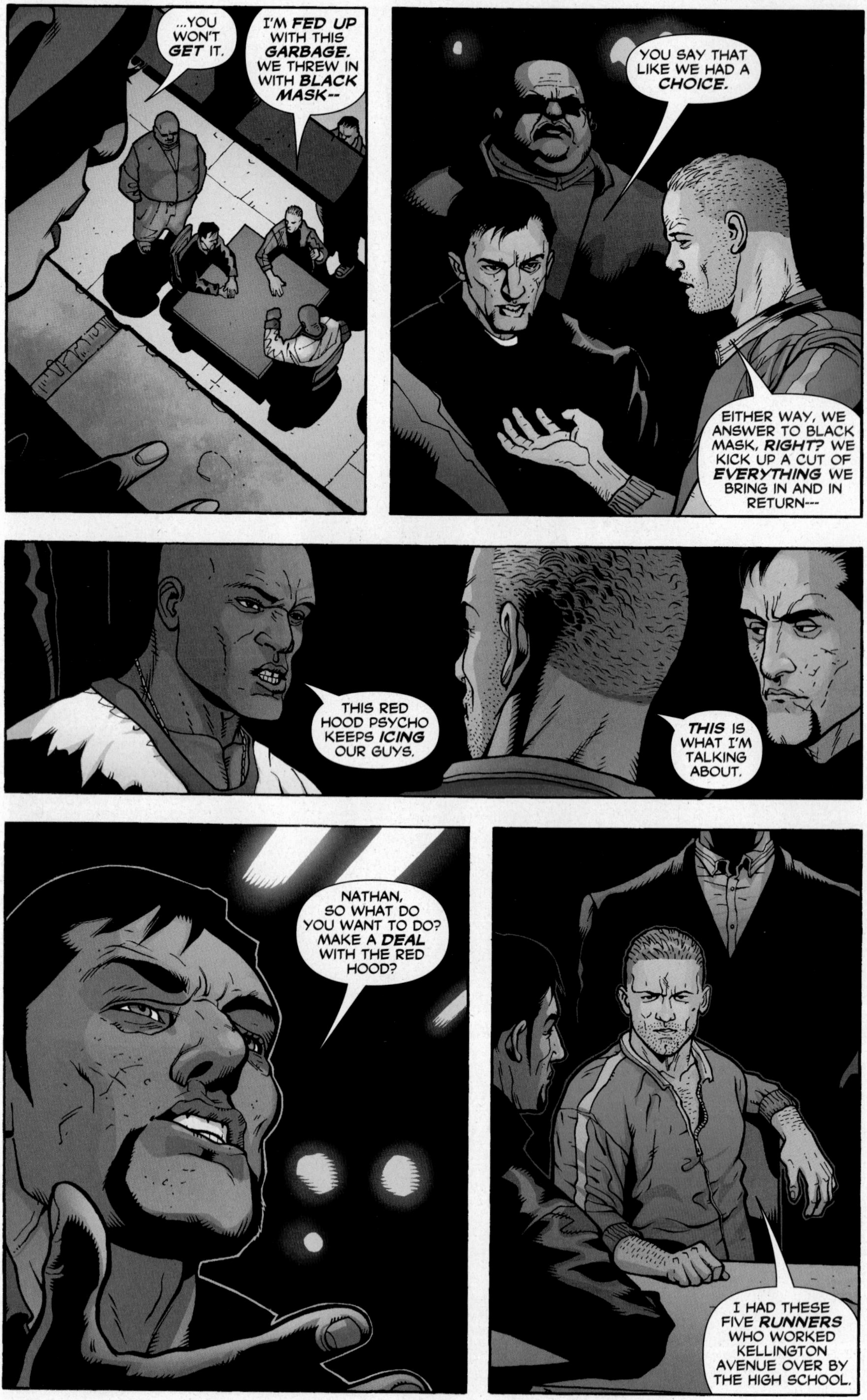
...YOU WON'T GET IT.
I'M FED UP WITH THIS GARBAGE. WE THREW IN WITH BLACK MASK--
YOU SAY THAT LIKE WE HAD A CHOICE.
EITHER WAY, WE ANSWER TO BLACK MASK, RIGHT? WE KICK UP A CUT OF EVERYTHING WE BRING IN AND IN RETURN---
THIS RED HOOD PSYCHO KEEPS ICING OUR GUYS.
THIS IS WHAT I'M TALKING ABOUT.
NATHAN, SO WHAT DO YOU WANT TO DO? MAKE A DEAL WITH THE RED HOOD?
I HAD THESE FIVE RUNNERS WHO WORKED KELLINGTON AVENUE OVER BY THE HIGH SCHOOL.

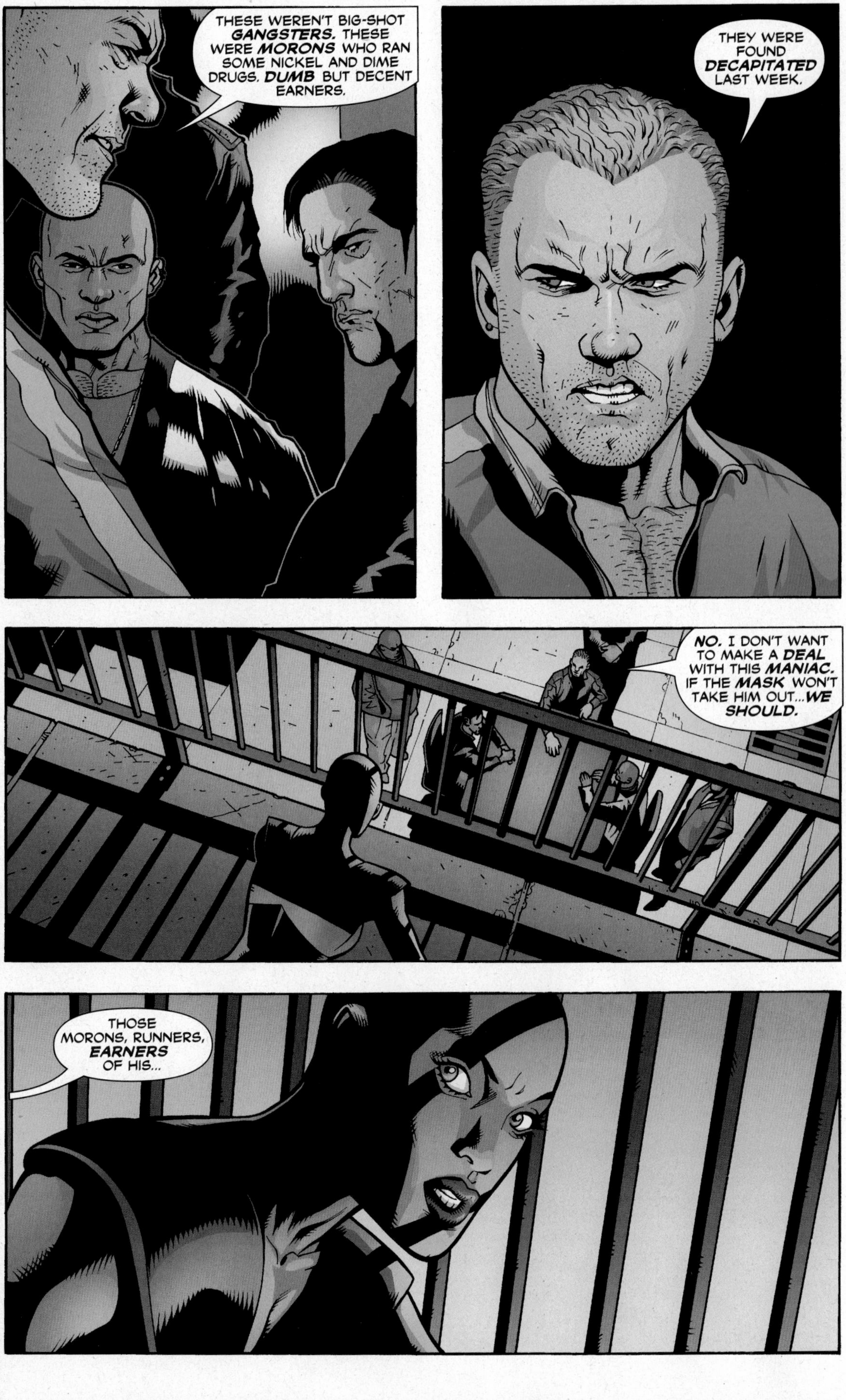
THESE WEREN'T BIG-SHOT GANGSTERS. THESE WERE MORONS WHO RAN SOME NICKEL AND DIME DRUGS. DUMB BUT DECENT EARNERS.
THEY WERE FOUND DECAPITATED LAST WEEK.
NO. I DON'T WANT TO MAKE A DEAL WITH THIS MANIAC. IF THE MASK WON'T TAKE HIM OUT...WE SHOULD.
THOSE MORONS, RUNNERS, EARNERS OF HIS...

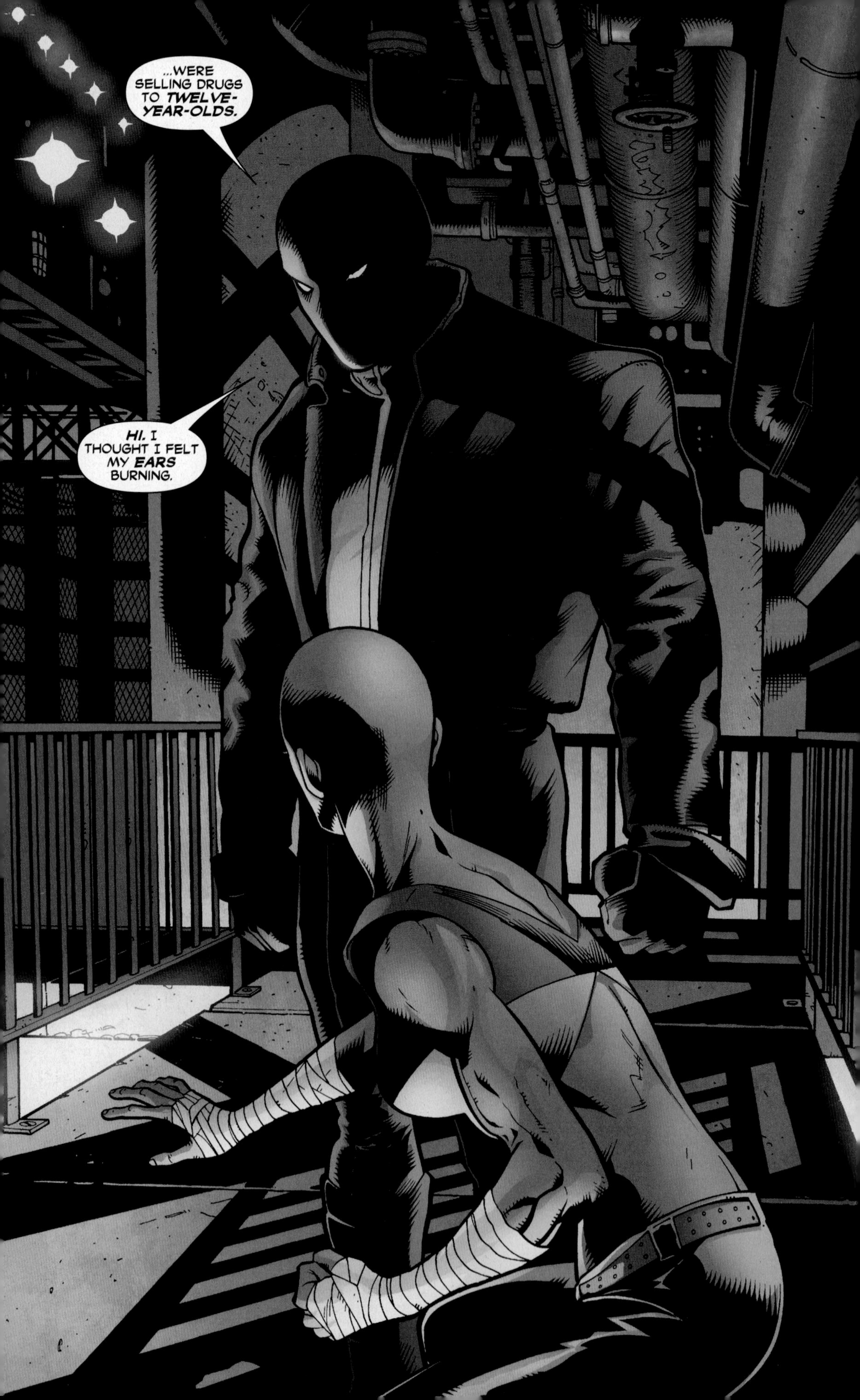
...WERE SELLING DRUGS TO *TWELVE-YEAR-OLDS.*
HI. I THOUGHT I FELT MY *EARS* BURNING.

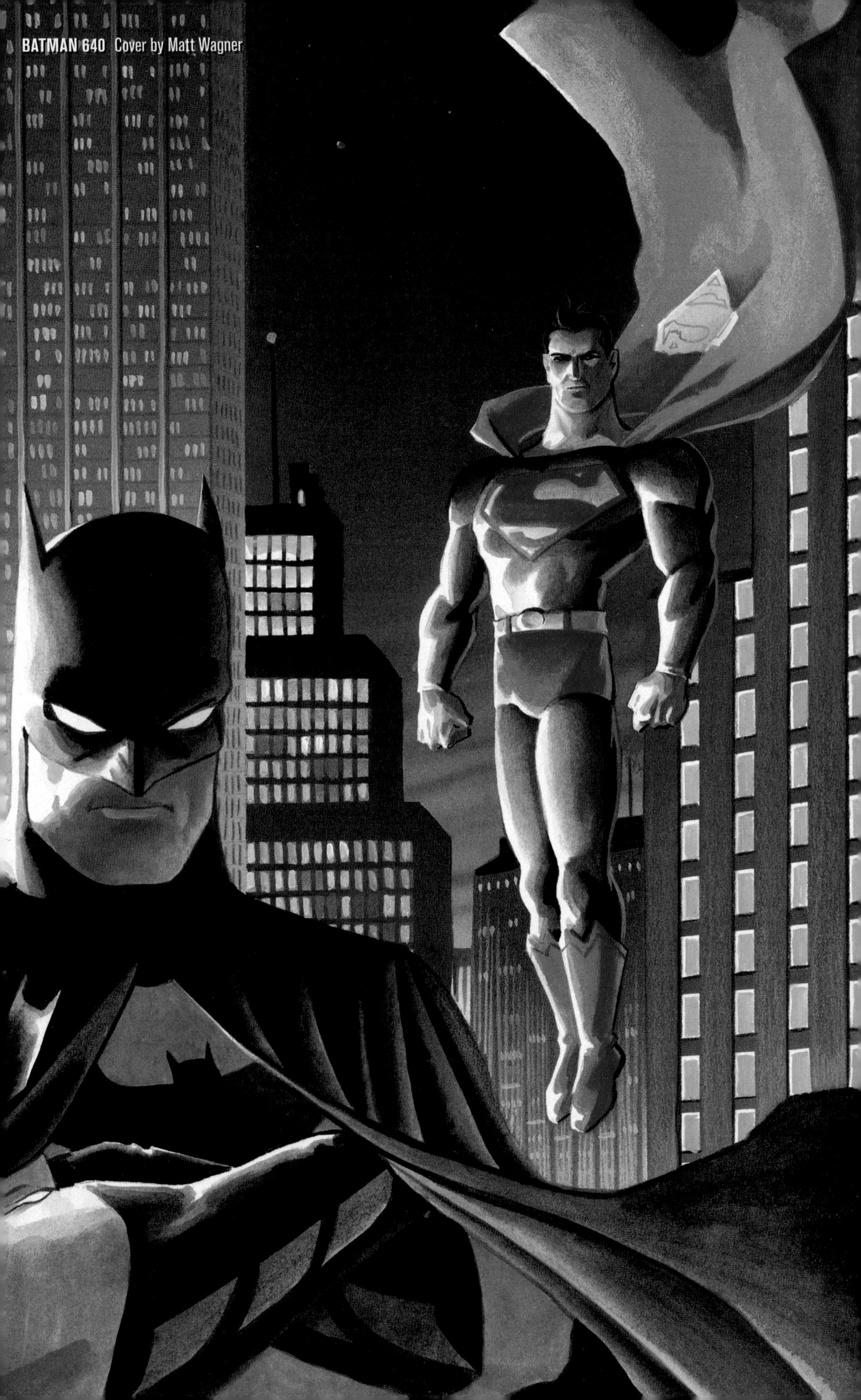

BATMAN 640 Cover by Matt Wagner

CHAPTER 6

WHILE THE CAT'S AWAY

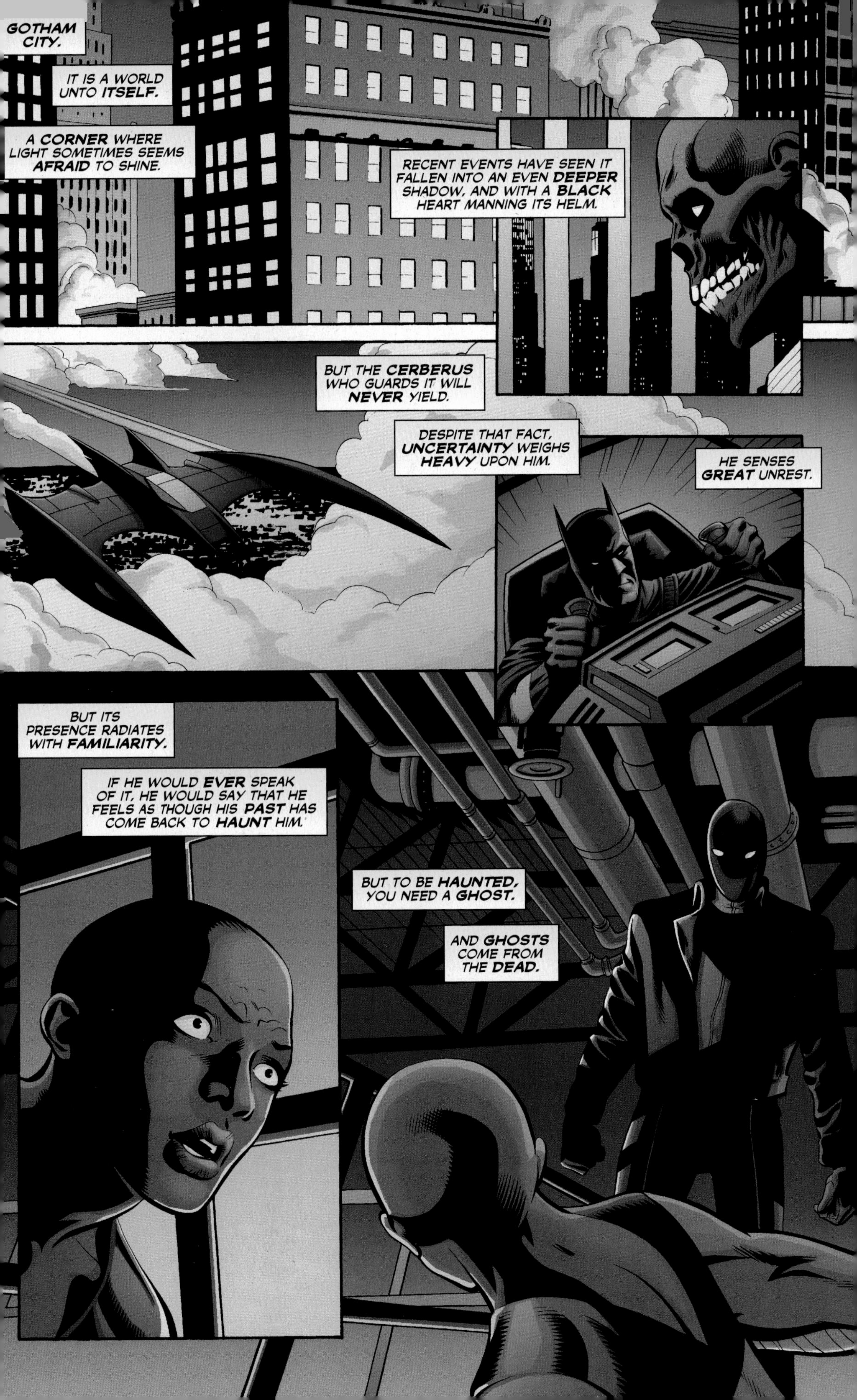
GOTHAM CITY.
IT IS A WORLD UNTO ITSELF.
A CORNER WHERE LIGHT SOMETIMES SEEMS AFRAID TO SHINE.
RECENT EVENTS HAVE SEEN IT FALLEN INTO AN EVEN DEEPER SHADOW, AND WITH A BLACK HEART MANNING ITS HELM.
BUT THE CERBERUS WHO GUARDS IT WILL NEVER YIELD.
DESPITE THAT FACT, UNCERTAINTY WEIGHS HEAVY UPON HIM.
HE SENSES GREAT UNREST.
BUT ITS PRESENCE RADIATES WITH FAMILIARITY.
IF HE WOULD EVER SPEAK OF IT, HE WOULD SAY THAT HE FEELS AS THOUGH HIS PAST HAS COME BACK TO HAUNT HIM.
BUT TO BE HAUNTED, YOU NEED A GHOST.
AND GHOSTS COME FROM THE DEAD.

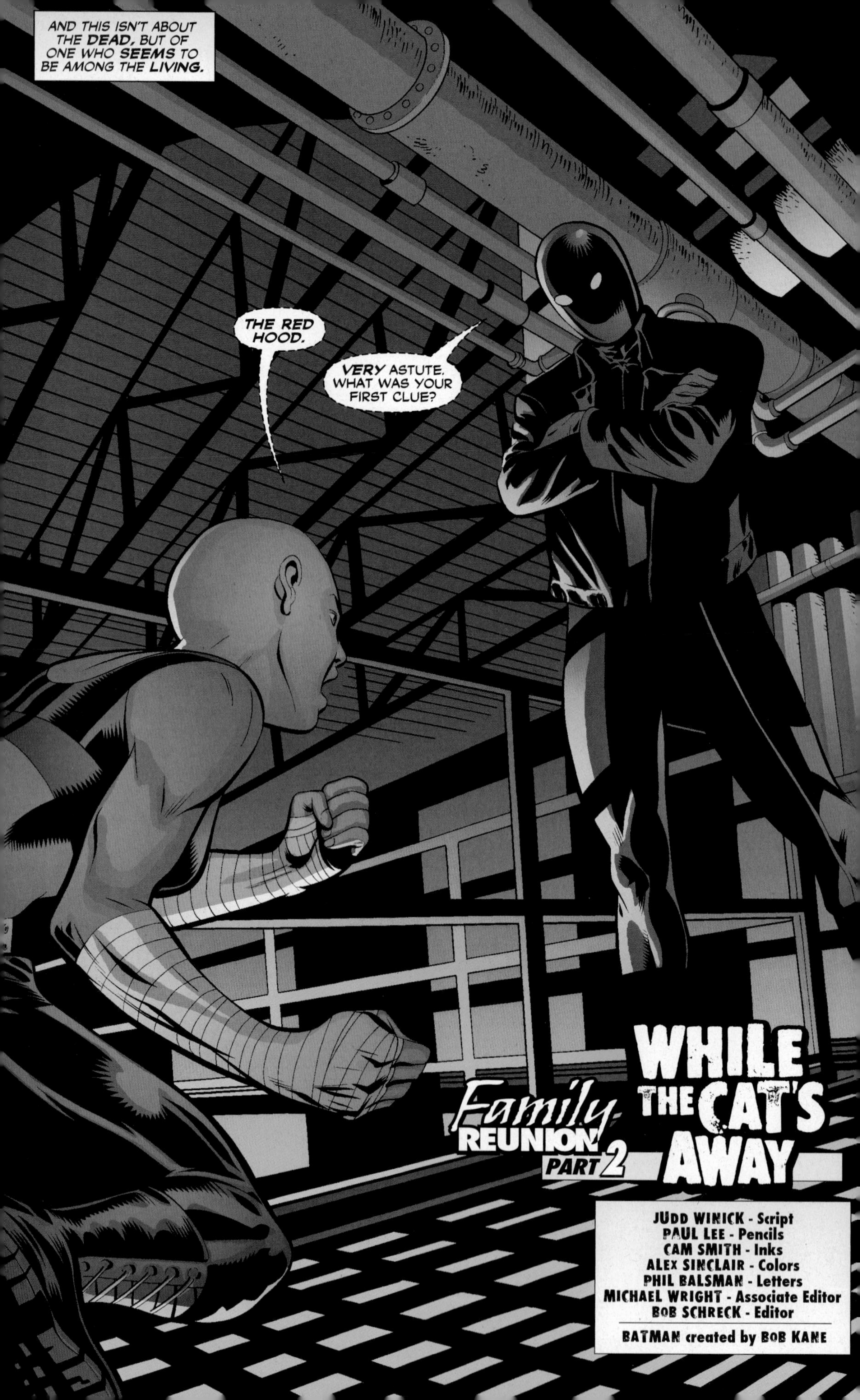
AND THIS ISN'T ABOUT THE DEAD, BUT OF ONE WHO SEEMS TO BE AMONG THE LIVING.
THE RED HOOD.
VERY ASTUTE. WHAT WAS YOUR FIRST CLUE?
Family REUNION PART 2
WHILE THE CAT'S AWAY
JUDD WINICK - Script
PAUL LEE - Pencils
CAM SMITH - Inks
ALEX SINCLAIR - Colors
PHIL BALSMAN - Letters
MICHAEL WRIGHT - Associate Editor
BOB SCHRECK - Editor
BATMAN created by BOB KANE

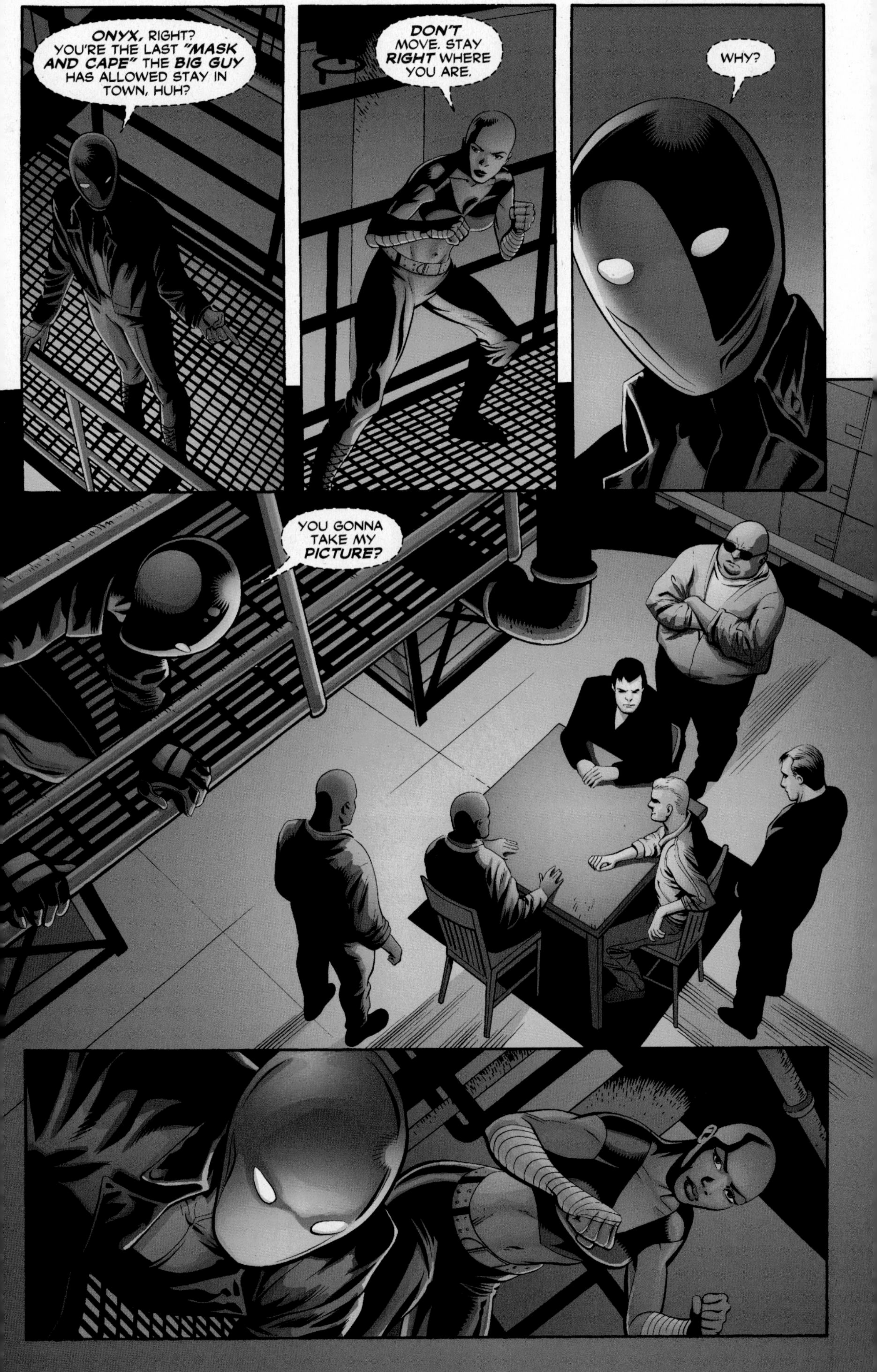
ONYX, RIGHT? YOU'RE THE LAST "MASK AND CAPE" THE BIG GUY HAS ALLOWED STAY IN TOWN, HUH?
DON'T MOVE. STAY RIGHT WHERE YOU ARE.
WHY?
YOU GONNA TAKE MY PICTURE?

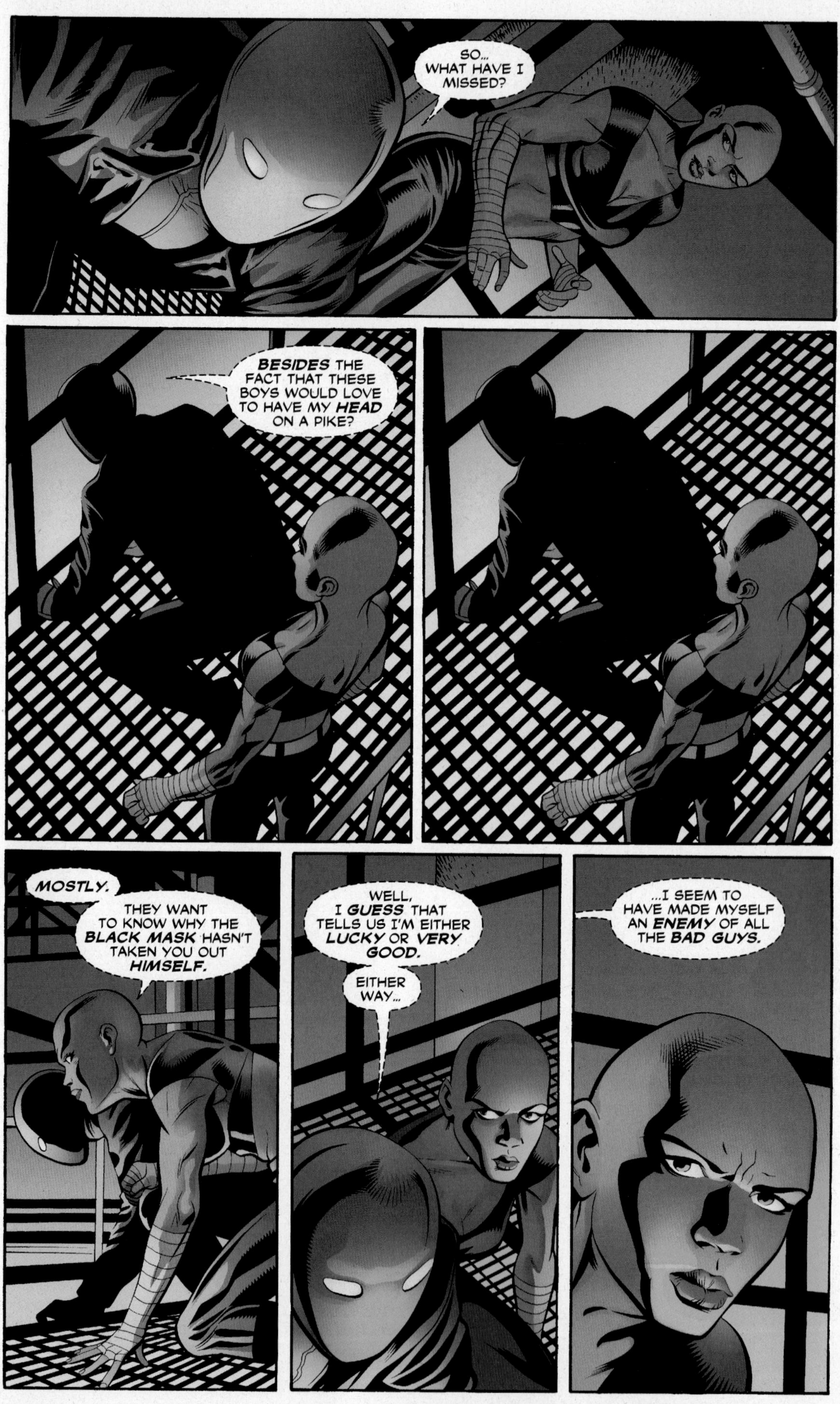
SO... WHAT HAVE I MISSED?
BESIDES THE FACT THAT THESE BOYS WOULD LOVE TO HAVE MY HEAD ON A PIKE?
MOSTLY.
THEY WANT TO KNOW WHY THE BLACK MASK HASN'T TAKEN YOU OUT HIMSELF.
WELL, I GUESS THAT TELLS US I'M EITHER LUCKY OR VERY GOOD.
EITHER WAY...
...I SEEM TO HAVE MADE MYSELF AN ENEMY OF ALL THE BAD GUYS.

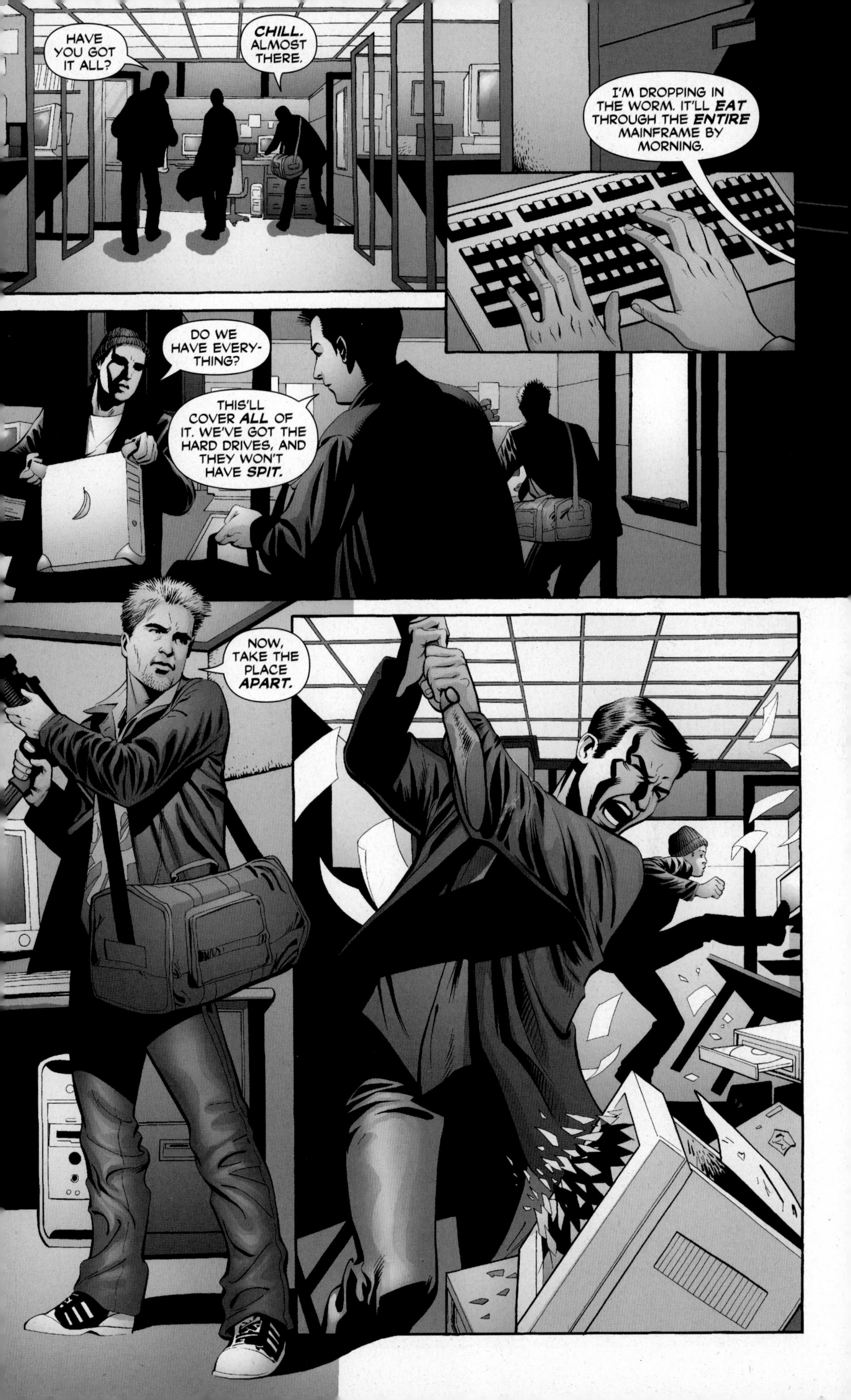
HAVE YOU GOT IT ALL?
CHILL. ALMOST THERE.
I'M DROPPING IN THE WORM. IT'LL EAT THROUGH THE ENTIRE MAINFRAME BY MORNING.
DO WE HAVE EVERY-THING?
THIS'LL COVER ALL OF IT. WE'VE GOT THE HARD DRIVES, AND THEY WON'T HAVE SPIT.
NOW, TAKE THE PLACE APART.

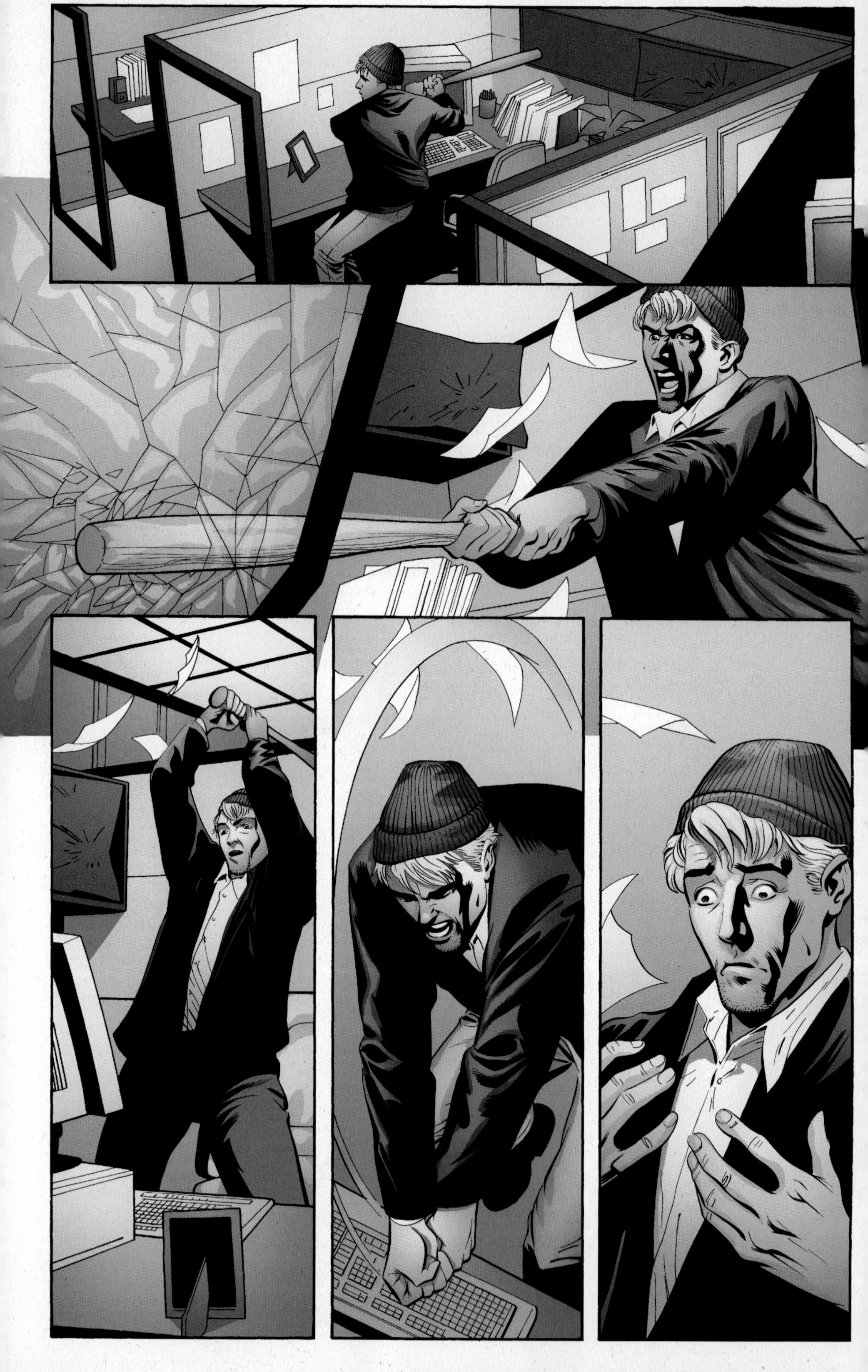

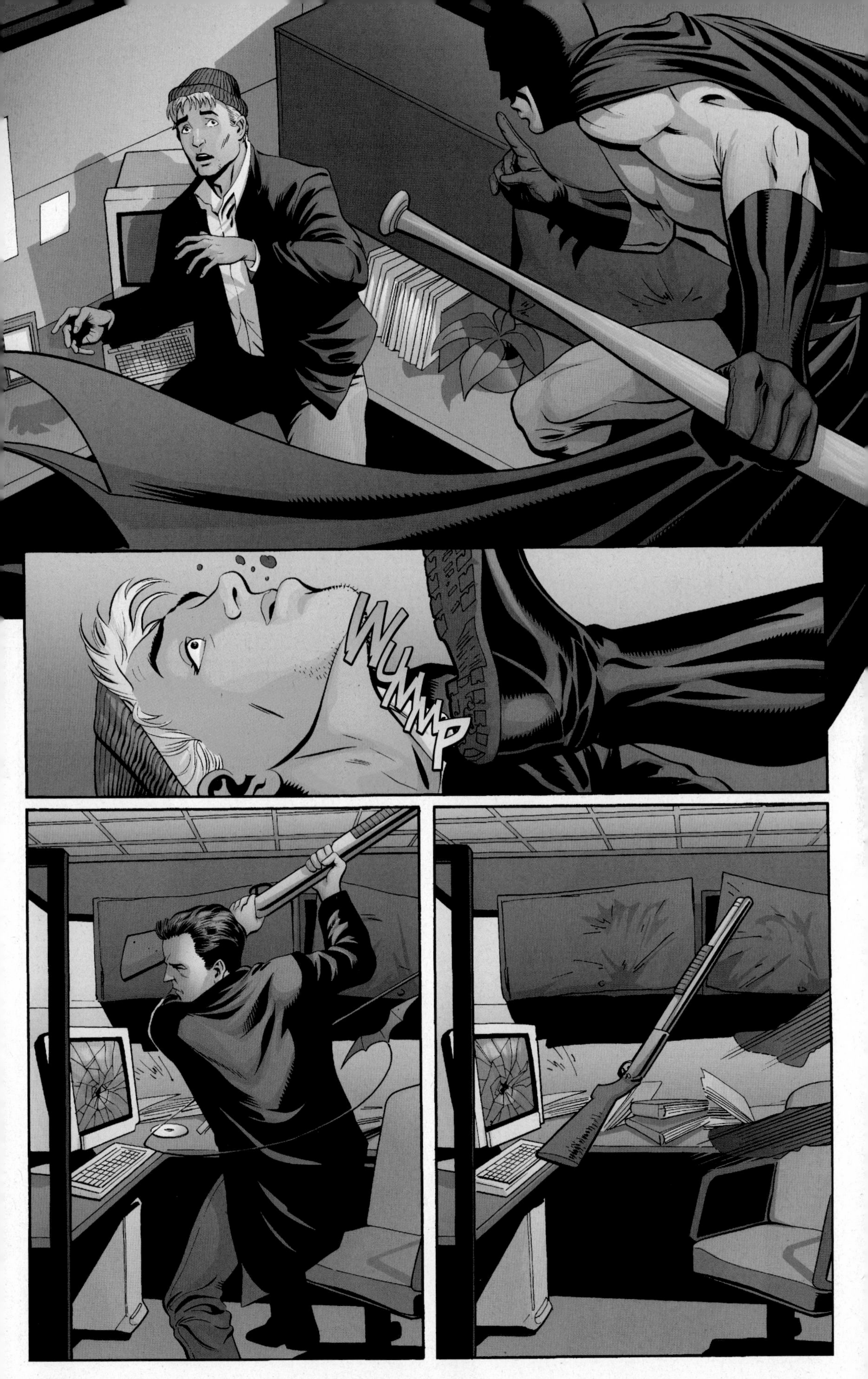
WUMMP

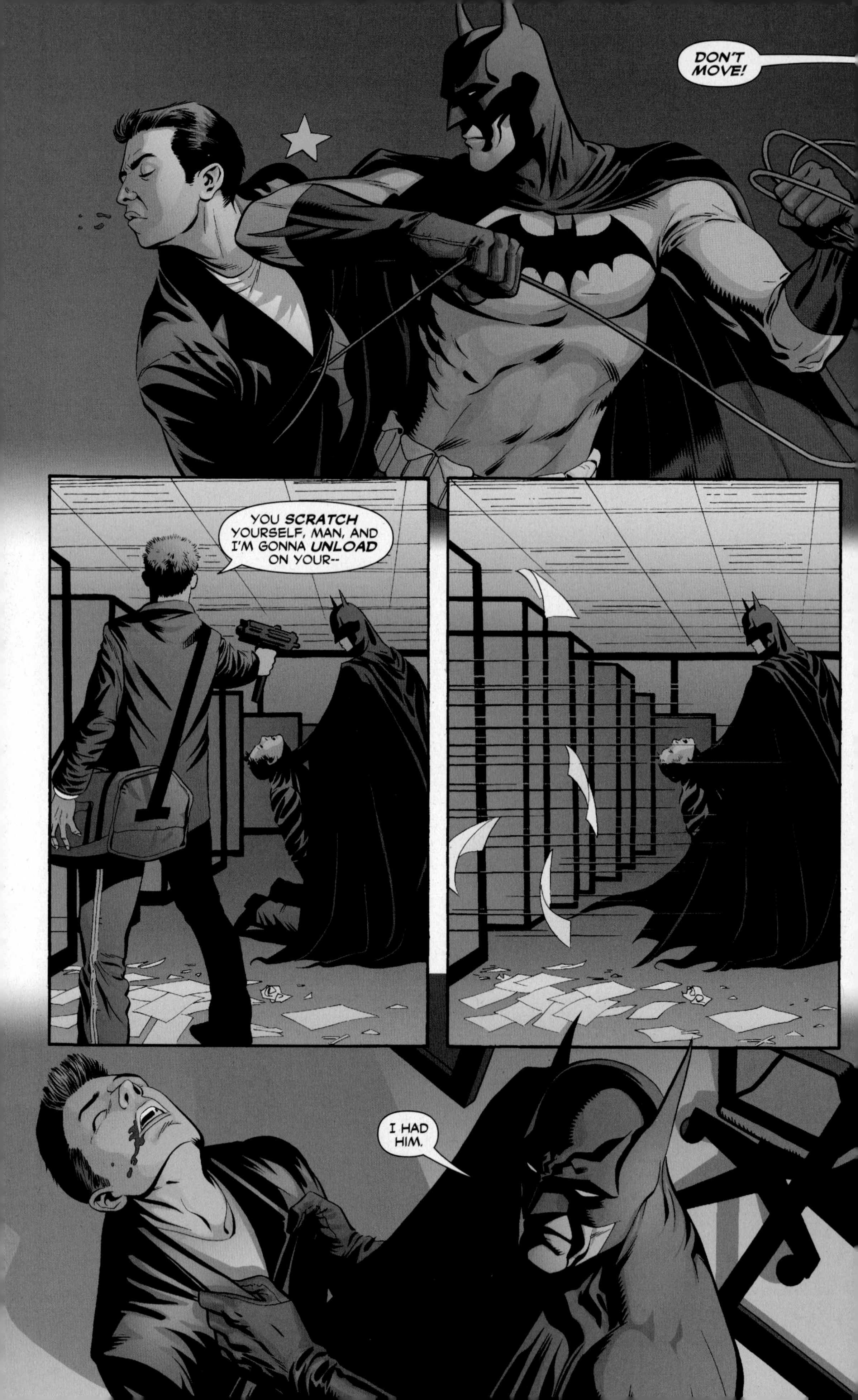
DON'T MOVE!
YOU SCRATCH YOURSELF, MAN, AND I'M GONNA UNLOAD ON YOUR--
I HAD HIM.

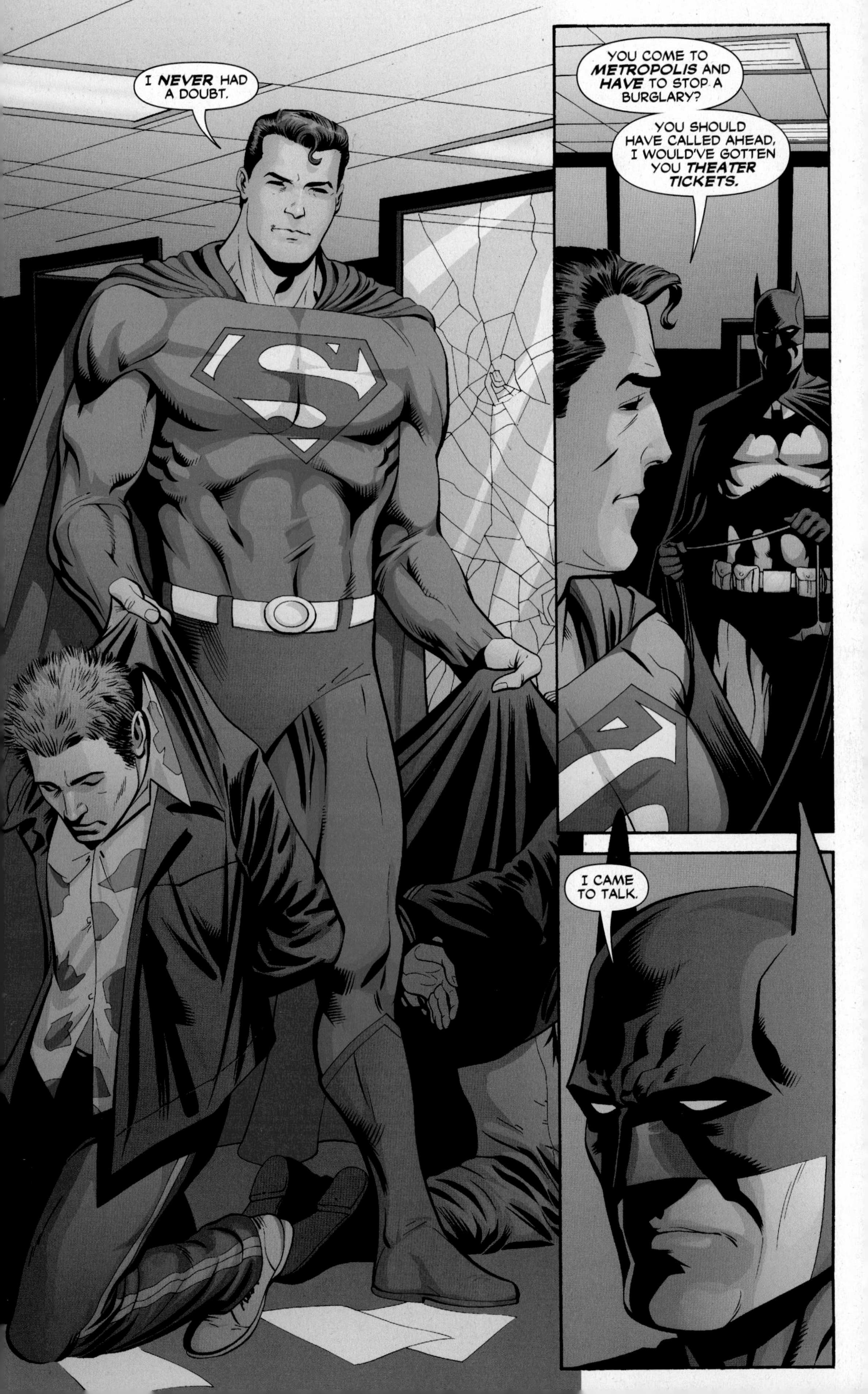
I NEVER HAD A DOUBT.
YOU COME TO METROPOLIS AND HAVE TO STOP A BURGLARY?
YOU SHOULD HAVE CALLED AHEAD, I WOULD'VE GOTTEN YOU THEATER TICKETS.
I CAME TO TALK.

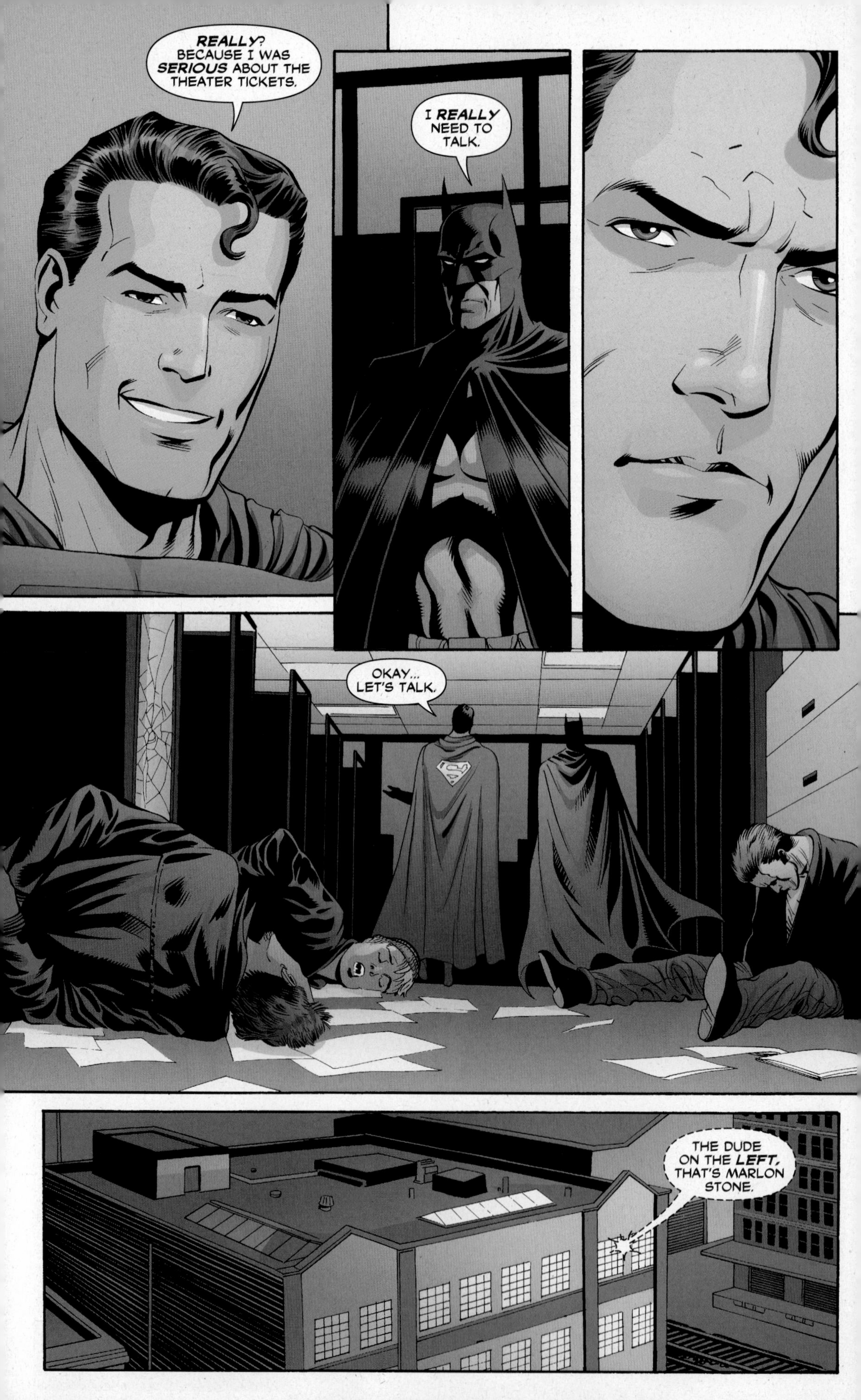
REALLY? BECAUSE I WAS SERIOUS ABOUT THE THEATER TICKETS.
I REALLY NEED TO TALK.
OKAY... LET'S TALK.
THE DUDE ON THE LEFT, THAT'S MARLON STONE.

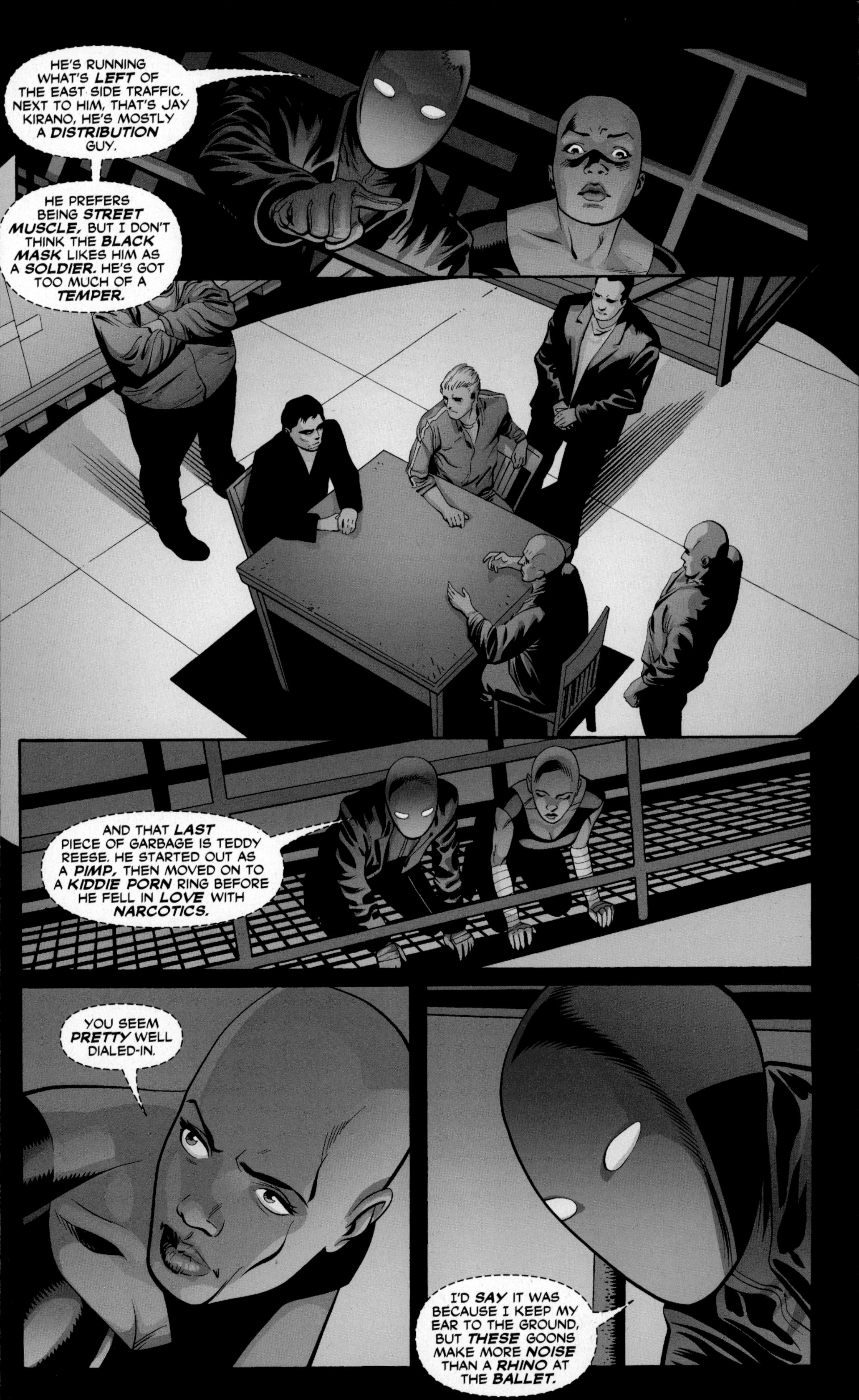

HE'S RUNNING WHAT'S LEFT OF THE EAST SIDE TRAFFIC. NEXT TO HIM, THAT'S JAY KIRANO, HE'S MOSTLY A DISTRIBUTION GUY.
HE PREFERS BEING STREET MUSCLE, BUT I DON'T THINK THE BLACK MASK LIKES HIM AS A SOLDIER. HE'S GOT TOO MUCH OF A TEMPER.
AND THAT LAST PIECE OF GARBAGE IS TEDDY REESE. HE STARTED OUT AS A PIMP, THEN MOVED ON TO A KIDDIE PORN RING BEFORE HE FELL IN LOVE WITH NARCOTICS.
YOU SEEM PRETTY WELL DIALED-IN.
I'D SAY IT WAS BECAUSE I KEEP MY EAR TO THE GROUND, BUT THESE GOONS MAKE MORE NOISE THAN A RHINO AT THE BALLET.

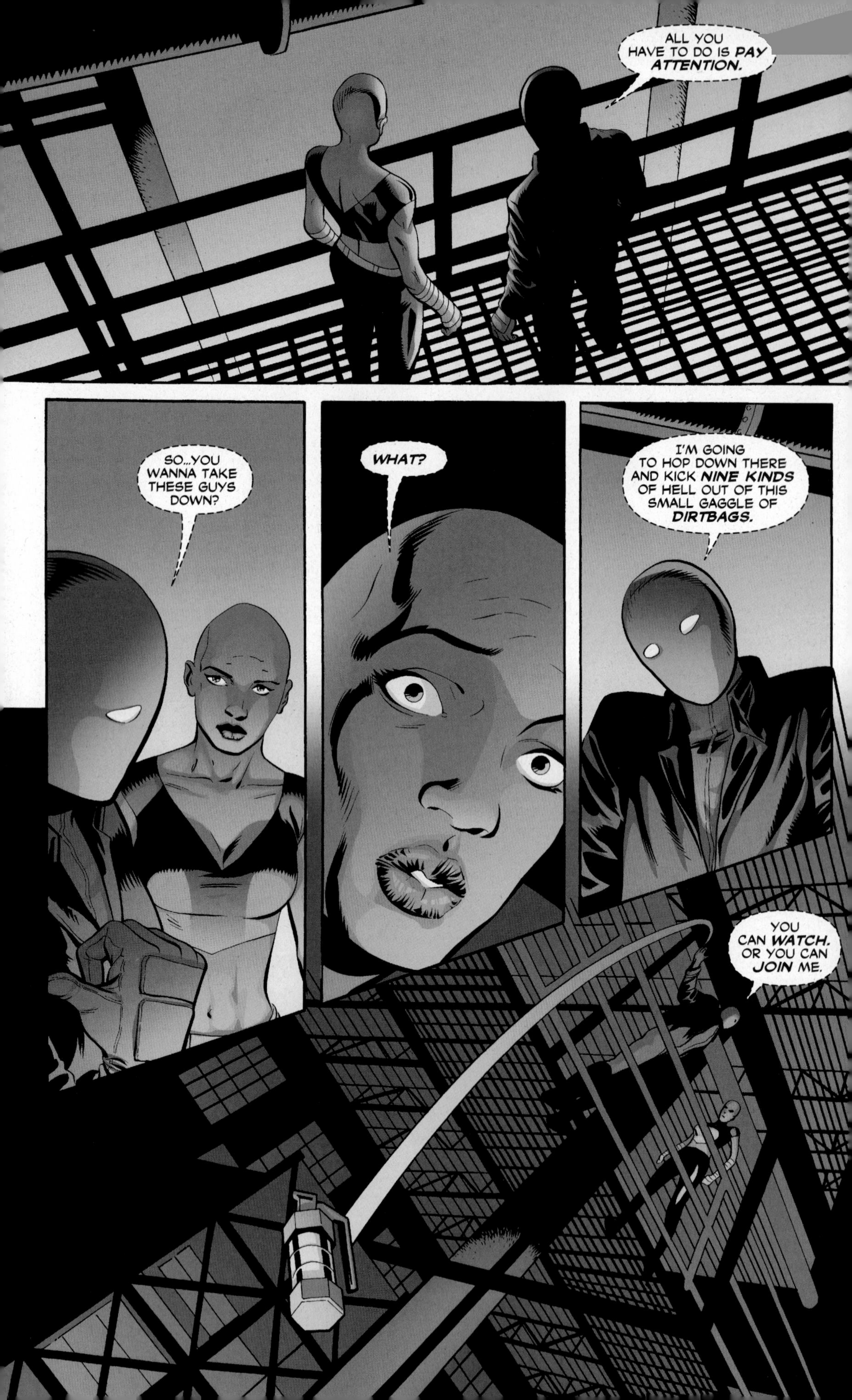
ALL YOU HAVE TO DO IS PAY ATTENTION.
SO...YOU WANNA TAKE THESE GUYS DOWN?
WHAT?
I'M GOING TO HOP DOWN THERE AND KICK NINE KINDS OF HELL OUT OF THIS SMALL GAGGLE OF DIRTBAGS.
YOU CAN WATCH. OR YOU CAN JOIN ME.

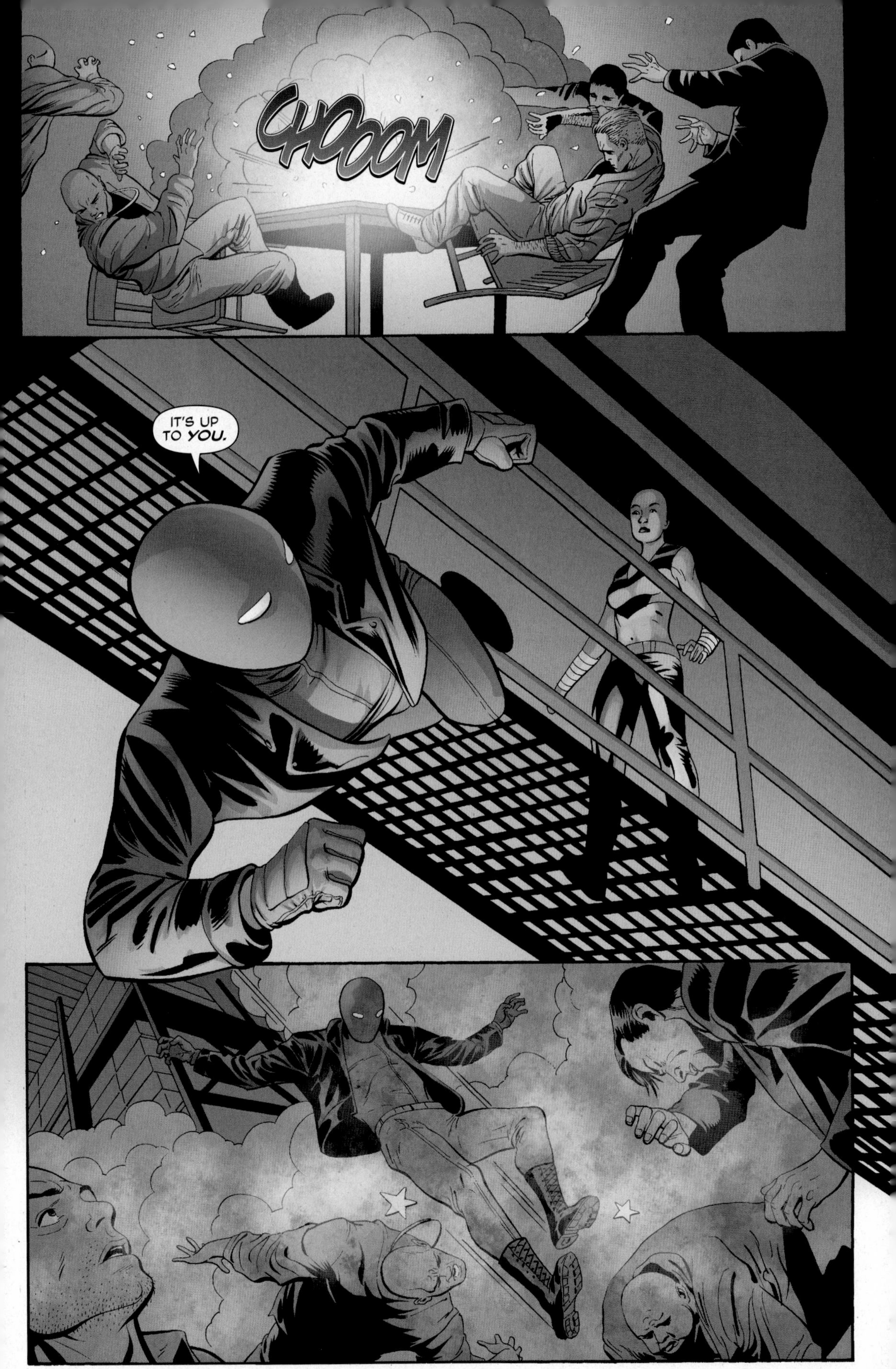
CHOOOM
IT'S UP TO YOU.

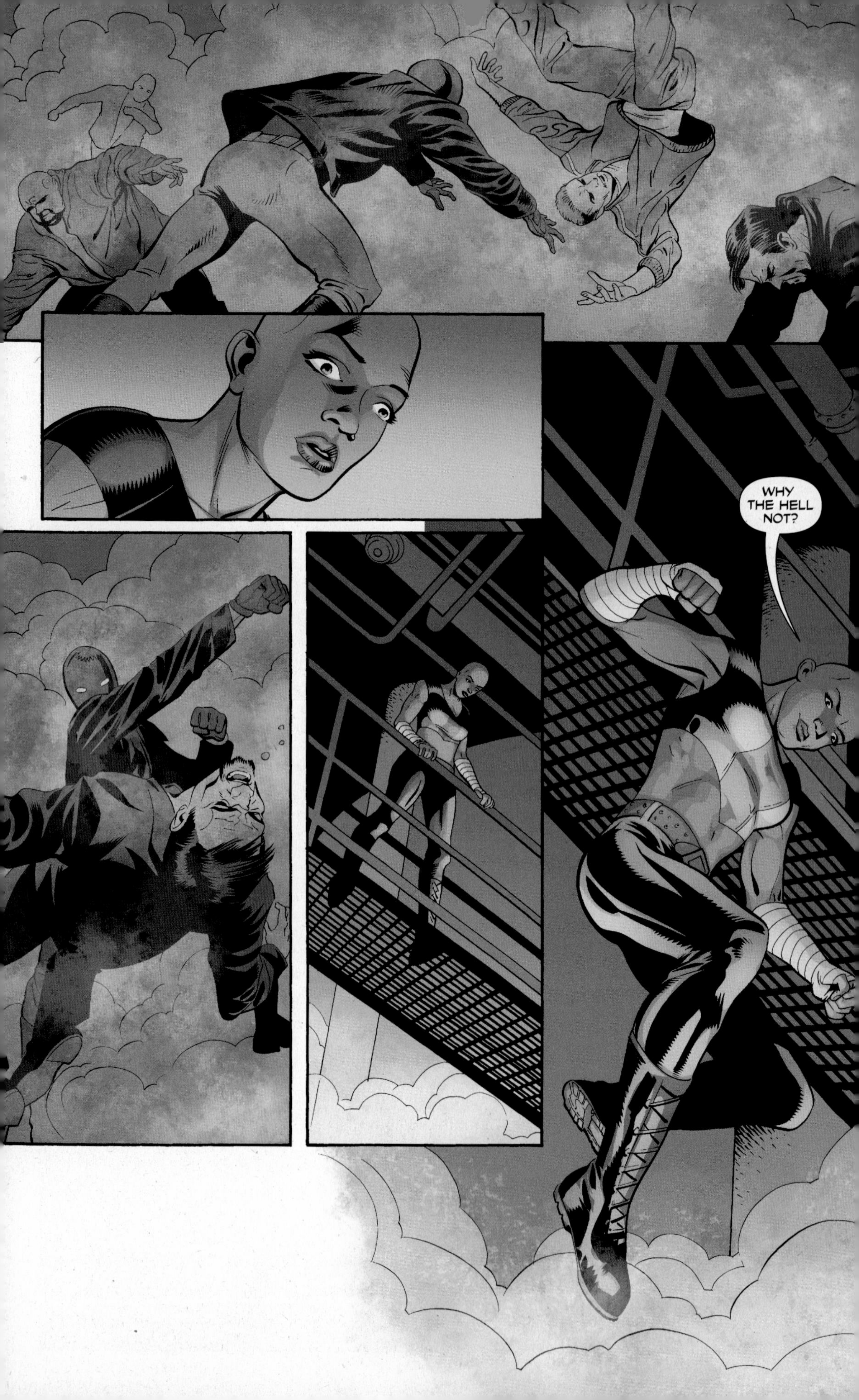
WHY THE HELL NOT?

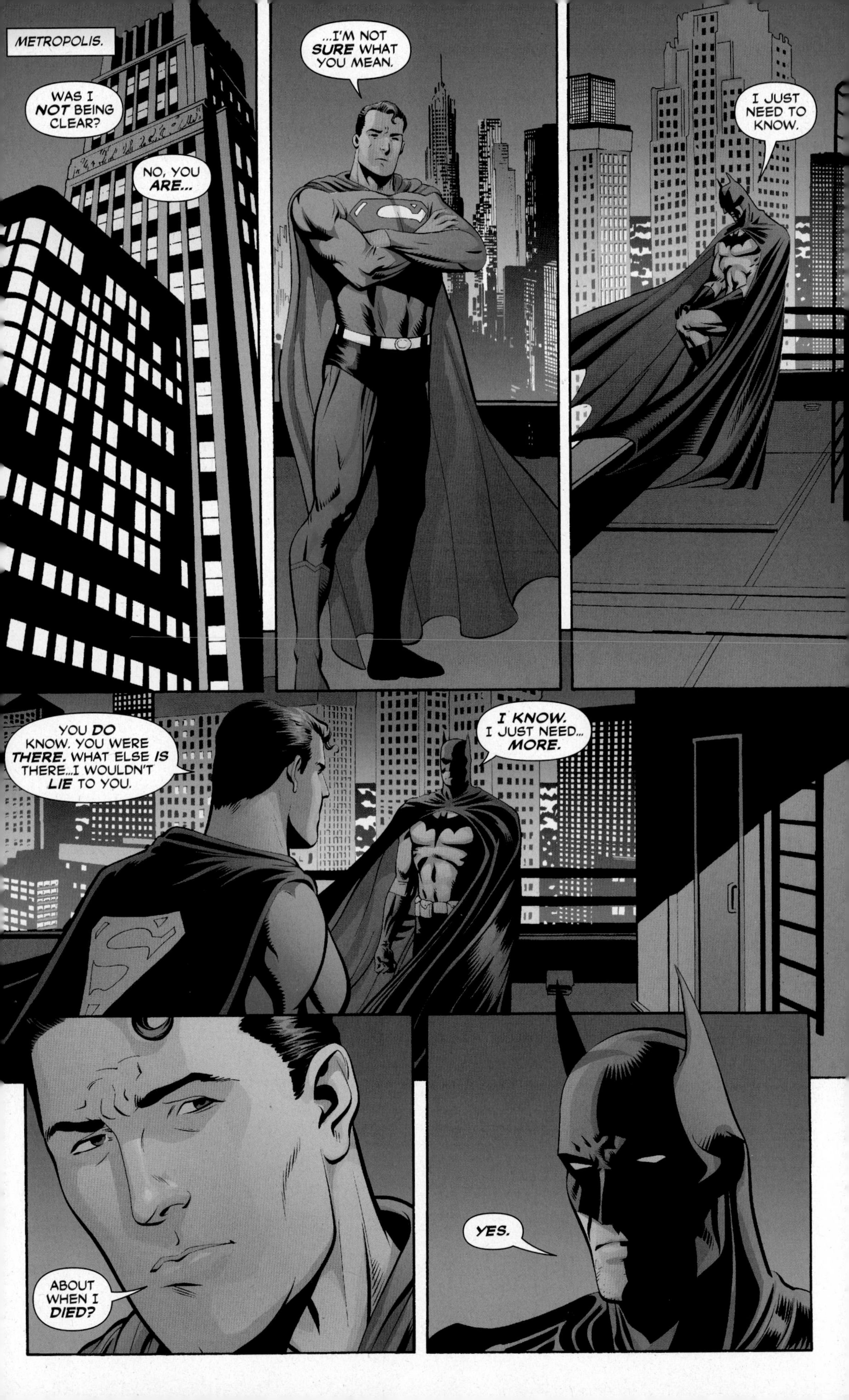
METROPOLIS.
WAS I NOT BEING CLEAR?
NO, YOU ARE...
...I'M NOT SURE WHAT YOU MEAN.
I JUST NEED TO KNOW.
YOU DO KNOW. YOU WERE THERE. WHAT ELSE IS THERE...I WOULDN'T LIE TO YOU.
I KNOW. I JUST NEED... MORE.
ABOUT WHEN I DIED?
YES.

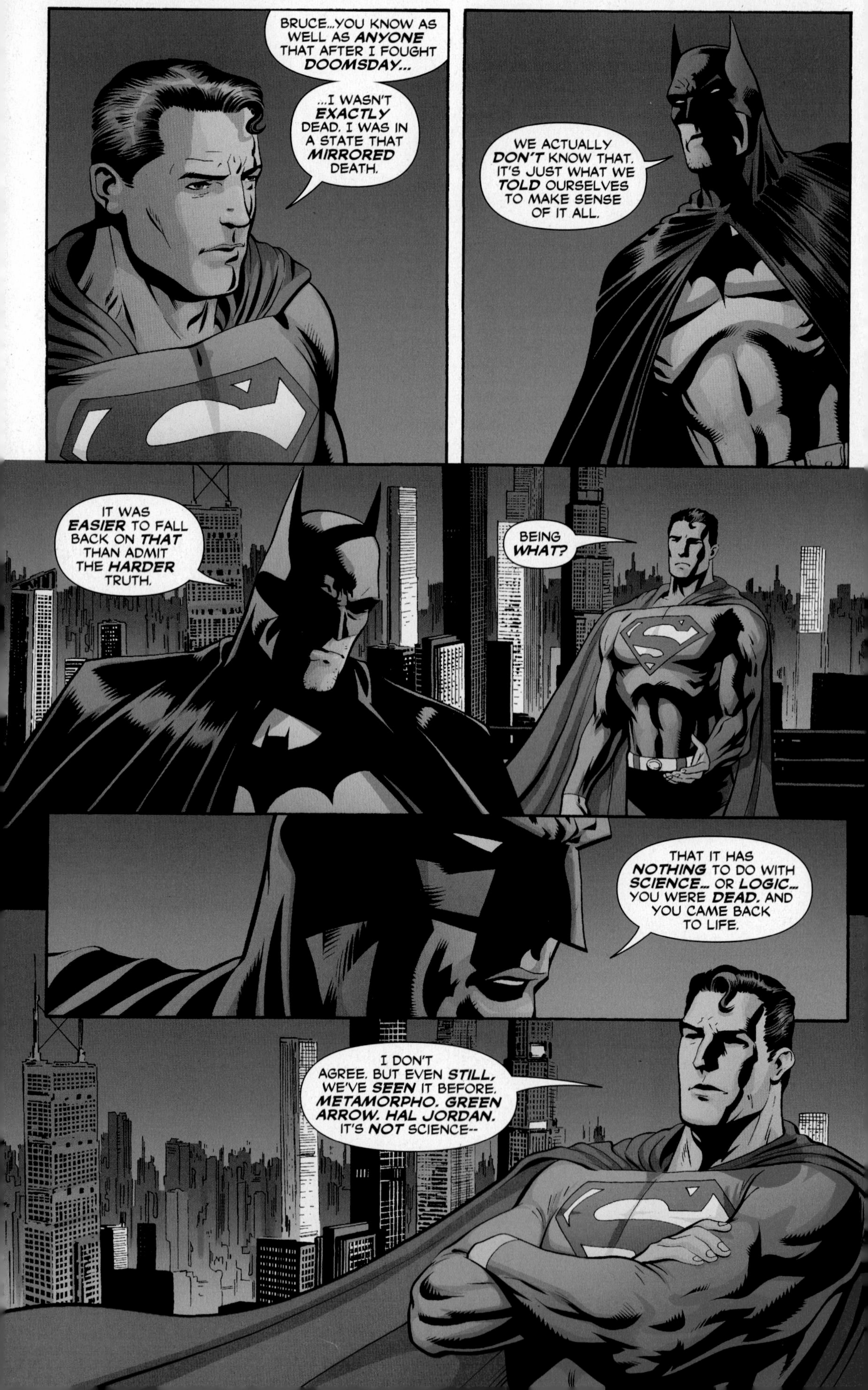
BRUCE...YOU KNOW AS WELL AS ANYONE THAT AFTER I FOUGHT DOOMSDAY...
...I WASN'T EXACTLY DEAD. I WAS IN A STATE THAT MIRRORED DEATH.
WE ACTUALLY DON'T KNOW THAT. IT'S JUST WHAT WE TOLD OURSELVES TO MAKE SENSE OF IT ALL.
IT WAS EASIER TO FALL BACK ON THAT THAN ADMIT THE HARDER TRUTH.
BEING WHAT?
THAT IT HAS NOTHING TO DO WITH SCIENCE... OR LOGIC... YOU WERE DEAD. AND YOU CAME BACK TO LIFE.
I DON'T AGREE. BUT EVEN STILL, WE'VE SEEN IT BEFORE. METAMORPHO. GREEN ARROW. HAL JORDAN. IT'S NOT SCIENCE--

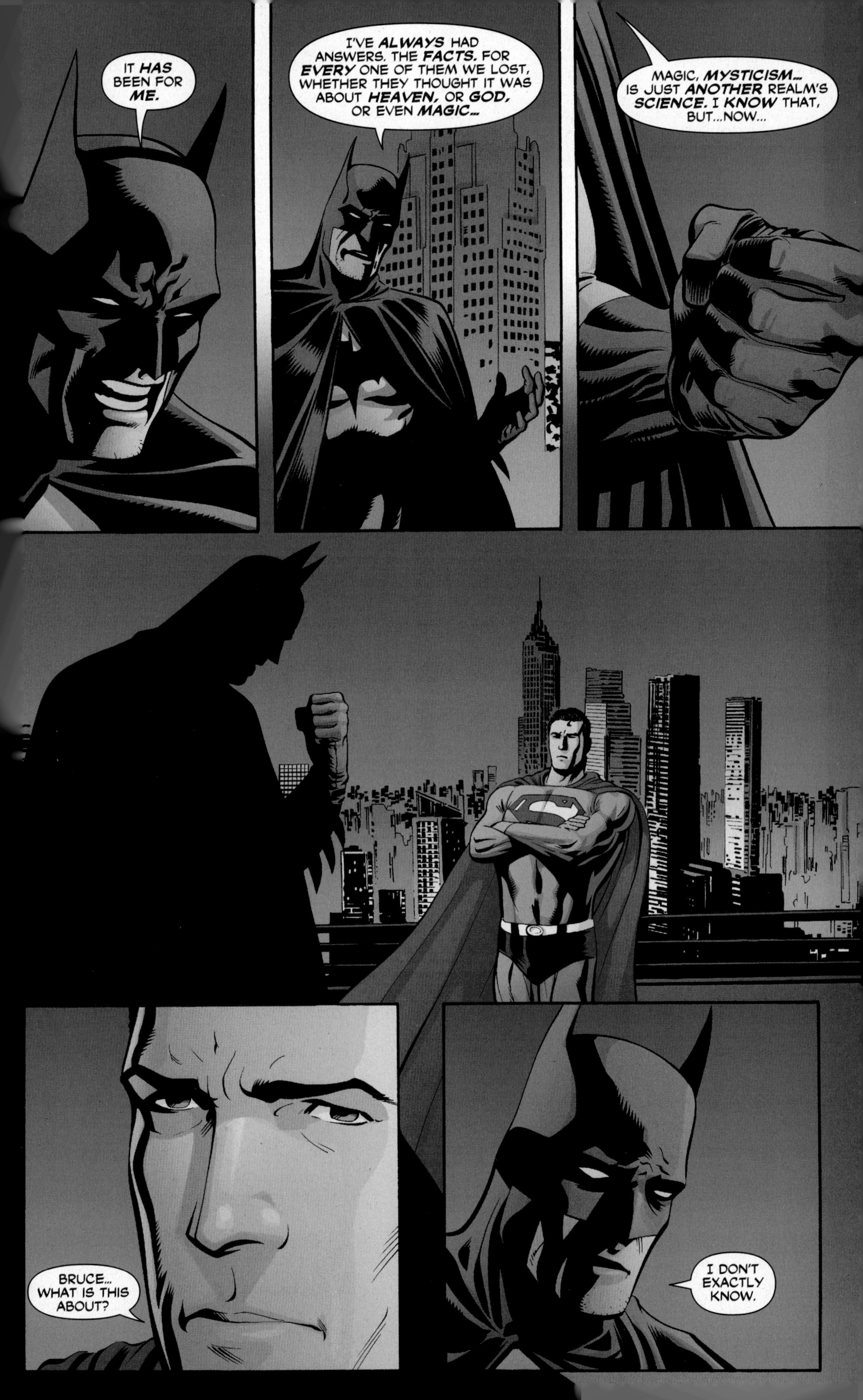
IT HAS BEEN FOR ME.
I'VE ALWAYS HAD ANSWERS. THE FACTS. FOR EVERY ONE OF THEM WE LOST, WHETHER THEY THOUGHT IT WAS ABOUT HEAVEN, OR GOD, OR EVEN MAGIC...
MAGIC, MYSTICISM... IS JUST ANOTHER REALM'S SCIENCE. I KNOW THAT, BUT...NOW...
BRUCE... WHAT IS THIS ABOUT?
I DON'T EXACTLY KNOW.

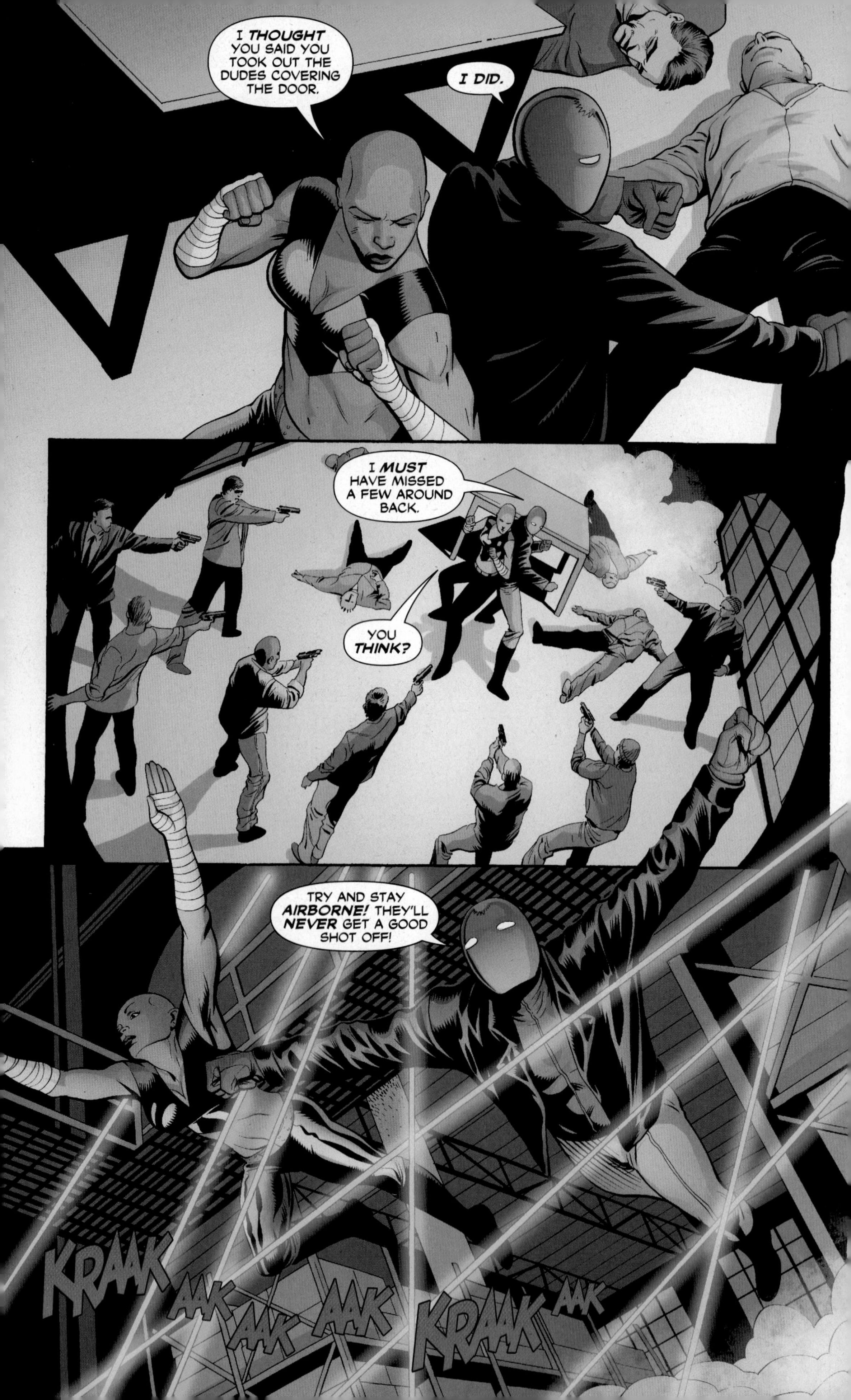
I THOUGHT YOU SAID YOU TOOK OUT THE DUDES COVERING THE DOOR.
I DID.
I MUST HAVE MISSED A FEW AROUND BACK.
YOU THINK?
TRY AND STAY AIRBORNE! THEY'LL NEVER GET A GOOD SHOT OFF!
KRAAK AAK AAK AAK KRAAK AAK

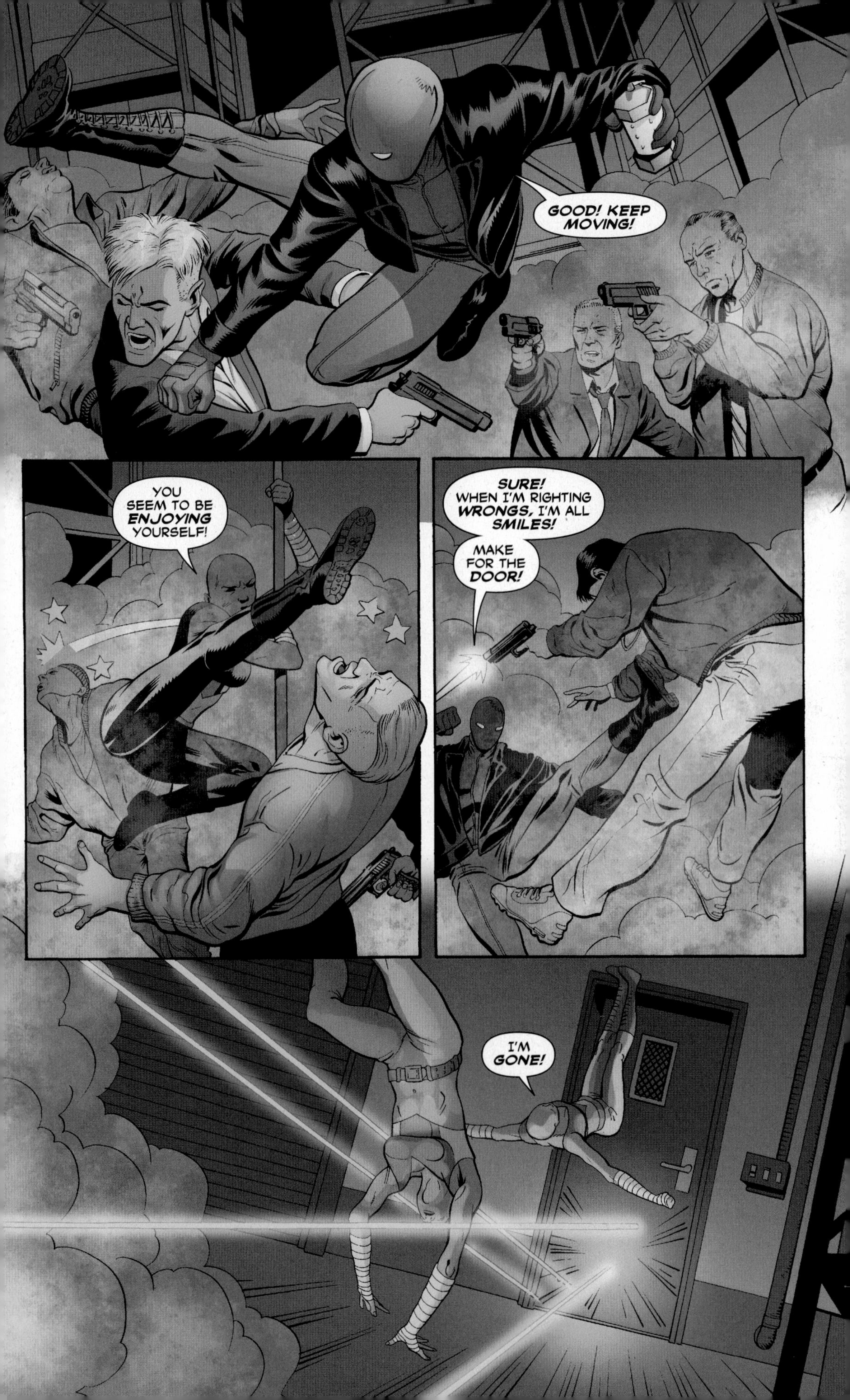
GOOD! KEEP MOVING!
YOU SEEM TO BE ENJOYING YOURSELF!
SURE! WHEN I'M RIGHTING WRONGS, I'M ALL SMILES!
MAKE FOR THE DOOR!
I'M GONE!

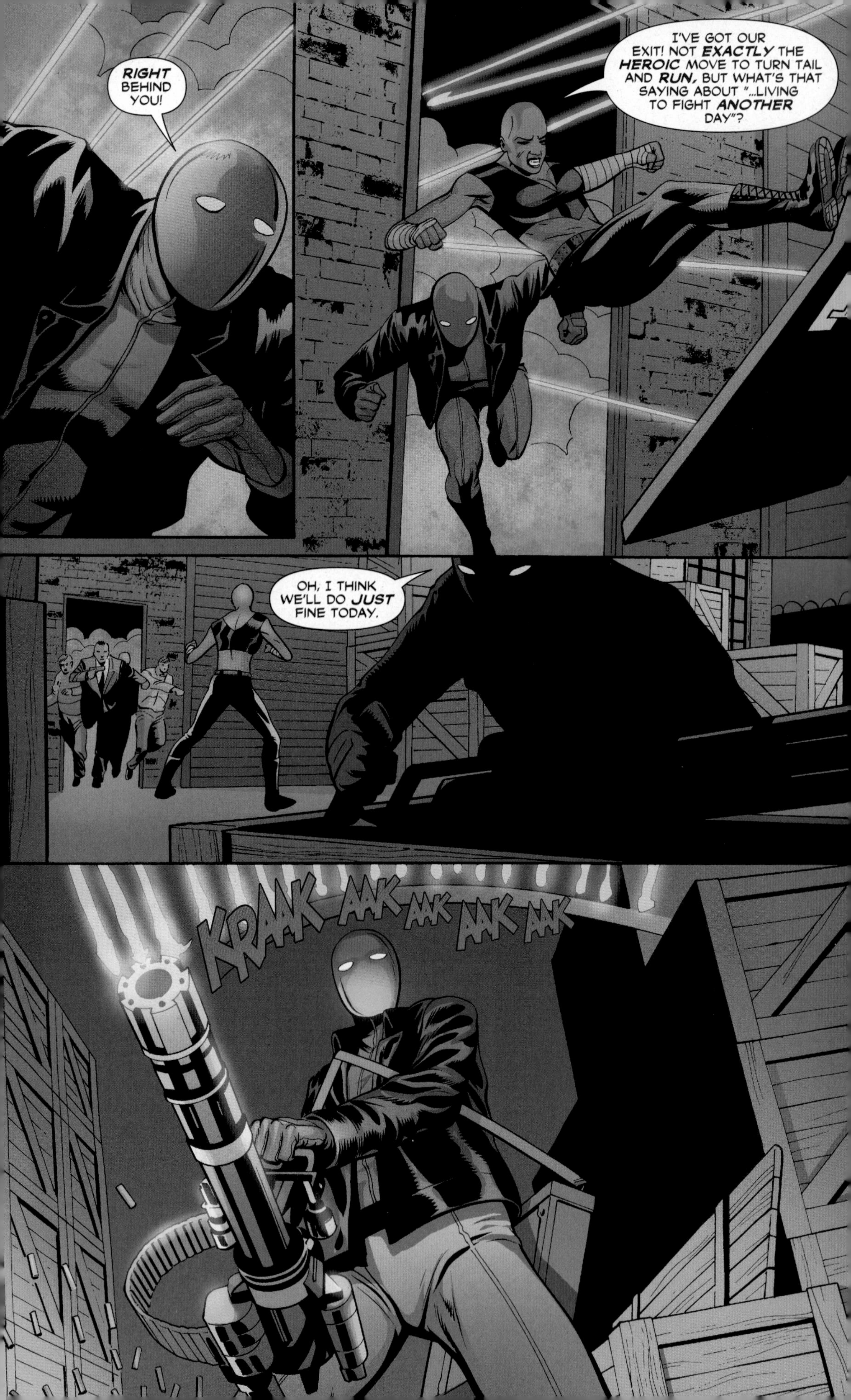
RIGHT BEHIND YOU!
I'VE GOT OUR EXIT! NOT EXACTLY THE HEROIC MOVE TO TURN TAIL AND RUN, BUT WHAT'S THAT SAYING ABOUT "...LIVING TO FIGHT ANOTHER DAY"?
OH, I THINK WE'LL DO JUST FINE TODAY.
KRAAK AAK AAK AAK AAK

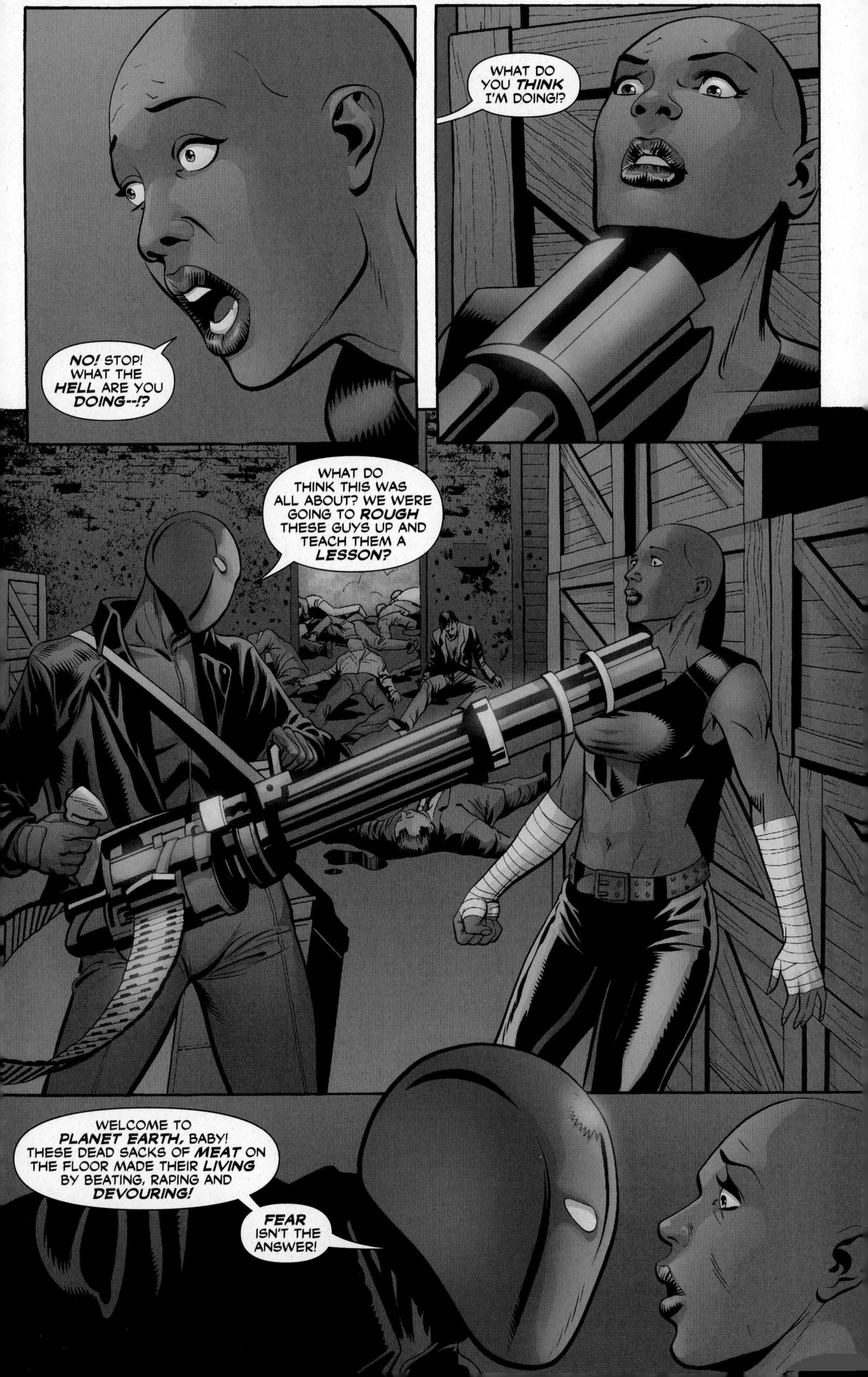
NO! STOP! WHAT THE HELL ARE YOU DOING--!?
WHAT DO YOU THINK I'M DOING!?
WHAT DO THINK THIS WAS ALL ABOUT? WE WERE GOING TO ROUGH THESE GUYS UP AND TEACH THEM A LESSON?
WELCOME TO PLANET EARTH, BABY! THESE DEAD SACKS OF MEAT ON THE FLOOR MADE THEIR LIVING BY BEATING, RAPING AND DEVOURING!
FEAR ISN'T THE ANSWER!

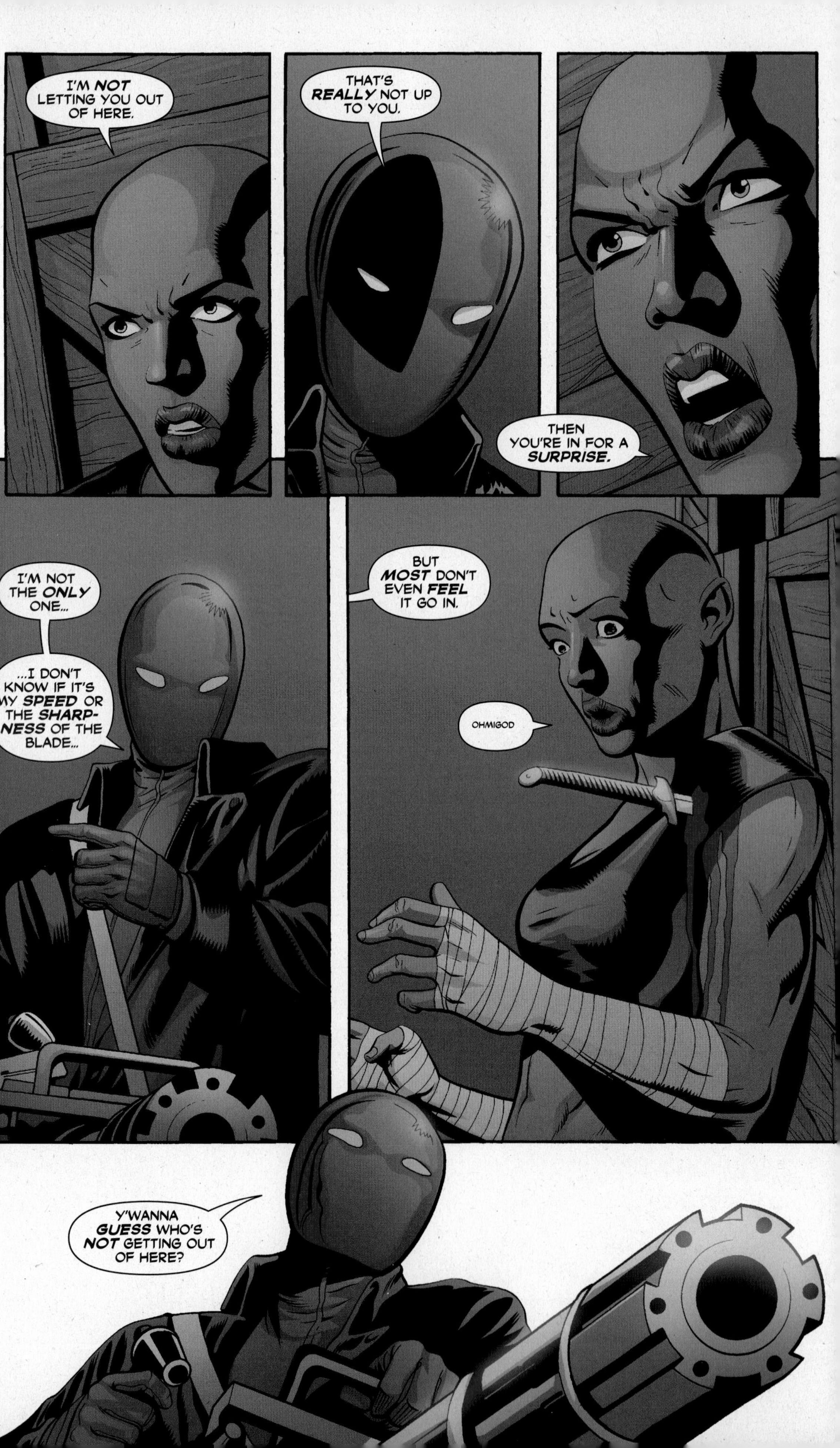
I'M NOT LETTING YOU OUT OF HERE.
THAT'S REALLY NOT UP TO YOU.
THEN YOU'RE IN FOR A SURPRISE.
I'M NOT THE ONLY ONE...
...I DON'T KNOW IF IT'S MY SPEED OR THE SHARPNESS OF THE BLADE...
BUT MOST DON'T EVEN FEEL IT GO IN.
OHMIGOD
Y'WANNA GUESS WHO'S NOT GETTING OUT OF HERE?

BATMAN 641 Cover by Matt Wagner

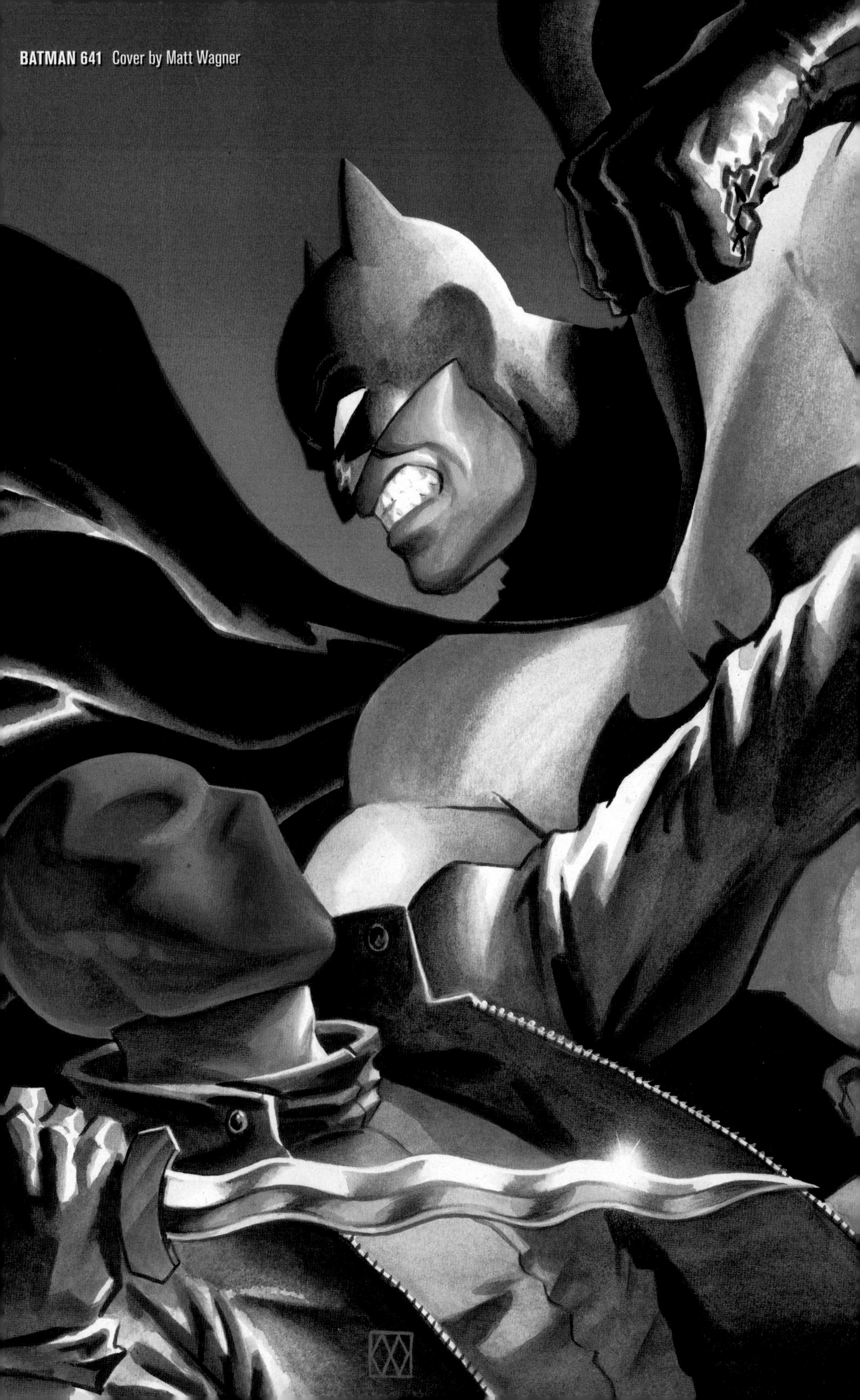

CHAPTER 7

FACE TO FACE

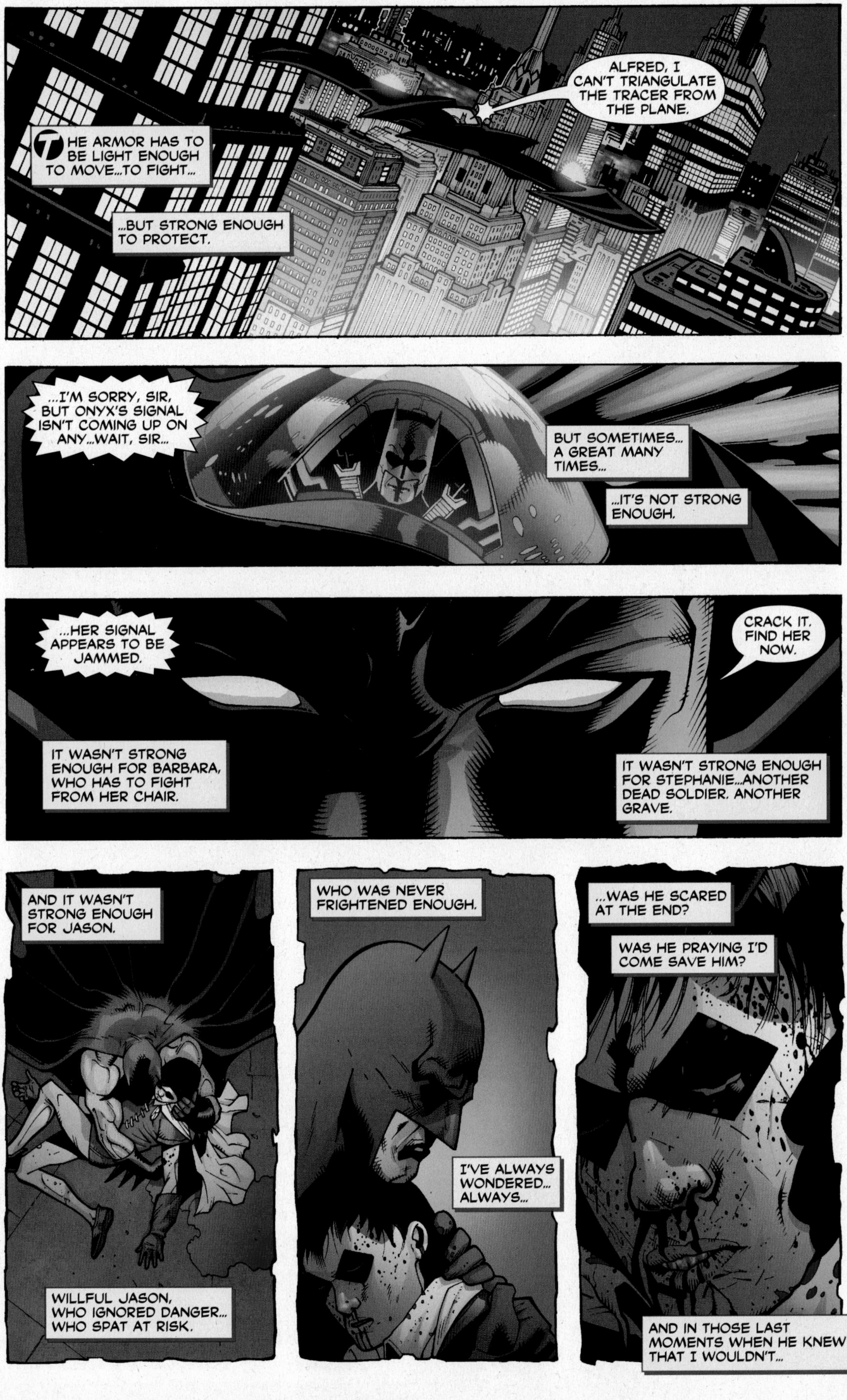
THE ARMOR HAS TO BE LIGHT ENOUGH TO MOVE...TO FIGHT...
ALFRED, I CAN'T TRIANGULATE THE TRACER FROM THE PLANE.
...BUT STRONG ENOUGH TO PROTECT.
...I'M SORRY, SIR, BUT ONYX'S SIGNAL ISN'T COMING UP ON ANY...WAIT, SIR...
BUT SOMETIMES... A GREAT MANY TIMES...
...IT'S NOT STRONG ENOUGH.
...HER SIGNAL APPEARS TO BE JAMMED.
CRACK IT. FIND HER NOW.
IT WASN'T STRONG ENOUGH FOR BARBARA, WHO HAS TO FIGHT FROM HER CHAIR.
IT WASN'T STRONG ENOUGH FOR STEPHANIE...ANOTHER DEAD SOLDIER. ANOTHER GRAVE.
AND IT WASN'T STRONG ENOUGH FOR JASON.
WILLFUL JASON, WHO IGNORED DANGER... WHO SPAT AT RISK.
WHO WAS NEVER FRIGHTENED ENOUGH.
I'VE ALWAYS WONDERED... ALWAYS...
...WAS HE SCARED AT THE END?
WAS HE PRAYING I'D COME SAVE HIM?
AND IN THOSE LAST MOMENTS WHEN HE KNEW THAT I WOULDN'T...

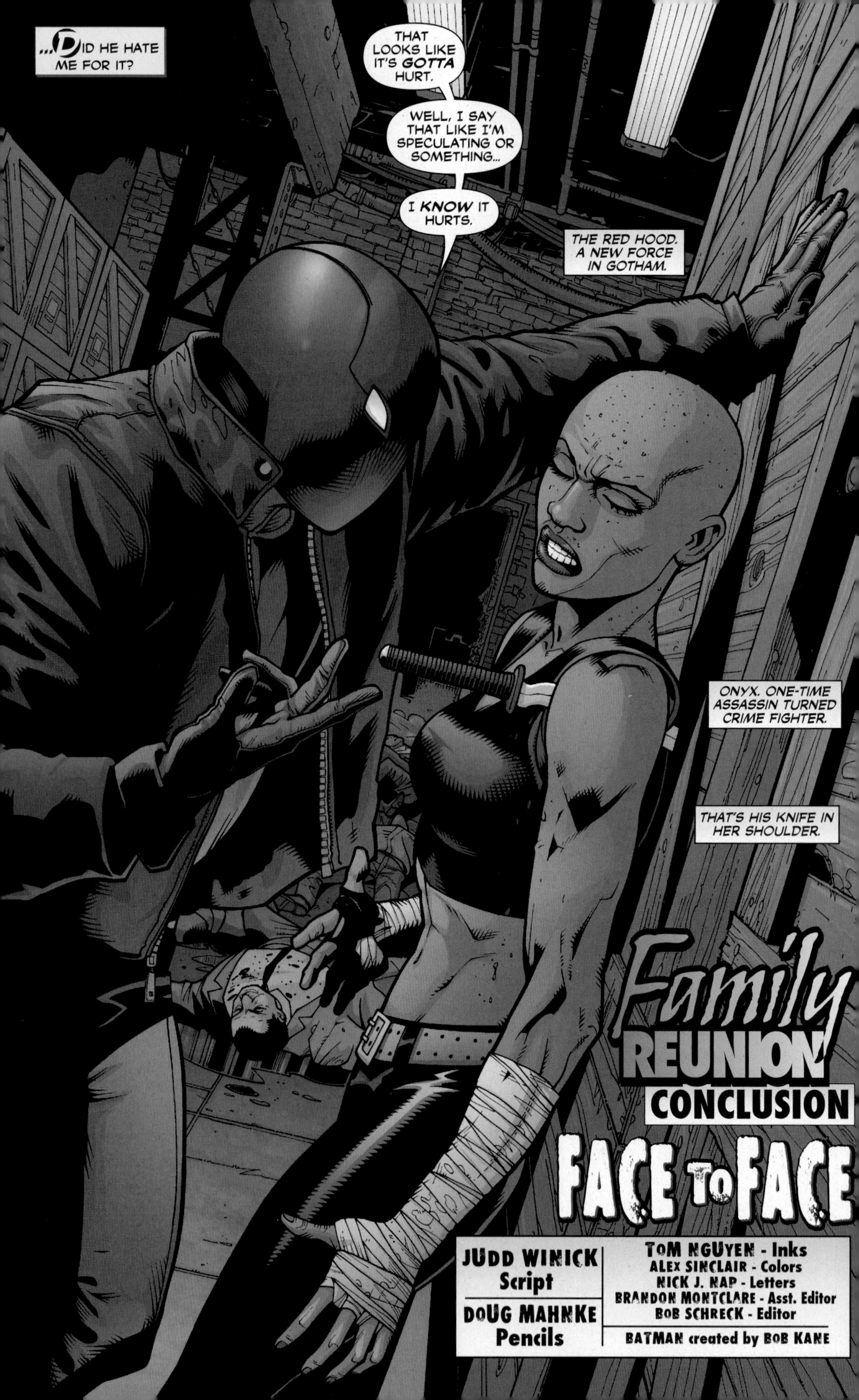

...DID HE HATE ME FOR IT?
THAT LOOKS LIKE IT'S GOTTA HURT.
WELL, I SAY THAT LIKE I'M SPECULATING OR SOMETHING...
I KNOW IT HURTS.
THE RED HOOD. A NEW FORCE IN GOTHAM.
ONYX. ONE-TIME ASSASSIN TURNED CRIME FIGHTER.
THAT'S HIS KNIFE IN HER SHOULDER.
Family REUNION CONCLUSION
FACE TO FACE
JUDD WINICK Script
DOUG MAHNKE Pencils
TOM NGUYEN - Inks
ALEX SINCLAIR - Colors
NICK J. NAP - Letters
BRANDON MONTCLARE - Asst. Editor
BOB SCHRECK - Editor
BATMAN created by BOB KANE

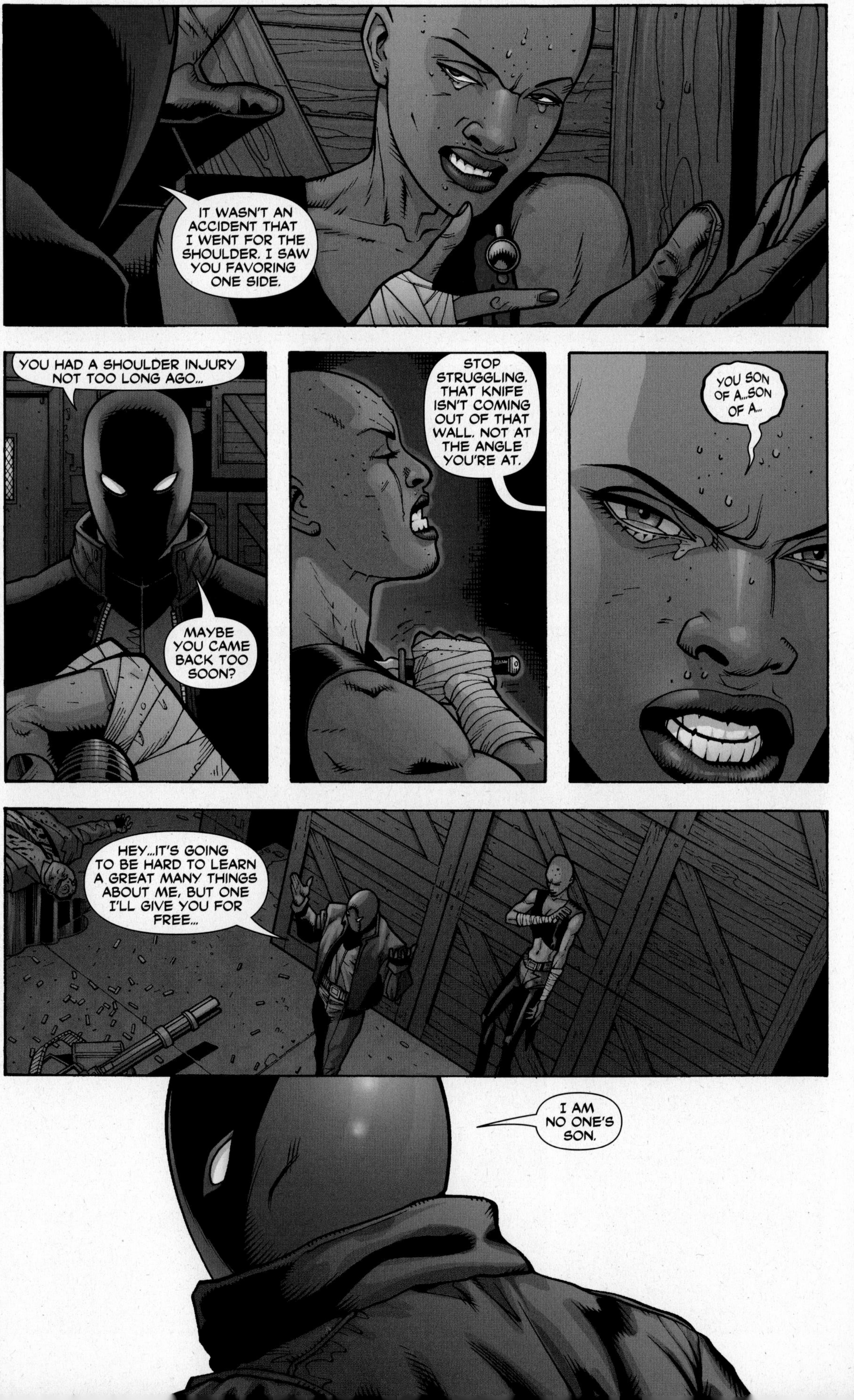
IT WASN'T AN ACCIDENT THAT I WENT FOR THE SHOULDER. I SAW YOU FAVORING ONE SIDE.
YOU HAD A SHOULDER INJURY NOT TOO LONG AGO...
MAYBE YOU CAME BACK TOO SOON?
STOP STRUGGLING. THAT KNIFE ISN'T COMING OUT OF THAT WALL. NOT AT THE ANGLE YOU'RE AT.
YOU SON OF A...SON OF A...
HEY...IT'S GOING TO BE HARD TO LEARN A GREAT MANY THINGS ABOUT ME, BUT ONE I'LL GIVE YOU FOR FREE...
I AM NO ONE'S SON.

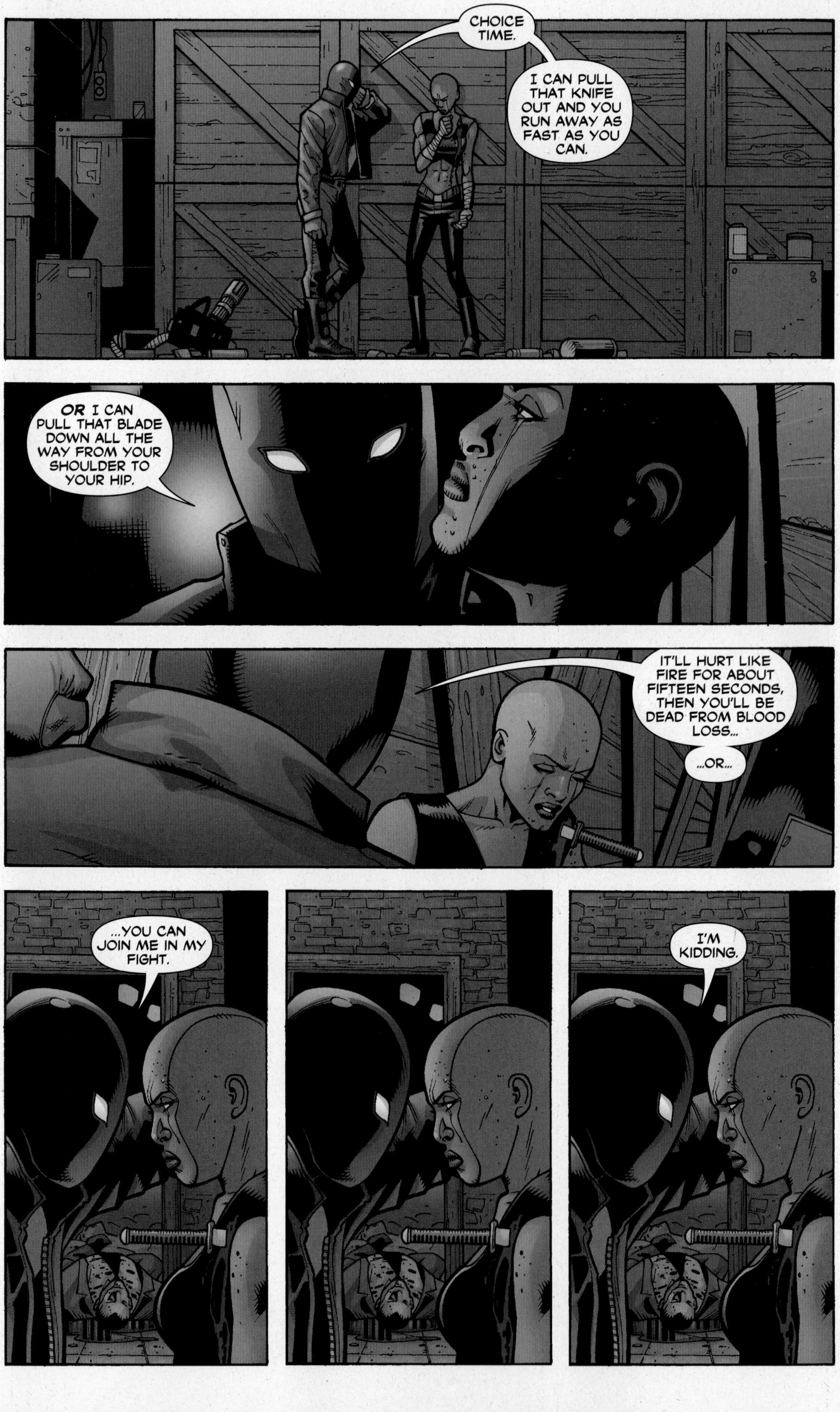
CHOICE TIME.
I CAN PULL THAT KNIFE OUT AND YOU RUN AWAY AS FAST AS YOU CAN.
OR I CAN PULL THAT BLADE DOWN ALL THE WAY FROM YOUR SHOULDER TO YOUR HIP.
IT'LL HURT LIKE FIRE FOR ABOUT FIFTEEN SECONDS, THEN YOU'LL BE DEAD FROM BLOOD LOSS...
...OR...
...YOU CAN JOIN ME IN MY FIGHT.
I'M KIDDING.

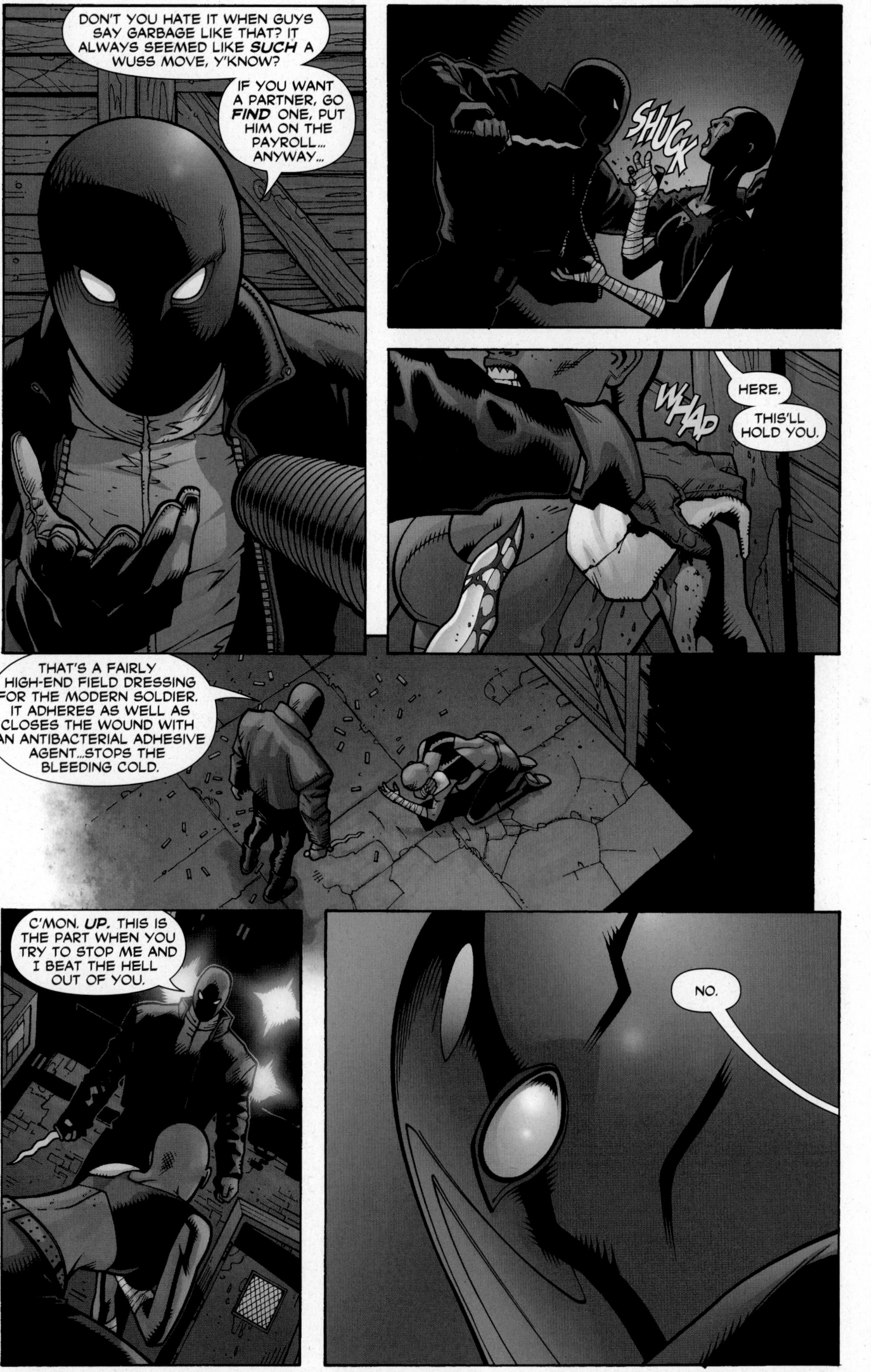
DON'T YOU HATE IT WHEN GUYS SAY GARBAGE LIKE THAT? IT ALWAYS SEEMED LIKE SUCH A WUSS MOVE, Y'KNOW?
IF YOU WANT A PARTNER, GO FIND ONE, PUT HIM ON THE PAYROLL... ANYWAY...
SHUCK
WHAP
HERE.
THIS'LL HOLD YOU.
THAT'S A FAIRLY HIGH-END FIELD DRESSING FOR THE MODERN SOLDIER. IT ADHERES AS WELL AS CLOSES THE WOUND WITH AN ANTIBACTERIAL ADHESIVE AGENT...STOPS THE BLEEDING COLD.
C'MON. UP. THIS IS THE PART WHEN YOU TRY TO STOP ME AND I BEAT THE HELL OUT OF YOU.
NO.

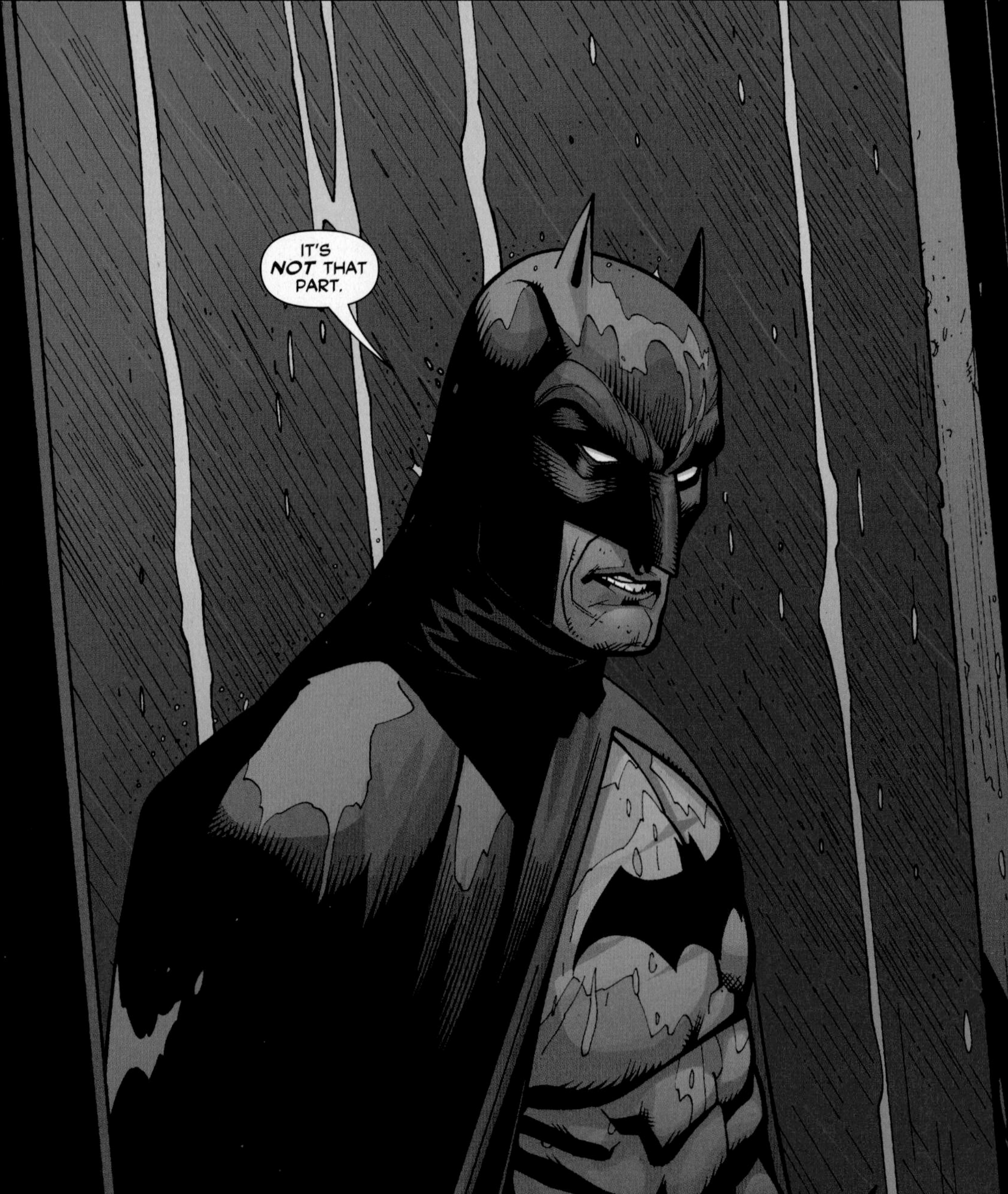
IT'S NOT THAT PART.

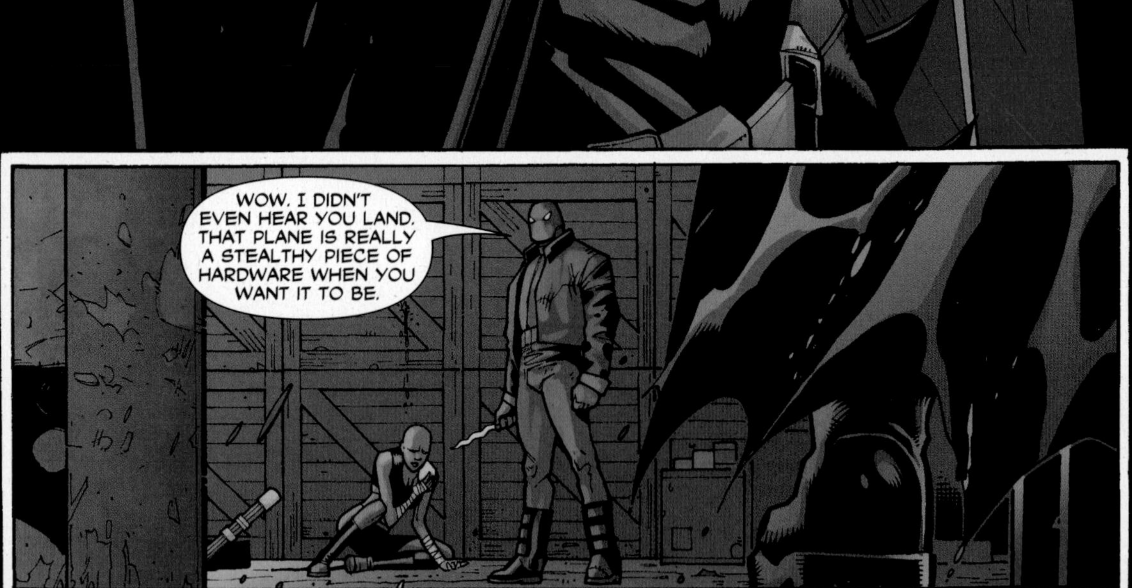
WOW. I DIDN'T EVEN HEAR YOU LAND. THAT PLANE IS REALLY A STEALTHY PIECE OF HARDWARE WHEN YOU WANT IT TO BE.

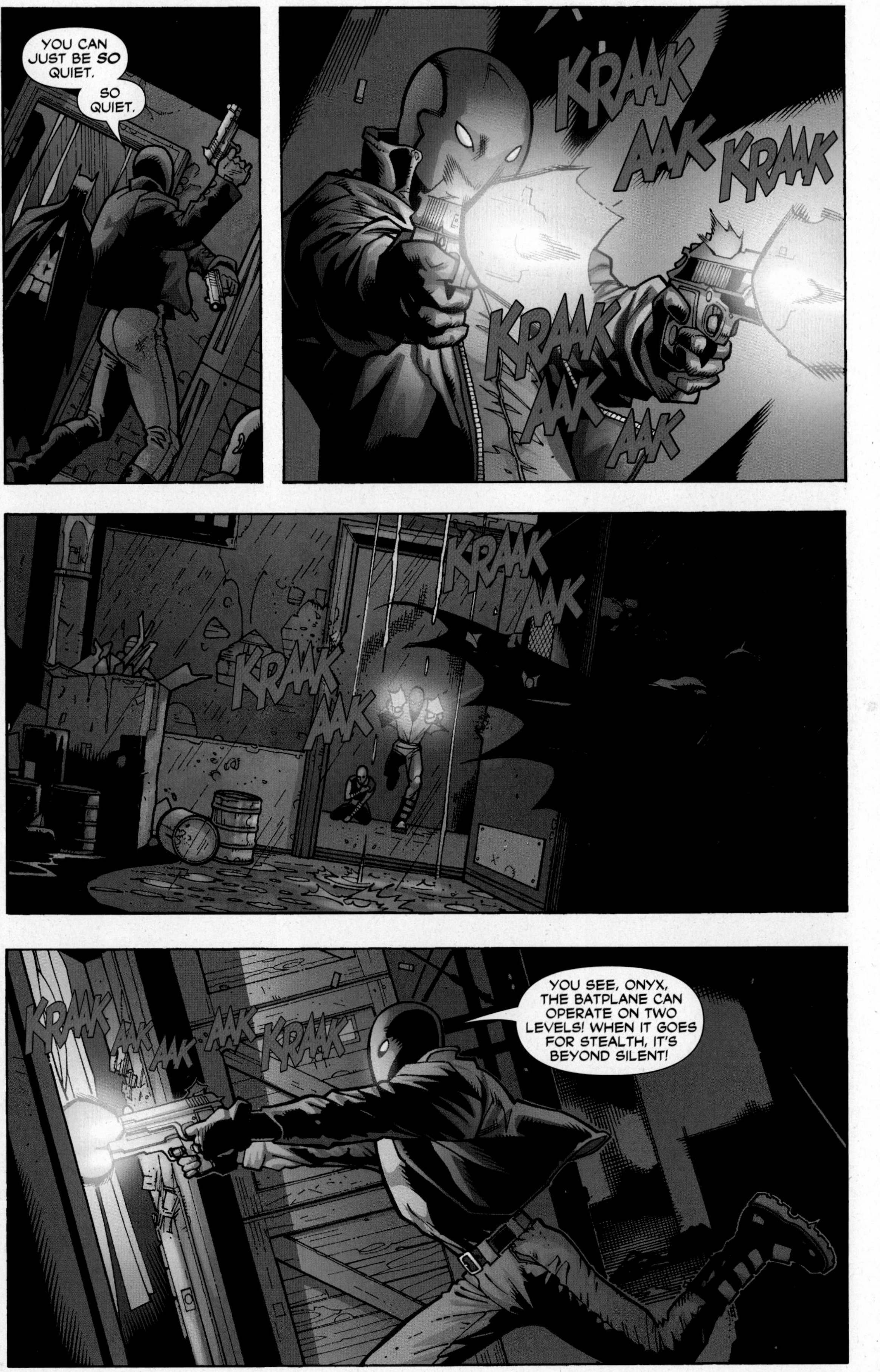
YOU CAN JUST BE SO QUIET.
SO QUIET.
KRAAK
AAK KRAAK
KRAAK
AAK
AAK
KRAAK
AAK
KRAAK
AAK
KRAAK AAK AAK AAK KRAAK
YOU SEE, ONYX, THE BATPLANE CAN OPERATE ON TWO LEVELS! WHEN IT GOES FOR STEALTH, IT'S BEYOND SILENT!

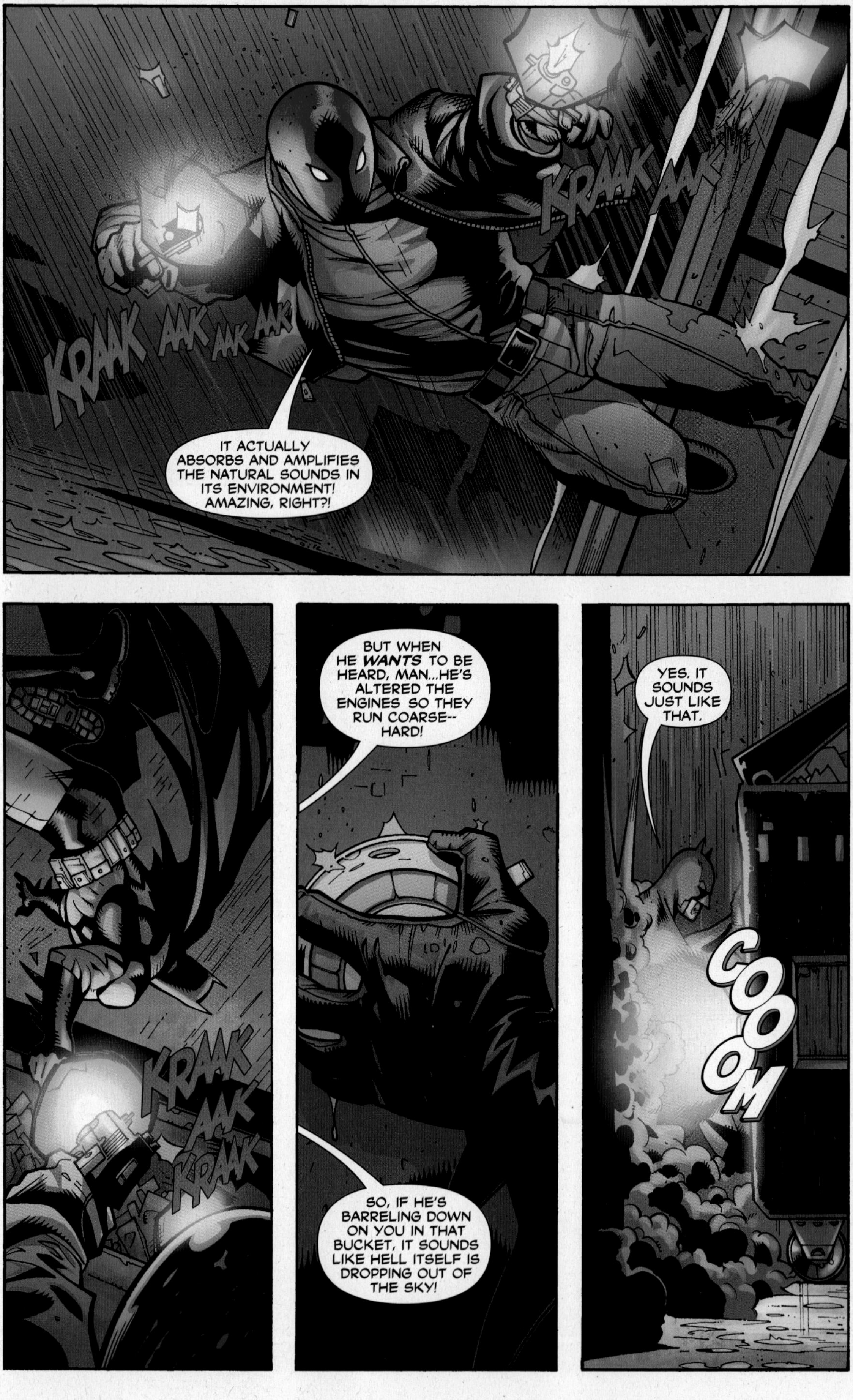
KRAAK AAK
KRAAK AAK AAK AAK
IT ACTUALLY ABSORBS AND AMPLIFIES THE NATURAL SOUNDS IN ITS ENVIRONMENT! AMAZING, RIGHT?!
KRAAK AAK KRAAK
BUT WHEN HE **WANTS** TO BE HEARD, MAN...HE'S ALTERED THE ENGINES SO THEY RUN COARSE-- HARD!
SO, IF HE'S BARRELING DOWN ON YOU IN THAT BUCKET, IT SOUNDS LIKE HELL ITSELF IS DROPPING OUT OF THE SKY!
YES. IT SOUNDS JUST LIKE THAT.
COOOM

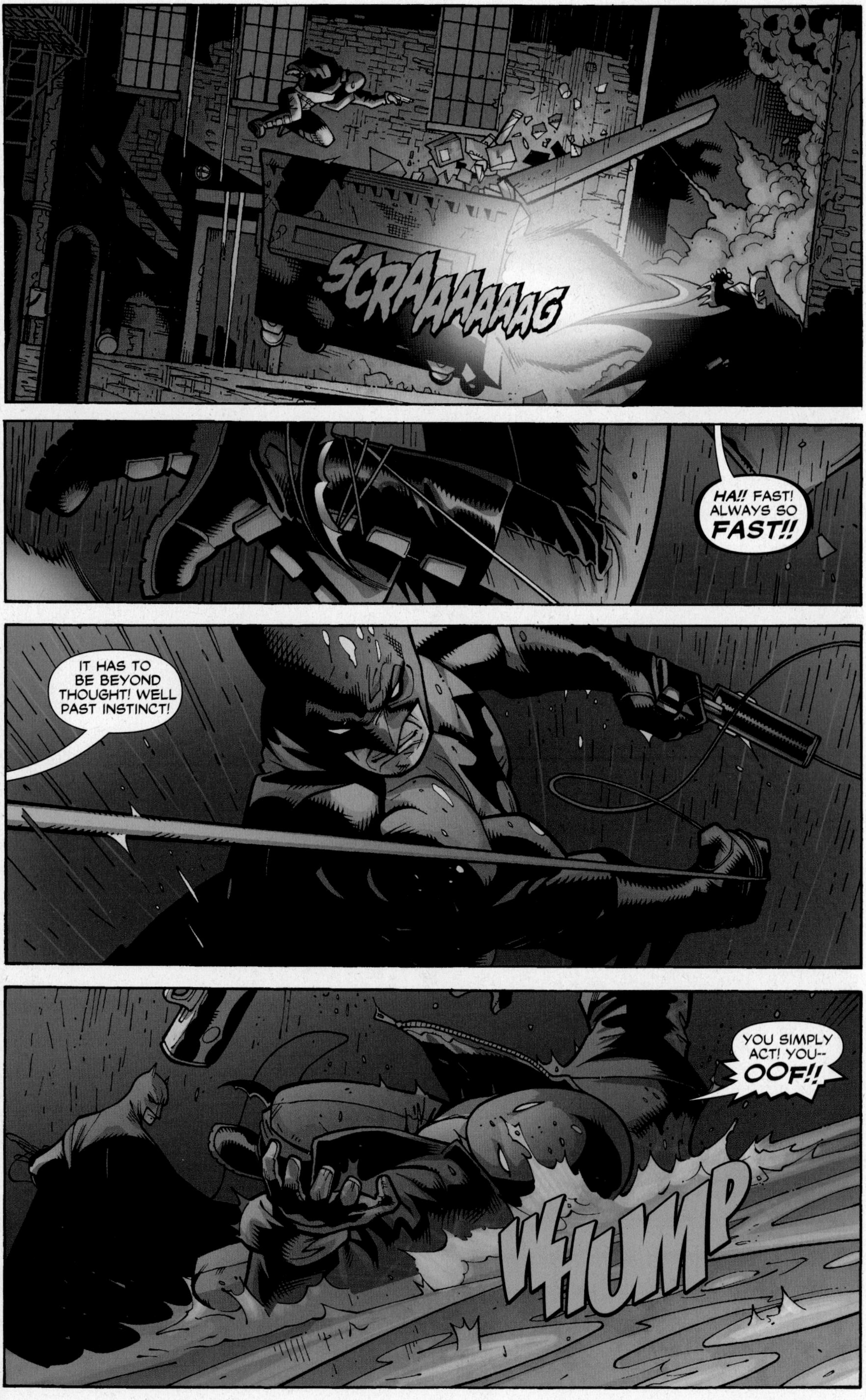
SCRAAAAAAG
HA!! FAST! ALWAYS SO FAST!!
IT HAS TO BE BEYOND THOUGHT! WELL PAST INSTINCT!
YOU SIMPLY ACT! YOU-- OOF!!
WHUMP

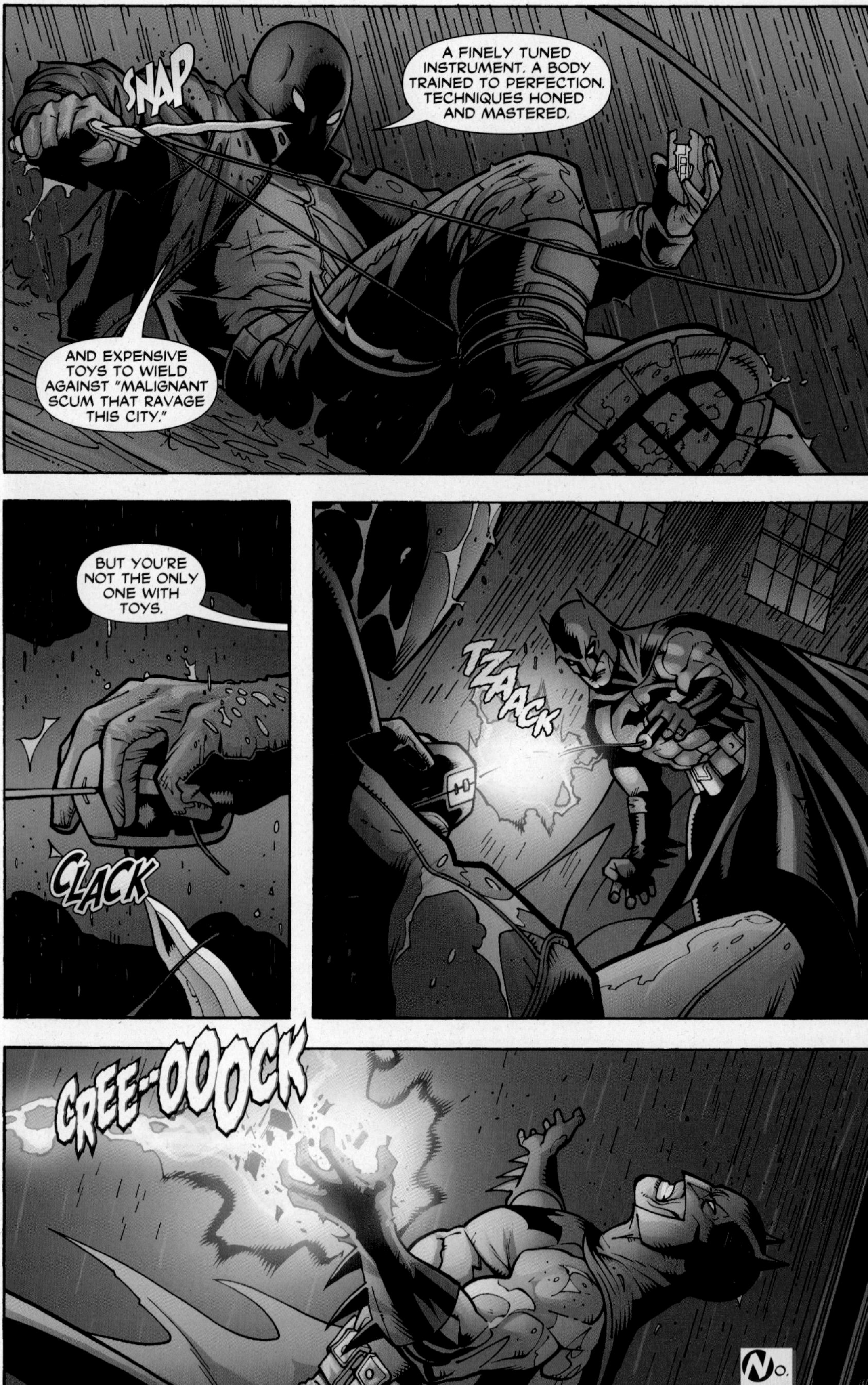

SNAP
A FINELY TUNED INSTRUMENT. A BODY TRAINED TO PERFECTION. TECHNIQUES HONED AND MASTERED.
AND EXPENSIVE TOYS TO WIELD AGAINST "MALIGNANT SCUM THAT RAVAGE THIS CITY."
BUT YOU'RE NOT THE ONLY ONE WITH TOYS.
CLACK
TZAACK
CREE-OOOCK

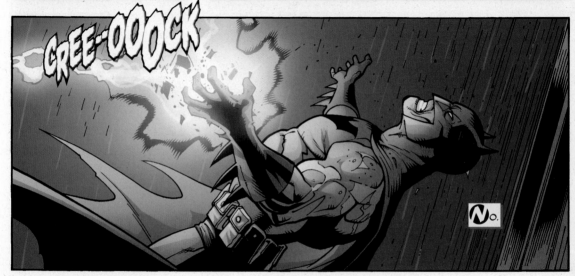

THAT DEVICE WAS FROM KORD INDUSTRIES. I SHOULD KNOW.

ORDERED IT "SPECIAL" FROM THEM.

DAMN IT.

HOW CAN *HE* HAVE IT?

BOOOOM

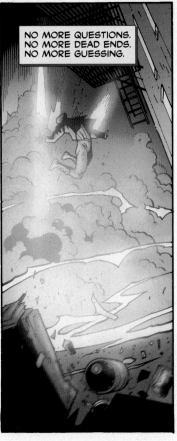

NO MORE QUESTIONS. NO MORE DEAD ENDS. NO MORE GUESSING.

TONIGHT I FIND WHAT IS PASSING FOR THE TRUTH.

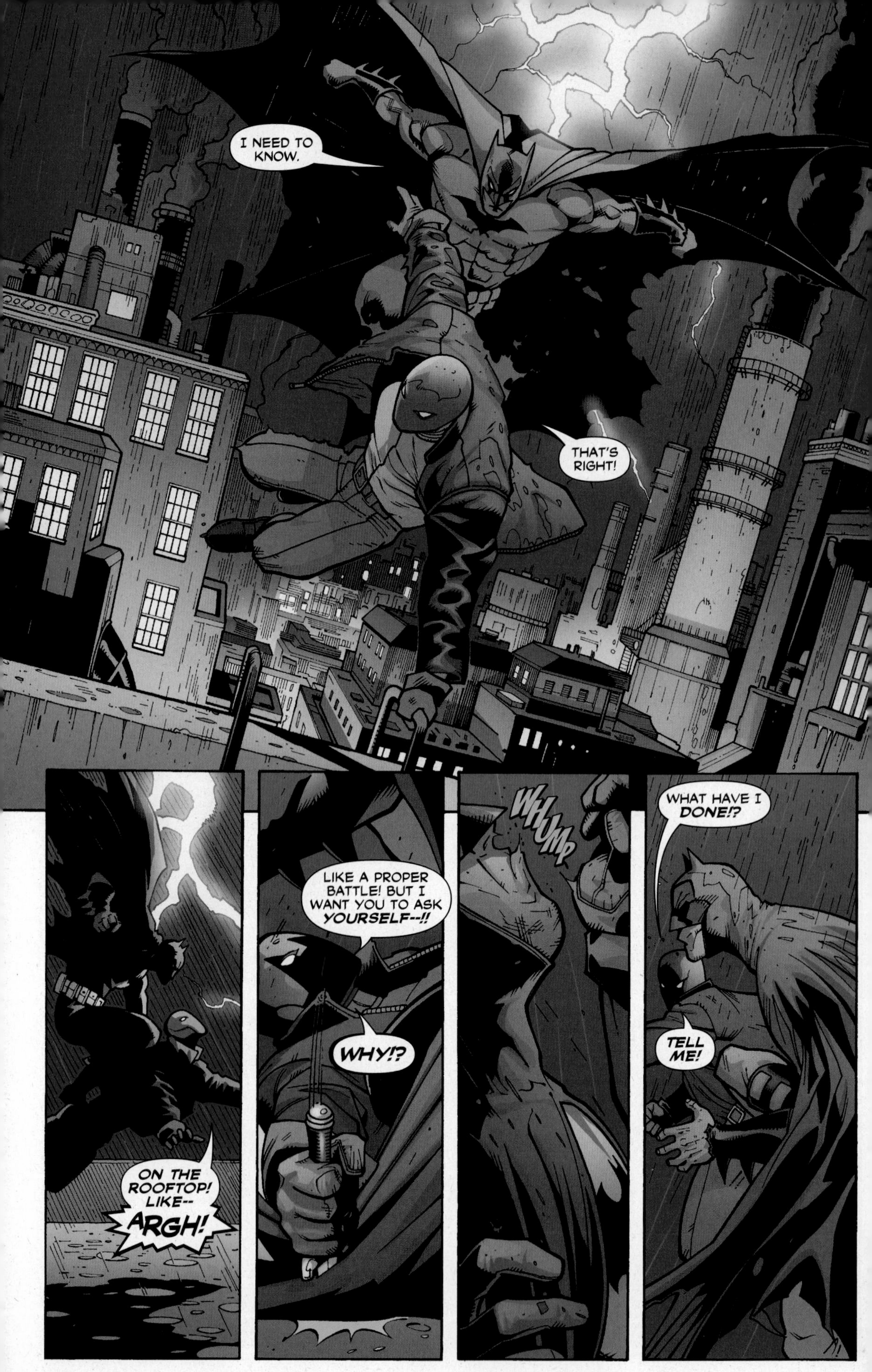
I NEED TO KNOW.
THAT'S RIGHT!
ON THE ROOFTOP! LIKE--
ARGH!
LIKE A PROPER BATTLE! BUT I WANT YOU TO ASK YOURSELF--!!
WHY!?
WHUMP
WHAT HAVE I DONE!?
TELL ME!

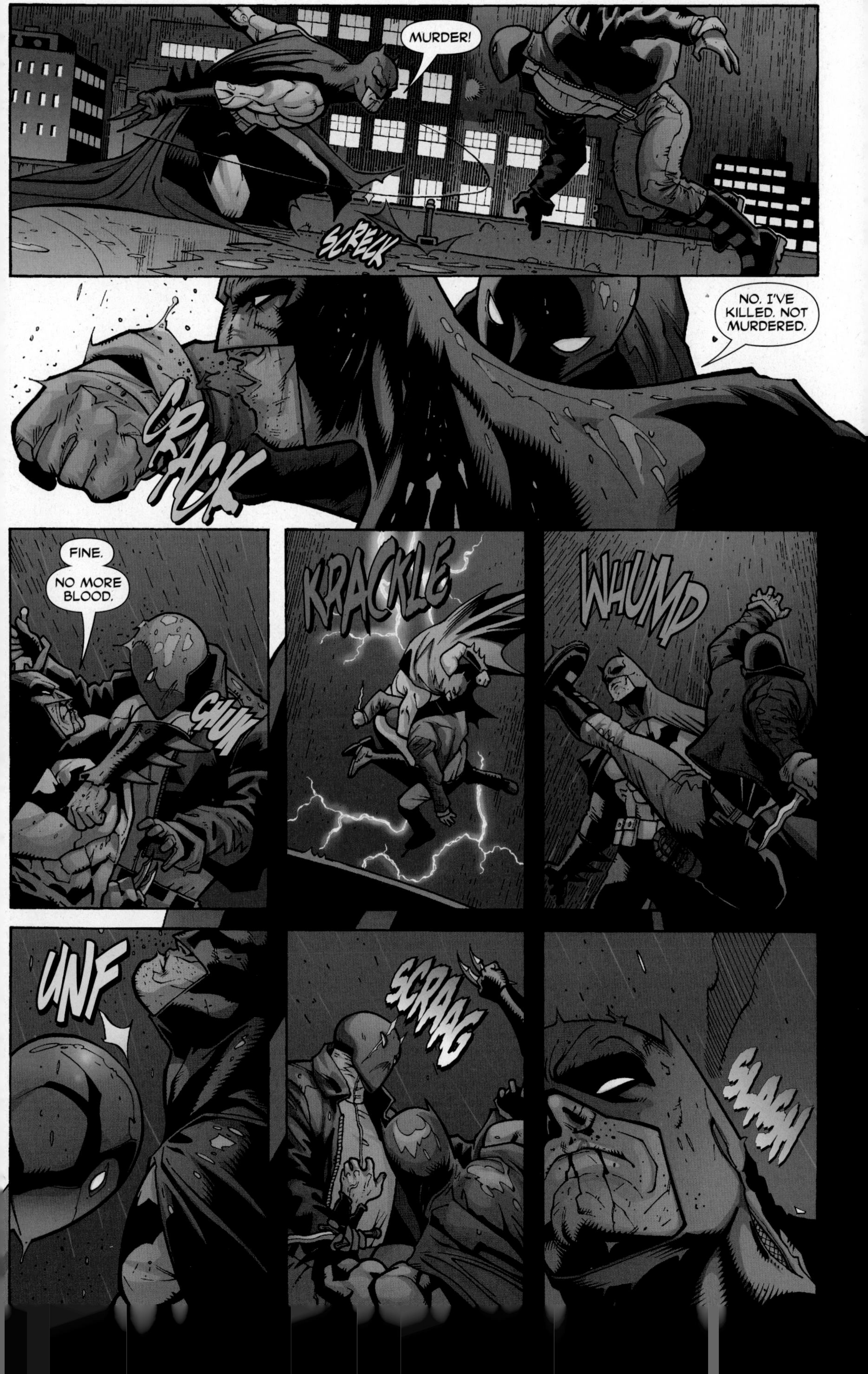
MURDER!
SCRECK
NO. I'VE KILLED. NOT MURDERED.
CRACK
FINE.
NO MORE BLOOD.
CHUK
KRACKLE
WHUMP
UNF
SCRAAG
SLASH

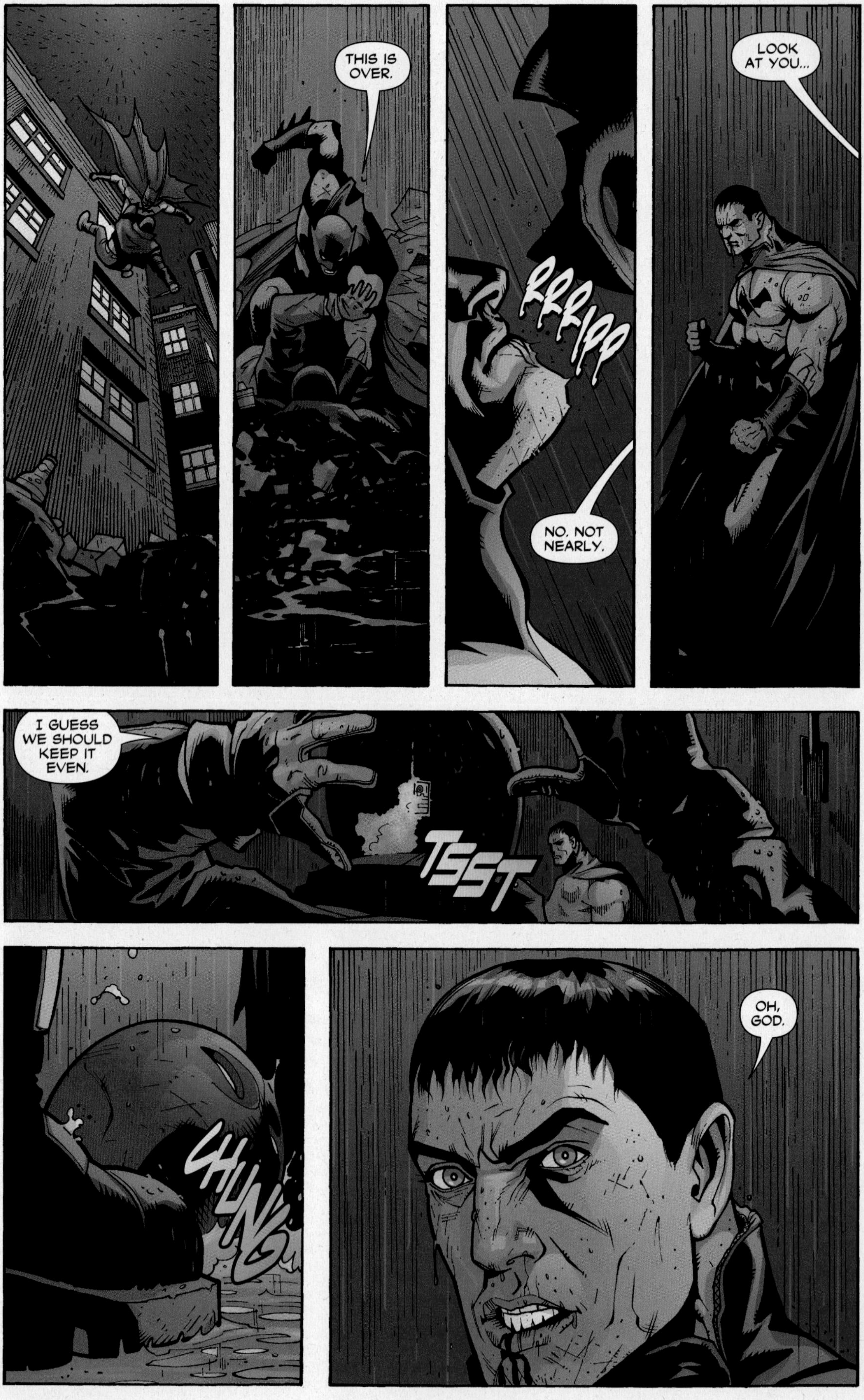
THIS IS OVER.
RRRIPP
NO, NOT NEARLY.
LOOK AT YOU...
I GUESS WE SHOULD KEEP IT EVEN.
TSST
CHUNG
OH, GOD.

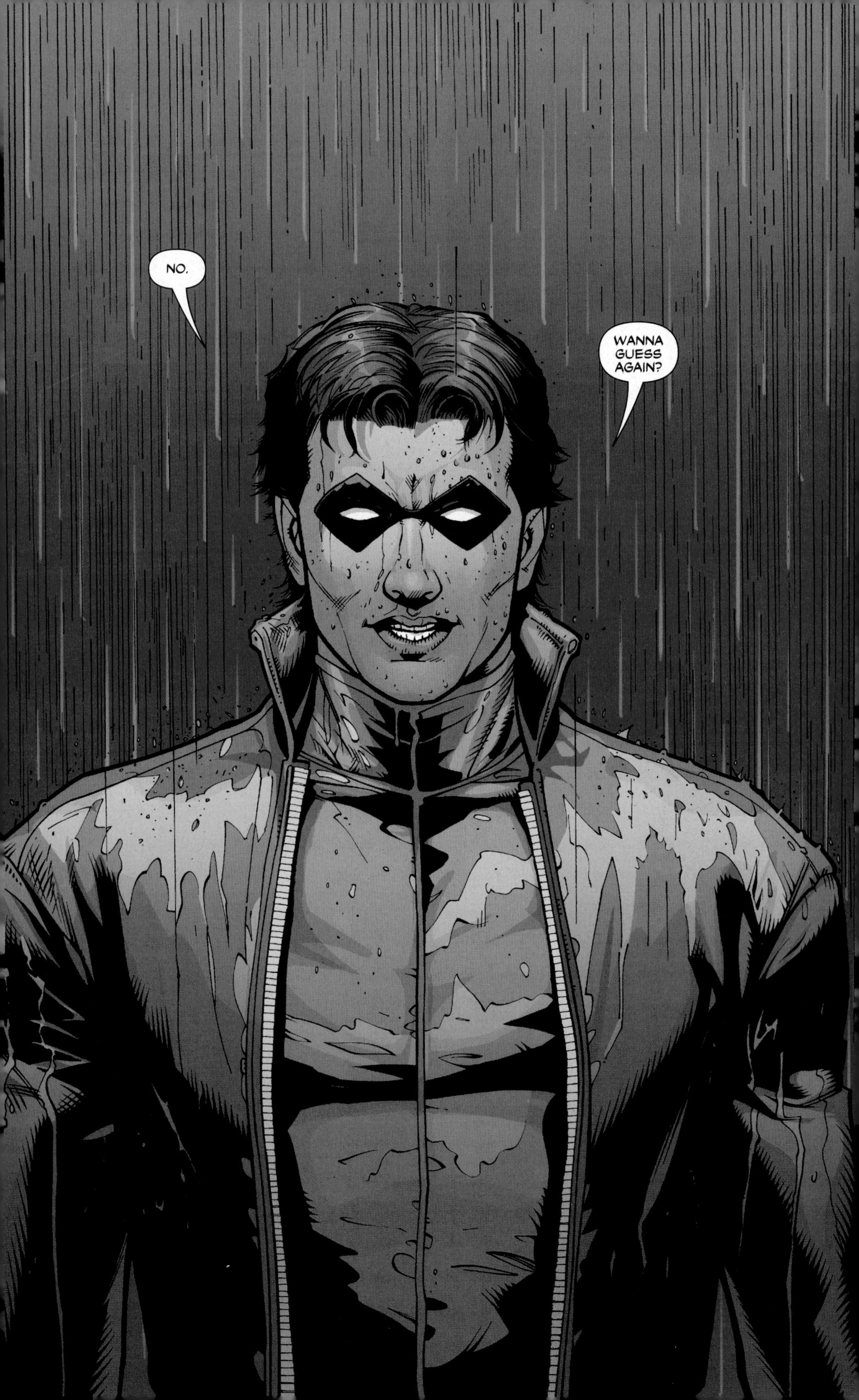
NO.
WANNA GUESS AGAIN?

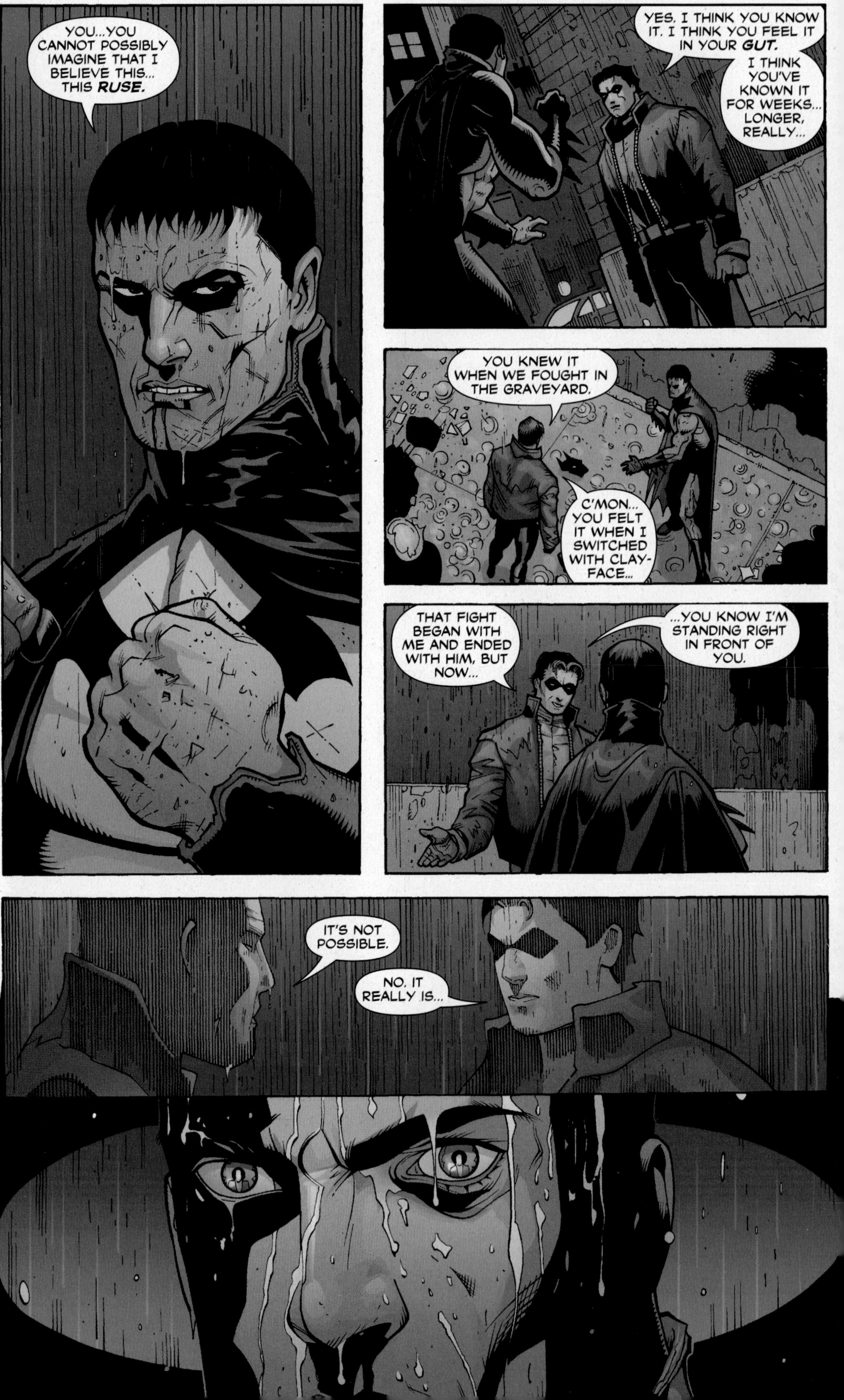
YOU...YOU CANNOT POSSIBLY IMAGINE THAT I BELIEVE THIS... THIS **RUSE.**
YES, I THINK YOU KNOW IT. I THINK YOU FEEL IT IN YOUR **GUT.**
I THINK YOU'VE KNOWN IT FOR WEEKS... LONGER, REALLY...
YOU KNEW IT WHEN WE FOUGHT IN THE GRAVEYARD.
C'MON... YOU FELT IT WHEN I SWITCHED WITH CLAY-FACE...
THAT FIGHT BEGAN WITH ME AND ENDED WITH HIM, BUT NOW...
...YOU KNOW I'M STANDING RIGHT IN FRONT OF YOU.
IT'S NOT POSSIBLE.
NO, IT REALLY IS...

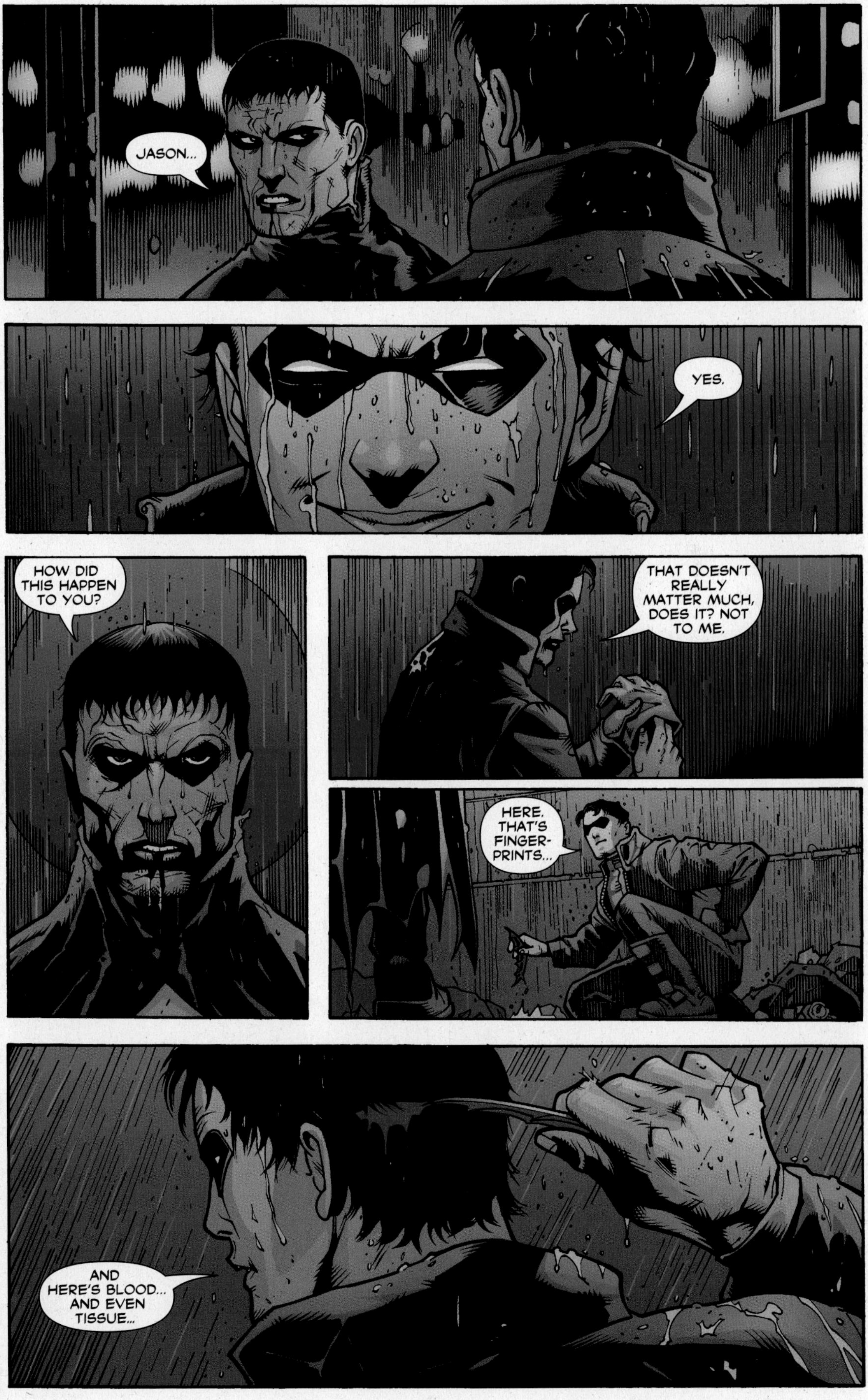
JASON...
YES.
HOW DID THIS HAPPEN TO YOU?
THAT DOESN'T REALLY MATTER MUCH, DOES IT? NOT TO ME.
HERE. THAT'S FINGER-PRINTS...
AND HERE'S BLOOD... AND EVEN TISSUE...

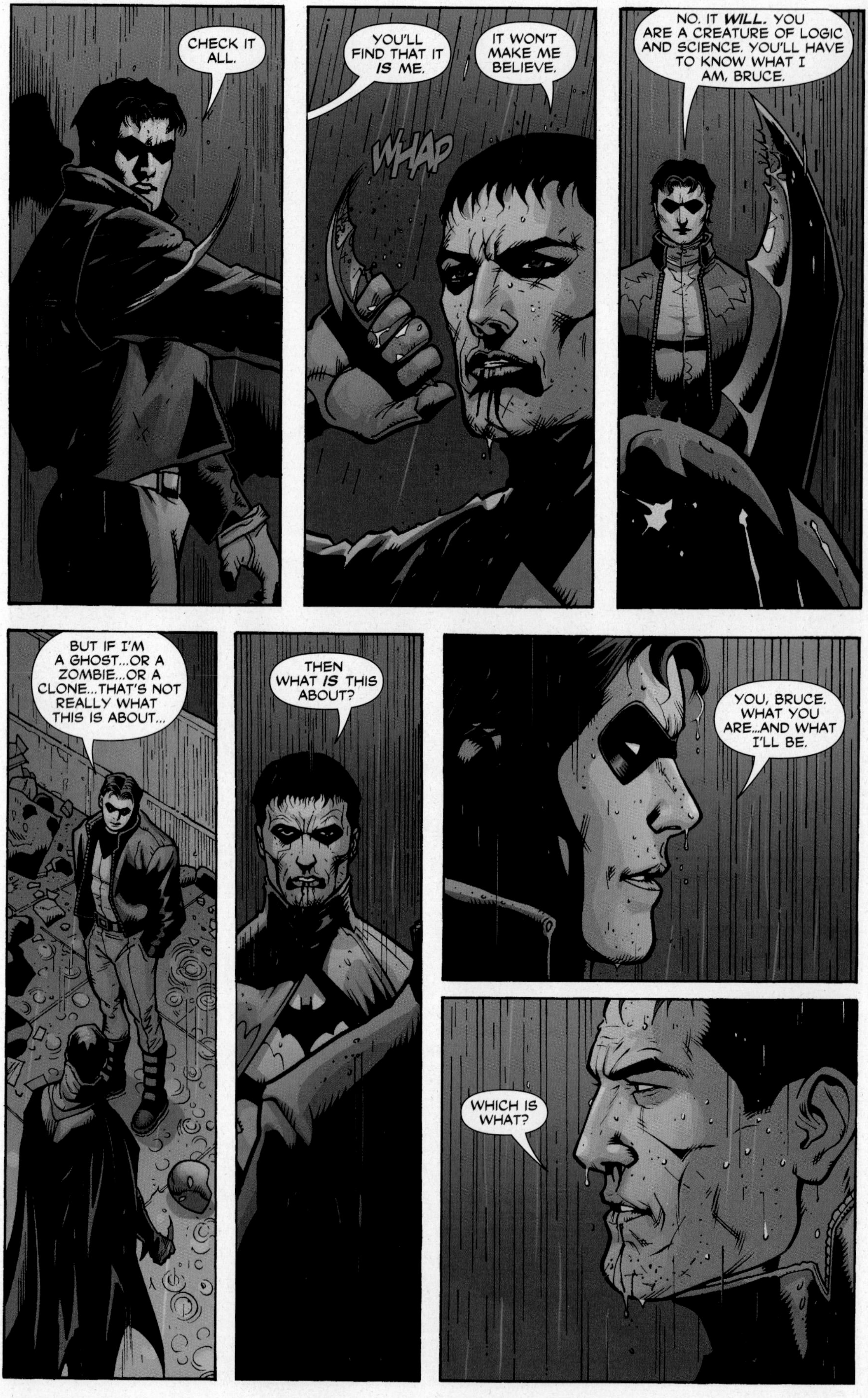
CHECK IT ALL.
YOU'LL FIND THAT IT *IS* ME.
IT WON'T MAKE ME BELIEVE.
WHAP
NO. IT *WILL.* YOU ARE A CREATURE OF LOGIC AND SCIENCE. YOU'LL HAVE TO KNOW WHAT I AM, BRUCE.
BUT IF I'M A GHOST...OR A ZOMBIE...OR A CLONE...THAT'S NOT REALLY WHAT THIS IS ABOUT...
THEN WHAT *IS* THIS ABOUT?
YOU, BRUCE. WHAT YOU ARE...AND WHAT I'LL BE.
WHICH IS WHAT?

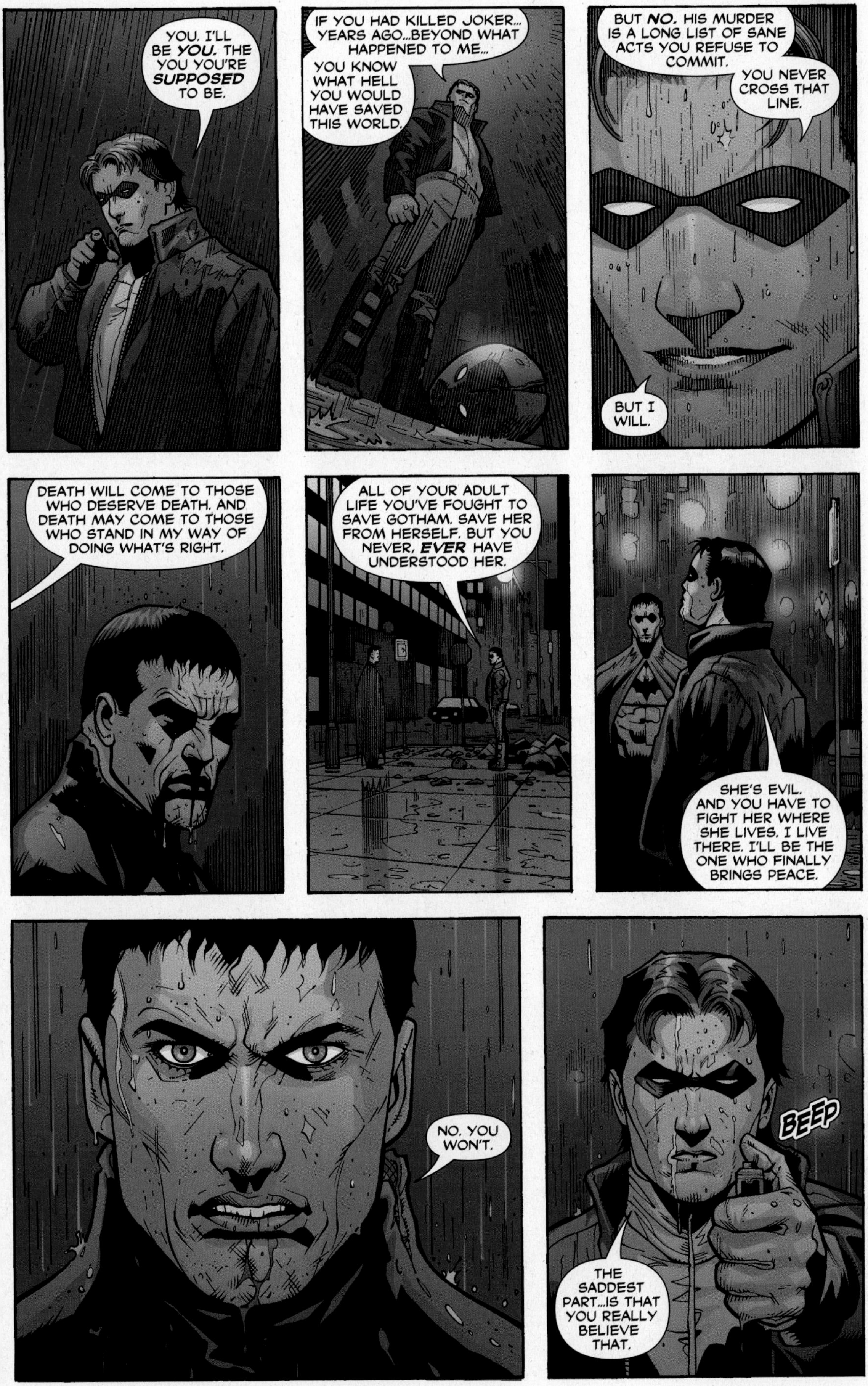
YOU. I'LL BE YOU. THE YOU YOU'RE SUPPOSED TO BE.
IF YOU HAD KILLED JOKER... YEARS AGO...BEYOND WHAT HAPPENED TO ME...
YOU KNOW WHAT HELL YOU WOULD HAVE SAVED THIS WORLD.
BUT NO. HIS MURDER IS A LONG LIST OF SANE ACTS YOU REFUSE TO COMMIT.
YOU NEVER CROSS THAT LINE.
BUT I WILL.
DEATH WILL COME TO THOSE WHO DESERVE DEATH. AND DEATH MAY COME TO THOSE WHO STAND IN MY WAY OF DOING WHAT'S RIGHT.
ALL OF YOUR ADULT LIFE YOU'VE FOUGHT TO SAVE GOTHAM. SAVE HER FROM HERSELF. BUT YOU NEVER, EVER HAVE UNDERSTOOD HER.
SHE'S EVIL. AND YOU HAVE TO FIGHT HER WHERE SHE LIVES. I LIVE THERE. I'LL BE THE ONE WHO FINALLY BRINGS PEACE.
NO. YOU WON'T.
BEEP
THE SADDEST PART...IS THAT YOU REALLY BELIEVE THAT.

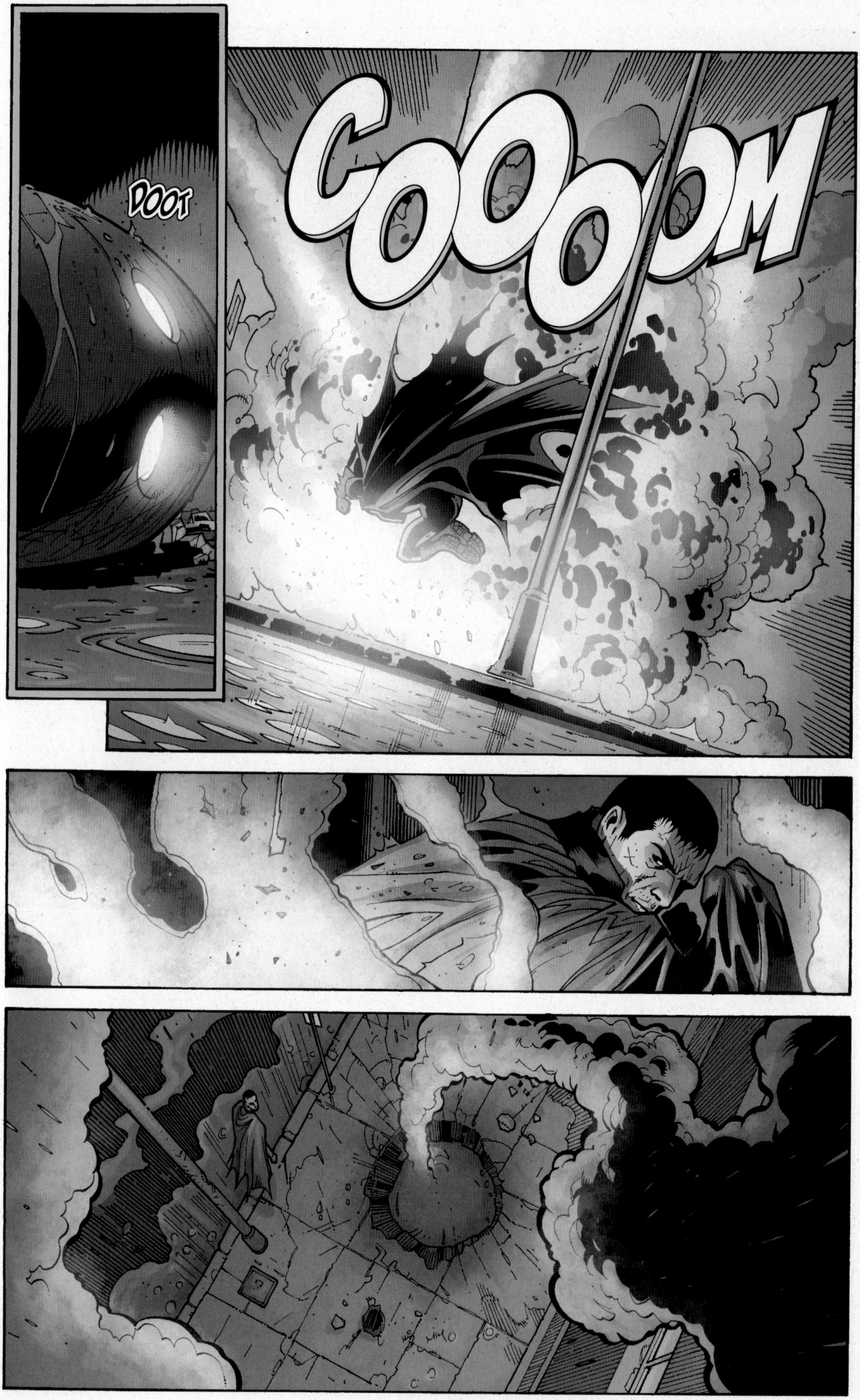
DOOT
COOOOOM

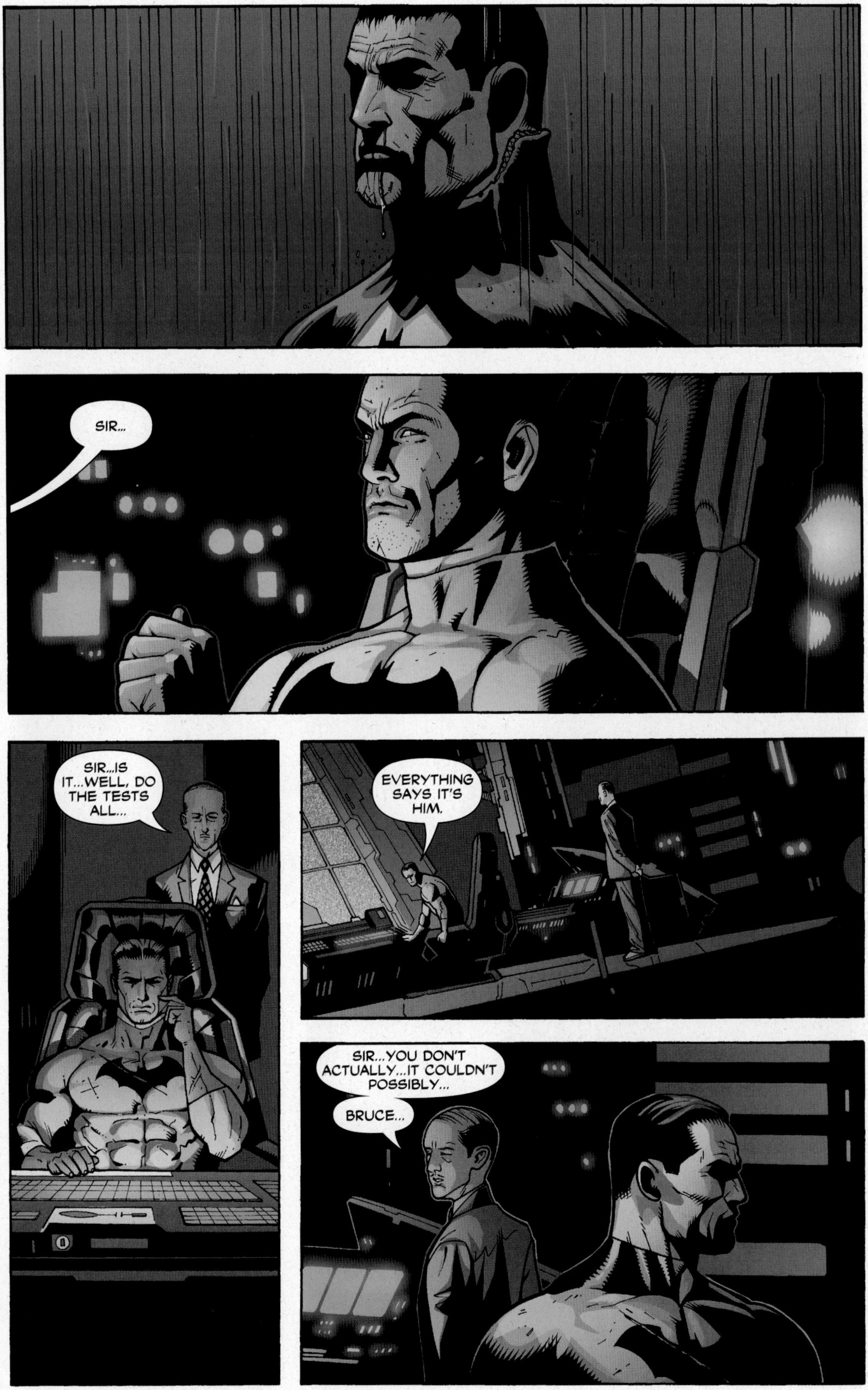
SIR...
SIR...IS IT...WELL, DO THE TESTS ALL...
EVERYTHING SAYS IT'S HIM.
SIR...YOU DON'T ACTUALLY...IT COULDN'T POSSIBLY...
BRUCE...

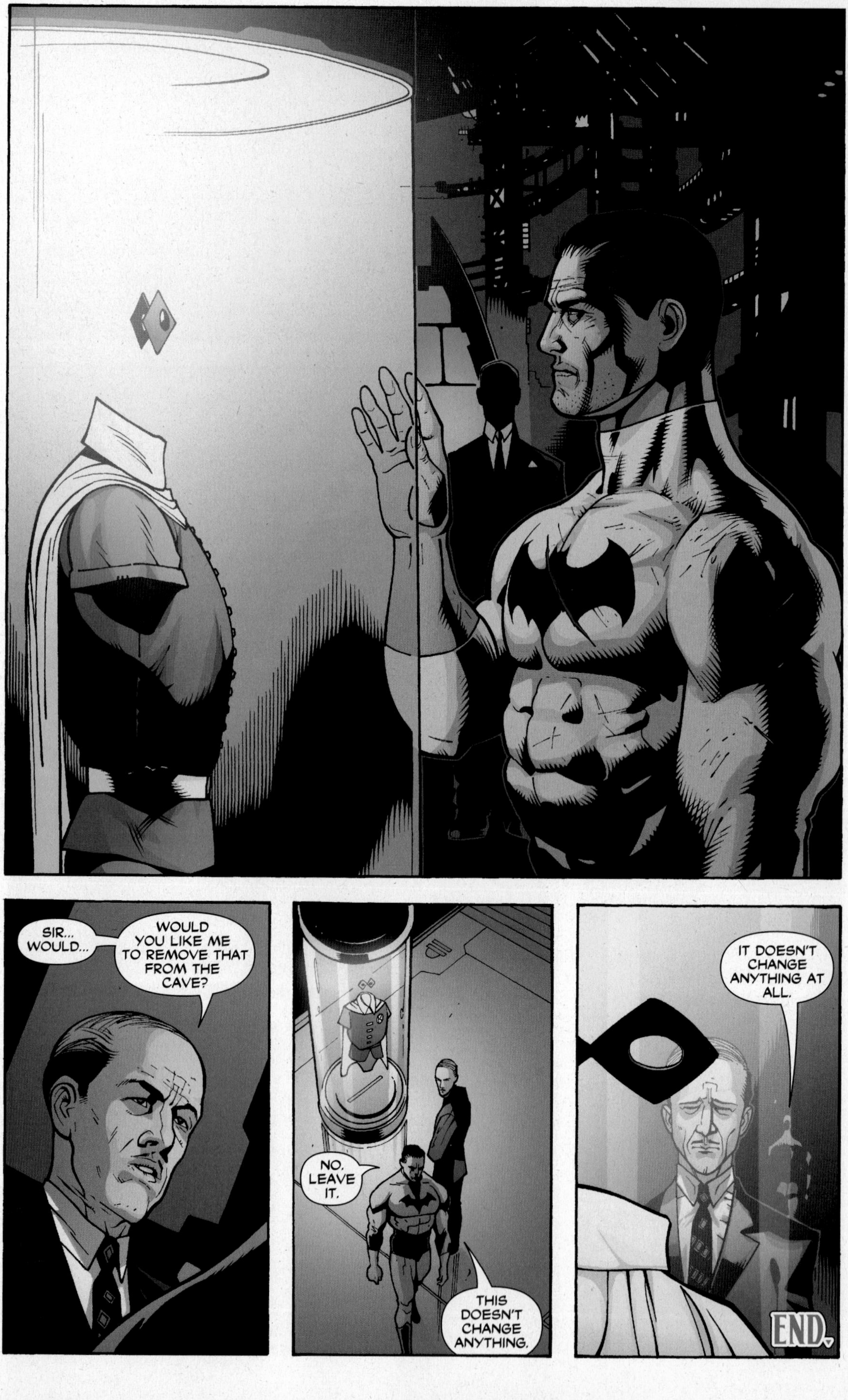
SIR... WOULD...
WOULD YOU LIKE ME TO REMOVE THAT FROM THE CAVE?
NO, LEAVE IT.
THIS DOESN'T CHANGE ANYTHING.
IT DOESN'T CHANGE ANYTHING AT ALL.
END.

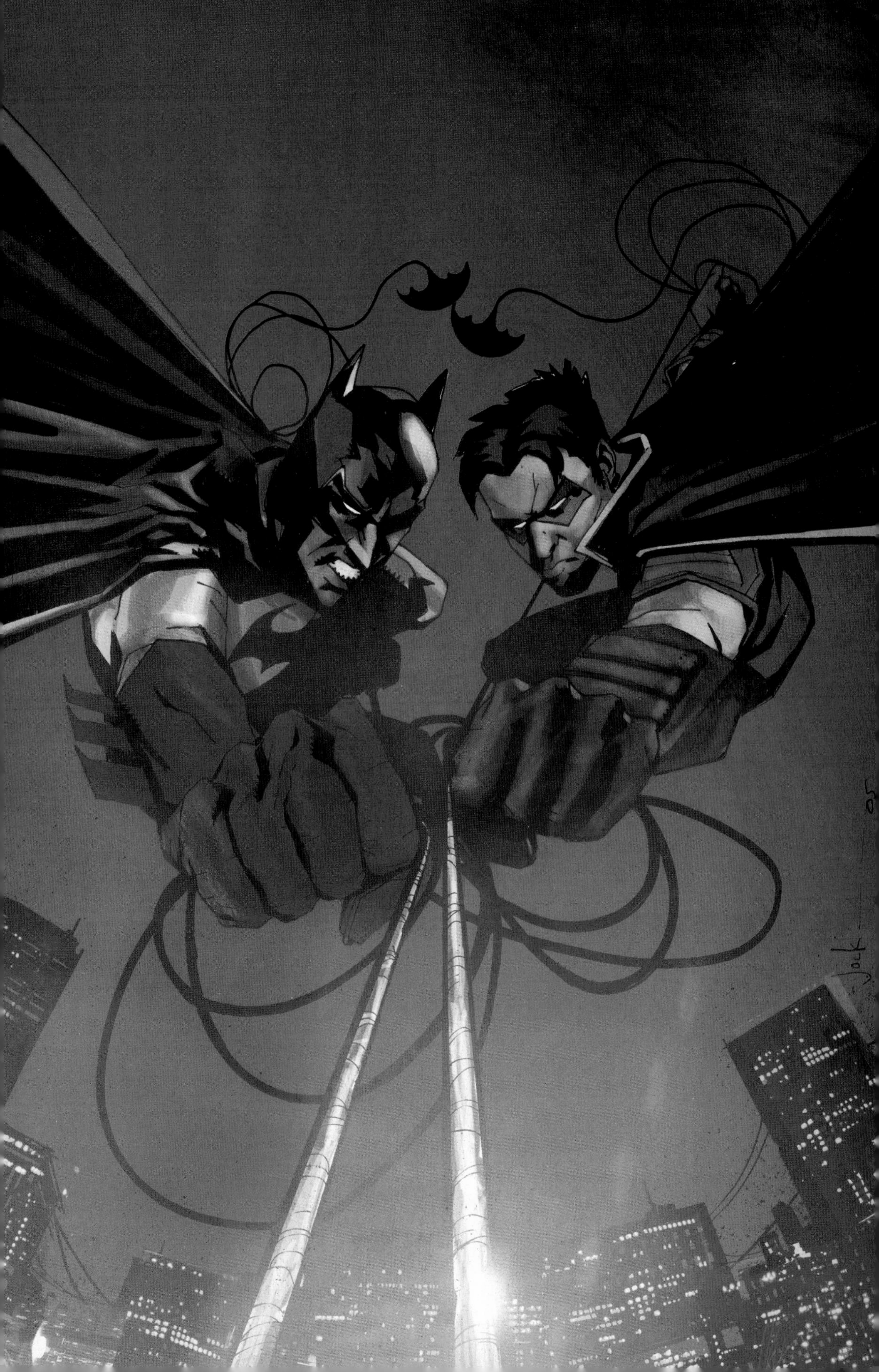
Jock
05

CHAPTER 8

SHOW ME YESTERDAY,
FOR I CAN'T FIND TODAY

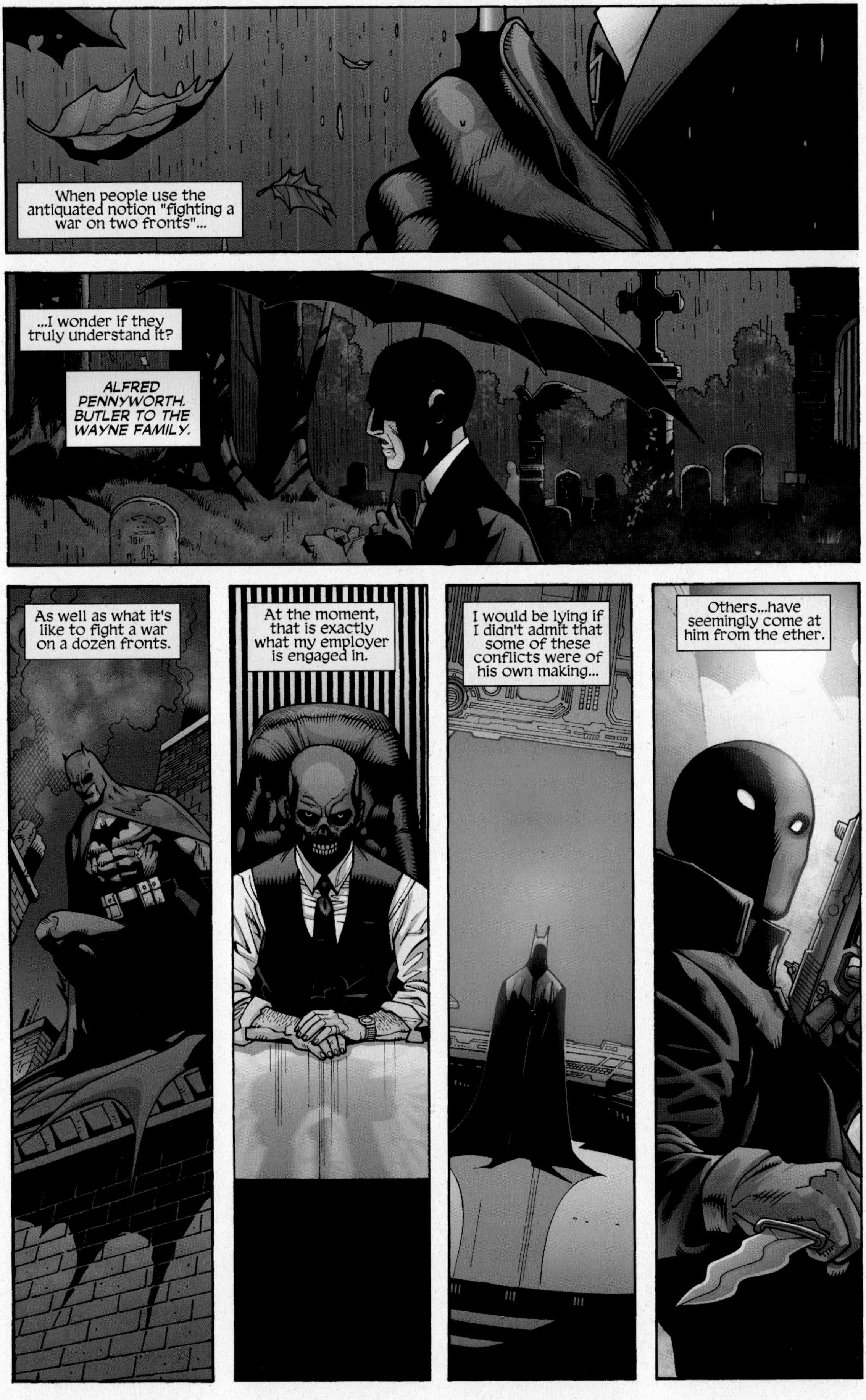
When people use the antiquated notion "fighting a war on two fronts"...
...I wonder if they truly understand it?
ALFRED PENNYWORTH. BUTLER TO THE WAYNE FAMILY.
As well as what it's like to fight a war on a dozen fronts.
At the moment, that is exactly what my employer is engaged in.
I would be lying if I didn't admit that some of these conflicts were of his own making...
Others...have seemingly come at him from the ether.

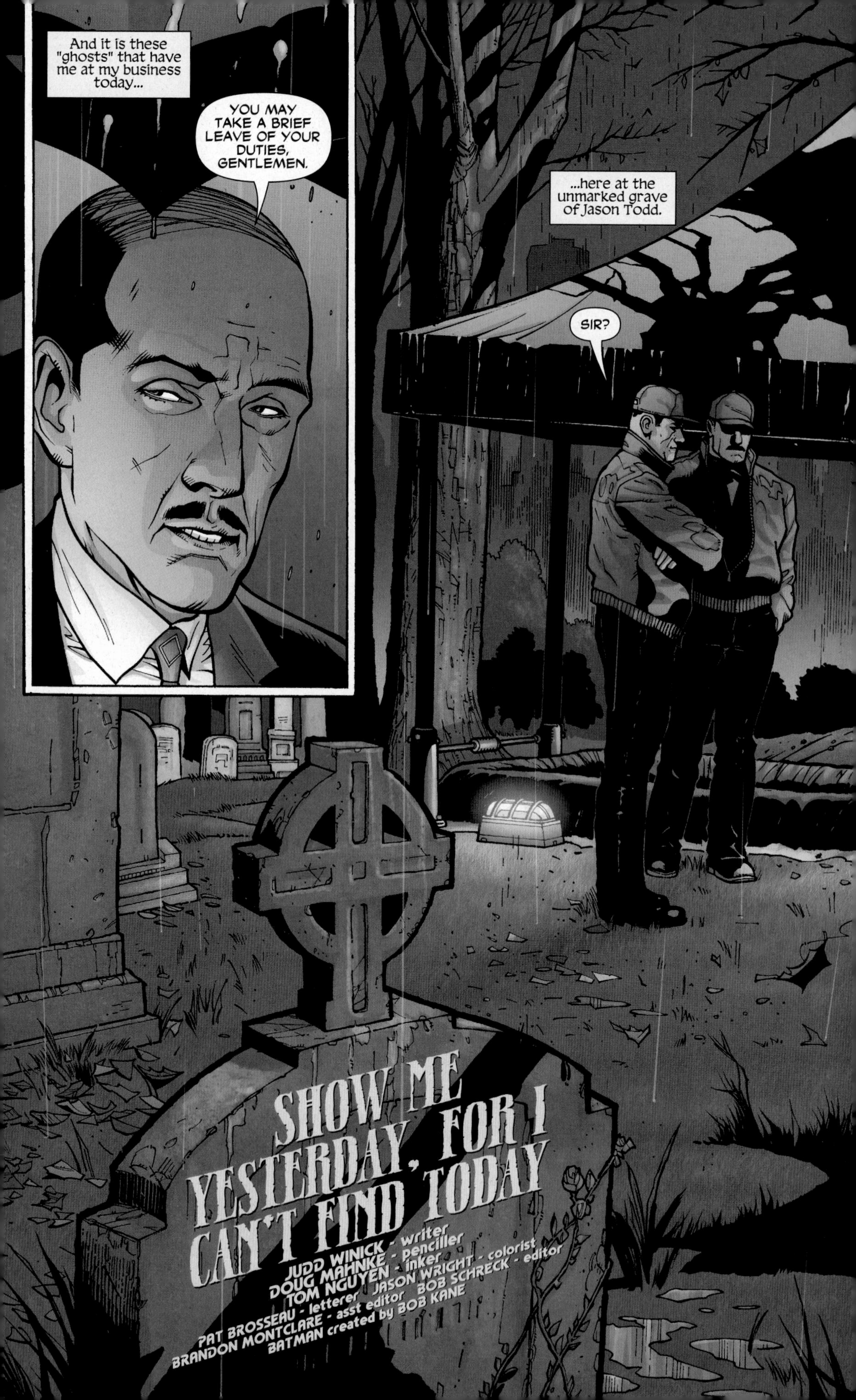
And it is these "ghosts" that have me at my business today...
YOU MAY TAKE A BRIEF LEAVE OF YOUR DUTIES, GENTLEMEN.
...here at the unmarked grave of Jason Todd.
SIR?
SHOW ME YESTERDAY, FOR I CAN'T FIND TODAY
JUDD WINICK - writer
DOUG MAHNKE - penciller
TOM NGUYEN - inker
PAT BROSSEAU - letterer JASON WRIGHT - colorist
BRANDON MONTCLARE - asst editor BOB SCHRECK - editor
BATMAN created by BOB KANE

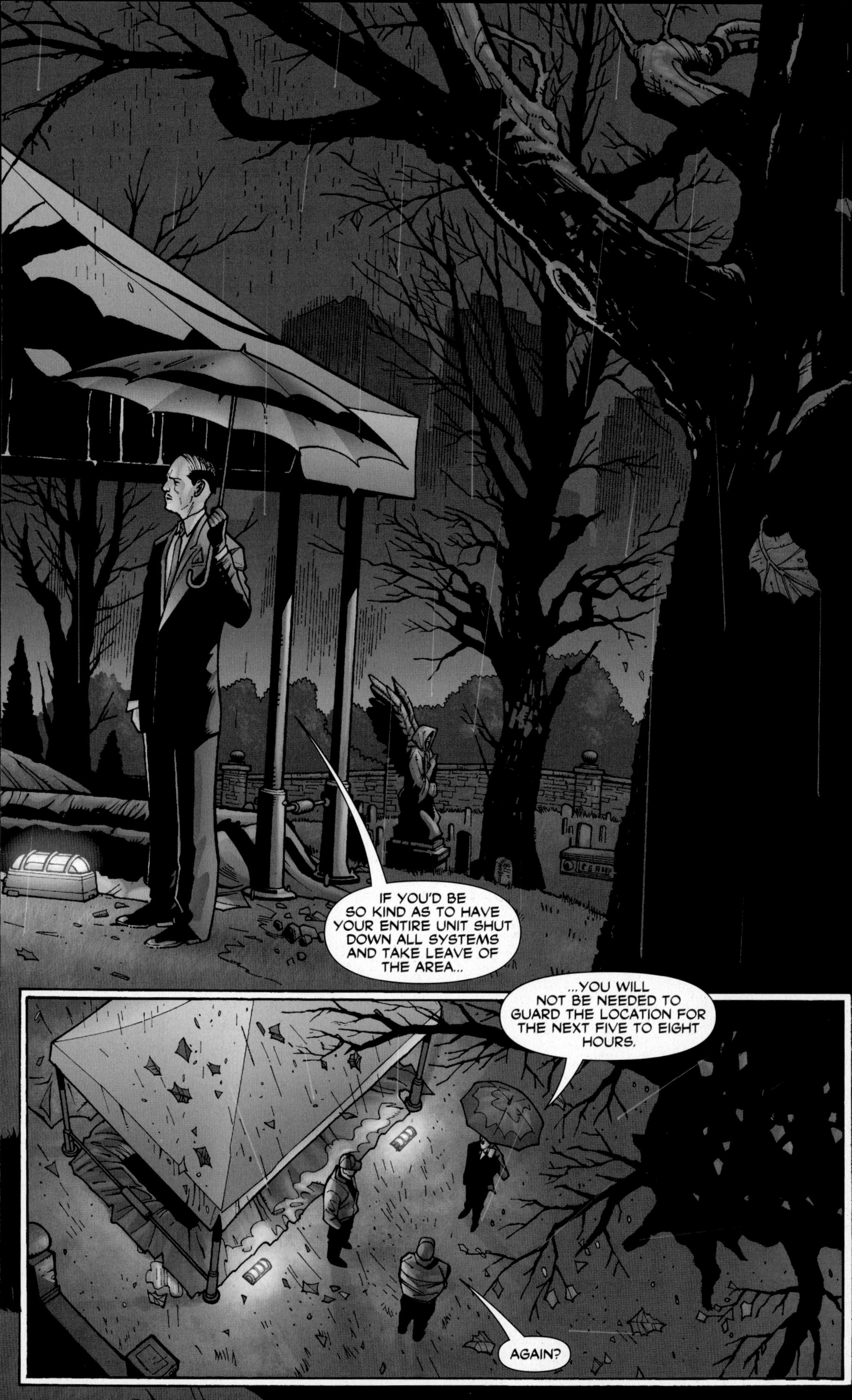
IF YOU'D BE SO KIND AS TO HAVE YOUR ENTIRE UNIT SHUT DOWN ALL SYSTEMS AND TAKE LEAVE OF THE AREA...
...YOU WILL NOT BE NEEDED TO GUARD THE LOCATION FOR THE NEXT FIVE TO EIGHT HOURS.
AGAIN?

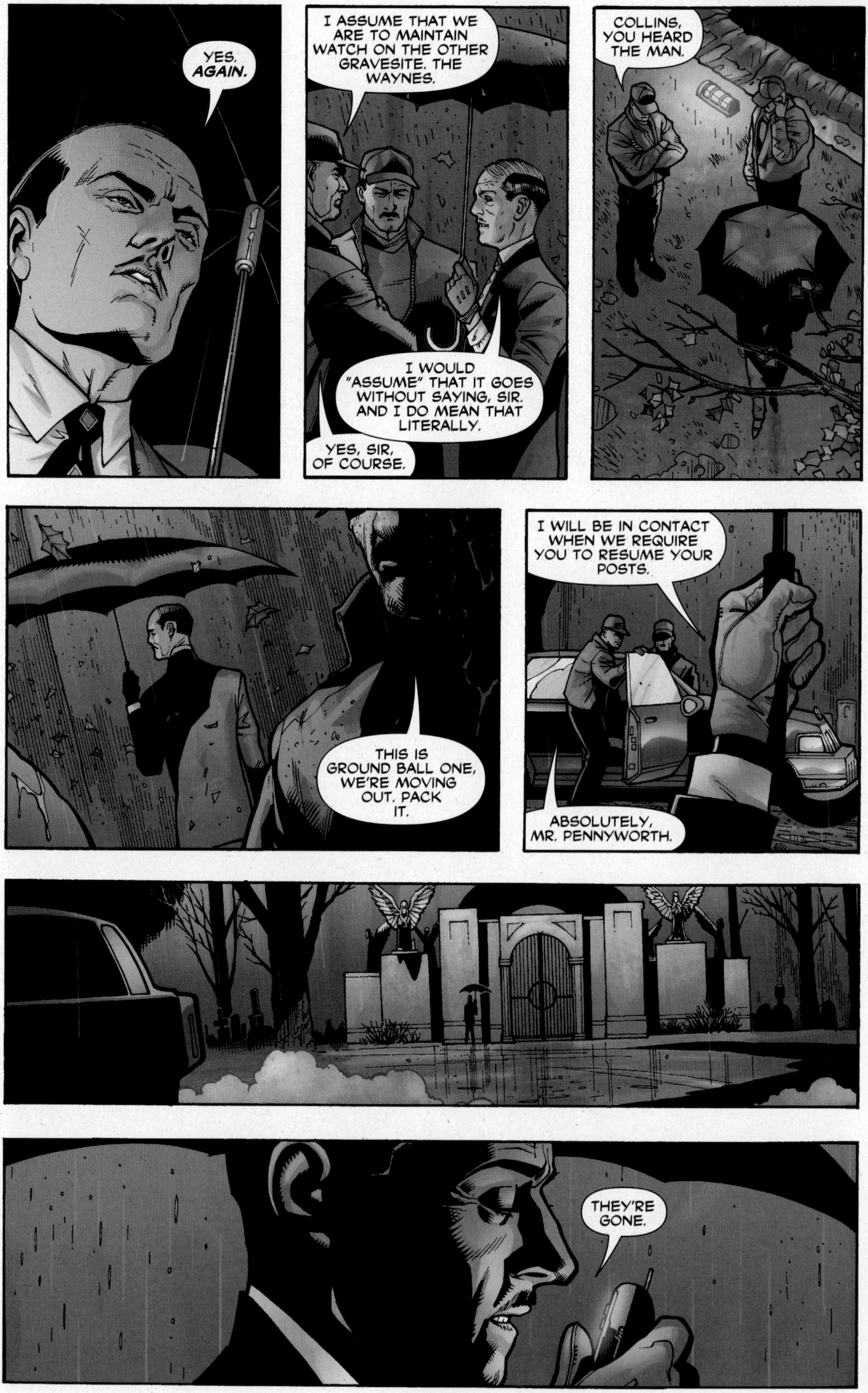
YES. AGAIN.
I ASSUME THAT WE ARE TO MAINTAIN WATCH ON THE OTHER GRAVESITE. THE WAYNES.
I WOULD "ASSUME" THAT IT GOES WITHOUT SAYING, SIR. AND I DO MEAN THAT LITERALLY.
YES, SIR, OF COURSE.
COLLINS, YOU HEARD THE MAN.
THIS IS GROUND BALL ONE, WE'RE MOVING OUT. PACK IT.
I WILL BE IN CONTACT WHEN WE REQUIRE YOU TO RESUME YOUR POSTS.
ABSOLUTELY, MR. PENNYWORTH.
THEY'RE GONE.

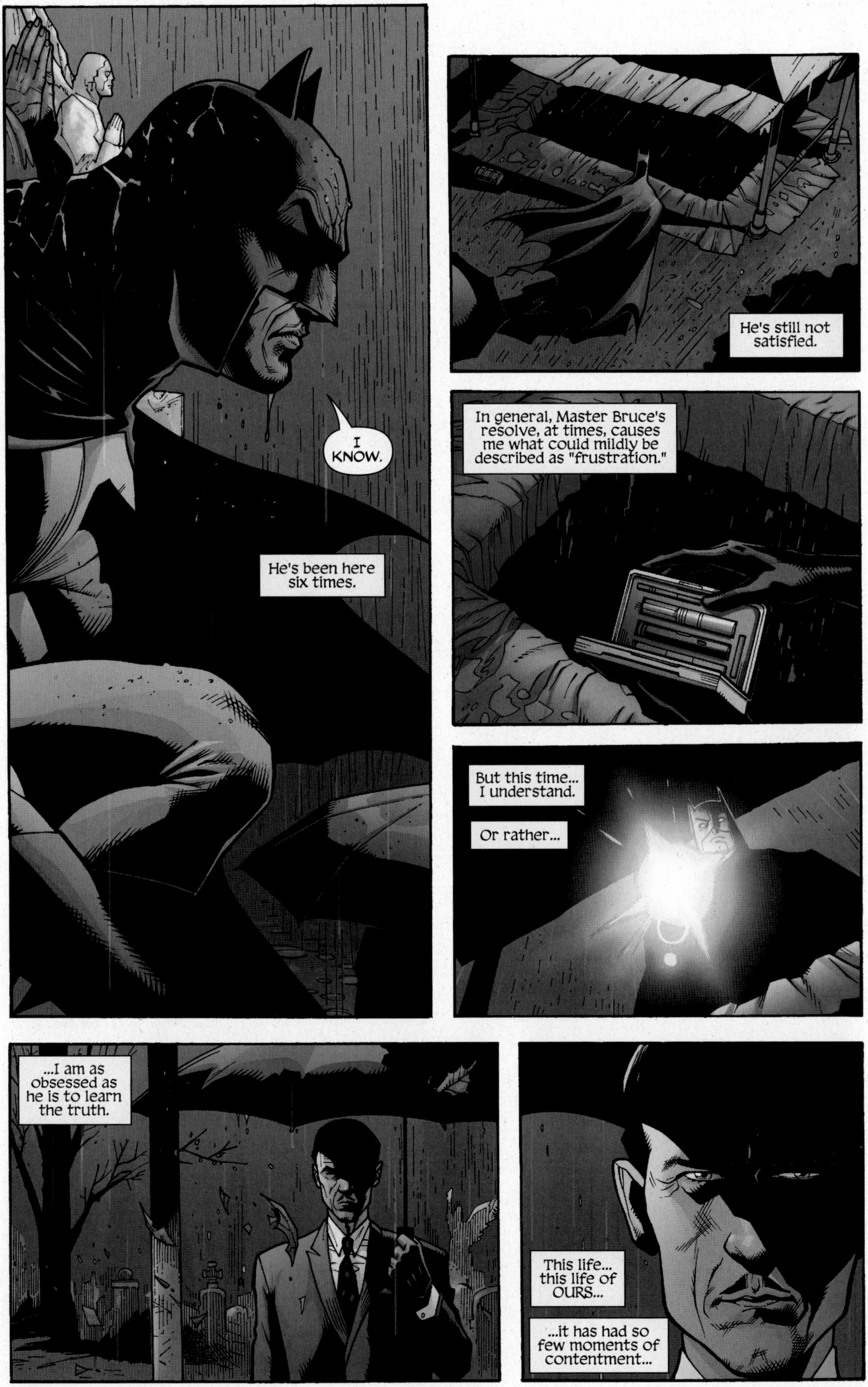
I KNOW.
He's been here six times.
He's still not satisfied.
In general, Master Bruce's resolve, at times, causes me what could mildly be described as "frustration."
But this time... I understand.
Or rather...
...I am as obsessed as he is to learn the truth.
This life... this life of OURS...
...it has had so few moments of contentment...

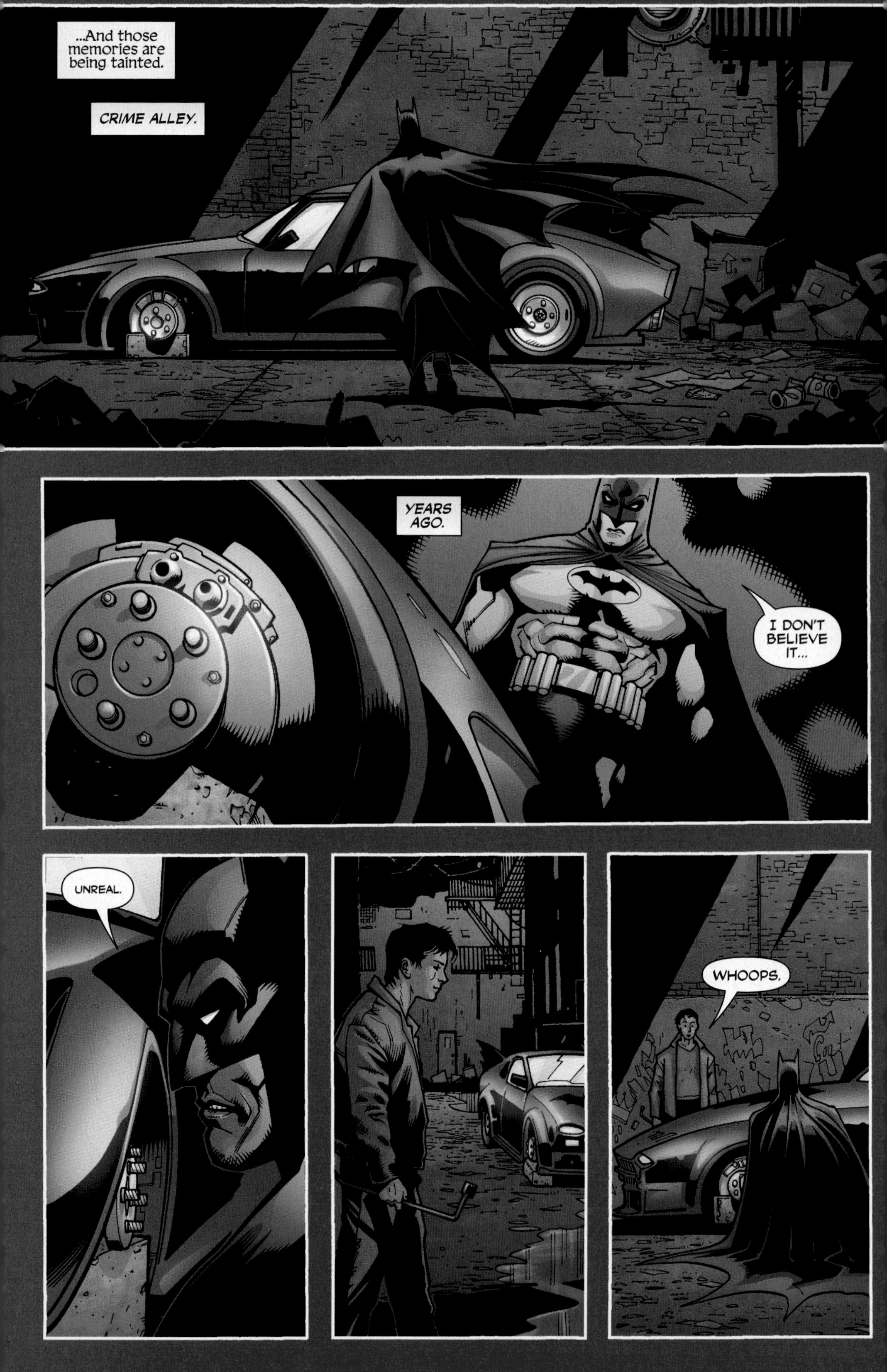
...And those memories are being tainted.
CRIME ALLEY.
YEARS AGO.
I DON'T BELIEVE IT...
UNREAL.
WHOOPS.

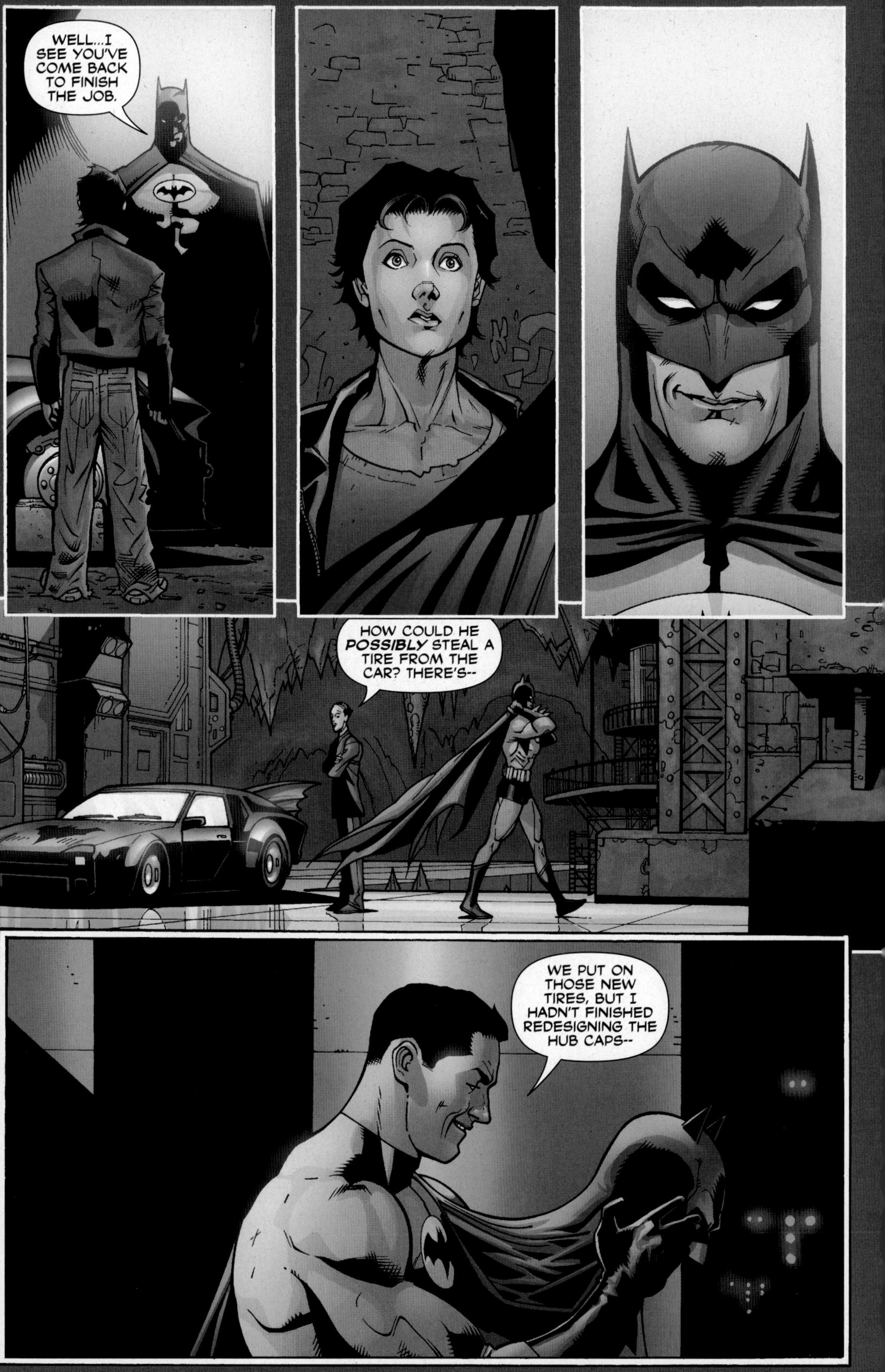
WELL...I SEE YOU'VE COME BACK TO FINISH THE JOB.
HOW COULD HE *POSSIBLY* STEAL A TIRE FROM THE CAR? THERE'S--
WE PUT ON THOSE NEW TIRES, BUT I HADN'T FINISHED REDESIGNING THE HUB CAPS--

--LEAVING THE LUG NUTS EXPOSED. OH, AND THE CAR'S SENSORS WERE STILL DOWN FROM THE ELECTRICAL SURGE YOU HAD LAST NIGHT...NO ALARMS.

THEREBY CREATING THE PERFECT OPPORTUNITY--

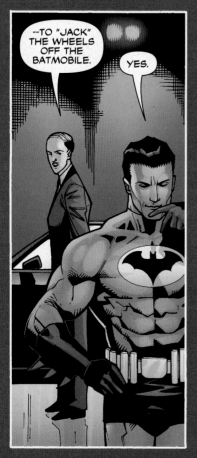

--TO "JACK" THE WHEELS OFF THE BATMOBILE.

YES.

IT SEEMS YOU TWO WERE FATED TO MEET.

YES...

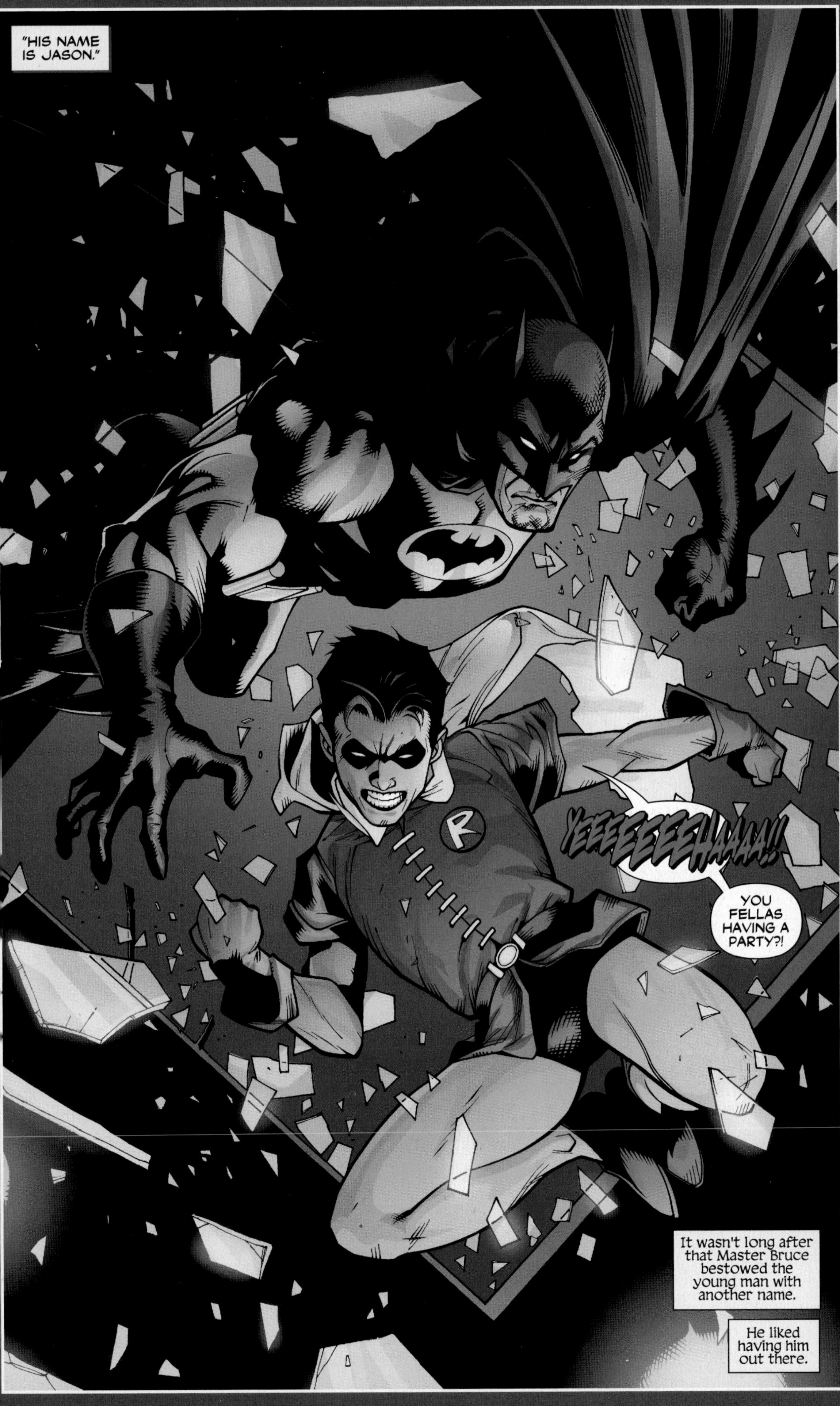
"HIS NAME IS JASON."
YEEEEEEEEHAAAA!!
YOU FELLAS HAVING A PARTY?!
It wasn't long after that Master Bruce bestowed the young man with another name.
He liked having him out there.

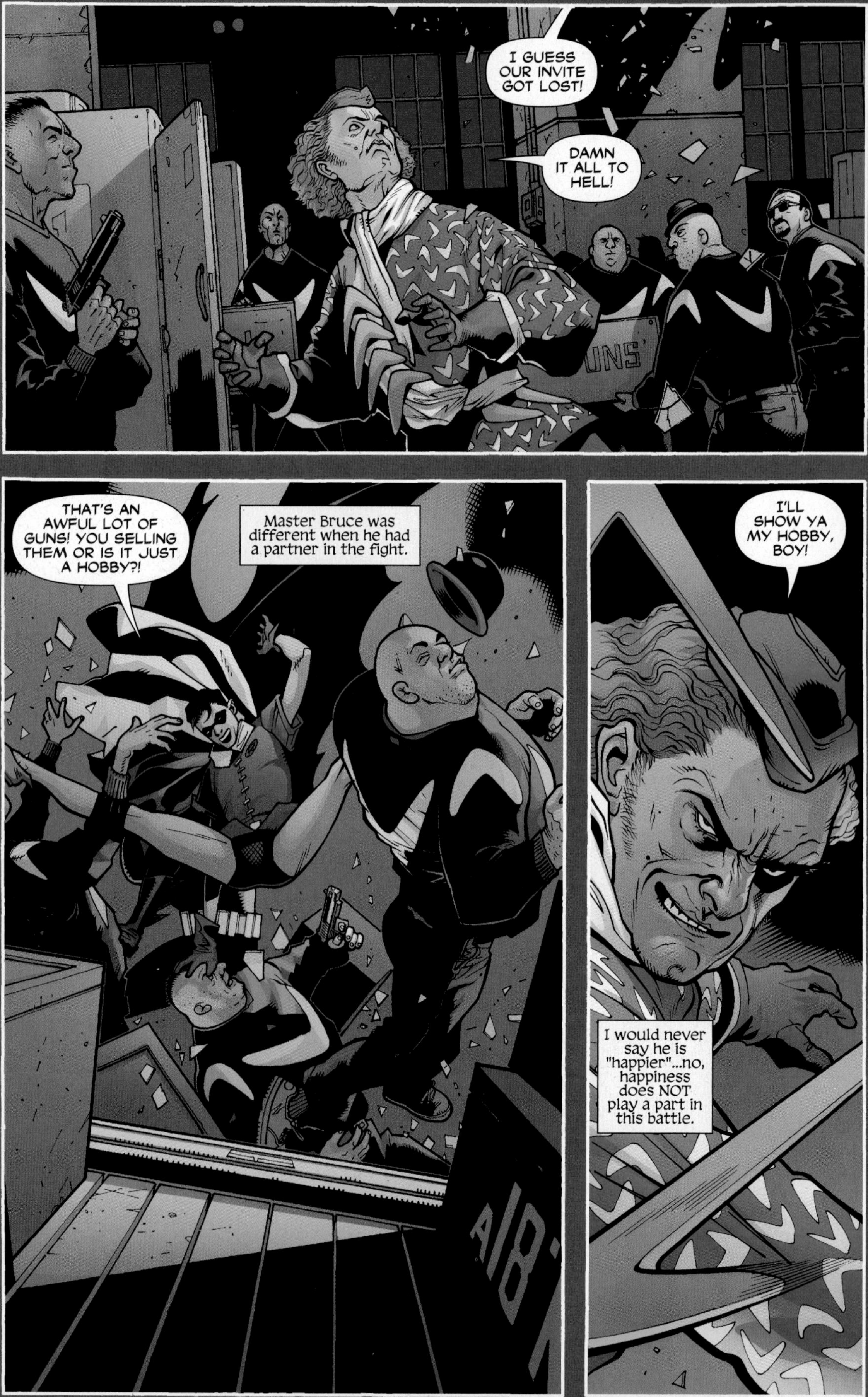
I GUESS OUR INVITE GOT LOST!
DAMN IT ALL TO HELL!
UNS
THAT'S AN AWFUL LOT OF GUNS! YOU SELLING THEM OR IS IT JUST A HOBBY?!
Master Bruce was different when he had a partner in the fight.
A18
I'LL SHOW YA MY HOBBY, BOY!
I would never say he is "happier"...no, happiness does NOT play a part in this battle.

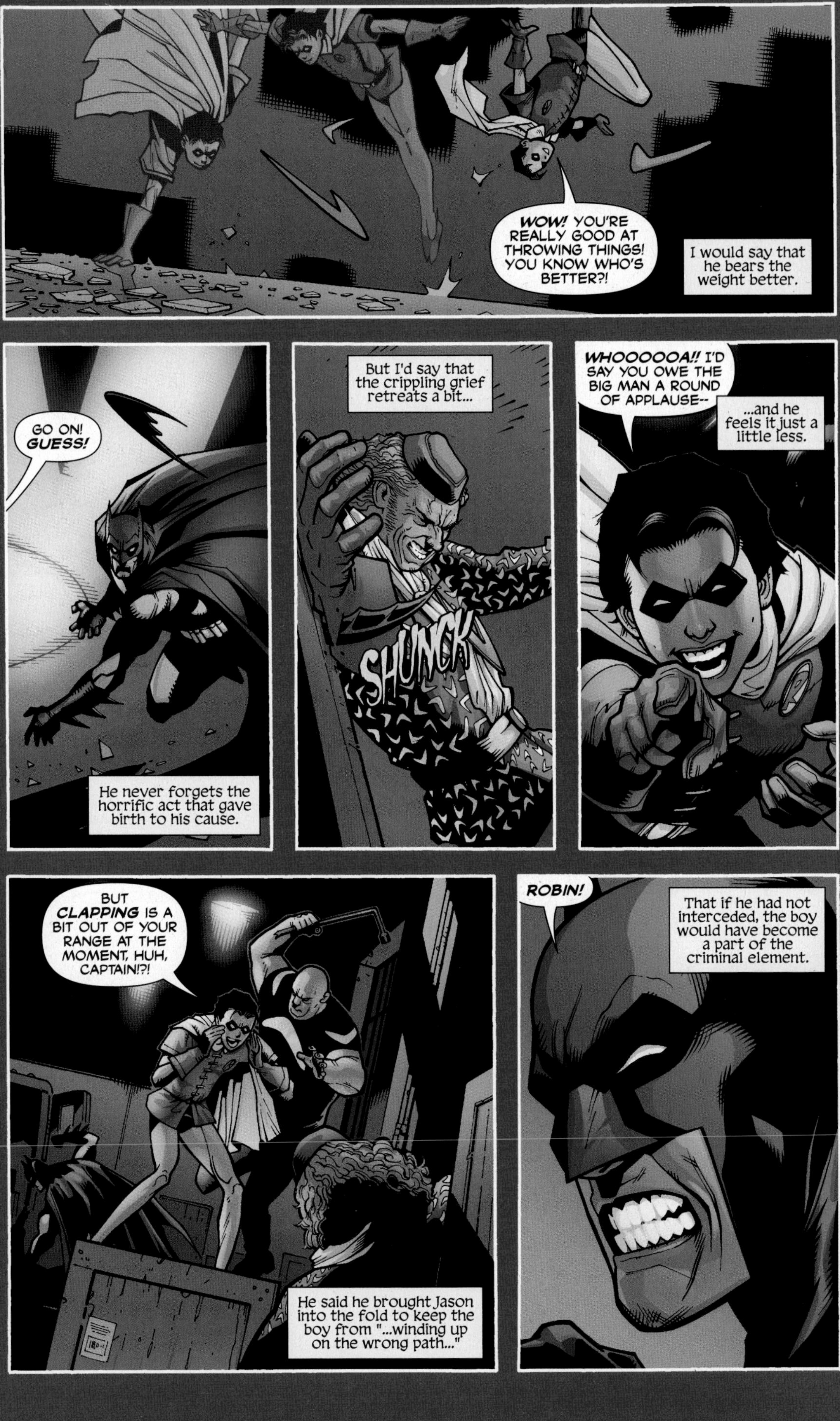
WOW! YOU'RE REALLY GOOD AT THROWING THINGS! YOU KNOW WHO'S BETTER?!
I would say that he bears the weight better.
GO ON! GUESS!
He never forgets the horrific act that gave birth to his cause.
But I'd say that the crippling grief retreats a bit...
SHUNCK
WHOOOOOA!! I'D SAY YOU OWE THE BIG MAN A ROUND OF APPLAUSE--
...and he feels it just a little less.
BUT CLAPPING IS A BIT OUT OF YOUR RANGE AT THE MOMENT, HUH, CAPTAIN!?!
He said he brought Jason into the fold to keep the boy from "...winding up on the wrong path..."
ROBIN!
That if he had not interceded, the boy would have become a part of the criminal element.

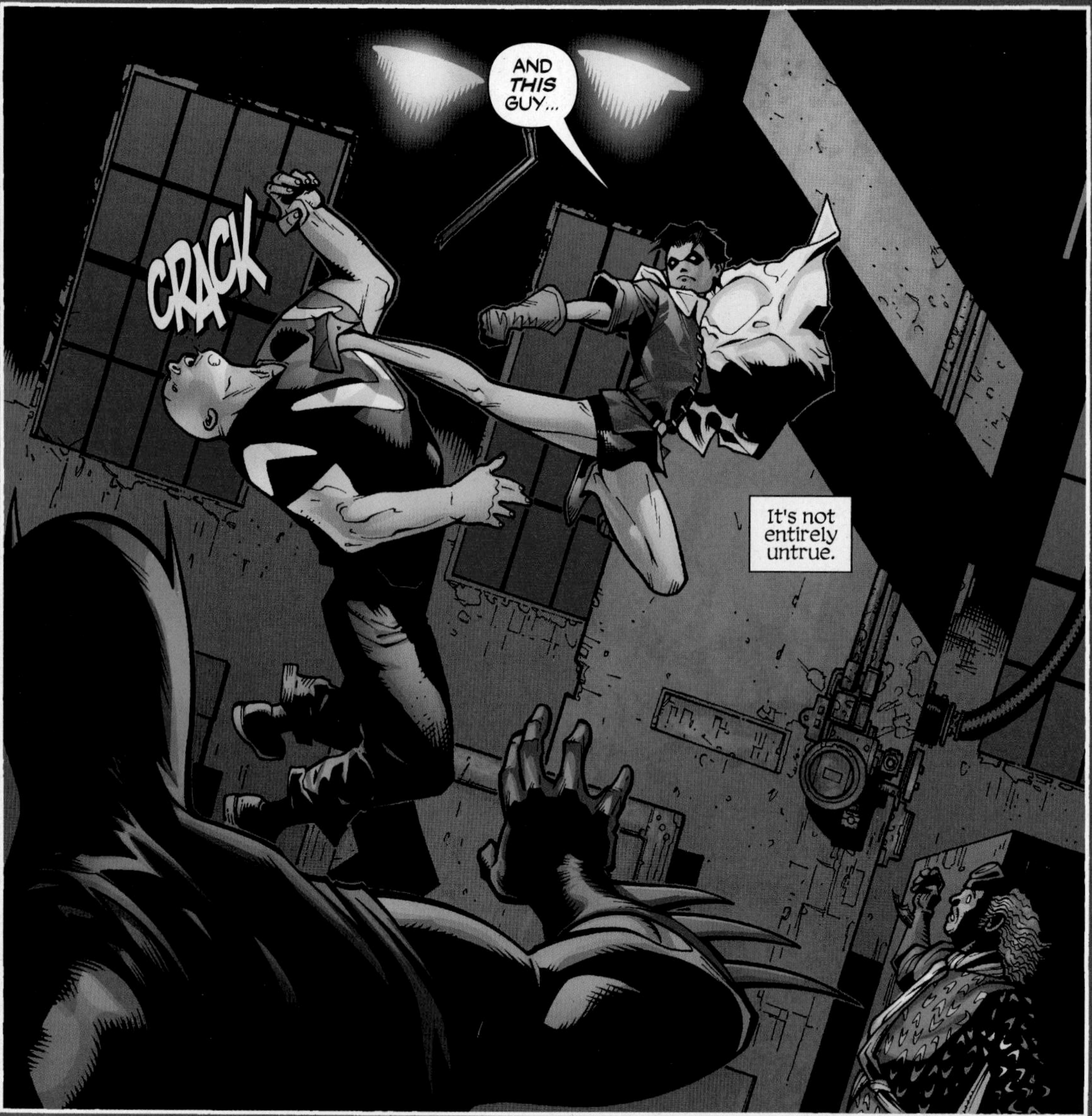
AND THIS GUY...
CRACK
It's not entirely untrue.

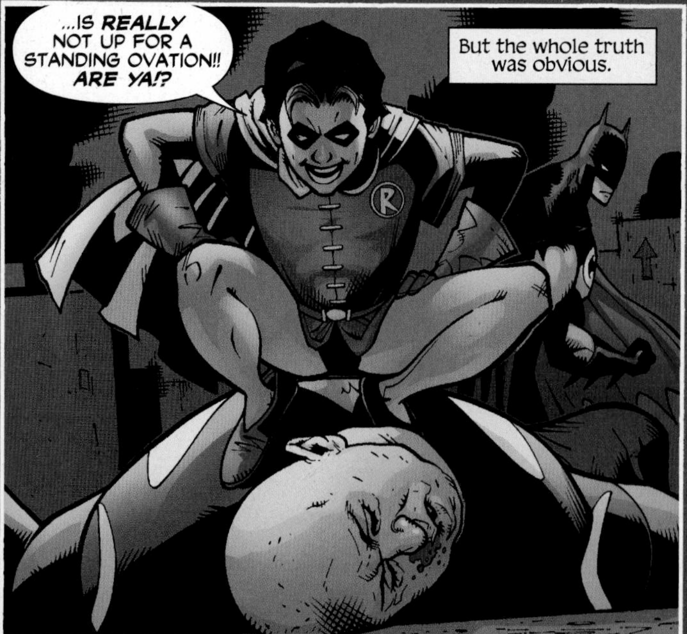
...IS REALLY NOT UP FOR A STANDING OVATION!! ARE YA!?
But the whole truth was obvious.

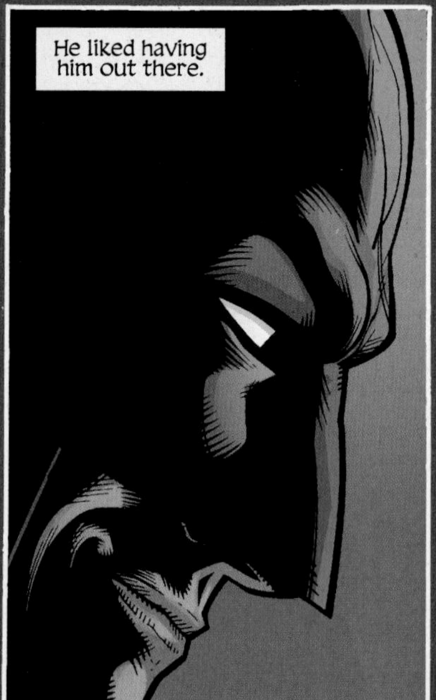
He liked having him out there.

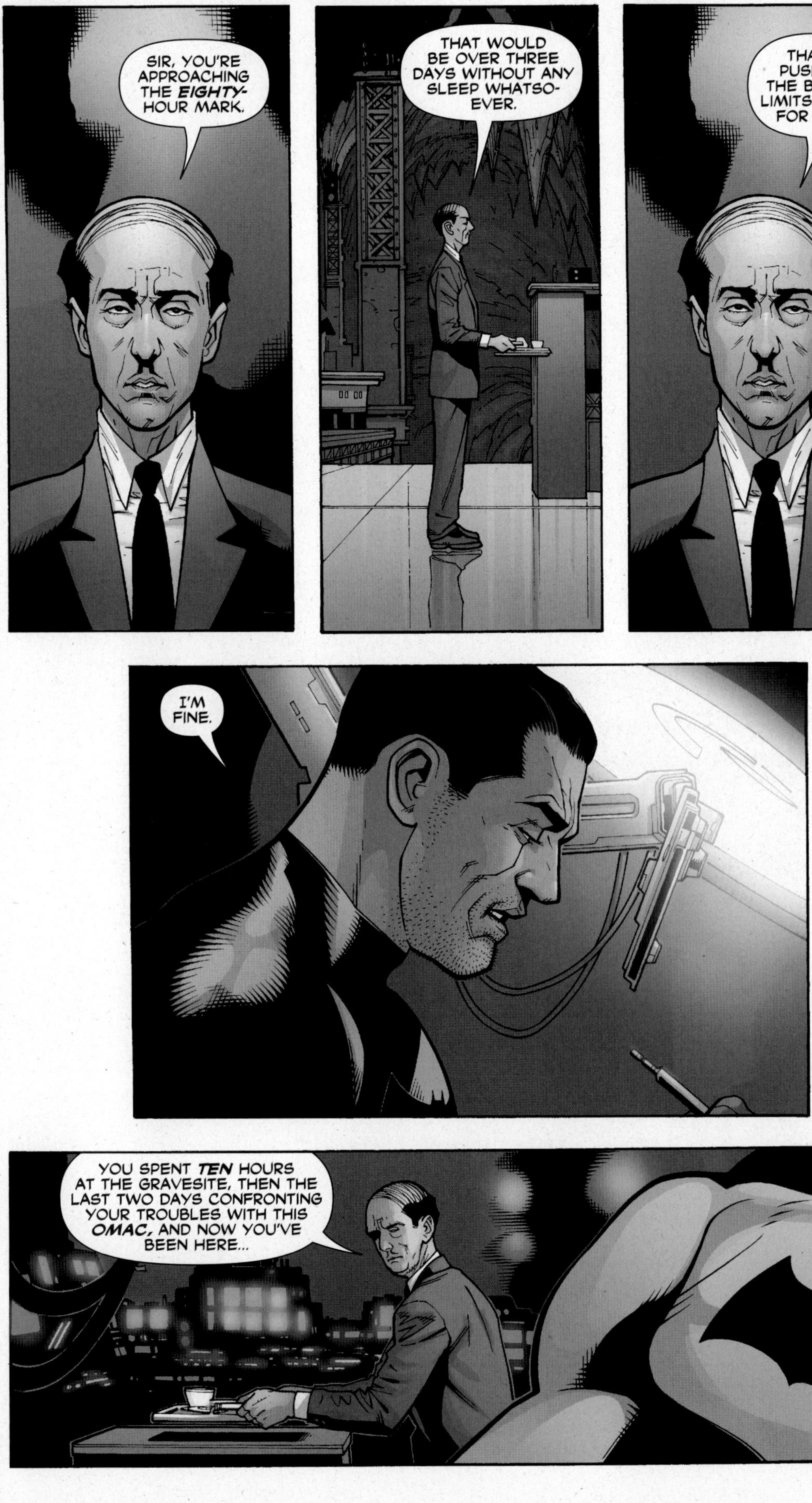
SIR, YOU'RE APPROACHING THE EIGHTY-HOUR MARK.
THAT WOULD BE OVER THREE DAYS WITHOUT ANY SLEEP WHATSO-EVER.
THAT'S PUSHING THE BODY'S LIMITS...EVEN FOR YOU.
I'M FINE.
YOU SPENT TEN HOURS AT THE GRAVESITE, THEN THE LAST TWO DAYS CONFRONTING YOUR TROUBLES WITH THIS OMAC, AND NOW YOU'VE BEEN HERE...

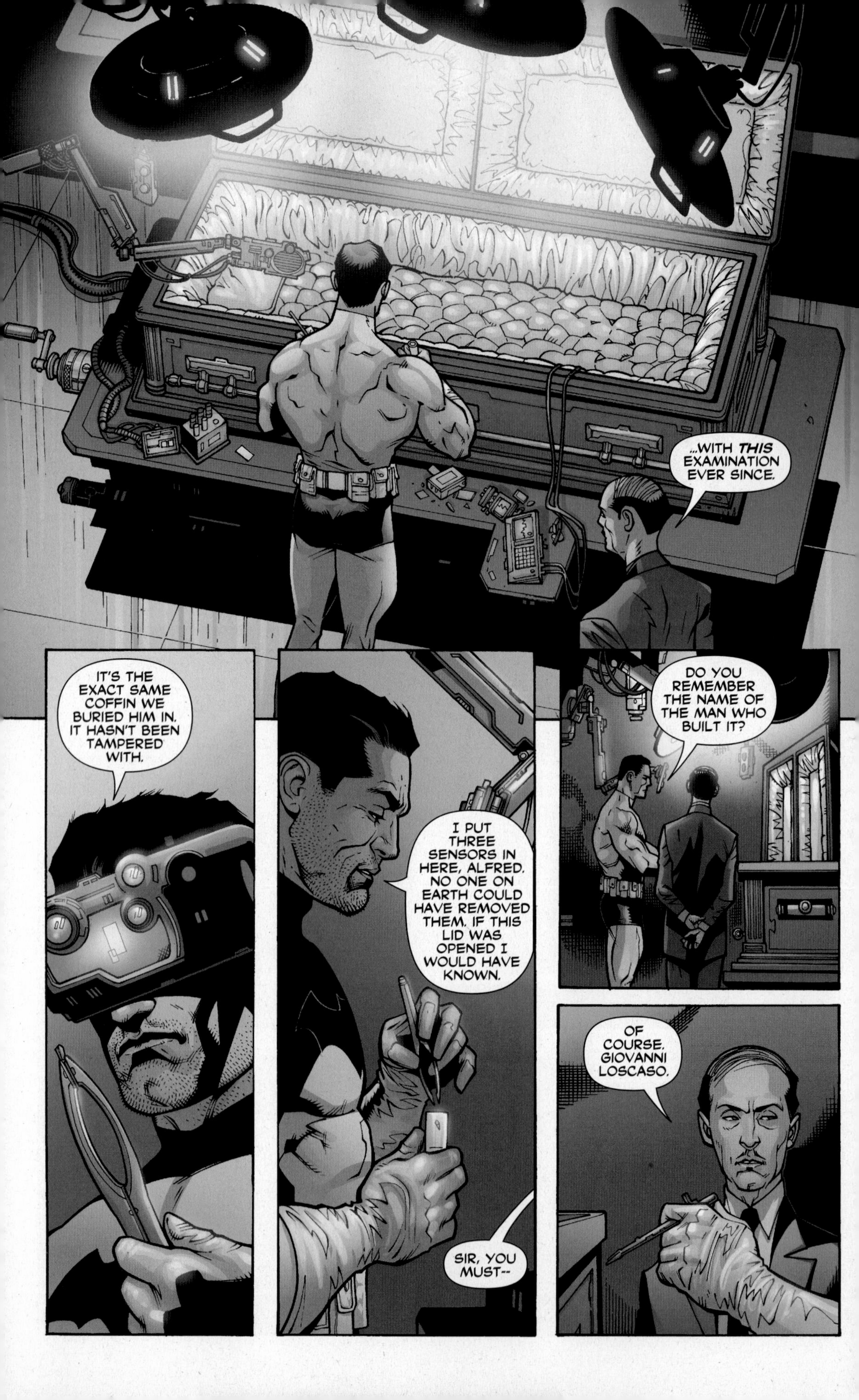
...WITH THIS EXAMINATION EVER SINCE.
IT'S THE EXACT SAME COFFIN WE BURIED HIM IN. IT HASN'T BEEN TAMPERED WITH.
I PUT THREE SENSORS IN HERE, ALFRED. NO ONE ON EARTH COULD HAVE REMOVED THEM. IF THIS LID WAS OPENED I WOULD HAVE KNOWN.
SIR, YOU MUST--
DO YOU REMEMBER THE NAME OF THE MAN WHO BUILT IT?
OF COURSE. GIOVANNI LOSCASO.

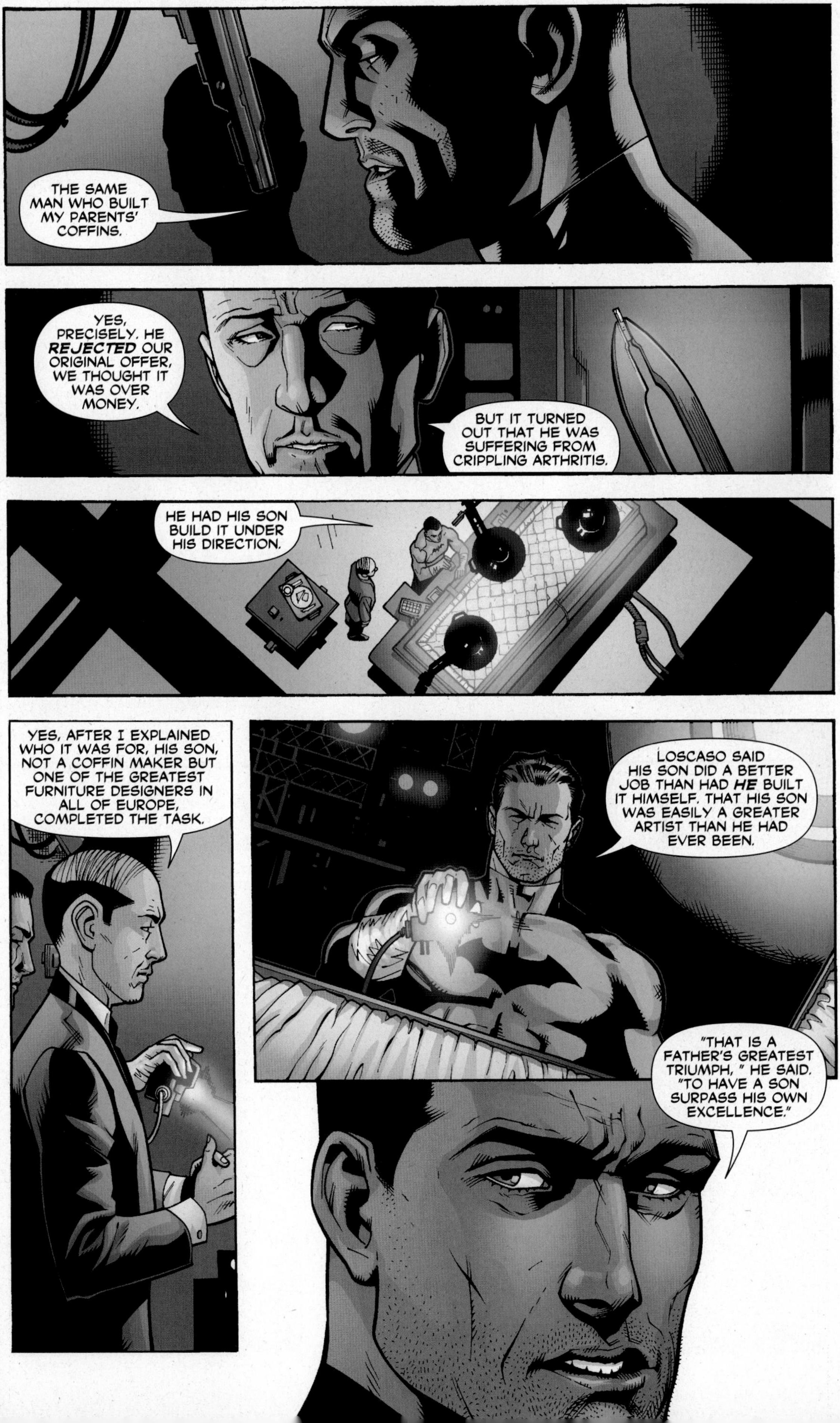
THE SAME MAN WHO BUILT MY PARENTS' COFFINS.
YES, PRECISELY. HE REJECTED OUR ORIGINAL OFFER, WE THOUGHT IT WAS OVER MONEY.
BUT IT TURNED OUT THAT HE WAS SUFFERING FROM CRIPPLING ARTHRITIS.
HE HAD HIS SON BUILD IT UNDER HIS DIRECTION.
YES, AFTER I EXPLAINED WHO IT WAS FOR, HIS SON, NOT A COFFIN MAKER BUT ONE OF THE GREATEST FURNITURE DESIGNERS IN ALL OF EUROPE, COMPLETED THE TASK.
LOSCASO SAID HIS SON DID A BETTER JOB THAN HAD HE BUILT IT HIMSELF. THAT HIS SON WAS EASILY A GREATER ARTIST THAN HE HAD EVER BEEN.
"THAT IS A FATHER'S GREATEST TRIUMPH," HE SAID. "TO HAVE A SON SURPASS HIS OWN EXCELLENCE."

SIR...THAT ISN'T...THIS BUSINESS WITH... IF THIS EVEN *IS* JASON...

HE ISN'T...HE HASN'T...

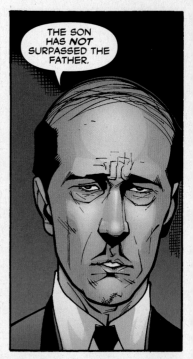

THE SON HAS *NOT* SURPASSED THE FATHER.

I'M STARTING OVER. I *MUST* HAVE MISSED SOMETHING.

YES, SIR. VERY GOOD, SIR.

BUMM

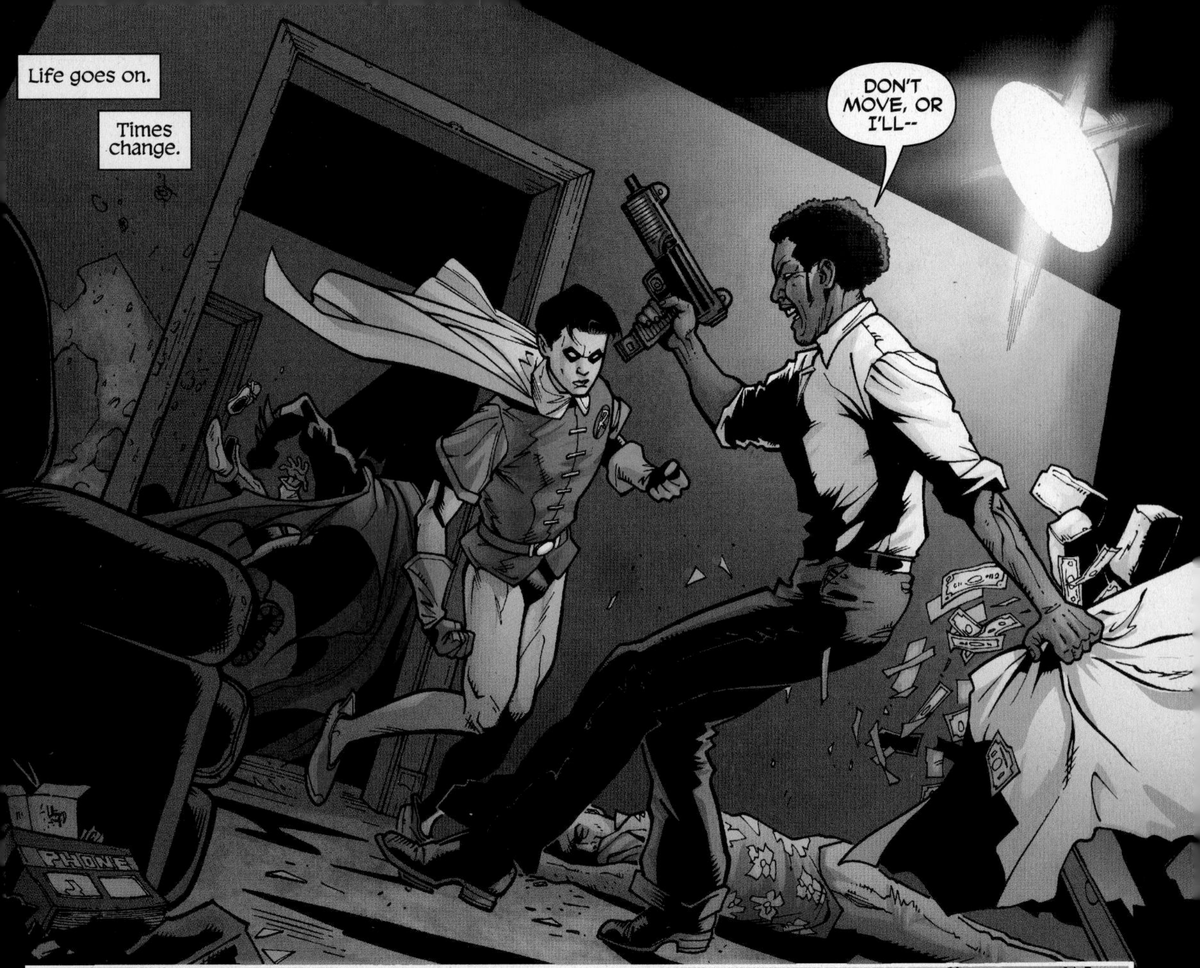
Life goes on.
Times change.
DON'T MOVE, OR I'LL--
PHONE

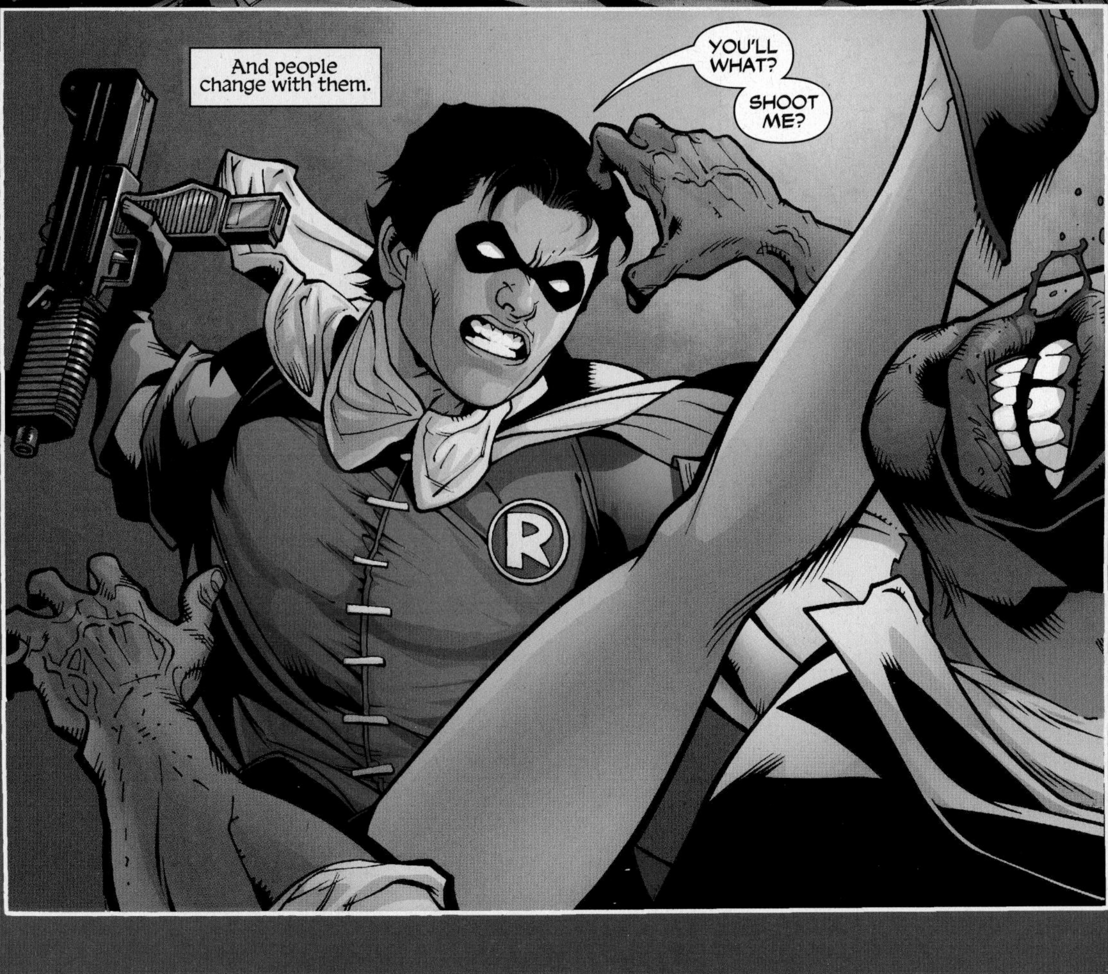
And people change with them.
YOU'LL WHAT?
SHOOT ME?

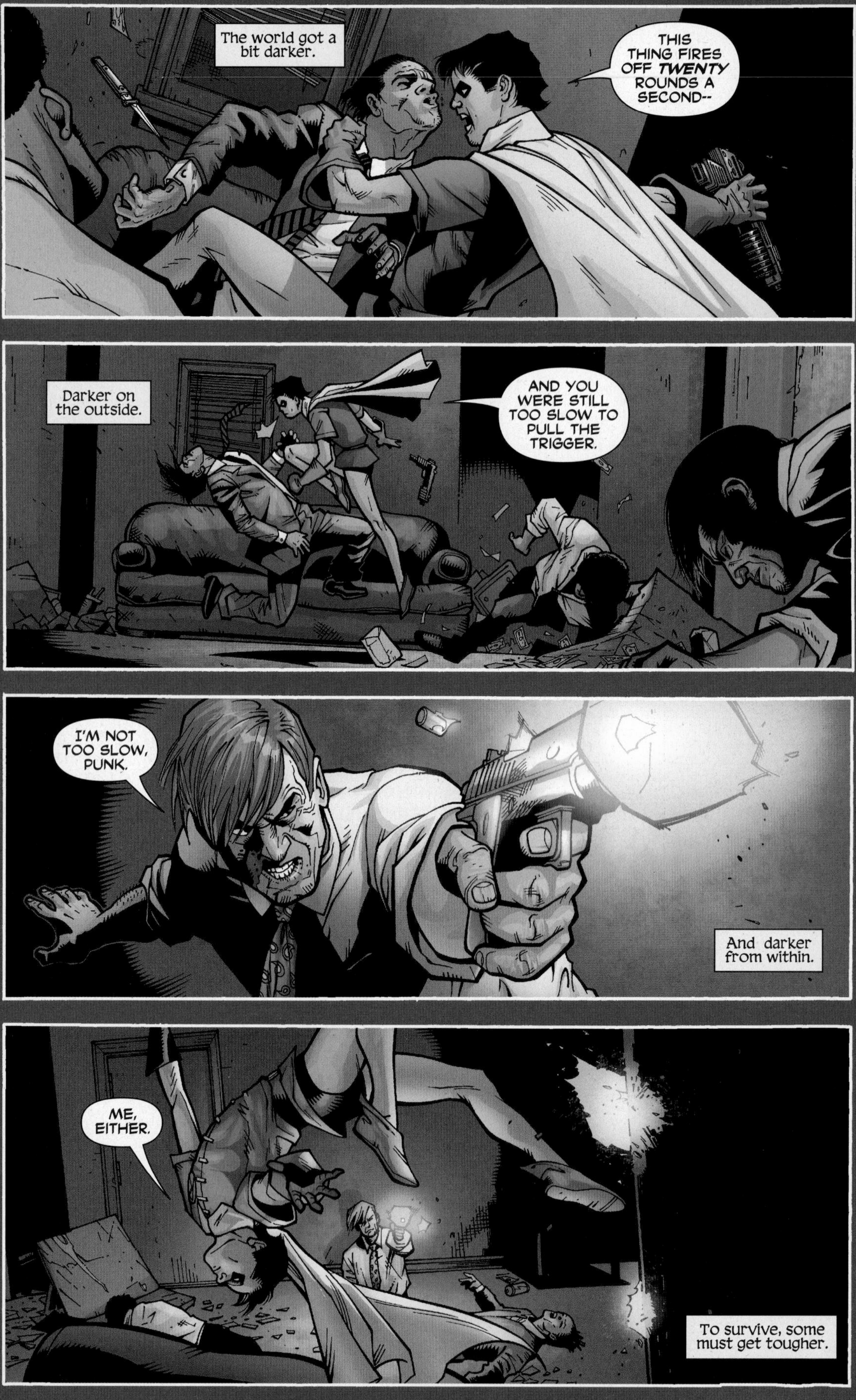
The world got a bit darker.
THIS THING FIRES OFF TWENTY ROUNDS A SECOND--
Darker on the outside.
AND YOU WERE STILL TOO SLOW TO PULL THE TRIGGER.
I'M NOT TOO SLOW, PUNK.
And darker from within.
ME, EITHER.
To survive, some must get tougher.

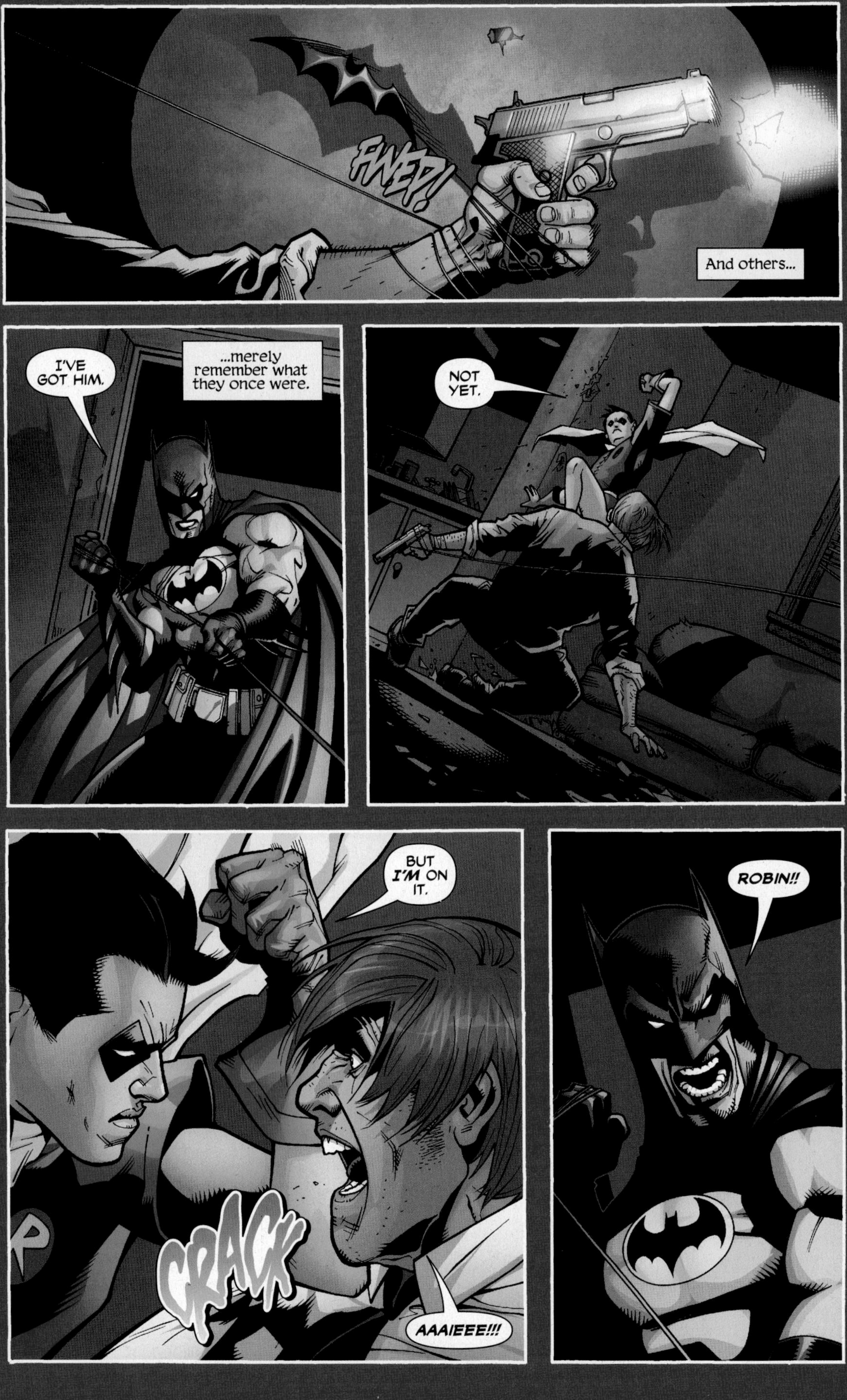
FWEP!
And others...
I'VE GOT HIM.
...merely remember what they once were.
NOT YET.
BUT I'M ON IT.
CRACK
AAAIEEE!!!
ROBIN!!

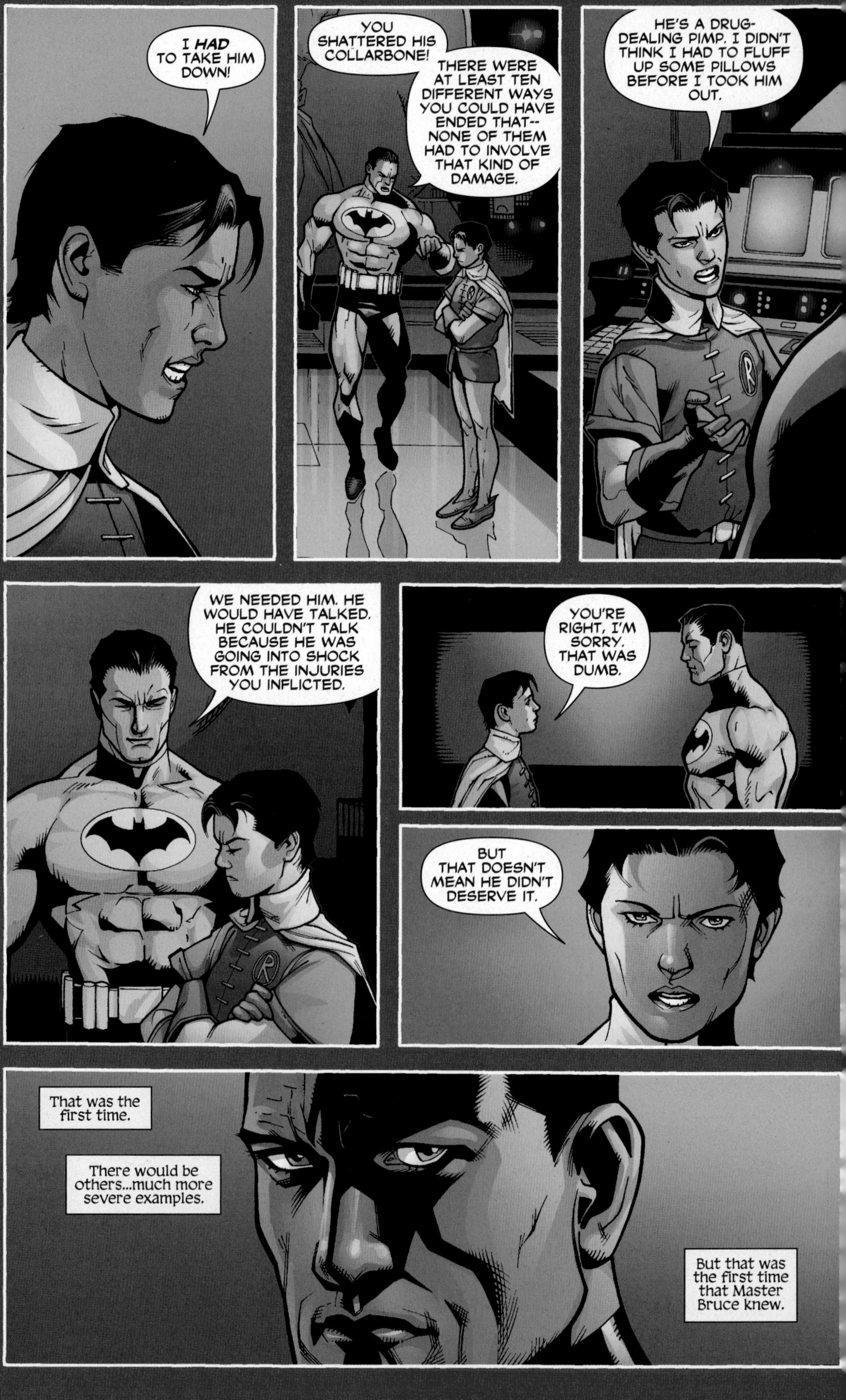
I *HAD* TO TAKE HIM DOWN!
YOU SHATTERED HIS COLLARBONE!
THERE WERE AT LEAST TEN DIFFERENT WAYS YOU COULD HAVE ENDED THAT-- NONE OF THEM HAD TO INVOLVE THAT KIND OF DAMAGE.
HE'S A DRUG-DEALING PIMP. I DIDN'T THINK I HAD TO FLUFF UP SOME PILLOWS BEFORE I TOOK HIM OUT.
WE NEEDED HIM. HE WOULD HAVE TALKED. HE COULDN'T TALK BECAUSE HE WAS GOING INTO SHOCK FROM THE INJURIES YOU INFLICTED.
YOU'RE RIGHT, I'M SORRY. THAT WAS DUMB.
BUT THAT DOESN'T MEAN HE DIDN'T DESERVE IT.
That was the first time.
There would be others...much more severe examples.
But that was the first time that Master Bruce knew.

He knew that Jason Todd was NOT Dick Grayson.

It wasn't about skill, or about endurance, or even their will to succeed.

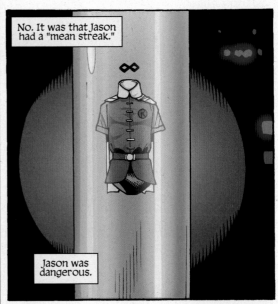

No. It was that Jason had a "mean streak."

Jason was dangerous.

And as a father... he was at a loss for what to do.

I'VE BEEN STUPID.

SIR?

BLIND, ARROGANT, CARELESS AND STUPID. I *KNOW* THIS IS THE SAME COFFIN...THIS IS THE VERY ONE WE BURIED HIM IN, BUT...

I'VE GONE OVER EVERY INCH OF IT, TRYING TO FIND ANY CLUE OF TAMPERING.

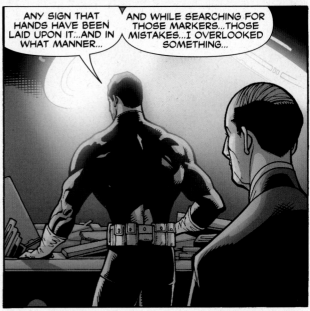

ANY SIGN THAT HANDS HAVE BEEN LAID UPON IT...AND IN WHAT MANNER...

AND WHILE SEARCHING FOR THOSE MARKERS...THOSE MISTAKES...I OVERLOOKED SOMETHING...

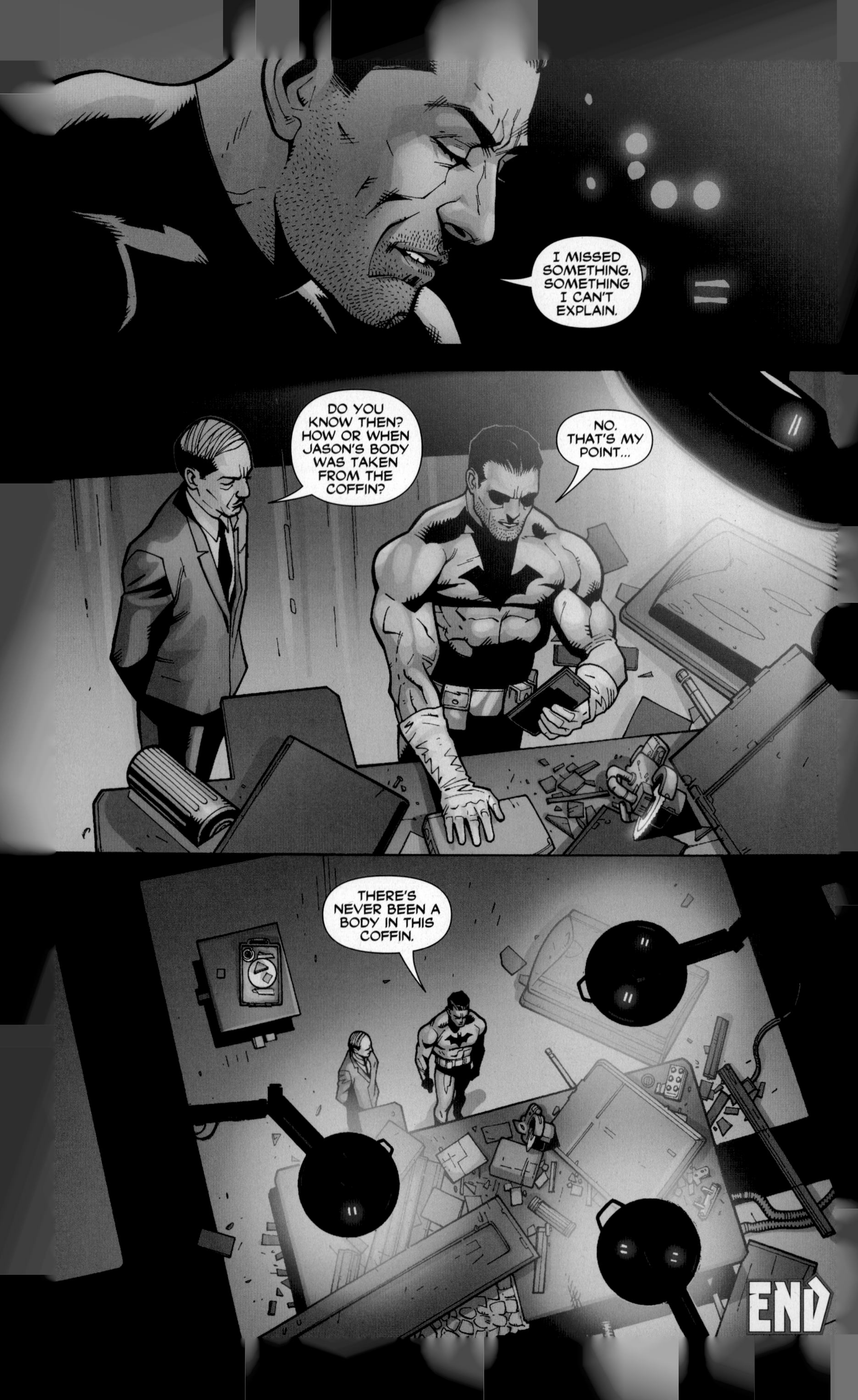
I MISSED SOMETHING. SOMETHING I CAN'T EXPLAIN.
DO YOU KNOW THEN? HOW OR WHEN JASON'S BODY WAS TAKEN FROM THE COFFIN?
NO. THAT'S MY POINT...
THERE'S NEVER BEEN A BODY IN THIS COFFIN.
END

BATMAN 646 Cover by Jock

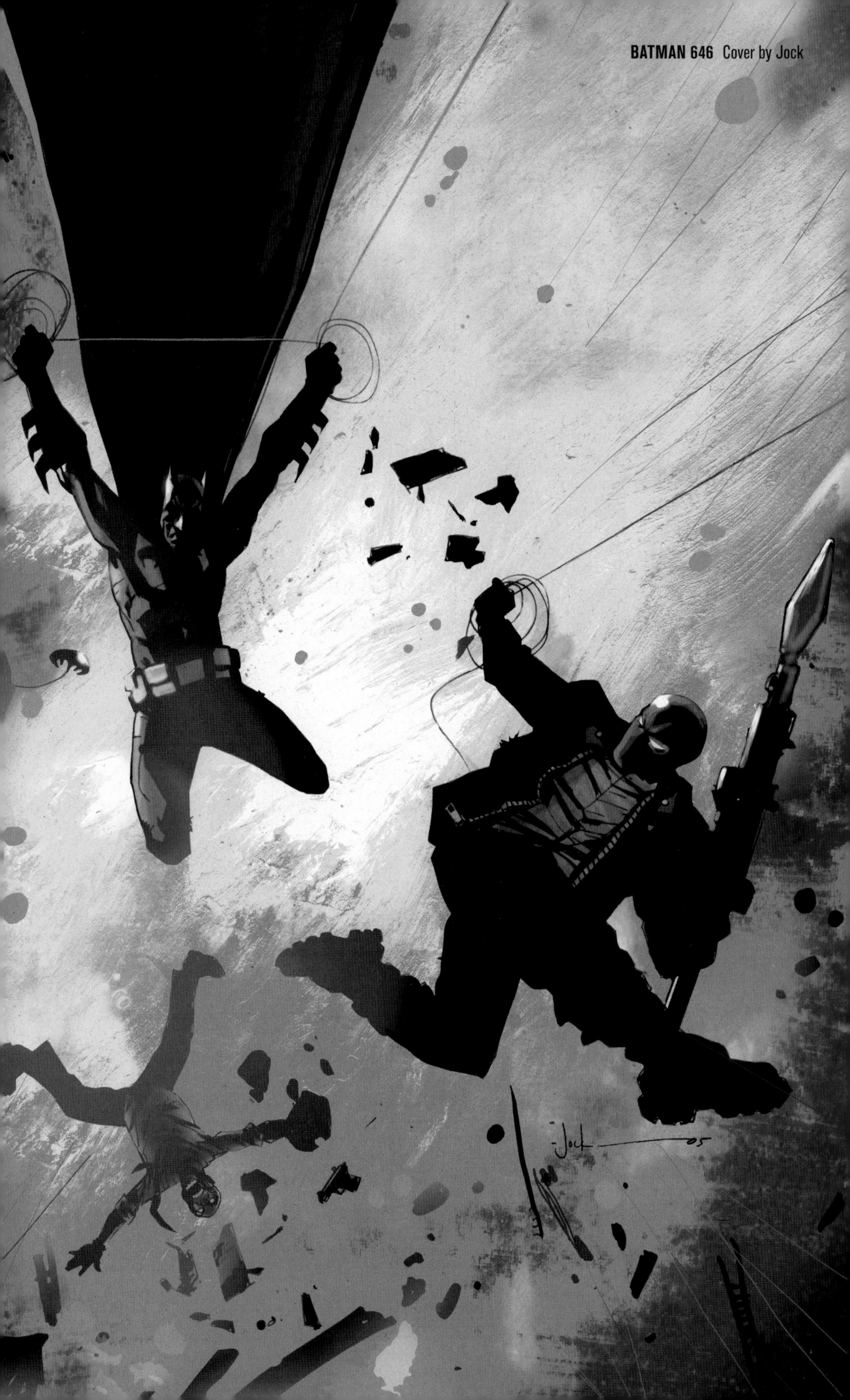
Jock 05

CHAPTER 9

FRANCHISE PART ONE:
SUPPLY SIDE
ECONOMICS

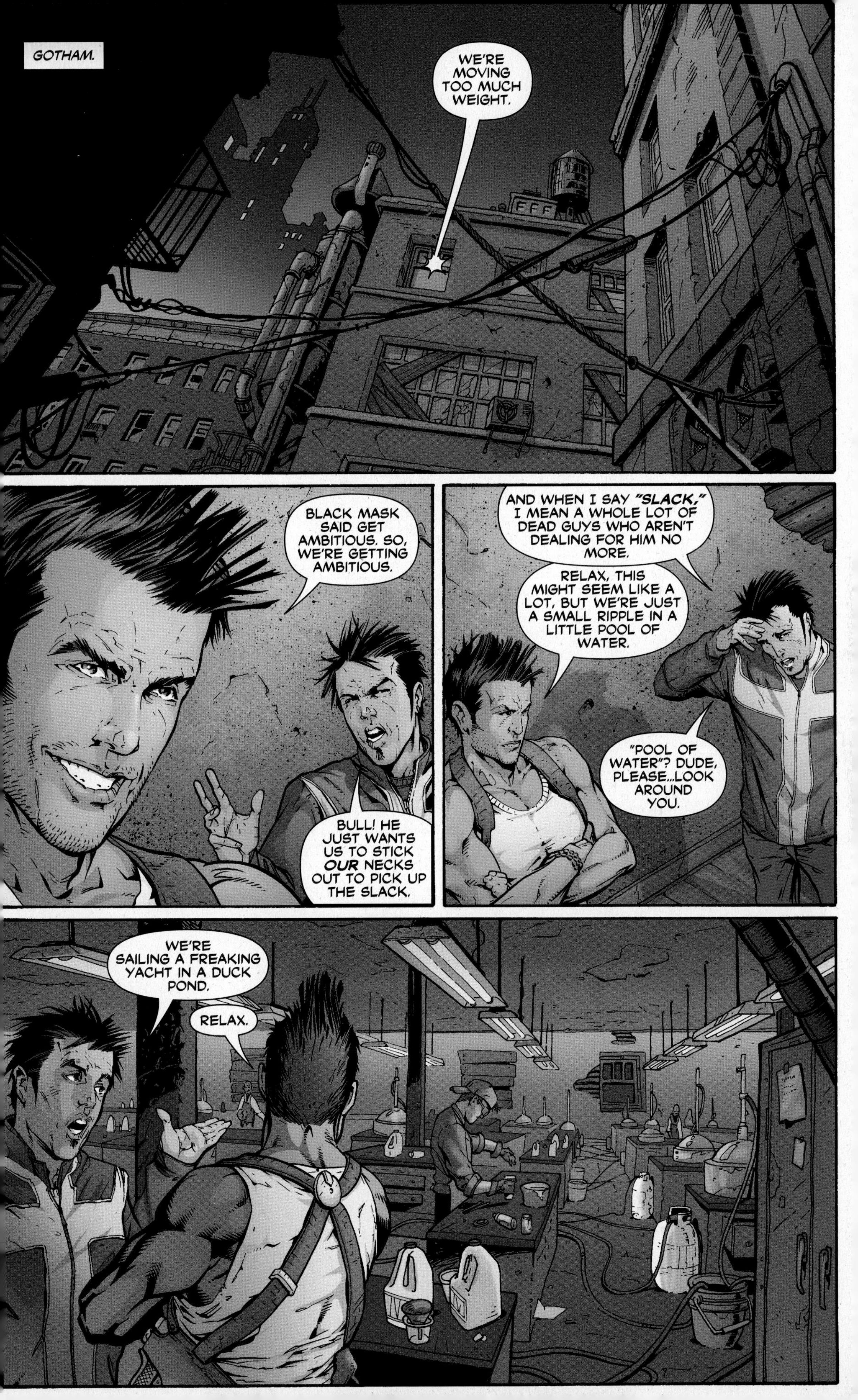
GOTHAM.
WE'RE MOVING TOO MUCH WEIGHT.
BLACK MASK SAID GET AMBITIOUS. SO, WE'RE GETTING AMBITIOUS.
BULL! HE JUST WANTS US TO STICK *OUR* NECKS OUT TO PICK UP THE SLACK.
AND WHEN I SAY *"SLACK,"* I MEAN A WHOLE LOT OF DEAD GUYS WHO AREN'T DEALING FOR HIM NO MORE.
RELAX, THIS MIGHT SEEM LIKE A LOT, BUT WE'RE JUST A SMALL RIPPLE IN A LITTLE POOL OF WATER.
"POOL OF WATER"? DUDE, PLEASE...LOOK AROUND YOU.
WE'RE SAILING A FREAKING YACHT IN A DUCK POND.
RELAX.

"RELAX?!" ARE YOU OFF YOUR NUT, MAN?!

YOU GOT A PROBLEM MAKING BANK?

NO, I'VE *GOT* A PROBLEM WITH RUNNING A METH LAB THE SIZE OF A FOOTBALL FIELD, WHEN THIS RED HOOD WHACK-JOB IS OFFING EVERYBODY!

WE'LL BE FINE.

WE'RE IN HIS TERRITORY!

WE'RE IN BLACK MASK'S TERRITORY.

THAT'S KIND OF A GRAY AREA. HE MIGHT KILL US FOR KICKING OUR TRIBUTES UP TO THE MASK. HE MIGHT WANT A CUT.

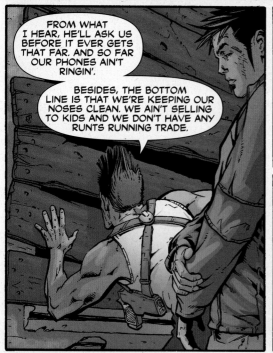

FROM WHAT I HEAR, HE'LL ASK US BEFORE IT EVER GETS THAT FAR. AND SO FAR OUR PHONES AIN'T RINGIN'.

BESIDES, THE BOTTOM LINE IS THAT WE'RE KEEPING OUR NOSES CLEAN. WE AIN'T SELLING TO KIDS AND WE DON'T HAVE ANY RUNTS RUNNING TRADE.

HE ONLY SEEMS TO BRING DOWN THE HAMMER IF YOU MESS WITH THE SHORTIES.

THAT'S KIND OF *GRAY AREA*, TOO.

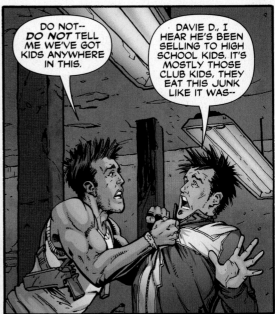

DO NOT-- *DO NOT* TELL ME WE'VE GOT KIDS ANYWHERE IN THIS.

DAVIE D., I HEAR HE'S BEEN SELLING TO HIGH SCHOOL KIDS. IT'S MOSTLY THOSE CLUB KIDS, THEY EAT THIS JUNK LIKE IT WAS--

WHAT!? *WHAT?!*

WE WERE STAYING *CLEAN!* CLEAN, YOU IDIOT!! NO KIDS!! *NO FREAKING KIDS!*

I KNOW, MAN. THAT'S WHAT I'VE BEEN TRYING TO TELL YOU. WE GOTTA BAIL OR WE'RE TEN KINDS OF DEAD MEAT.

OKAY...OKAY... WE GOTTA BE COOL. FIND DAVIE D--PUT HIM IN THE GROUND. MAKE A BIG SHOW OF IT. LET EVERYBODY KNOW THAT THIS KIND OF GARBAGE DOESN'T PLAY WITH US.

WILL THAT WORK? THAT'LL KEEP THE *RED HOOD* OFF OF US?

MAYBE. WE'VE BEEN LUCKY SO FAR.

FLAME

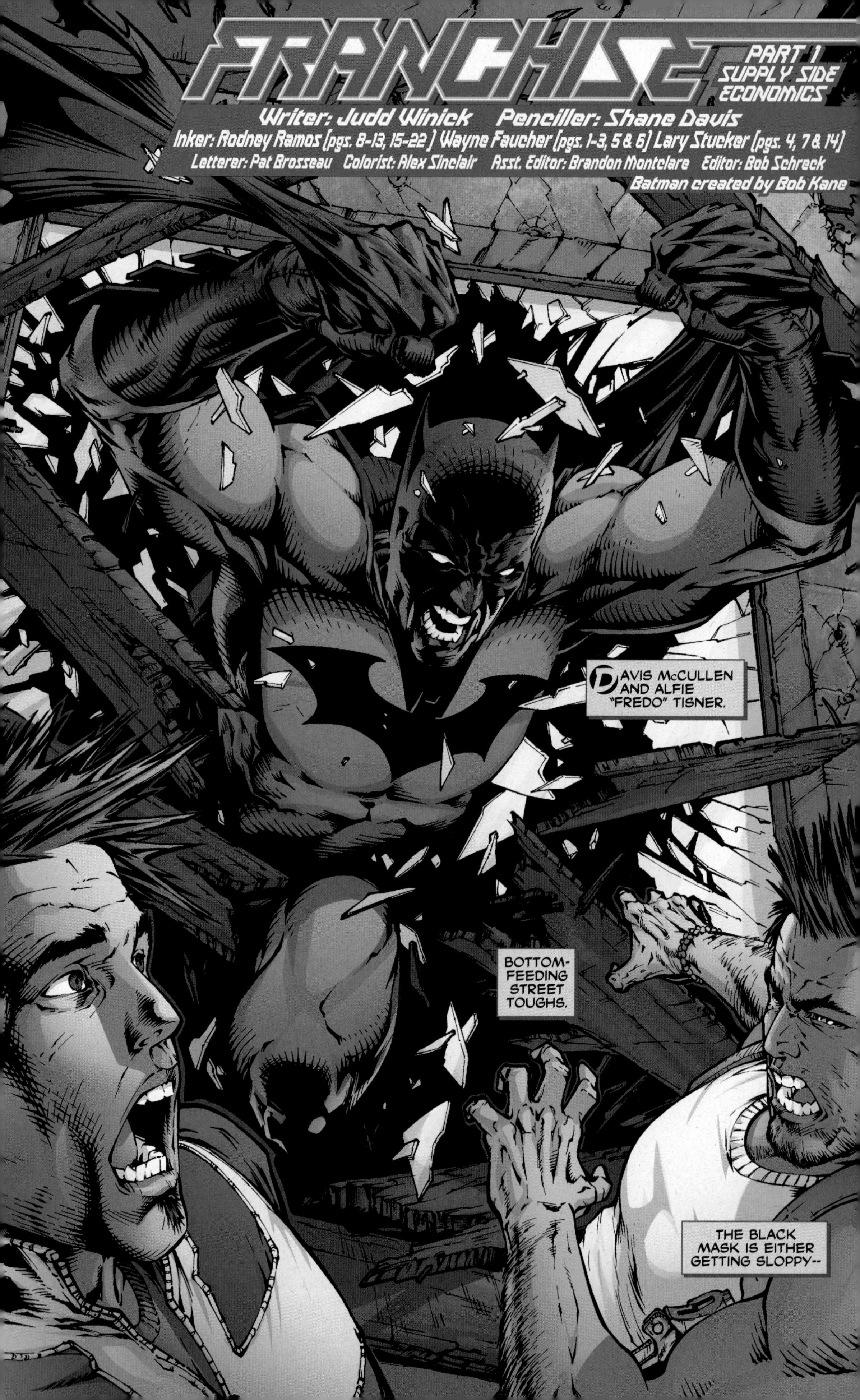
FRANCHISE
PART 1
SUPPLY SIDE ECONOMICS
Writer: Judd Winick Penciller: Shane Davis
Inker: Rodney Ramos (pgs. 8-13, 15-22) Wayne Faucher (pgs. 1-3, 5 & 6) Lary Stucker (pgs. 4, 7 & 14)
Letterer: Pat Brosseau Colorist: Alex Sinclair Asst. Editor: Brandon Montclare Editor: Bob Schreck
Batman created by Bob Kane
DAVIS McCULLEN AND ALFIE "FREDO" TISNER.
BOTTOM-FEEDING STREET TOUGHS.
THE BLACK MASK IS EITHER GETTING SLOPPY--

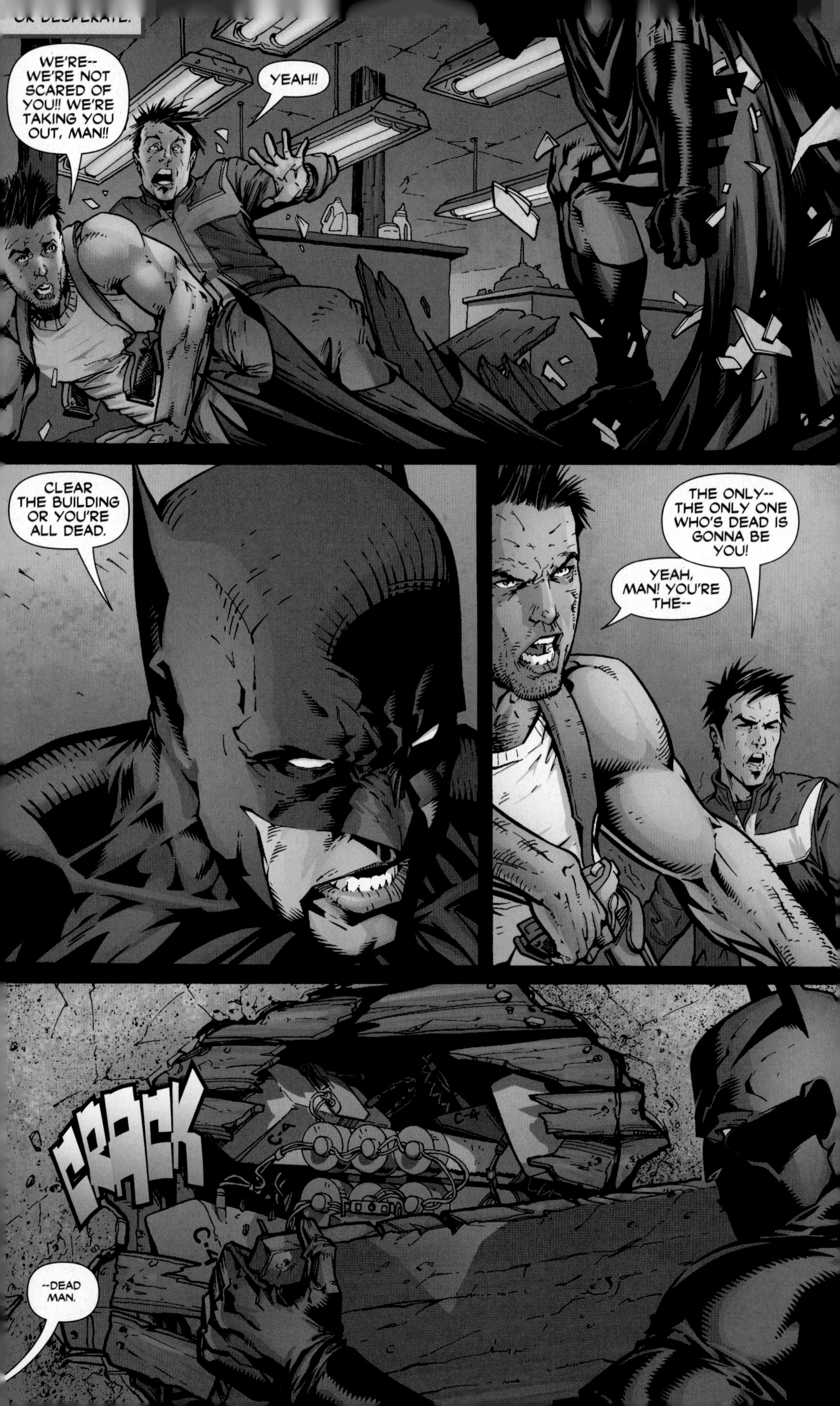

WE'RE-- WE'RE NOT SCARED OF YOU!! WE'RE TAKING YOU OUT, MAN!!
YEAH!!
CLEAR THE BUILDING OR YOU'RE ALL DEAD.
THE ONLY-- THE ONLY ONE WHO'S DEAD IS GONNA BE YOU!
YEAH, MAN! YOU'RE THE--
CRACK
--DEAD MAN.

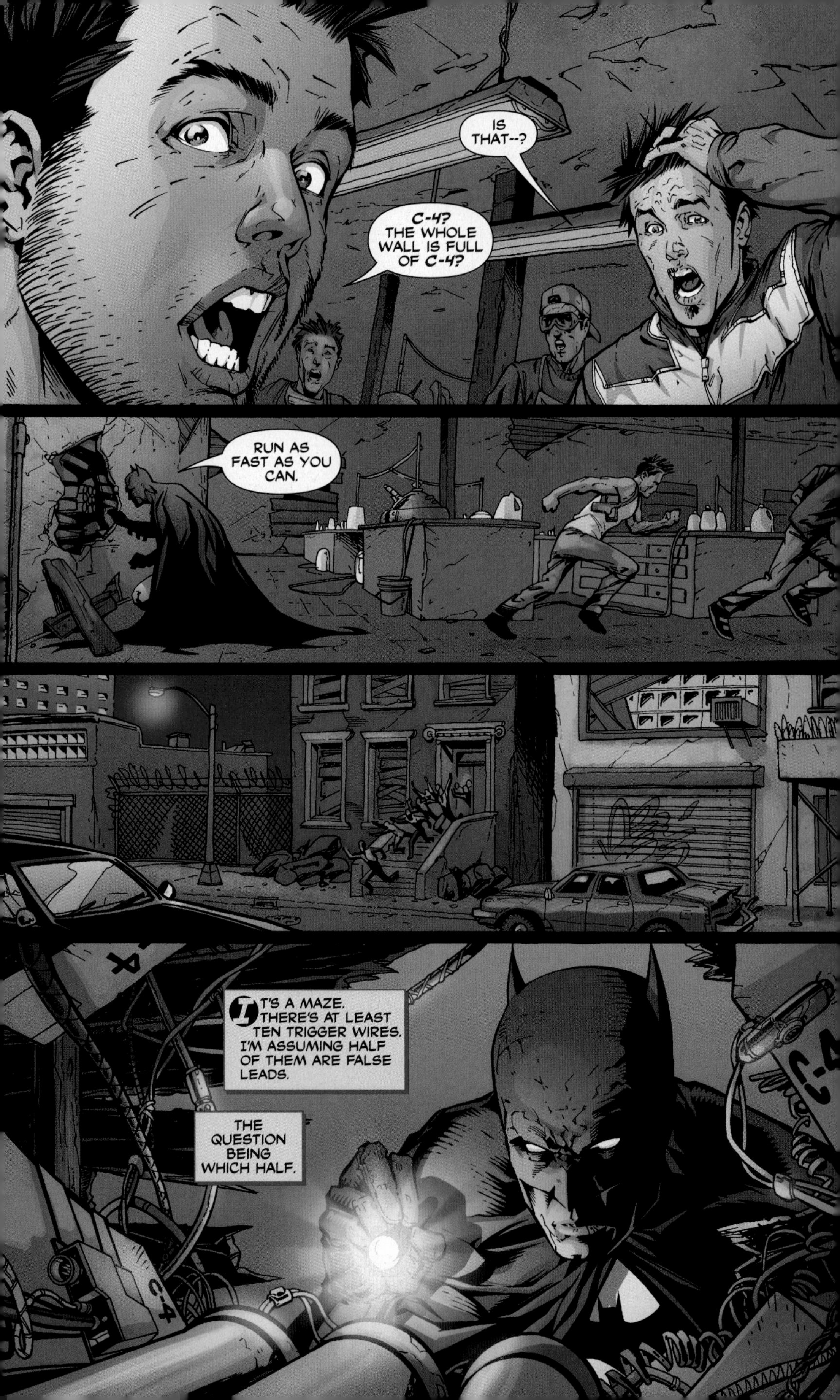
IS THAT--?
C-4? THE WHOLE WALL IS FULL OF C-4?
RUN AS FAST AS YOU CAN.
IT'S A MAZE. THERE'S AT LEAST TEN TRIGGER WIRES. I'M ASSUMING HALF OF THEM ARE FALSE LEADS.
THE QUESTION BEING WHICH HALF.
C-4
C-4

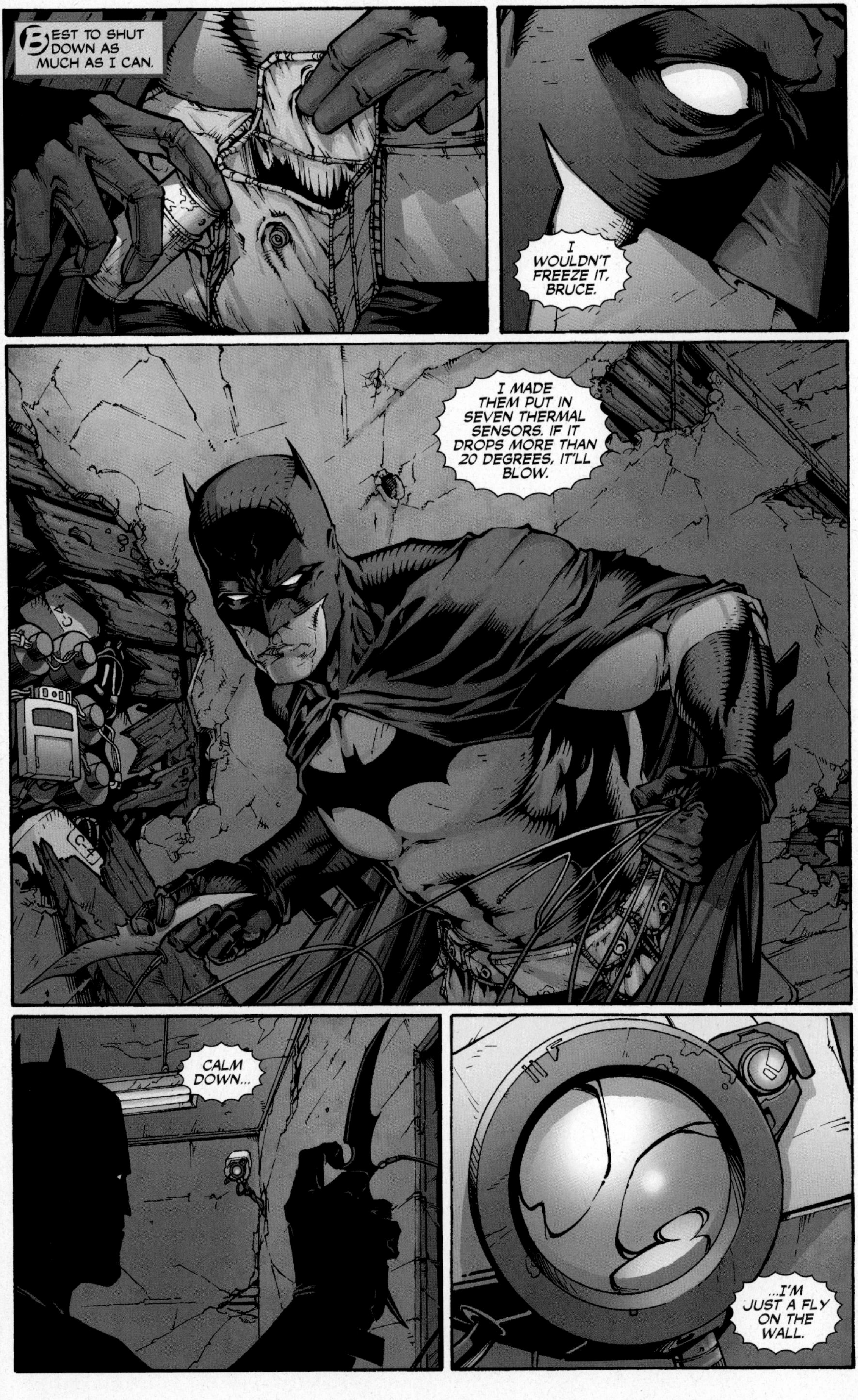
BEST TO SHUT DOWN AS MUCH AS I CAN.
I WOULDN'T FREEZE IT, BRUCE.
I MADE THEM PUT IN SEVEN THERMAL SENSORS. IF IT DROPS MORE THAN 20 DEGREES, IT'LL BLOW.
C-4
C-4
CALM DOWN...
...I'M JUST A FLY ON THE WALL.

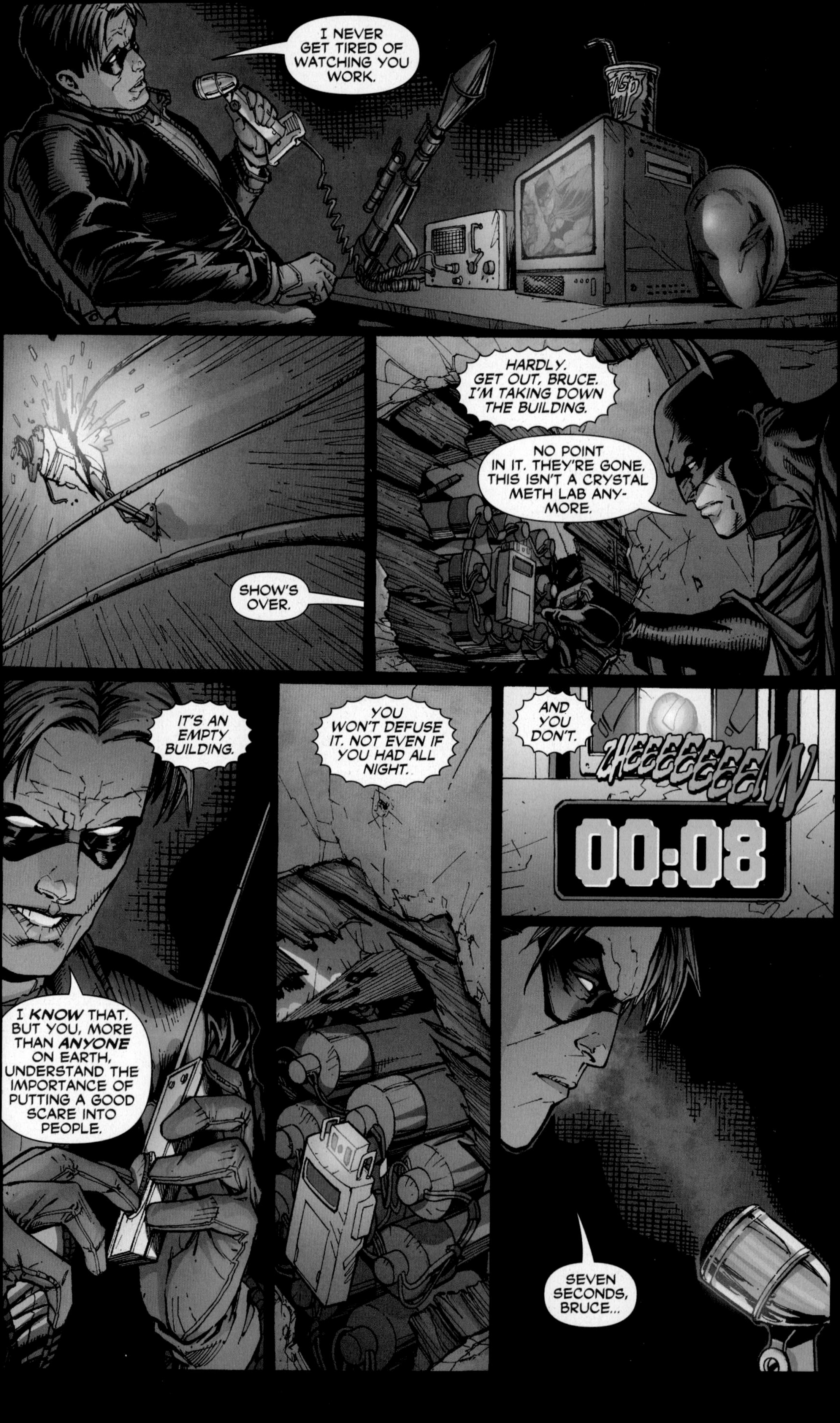
I NEVER GET TIRED OF WATCHING YOU WORK.
SHOW'S OVER.
HARDLY. GET OUT, BRUCE. I'M TAKING DOWN THE BUILDING.
NO POINT IN IT. THEY'RE GONE. THIS ISN'T A CRYSTAL METH LAB ANY-MORE.
IT'S AN EMPTY BUILDING.
I KNOW THAT. BUT YOU, MORE THAN ANYONE ON EARTH, UNDERSTAND THE IMPORTANCE OF PUTTING A GOOD SCARE INTO PEOPLE.
YOU WON'T DEFUSE IT. NOT EVEN IF YOU HAD ALL NIGHT.
AND YOU DON'T.
ZHEEEEEEEMN
00:08
SEVEN SECONDS, BRUCE...

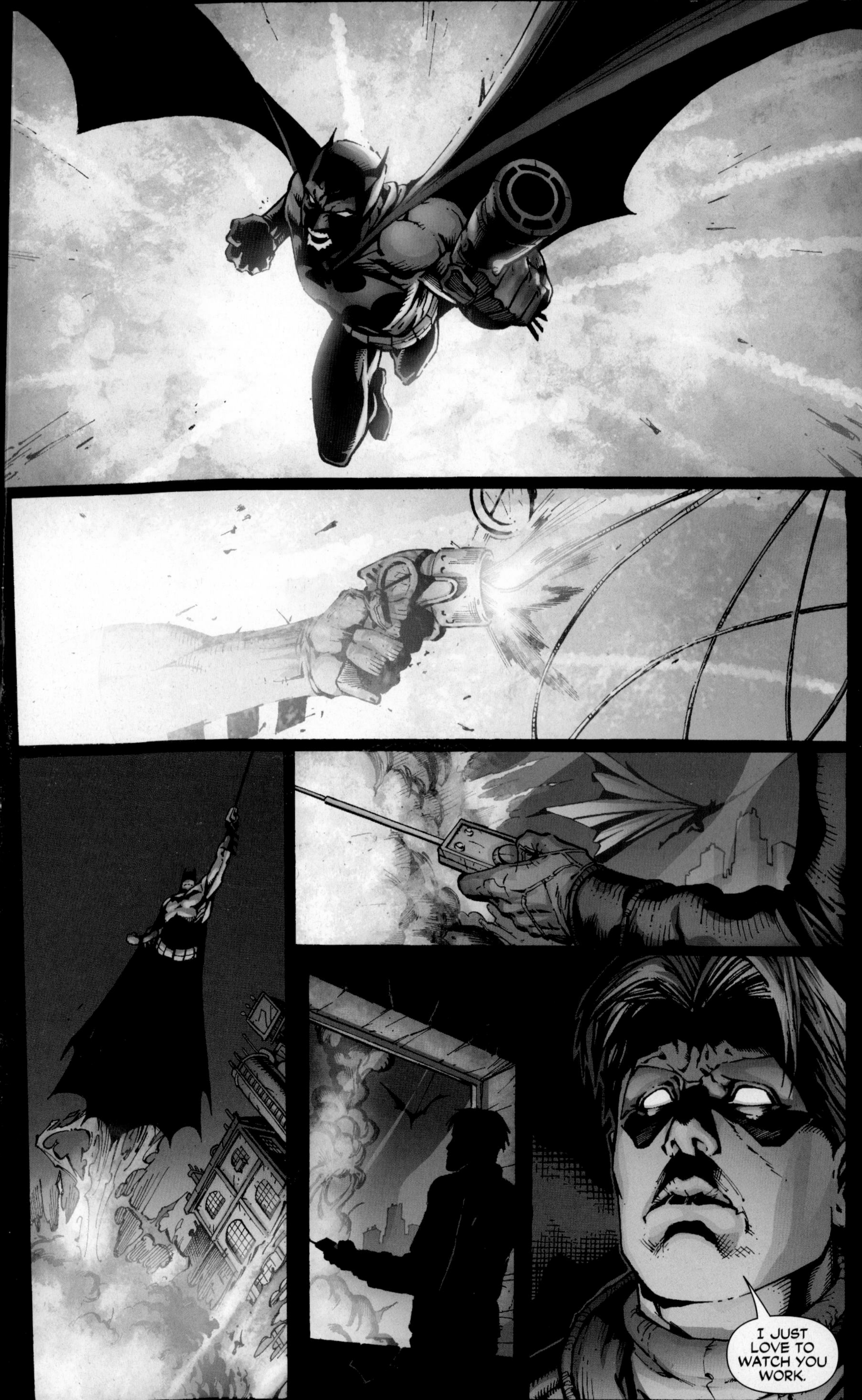
I JUST LOVE TO WATCH YOU WORK.

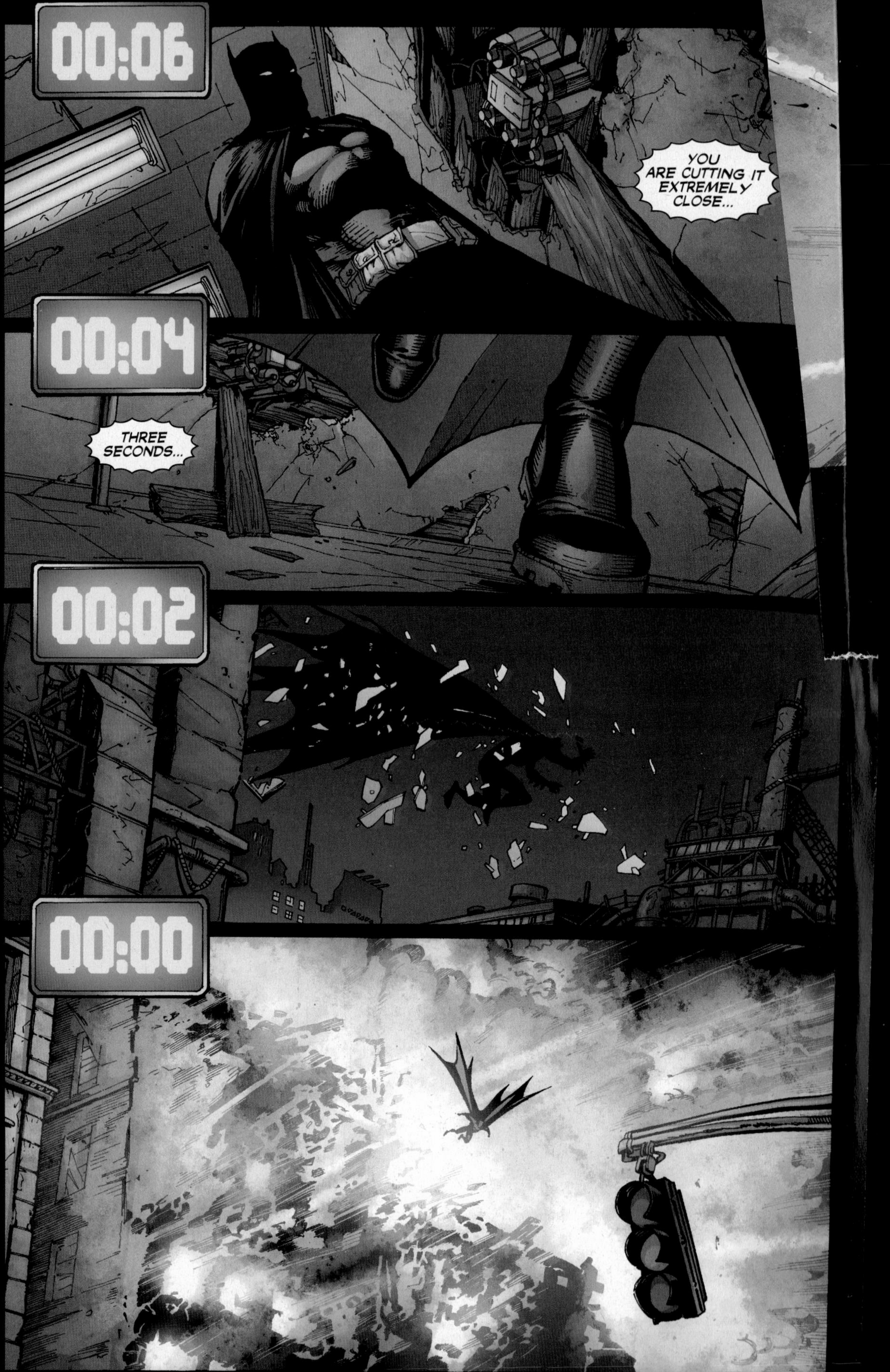
00:06
YOU ARE CUTTING IT EXTREMELY CLOSE...
00:04
THREE SECONDS...
00:02
00:00

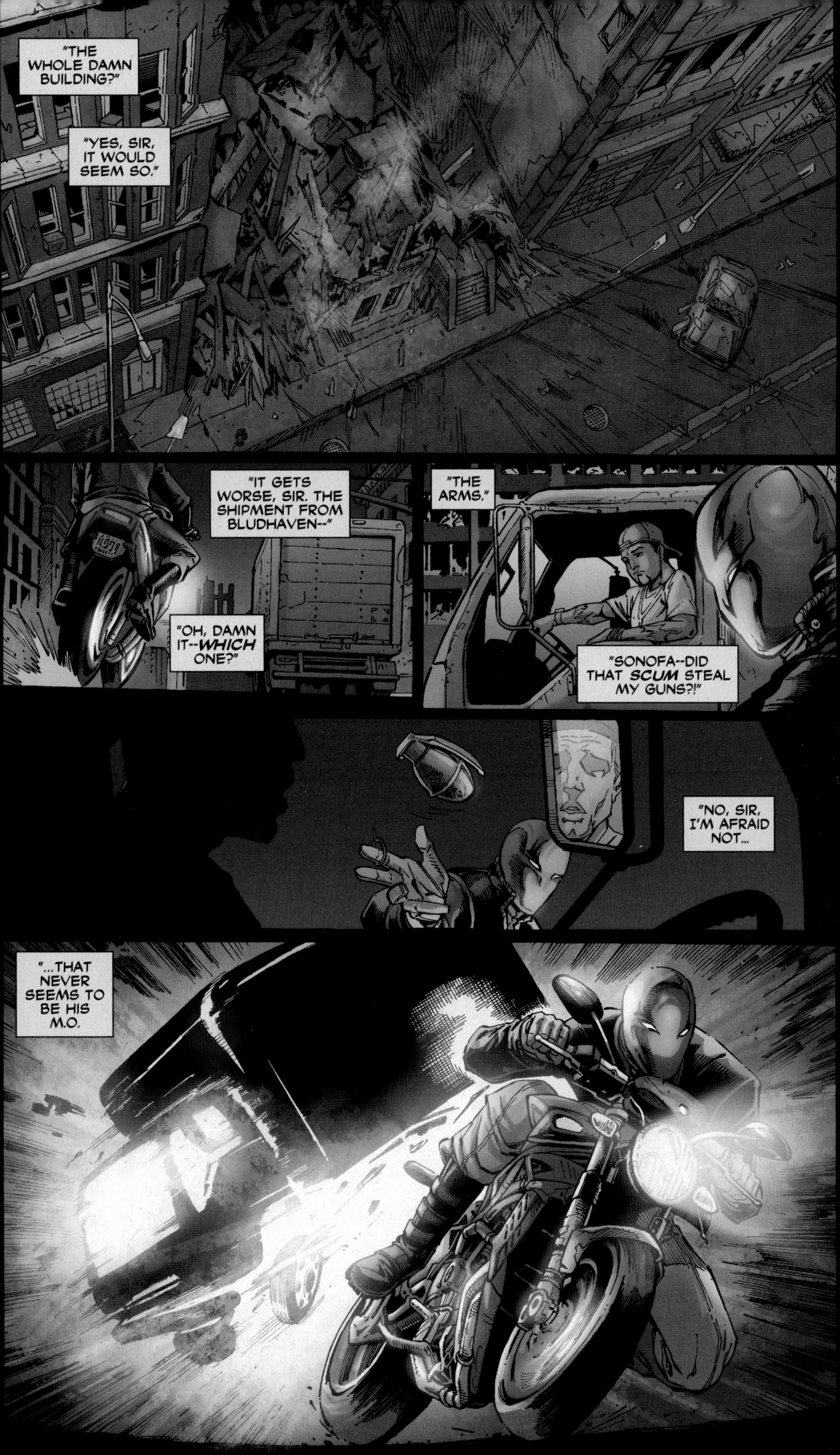
"THE WHOLE DAMN BUILDING?"
"YES, SIR, IT WOULD SEEM SO."
"IT GETS WORSE, SIR. THE SHIPMENT FROM BLUDHAVEN--"
"OH, DAMN IT--WHICH ONE?"
"THE ARMS."
"SONOFA--DID THAT SCUM STEAL MY GUNS?!"
"NO, SIR, I'M AFRAID NOT...
"...THAT NEVER SEEMS TO BE HIS M.O.

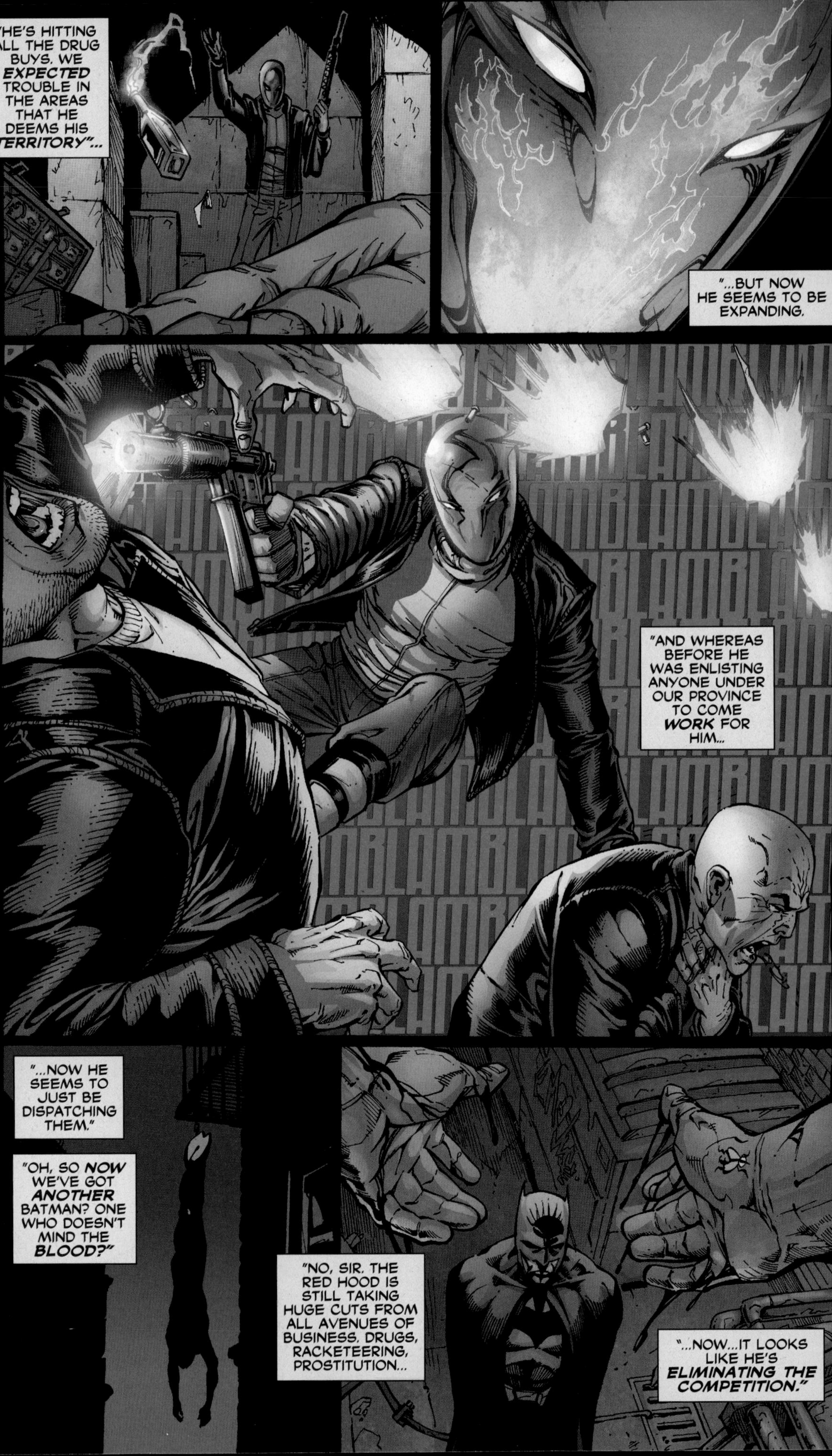
"HE'S HITTING ALL THE DRUG BUYS. WE EXPECTED TROUBLE IN THE AREAS THAT HE DEEMS HIS "TERRITORY"...
"...BUT NOW HE SEEMS TO BE EXPANDING.
"AND WHEREAS BEFORE HE WAS ENLISTING ANYONE UNDER OUR PROVINCE TO COME WORK FOR HIM...
"...NOW HE SEEMS TO JUST BE DISPATCHING THEM."
"OH, SO NOW WE'VE GOT ANOTHER BATMAN? ONE WHO DOESN'T MIND THE BLOOD?"
"NO, SIR. THE RED HOOD IS STILL TAKING HUGE CUTS FROM ALL AVENUES OF BUSINESS. DRUGS, RACKETEERING, PROSTITUTION...
"...NOW...IT LOOKS LIKE HE'S ELIMINATING THE COMPETITION."

YOU WANNA TELL ME WHY THIS GUY AIN'T DEAD!??

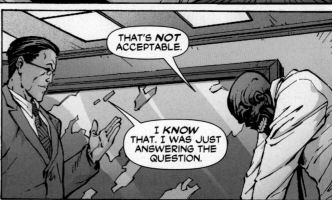

TRUTH? HE'S BETTER THAN ANYTHING WE HAVE ON THE STREET.

THAT'S *NOT* ACCEPTABLE.

I *KNOW* THAT. I WAS JUST ANSWERING THE QUESTION.

AND *WHY* IN THE BLUE HELL HASN'T BATMAN WIPED THIS LITTLE SMEAR OFF THE FACE OF THE PLANET?

MAYBE HE DOESN'T *WANT* TO.

EXCUSE ME?

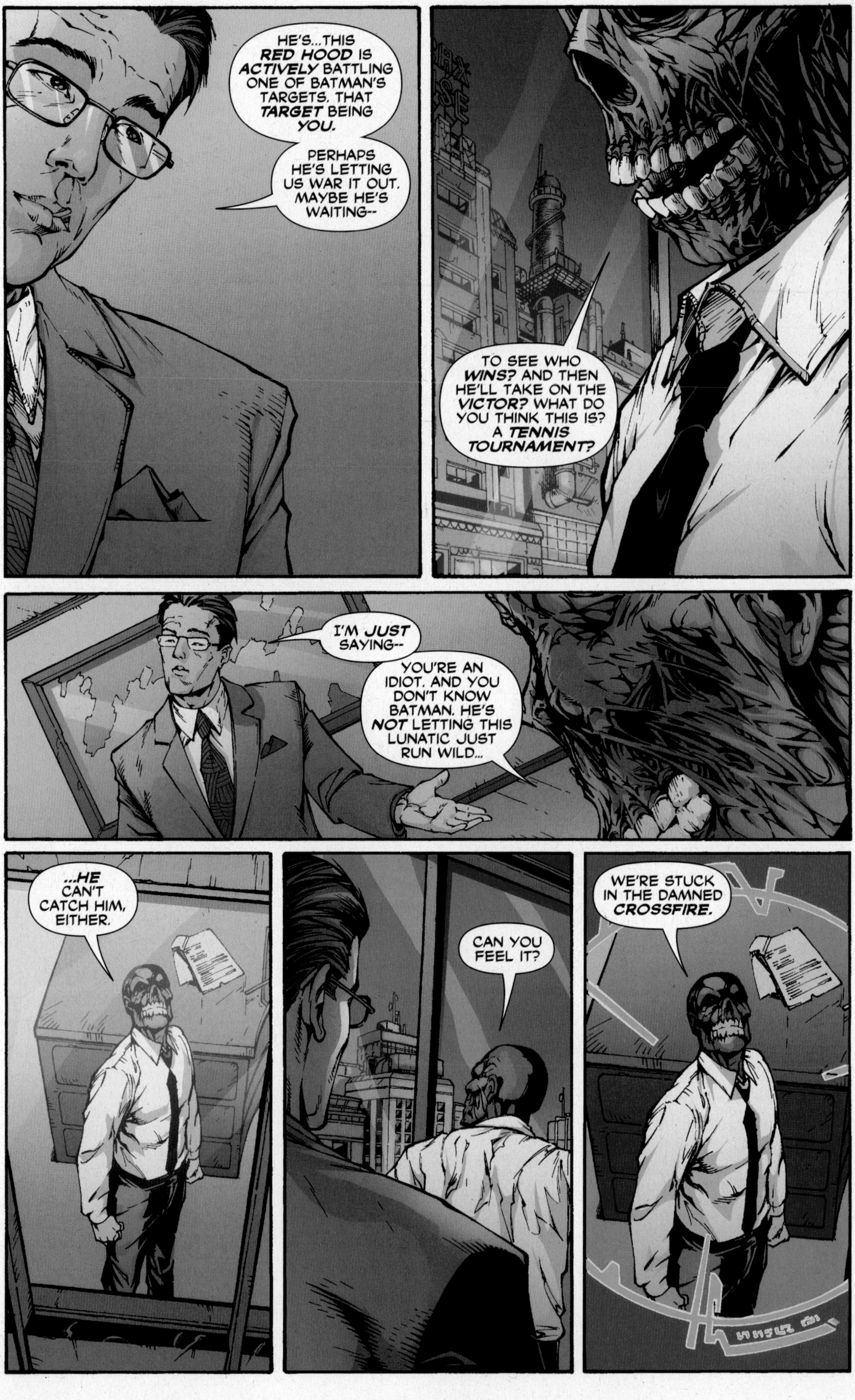
HE'S...THIS RED HOOD IS ACTIVELY BATTLING ONE OF BATMAN'S TARGETS. THAT TARGET BEING YOU.
PERHAPS HE'S LETTING US WAR IT OUT. MAYBE HE'S WAITING--
TO SEE WHO WINS? AND THEN HE'LL TAKE ON THE VICTOR? WHAT DO YOU THINK THIS IS? A TENNIS TOURNAMENT?
I'M JUST SAYING--
YOU'RE AN IDIOT. AND YOU DON'T KNOW BATMAN. HE'S NOT LETTING THIS LUNATIC JUST RUN WILD...
...HE CAN'T CATCH HIM, EITHER.
CAN YOU FEEL IT?
WE'RE STUCK IN THE DAMNED CROSSFIRE.

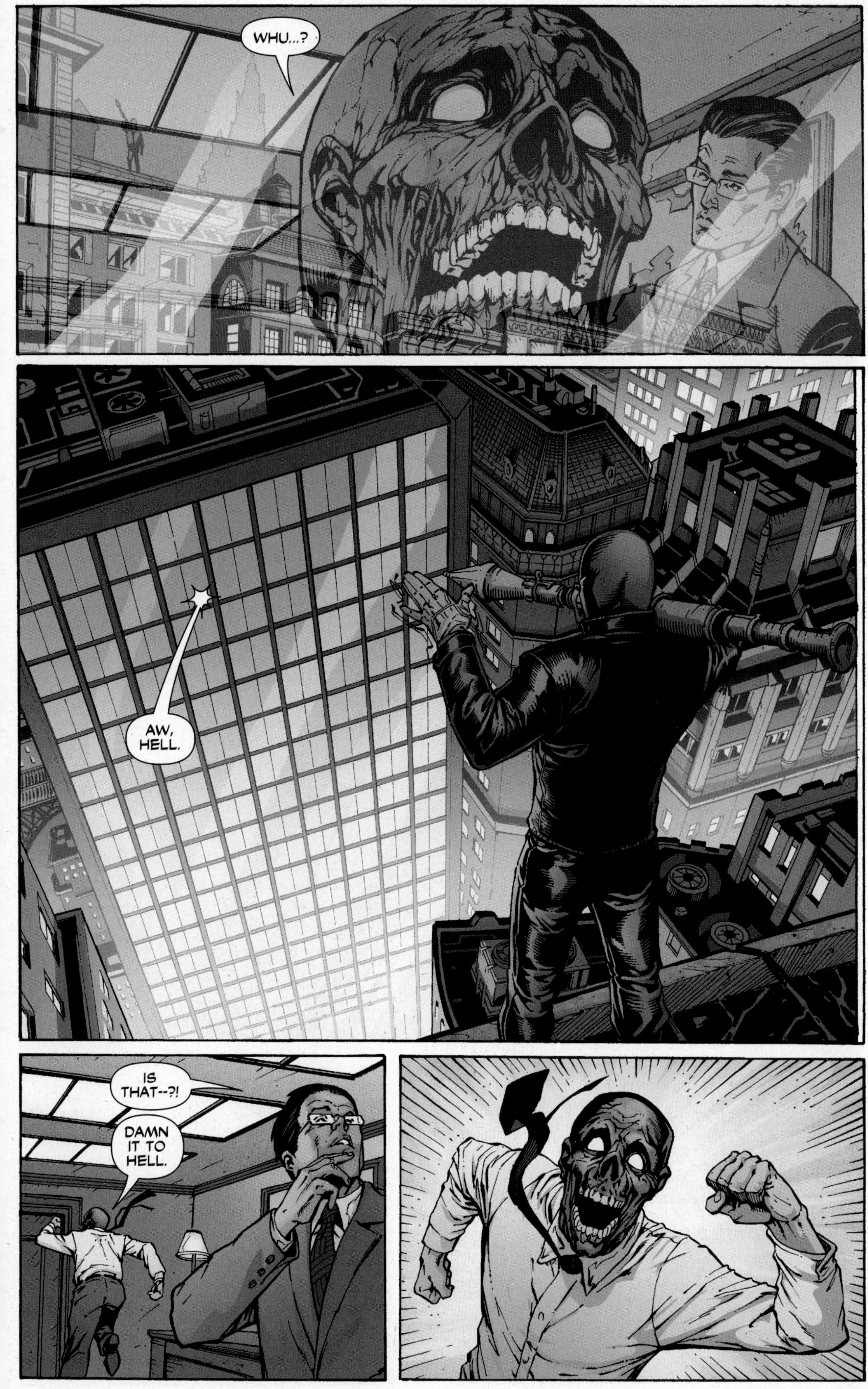
WHU...?
AW, HELL.
IS THAT--?!
DAMN IT TO HELL.

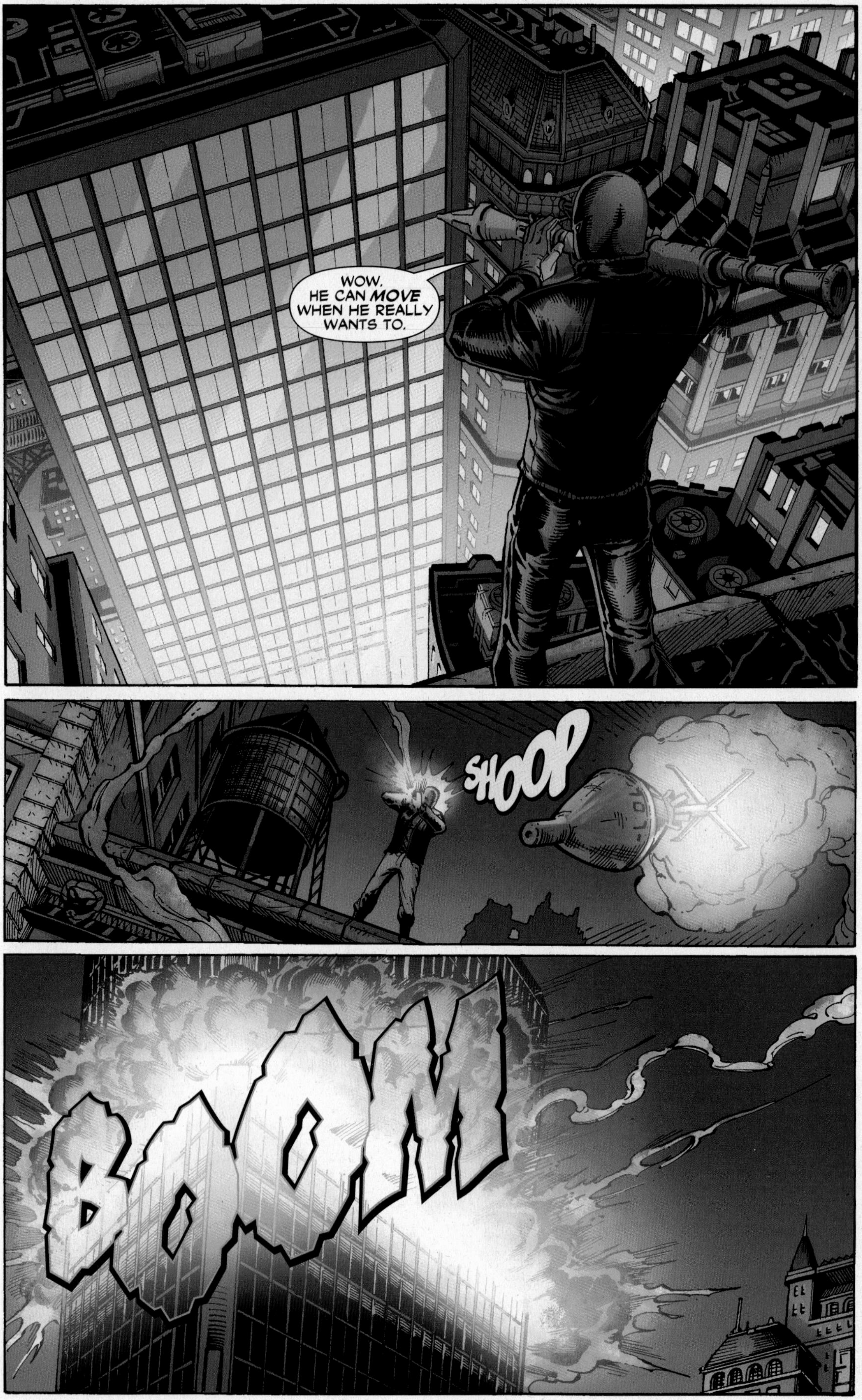
WOW, HE CAN MOVE WHEN HE REALLY WANTS TO.
SHOOP
BOOM

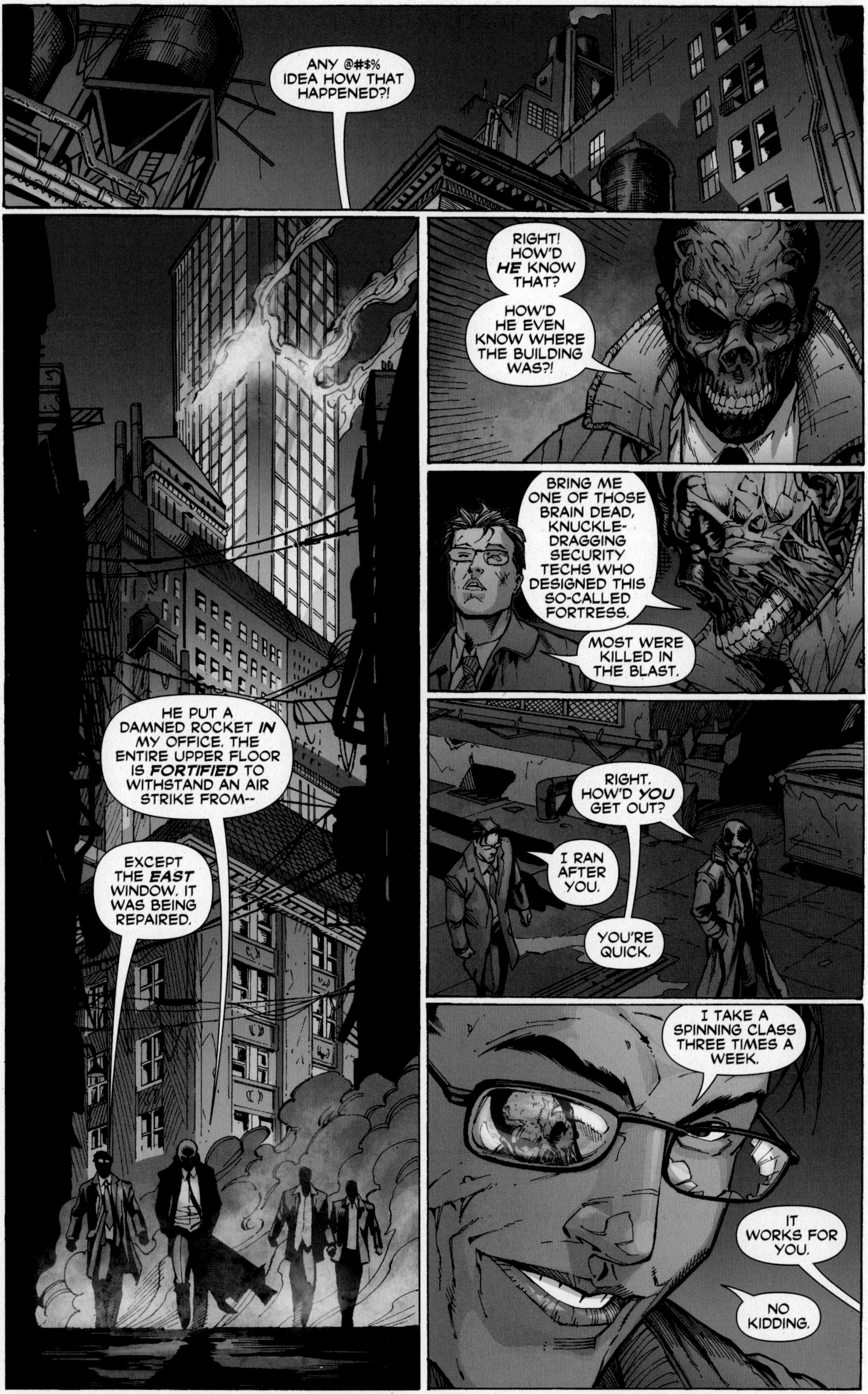
ANY @#$% IDEA HOW THAT HAPPENED?!
HE PUT A DAMNED ROCKET IN MY OFFICE. THE ENTIRE UPPER FLOOR IS FORTIFIED TO WITHSTAND AN AIR STRIKE FROM--
EXCEPT THE EAST WINDOW. IT WAS BEING REPAIRED.
RIGHT! HOW'D HE KNOW THAT?
HOW'D HE EVEN KNOW WHERE THE BUILDING WAS?!
BRING ME ONE OF THOSE BRAIN DEAD, KNUCKLE-DRAGGING SECURITY TECHS WHO DESIGNED THIS SO-CALLED FORTRESS.
MOST WERE KILLED IN THE BLAST.
RIGHT. HOW'D YOU GET OUT?
I RAN AFTER YOU.
YOU'RE QUICK.
I TAKE A SPINNING CLASS THREE TIMES A WEEK.
IT WORKS FOR YOU.
NO KIDDING.

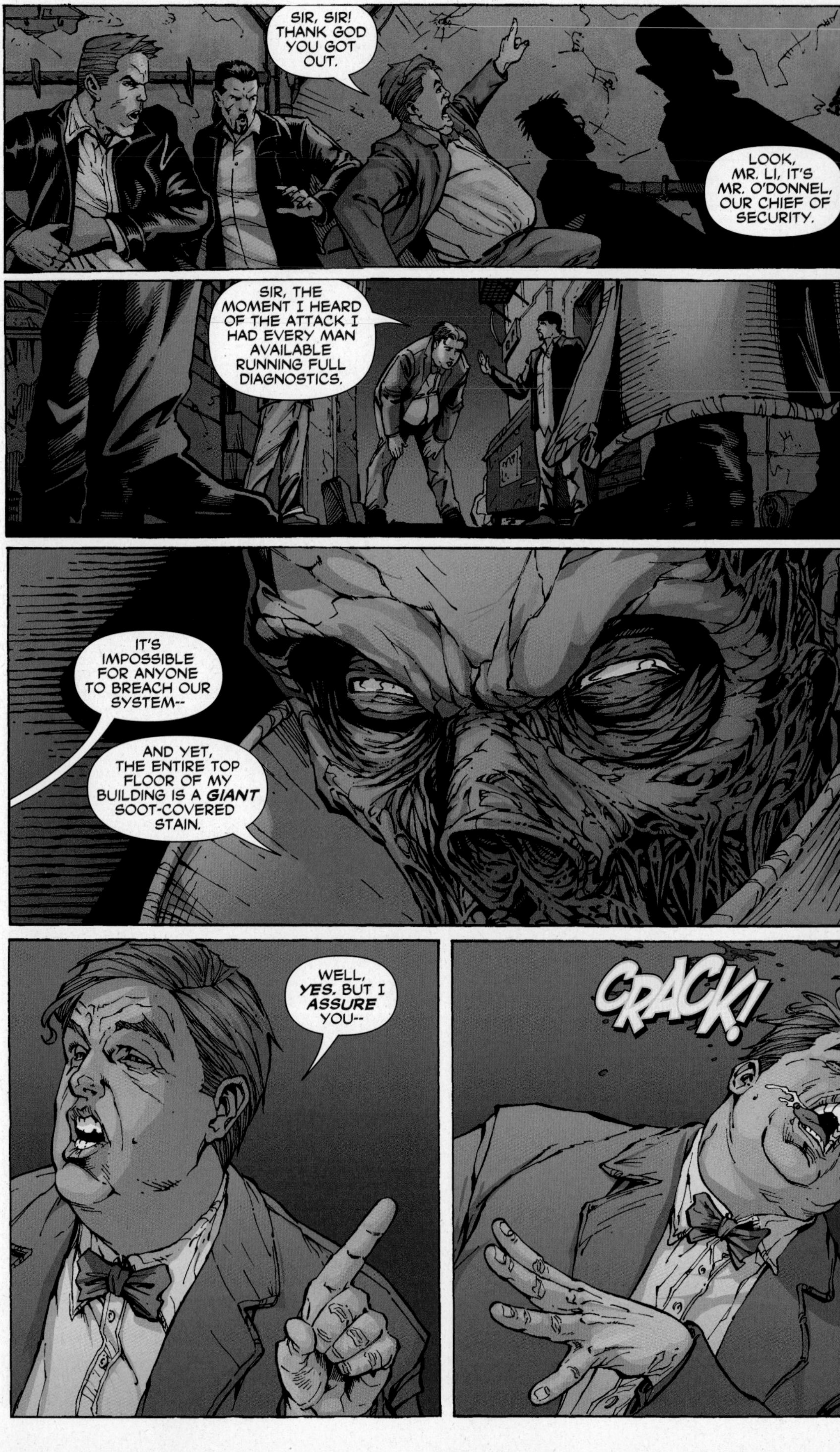
SIR, SIR! THANK GOD YOU GOT OUT.
LOOK, MR. LI, IT'S MR. O'DONNEL, OUR CHIEF OF SECURITY.
SIR, THE MOMENT I HEARD OF THE ATTACK I HAD EVERY MAN AVAILABLE RUNNING FULL DIAGNOSTICS.
IT'S IMPOSSIBLE FOR ANYONE TO BREACH OUR SYSTEM--
AND YET, THE ENTIRE TOP FLOOR OF MY BUILDING IS A GIANT SOOT-COVERED STAIN.
WELL, YES. BUT I ASSURE YOU--
CRACK!

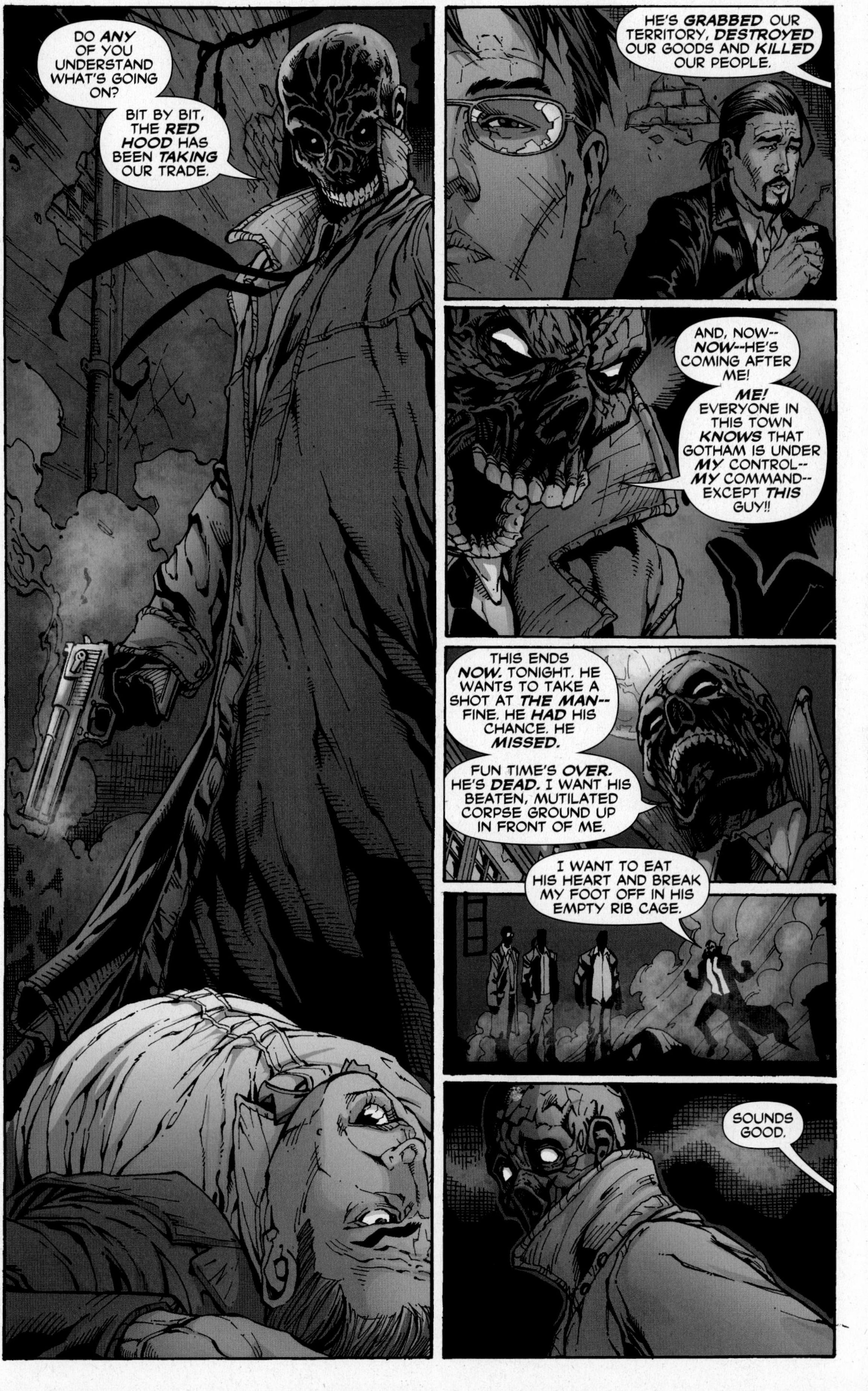
DO ANY OF YOU UNDERSTAND WHAT'S GOING ON?
BIT BY BIT, THE RED HOOD HAS BEEN TAKING OUR TRADE.
HE'S GRABBED OUR TERRITORY, DESTROYED OUR GOODS AND KILLED OUR PEOPLE.
AND, NOW-- NOW--HE'S COMING AFTER ME!
ME! EVERYONE IN THIS TOWN KNOWS THAT GOTHAM IS UNDER MY CONTROL-- MY COMMAND-- EXCEPT THIS GUY!!
THIS ENDS NOW. TONIGHT. HE WANTS TO TAKE A SHOT AT THE MAN-- FINE. HE HAD HIS CHANCE. HE MISSED.
FUN TIME'S OVER. HE'S DEAD. I WANT HIS BEATEN, MUTILATED CORPSE GROUND UP IN FRONT OF ME.
I WANT TO EAT HIS HEART AND BREAK MY FOOT OFF IN HIS EMPTY RIB CAGE.
SOUNDS GOOD.

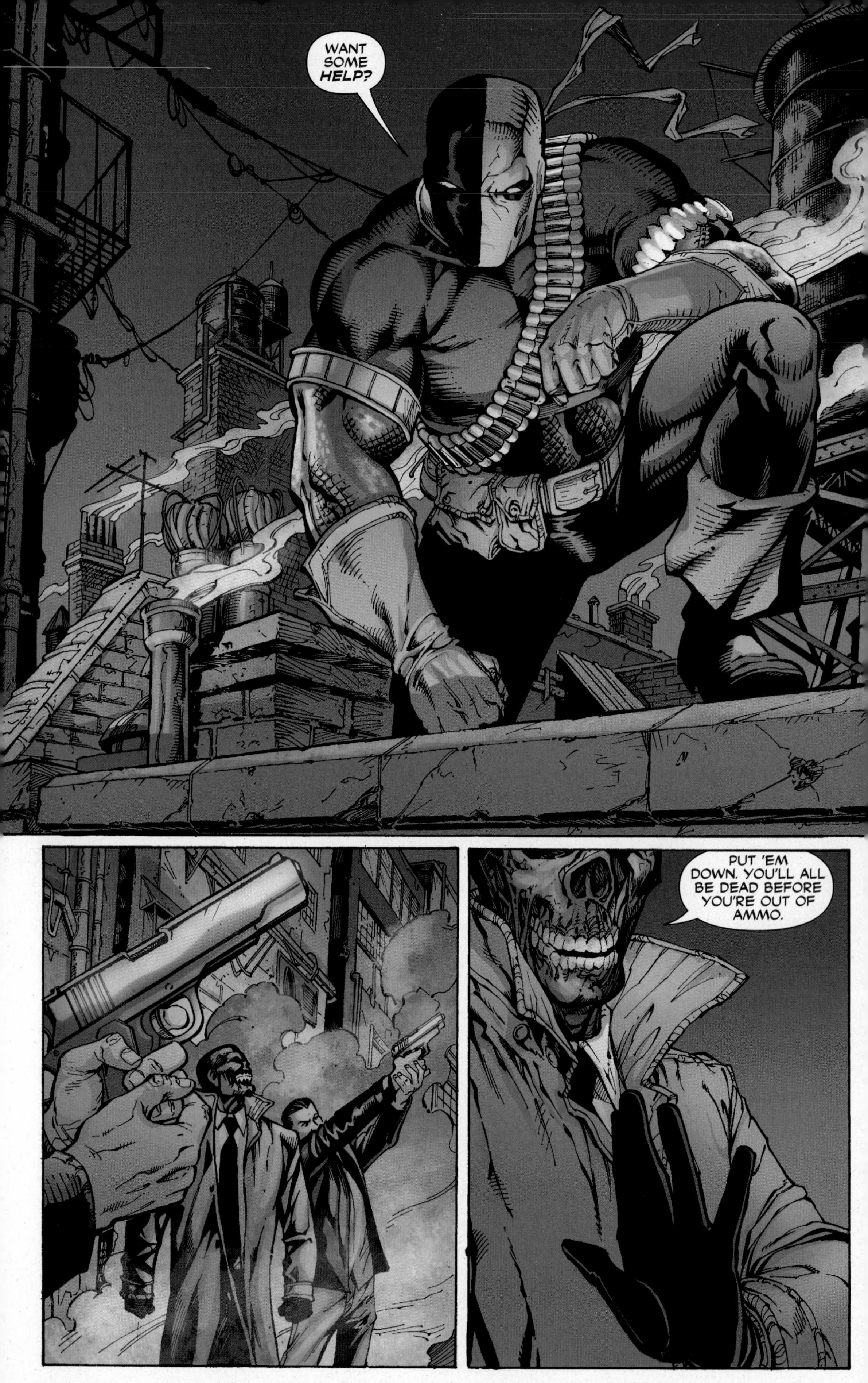
WANT SOME HELP?
PUT 'EM DOWN. YOU'LL ALL BE DEAD BEFORE YOU'RE OUT OF AMMO.

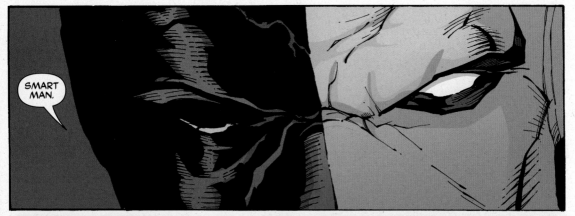

SMART MAN.

YEAH. IT TAKES A *MENSA* MEMBER TO KNOW THAT DEATHSTROKE, THE MASTER ASSASSIN, COULD ICE ALL THESE IDIOTS.

YOU GOT SOMETHING TO SAY?

YES. THERE'S A *COLLECTIVE.* IT'S CALLED THE *SOCIETY.*

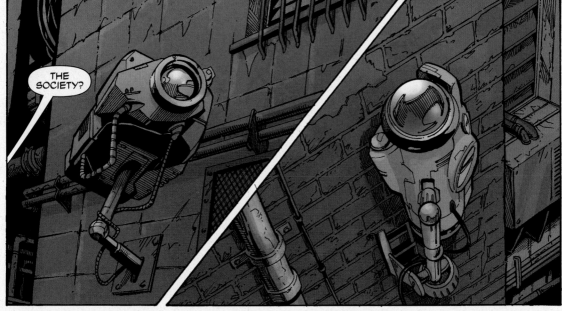

THE SOCIETY?

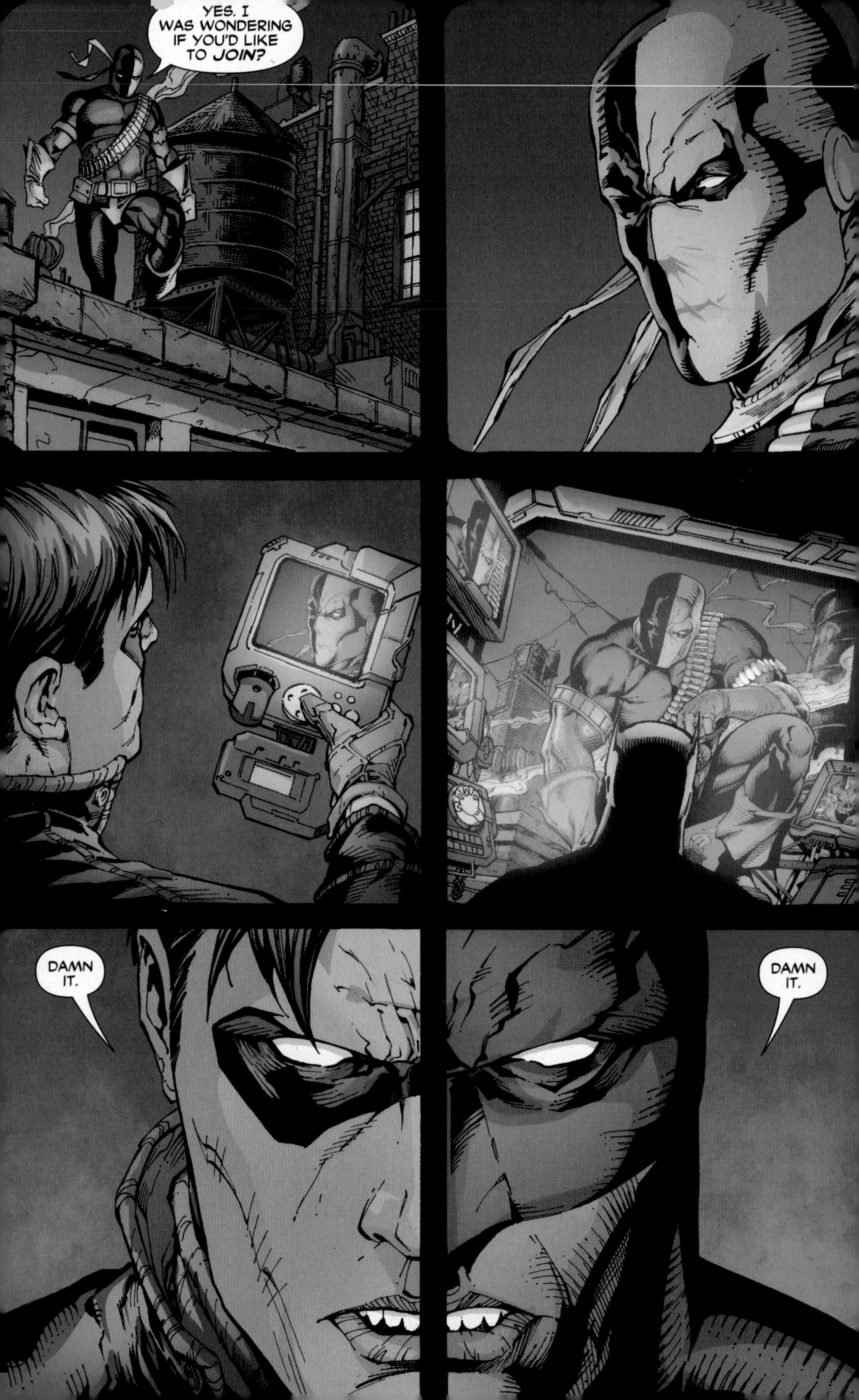
YES, I WAS WONDERING IF YOU'D LIKE TO JOIN?
DAMN IT.
DAMN IT.

BATMAN 647 Cover by Jock

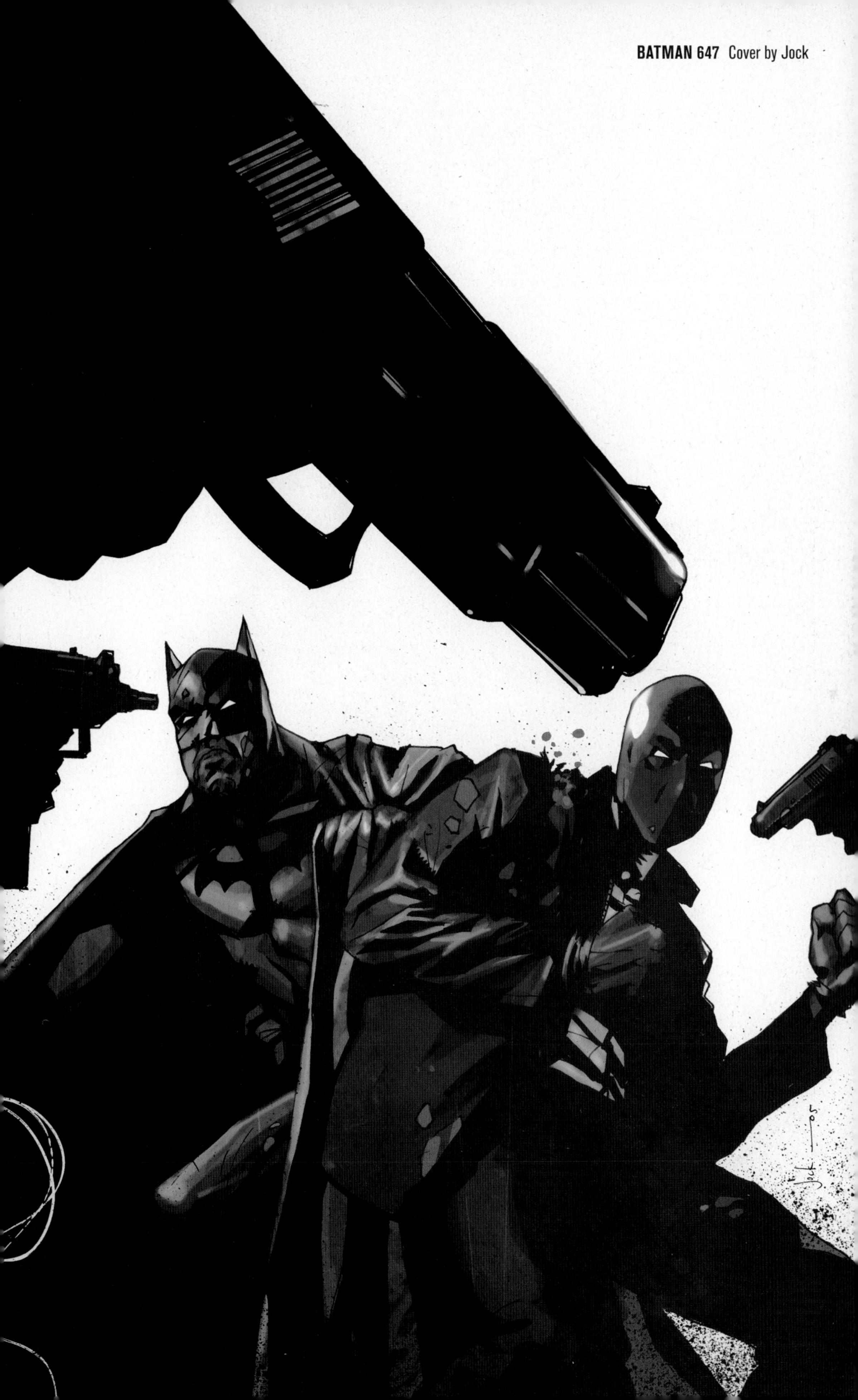

Jock 05

CHAPTER 10

FRANCHISE PART TWO:

THE
AWAY TEAM

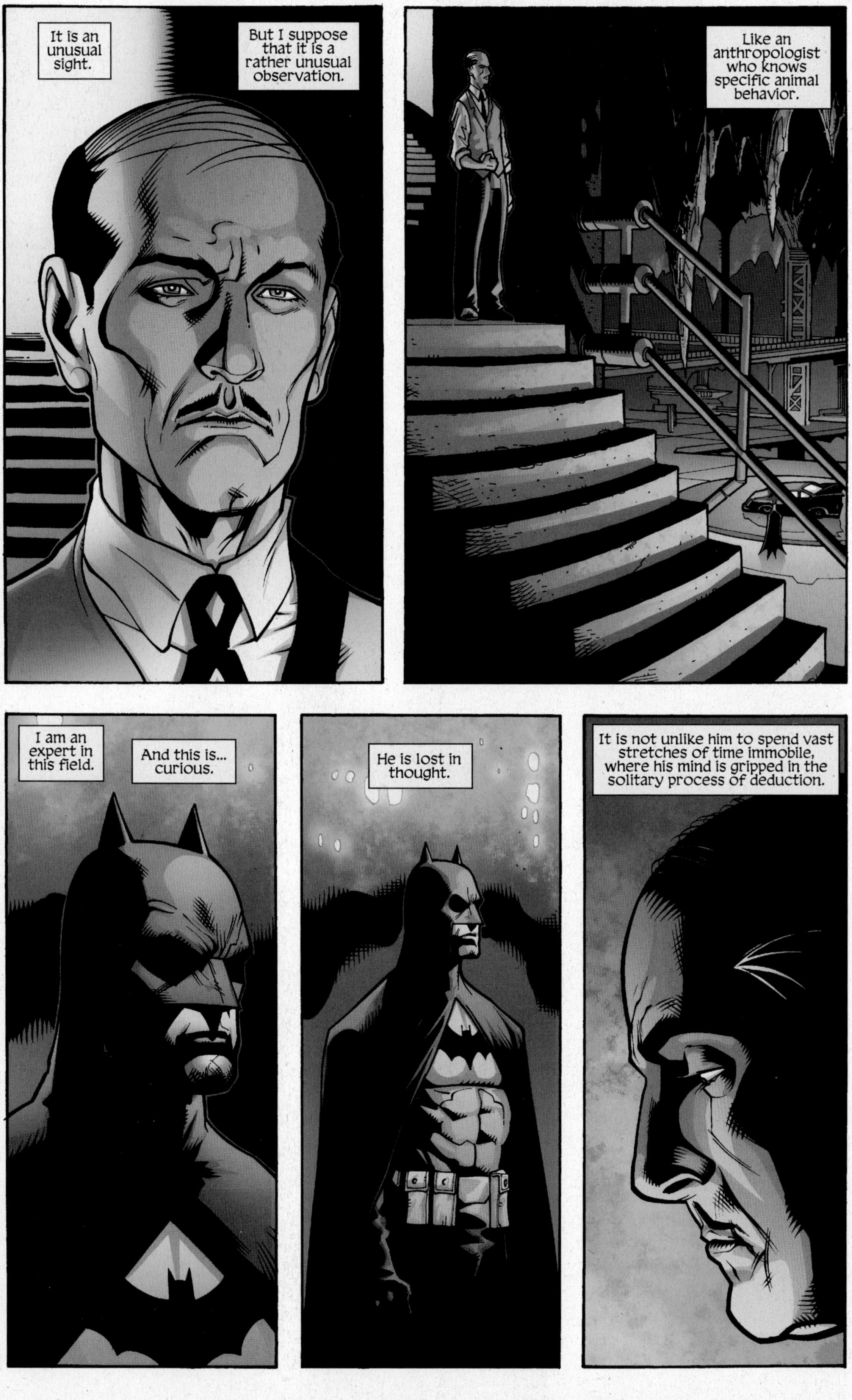
It is an unusual sight.
But I suppose that it is a rather unusual observation.
Like an anthropologist who knows specific animal behavior.
I am an expert in this field.
And this is... curious.
He is lost in thought.
It is not unlike him to spend vast stretches of time immobile, where his mind is gripped in the solitary process of deduction.

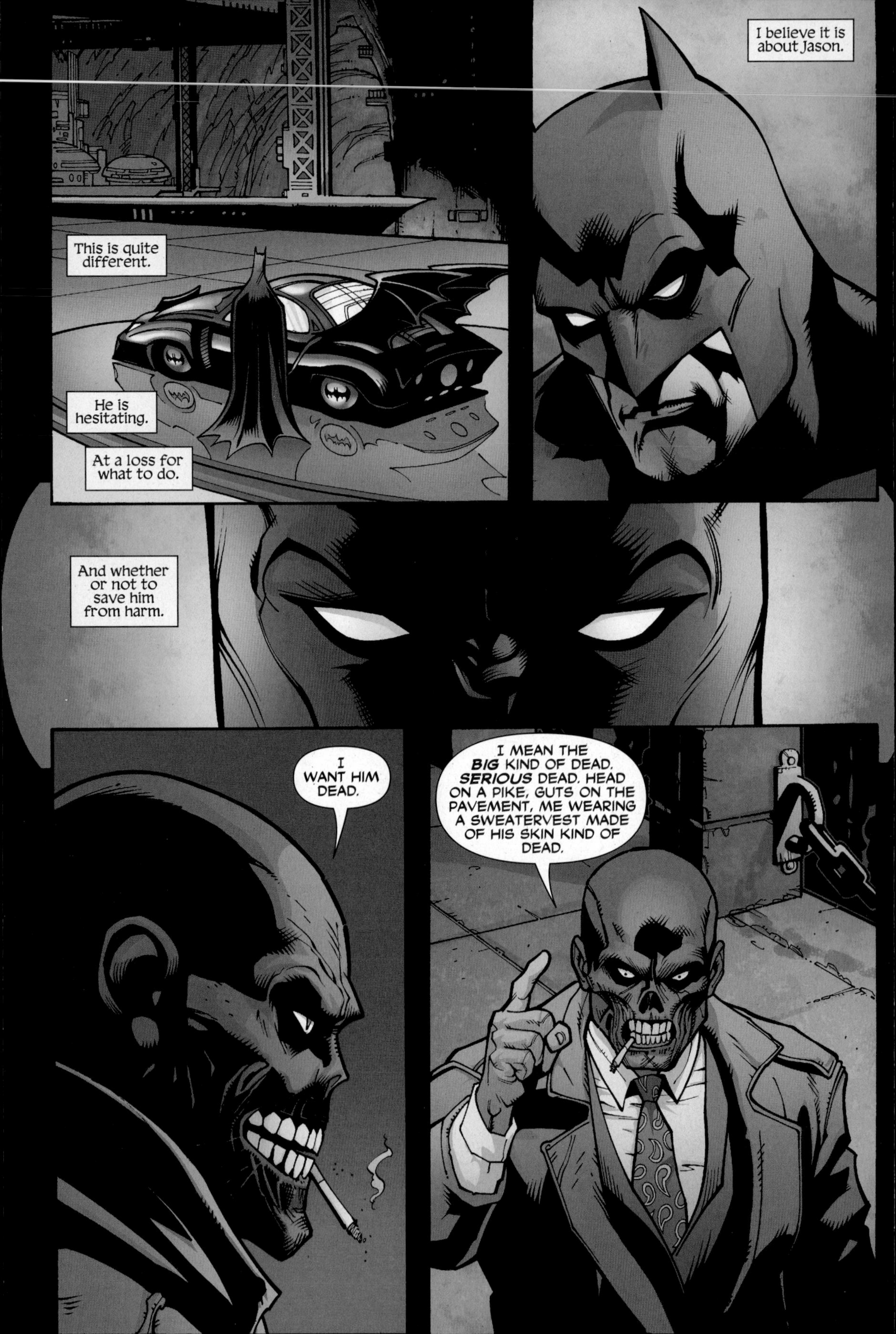

This is quite different.
He is hesitating.
At a loss for what to do.
I believe it is about Jason.
And whether or not to save him from harm.
I WANT HIM DEAD.
I MEAN THE BIG KIND OF DEAD. SERIOUS DEAD. HEAD ON A PIKE, GUTS ON THE PAVEMENT, ME WEARING A SWEATERVEST MADE OF HIS SKIN KIND OF DEAD.

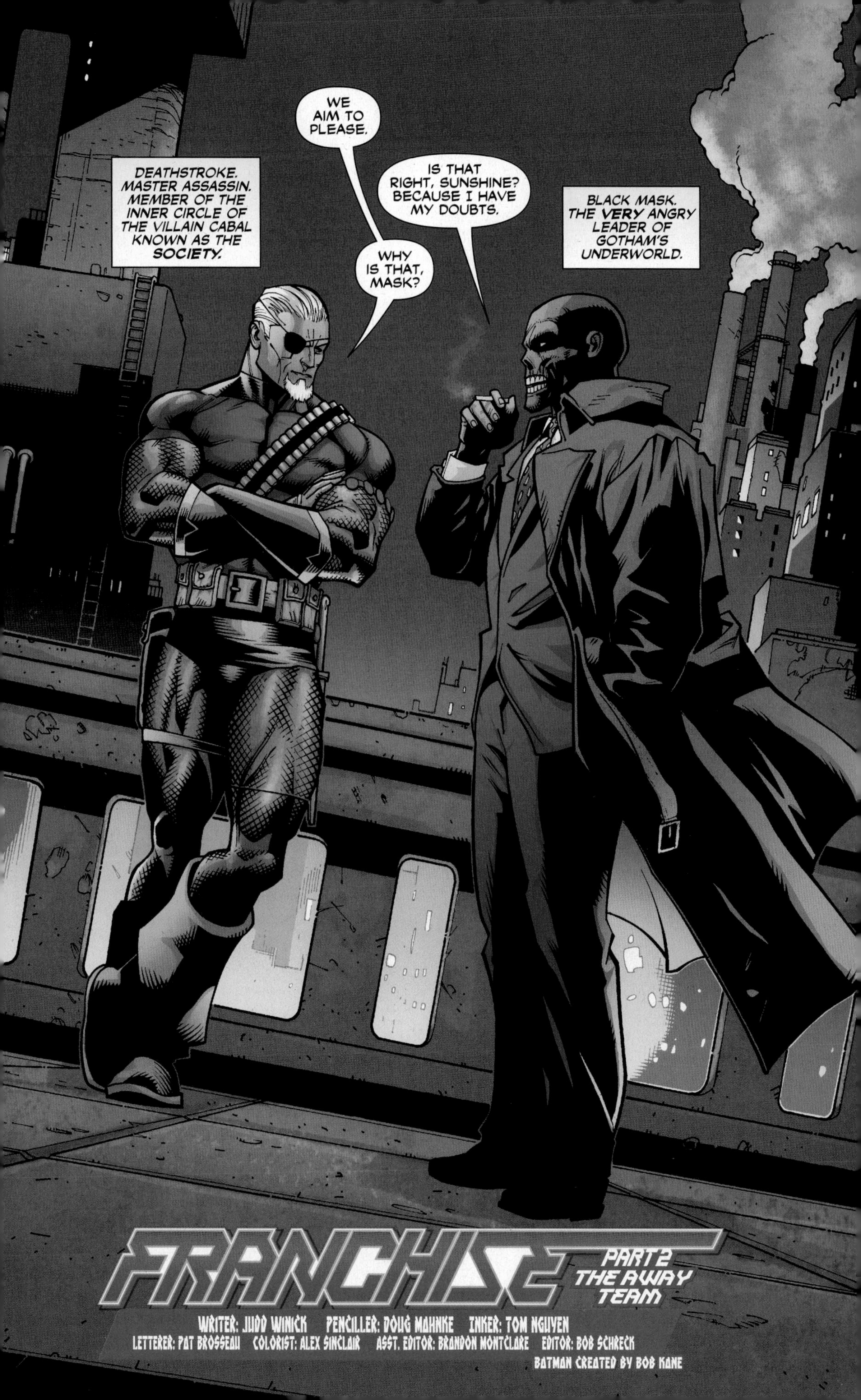
DEATHSTROKE. MASTER ASSASSIN. MEMBER OF THE INNER CIRCLE OF THE VILLAIN CABAL KNOWN AS THE SOCIETY.
WE AIM TO PLEASE.
IS THAT RIGHT, SUNSHINE? BECAUSE I HAVE MY DOUBTS.
WHY IS THAT, MASK?
BLACK MASK. THE VERY ANGRY LEADER OF GOTHAM'S UNDERWORLD.
FRANCHISE
PART 2 THE AWAY TEAM
WRITER: JUDD WINICK PENCILLER: DOUG MAHNKE INKER: TOM NGUYEN
LETTERER: PAT BROSSEAU COLORIST: ALEX SINCLAIR ASST. EDITOR: BRANDON MONTCLARE EDITOR: BOB SCHRECK
BATMAN CREATED BY BOB KANE

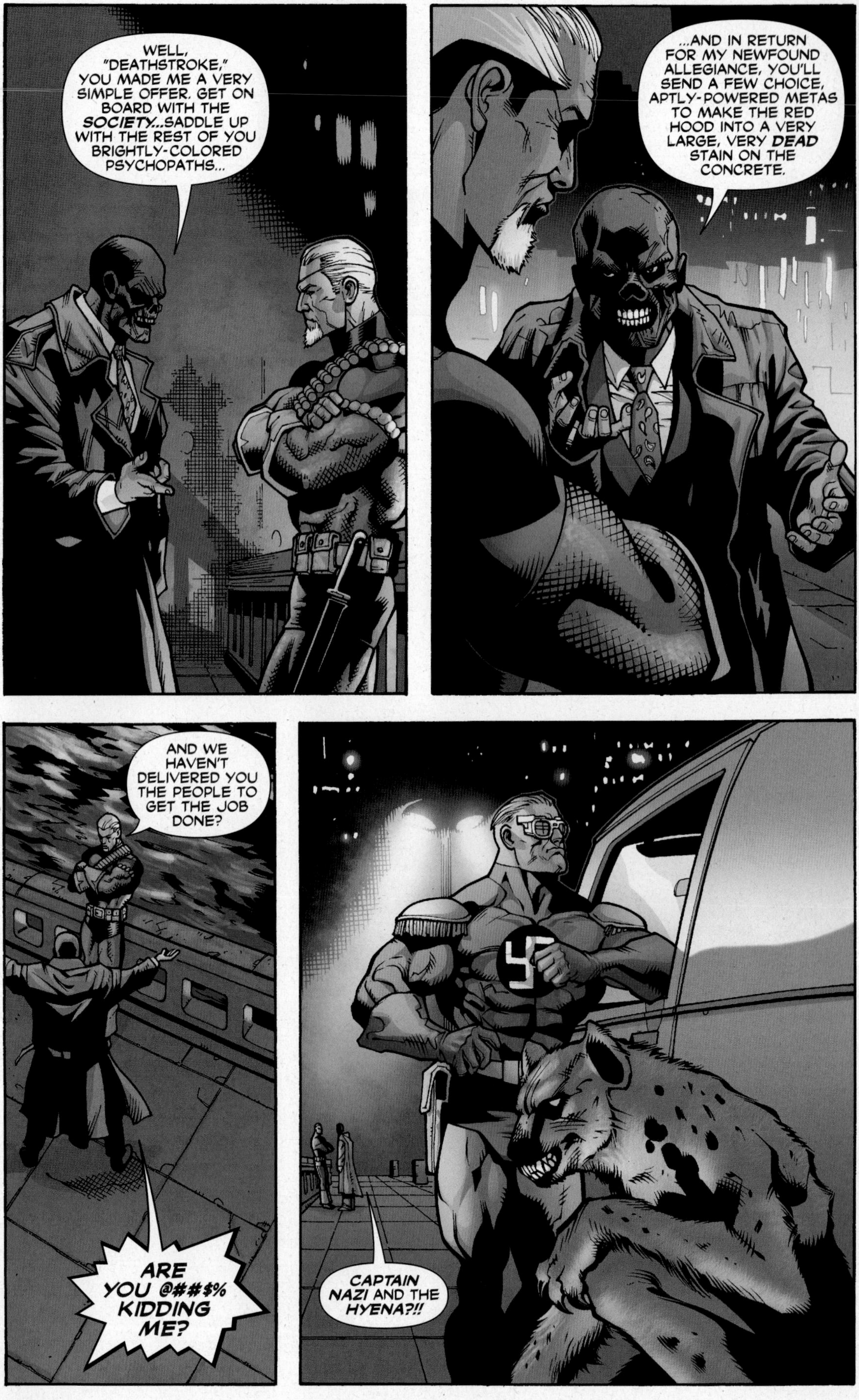
WELL, "DEATHSTROKE," YOU MADE ME A VERY SIMPLE OFFER. GET ON BOARD WITH THE SOCIETY...SADDLE UP WITH THE REST OF YOU BRIGHTLY-COLORED PSYCHOPATHS...
...AND IN RETURN FOR MY NEWFOUND ALLEGIANCE, YOU'LL SEND A FEW CHOICE, APTLY-POWERED METAS TO MAKE THE RED HOOD INTO A VERY LARGE, VERY DEAD STAIN ON THE CONCRETE.
AND WE HAVEN'T DELIVERED YOU THE PEOPLE TO GET THE JOB DONE?
ARE YOU @##$% KIDDING ME?
CAPTAIN NAZI AND THE HYENA?!!

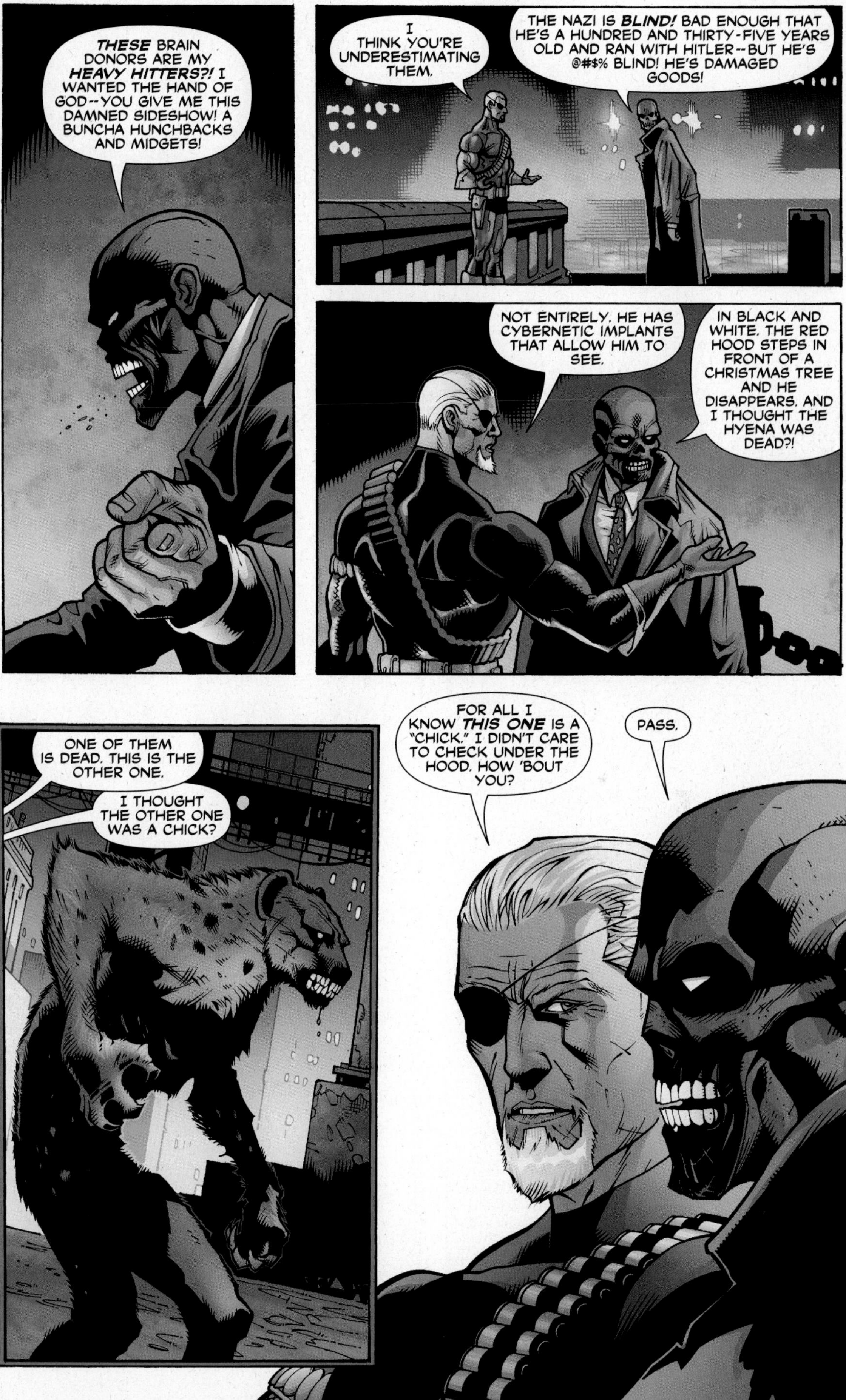
THESE BRAIN DONORS ARE MY HEAVY HITTERS?! I WANTED THE HAND OF GOD--YOU GIVE ME THIS DAMNED SIDESHOW! A BUNCHA HUNCHBACKS AND MIDGETS!
I THINK YOU'RE UNDERESTIMATING THEM.
THE NAZI IS BLIND! BAD ENOUGH THAT HE'S A HUNDRED AND THIRTY-FIVE YEARS OLD AND RAN WITH HITLER--BUT HE'S @#$% BLIND! HE'S DAMAGED GOODS!
NOT ENTIRELY. HE HAS CYBERNETIC IMPLANTS THAT ALLOW HIM TO SEE.
IN BLACK AND WHITE. THE RED HOOD STEPS IN FRONT OF A CHRISTMAS TREE AND HE DISAPPEARS. AND I THOUGHT THE HYENA WAS DEAD?!
ONE OF THEM IS DEAD. THIS IS THE OTHER ONE.
I THOUGHT THE OTHER ONE WAS A CHICK?
FOR ALL I KNOW THIS ONE IS A "CHICK." I DIDN'T CARE TO CHECK UNDER THE HOOD. HOW 'BOUT YOU?
PASS.

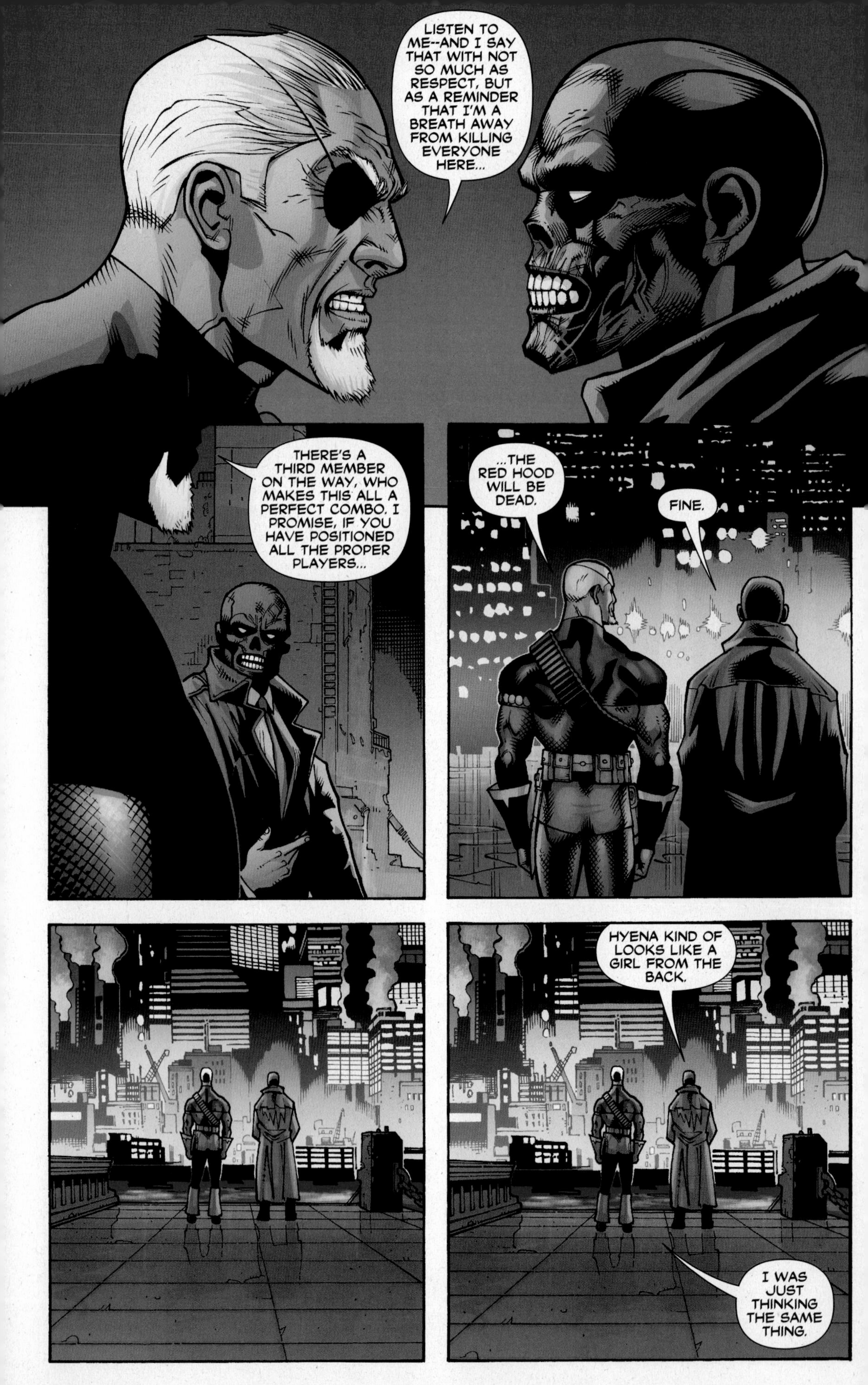
LISTEN TO ME--AND I SAY THAT WITH NOT SO MUCH AS RESPECT, BUT AS A REMINDER THAT I'M A BREATH AWAY FROM KILLING EVERYONE HERE...
THERE'S A THIRD MEMBER ON THE WAY, WHO MAKES THIS ALL A PERFECT COMBO. I PROMISE, IF YOU HAVE POSITIONED ALL THE PROPER PLAYERS...
...THE RED HOOD WILL BE DEAD.
FINE.
HYENA KIND OF LOOKS LIKE A GIRL FROM THE BACK.
I WAS JUST THINKING THE SAME THING.

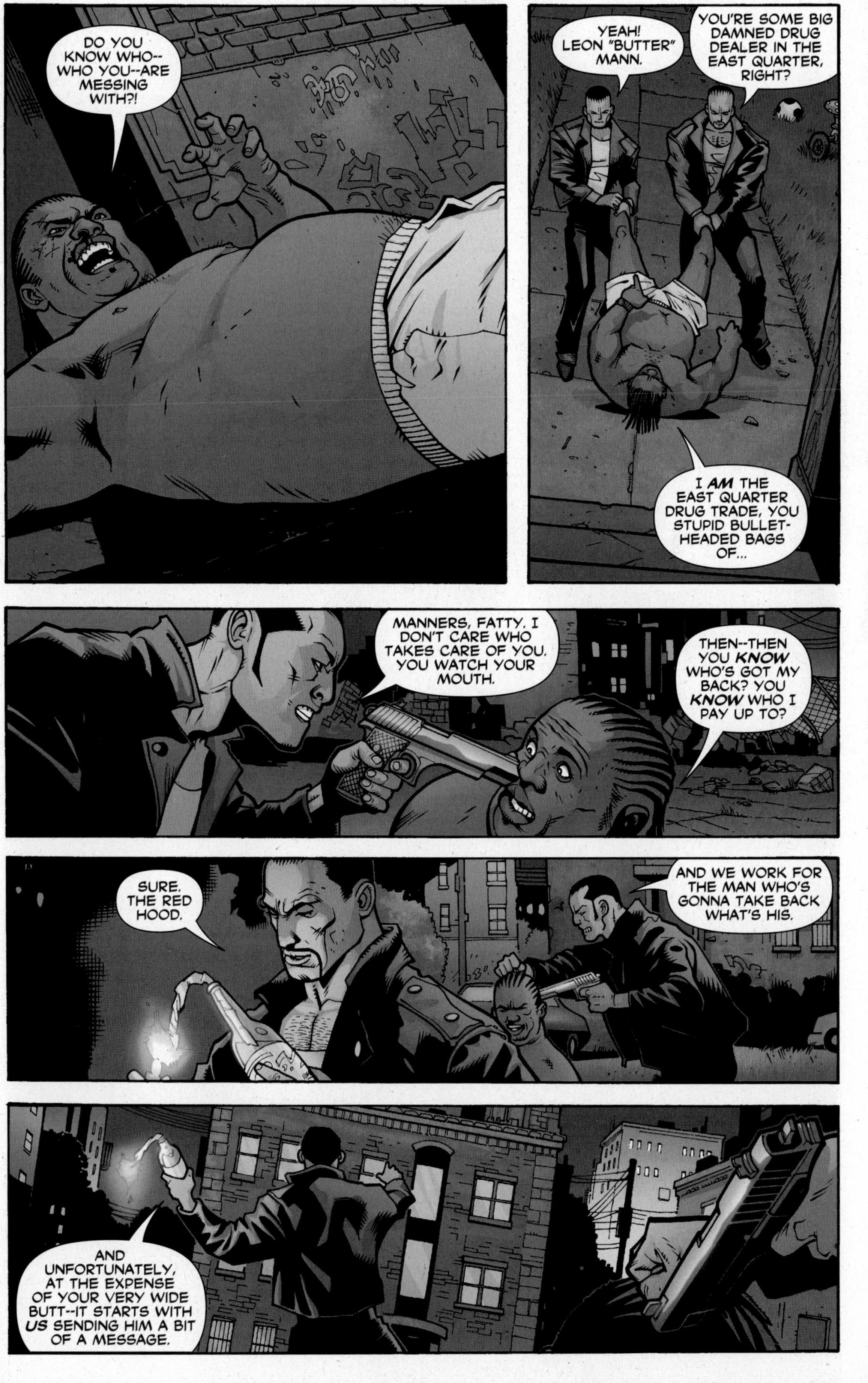
DO YOU KNOW WHO-- WHO YOU--ARE MESSING WITH?!
YEAH! LEON "BUTTER" MANN.
YOU'RE SOME BIG DAMNED DRUG DEALER IN THE EAST QUARTER, RIGHT?
I AM THE EAST QUARTER DRUG TRADE, YOU STUPID BULLET-HEADED BAGS OF...
MANNERS, FATTY. I DON'T CARE WHO TAKES CARE OF YOU. YOU WATCH YOUR MOUTH.
THEN--THEN YOU KNOW WHO'S GOT MY BACK? YOU KNOW WHO I PAY UP TO?
SURE. THE RED HOOD.
AND WE WORK FOR THE MAN WHO'S GONNA TAKE BACK WHAT'S HIS.
AND UNFORTUNATELY, AT THE EXPENSE OF YOUR VERY WIDE BUTT--IT STARTS WITH US SENDING HIM A BIT OF A MESSAGE.

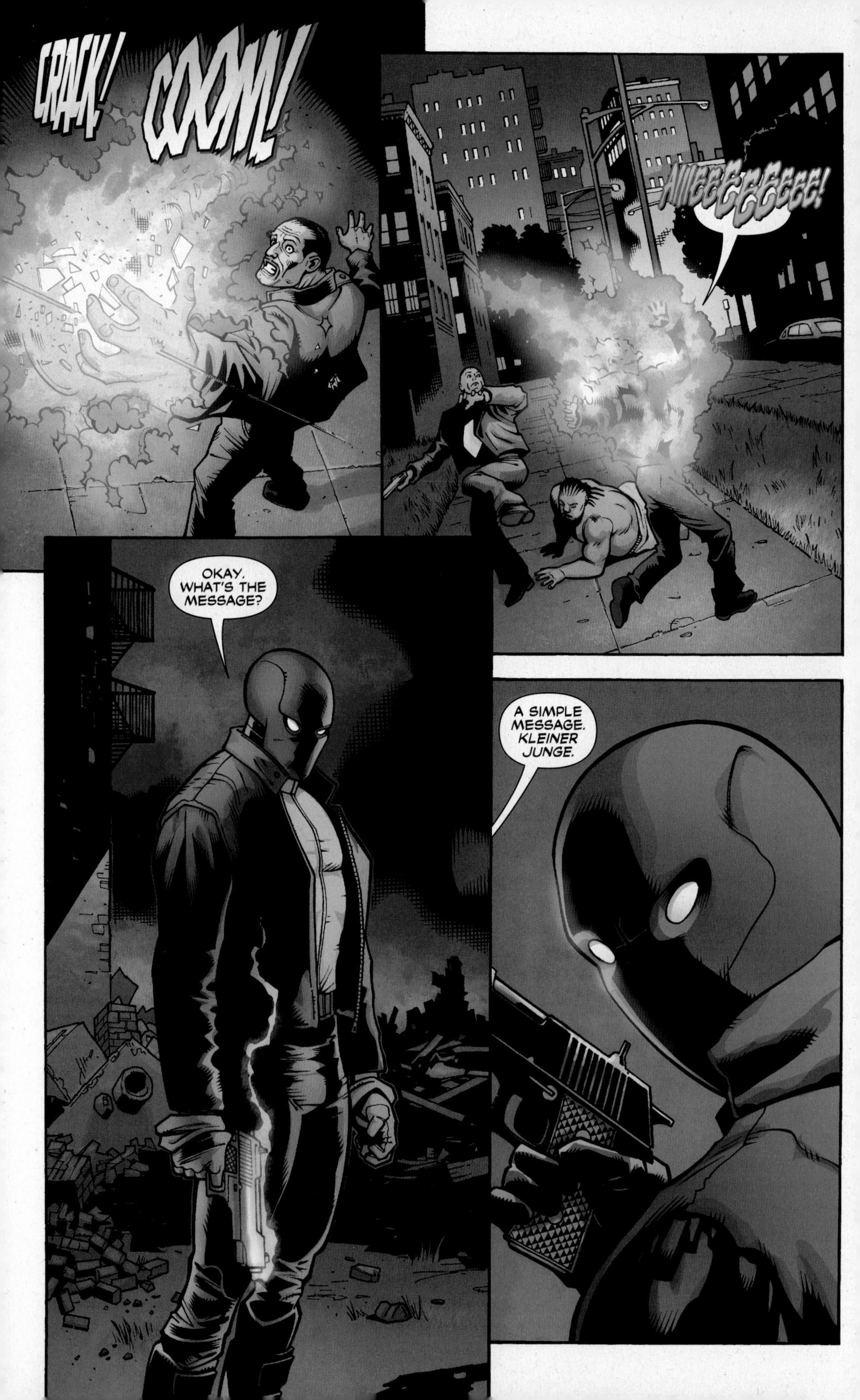
CRACK! COOM!
AIIIEEEEEEEeee!
OKAY. WHAT'S THE MESSAGE?
A SIMPLE MESSAGE. KLEINER JUNGE.

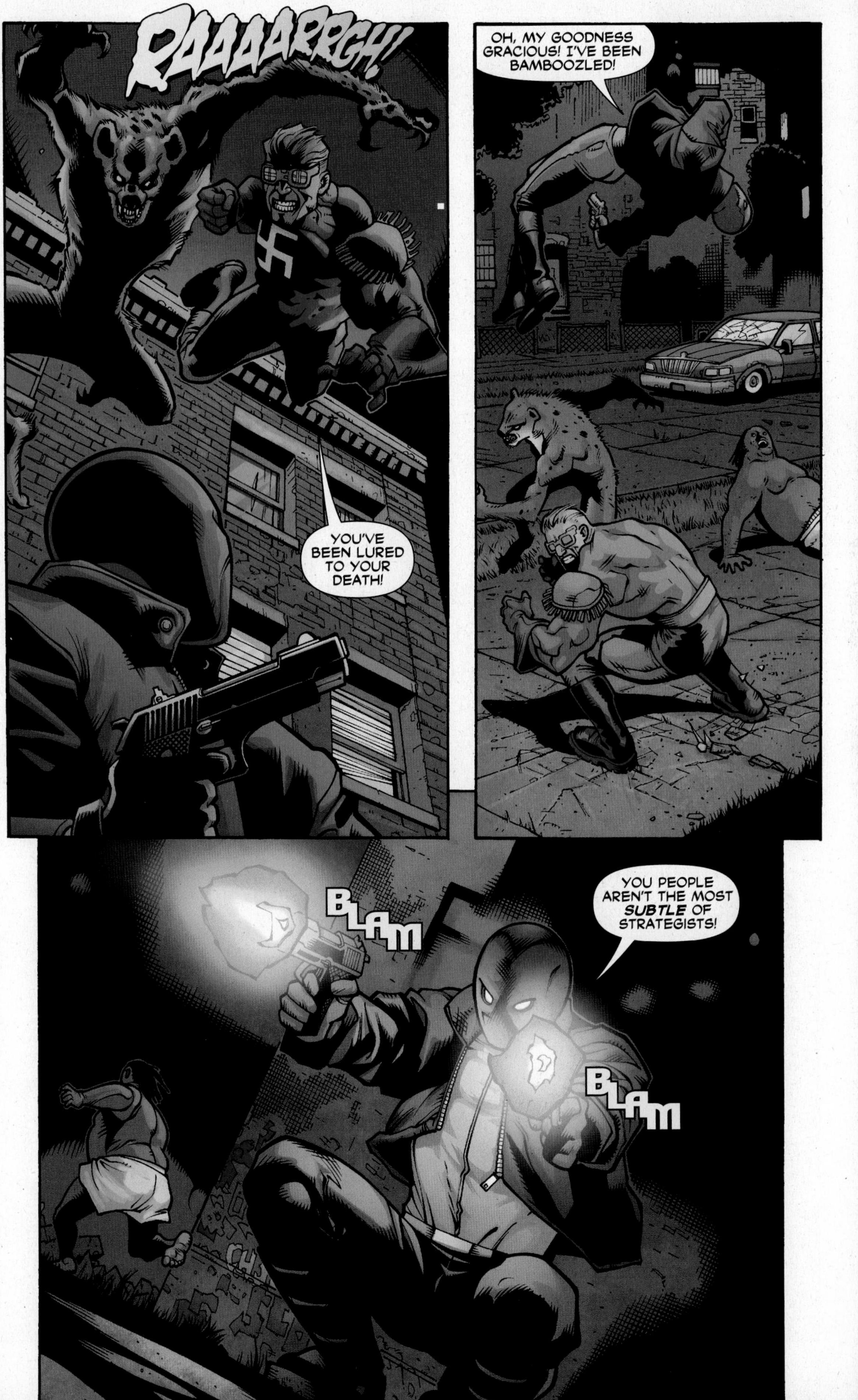
RAAAARRGH!!
YOU'VE BEEN LURED TO YOUR DEATH!
OH, MY GOODNESS GRACIOUS! I'VE BEEN BAMBOOZLED!
BLAM
YOU PEOPLE AREN'T THE MOST SUBTLE OF STRATEGISTS!
BLAM

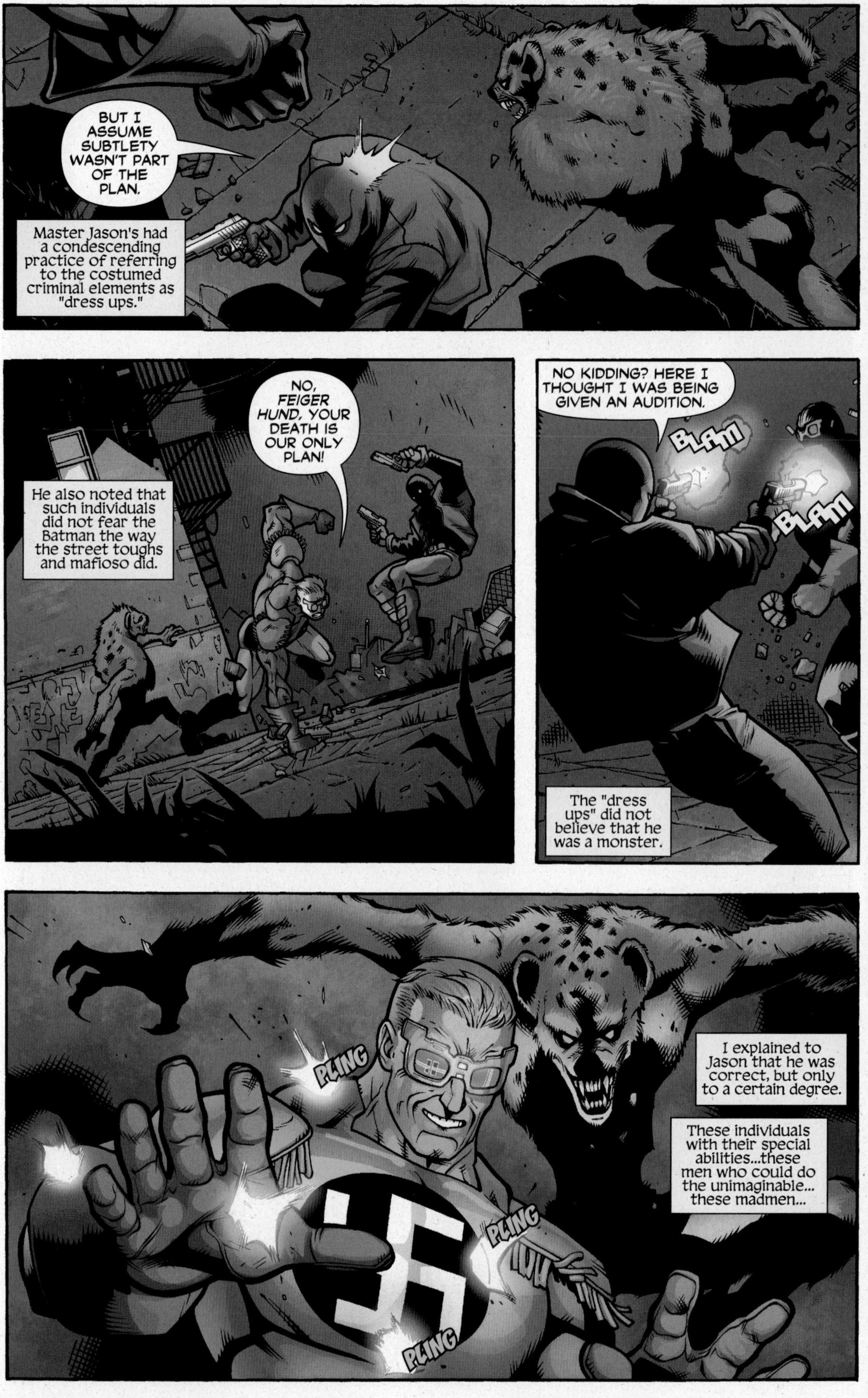
BUT I ASSUME SUBTLETY WASN'T PART OF THE PLAN.
Master Jason's had a condescending practice of referring to the costumed criminal elements as "dress ups."
He also noted that such individuals did not fear the Batman the way the street toughs and mafioso did.
NO, FEIGER HUND, YOUR DEATH IS OUR ONLY PLAN!
NO KIDDING? HERE I THOUGHT I WAS BEING GIVEN AN AUDITION.
BLAM
BLAM
The "dress ups" did not believe that he was a monster.
PLING
I explained to Jason that he was correct, but only to a certain degree.
These individuals with their special abilities...these men who could do the unimaginable... these madmen...
PLING
PLING

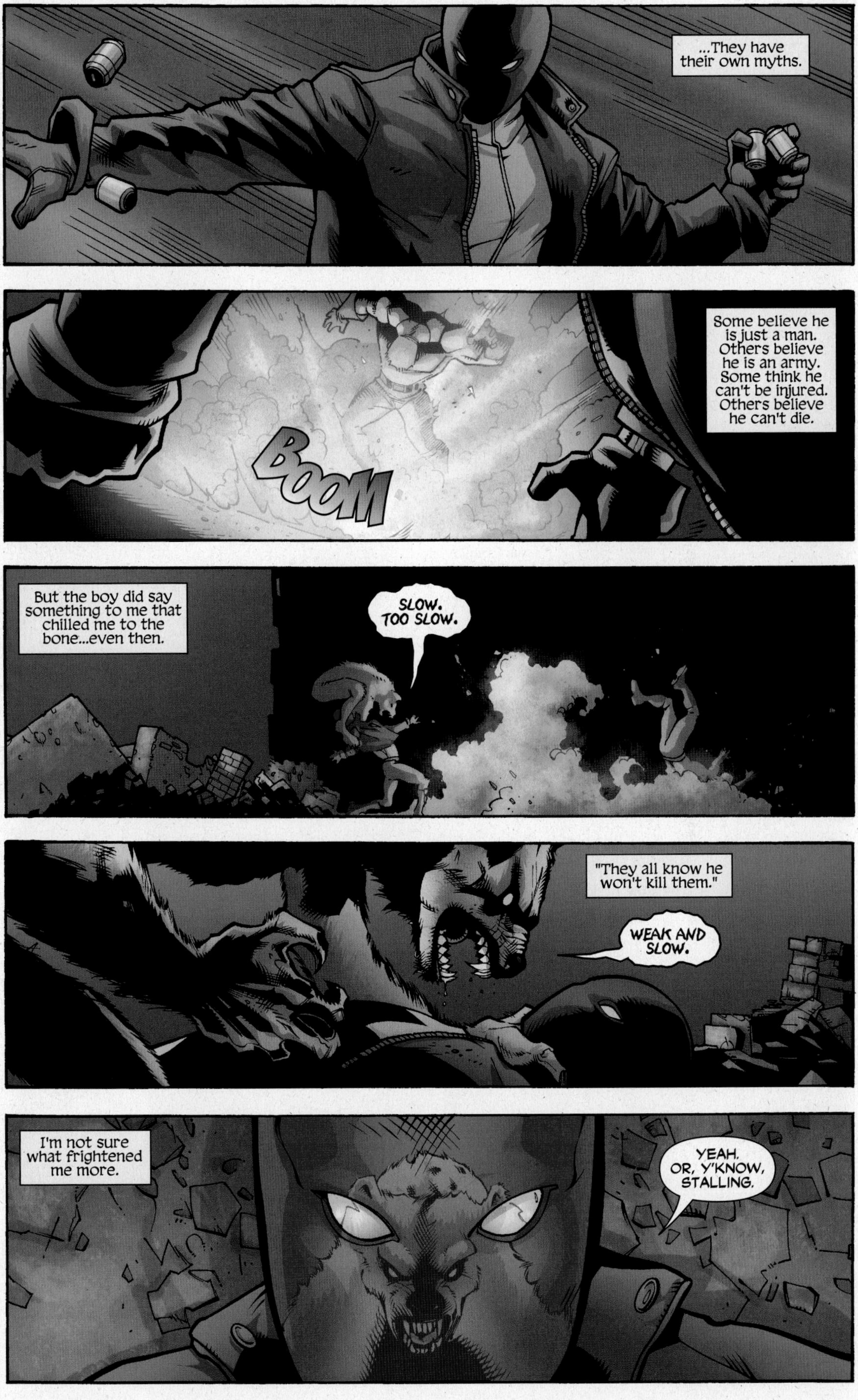
...They have their own myths.
Some believe he is just a man. Others believe he is an army. Some think he can't be injured. Others believe he can't die.
BOOM
But the boy did say something to me that chilled me to the bone...even then.
SLOW. TOO SLOW.
"They all know he won't kill them."
WEAK AND SLOW.
I'm not sure what frightened me more.
YEAH. OR, Y'KNOW, STALLING.

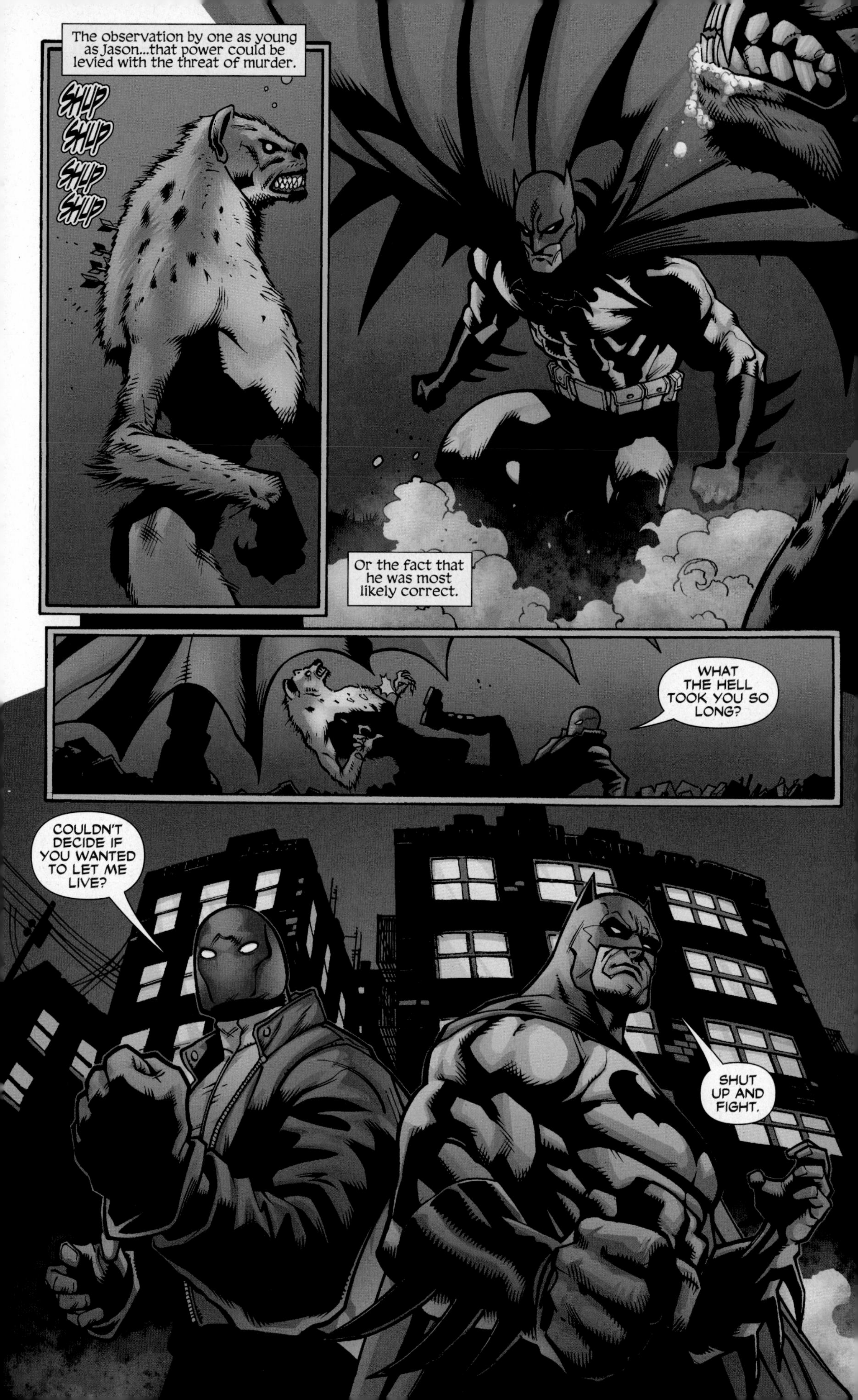
The observation by one as young as Jason...that power could be levied with the threat of murder.
SHLIP SHLIP SHLIP SHLIP
Or the fact that he was most likely correct.
WHAT THE HELL TOOK YOU SO LONG?
COULDN'T DECIDE IF YOU WANTED TO LET ME LIVE?
SHUT UP AND FIGHT.

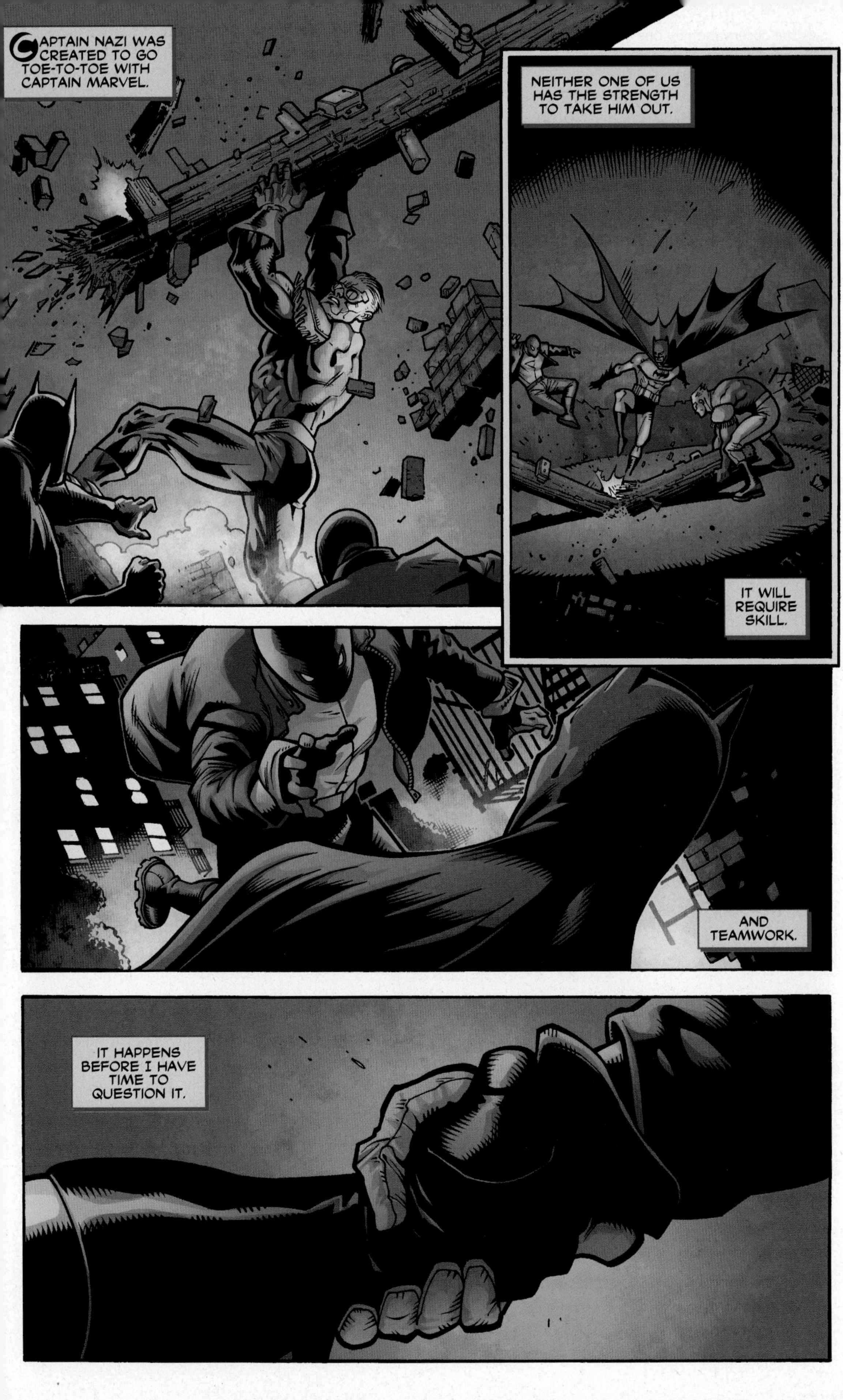
CAPTAIN NAZI WAS CREATED TO GO TOE-TO-TOE WITH CAPTAIN MARVEL.
NEITHER ONE OF US HAS THE STRENGTH TO TAKE HIM OUT.
IT WILL REQUIRE SKILL.
AND TEAMWORK.
IT HAPPENS BEFORE I HAVE TIME TO QUESTION IT.

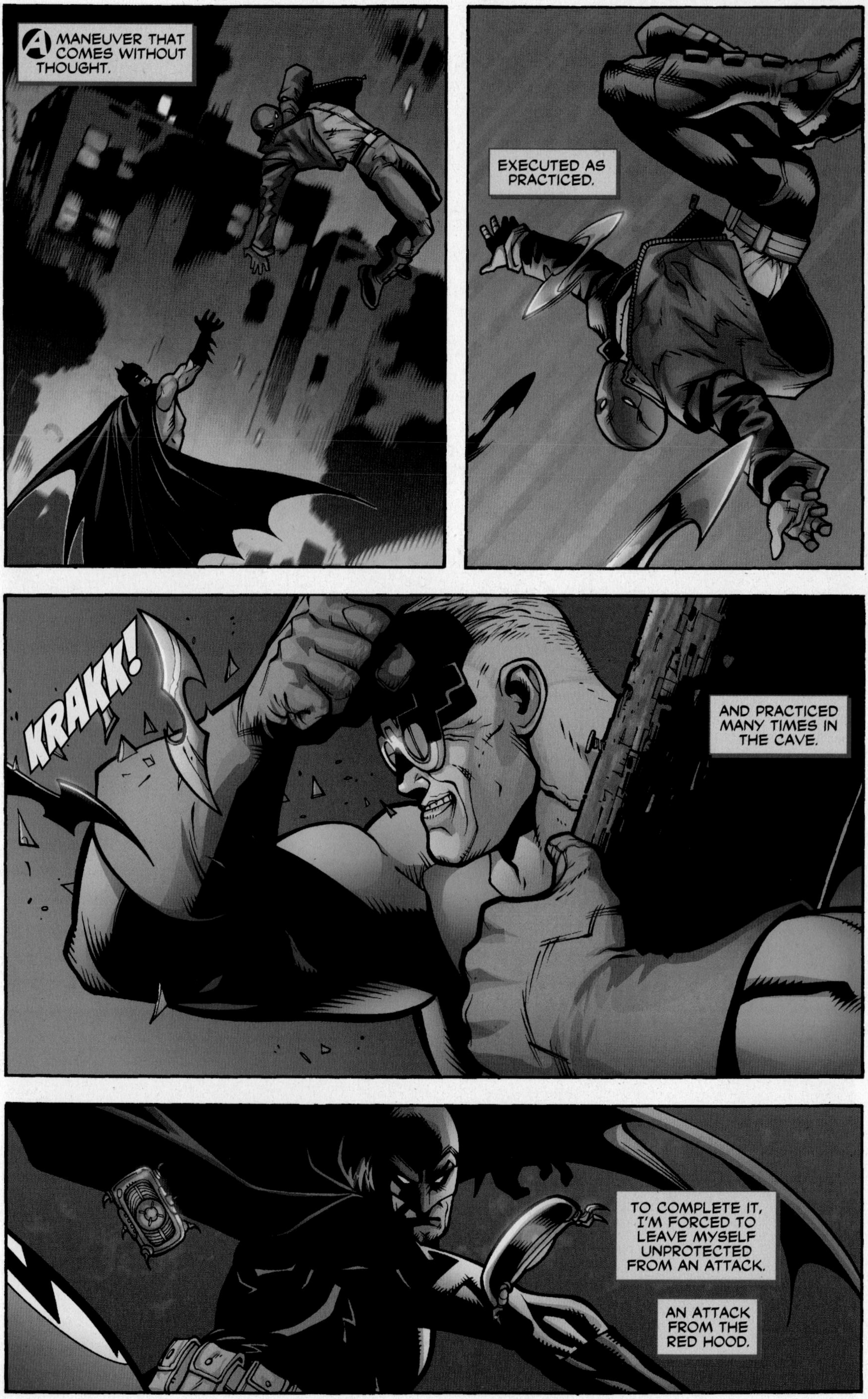
A MANEUVER THAT COMES WITHOUT THOUGHT.
EXECUTED AS PRACTICED.
KRAKK!
AND PRACTICED MANY TIMES IN THE CAVE.
TO COMPLETE IT, I'M FORCED TO LEAVE MYSELF UNPROTECTED FROM AN ATTACK.
AN ATTACK FROM THE RED HOOD.

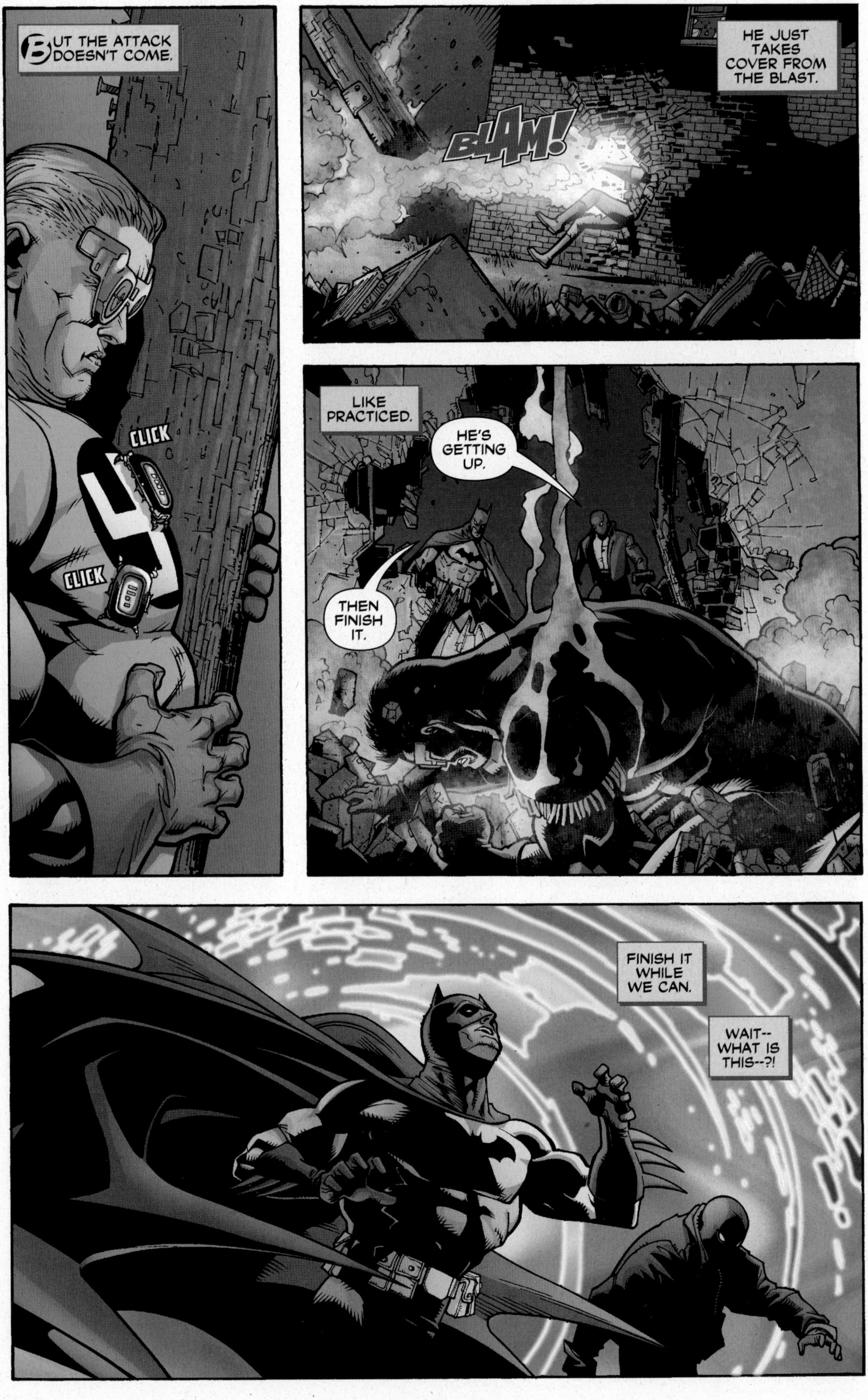
BUT THE ATTACK DOESN'T COME.
CLICK
CLICK
HE JUST TAKES COVER FROM THE BLAST.
BLAM!
LIKE PRACTICED.
HE'S GETTING UP.
THEN FINISH IT.
FINISH IT WHILE WE CAN.
WAIT-- WHAT IS THIS--?!

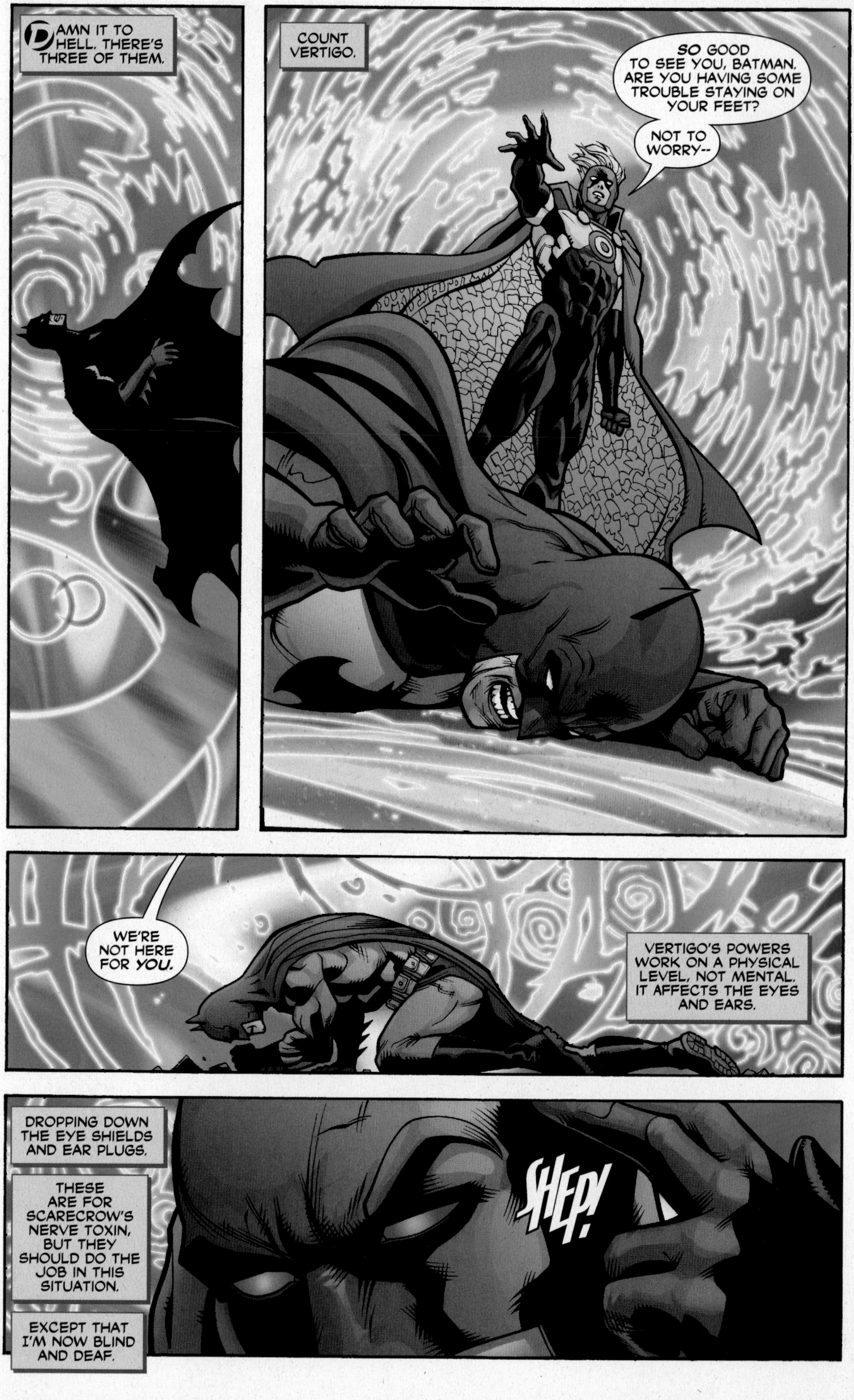
DAMN IT TO HELL. THERE'S THREE OF THEM.
COUNT VERTIGO.
SO GOOD TO SEE YOU, BATMAN. ARE YOU HAVING SOME TROUBLE STAYING ON YOUR FEET?
NOT TO WORRY--
WE'RE NOT HERE FOR YOU.
VERTIGO'S POWERS WORK ON A PHYSICAL LEVEL, NOT MENTAL. IT AFFECTS THE EYES AND EARS.
DROPPING DOWN THE EYE SHIELDS AND EAR PLUGS.
THESE ARE FOR SCARECROW'S NERVE TOXIN, BUT THEY SHOULD DO THE JOB IN THIS SITUATION.
SHEP!
EXCEPT THAT I'M NOW BLIND AND DEAF.

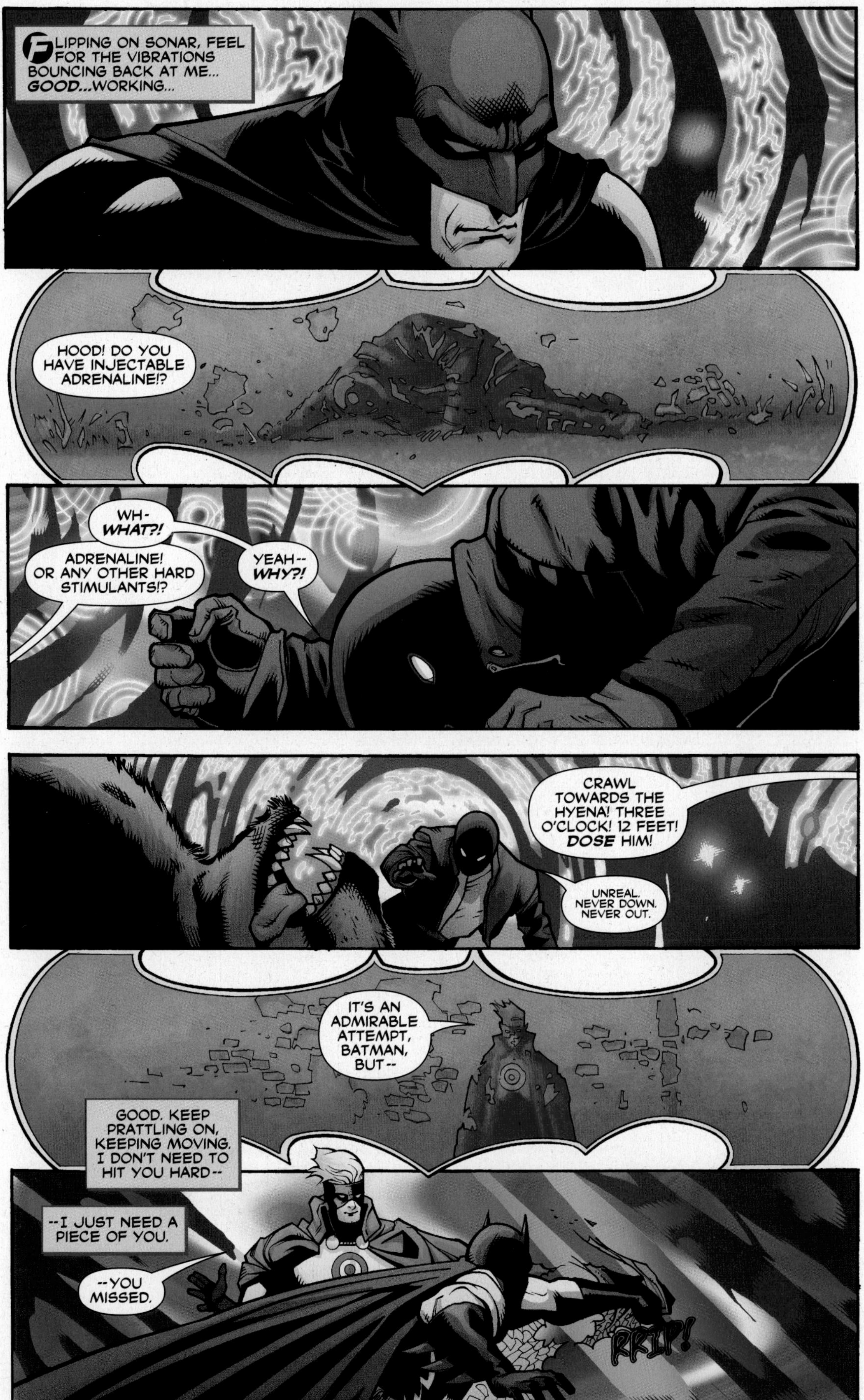
FLIPPING ON SONAR, FEEL FOR THE VIBRATIONS BOUNCING BACK AT ME... GOOD...WORKING...
HOOD! DO YOU HAVE INJECTABLE ADRENALINE!?
WH- WHAT?!
ADRENALINE! OR ANY OTHER HARD STIMULANTS!?
YEAH-- WHY?!
CRAWL TOWARDS THE HYENA! THREE O'CLOCK! 12 FEET! DOSE HIM!
UNREAL. NEVER DOWN. NEVER OUT.
IT'S AN ADMIRABLE ATTEMPT, BATMAN, BUT--
GOOD. KEEP PRATTLING ON, KEEPING MOVING. I DON'T NEED TO HIT YOU HARD--
--I JUST NEED A PIECE OF YOU.
--YOU MISSED.
RRIP!

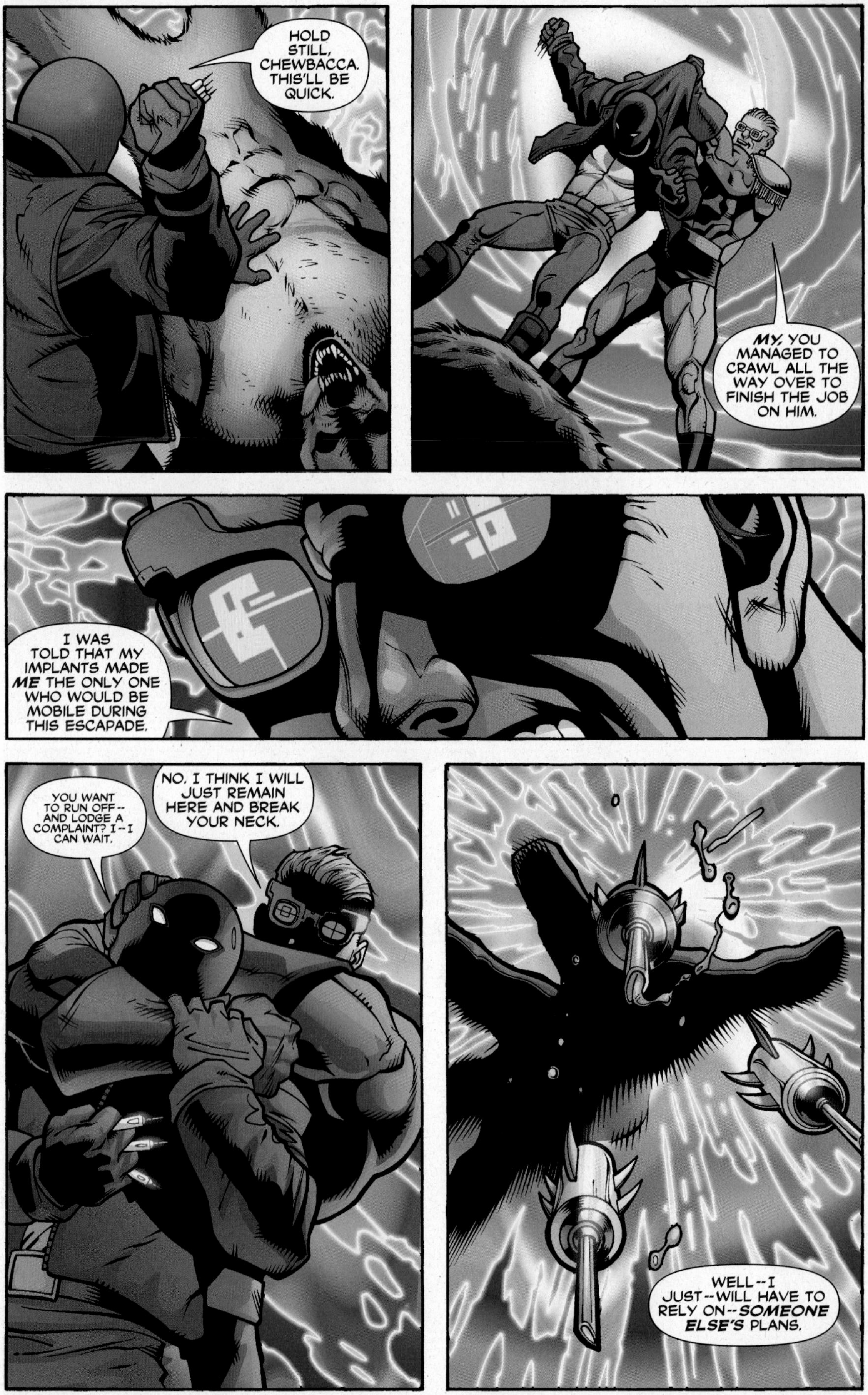
HOLD STILL, CHEWBACCA. THIS'LL BE QUICK.
MY, YOU MANAGED TO CRAWL ALL THE WAY OVER TO FINISH THE JOB ON HIM.
I WAS TOLD THAT MY IMPLANTS MADE ME THE ONLY ONE WHO WOULD BE MOBILE DURING THIS ESCAPADE.
YOU WANT TO RUN OFF-- AND LODGE A COMPLAINT? I--I CAN WAIT.
NO. I THINK I WILL JUST REMAIN HERE AND BREAK YOUR NECK.
WELL--I JUST--WILL HAVE TO RELY ON--SOMEONE ELSE'S PLANS.

SHUP!

WELL DONE, JASON. HYENA IS LITTLE MORE THAN A RABID DOG.

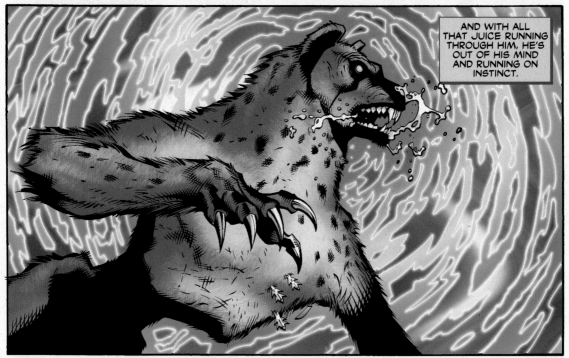

AND WITH ALL THAT JUICE RUNNING THROUGH HIM, HE'S OUT OF HIS MIND AND RUNNING ON INSTINCT.

LET'S SEE WHAT HAPPENS WHEN WE GIVE HIM A FEW VERY PAINFUL BLOWS--

--WRAPPED IN COUNT VERTIGO'S SCENT.

RAAAARGH!

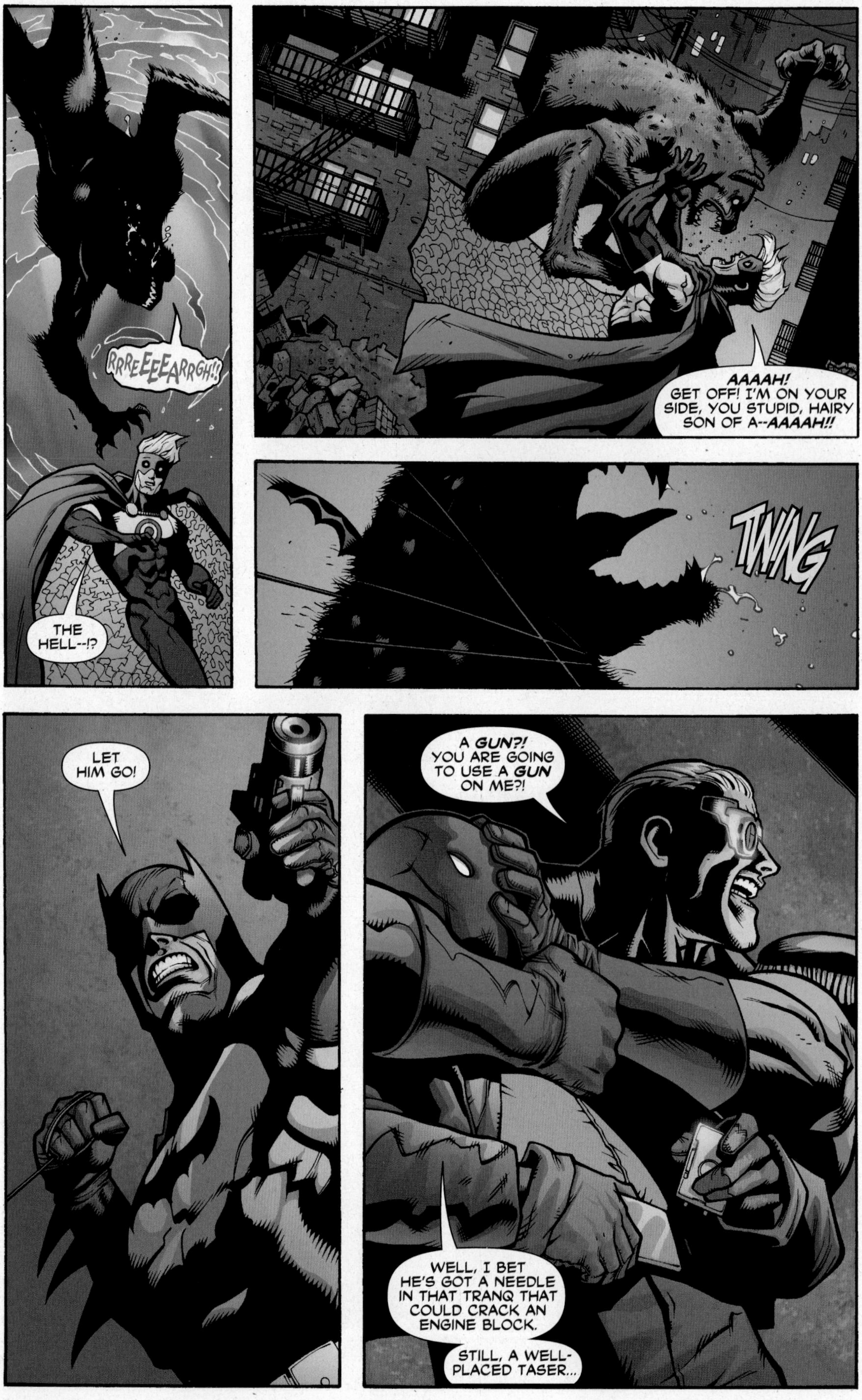
RRREEEEARRGH!!
THE HELL--!?
AAAAH! GET OFF! I'M ON YOUR SIDE, YOU STUPID, HAIRY SON OF A--AAAAH!!
TWING
LET HIM GO!
A GUN?! YOU ARE GOING TO USE A GUN ON ME?!
WELL, I BET HE'S GOT A NEEDLE IN THAT TRANQ THAT COULD CRACK AN ENGINE BLOCK.
STILL, A WELL-PLACED TASER...

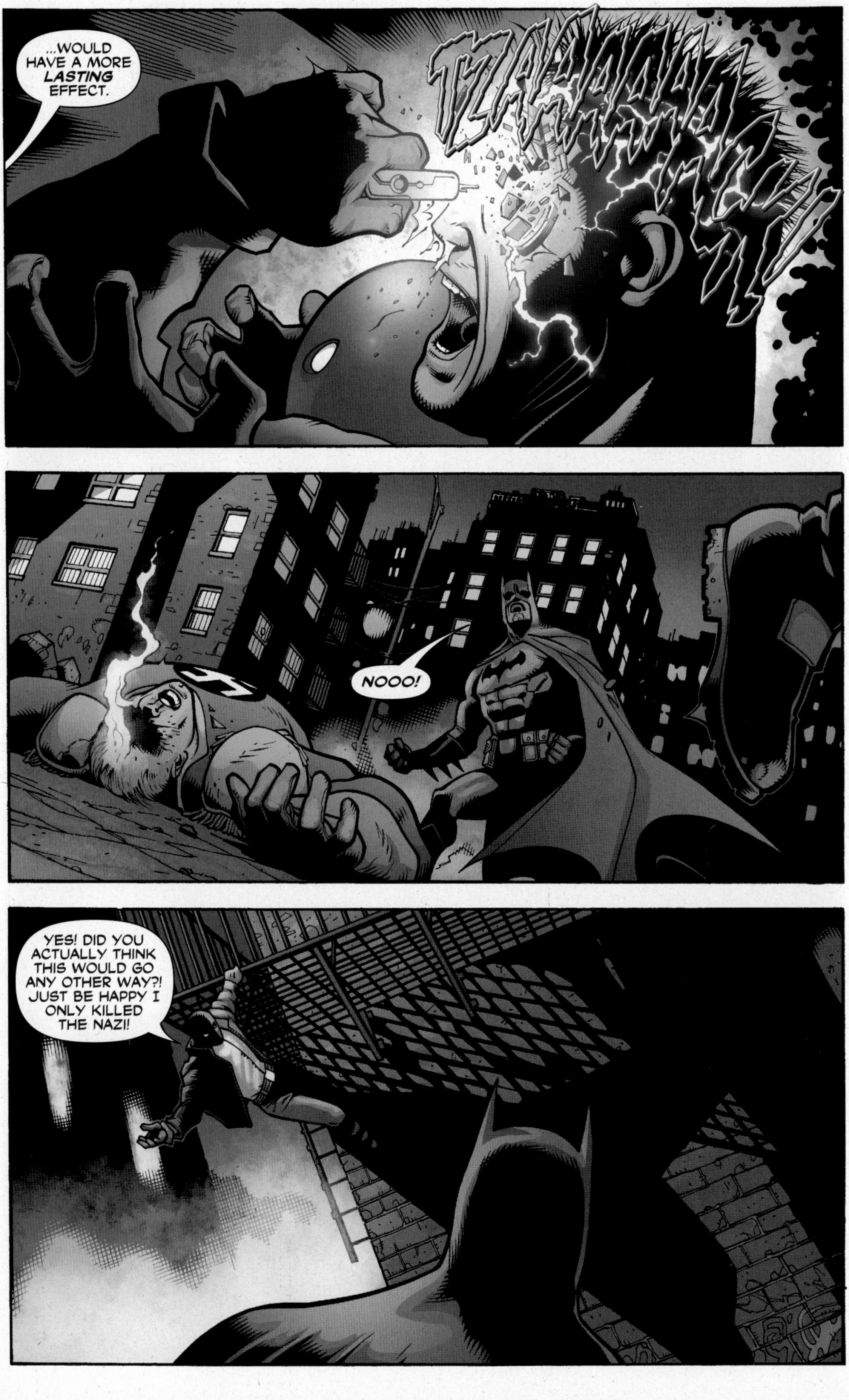
...WOULD HAVE A MORE *LASTING* EFFECT.
NOOO!
YES! DID YOU ACTUALLY THINK THIS WOULD GO ANY OTHER WAY?! JUST BE HAPPY I ONLY KILLED THE NAZI!

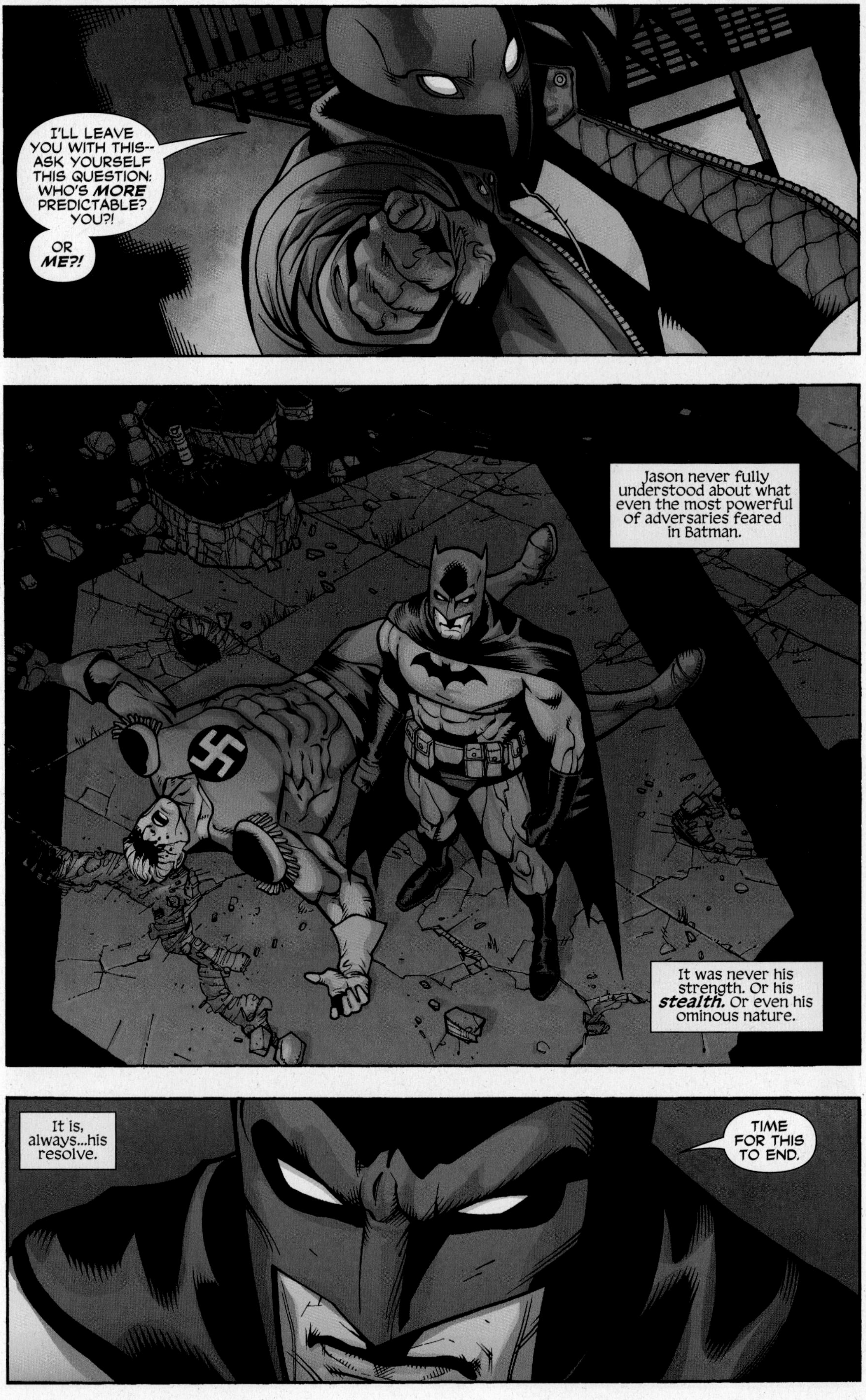
I'LL LEAVE YOU WITH THIS-- ASK YOURSELF THIS QUESTION: WHO'S MORE PREDICTABLE? YOU?!
OR ME?!
Jason never fully understood about what even the most powerful of adversaries feared in Batman.
It was never his strength. Or his stealth. Or even his ominous nature.
It is, always...his resolve.
TIME FOR THIS TO END.

BATMAN 648 Cover by Jock

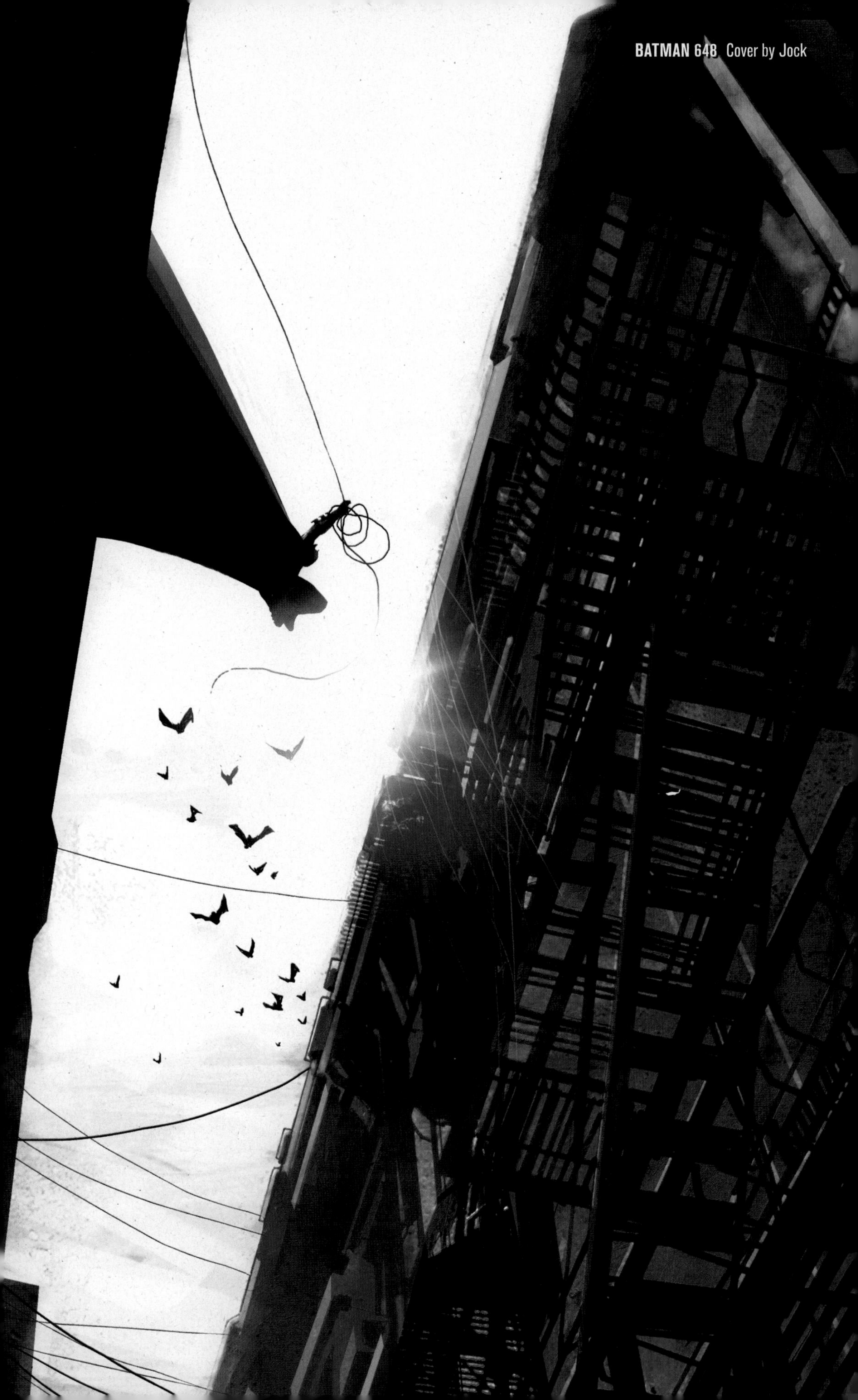

CHAPTER 11

ALL THEY DO IS WATCH US KILL

PART ONE

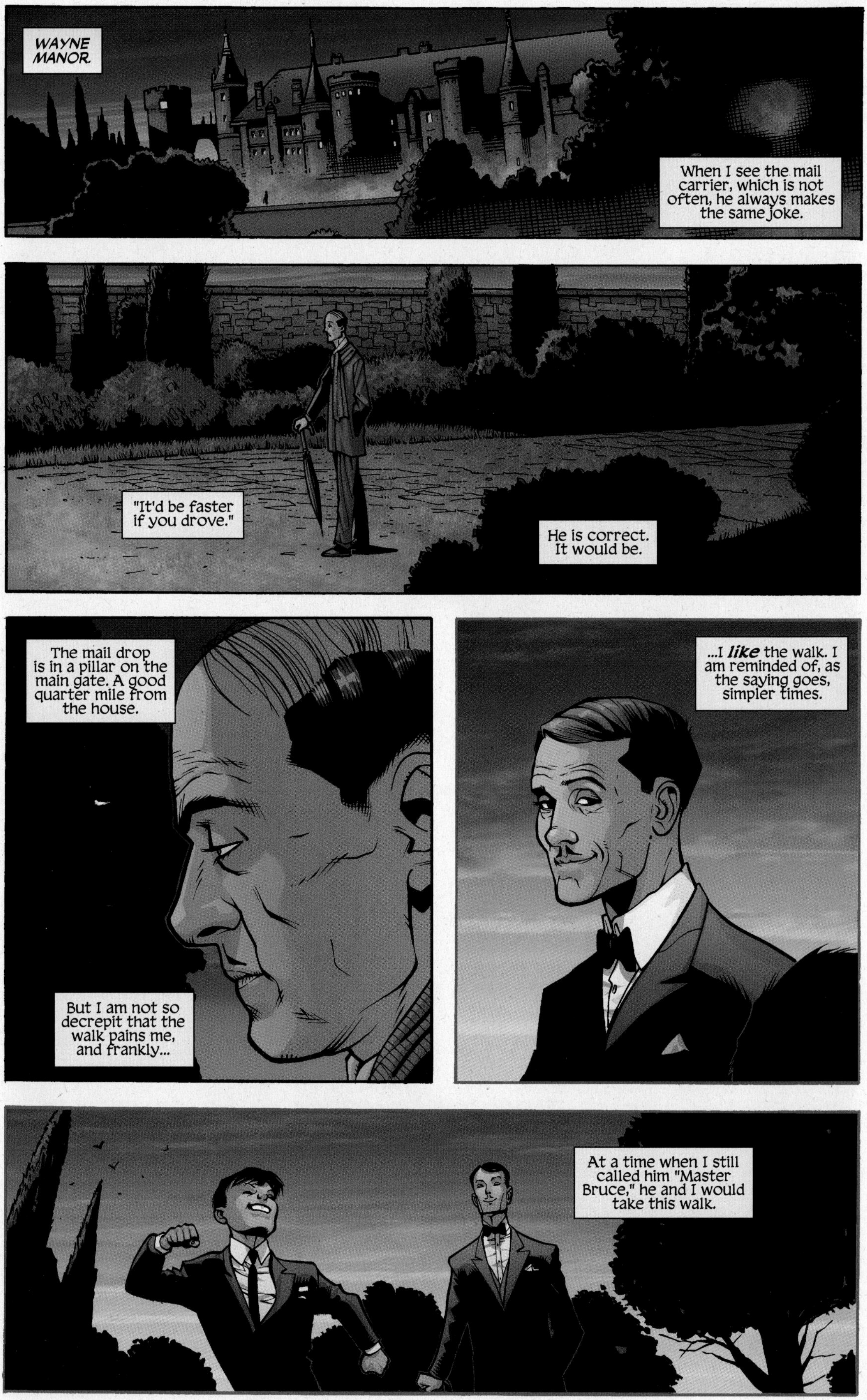
WAYNE MANOR.
When I see the mail carrier, which is not often, he always makes the same joke.
"It'd be faster if you drove."
He is correct. It would be.
The mail drop is in a pillar on the main gate. A good quarter mile from the house.
But I am not so decrepit that the walk pains me, and frankly...
...I *like* the walk. I am reminded of, as the saying goes, simpler times.
At a time when I still called him "Master Bruce," he and I would take this walk.

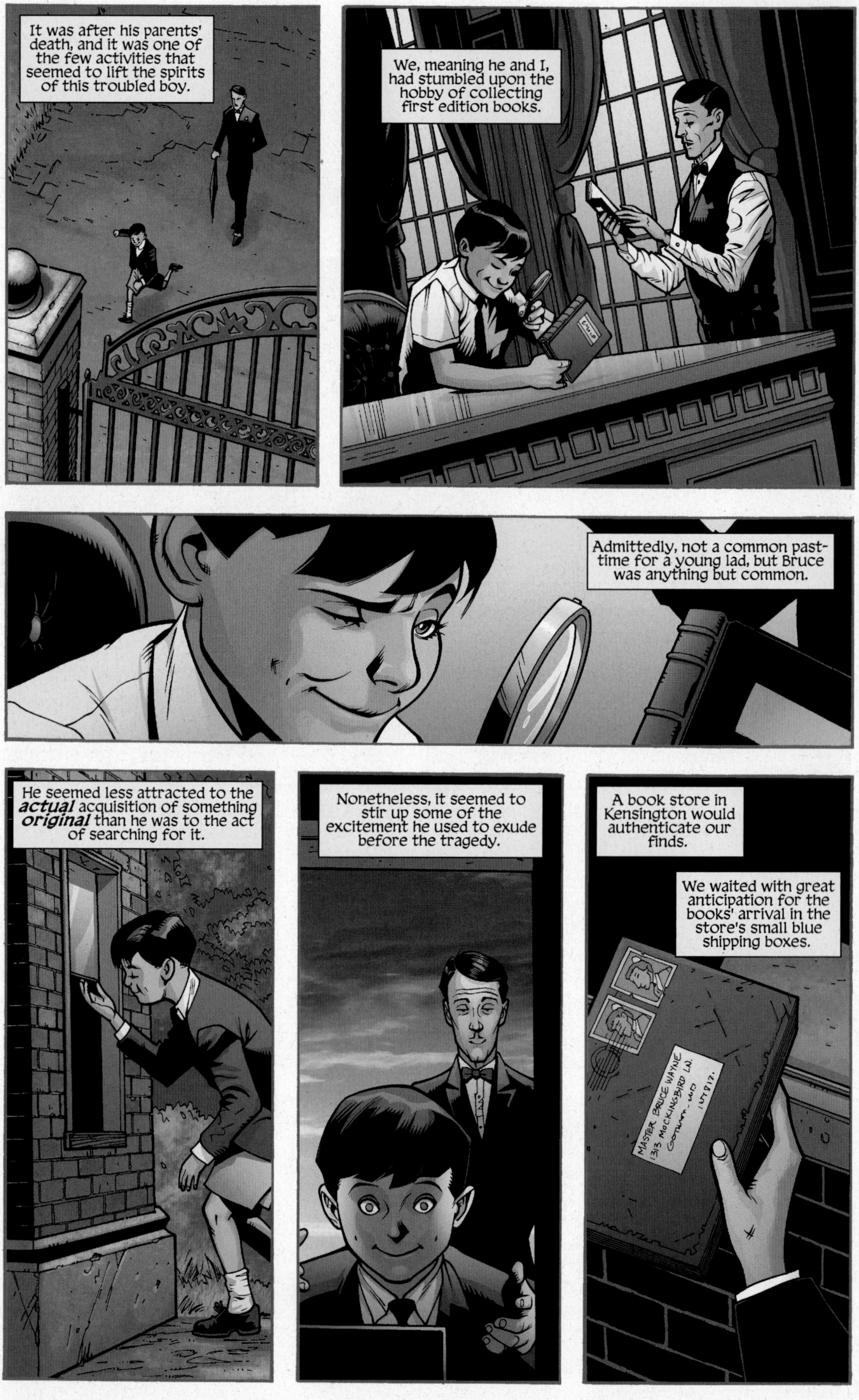
It was after his parents' death, and it was one of the few activities that seemed to lift the spirits of this troubled boy.
We, meaning he and I, had stumbled upon the hobby of collecting first edition books.
Admittedly, not a common past-time for a young lad, but Bruce was anything but common.
He seemed less attracted to the *actual* acquisition of something *original* than he was to the act of searching for it.
Nonetheless, it seemed to stir up some of the excitement he used to exude before the tragedy.
A book store in Kensington would authenticate our finds.
We waited with great anticipation for the books' arrival in the store's small blue shipping boxes.
MASTER BRUCE WAYNE
1313 MOCKINGBIRD LN.

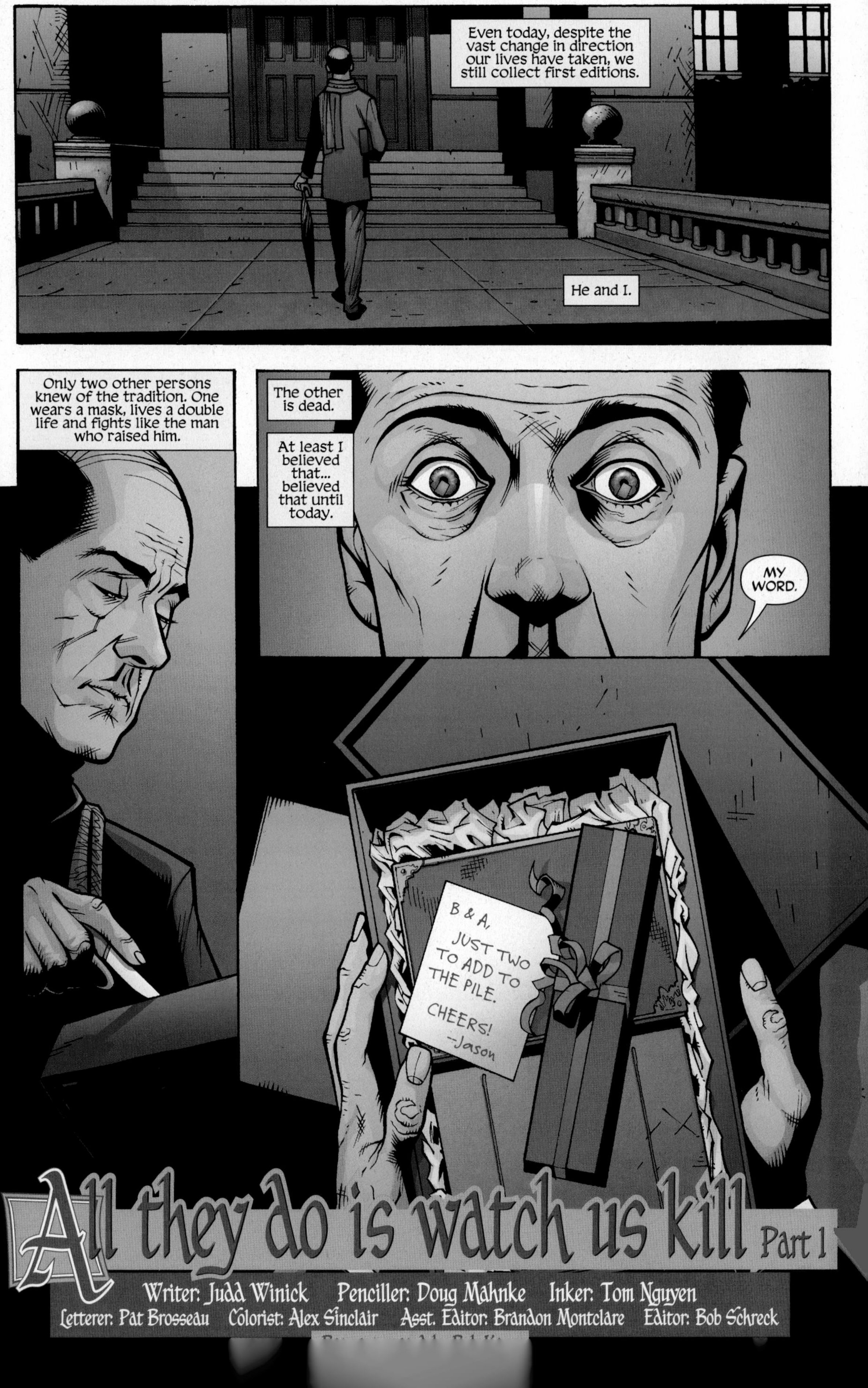
Even today, despite the vast change in direction our lives have taken, we still collect first editions.
He and I.
Only two other persons knew of the tradition. One wears a mask, lives a double life and fights like the man who raised him.
The other is dead.
At least I believed that... believed that until today.
MY WORD.
B & A, JUST TWO TO ADD TO THE PILE. CHEERS! -Jason
All they do is watch us kill Part 1
Writer: Judd Winick Penciller: Doug Mahnke Inker: Tom Nguyen
Letterer: Pat Brosseau Colorist: Alex Sinclair Asst. Editor: Brandon Montclare Editor: Bob Schreck

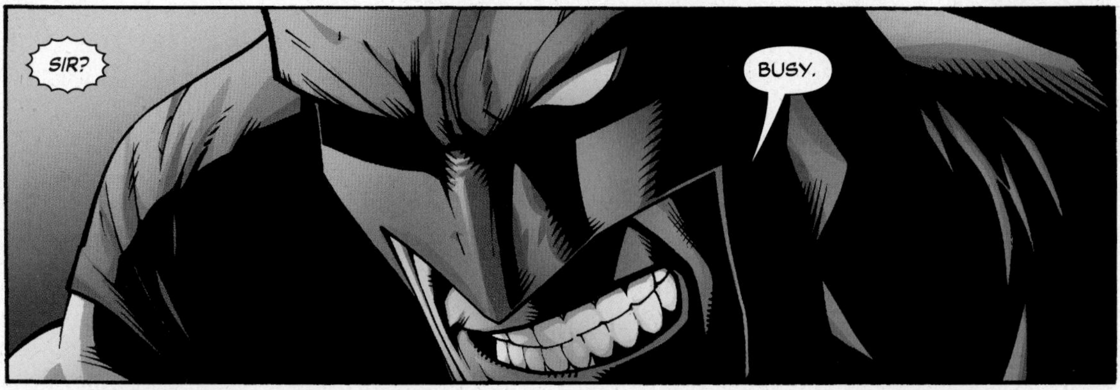
SIR?
BUSY.

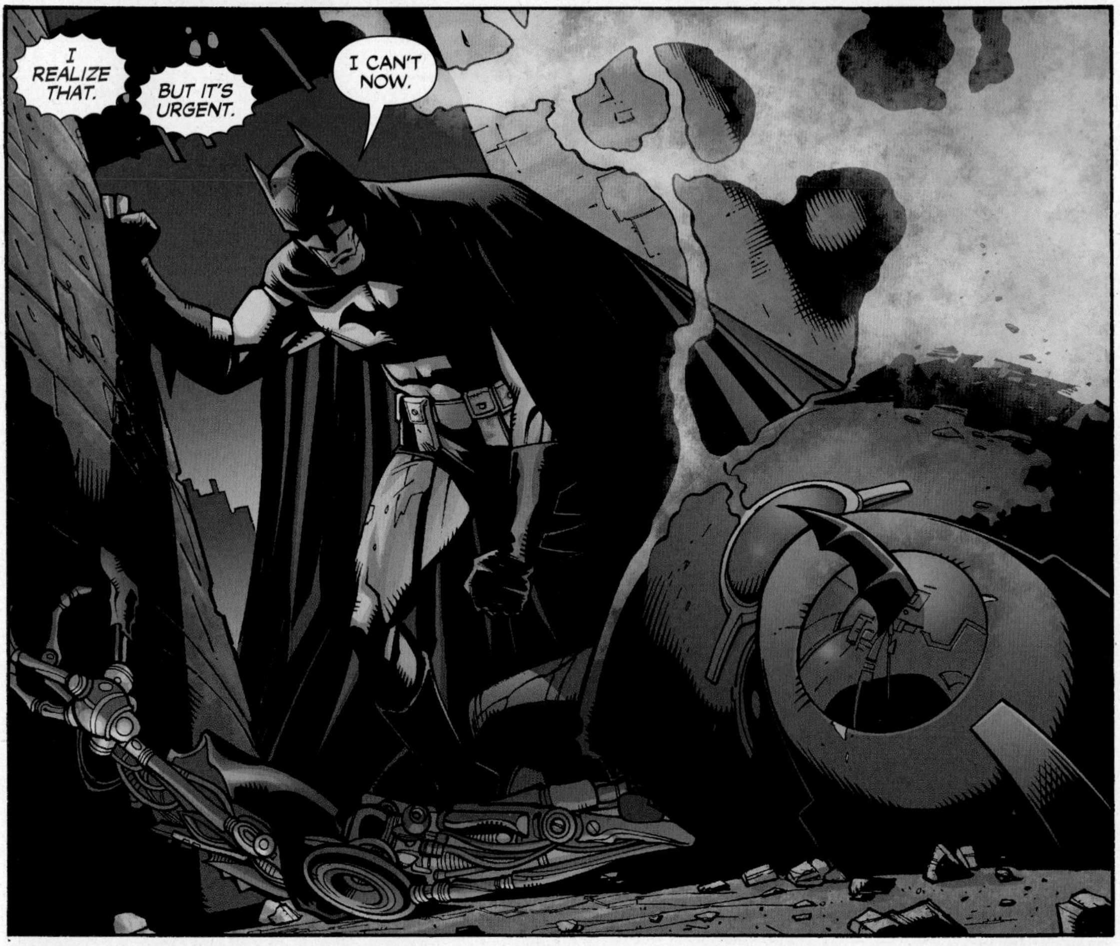
I REALIZE THAT.
BUT IT'S URGENT.
I CAN'T NOW.

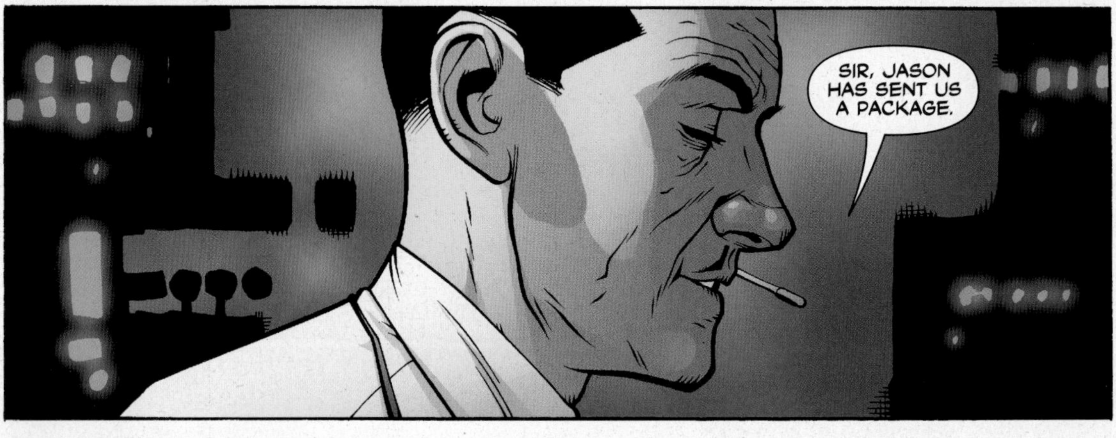
SIR, JASON HAS SENT US A PACKAGE.

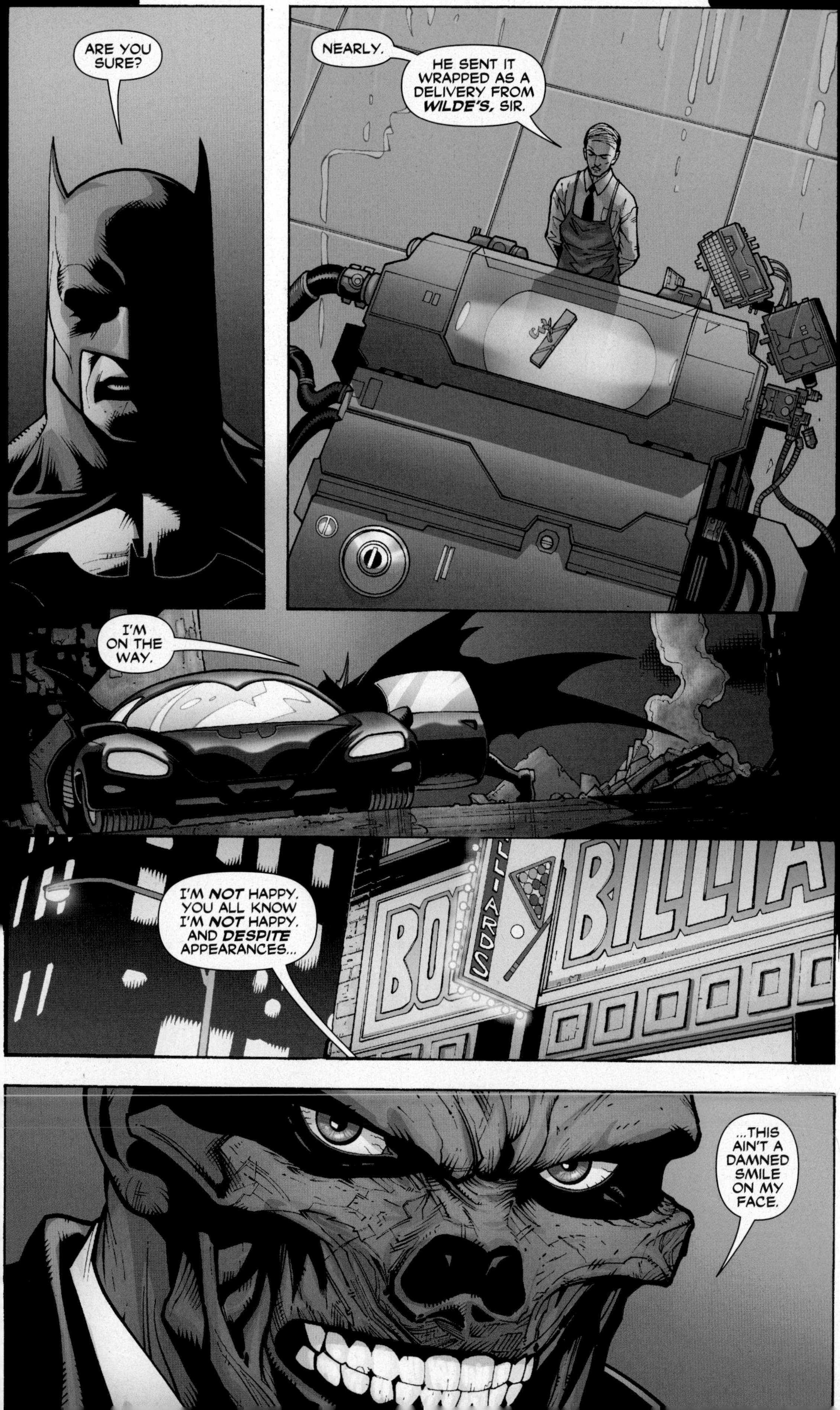
ARE YOU SURE?
NEARLY.
HE SENT IT WRAPPED AS A DELIVERY FROM *WILDE'S,* SIR.
I'M ON THE WAY.
BILLIARDS
I'M *NOT* HAPPY. YOU ALL KNOW I'M *NOT* HAPPY. AND *DESPITE* APPEARANCES...
...THIS AIN'T A DAMNED SMILE ON MY FACE.

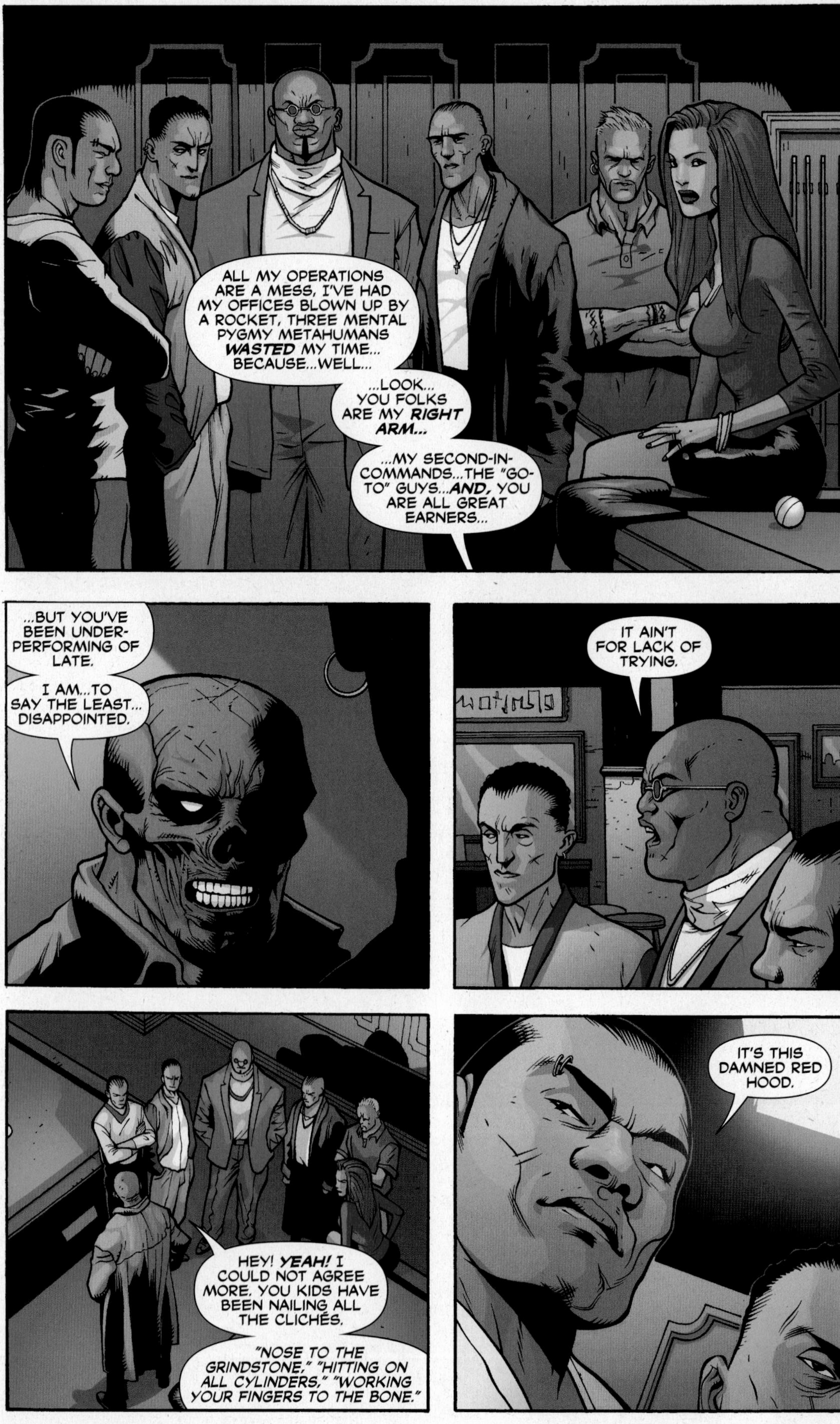
ALL MY OPERATIONS ARE A MESS, I'VE HAD MY OFFICES BLOWN UP BY A ROCKET, THREE MENTAL PYGMY METAHUMANS **WASTED** MY TIME... BECAUSE...WELL...
...LOOK... YOU FOLKS ARE MY **RIGHT ARM...**
...MY SECOND-IN-COMMANDS...THE "GO-TO" GUYS...**AND,** YOU ARE ALL GREAT EARNERS...
...BUT YOU'VE BEEN UNDER-PERFORMING OF LATE.
I AM...TO SAY THE LEAST... DISAPPOINTED.
IT AIN'T FOR LACK OF TRYING.
HEY! **YEAH!** I COULD NOT AGREE MORE. YOU KIDS HAVE BEEN NAILING ALL THE CLICHÉS.
"NOSE TO THE GRINDSTONE," "HITTING ON ALL CYLINDERS," "WORKING YOUR FINGERS TO THE BONE."
IT'S THIS DAMNED RED HOOD.

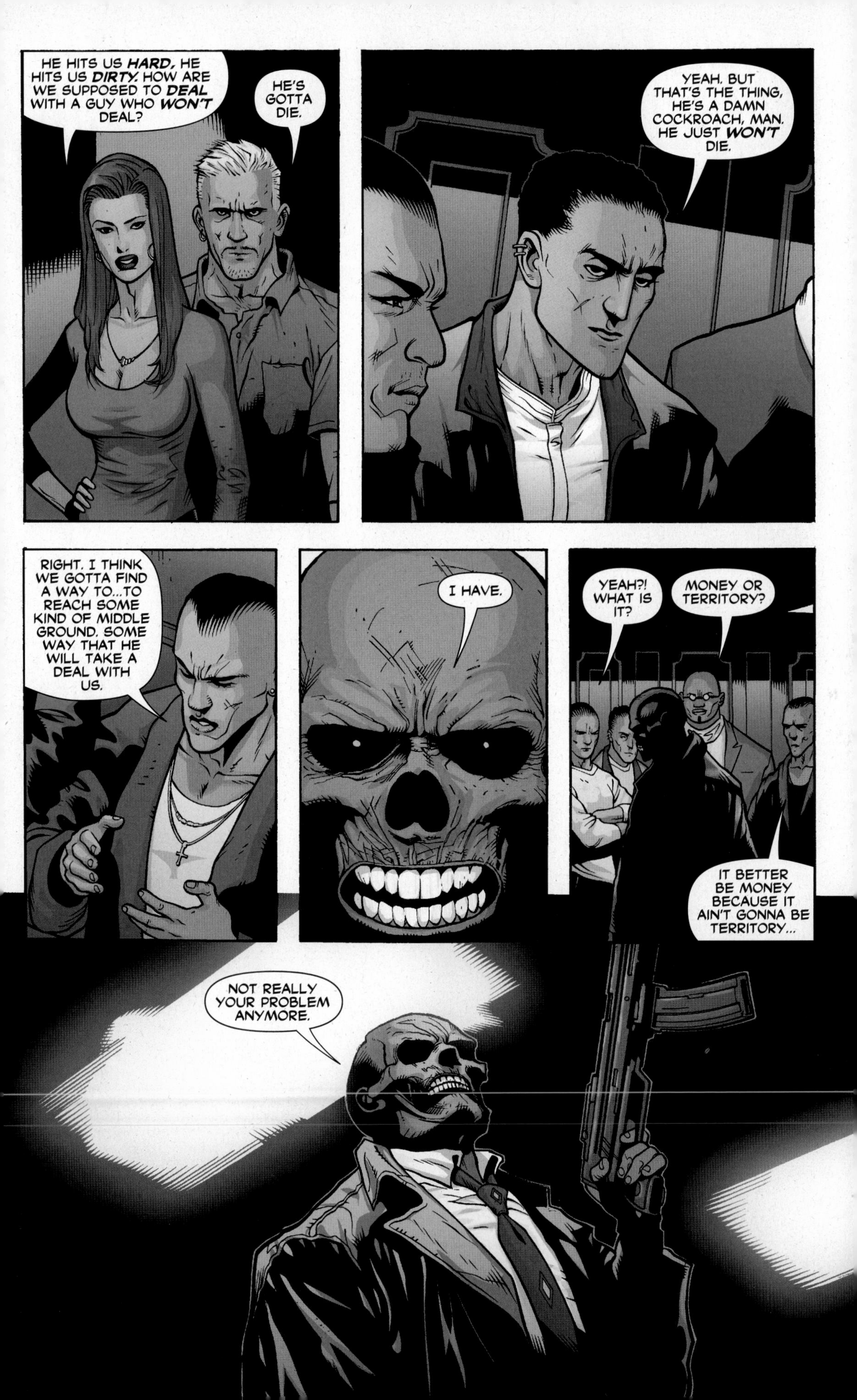

HE HITS US HARD, HE HITS US DIRTY. HOW ARE WE SUPPOSED TO DEAL WITH A GUY WHO WON'T DEAL?
HE'S GOTTA DIE.
YEAH. BUT THAT'S THE THING, HE'S A DAMN COCKROACH, MAN. HE JUST WON'T DIE.
RIGHT. I THINK WE GOTTA FIND A WAY TO...TO REACH SOME KIND OF MIDDLE GROUND. SOME WAY THAT HE WILL TAKE A DEAL WITH US.
I HAVE.
YEAH?! WHAT IS IT?
MONEY OR TERRITORY?
IT BETTER BE MONEY BECAUSE IT AIN'T GONNA BE TERRITORY...
NOT REALLY YOUR PROBLEM ANYMORE.

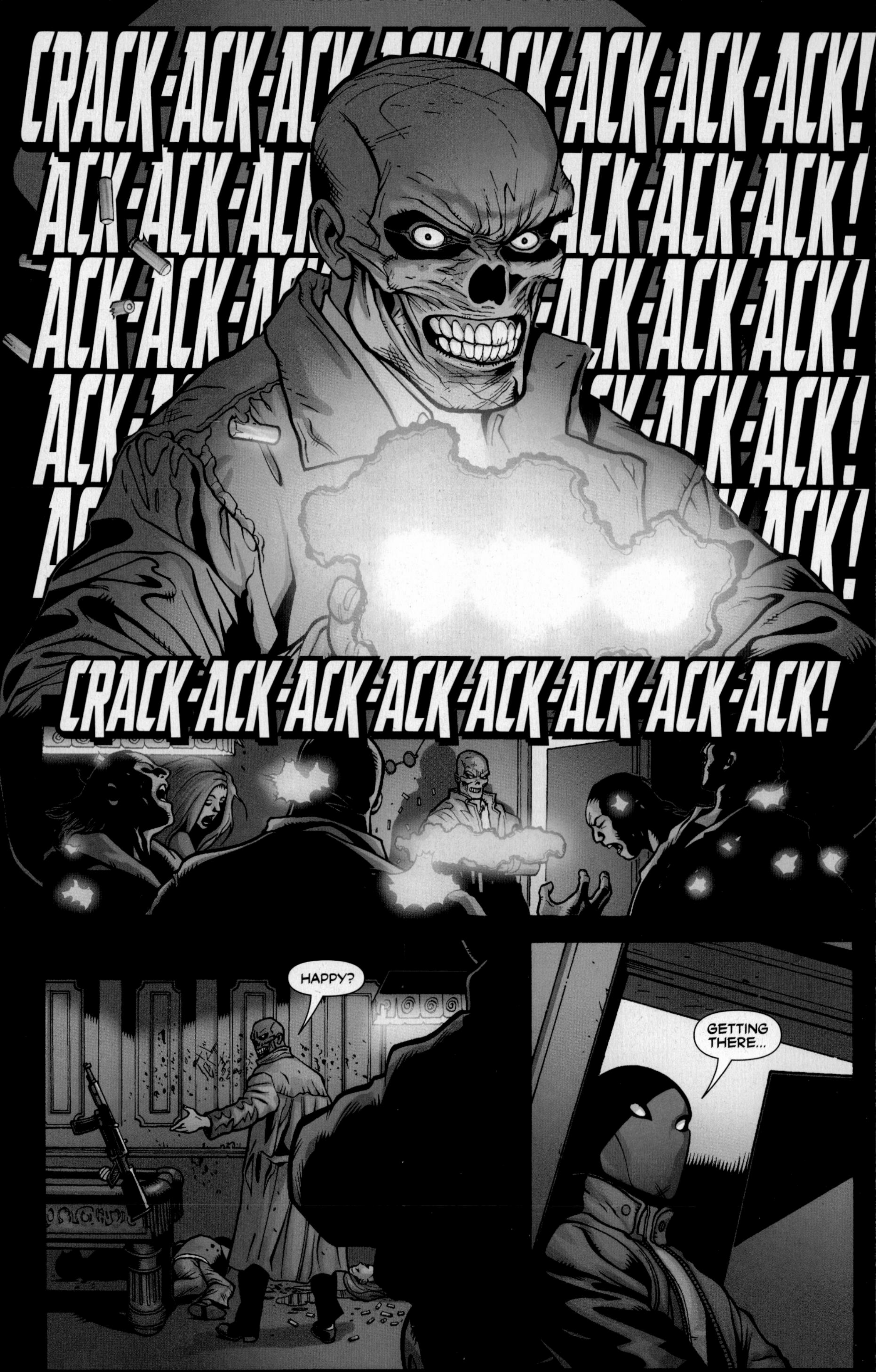
CRACK-ACK-ACK-ACK-ACK-ACK-ACK-ACK!
ACK-ACK-ACK-ACK-ACK-ACK!
ACK-ACK-ACK-ACK-ACK-ACK!
ACK-ACK-ACK-ACK!
ACK!
CRACK-ACK-ACK-ACK-ACK-ACK-ACK-ACK!
HAPPY?
GETTING THERE...

ALFRED, WE SHOULDN'T WASTE TIME.

I'M GOING TO NEED YOU TO--

YES, SIR, OPEN THE REMAINING BOX.

BE SURE TO--

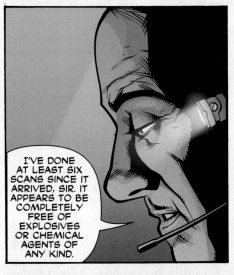

I'VE DONE AT LEAST SIX SCANS SINCE IT ARRIVED, SIR. IT APPEARS TO BE COMPLETELY FREE OF EXPLOSIVES OR CHEMICAL AGENTS OF ANY KIND.

AND AS YOU KNOW, SIR, I AM QUITE ADEPT WITH INCENDIARIES.

I KNOW.

I'M OPENING THE BOX, SIR... I...

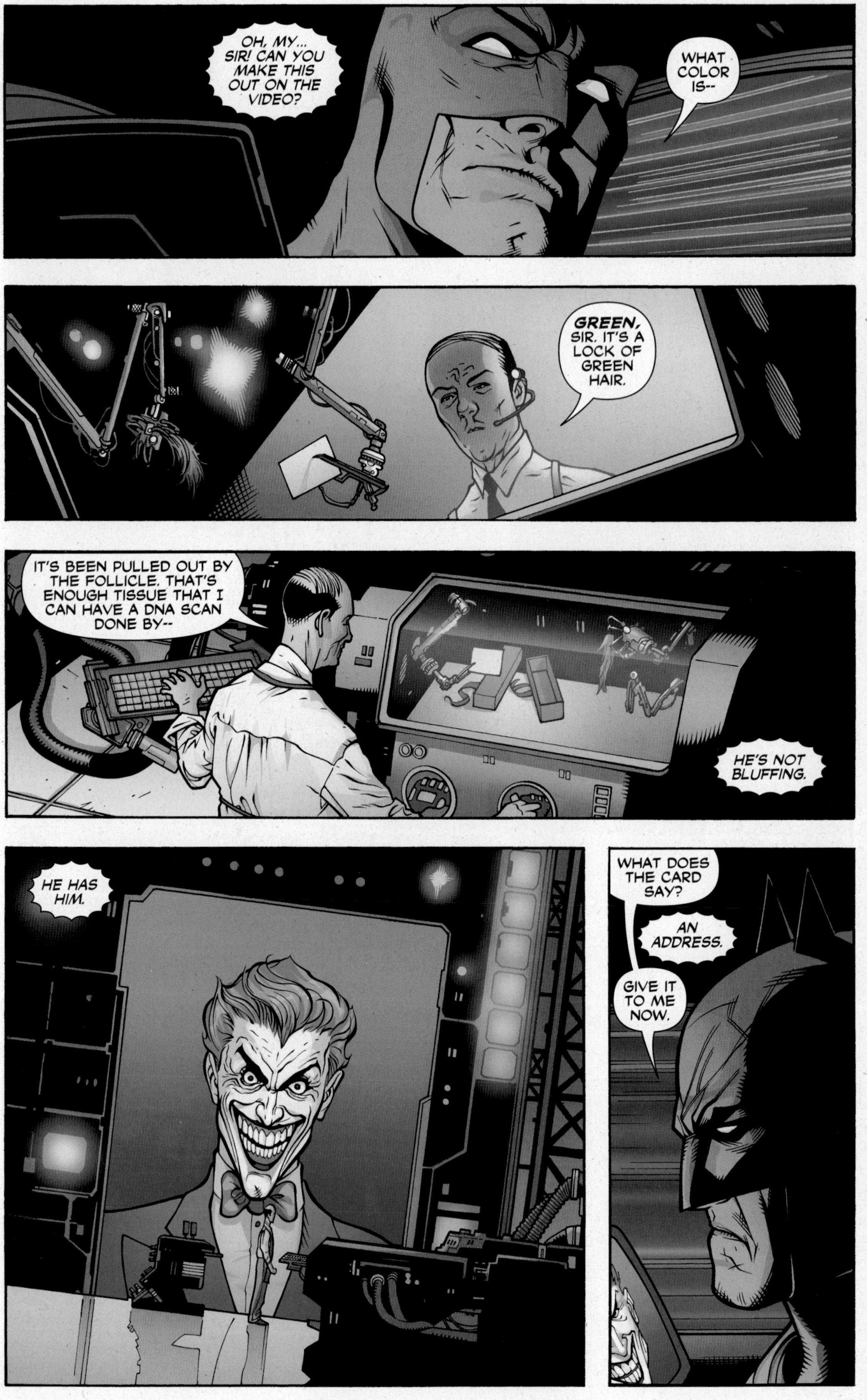
OH, MY... SIR! CAN YOU MAKE THIS OUT ON THE VIDEO?
WHAT COLOR IS--
GREEN, SIR. IT'S A LOCK OF GREEN HAIR.
IT'S BEEN PULLED OUT BY THE FOLLICLE. THAT'S ENOUGH TISSUE THAT I CAN HAVE A DNA SCAN DONE BY--
HE'S NOT BLUFFING.
HE HAS HIM.
WHAT DOES THE CARD SAY?
AN ADDRESS.
GIVE IT TO ME NOW.

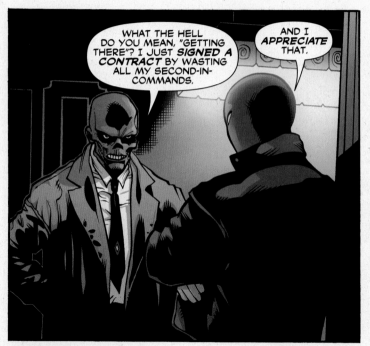

WHAT THE HELL DO YOU MEAN, "GETTING THERE"? I JUST *SIGNED A CONTRACT* BY WASTING ALL MY SECOND-IN-COMMANDS.

AND I *APPRECIATE* THAT.

I DON'T WANT YOUR *DAMNED* APPRECIATION. I *EXPECT* YOUR *OBEDIENCE.*

THIS IS CALLED DETENTE, YOU SICK, DEMENTED MORON.

I THINK YOU MAY HAVE MISUNDERSTOOD THE TERMS OF OUR--

ARE YOU COMPLETELY OFF YOUR BULLET-HEADED NUT?! *YOU* CAME TO ME--*TO ME*--WANTING TO PUT AN END TO THIS!

"REALLY, MASK," YOU SAID. "I'M ALL DONE WITH THE WHACKED-OUT MAD BOMBER ROUTINE. I WANT A SEAT AT THE TABLE."

"GO TO HELL," I SAY. "DESPITE THE FACT THAT I'D RATHER TAKE ALL MY CAPOS, SET THEM ON FIRE AND PITCH THEM OUT OF AN AIRPLANE--I *NEED* THEM."

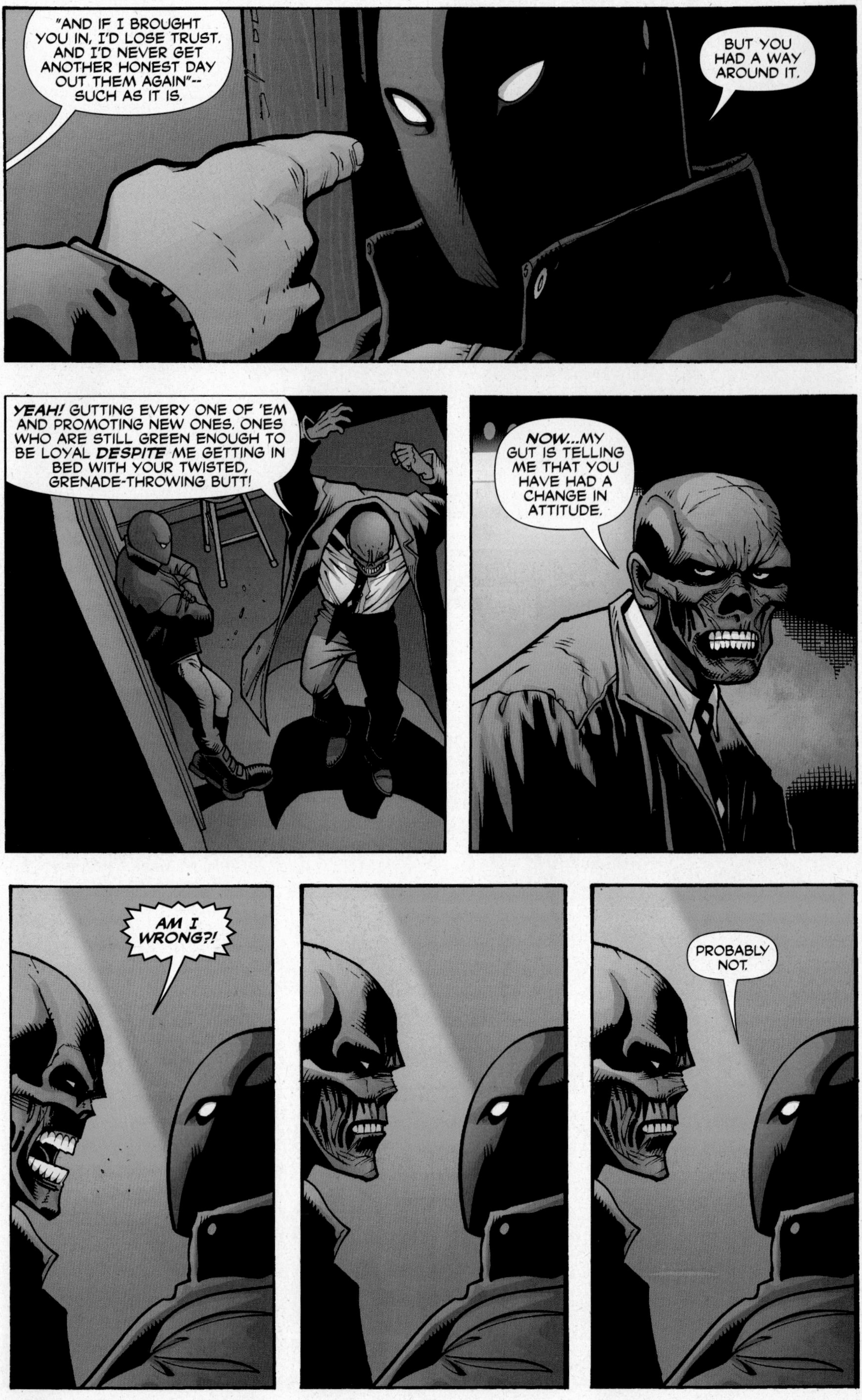
"AND IF I BROUGHT YOU IN, I'D LOSE TRUST. AND I'D NEVER GET ANOTHER HONEST DAY OUT THEM AGAIN"-- SUCH AS IT IS.
BUT YOU HAD A WAY AROUND IT.
YEAH! GUTTING EVERY ONE OF 'EM AND PROMOTING NEW ONES. ONES WHO ARE STILL GREEN ENOUGH TO BE LOYAL DESPITE ME GETTING IN BED WITH YOUR TWISTED, GRENADE-THROWING BUTT!
NOW...MY GUT IS TELLING ME THAT YOU HAVE HAD A CHANGE IN ATTITUDE.
AM I WRONG?!
PROBABLY NOT.

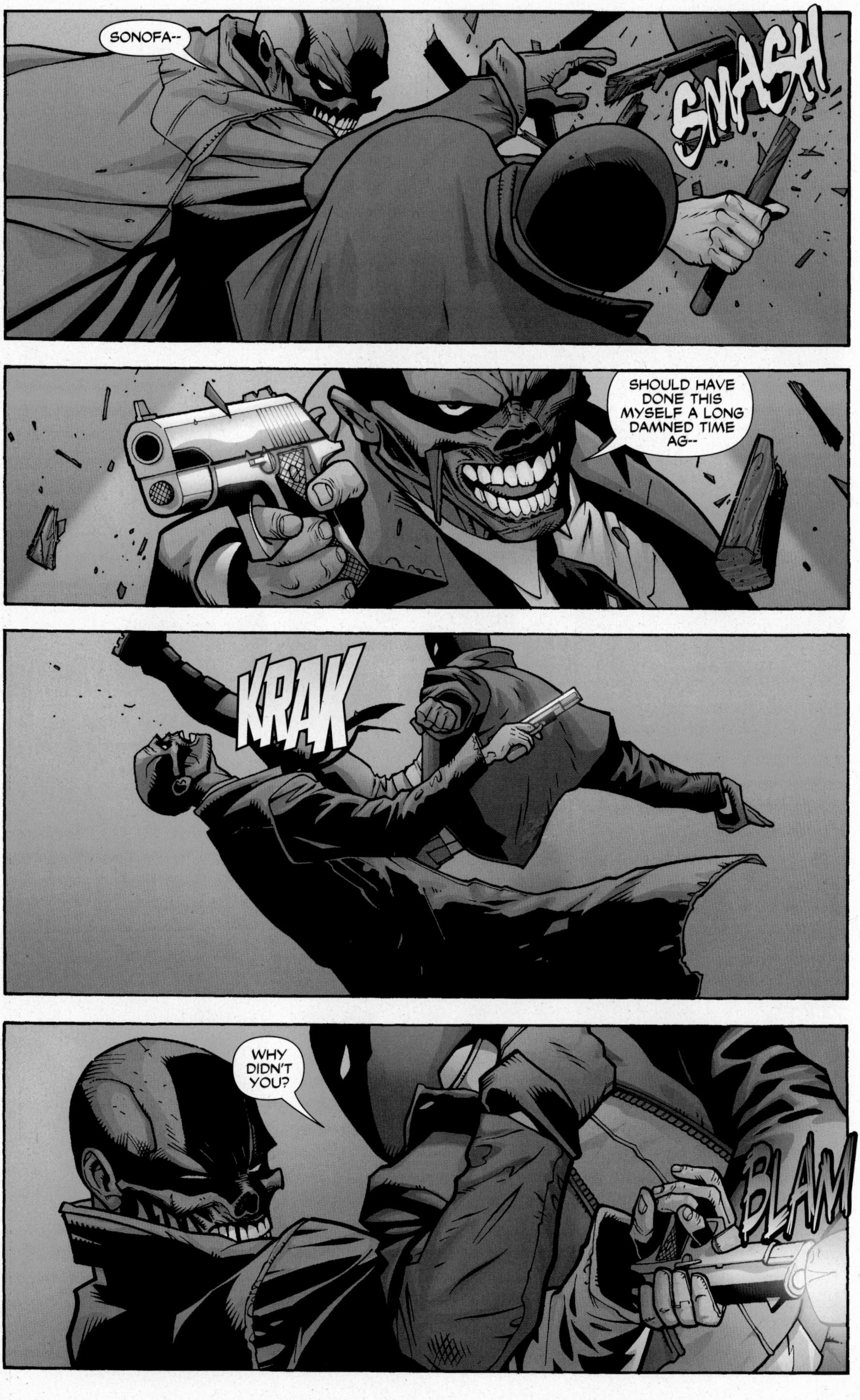
SONOFA--
SMASH
SHOULD HAVE DONE THIS MYSELF A LONG DAMNED TIME AG--
KRAK
WHY DIDN'T YOU?
BLAM

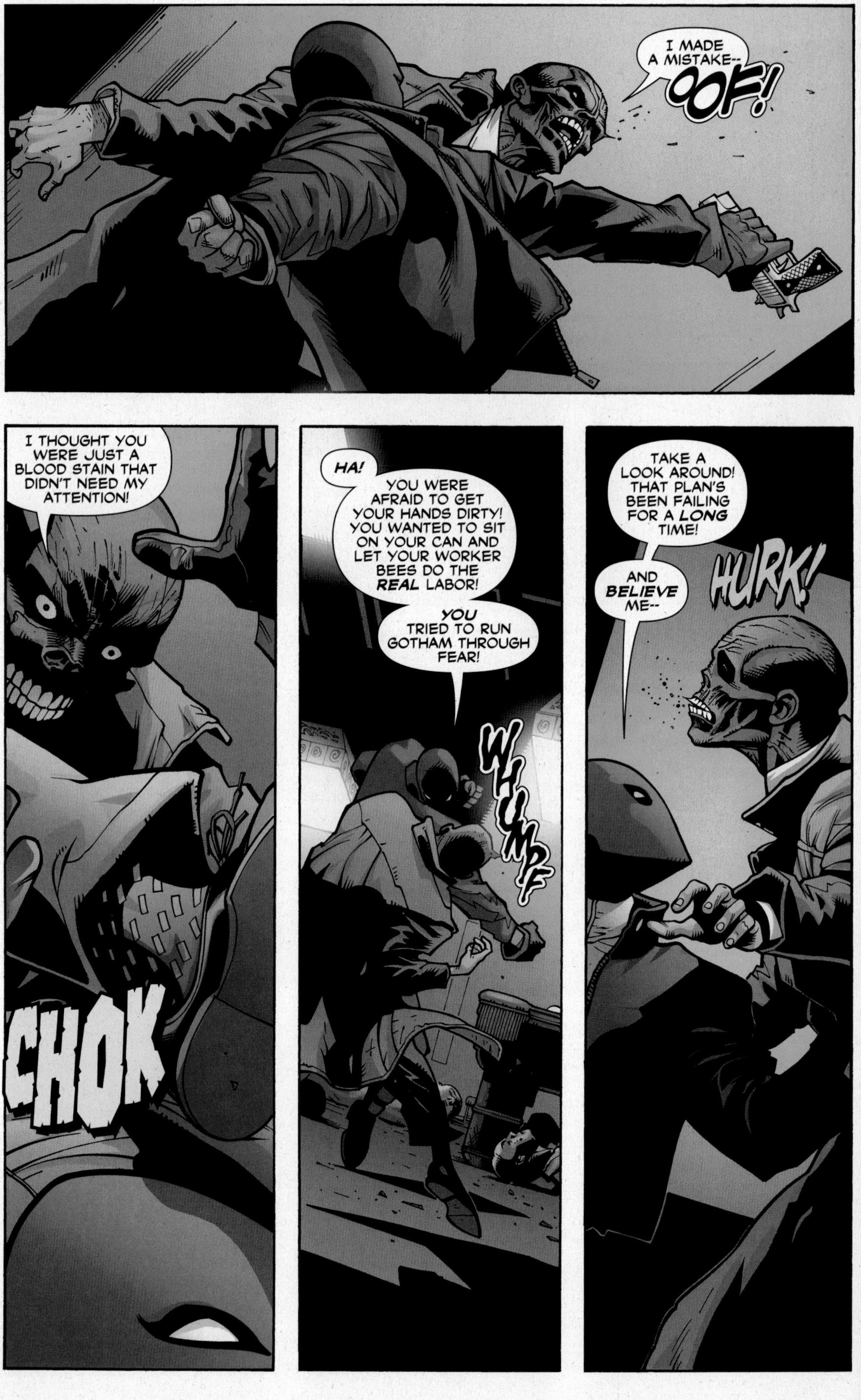
I MADE A MISTAKE--
OOF!
I THOUGHT YOU WERE JUST A BLOOD STAIN THAT DIDN'T NEED MY ATTENTION!
CHOK
HA!
YOU WERE AFRAID TO GET YOUR HANDS DIRTY! YOU WANTED TO SIT ON YOUR CAN AND LET YOUR WORKER BEES DO THE REAL LABOR!
YOU TRIED TO RUN GOTHAM THROUGH FEAR!
WHUMPF
TAKE A LOOK AROUND! THAT PLAN'S BEEN FAILING FOR A LONG TIME!
AND BELIEVE ME--
HURK!

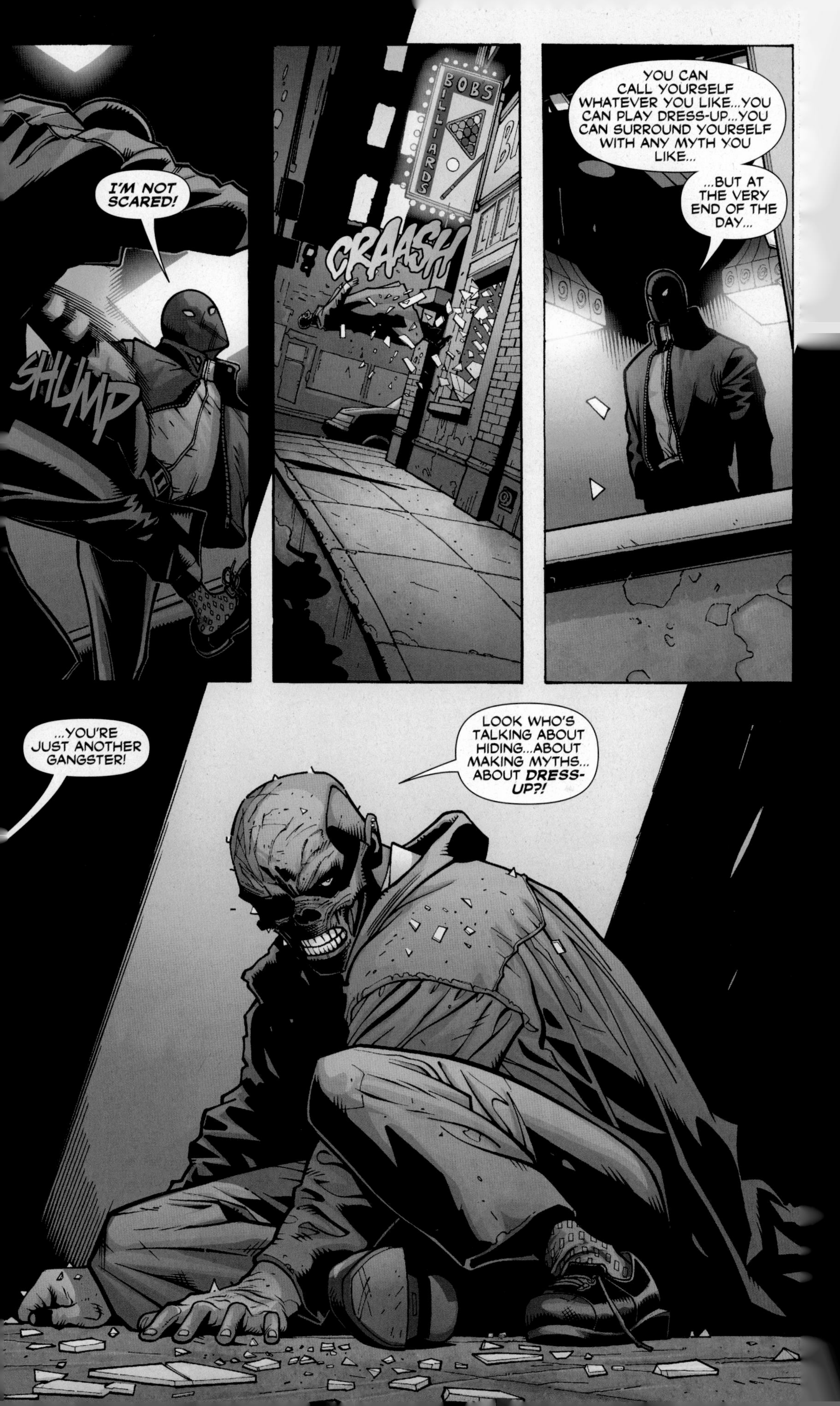
I'M NOT SCARED!
SHUMP
BOBS BILLIARDS
CRAASH
YOU CAN CALL YOURSELF WHATEVER YOU LIKE...YOU CAN PLAY DRESS-UP...YOU CAN SURROUND YOURSELF WITH ANY MYTH YOU LIKE...
...BUT AT THE VERY END OF THE DAY...
...YOU'RE JUST ANOTHER GANGSTER!
LOOK WHO'S TALKING ABOUT HIDING...ABOUT MAKING MYTHS... ABOUT DRESS-UP?!

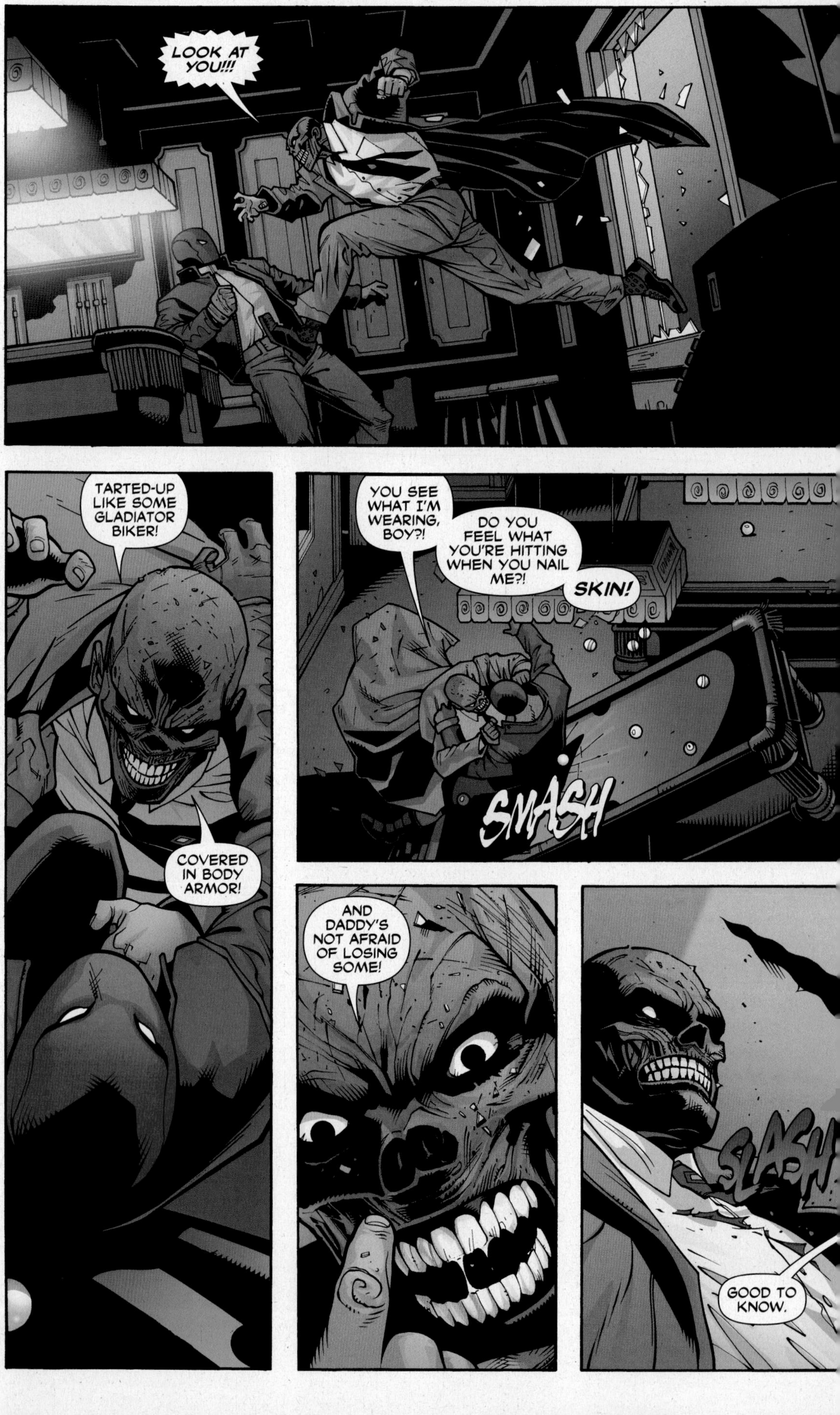
LOOK AT YOU!!!
TARTED-UP LIKE SOME GLADIATOR BIKER!
COVERED IN BODY ARMOR!
YOU SEE WHAT I'M WEARING, BOY?!
DO YOU FEEL WHAT YOU'RE HITTING WHEN YOU NAIL ME?!
SKIN!
SMASH
AND DADDY'S NOT AFRAID OF LOSING SOME!
SLASH
GOOD TO KNOW.

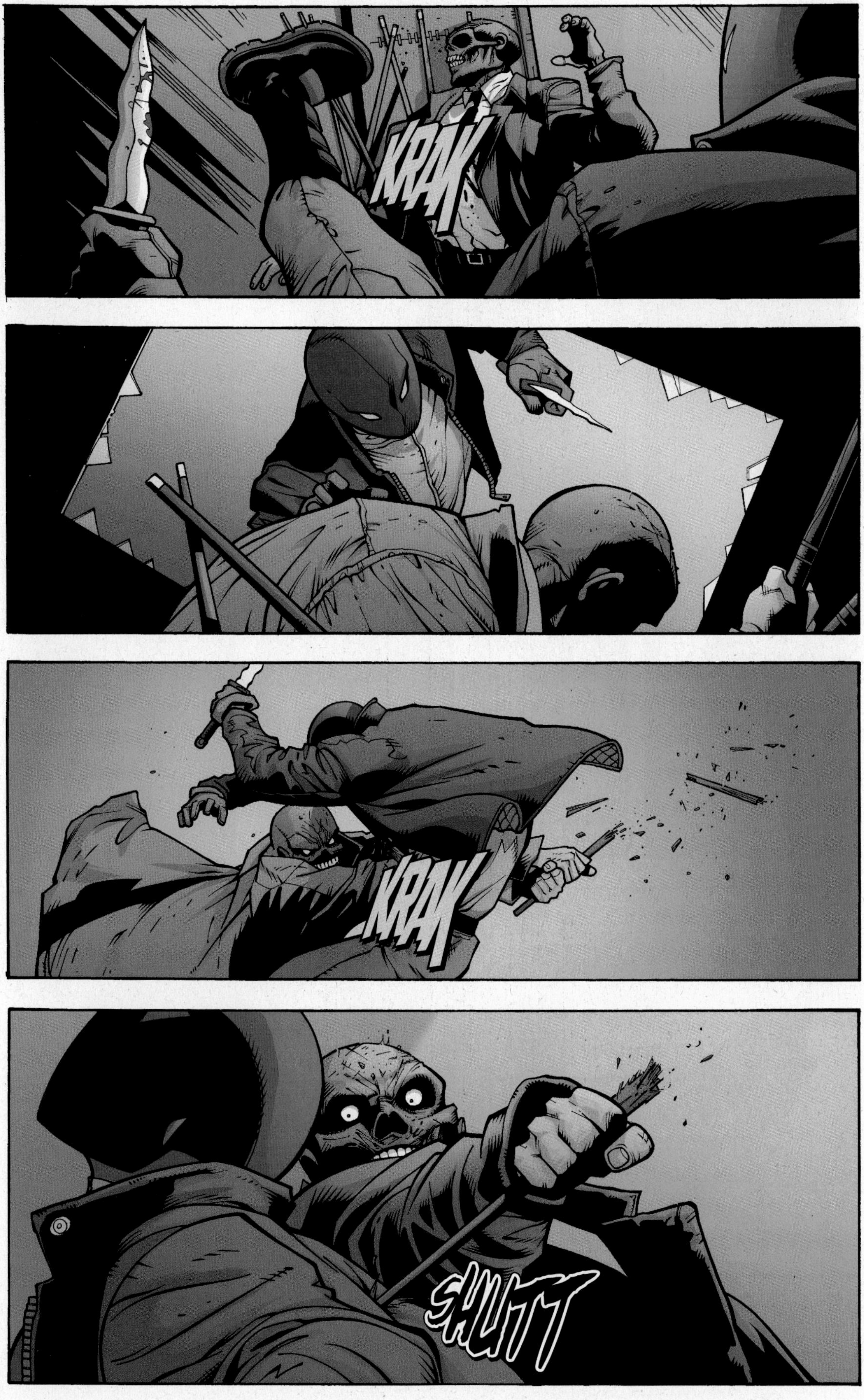
KRAK
KRAK
SHUTT

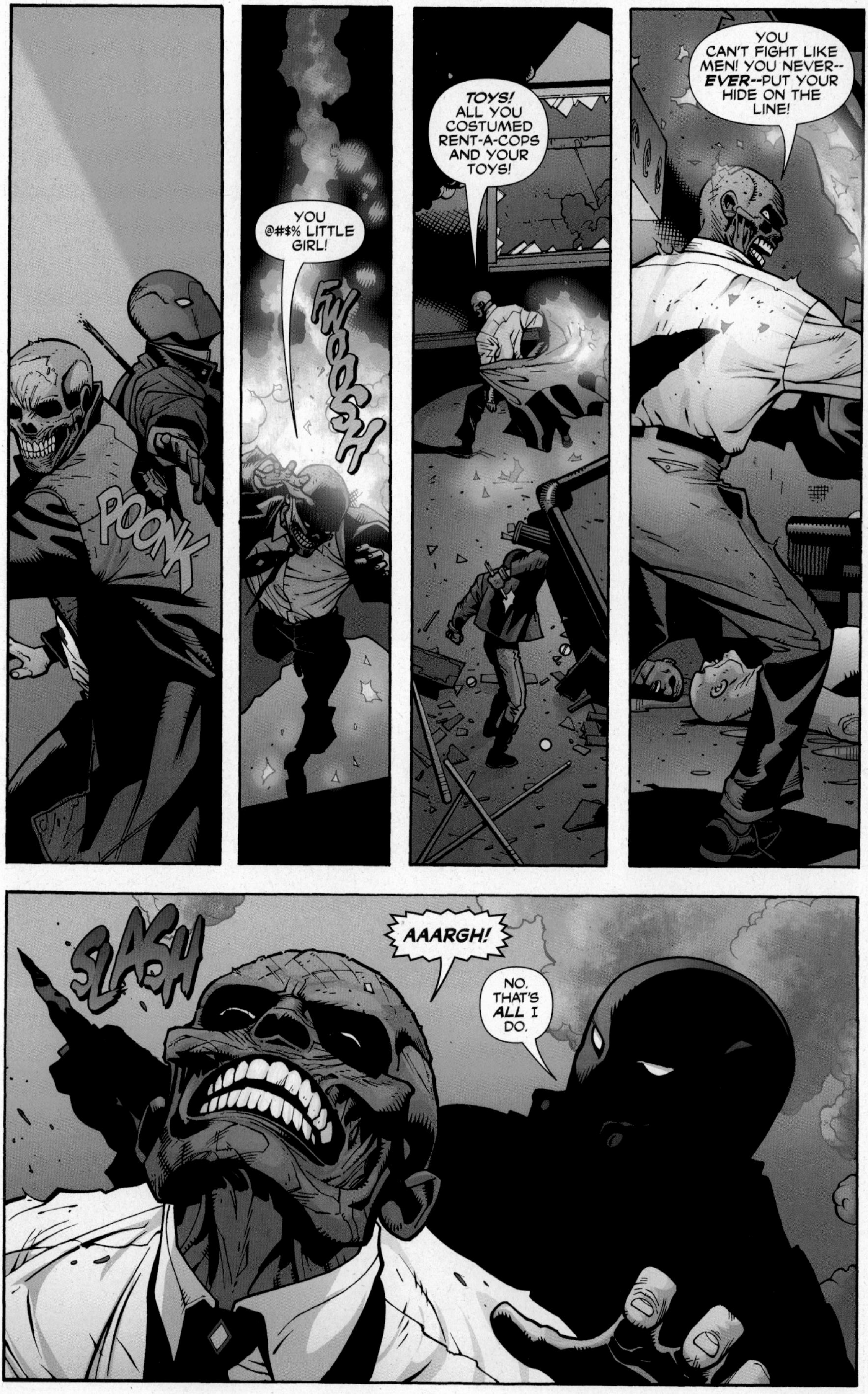
POONK
YOU @#$% LITTLE GIRL!
FWOOOSH
TOYS! ALL YOU COSTUMED RENT-A-COPS AND YOUR TOYS!
YOU CAN'T FIGHT LIKE MEN! YOU NEVER-- EVER--PUT YOUR HIDE ON THE LINE!
SLASH
AAARGH!
NO. THAT'S ALL I DO.

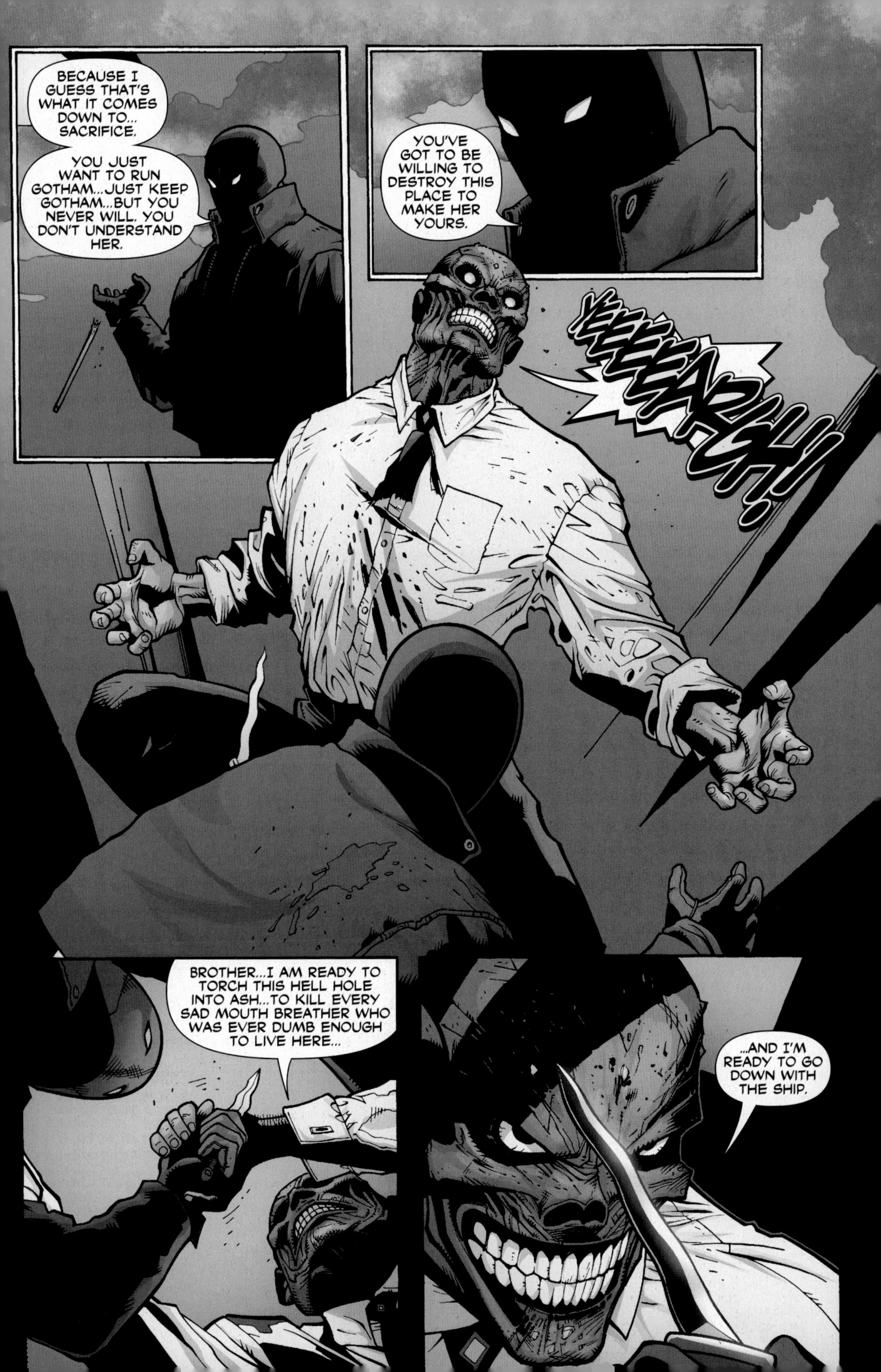
BECAUSE I GUESS THAT'S WHAT IT COMES DOWN TO... SACRIFICE.
YOU JUST WANT TO RUN GOTHAM...JUST KEEP GOTHAM...BUT YOU NEVER WILL. YOU DON'T UNDERSTAND HER.
YOU'VE GOT TO BE WILLING TO DESTROY THIS PLACE TO MAKE HER YOURS.
YEEEEAAARGH!!
BROTHER...I AM READY TO TORCH THIS HELL HOLE INTO ASH...TO KILL EVERY SAD MOUTH BREATHER WHO WAS EVER DUMB ENOUGH TO LIVE HERE...
...AND I'M READY TO GO DOWN WITH THE SHIP.

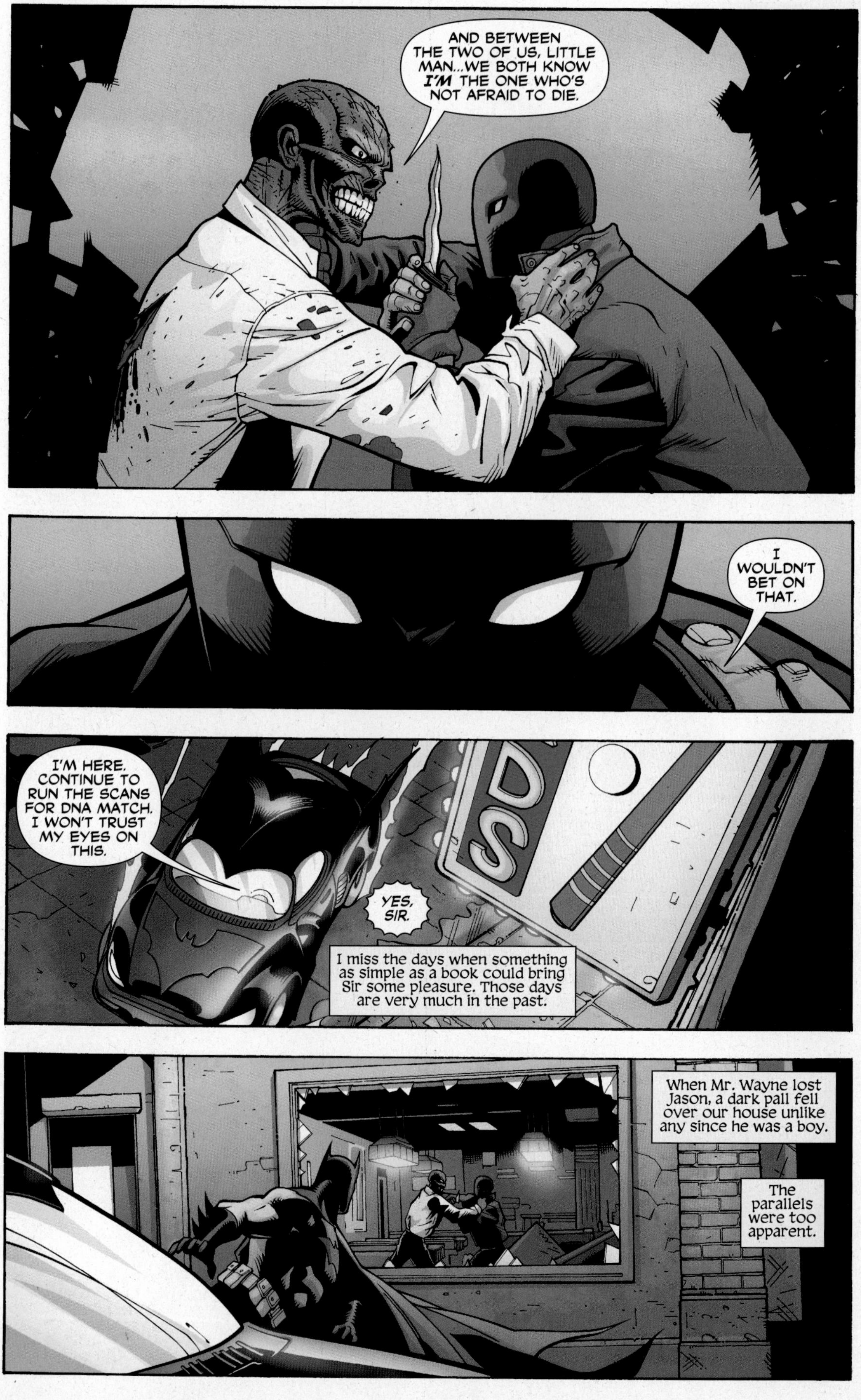
AND BETWEEN THE TWO OF US, LITTLE MAN...WE BOTH KNOW I'M THE ONE WHO'S NOT AFRAID TO DIE.
I WOULDN'T BET ON THAT.
I'M HERE. CONTINUE TO RUN THE SCANS FOR DNA MATCH. I WON'T TRUST MY EYES ON THIS.
YES, SIR.
I miss the days when something as simple as a book could bring Sir some pleasure. Those days are very much in the past.
When Mr. Wayne lost Jason, a dark pall fell over our house unlike any since he was a boy.
The parallels were too apparent.

Again he was gripped with the same guilt...the same shame.

But for Bruce it was the differences between these two tragedies that cut him.

HURK!

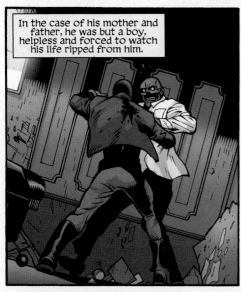

In the case of his mother and father, he was but a boy, helpless and forced to watch his life ripped from him.

With Jason, he was a champion, a skilled warrior with more abilities than maybe any normal living man.

He had every means at his disposal to rescue Jason from death...

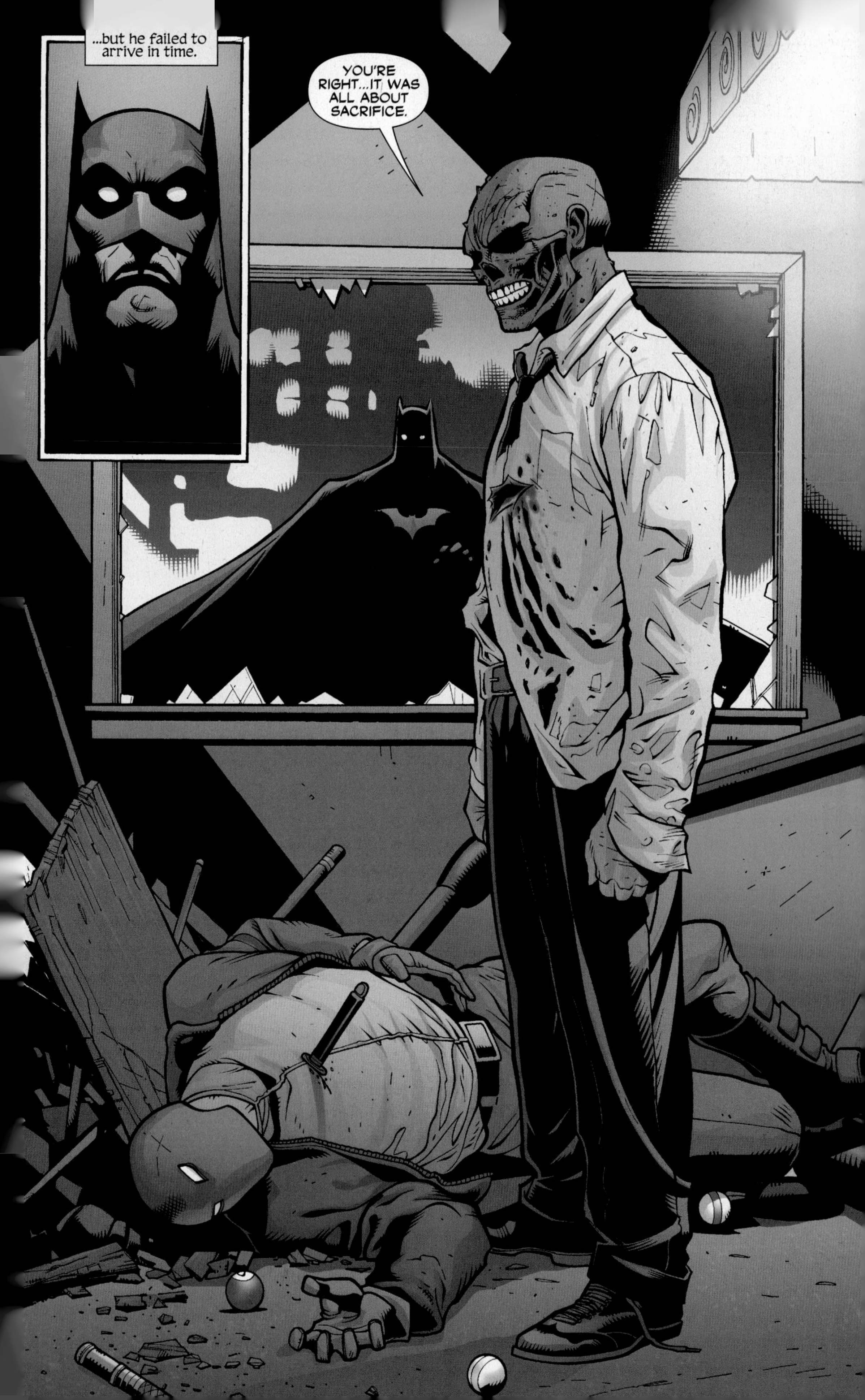

...but he failed to arrive in time.
YOU'RE RIGHT...IT WAS ALL ABOUT SACRIFICE.

BATMAN 649 Cover by Jock

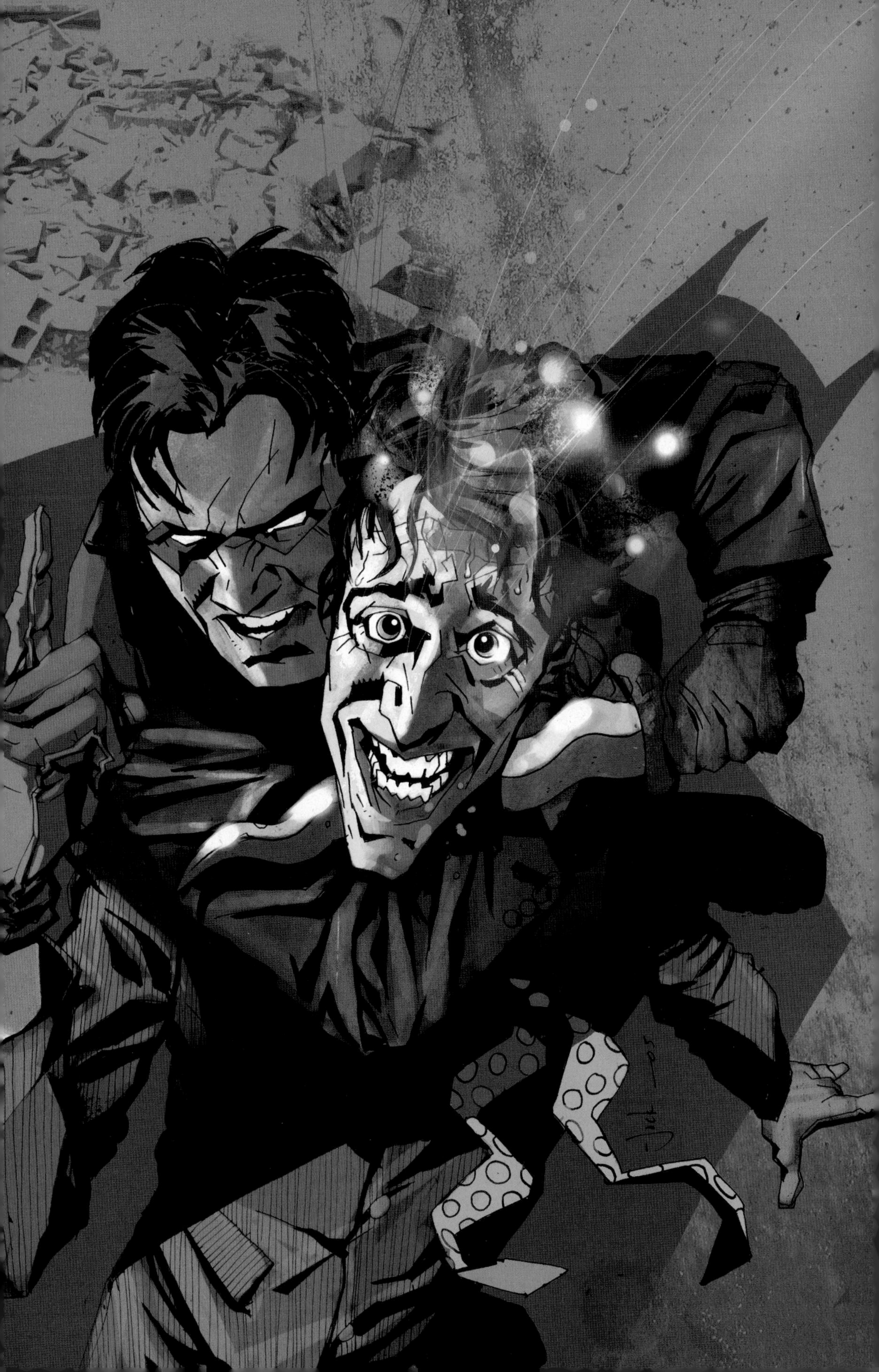

CHAPTER 12
ALL THEY DO IS WATCH US KILL
PART TWO

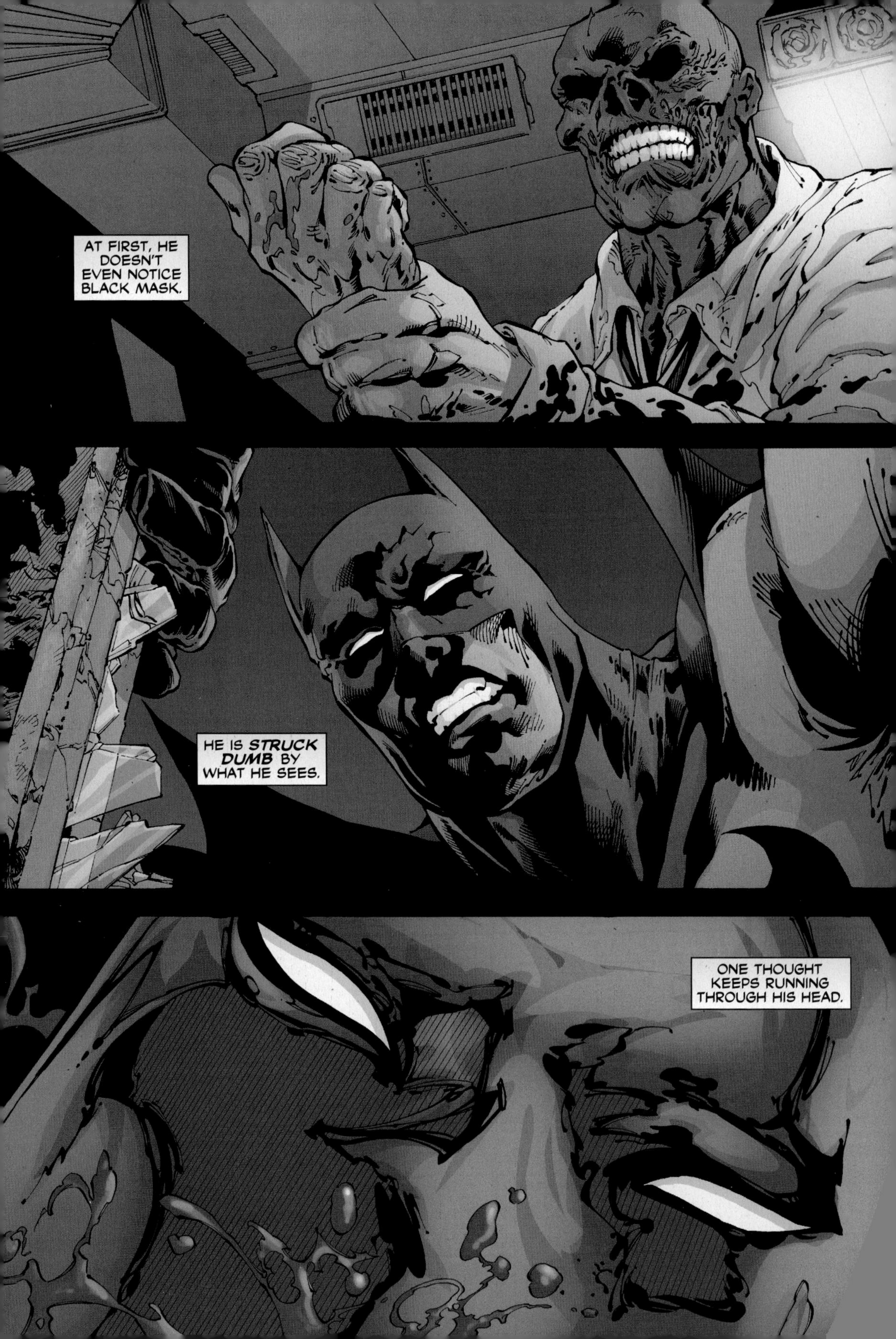
AT FIRST, HE DOESN'T EVEN NOTICE BLACK MASK.
HE IS *STRUCK DUMB* BY WHAT HE SEES.
ONE THOUGHT KEEPS RUNNING THROUGH HIS HEAD.

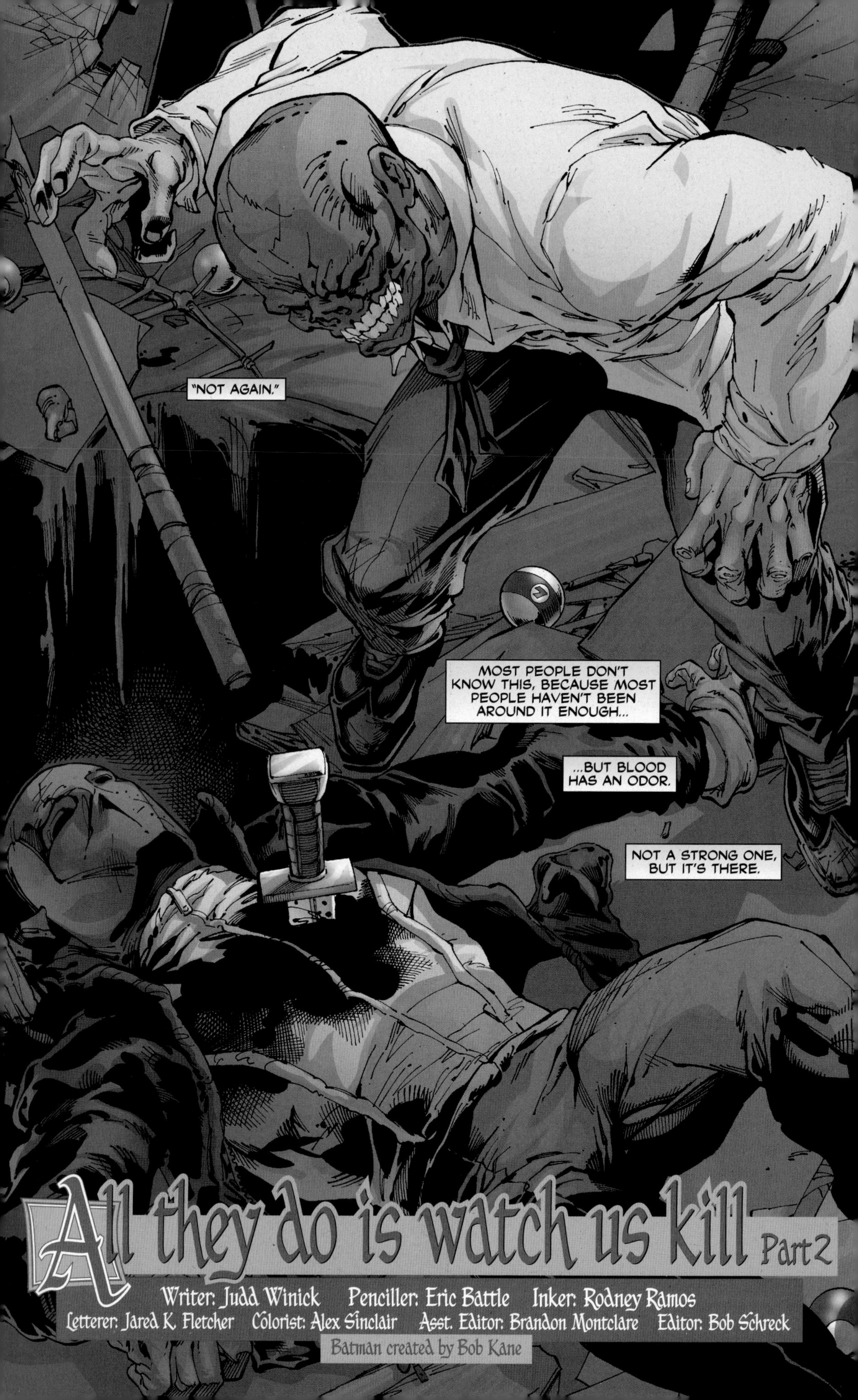
"NOT AGAIN."
MOST PEOPLE DON'T KNOW THIS, BECAUSE MOST PEOPLE HAVEN'T BEEN AROUND IT ENOUGH...
...BUT BLOOD HAS AN ODOR.
NOT A STRONG ONE, BUT IT'S THERE.
All they do is watch us kill Part 2
Writer: Judd Winick Penciller: Eric Battle Inker: Rodney Ramos
Letterer: Jared K. Fletcher Colorist: Alex Sinclair Asst. Editor: Brandon Montclare Editor: Bob Schreck
Batman created by Bob Kane

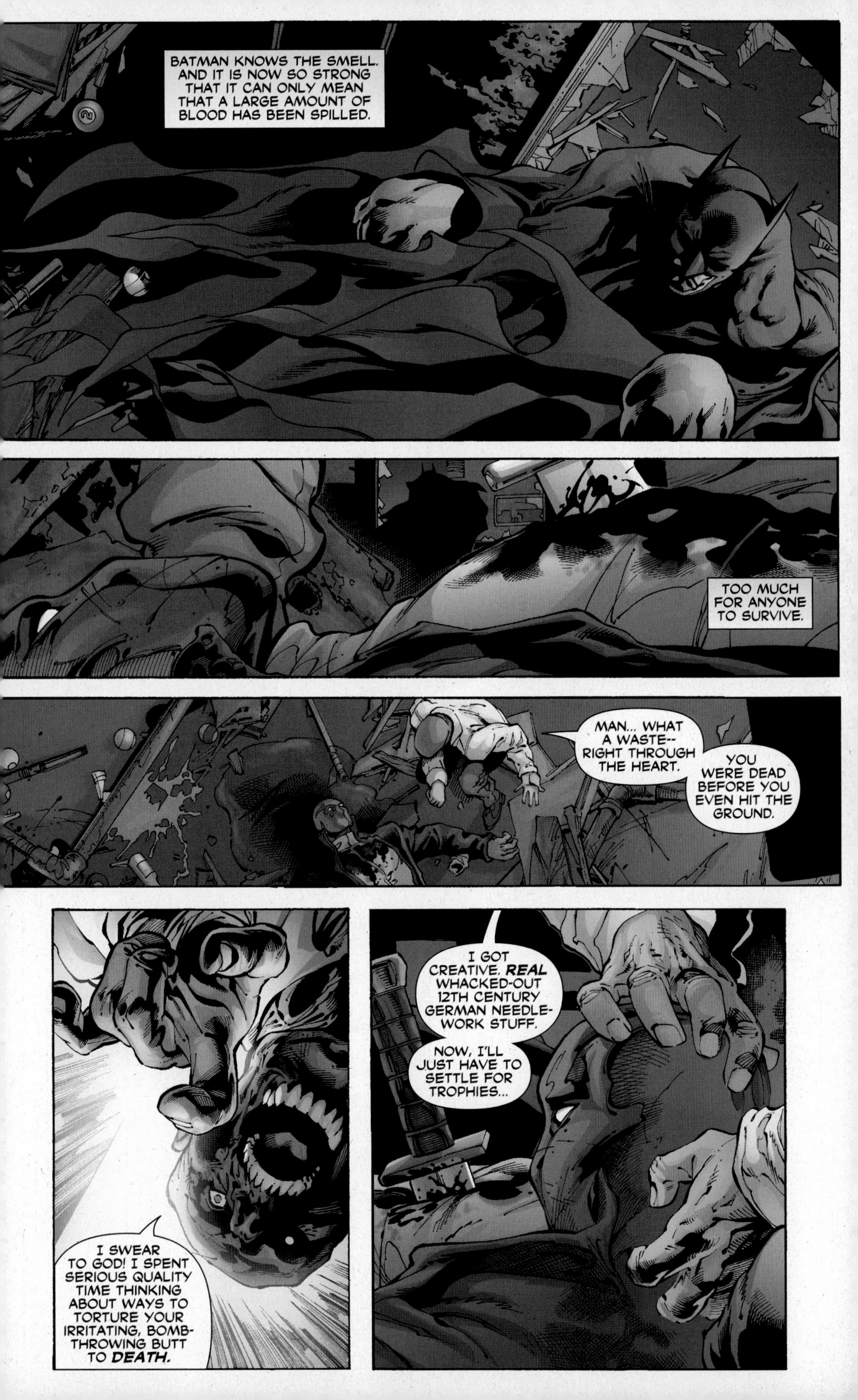
BATMAN KNOWS THE SMELL. AND IT IS NOW SO STRONG THAT IT CAN ONLY MEAN THAT A LARGE AMOUNT OF BLOOD HAS BEEN SPILLED.
TOO MUCH FOR ANYONE TO SURVIVE.
MAN... WHAT A WASTE-- RIGHT THROUGH THE HEART.
YOU WERE DEAD BEFORE YOU EVEN HIT THE GROUND.
I SWEAR TO GOD! I SPENT SERIOUS QUALITY TIME THINKING ABOUT WAYS TO TORTURE YOUR IRRITATING, BOMB-THROWING BUTT TO **DEATH.**
I GOT CREATIVE. **REAL** WHACKED-OUT 12TH CENTURY GERMAN NEEDLE-WORK STUFF.
NOW, I'LL JUST HAVE TO SETTLE FOR TROPHIES...

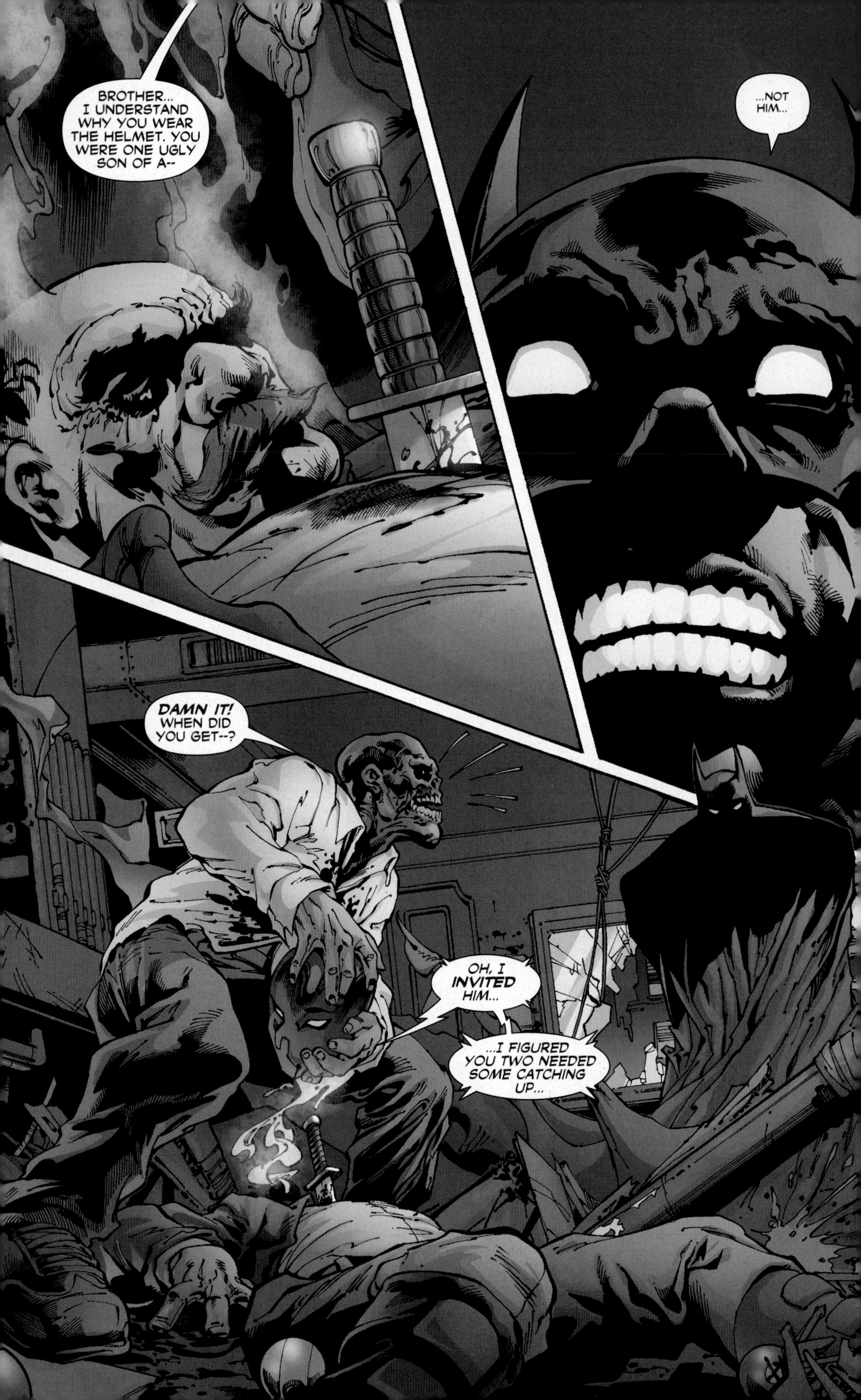
BROTHER... I UNDERSTAND WHY YOU WEAR THE HELMET. YOU WERE ONE UGLY SON OF A--
...NOT HIM...
DAMN IT! WHEN DID YOU GET--?
OH, I INVITED HIM...
...I FIGURED YOU TWO NEEDED SOME CATCHING UP...

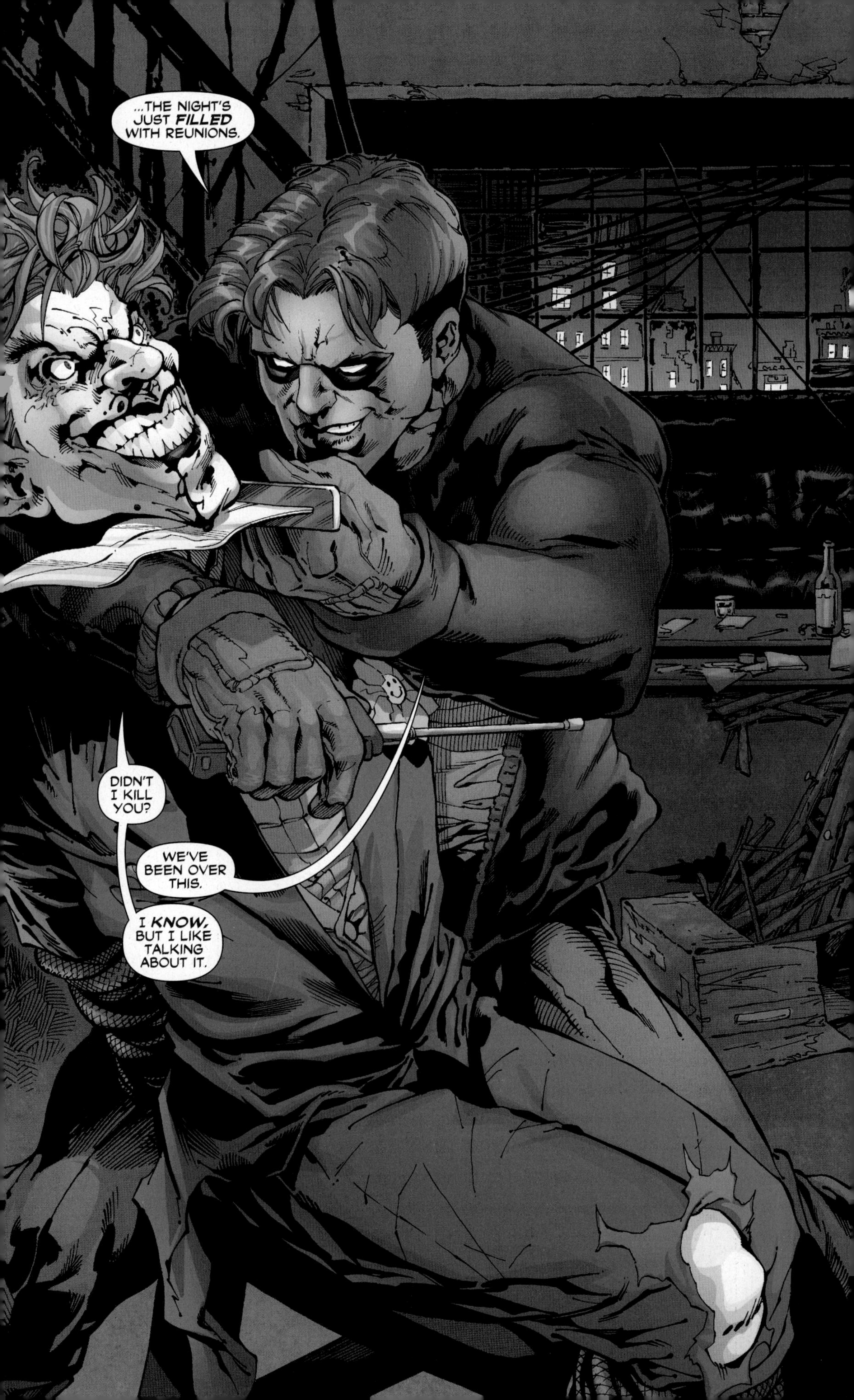
...THE NIGHT'S JUST FILLED WITH REUNIONS.
DIDN'T I KILL YOU?
WE'VE BEEN OVER THIS.
I KNOW, BUT I LIKE TALKING ABOUT IT.

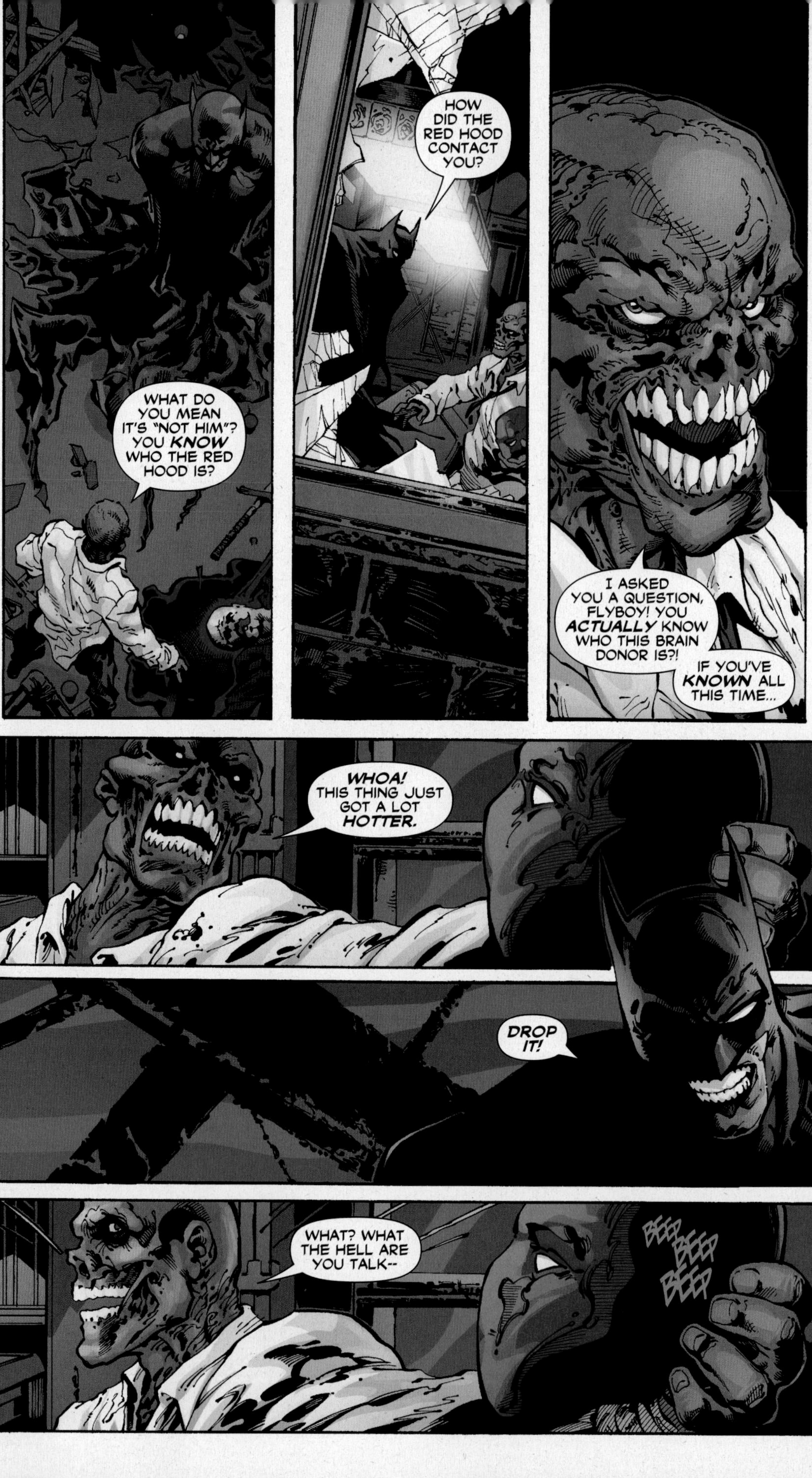
WHAT DO YOU MEAN IT'S "NOT HIM"? YOU KNOW WHO THE RED HOOD IS?
HOW DID THE RED HOOD CONTACT YOU?
I ASKED YOU A QUESTION, FLYBOY! YOU ACTUALLY KNOW WHO THIS BRAIN DONOR IS?!
IF YOU'VE KNOWN ALL THIS TIME...
WHOA! THIS THING JUST GOT A LOT HOTTER.
DROP IT!
WHAT? WHAT THE HELL ARE YOU TALK--
BEEP BEEP BEEP

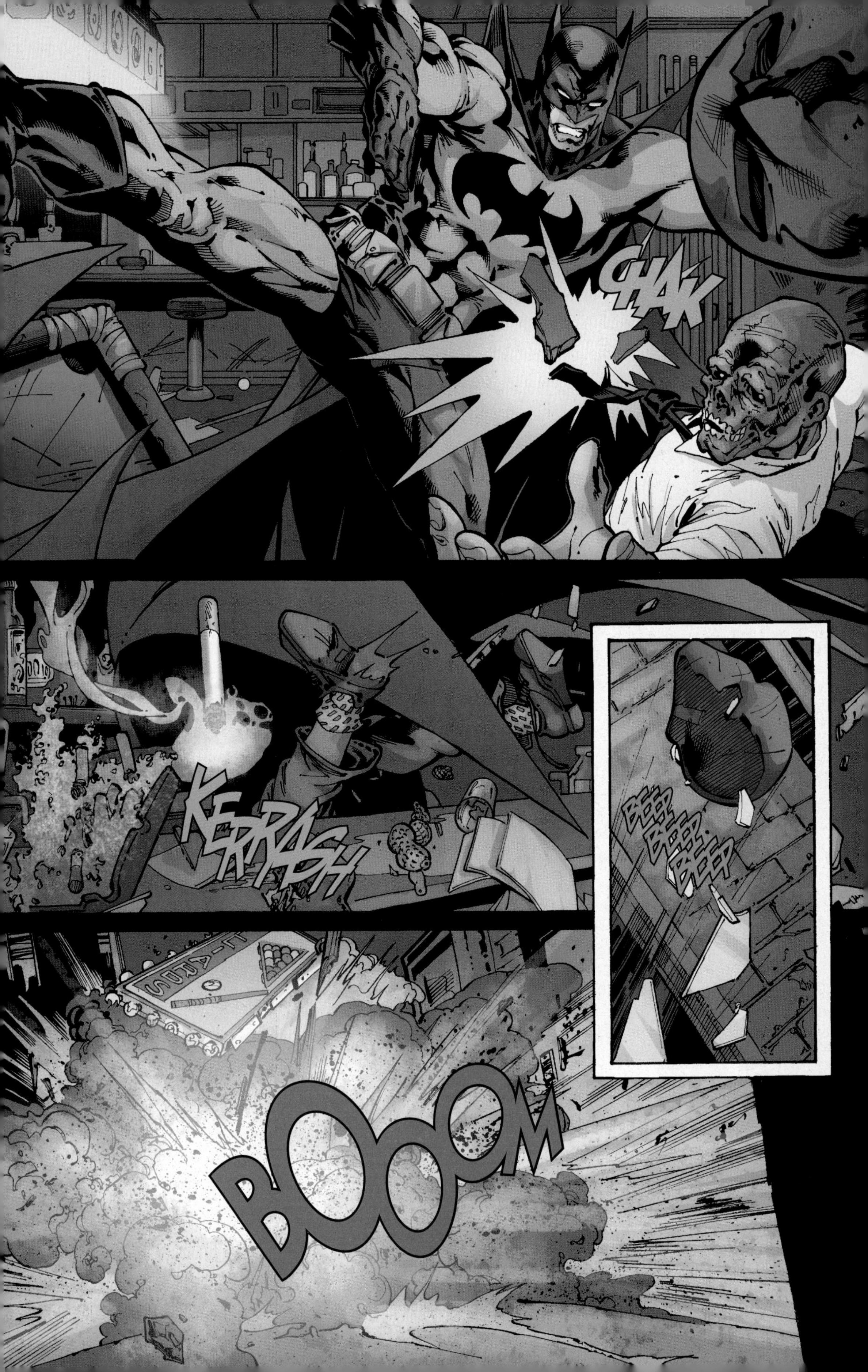
CHAK
KERRASH
BEEP BEEP BEEP
BOOOM

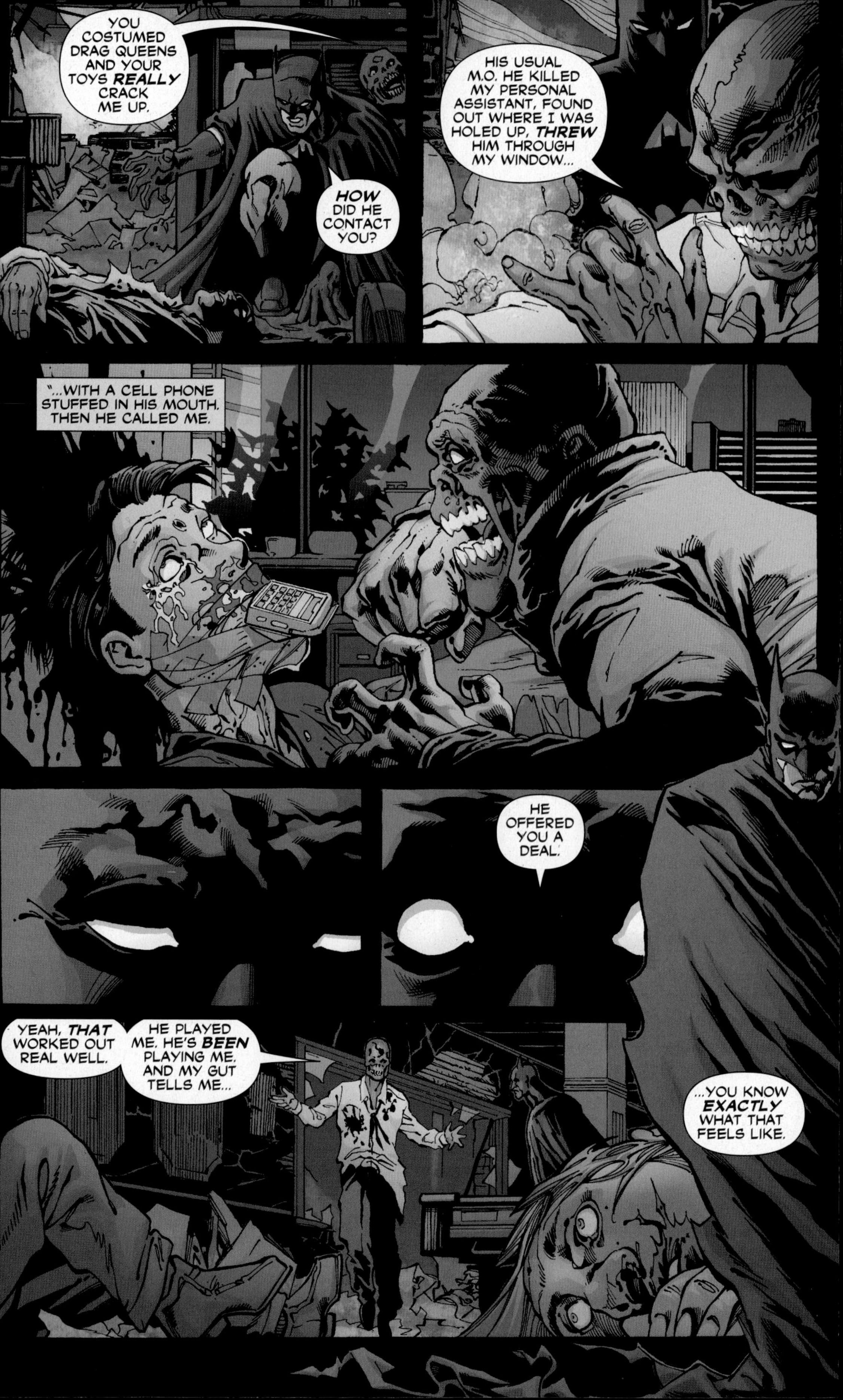

YOU COSTUMED DRAG QUEENS AND YOUR TOYS REALLY CRACK ME UP.
HOW DID HE CONTACT YOU?
HIS USUAL M.O. HE KILLED MY PERSONAL ASSISTANT, FOUND OUT WHERE I WAS HOLED UP, THREW HIM THROUGH MY WINDOW...
"...WITH A CELL PHONE STUFFED IN HIS MOUTH. THEN HE CALLED ME.
HE OFFERED YOU A DEAL.
YEAH, THAT WORKED OUT REAL WELL.
HE PLAYED ME. HE'S BEEN PLAYING ME. AND MY GUT TELLS ME...
...YOU KNOW EXACTLY WHAT THAT FEELS LIKE.

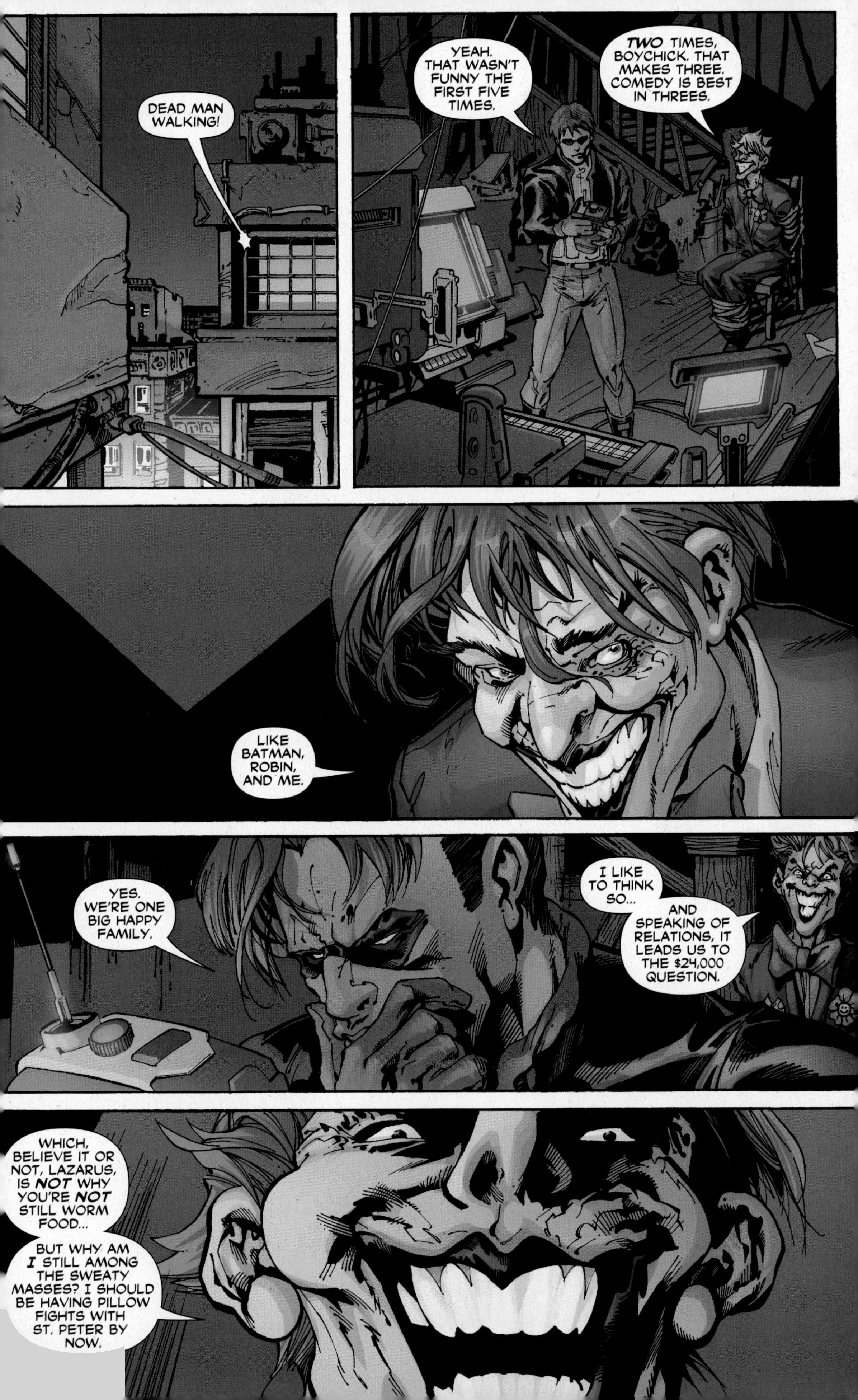
DEAD MAN WALKING!
YEAH. THAT WASN'T FUNNY THE FIRST FIVE TIMES.
TWO TIMES, BOYCHICK. THAT MAKES THREE. COMEDY IS BEST IN THREES.
LIKE BATMAN, ROBIN, AND ME.
YES. WE'RE ONE BIG HAPPY FAMILY.
I LIKE TO THINK SO...
AND SPEAKING OF RELATIONS, IT LEADS US TO THE $24,000 QUESTION.
WHICH, BELIEVE IT OR NOT, LAZARUS, IS NOT WHY YOU'RE NOT STILL WORM FOOD...
BUT WHY AM I STILL AMONG THE SWEATY MASSES? I SHOULD BE HAVING PILLOW FIGHTS WITH ST. PETER BY NOW.

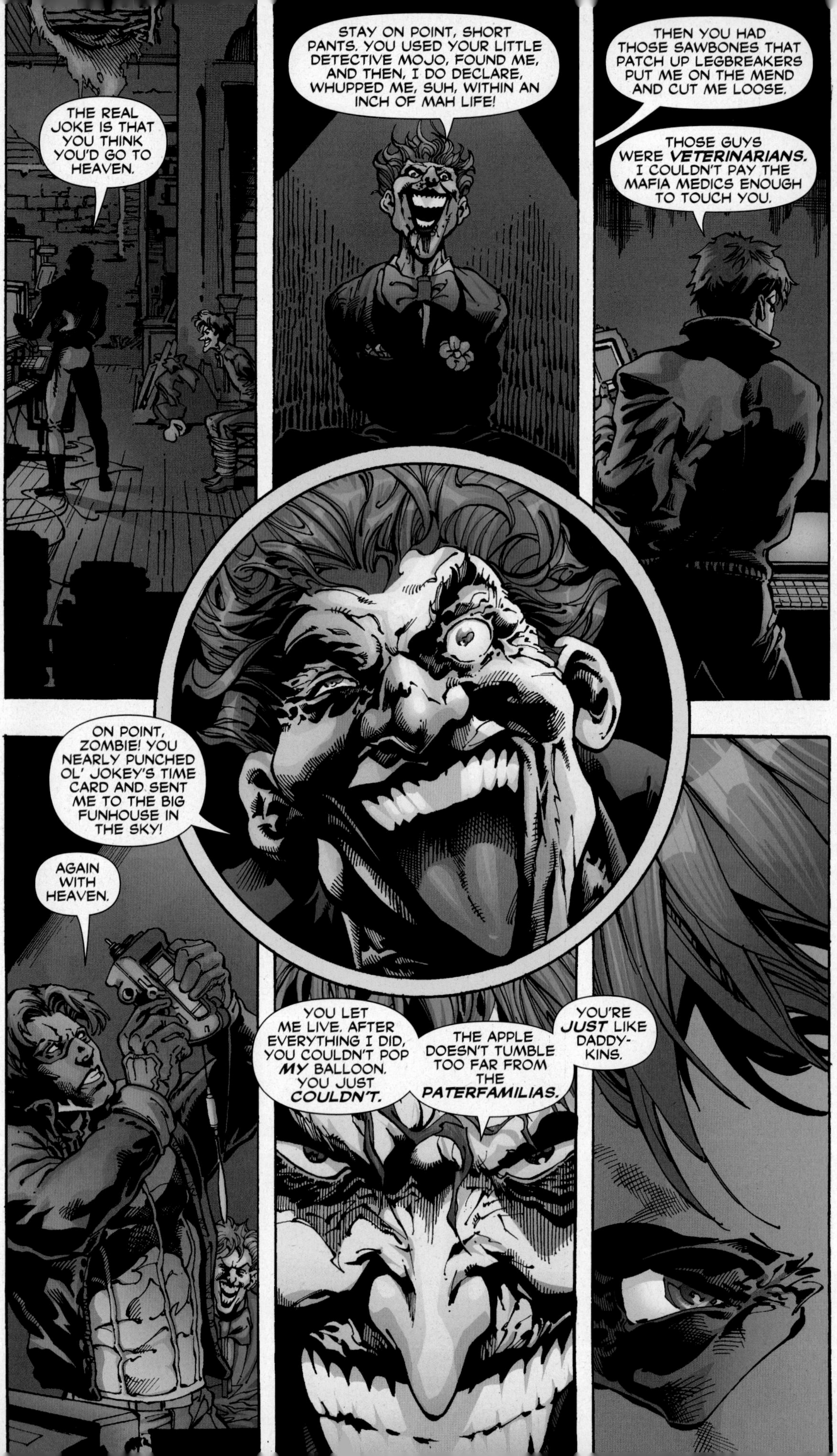
THE REAL JOKE IS THAT YOU THINK YOU'D GO TO HEAVEN.
STAY ON POINT, SHORT PANTS. YOU USED YOUR LITTLE DETECTIVE MOJO, FOUND ME, AND THEN, I DO DECLARE, WHUPPED ME, SUH, WITHIN AN INCH OF MAH LIFE!
THEN YOU HAD THOSE SAWBONES THAT PATCH UP LEGBREAKERS PUT ME ON THE MEND AND CUT ME LOOSE.
THOSE GUYS WERE *VETERINARIANS.* I COULDN'T PAY THE MAFIA MEDICS ENOUGH TO TOUCH YOU.
ON POINT, ZOMBIE! YOU NEARLY PUNCHED OL' JOKEY'S TIME CARD AND SENT ME TO THE BIG FUNHOUSE IN THE SKY!
AGAIN WITH HEAVEN.
YOU LET ME LIVE. AFTER EVERYTHING I DID, YOU COULDN'T POP *MY* BALLOON. YOU JUST *COULDN'T.*
THE APPLE DOESN'T TUMBLE TOO FAR FROM THE *PATERFAMILIAS.*
YOU'RE *JUST* LIKE DADDY-KINS.

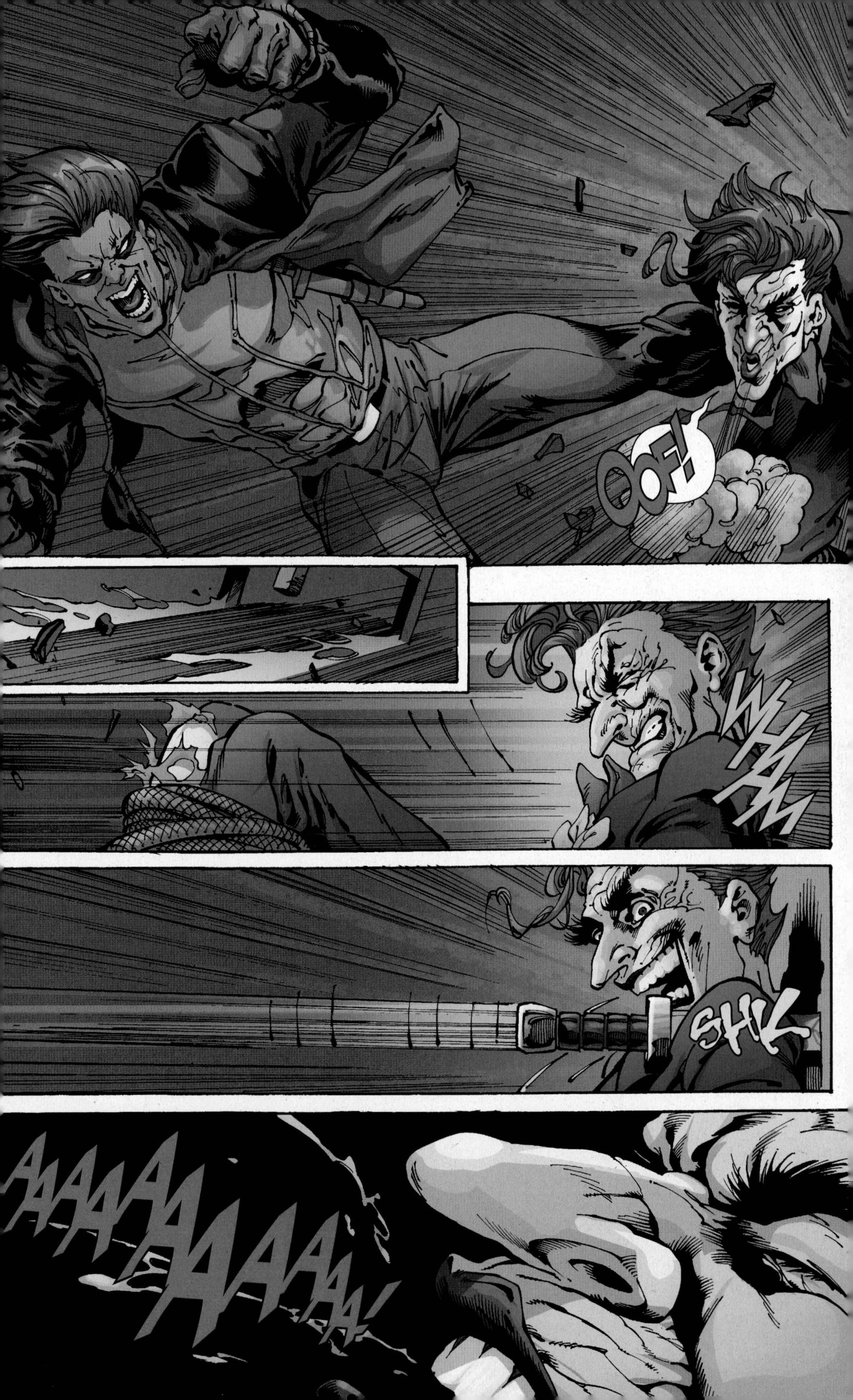
OOF!
WHAM
SHK
AAAAAAAAAAAA!

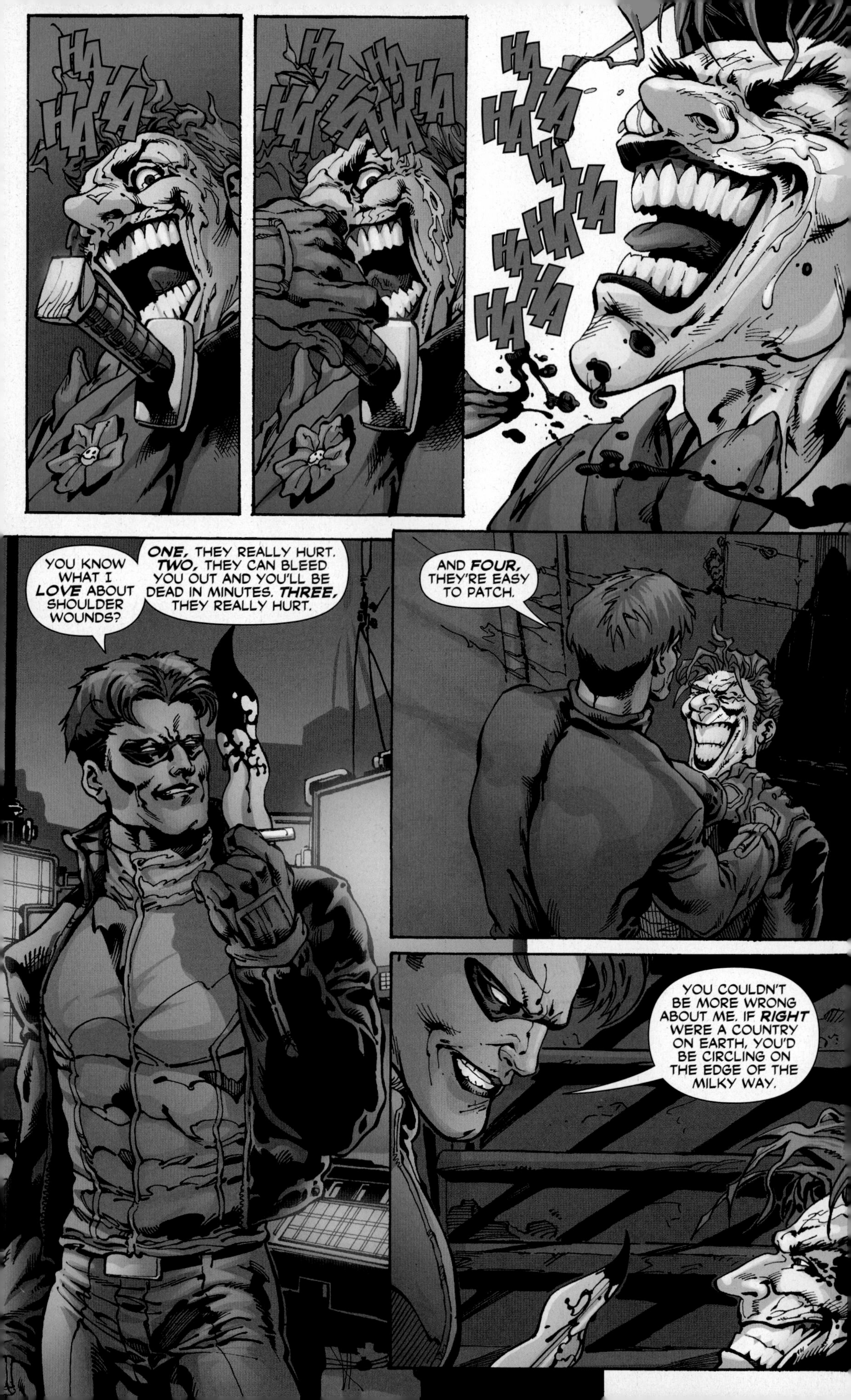
HA HA HA HA
HA HA HA HA HA HA HA HA
HA HA HA HA HA HA HA HA HA HA
YOU KNOW WHAT I LOVE ABOUT SHOULDER WOUNDS?
ONE, THEY REALLY HURT. TWO, THEY CAN BLEED YOU OUT AND YOU'LL BE DEAD IN MINUTES. THREE, THEY REALLY HURT.
AND FOUR, THEY'RE EASY TO PATCH.
YOU COULDN'T BE MORE WRONG ABOUT ME. IF RIGHT WERE A COUNTRY ON EARTH, YOU'D BE CIRCLING ON THE EDGE OF THE MILKY WAY.

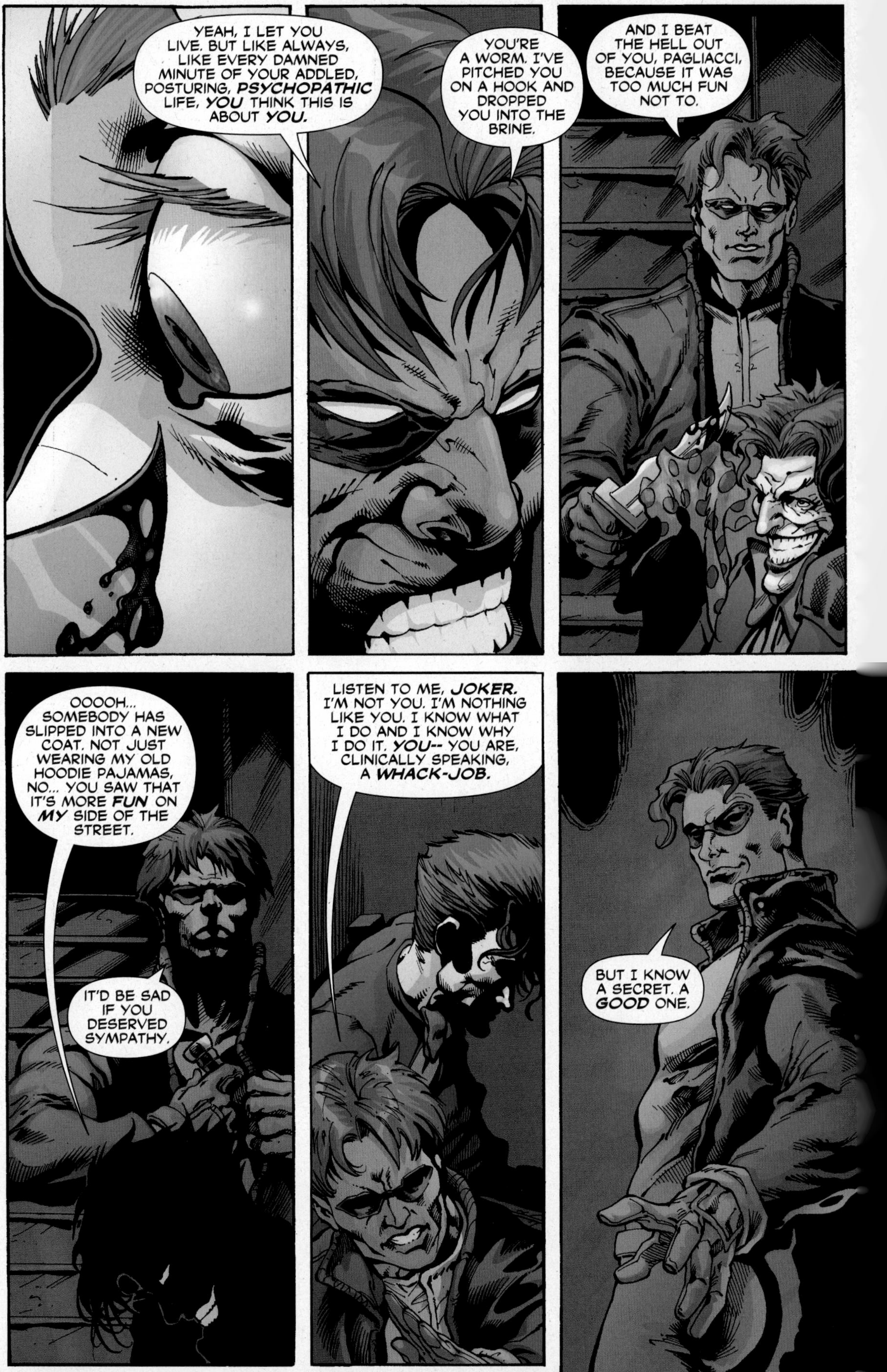
YEAH, I LET YOU LIVE. BUT LIKE ALWAYS, LIKE EVERY DAMNED MINUTE OF YOUR ADDLED, POSTURING, PSYCHOPATHIC LIFE, YOU THINK THIS IS ABOUT YOU.
YOU'RE A WORM. I'VE PITCHED YOU ON A HOOK AND DROPPED YOU INTO THE BRINE.
AND I BEAT THE HELL OUT OF YOU, PAGLIACCI, BECAUSE IT WAS TOO MUCH FUN NOT TO.
OOOOH... SOMEBODY HAS SLIPPED INTO A NEW COAT. NOT JUST WEARING MY OLD HOODIE PAJAMAS, NO... YOU SAW THAT IT'S MORE FUN ON MY SIDE OF THE STREET.
IT'D BE SAD IF YOU DESERVED SYMPATHY.
LISTEN TO ME, JOKER. I'M NOT YOU. I'M NOTHING LIKE YOU. I KNOW WHAT I DO AND I KNOW WHY I DO IT. YOU-- YOU ARE, CLINICALLY SPEAKING, A WHACK-JOB.
BUT I KNOW A SECRET. A GOOD ONE.

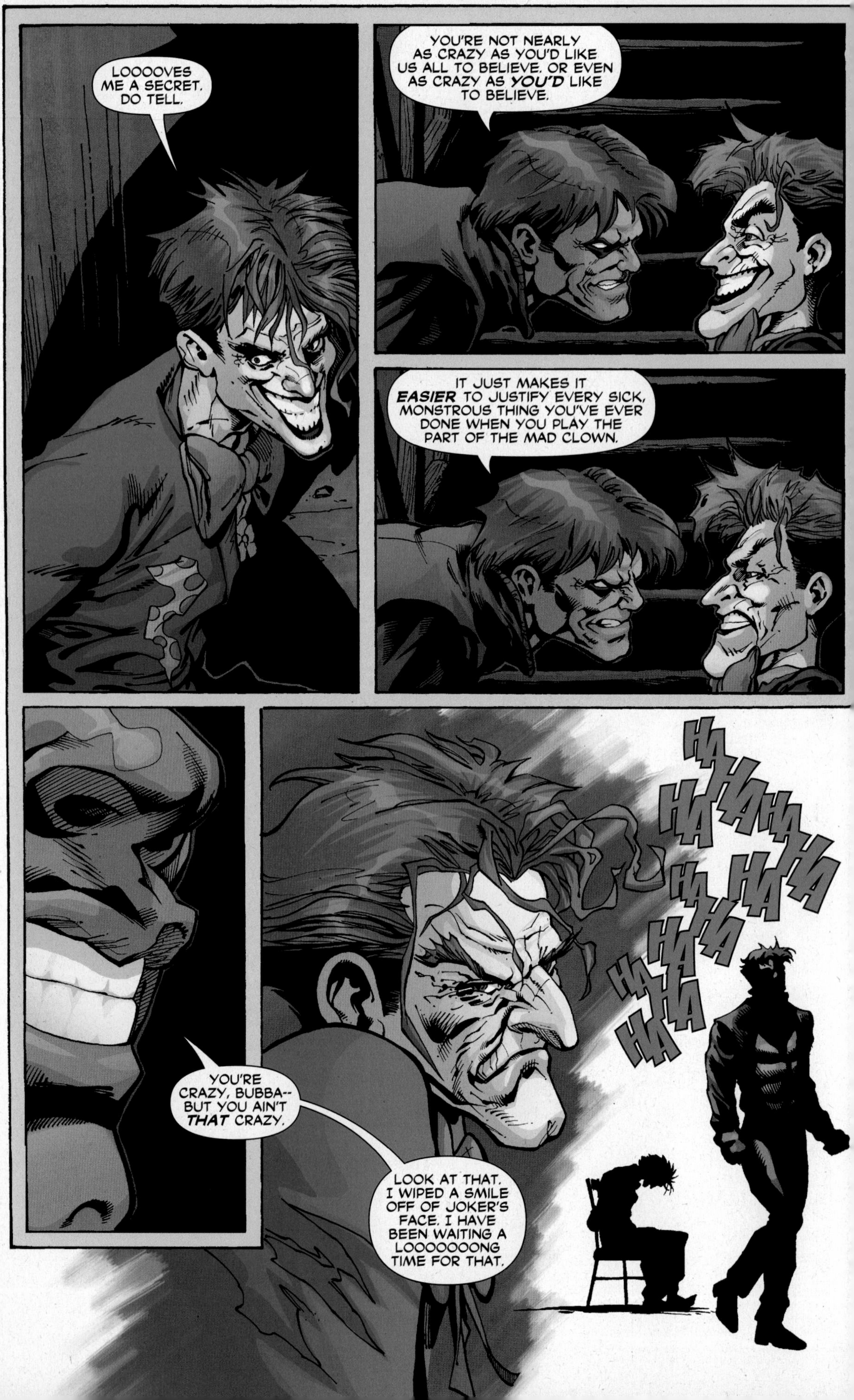

LOOOOVES ME A SECRET. DO TELL.
YOU'RE NOT NEARLY AS CRAZY AS YOU'D LIKE US ALL TO BELIEVE. OR EVEN AS CRAZY AS *YOU'D* LIKE TO BELIEVE.
IT JUST MAKES IT *EASIER* TO JUSTIFY EVERY SICK, MONSTROUS THING YOU'VE EVER DONE WHEN YOU PLAY THE PART OF THE MAD CLOWN.
YOU'RE CRAZY, BUBBA-- BUT YOU AIN'T *THAT* CRAZY.
LOOK AT THAT. I WIPED A SMILE OFF OF JOKER'S FACE. I HAVE BEEN WAITING A LOOOOOOONG TIME FOR THAT.
HA HA HA HA HA HA HA HA HA HA HA HA HA HA HA HA HA

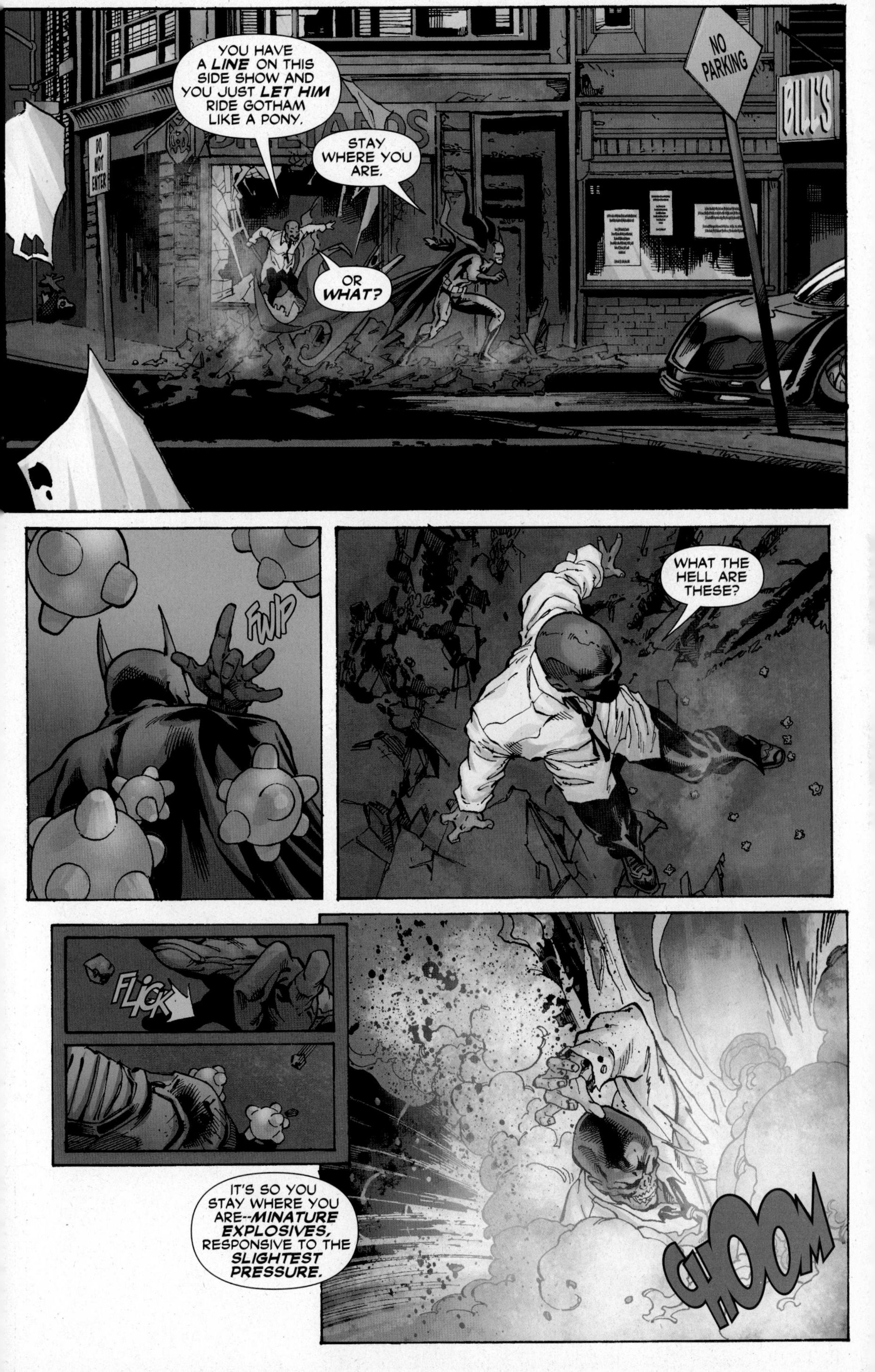

NO PARKING
BILL'S
DO NOT ENTER
YOU HAVE A LINE ON THIS SIDE SHOW AND YOU JUST LET HIM RIDE GOTHAM LIKE A PONY.
STAY WHERE YOU ARE.
OR WHAT?
FWIP
WHAT THE HELL ARE THESE?
FLICK
IT'S SO YOU STAY WHERE YOU ARE--MINATURE EXPLOSIVES, RESPONSIVE TO THE SLIGHTEST PRESSURE.
CHOOM

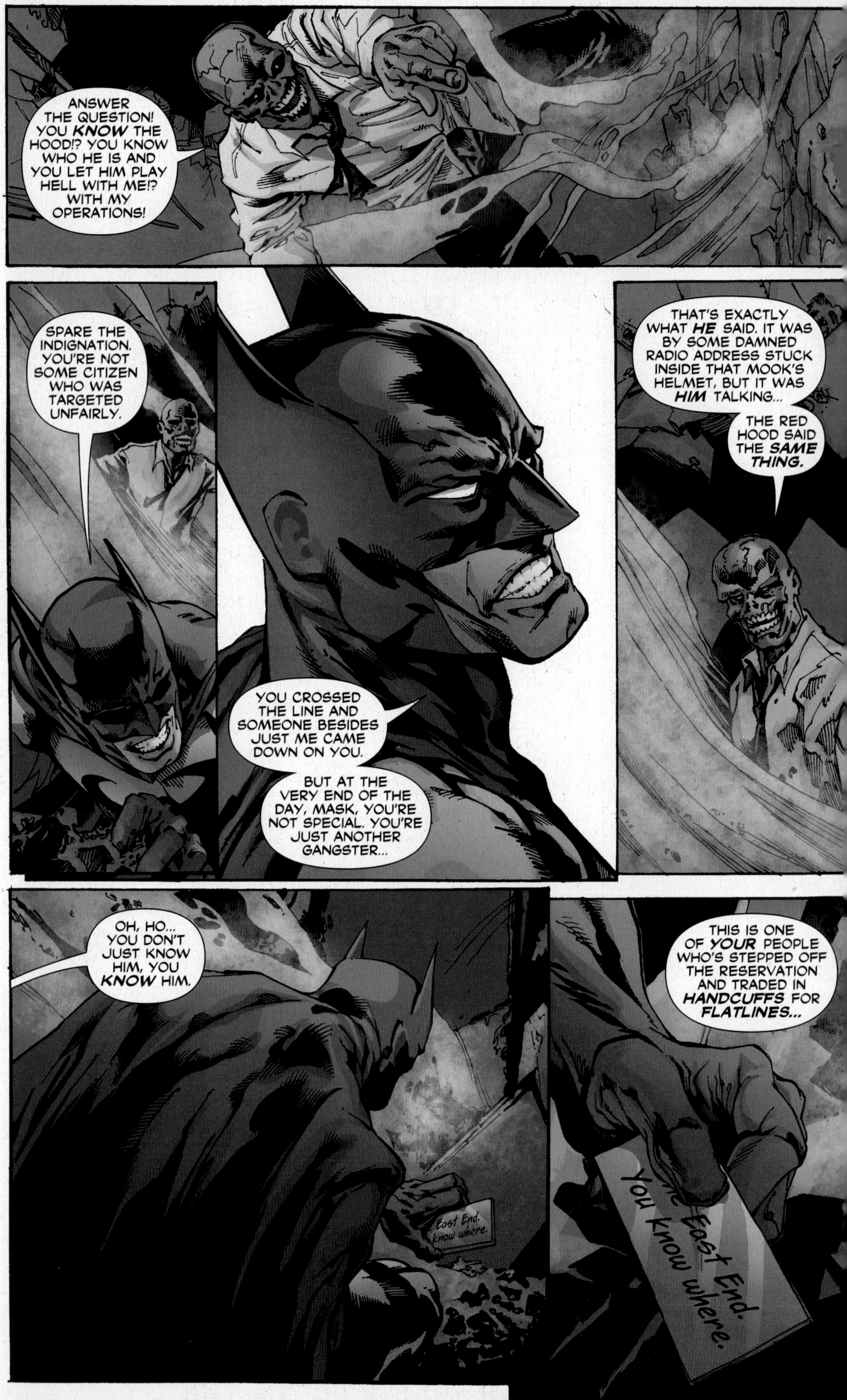

ANSWER THE QUESTION! YOU **KNOW** THE HOOD!? YOU KNOW WHO HE IS AND YOU LET HIM PLAY HELL WITH ME!? WITH MY OPERATIONS!
SPARE THE INDIGNATION. YOU'RE NOT SOME CITIZEN WHO WAS TARGETED UNFAIRLY.
YOU CROSSED THE LINE AND SOMEONE BESIDES JUST ME CAME DOWN ON YOU.
BUT AT THE VERY END OF THE DAY, MASK, YOU'RE NOT SPECIAL. YOU'RE JUST ANOTHER GANGSTER...
THAT'S EXACTLY WHAT **HE** SAID. IT WAS BY SOME DAMNED RADIO ADDRESS STUCK INSIDE THAT MOOK'S HELMET, BUT IT WAS **HIM** TALKING...
THE RED HOOD SAID THE ***SAME THING.***
OH, HO... YOU DON'T JUST KNOW HIM, YOU **KNOW** HIM.
East End.
know where.
THIS IS ONE OF **YOUR** PEOPLE WHO'S STEPPED OFF THE RESERVATION AND TRADED IN ***HANDCUFFS*** FOR ***FLATLINES...***
East End.
You know where.

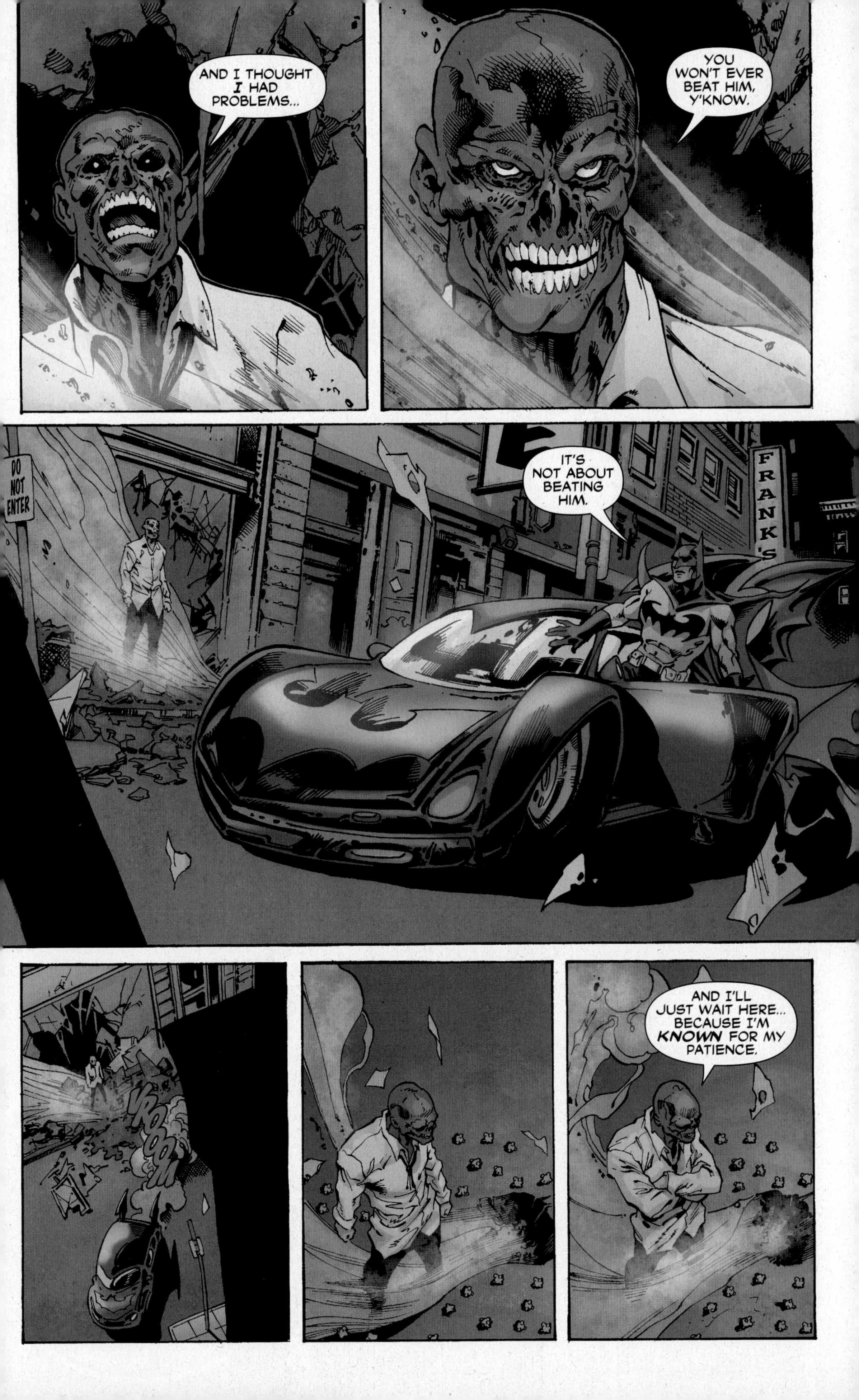
AND I THOUGHT *I* HAD PROBLEMS...
YOU WON'T EVER BEAT HIM, Y'KNOW.
DO NOT ENTER
FRANK'S
IT'S NOT ABOUT BEATING HIM.
VROOOM
AND I'LL JUST WAIT HERE... BECAUSE I'M *KNOWN* FOR MY PATIENCE.

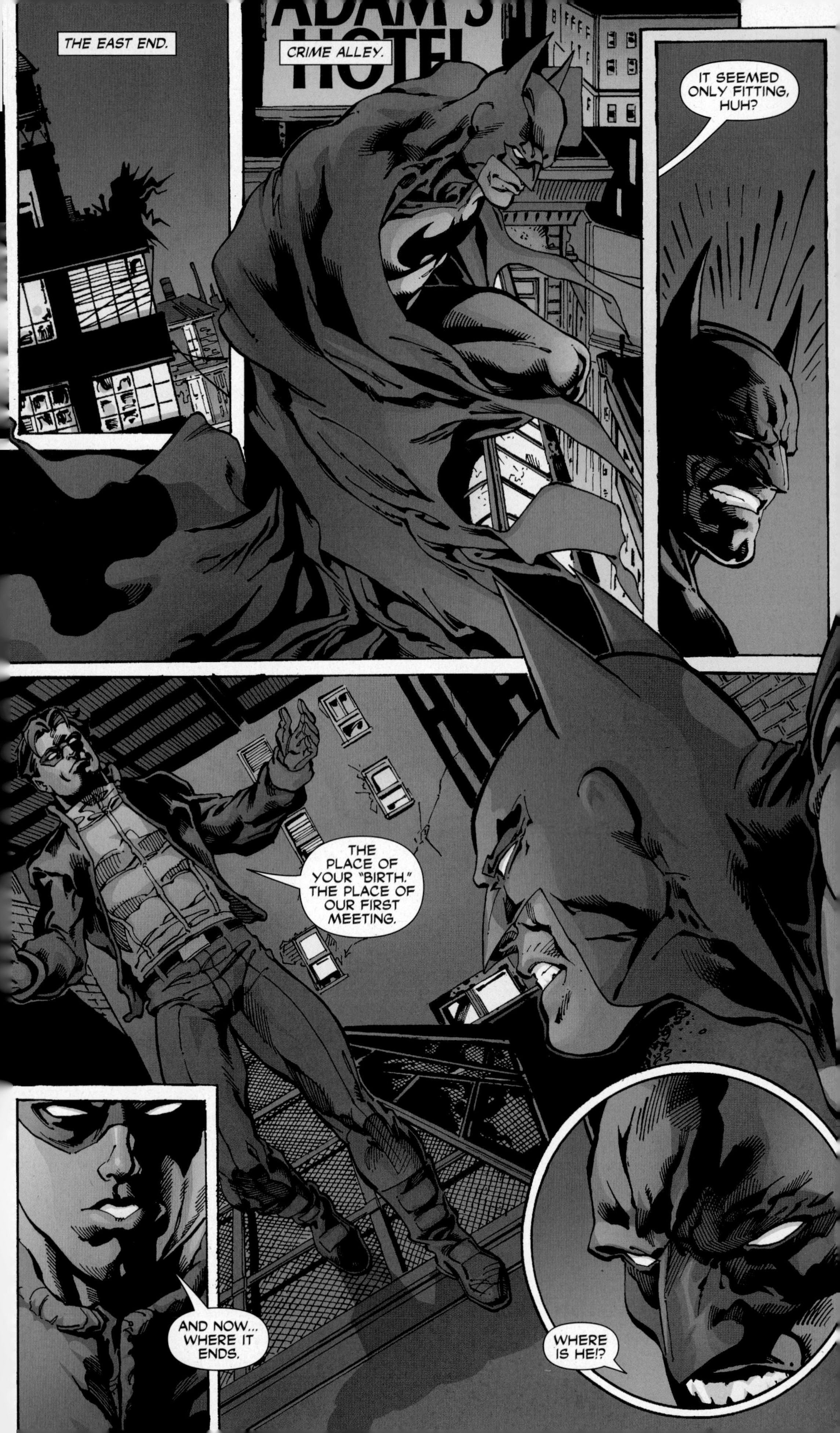
THE EAST END.
CRIME ALLEY.
ADAM'S HOTEL
IT SEEMED ONLY FITTING, HUH?
THE PLACE OF YOUR "BIRTH." THE PLACE OF OUR FIRST MEETING.
AND NOW... WHERE IT ENDS.
WHERE IS HE!?

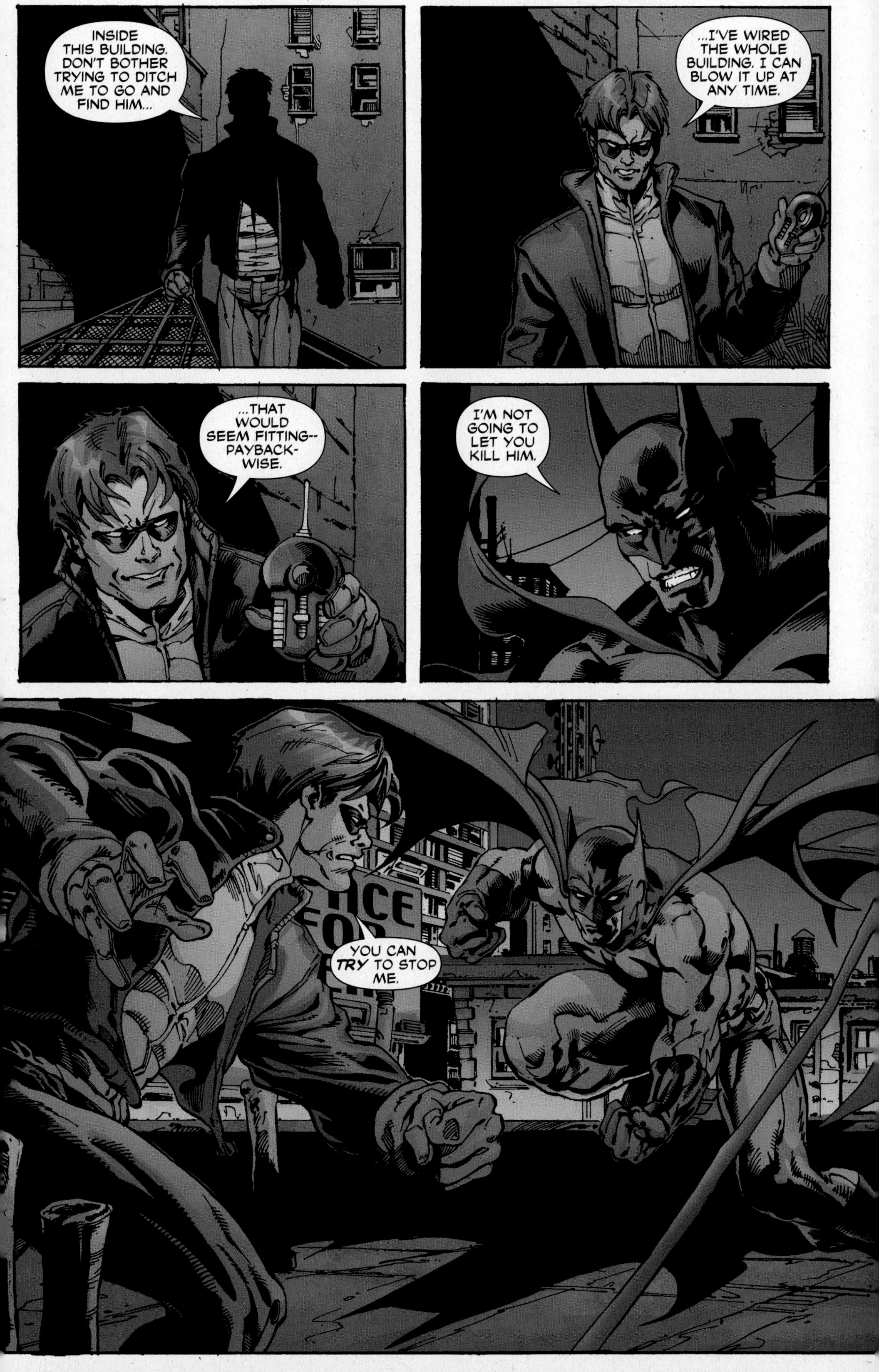
INSIDE THIS BUILDING. DON'T BOTHER TRYING TO DITCH ME TO GO AND FIND HIM...
...I'VE WIRED THE WHOLE BUILDING. I CAN BLOW IT UP AT ANY TIME.
...THAT WOULD SEEM FITTING-- PAYBACK-WISE.
I'M NOT GOING TO LET YOU KILL HIM.
YOU CAN TRY TO STOP ME.

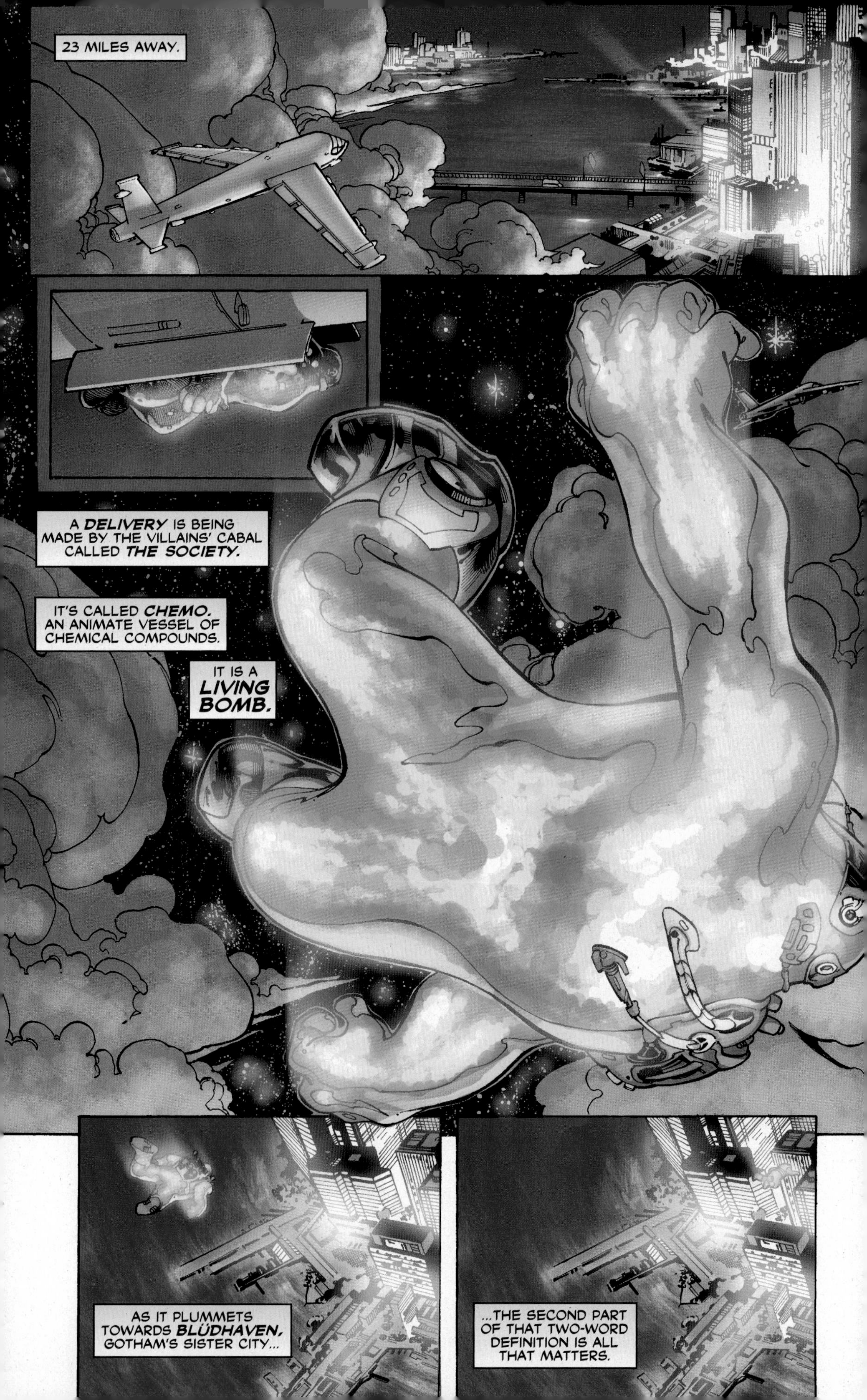
23 MILES AWAY.
A DELIVERY IS BEING MADE BY THE VILLAINS' CABAL CALLED THE SOCIETY.
IT'S CALLED CHEMO. AN ANIMATE VESSEL OF CHEMICAL COMPOUNDS.
IT IS A LIVING BOMB.
AS IT PLUMMETS TOWARDS BLÜDHAVEN, GOTHAM'S SISTER CITY...
...THE SECOND PART OF THAT TWO-WORD DEFINITION IS ALL THAT MATTERS.

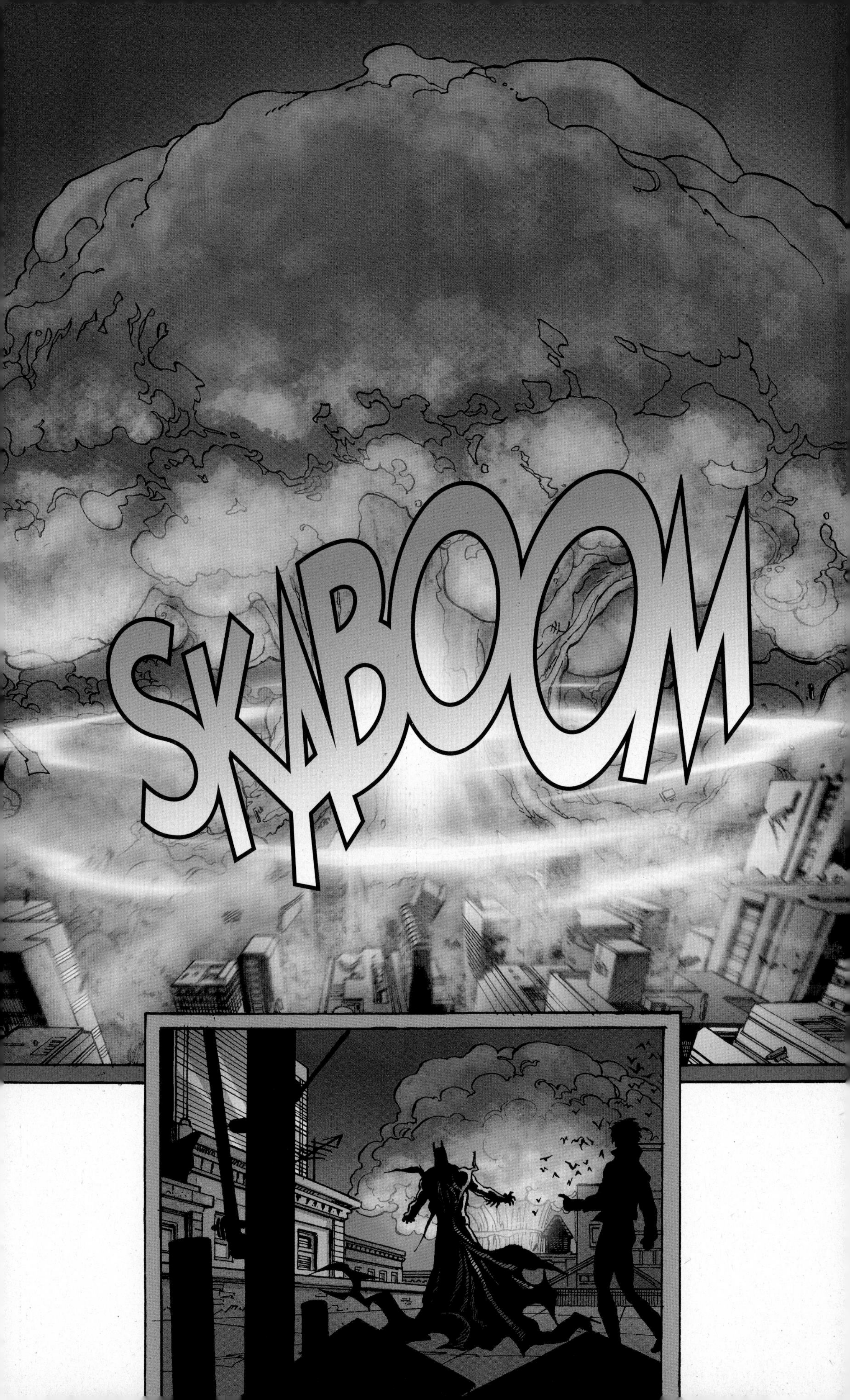
SKABOOM

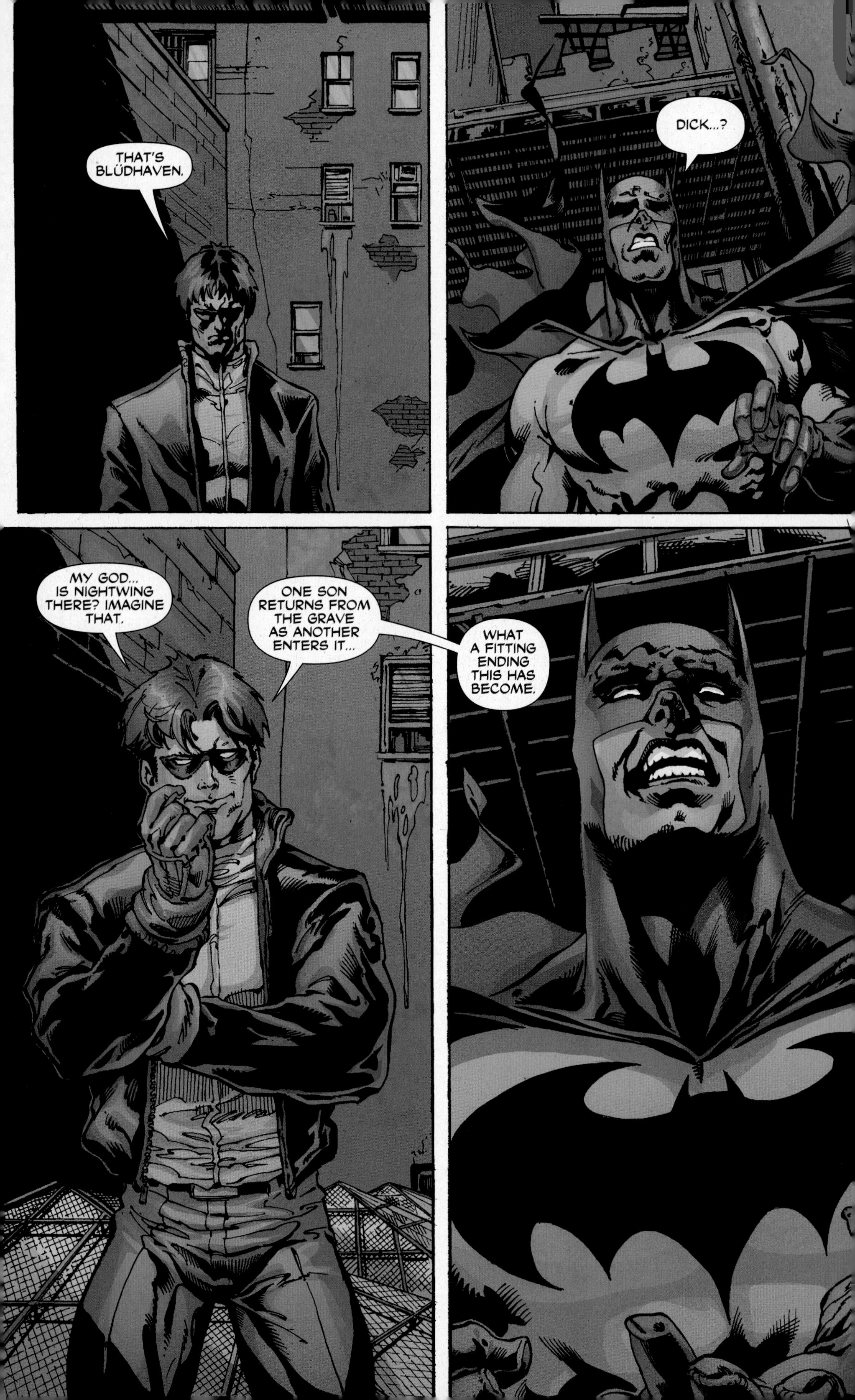
THAT'S BLÜDHAVEN.
DICK...?
MY GOD... IS NIGHTWING THERE? IMAGINE THAT.
ONE SON RETURNS FROM THE GRAVE AS ANOTHER ENTERS IT...
WHAT A FITTING ENDING THIS HAS BECOME.

BATMAN 650 Cover by Jock

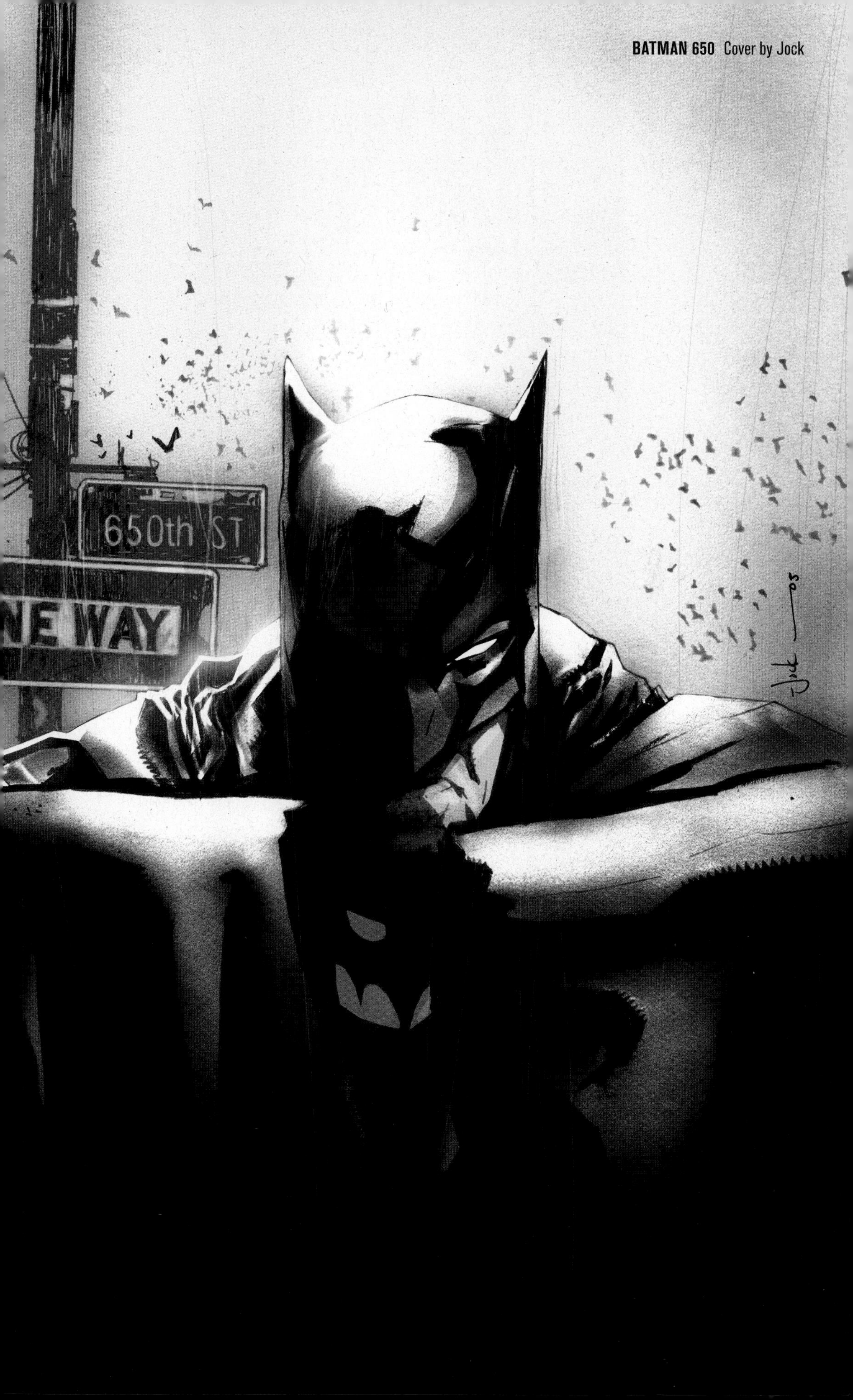
650th ST
NE WAY

CHAPTER 13

ALL THEY DO IS WATCH US KILL

PART THREE

CRIME ALLEY.

MARRED BY WRONGDOING AND BY DEATH, IT HAS BECOME A "BIRTH PLACE" OF SORTS.

IT IS WHERE THESE TWO FORMER PARTNERS...STUDENT AND TEACHER...ALLY AND FOE...FATHER AND SON...

...HAVE COME TO SETTLE THEIR DIFFERENCES-- ONCE AND FOR ALL.

THEN THE ENTIRE CITY OF BLÜDHAVEN IS VAPORIZED BEFORE THEIR EYES IN A NUCLEAR EXPLOSION.

BLÜDHAVEN. PROTECTED BY THE COSTUMED VIGILANTE NIGHTWING.

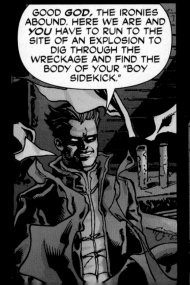

GOOD *GOD*, THE IRONIES ABOUND. HERE WE ARE AND *YOU* HAVE TO RUN TO THE SITE OF AN EXPLOSION TO DIG THROUGH THE WRECKAGE AND FIND THE BODY OF YOUR "BOY SIDEKICK."

IF HE'S THERE, BRUCE... YOU'RE TOO LATE.

AGAIN.

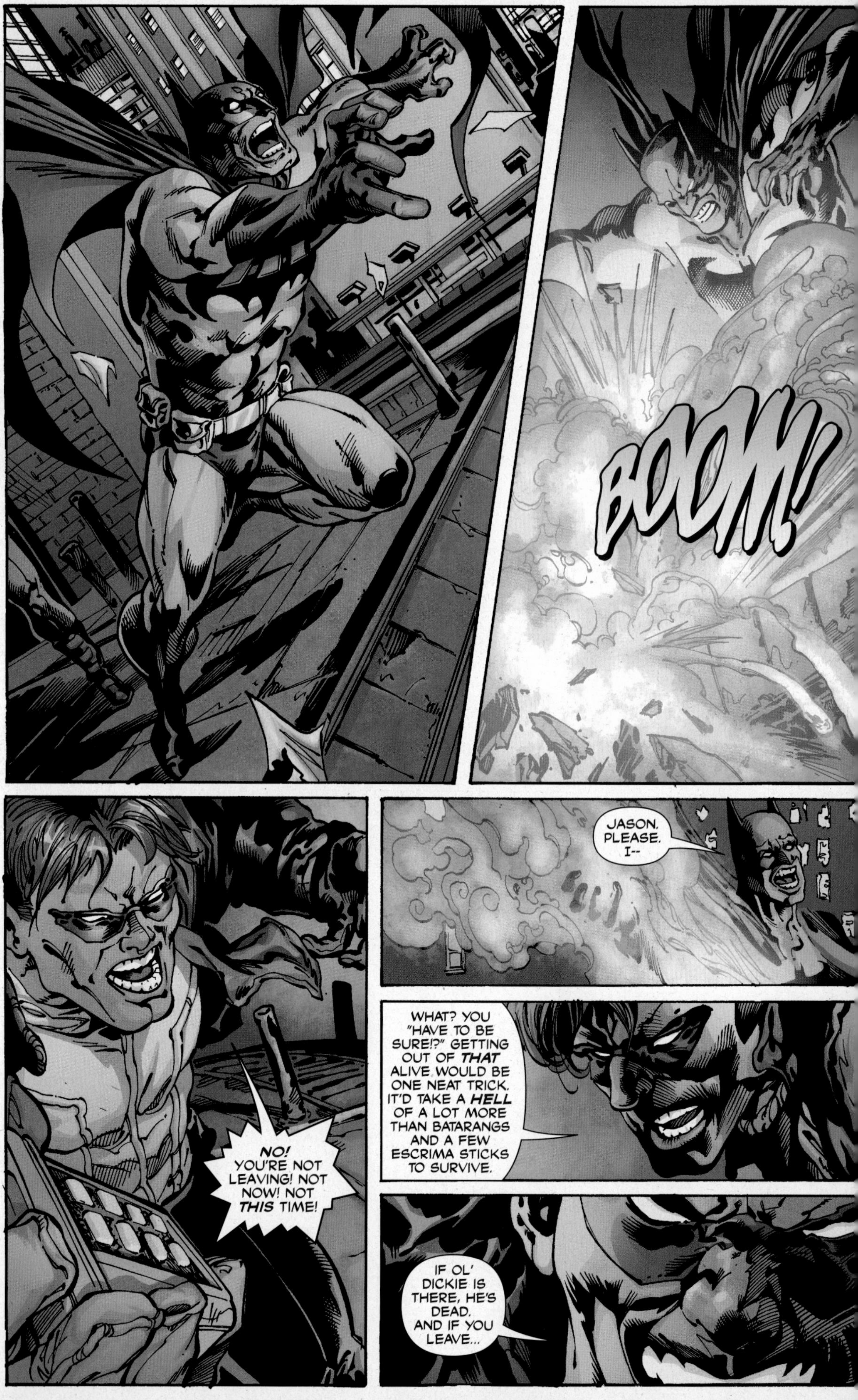
BOOM!
JASON. PLEASE. I--
WHAT? YOU "HAVE TO BE SURE!?" GETTING OUT OF *THAT* ALIVE WOULD BE ONE NEAT TRICK. IT'D TAKE A *HELL* OF A LOT MORE THAN BATARANGS AND A FEW ESCRIMA STICKS TO SURVIVE.
IF OL' DICKIE IS THERE, HE'S DEAD. AND IF YOU LEAVE...
NO! YOU'RE NOT LEAVING! NOT NOW! NOT *THIS* TIME!

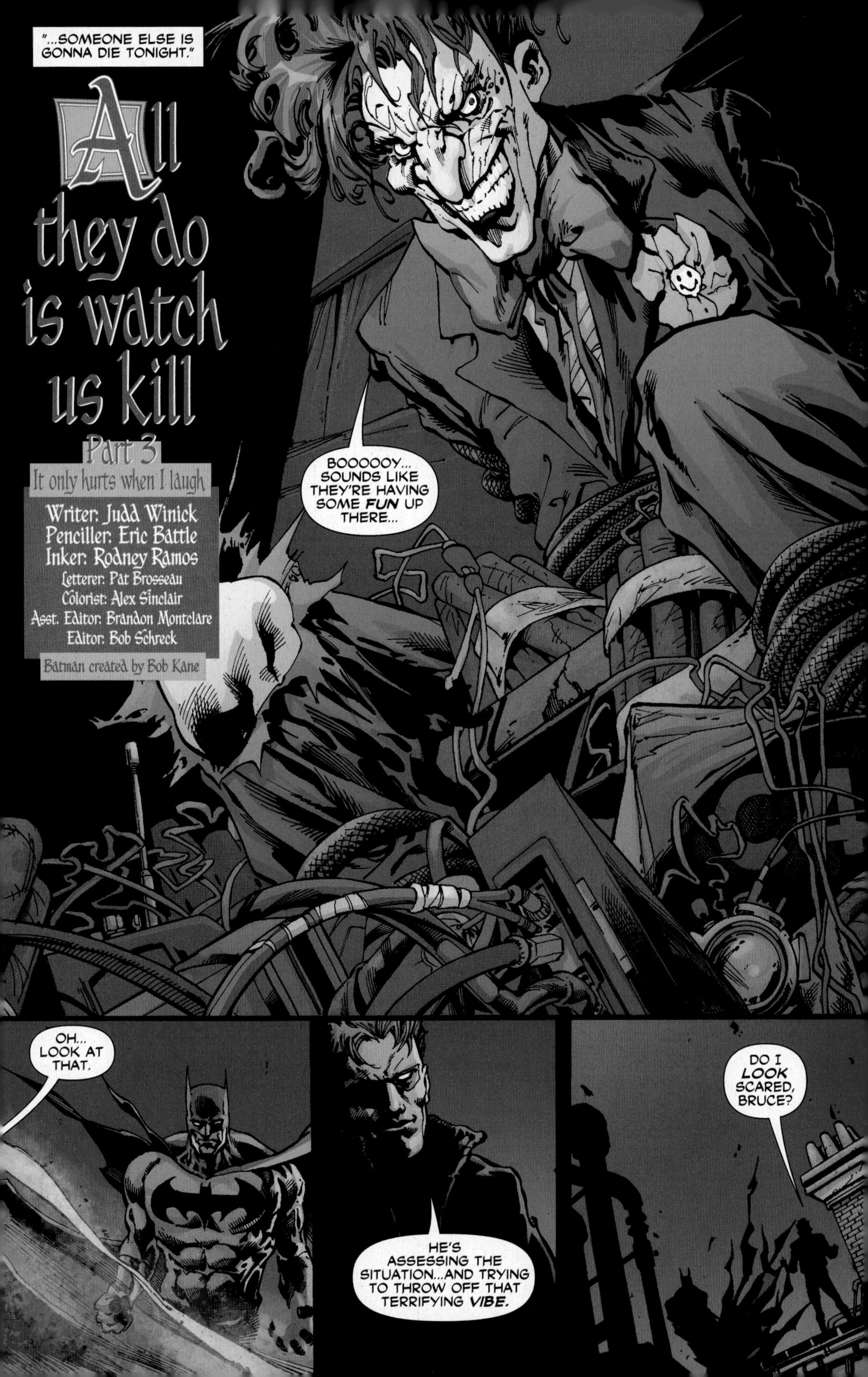
"...SOMEONE ELSE IS GONNA DIE TONIGHT."
All they do is watch us kill
Part 3
It only hurts when I laugh
Writer: Judd Winick
Penciller: Eric Battle
Inker: Rodney Ramos
Letterer: Pat Brosseau
Colorist: Alex Sinclair
Asst. Editor: Brandon Montclare
Editor: Bob Schreck
Batman created by Bob Kane
BOOOOOY... SOUNDS LIKE THEY'RE HAVING SOME FUN UP THERE...
OH... LOOK AT THAT.
HE'S ASSESSING THE SITUATION...AND TRYING TO THROW OFF THAT TERRIFYING VIBE.
DO I LOOK SCARED, BRUCE?

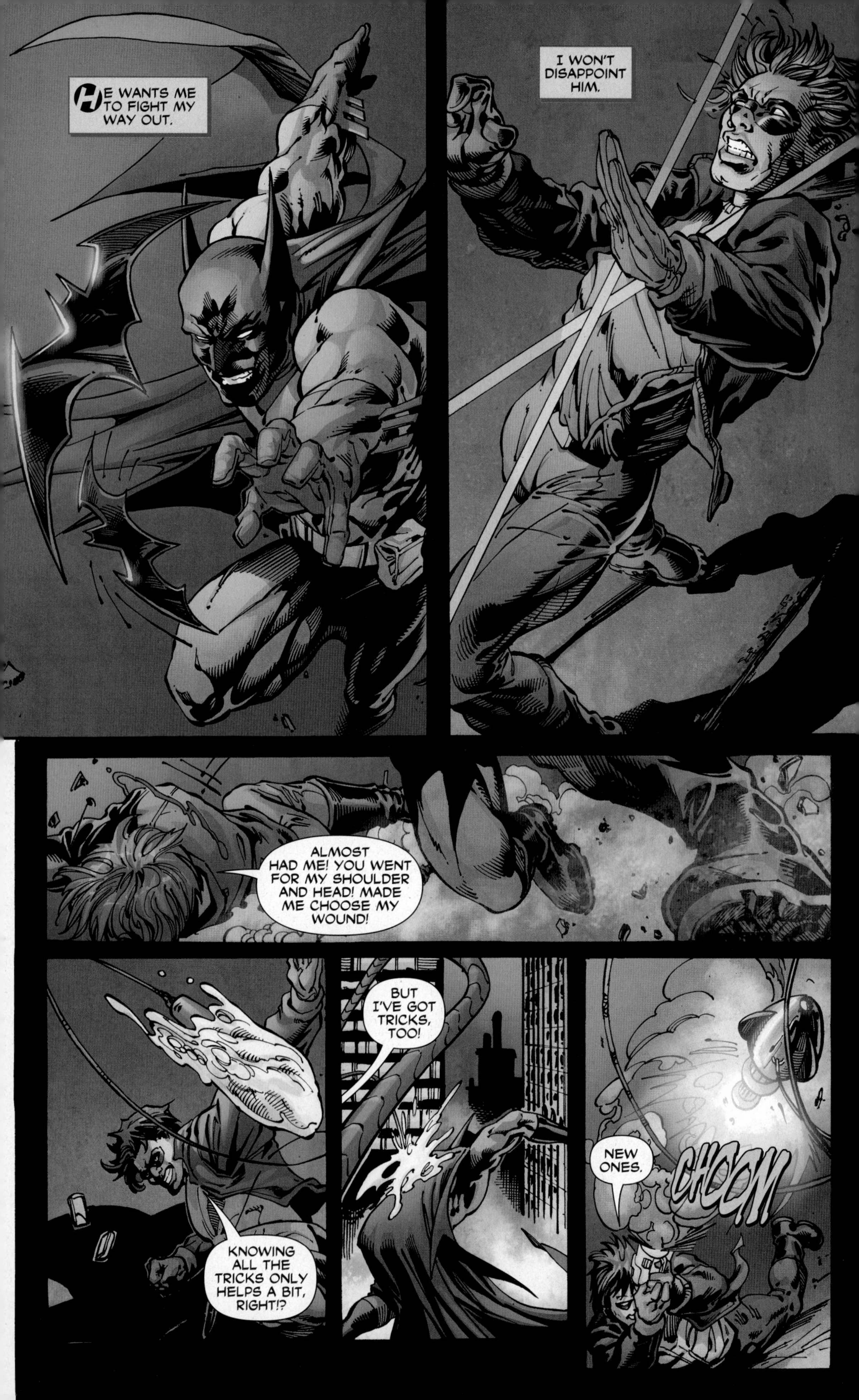
HE WANTS ME TO FIGHT MY WAY OUT.
I WON'T DISAPPOINT HIM.
ALMOST HAD ME! YOU WENT FOR MY SHOULDER AND HEAD! MADE ME CHOOSE MY WOUND!
KNOWING ALL THE TRICKS ONLY HELPS A BIT, RIGHT!?
BUT I'VE GOT TRICKS, TOO!
NEW ONES.
CHOOM

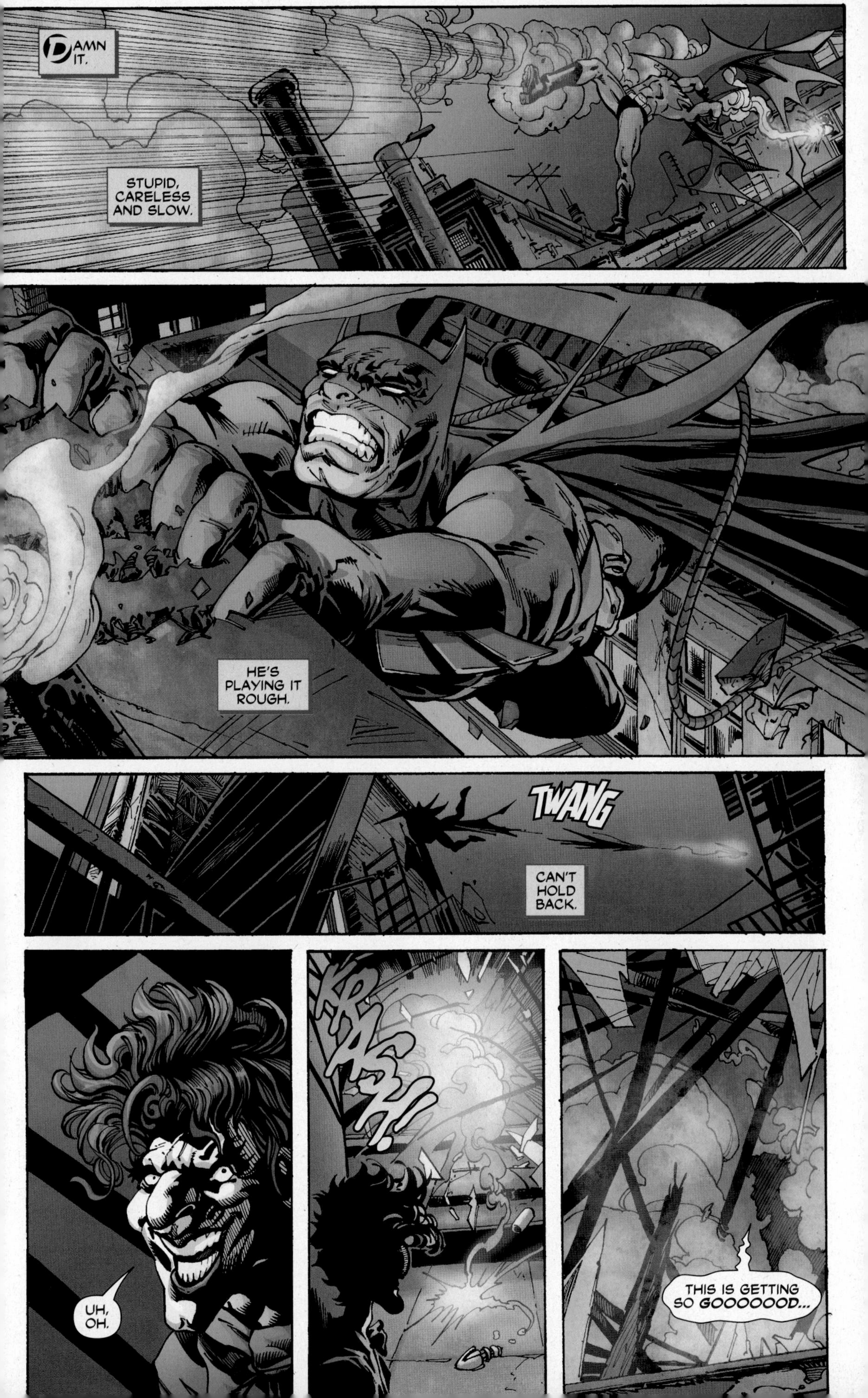
DAMN IT.
STUPID, CARELESS AND SLOW.
HE'S PLAYING IT ROUGH.
TWANG
CAN'T HOLD BACK.
UH, OH.
KRASH!!
THIS IS GETTING SO GOOOOOOD...

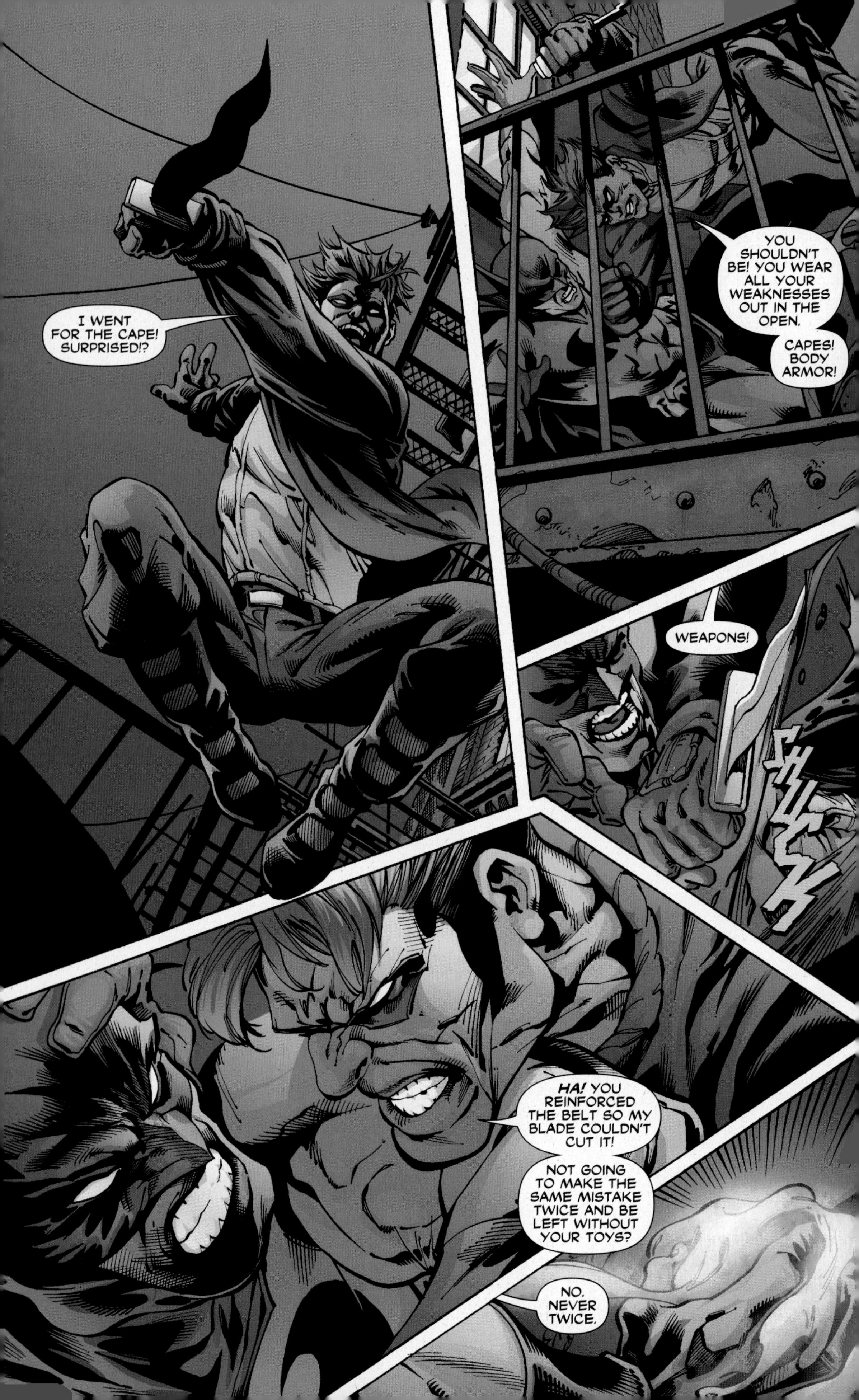
I WENT FOR THE CAPE! SURPRISED!?
YOU SHOULDN'T BE! YOU WEAR ALL YOUR WEAKNESSES OUT IN THE OPEN.
CAPES! BODY ARMOR!
WEAPONS!
SHUNK
HA! YOU REINFORCED THE BELT SO MY BLADE COULDN'T CUT IT!
NOT GOING TO MAKE THE SAME MISTAKE TWICE AND BE LEFT WITHOUT YOUR TOYS?
NO. NEVER TWICE.

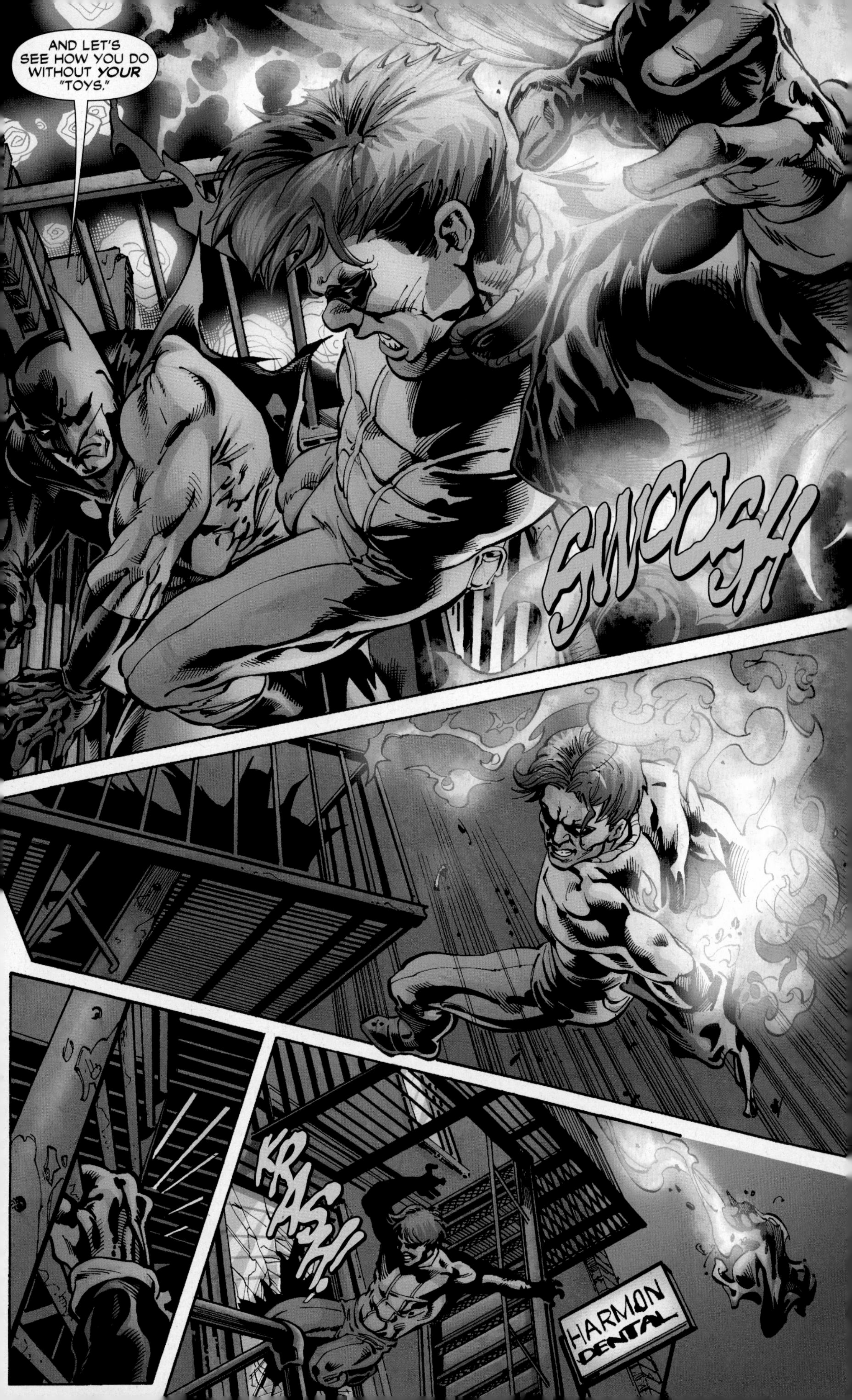
AND LET'S SEE HOW YOU DO WITHOUT *YOUR* "TOYS."
SWOOSH
KRASH!
HARMON DENTAL

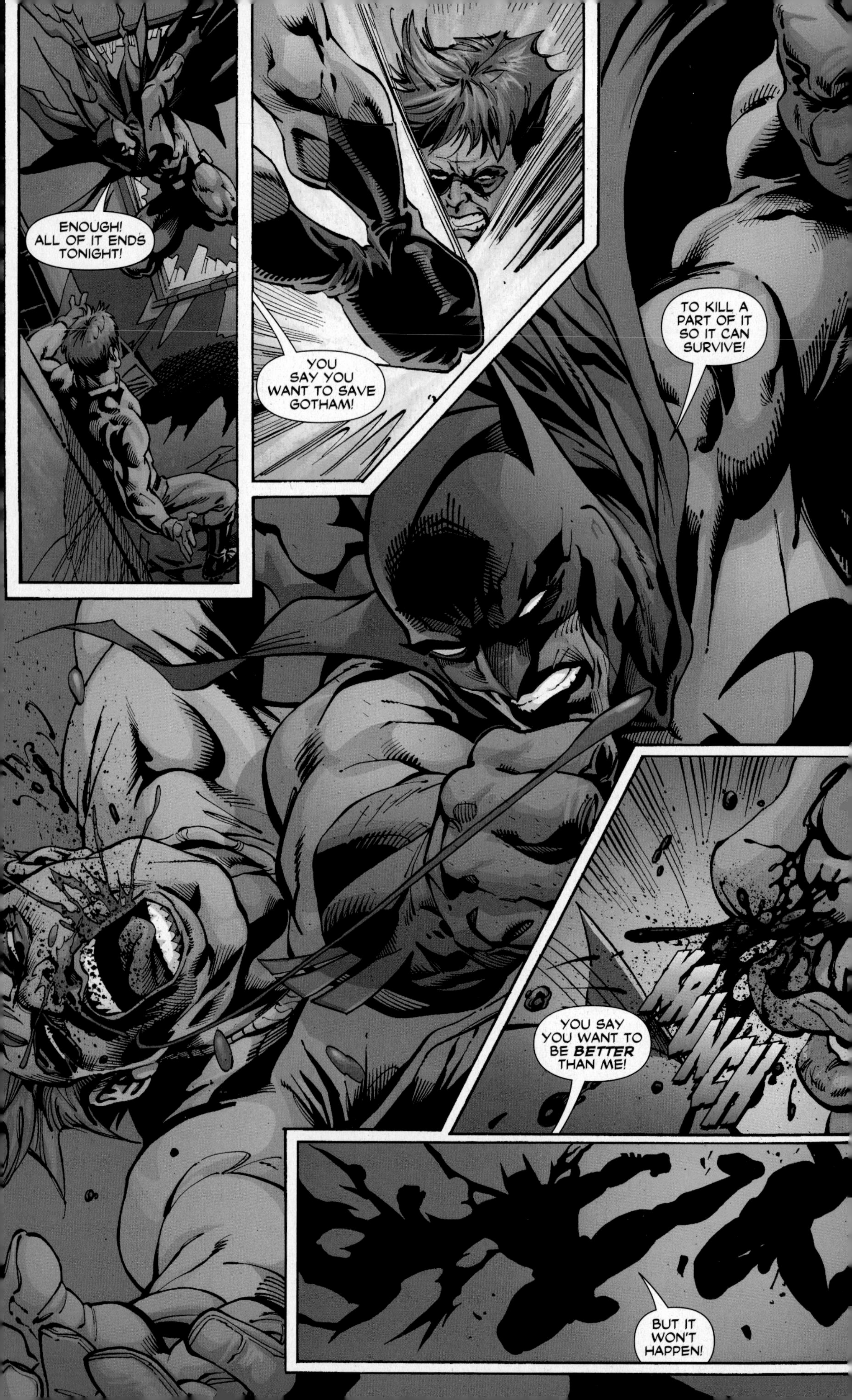
ENOUGH! ALL OF IT ENDS TONIGHT!
YOU SAY YOU WANT TO SAVE GOTHAM!
TO KILL A PART OF IT SO IT CAN SURVIVE!
KRUNCH
YOU SAY YOU WANT TO BE BETTER THAN ME!
BUT IT WON'T HAPPEN!

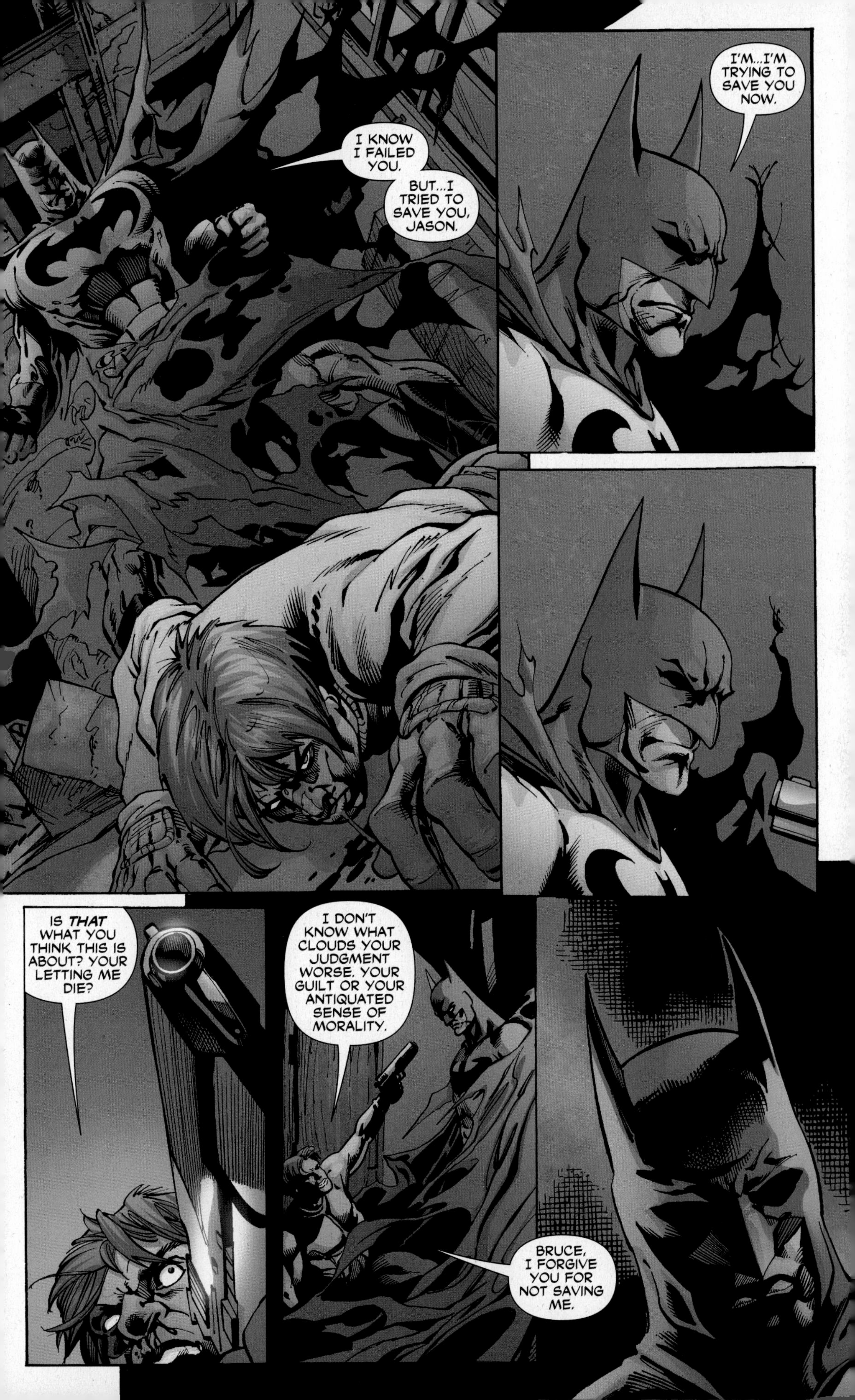
I KNOW I FAILED YOU.
BUT...I TRIED TO SAVE YOU, JASON.
I'M...I'M TRYING TO SAVE YOU NOW.
IS *THAT* WHAT YOU THINK THIS IS ABOUT? YOUR LETTING ME DIE?
I DON'T KNOW WHAT CLOUDS YOUR JUDGMENT WORSE. YOUR GUILT OR YOUR ANTIQUATED SENSE OF MORALITY.
BRUCE, I FORGIVE YOU FOR NOT SAVING ME.

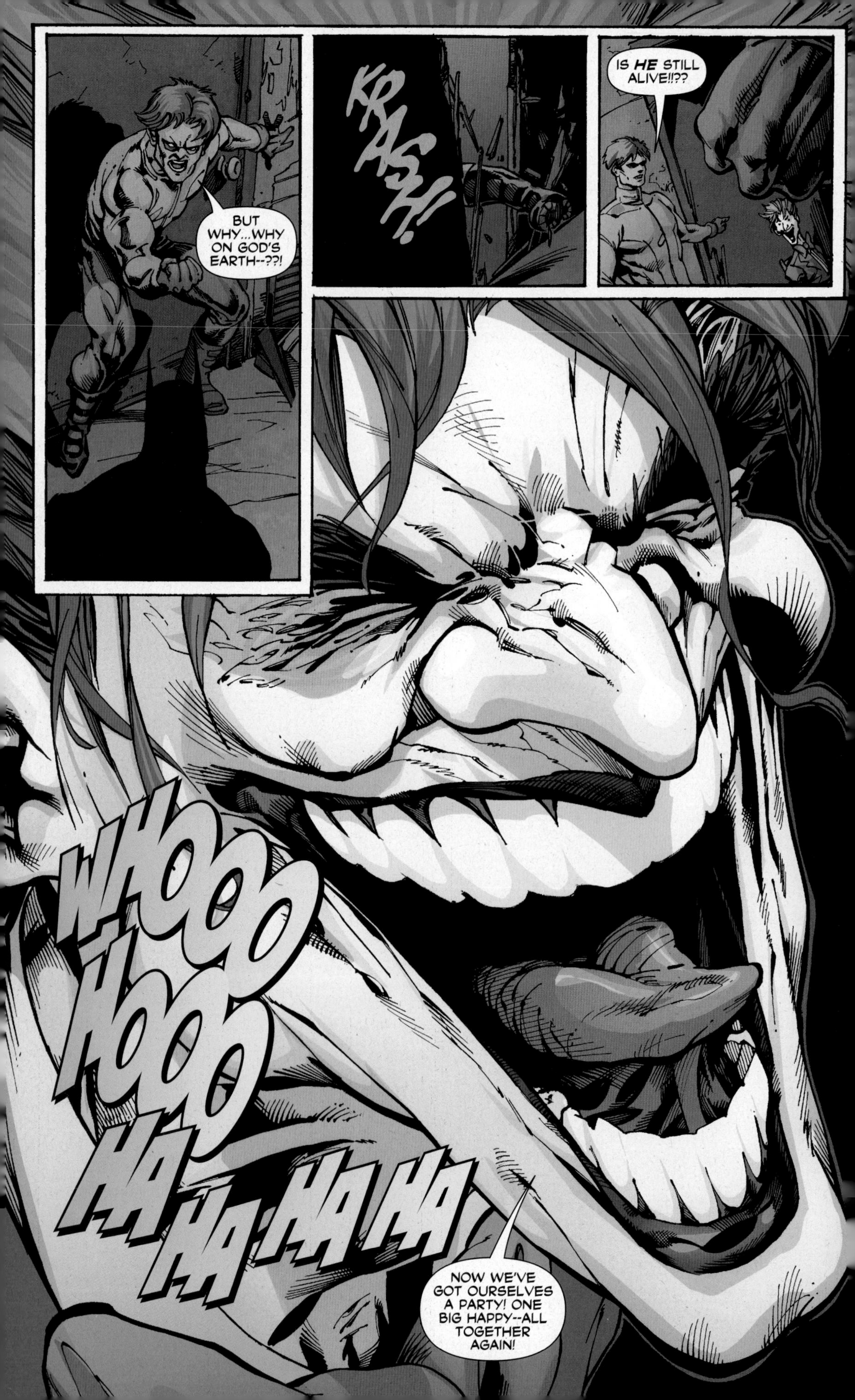
BUT WHY...WHY ON GOD'S EARTH--??!
KRASH!!
IS HE STILL ALIVE!!??
WHOOO HOOO HA HA HA HA HA
NOW WE'VE GOT OURSELVES A PARTY! ONE BIG HAPPY--ALL TOGETHER AGAIN!

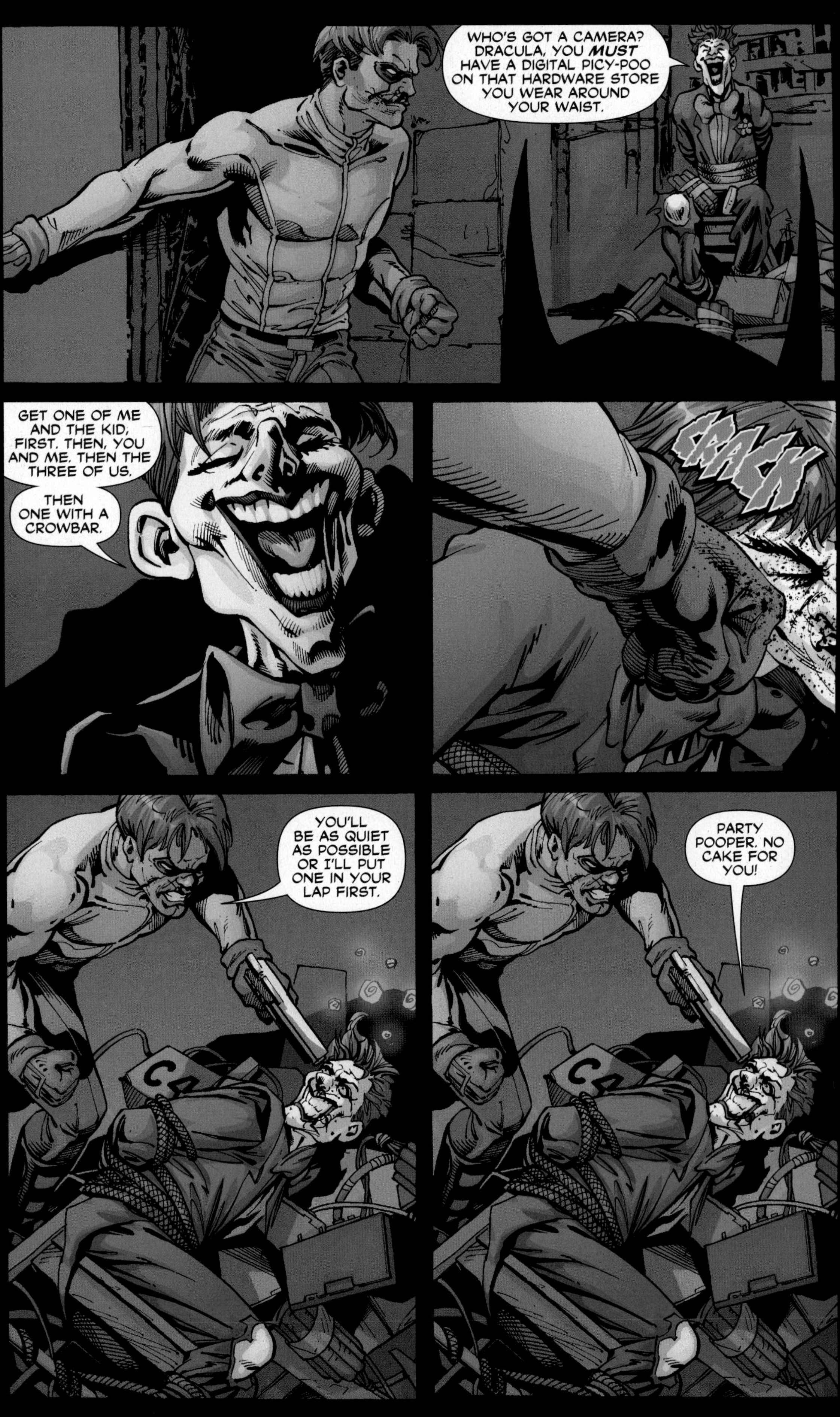
WHO'S GOT A CAMERA? DRACULA, YOU MUST HAVE A DIGITAL PICY-POO ON THAT HARDWARE STORE YOU WEAR AROUND YOUR WAIST.
GET ONE OF ME AND THE KID, FIRST. THEN, YOU AND ME. THEN THE THREE OF US.
THEN ONE WITH A CROWBAR.
CRACK
YOU'LL BE AS QUIET AS POSSIBLE OR I'LL PUT ONE IN YOUR LAP FIRST.
PARTY POOPER. NO CAKE FOR YOU!

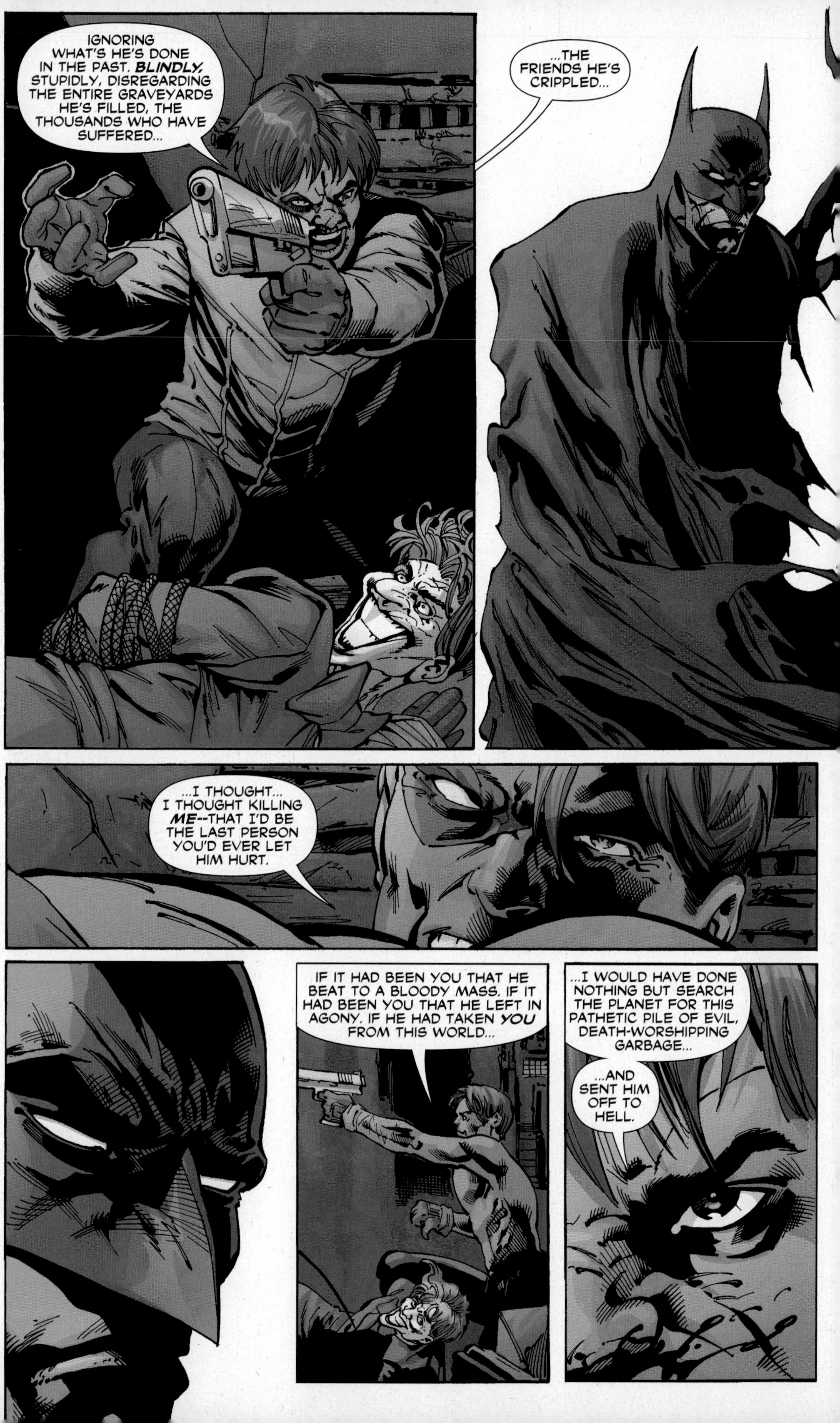
IGNORING WHAT'S HE'S DONE IN THE PAST. BLINDLY, STUPIDLY, DISREGARDING THE ENTIRE GRAVEYARDS HE'S FILLED, THE THOUSANDS WHO HAVE SUFFERED...
...THE FRIENDS HE'S CRIPPLED...
...I THOUGHT... I THOUGHT KILLING ME--THAT I'D BE THE LAST PERSON YOU'D EVER LET HIM HURT.
IF IT HAD BEEN YOU THAT HE BEAT TO A BLOODY MASS, IF IT HAD BEEN YOU THAT HE LEFT IN AGONY, IF HE HAD TAKEN YOU FROM THIS WORLD...
...I WOULD HAVE DONE NOTHING BUT SEARCH THE PLANET FOR THIS PATHETIC PILE OF EVIL, DEATH-WORSHIPPING GARBAGE...
...AND SENT HIM OFF TO HELL.

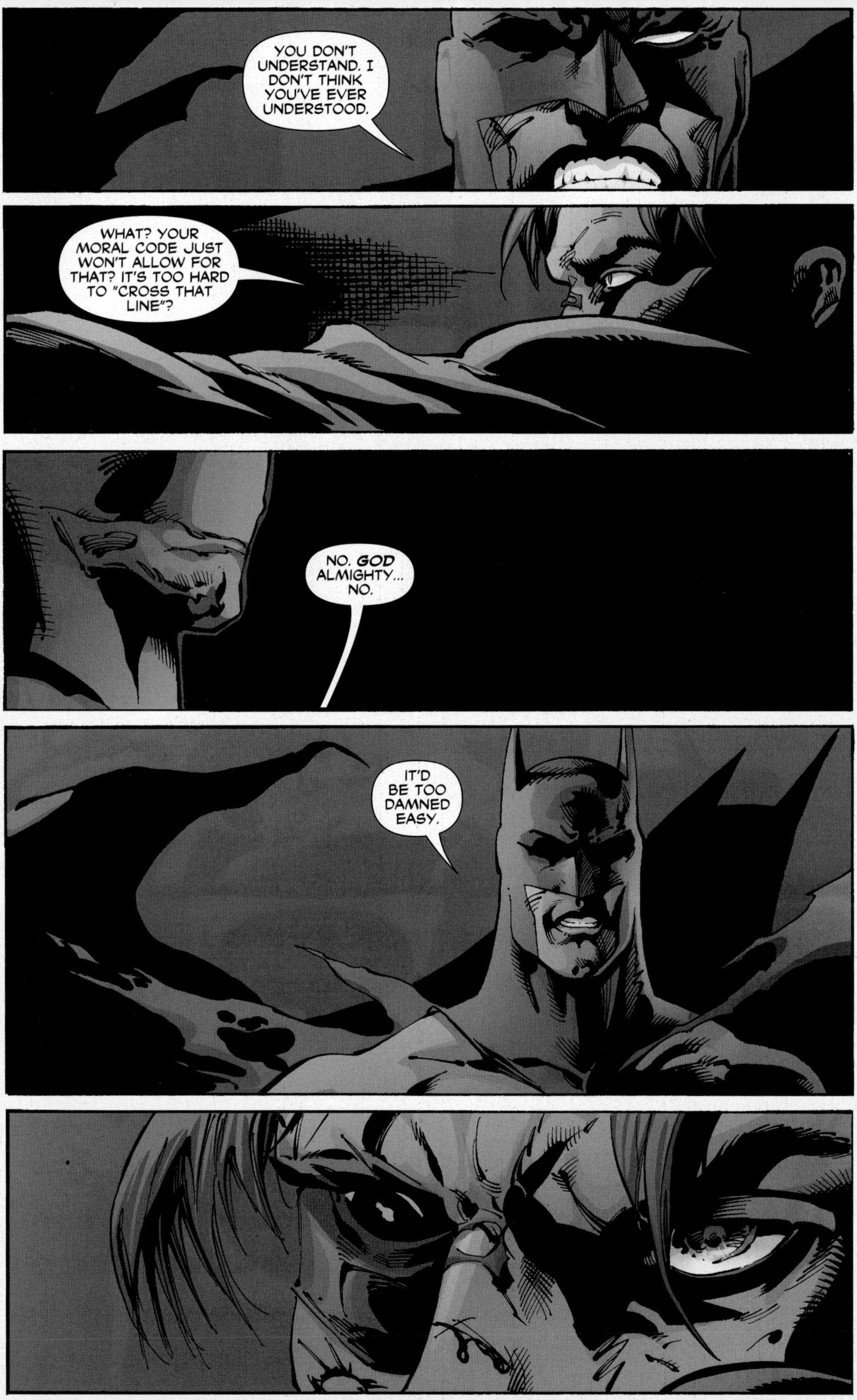
YOU DON'T UNDERSTAND. I DON'T THINK YOU'VE EVER UNDERSTOOD.
WHAT? YOUR MORAL CODE JUST WON'T ALLOW FOR THAT? IT'S TOO HARD TO "CROSS THAT LINE"?
NO. GOD ALMIGHTY... NO.
IT'D BE TOO DAMNED EASY.

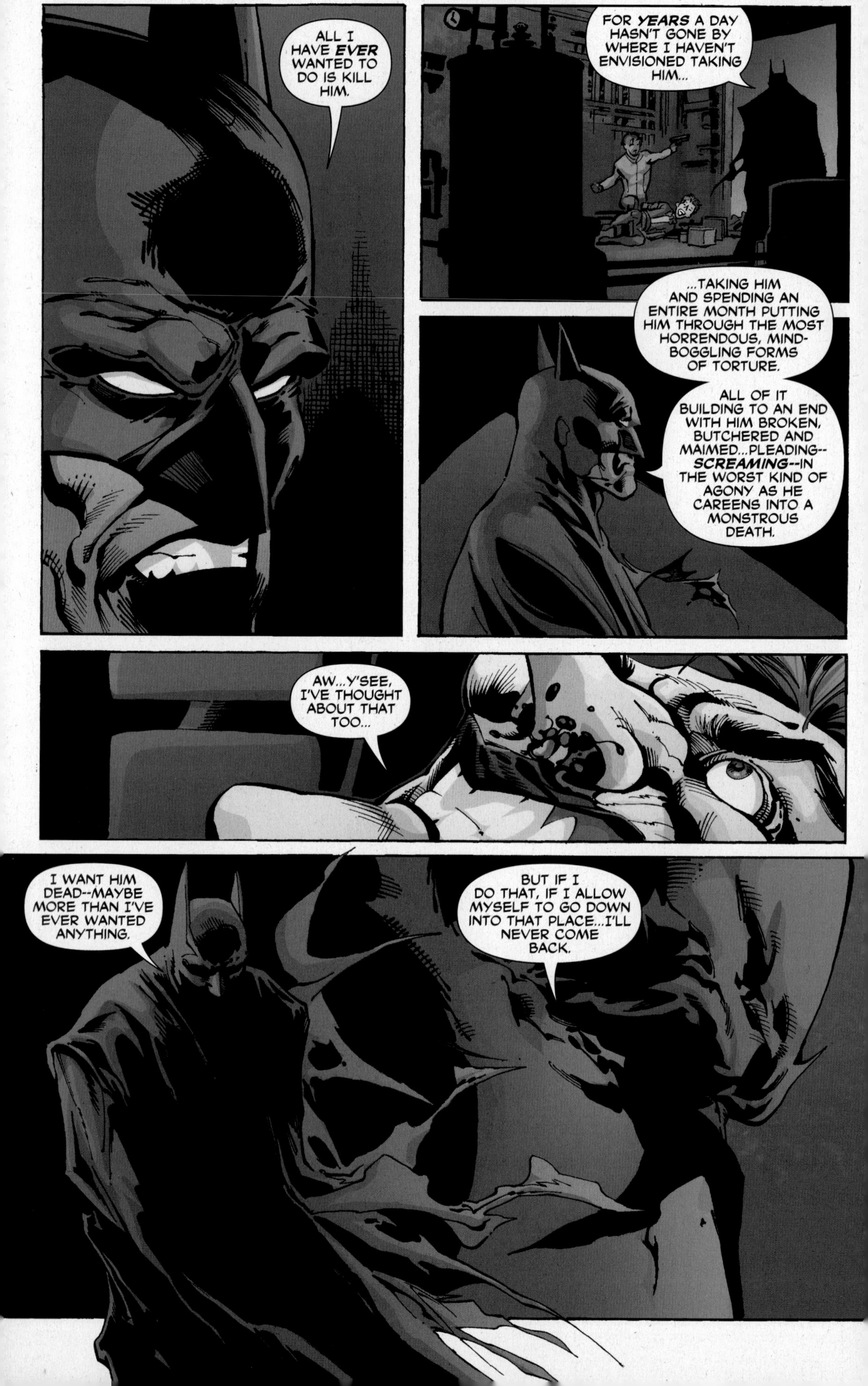
ALL I HAVE *EVER* WANTED TO DO IS KILL HIM.
FOR *YEARS* A DAY HASN'T GONE BY WHERE I HAVEN'T ENVISIONED TAKING HIM...
...TAKING HIM AND SPENDING AN ENTIRE MONTH PUTTING HIM THROUGH THE MOST HORRENDOUS, MIND-BOGGLING FORMS OF TORTURE.
ALL OF IT BUILDING TO AN END WITH HIM BROKEN, BUTCHERED AND MAIMED...PLEADING--*SCREAMING*--IN THE WORST KIND OF AGONY AS HE CAREENS INTO A MONSTROUS DEATH.
AW...Y'SEE, I'VE THOUGHT ABOUT THAT TOO...
I WANT HIM DEAD--MAYBE MORE THAN I'VE EVER WANTED ANYTHING.
BUT IF I DO THAT, IF I ALLOW MYSELF TO GO DOWN INTO THAT PLACE...I'LL NEVER COME BACK.

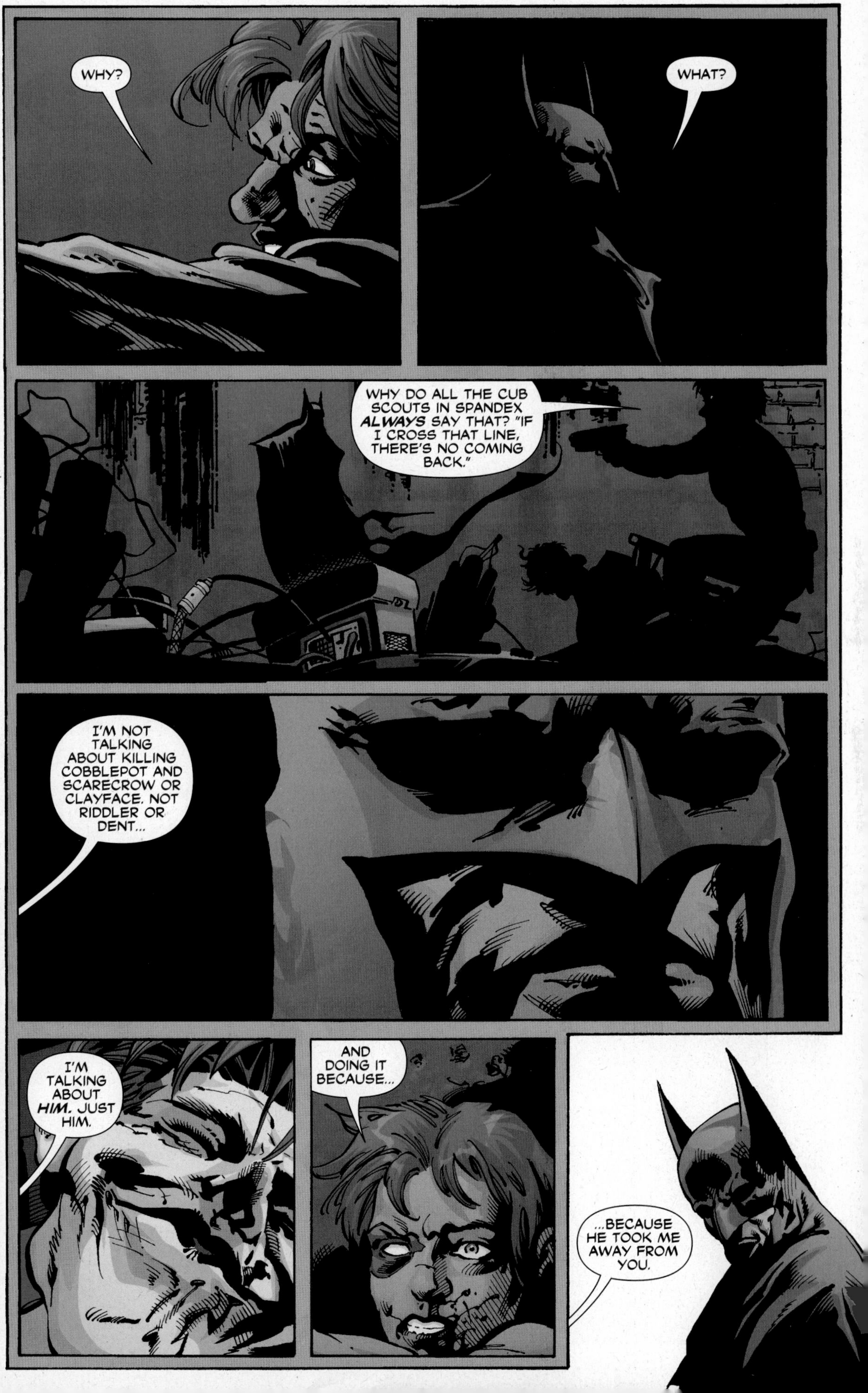

WHY?
WHAT?
WHY DO ALL THE CUB SCOUTS IN SPANDEX ALWAYS SAY THAT? "IF I CROSS THAT LINE, THERE'S NO COMING BACK."
I'M NOT TALKING ABOUT KILLING COBBLEPOT AND SCARECROW OR CLAYFACE. NOT RIDDLER OR DENT...
I'M TALKING ABOUT HIM. JUST HIM.
AND DOING IT BECAUSE...
...BECAUSE HE TOOK ME AWAY FROM YOU.

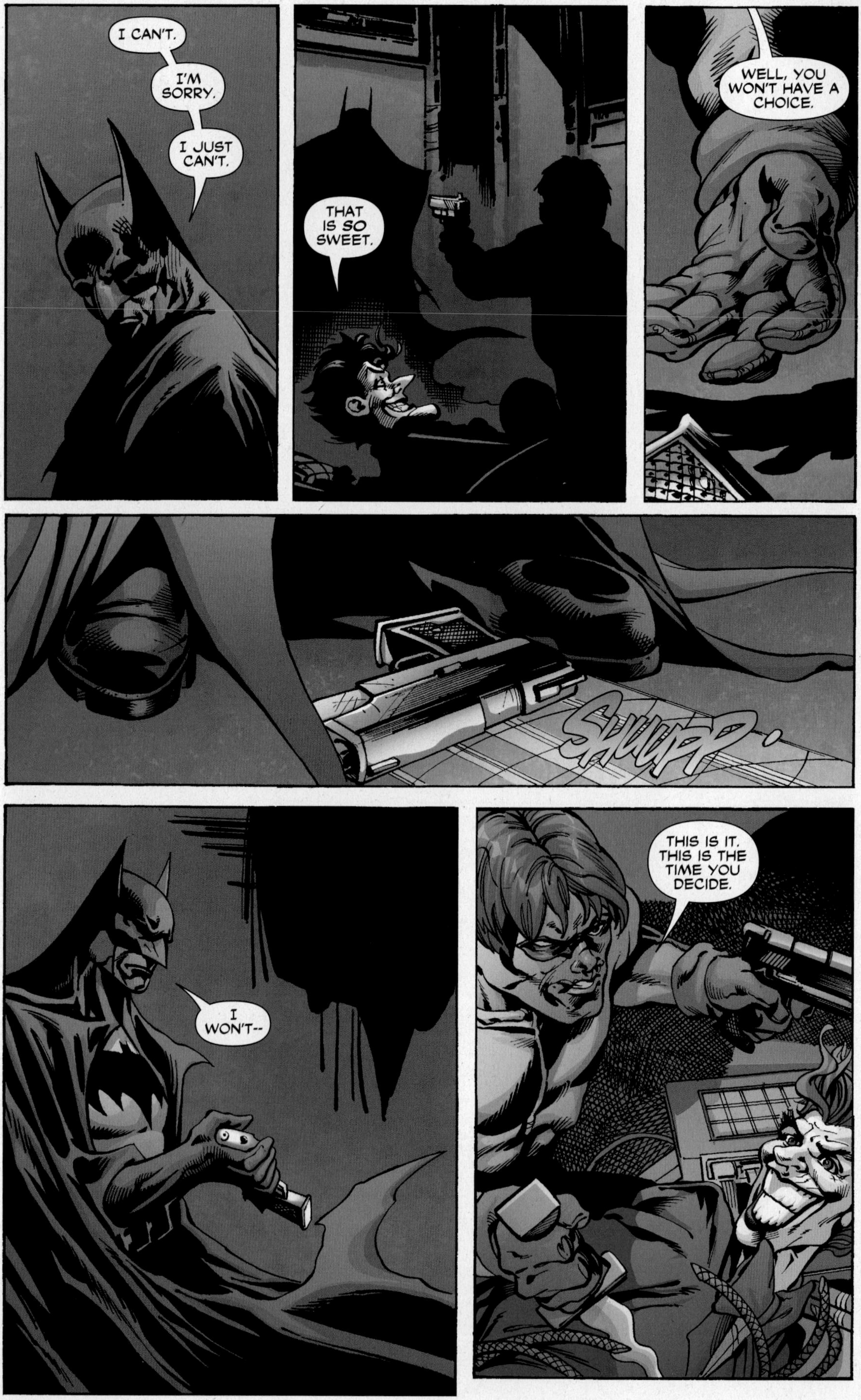
I CAN'T.
I'M SORRY.
I JUST CAN'T.
THAT IS SO SWEET.
WELL, YOU WON'T HAVE A CHOICE.
SHUPP
I WON'T--
THIS IS IT. THIS IS THE TIME YOU DECIDE.

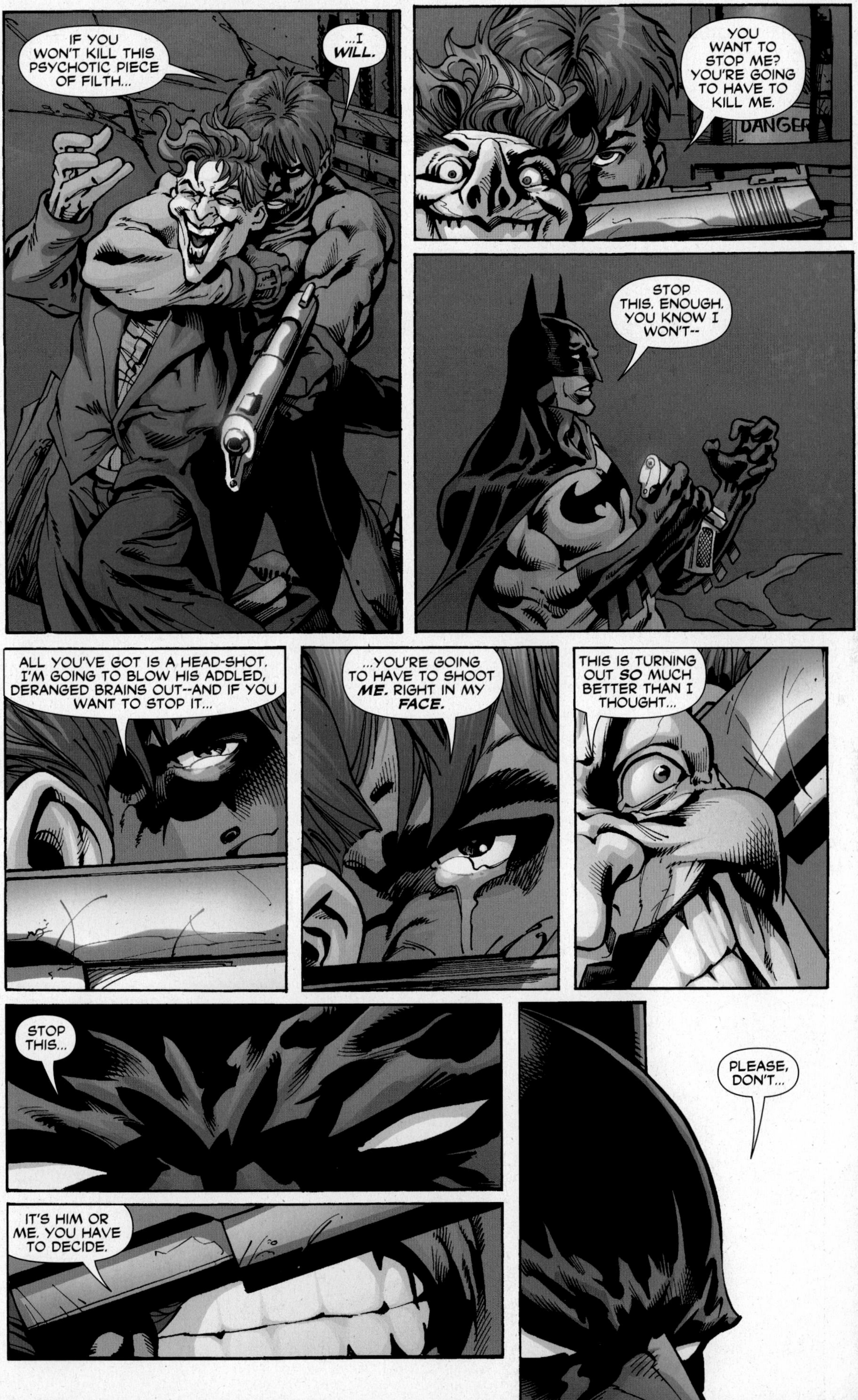
IF YOU WON'T KILL THIS PSYCHOTIC PIECE OF FILTH...
...I WILL.
YOU WANT TO STOP ME? YOU'RE GOING TO HAVE TO KILL ME.
DANGER
STOP THIS. ENOUGH. YOU KNOW I WON'T--
ALL YOU'VE GOT IS A HEAD-SHOT. I'M GOING TO BLOW HIS ADDLED, DERANGED BRAINS OUT--AND IF YOU WANT TO STOP IT...
...YOU'RE GOING TO HAVE TO SHOOT ME. RIGHT IN MY FACE.
THIS IS TURNING OUT SO MUCH BETTER THAN I THOUGHT...
STOP THIS...
IT'S HIM OR ME. YOU HAVE TO DECIDE.
PLEASE, DON'T...

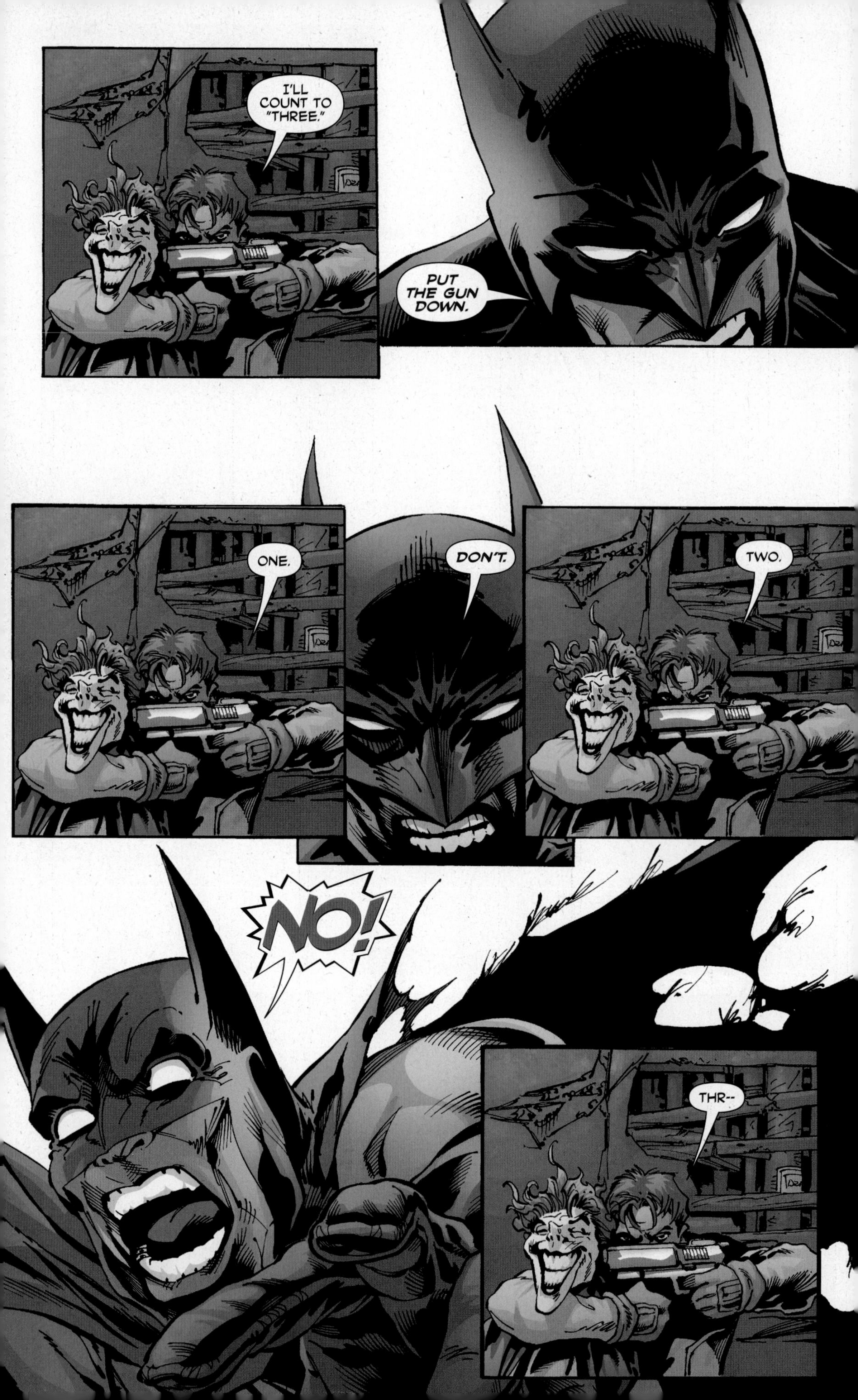
I'LL COUNT TO "THREE."
PUT THE GUN DOWN.
ONE.
DON'T.
TWO.
NO!
THR--

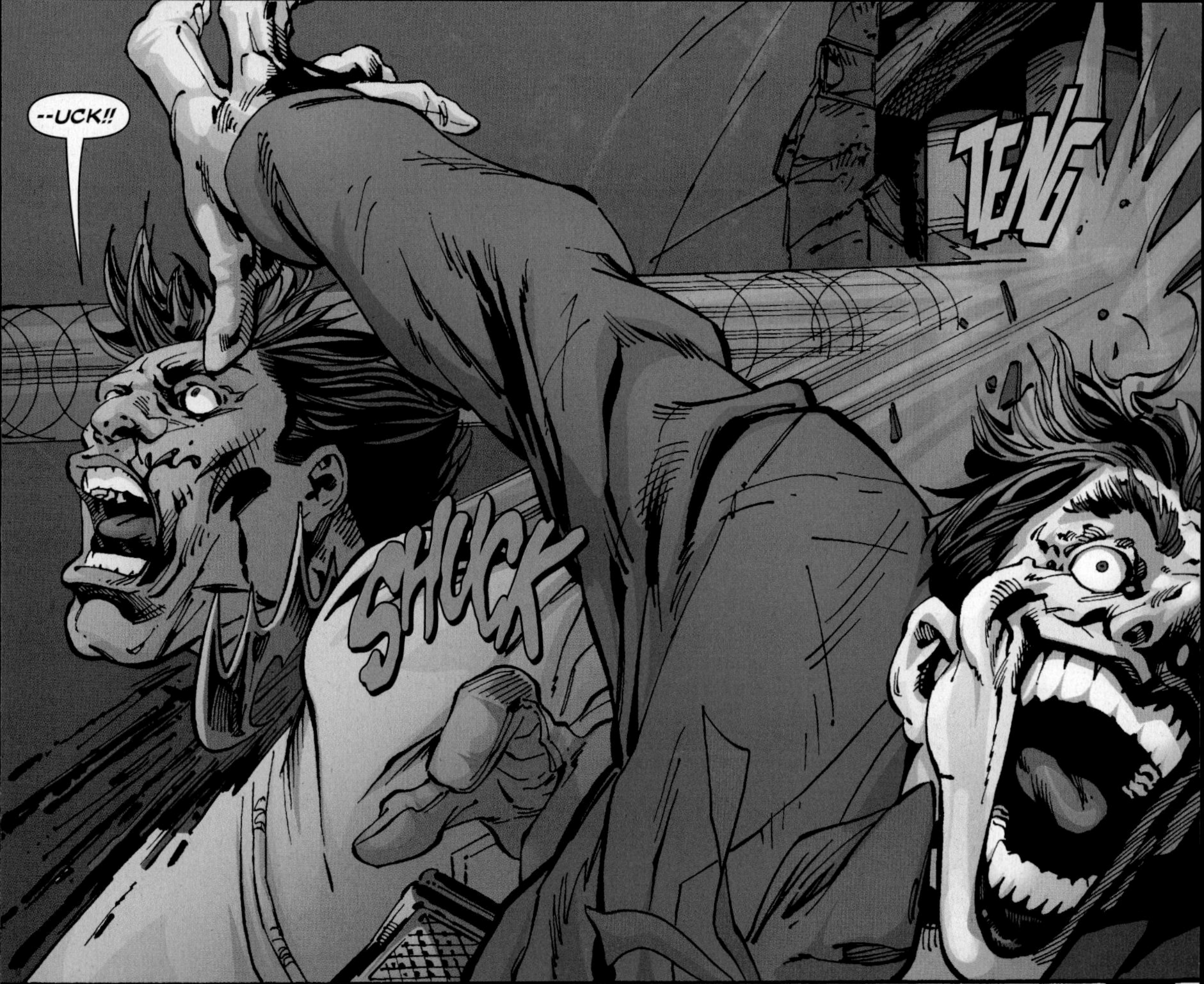
--UCK!!
TENG
SHUCK

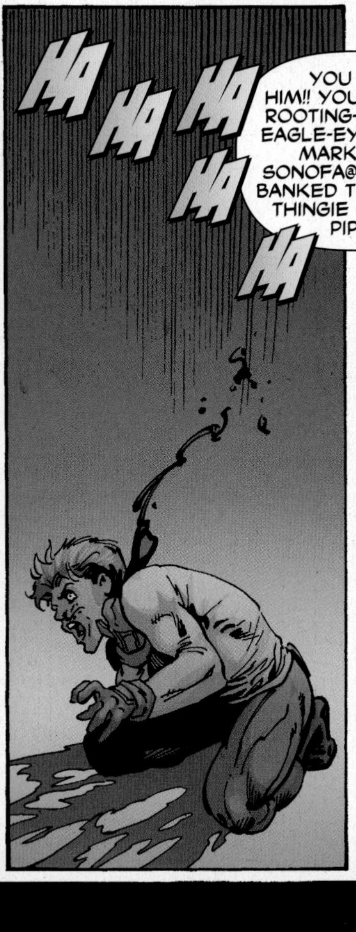
HA HA HA HA HA
YOU GOT HIM!! YOU EXPERT, ROOTING-TOOTING, EAGLE-EYED, GOTH MARKSMAN SONOFA@##$% ! YA BANKED THAT BATA-THINGIE OFF THE PIPE!!!

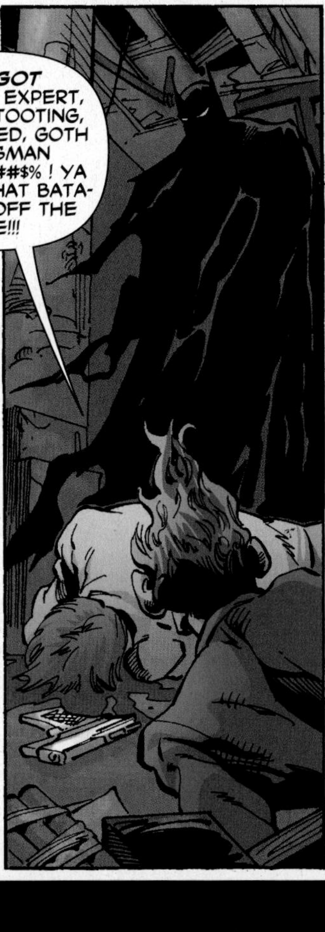

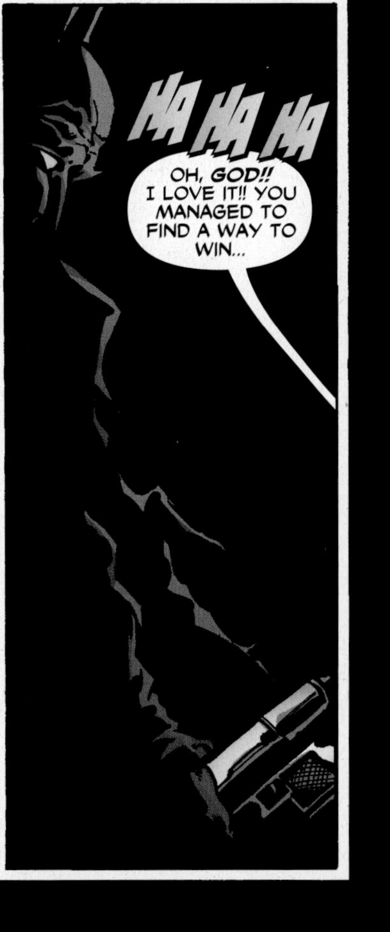
HA HA HA
OH, GOD!! I LOVE IT!! YOU MANAGED TO FIND A WAY TO WIN...

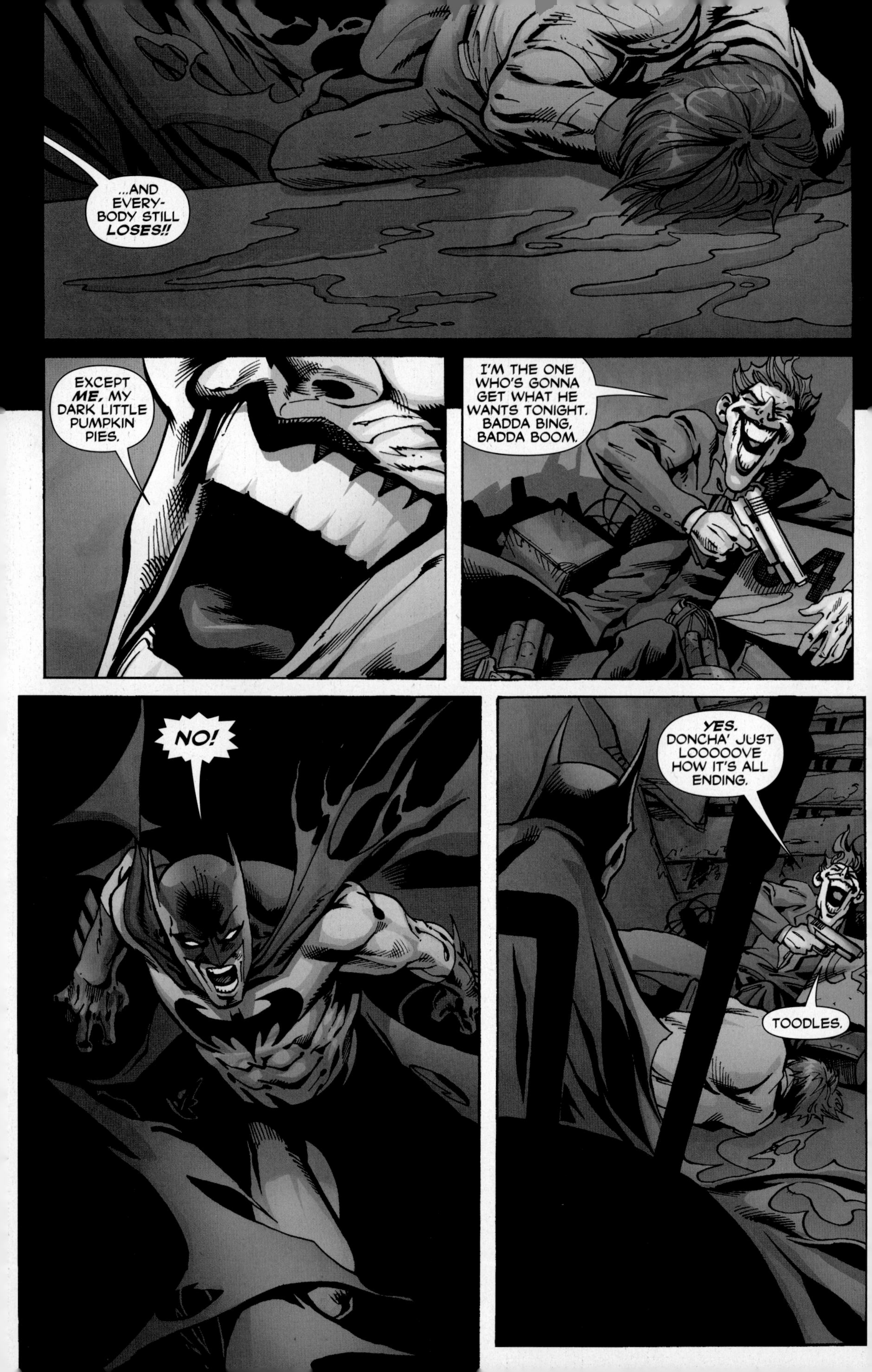
...AND EVERY- BODY STILL LOSES!!
EXCEPT ME, MY DARK LITTLE PUMPKIN PIES.
I'M THE ONE WHO'S GONNA GET WHAT HE WANTS TONIGHT. BADDA BING, BADDA BOOM.
NO!
YES. DONCHA' JUST LOOOOOVE HOW IT'S ALL ENDING.
TOODLES.

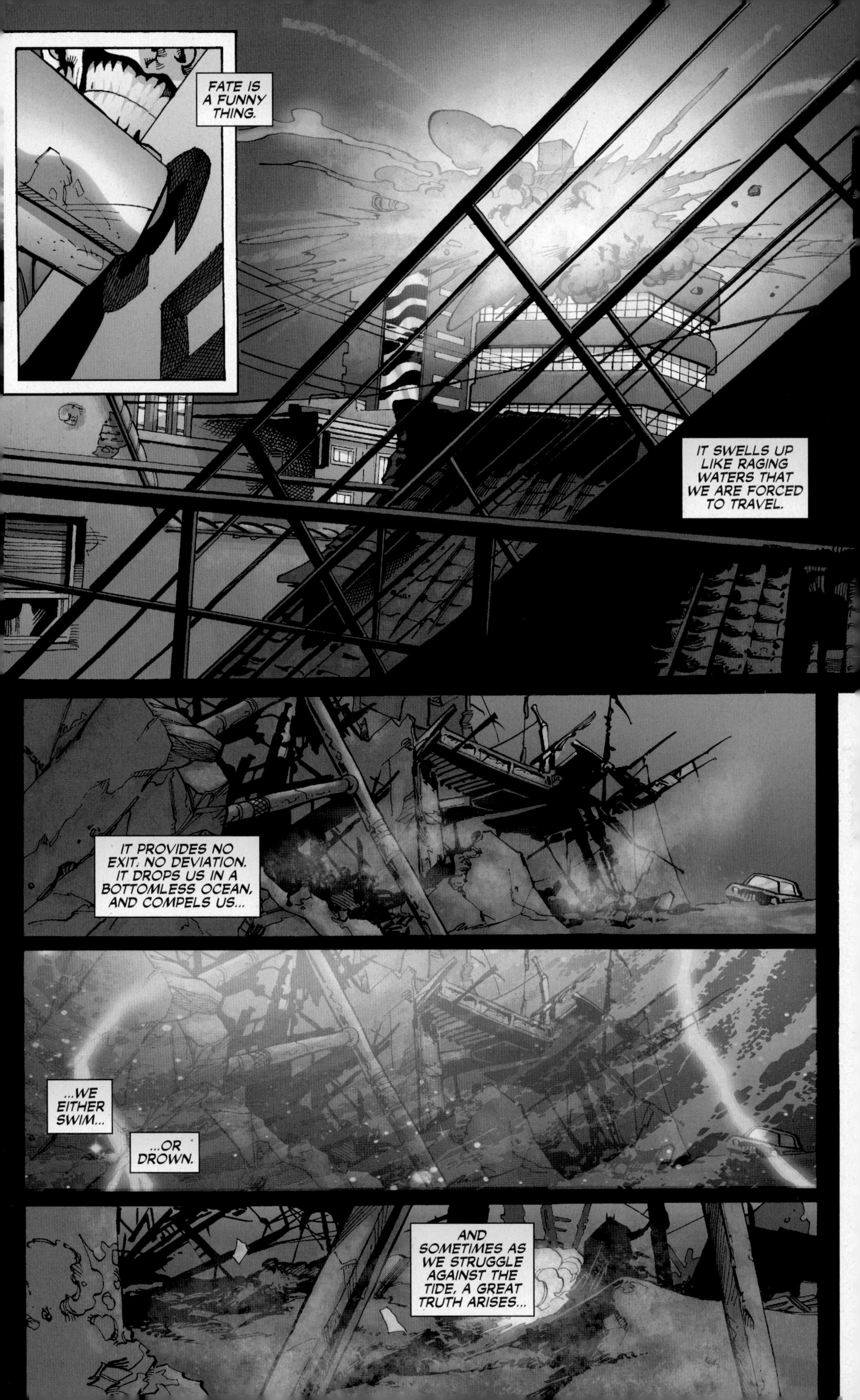
FATE IS A FUNNY THING.
IT SWELLS UP LIKE RAGING WATERS THAT WE ARE FORCED TO TRAVEL.
IT PROVIDES NO EXIT. NO DEVIATION. IT DROPS US IN A BOTTOMLESS OCEAN, AND COMPELS US...
...WE EITHER SWIM...
...OR DROWN.
AND SOMETIMES AS WE STRUGGLE AGAINST THE TIDE, A GREAT TRUTH ARISES...

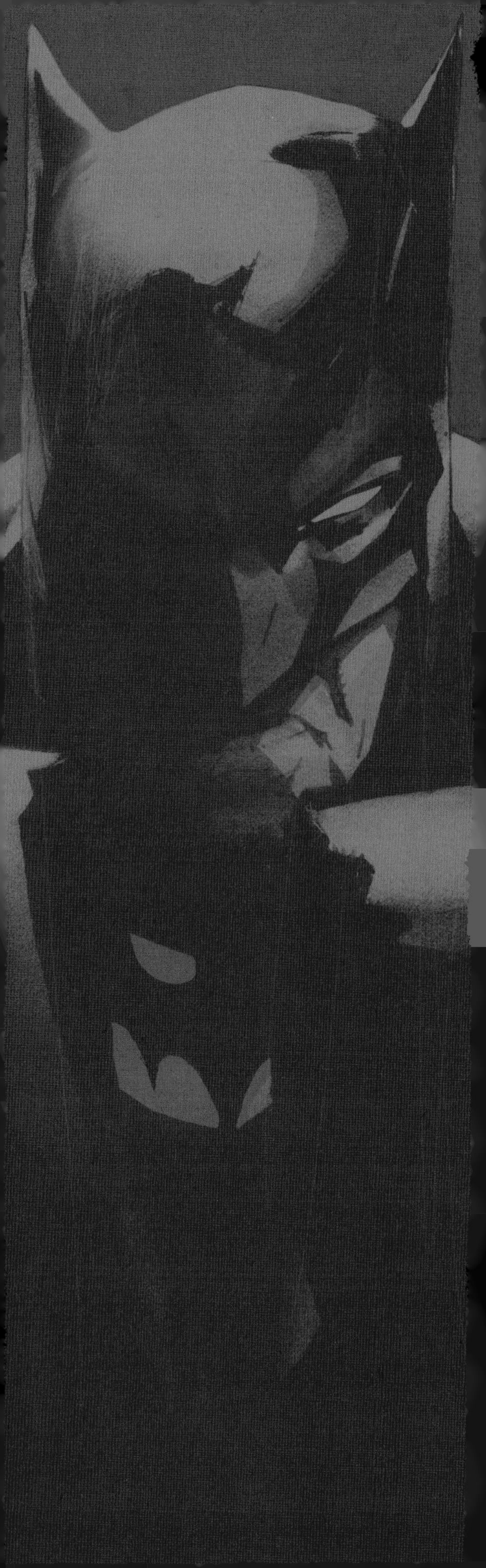

BATMAN ANNUAL 25 Cover by Jock after Jim Aparo

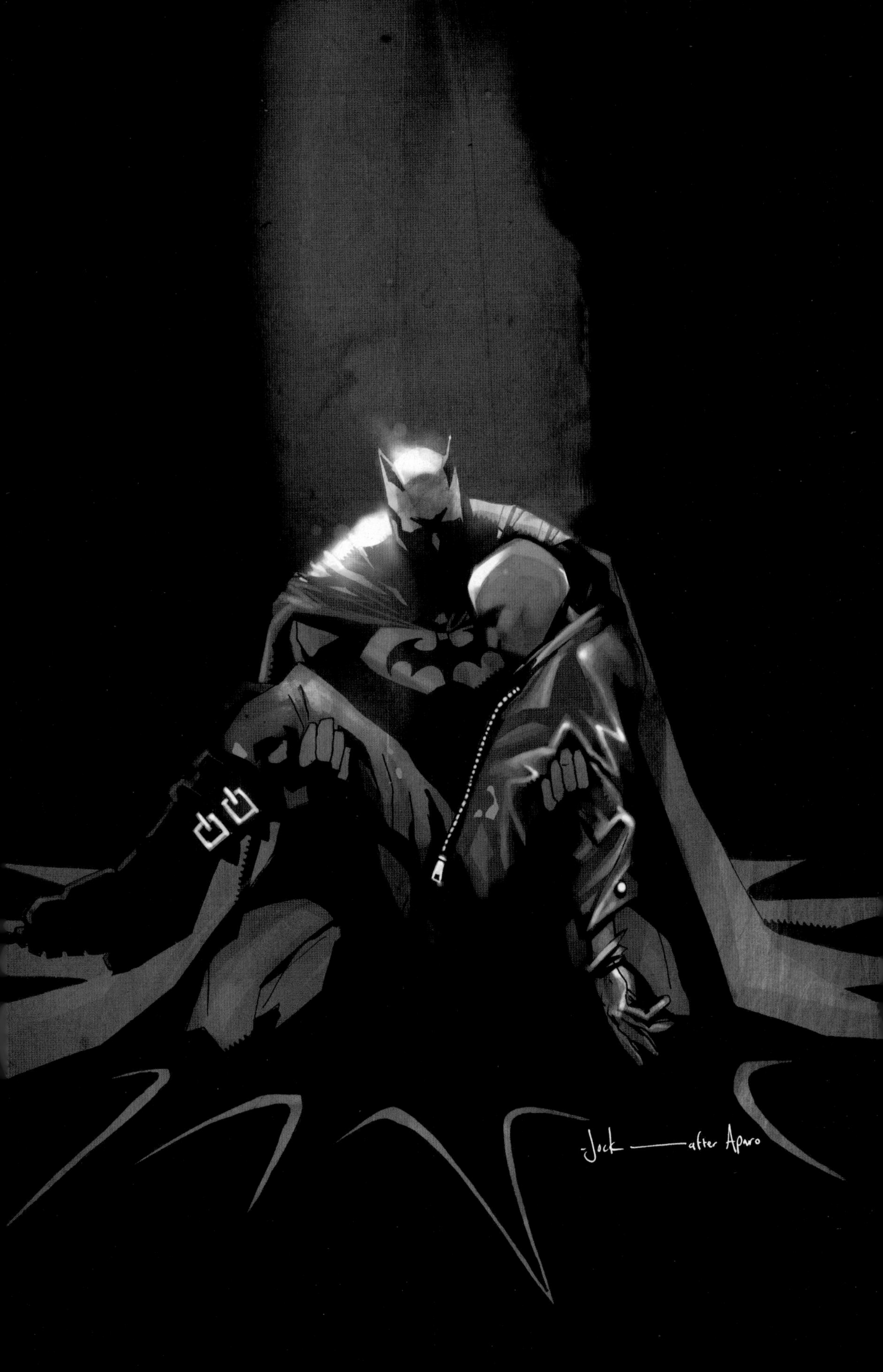
-Jock —— after Aparo

DAEDALUS AND ICARUS

THE RETURN OF JASON TODD

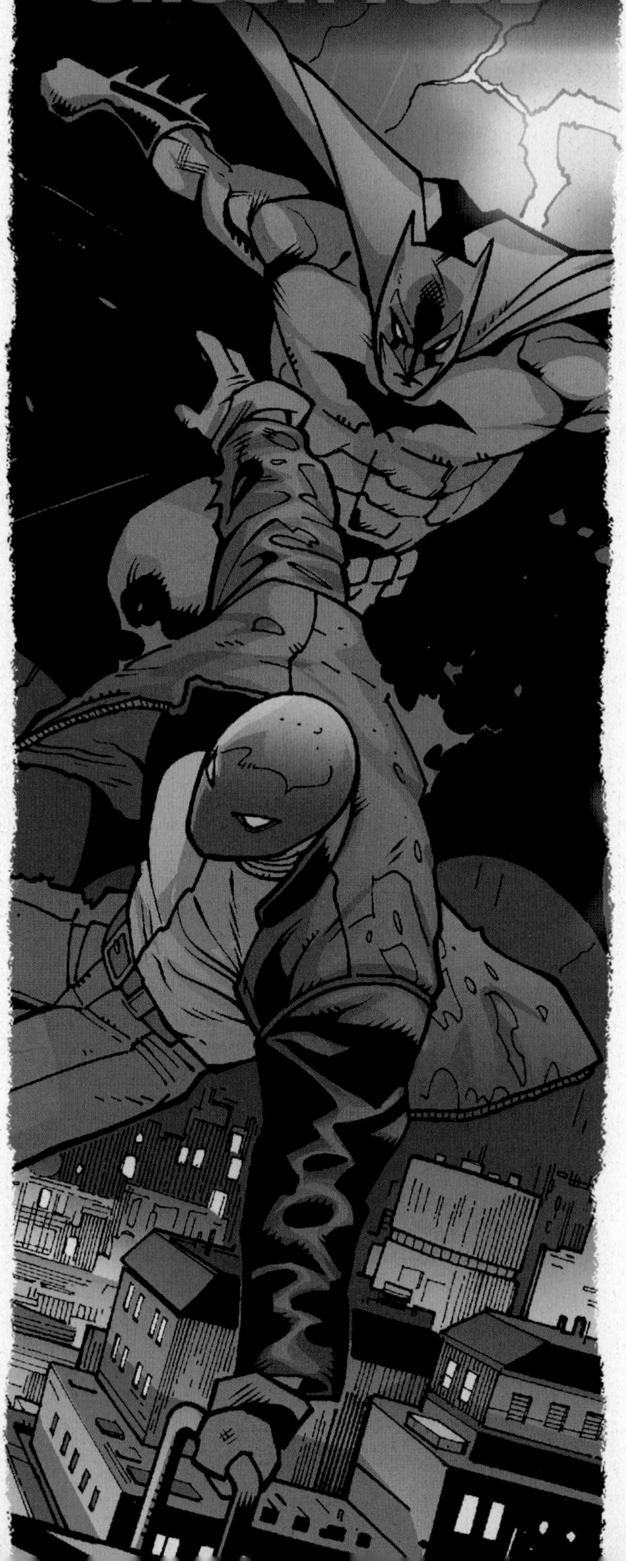

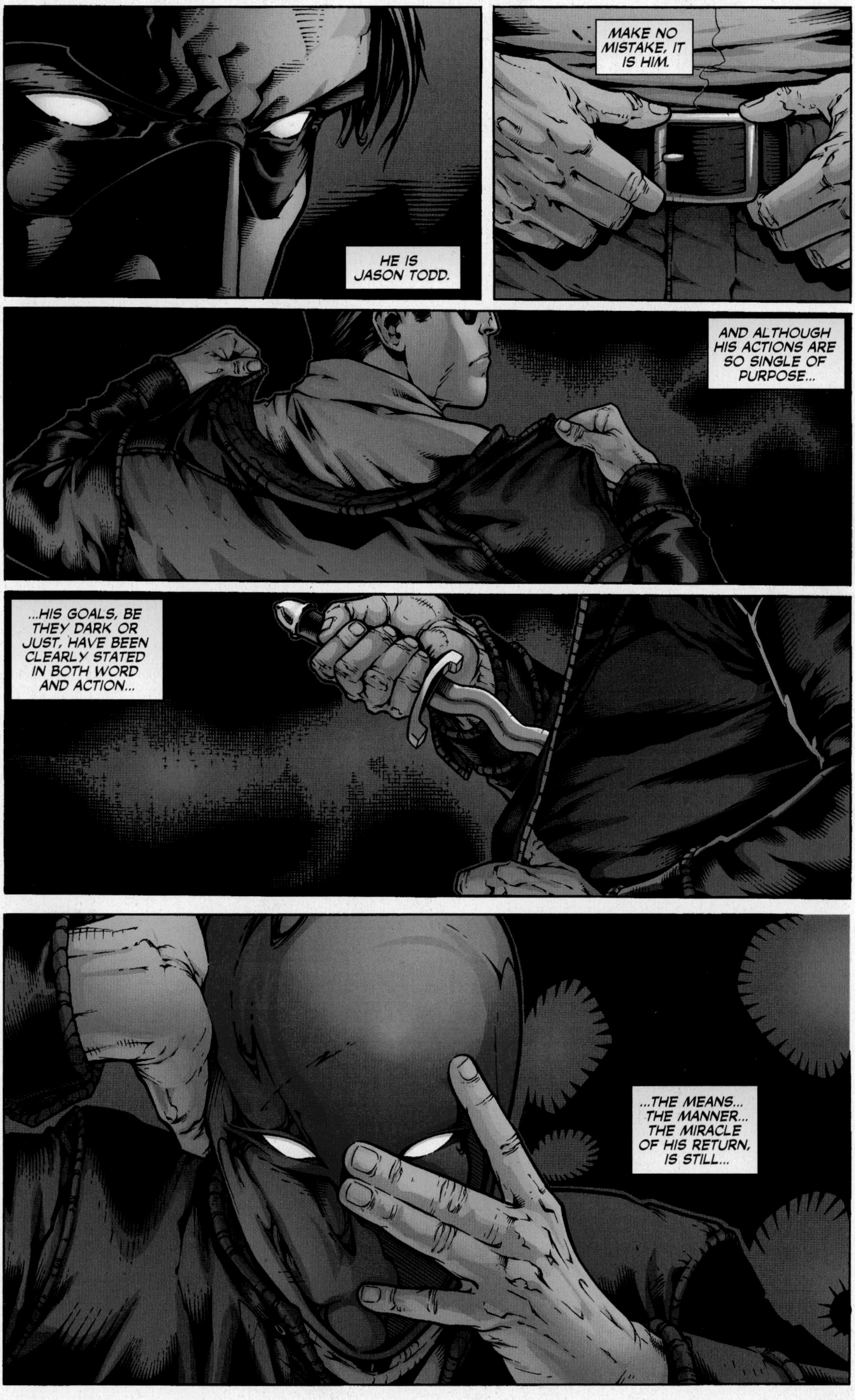
HE IS JASON TODD.
MAKE NO MISTAKE, IT IS HIM.
AND ALTHOUGH HIS ACTIONS ARE SO SINGLE OF PURPOSE...
...HIS GOALS, BE THEY DARK OR JUST, HAVE BEEN CLEARLY STATED IN BOTH WORD AND ACTION...
...THE MEANS... THE MANNER... THE MIRACLE OF HIS RETURN, IS STILL...

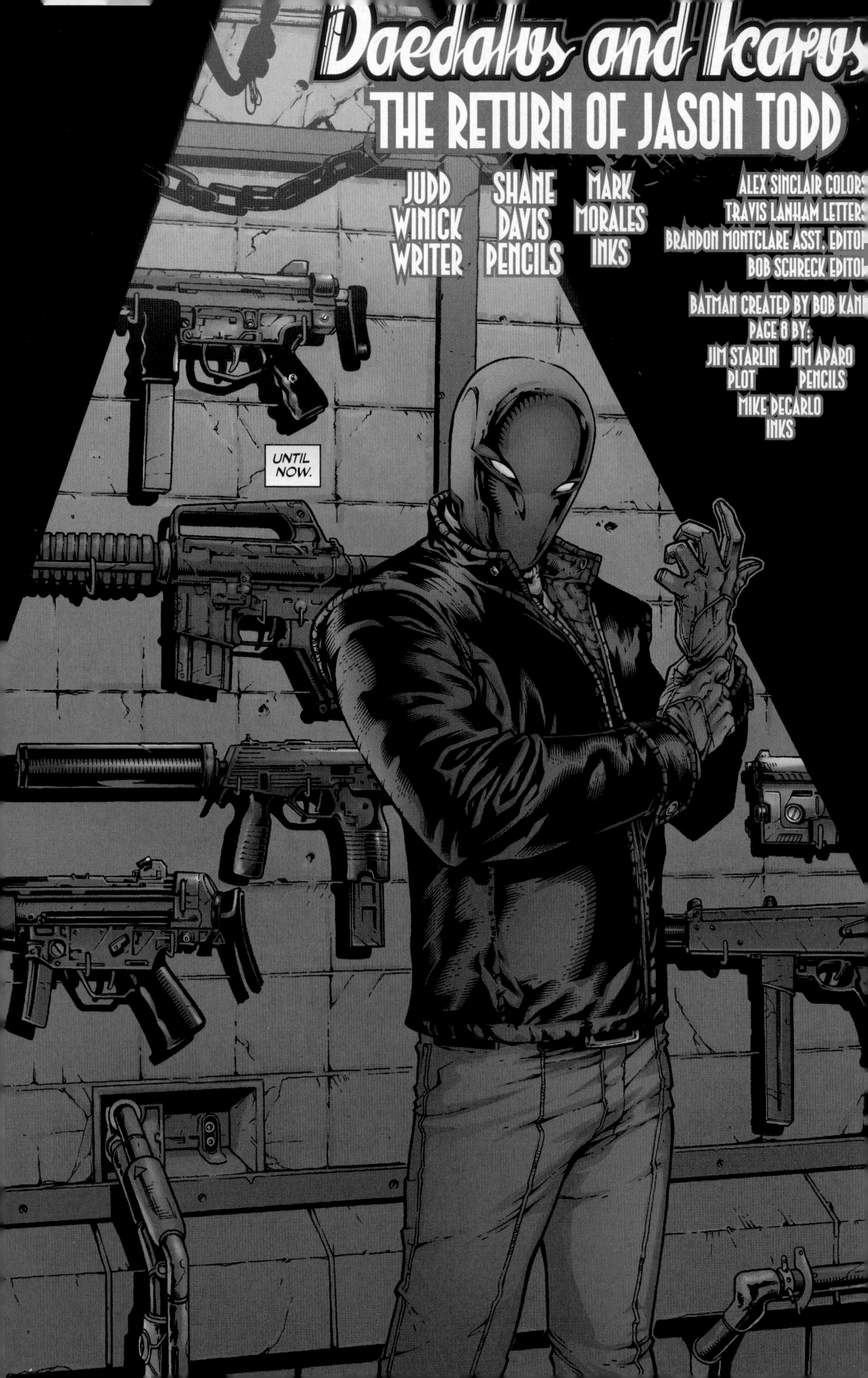
Daedalus and Icarus
THE RETURN OF JASON TODD
JUDD WINICK WRITER
SHANE DAVIS PENCILS
MARK MORALES INKS
ALEX SINCLAIR COLORS
TRAVIS LANHAM LETTERS
BRANDON MONTCLARE ASST. EDITOR
BOB SCHRECK EDITOR
BATMAN CREATED BY BOB KANE
PAGE 8 BY:
JIM STARLIN PLOT
JIM APARO PENCILS
MIKE DECARLO INKS
UNTIL NOW.

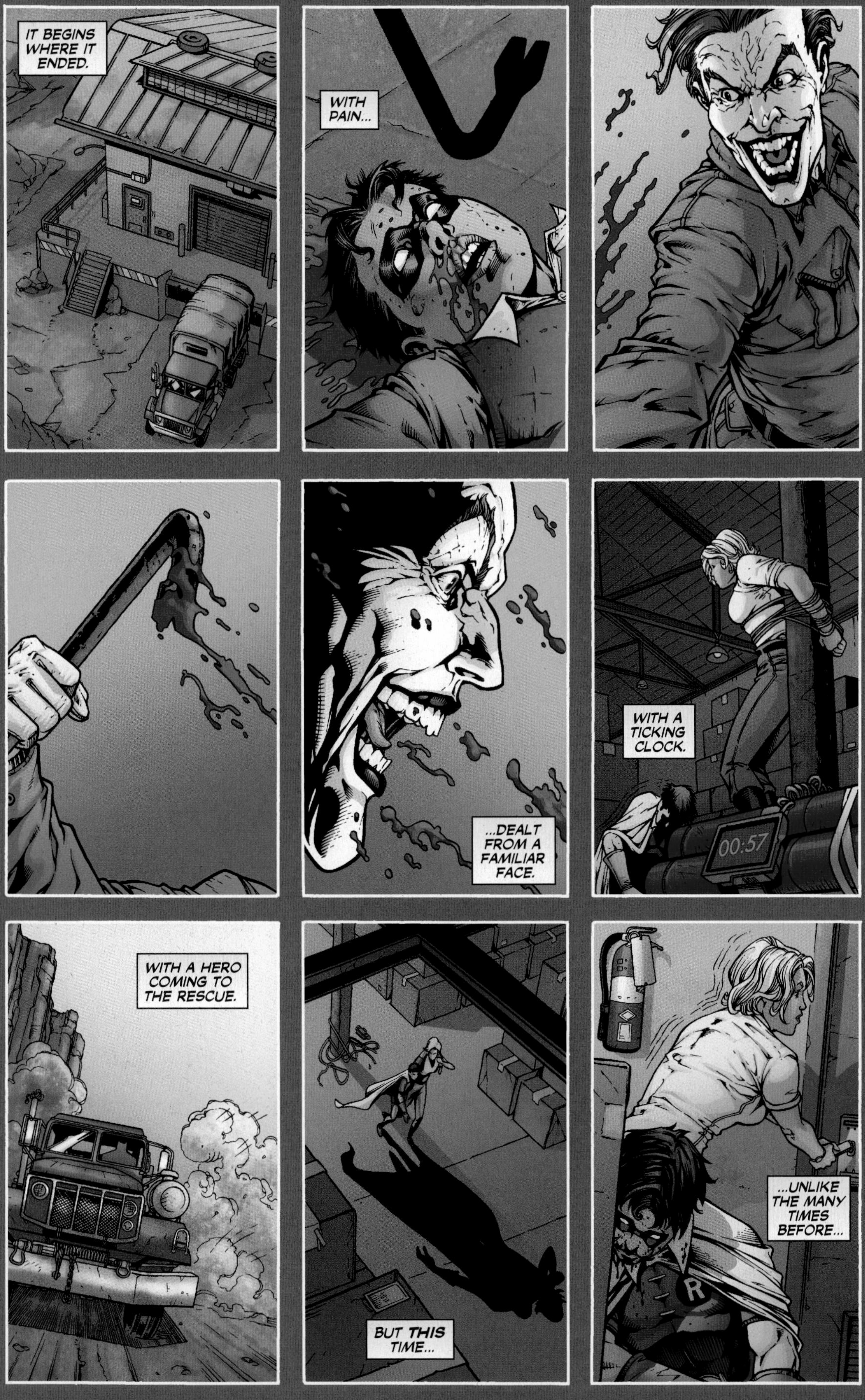
IT BEGINS WHERE IT ENDED.
WITH PAIN...
WITH A TICKING CLOCK.
00:57
...DEALT FROM A FAMILIAR FACE.
WITH A HERO COMING TO THE RESCUE.
BUT THIS TIME...
...UNLIKE THE MANY TIMES BEFORE...
R

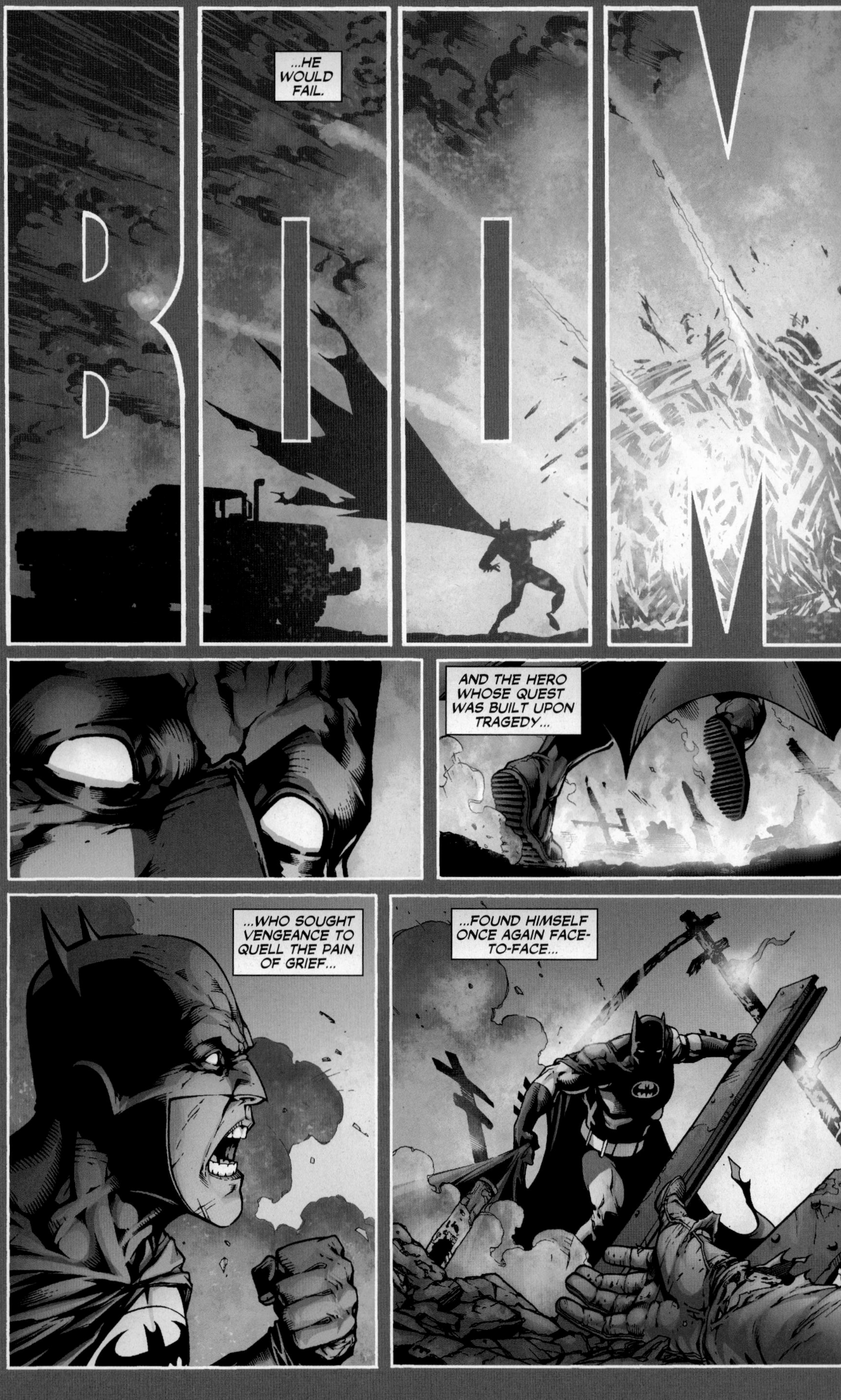
...HE WOULD FAIL.
BOOM
AND THE HERO WHOSE QUEST WAS BUILT UPON TRAGEDY...
...WHO SOUGHT VENGEANCE TO QUELL THE PAIN OF GRIEF...
...FOUND HIMSELF ONCE AGAIN FACE-TO-FACE...

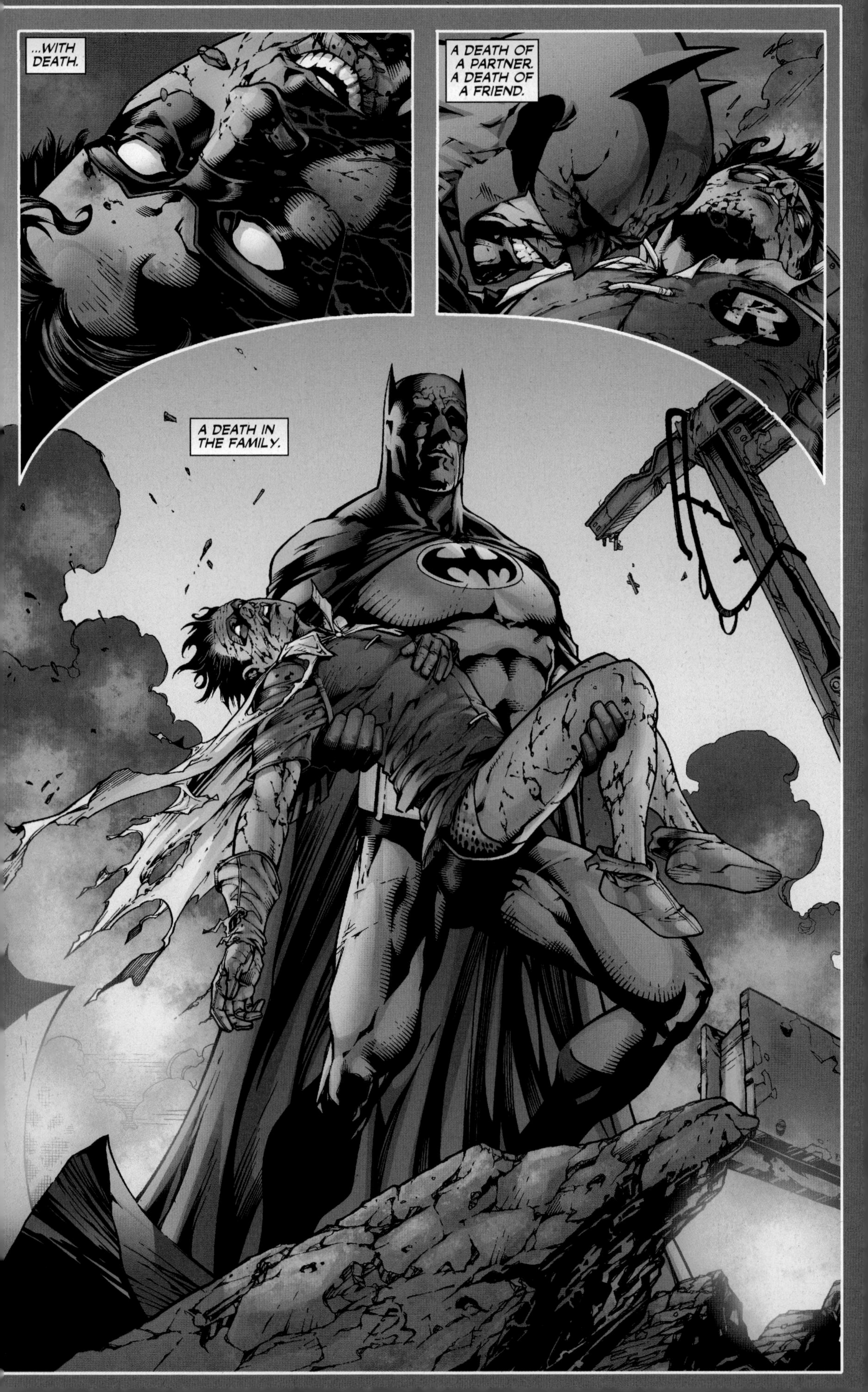
...WITH DEATH.
A DEATH OF A PARTNER. A DEATH OF A FRIEND.
A DEATH IN THE FAMILY.

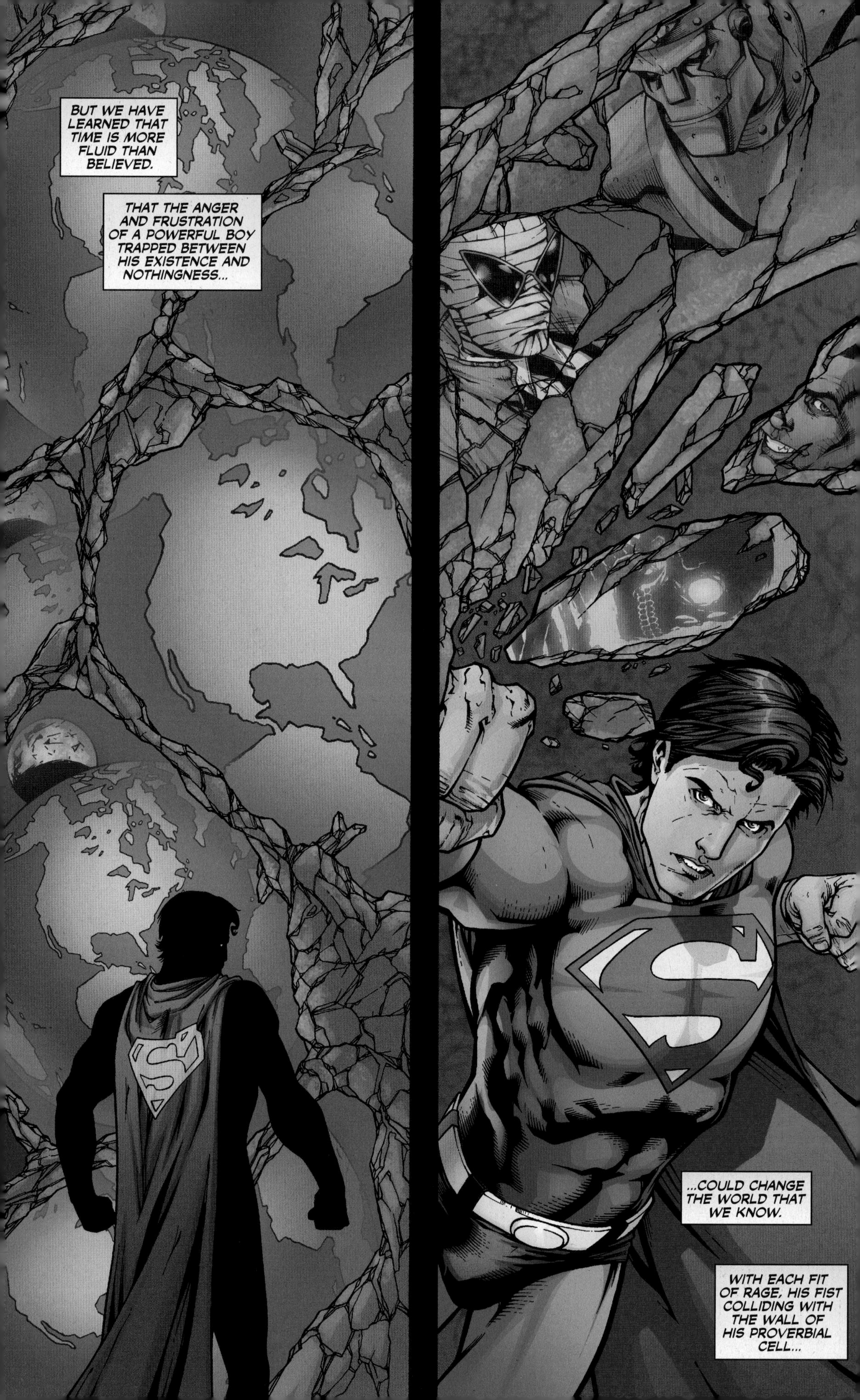
BUT WE HAVE LEARNED THAT TIME IS MORE FLUID THAN BELIEVED.
THAT THE ANGER AND FRUSTRATION OF A POWERFUL BOY TRAPPED BETWEEN HIS EXISTENCE AND NOTHINGNESS...
...COULD CHANGE THE WORLD THAT WE KNOW.
WITH EACH FIT OF RAGE, HIS FIST COLLIDING WITH THE WALL OF HIS PROVERBIAL CELL...

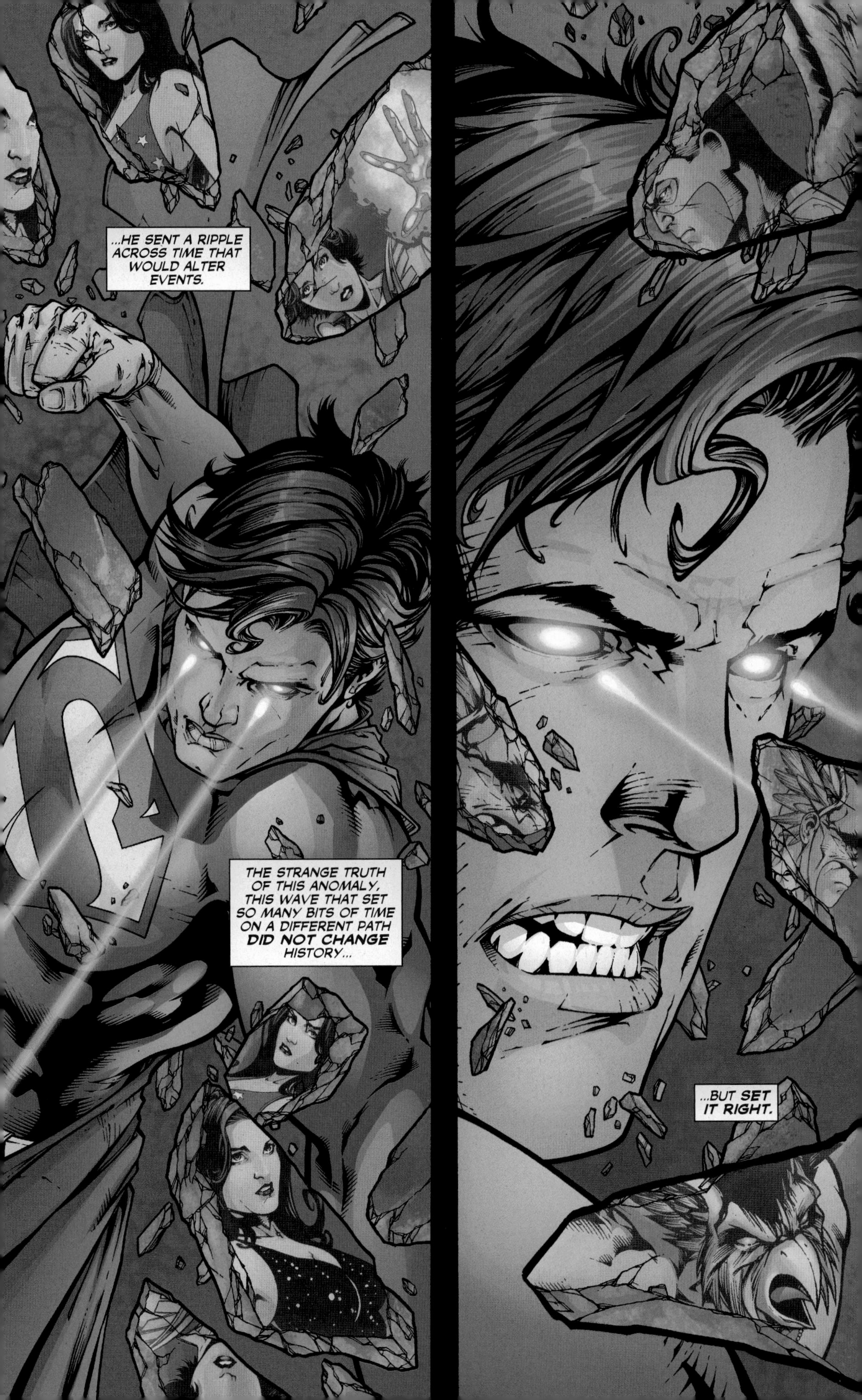
...HE SENT A RIPPLE ACROSS TIME THAT WOULD ALTER EVENTS.
THE STRANGE TRUTH OF THIS ANOMALY, THIS WAVE THAT SET SO MANY BITS OF TIME ON A DIFFERENT PATH **DID NOT CHANGE** HISTORY...
...BUT **SET IT RIGHT.**

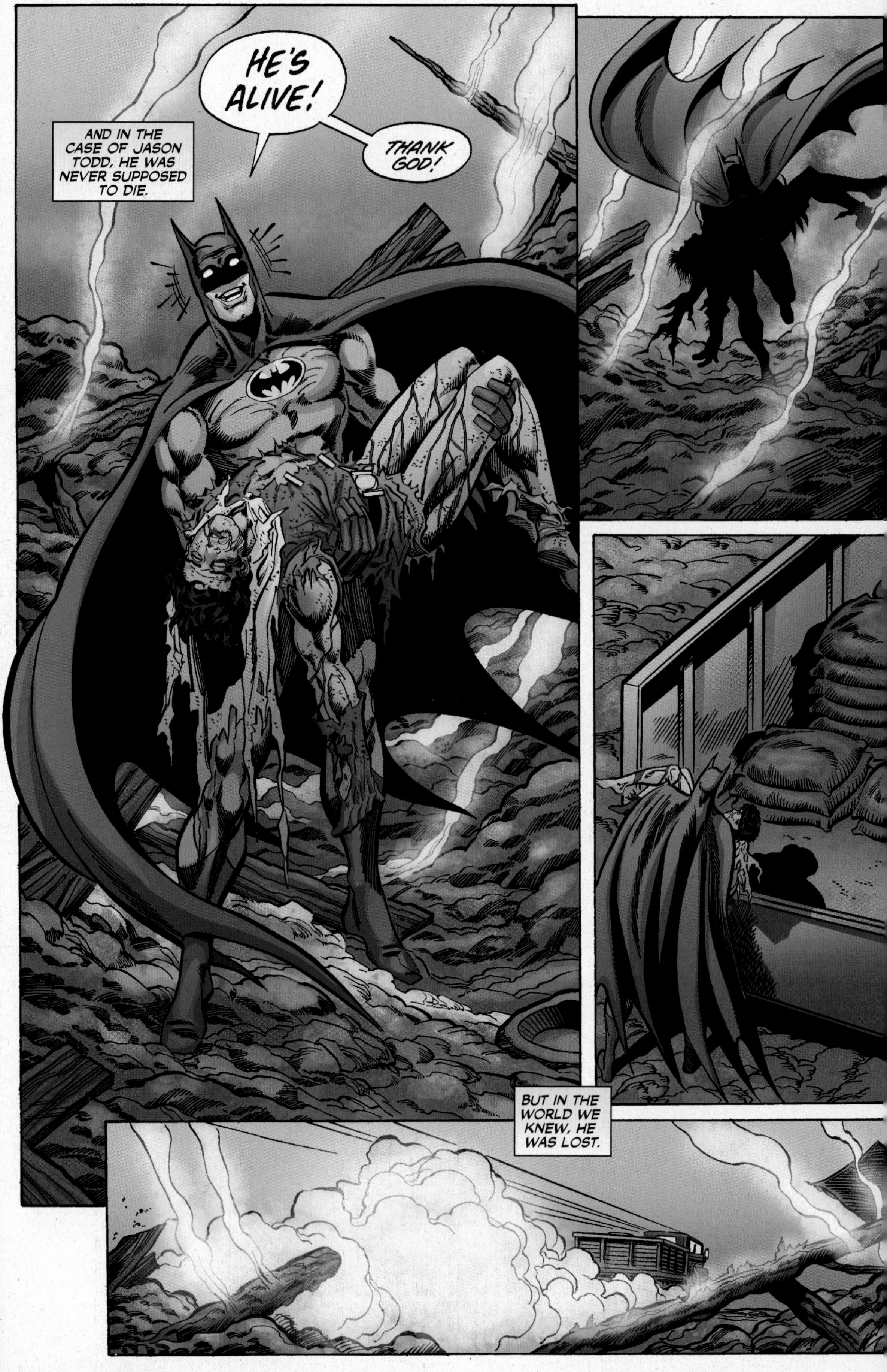
AND IN THE CASE OF JASON TODD, HE WAS NEVER SUPPOSED TO DIE.
HE'S ALIVE!
THANK GOD!
BUT IN THE WORLD WE KNEW, HE WAS LOST.

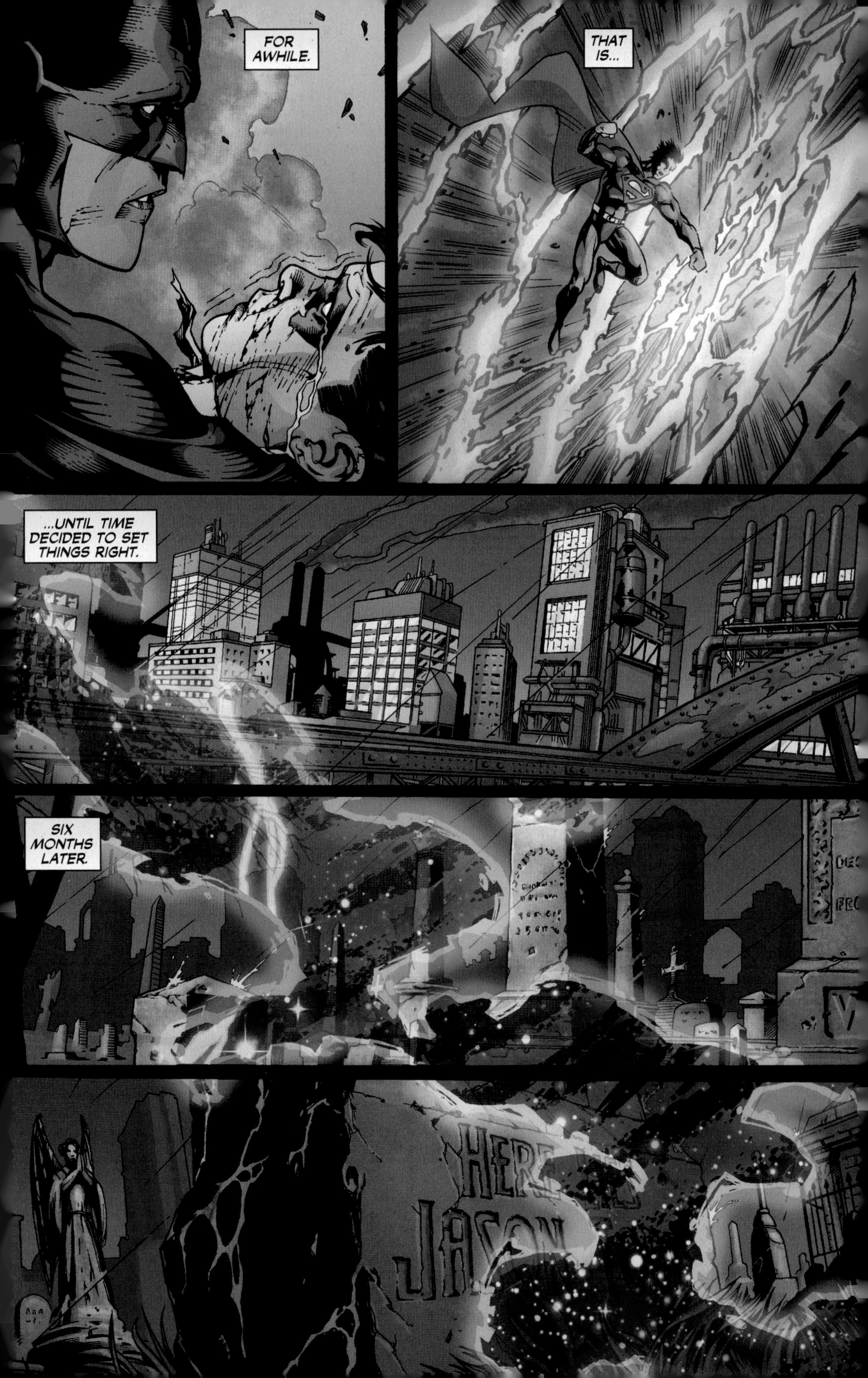
FOR AWHILE.
THAT IS...
...UNTIL TIME DECIDED TO SET THINGS RIGHT.
SIX MONTHS LATER.
HERE
JASON

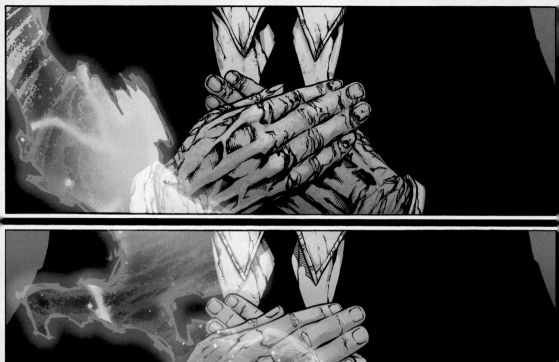

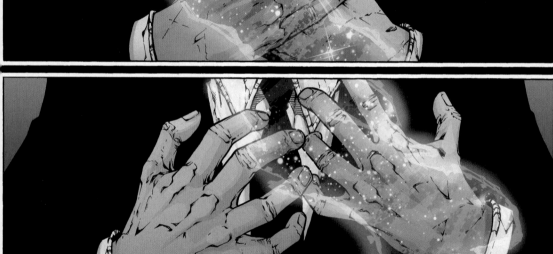

UUGH!!
UH-UH-UH-
UH-UH!!

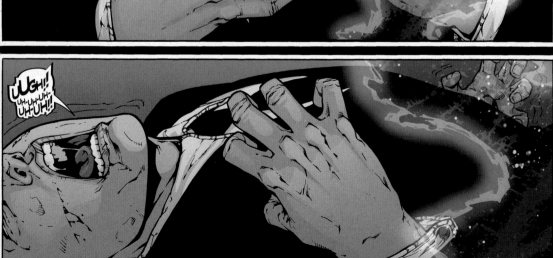

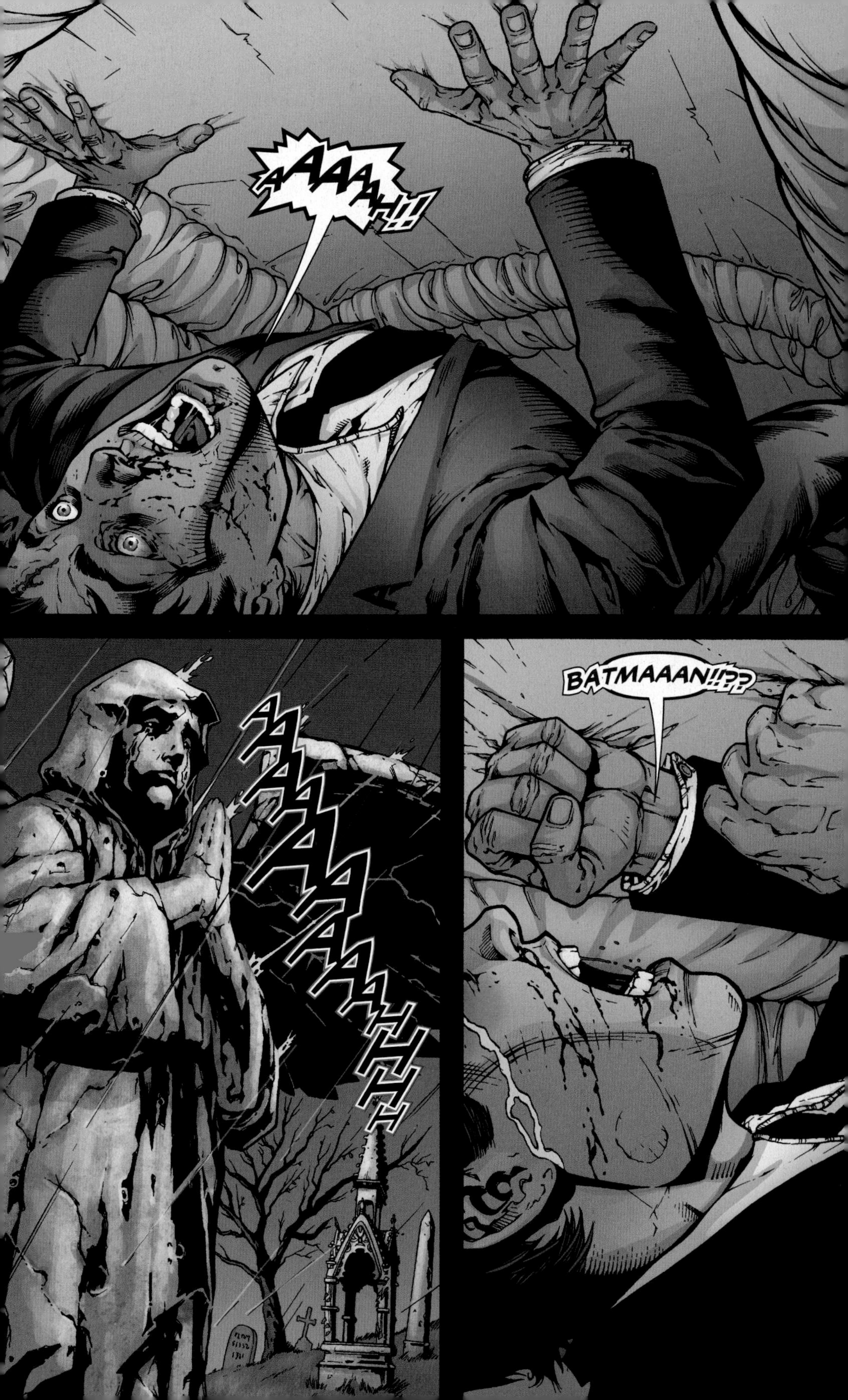
AAAAAH!!
AAAAAAAAAAAHHHH
BATMAAAN!!??

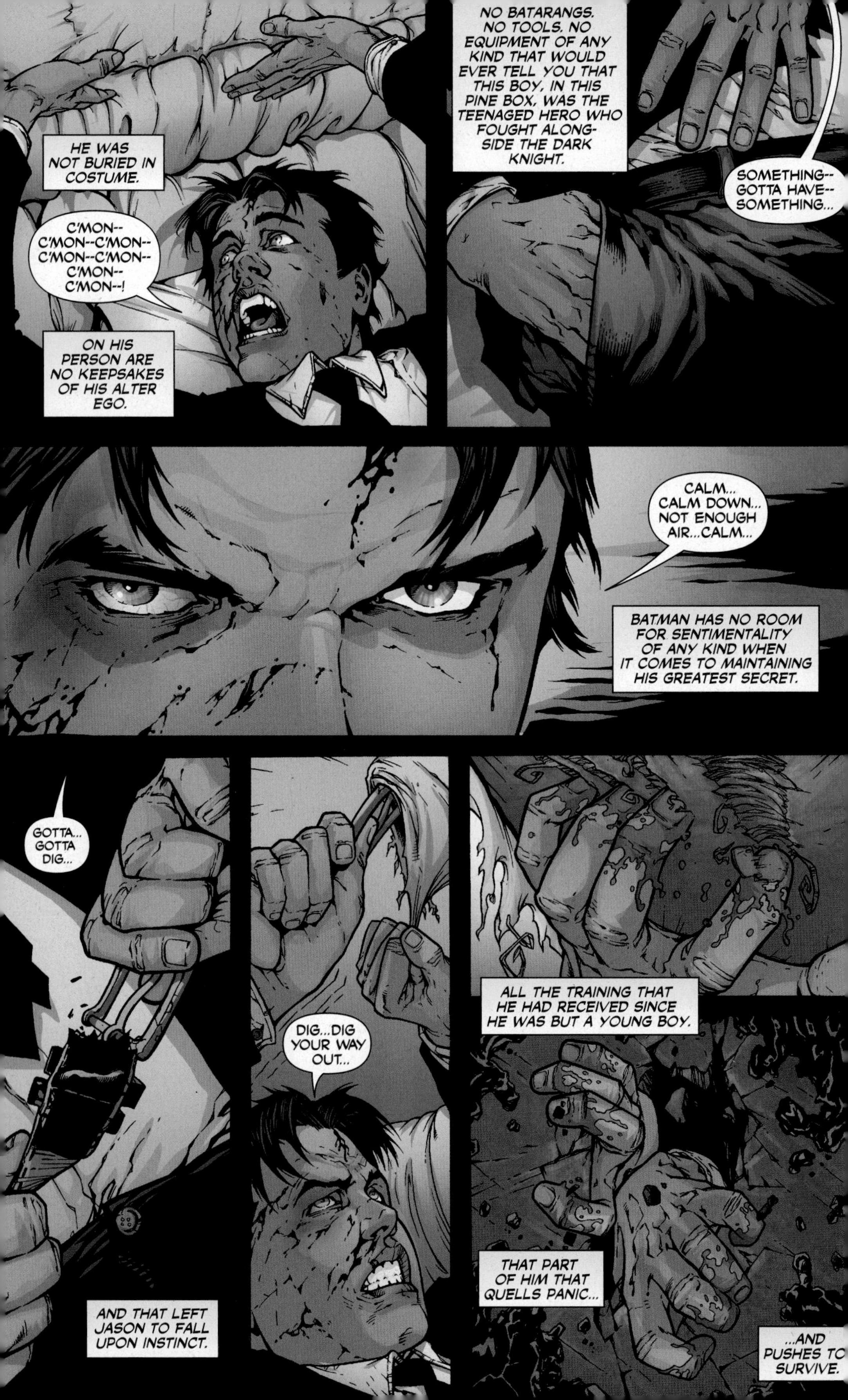

HE WAS NOT BURIED IN COSTUME.
C'MON-- C'MON--C'MON-- C'MON--C'MON-- C'MON-- C'MON--!
ON HIS PERSON ARE NO KEEPSAKES OF HIS ALTER EGO.
NO BATARANGS. NO TOOLS. NO EQUIPMENT OF ANY KIND THAT WOULD EVER TELL YOU THAT THIS BOY, IN THIS PINE BOX, WAS THE TEENAGED HERO WHO FOUGHT ALONG-SIDE THE DARK KNIGHT.
SOMETHING-- GOTTA HAVE-- SOMETHING...
CALM... CALM DOWN... NOT ENOUGH AIR...CALM...
BATMAN HAS NO ROOM FOR SENTIMENTALITY OF ANY KIND WHEN IT COMES TO MAINTAINING HIS GREATEST SECRET.
GOTTA... GOTTA DIG...
AND THAT LEFT JASON TO FALL UPON INSTINCT.
DIG...DIG YOUR WAY OUT...
ALL THE TRAINING THAT HE HAD RECEIVED SINCE HE WAS BUT A YOUNG BOY.
THAT PART OF HIM THAT QUELLS PANIC...
...AND PUSHES TO SURVIVE.

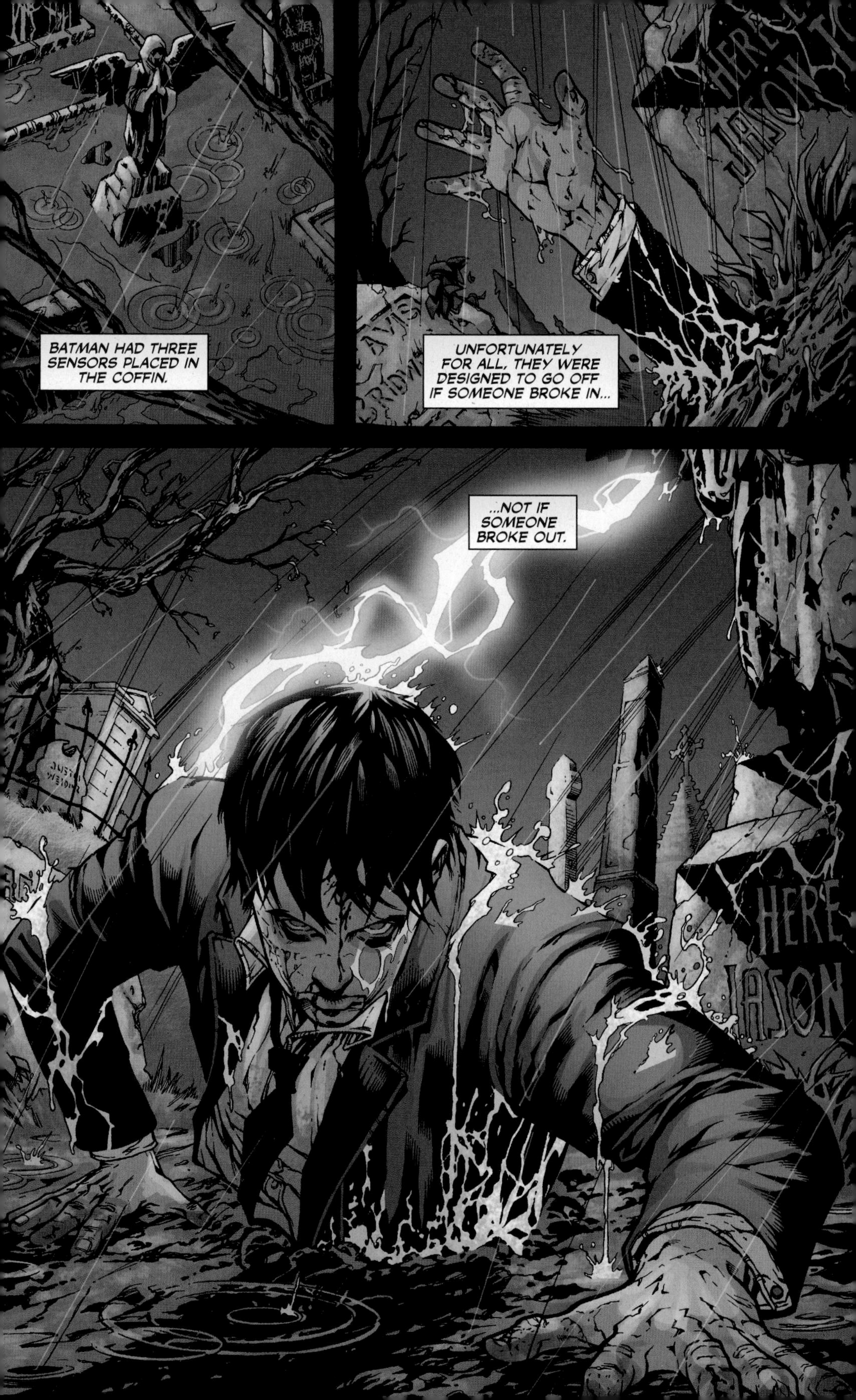
BATMAN HAD THREE SENSORS PLACED IN THE COFFIN.
UNFORTUNATELY FOR ALL, THEY WERE DESIGNED TO GO OFF IF SOMEONE BROKE IN...
...NOT IF SOMEONE BROKE OUT.
HERE
JASON

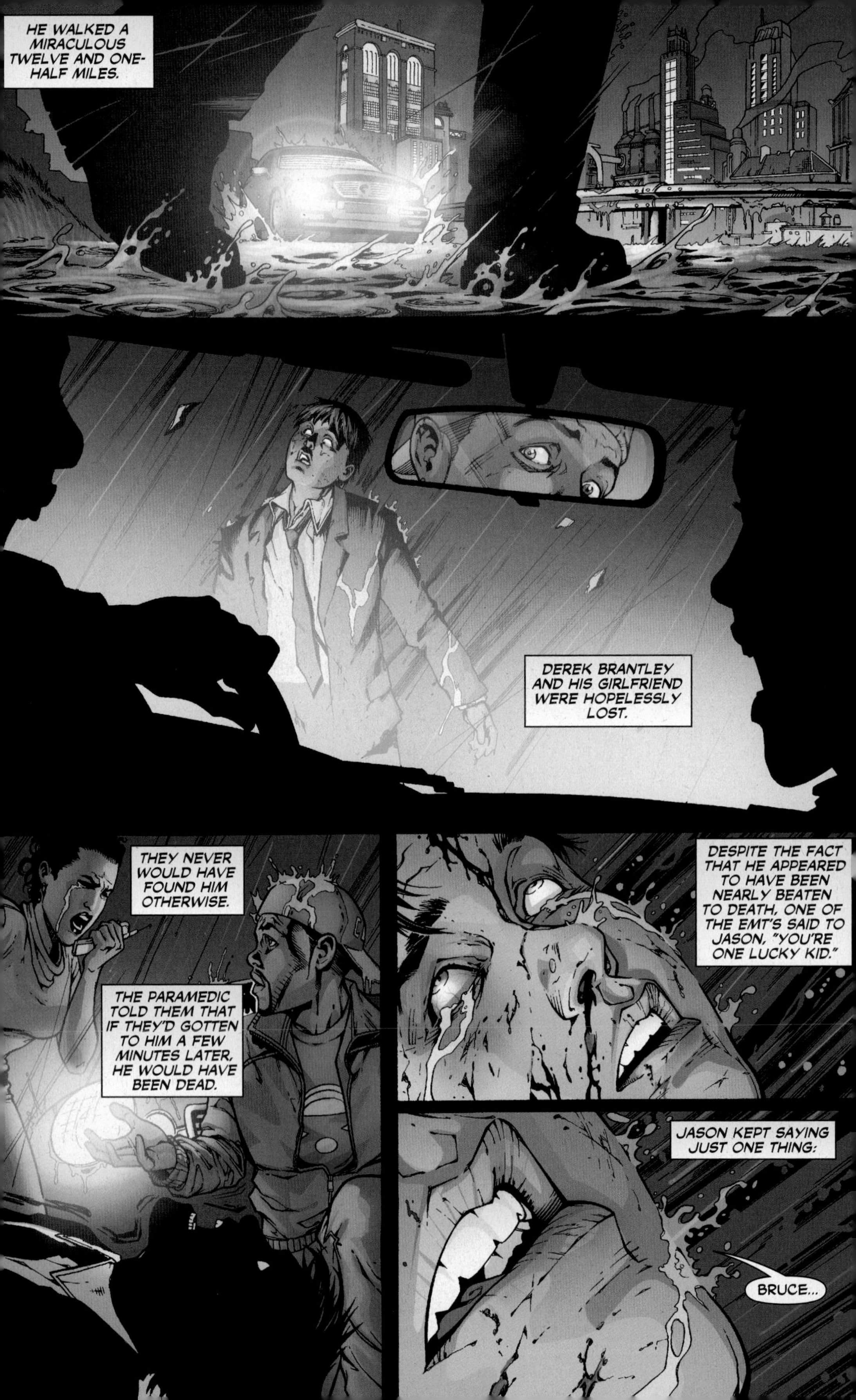
HE WALKED A MIRACULOUS TWELVE AND ONE-HALF MILES.
DEREK BRANTLEY AND HIS GIRLFRIEND WERE HOPELESSLY LOST.
THEY NEVER WOULD HAVE FOUND HIM OTHERWISE.
THE PARAMEDIC TOLD THEM THAT IF THEY'D GOTTEN TO HIM A FEW MINUTES LATER, HE WOULD HAVE BEEN DEAD.
DESPITE THE FACT THAT HE APPEARED TO HAVE BEEN NEARLY BEATEN TO DEATH, ONE OF THE EMT'S SAID TO JASON, "YOU'RE ONE LUCKY KID."
JASON KEPT SAYING JUST ONE THING:
BRUCE...

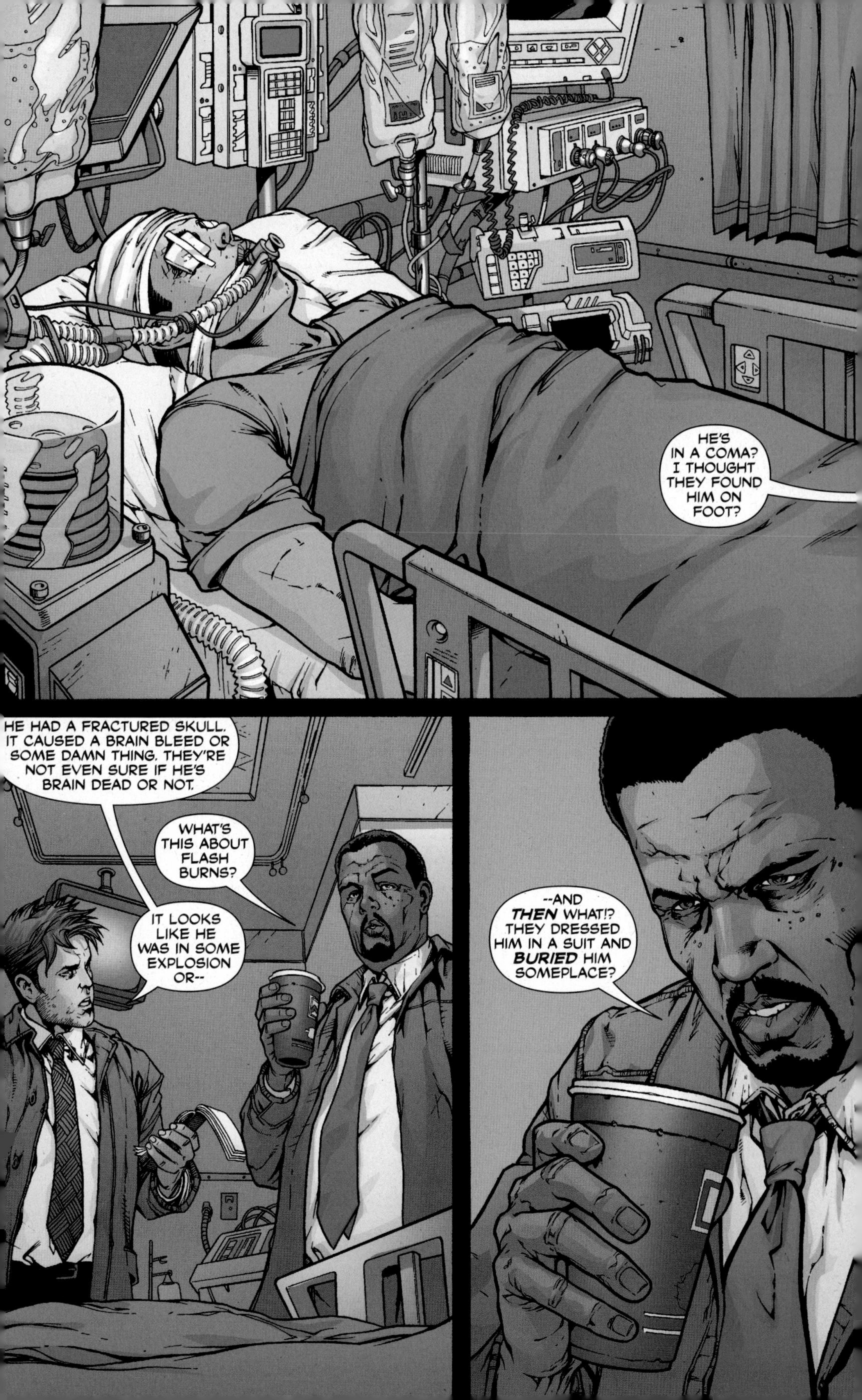
HE'S IN A COMA? I THOUGHT THEY FOUND HIM ON FOOT?
HE HAD A FRACTURED SKULL. IT CAUSED A BRAIN BLEED OR SOME DAMN THING. THEY'RE NOT EVEN SURE IF HE'S BRAIN DEAD OR NOT.
WHAT'S THIS ABOUT FLASH BURNS?
IT LOOKS LIKE HE WAS IN SOME EXPLOSION OR--
--AND *THEN* WHAT!? THEY DRESSED HIM IN A SUIT AND *BURIED* HIM SOMEPLACE?

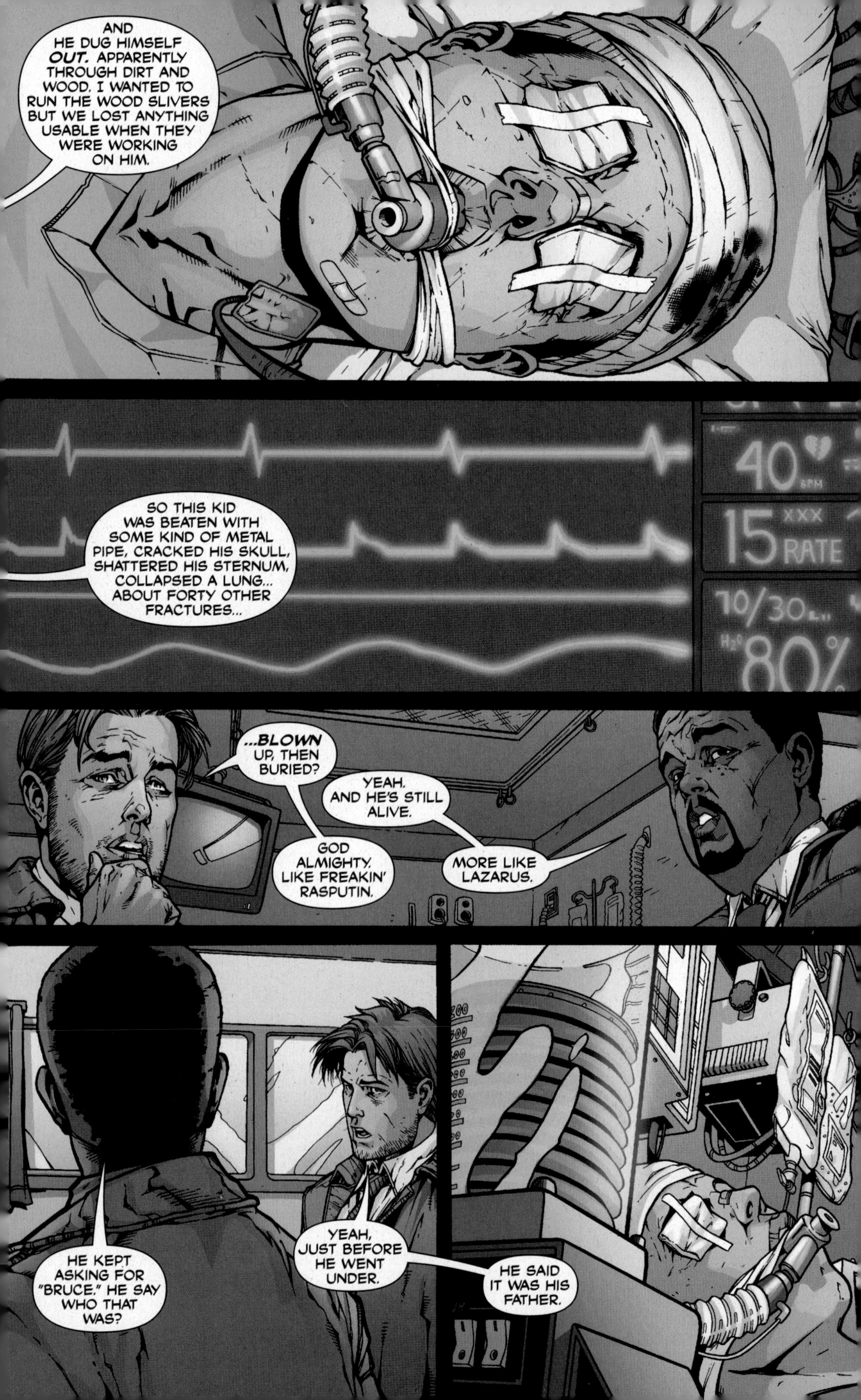
AND HE DUG HIMSELF *OUT.* APPARENTLY THROUGH DIRT AND WOOD. I WANTED TO RUN THE WOOD SLIVERS BUT WE LOST ANYTHING USABLE WHEN THEY WERE WORKING ON HIM.
40 BPM
15 RATE
70/30
80%
SO THIS KID WAS BEATEN WITH SOME KIND OF METAL PIPE, CRACKED HIS SKULL, SHATTERED HIS STERNUM, COLLAPSED A LUNG... ABOUT FORTY OTHER FRACTURES...
...BLOWN UP, THEN BURIED?
YEAH. AND HE'S STILL ALIVE.
GOD ALMIGHTY. LIKE FREAKIN' RASPUTIN.
MORE LIKE LAZARUS.
HE KEPT ASKING FOR "BRUCE." HE SAY WHO THAT WAS?
YEAH, JUST BEFORE HE WENT UNDER.
HE SAID IT WAS HIS FATHER.

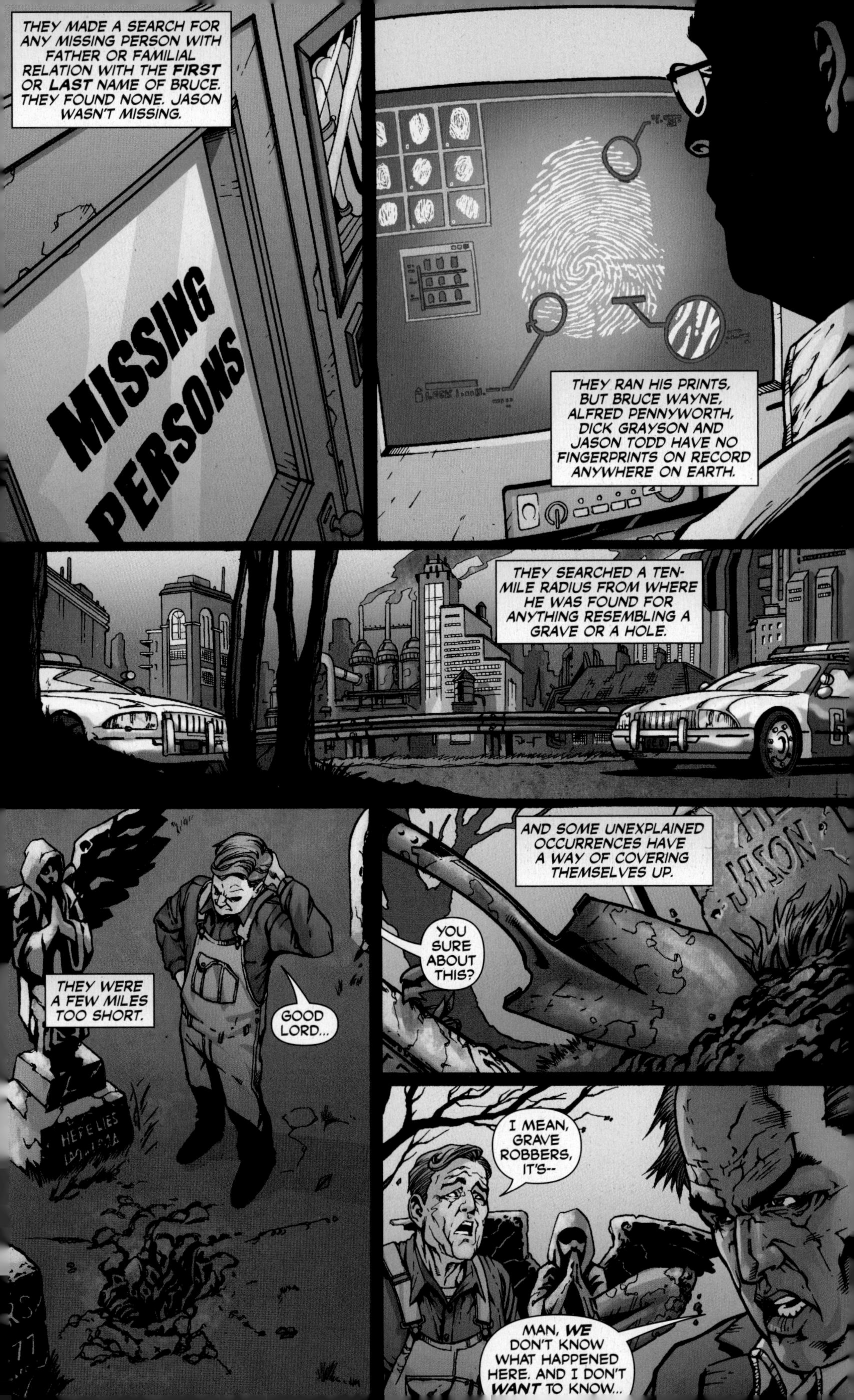
THEY MADE A SEARCH FOR ANY MISSING PERSON WITH FATHER OR FAMILIAL RELATION WITH THE **FIRST** OR **LAST** NAME OF BRUCE. THEY FOUND NONE. JASON WASN'T MISSING.
MISSING PERSONS
THEY RAN HIS PRINTS, BUT BRUCE WAYNE, ALFRED PENNYWORTH, DICK GRAYSON AND JASON TODD HAVE NO FINGERPRINTS ON RECORD ANYWHERE ON EARTH.
THEY SEARCHED A TEN-MILE RADIUS FROM WHERE HE WAS FOUND FOR ANYTHING RESEMBLING A GRAVE OR A HOLE.
THEY WERE A FEW MILES TOO SHORT.
GOOD LORD...
AND SOME UNEXPLAINED OCCURRENCES HAVE A WAY OF COVERING THEMSELVES UP.
YOU SURE ABOUT THIS?
JASON
I MEAN, GRAVE ROBBERS, IT'S--
MAN, **WE** DON'T KNOW WHAT HAPPENED HERE. AND I DON'T **WANT** TO KNOW...

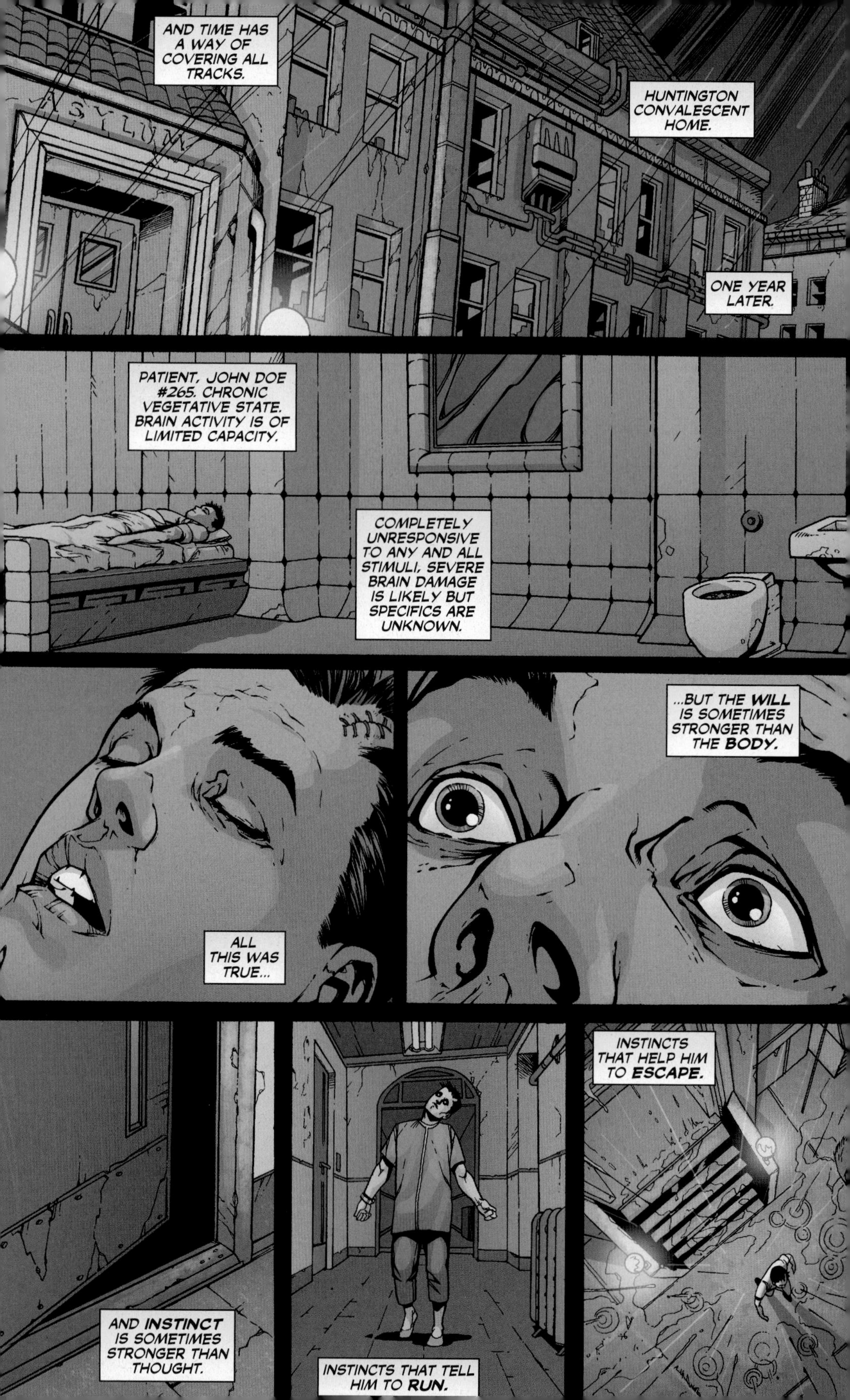
AND TIME HAS A WAY OF COVERING ALL TRACKS.
HUNTINGTON CONVALESCENT HOME.
ONE YEAR LATER.
PATIENT, JOHN DOE #265. CHRONIC VEGETATIVE STATE. BRAIN ACTIVITY IS OF LIMITED CAPACITY.
COMPLETELY UNRESPONSIVE TO ANY AND ALL STIMULI, SEVERE BRAIN DAMAGE IS LIKELY BUT SPECIFICS ARE UNKNOWN.
ALL THIS WAS TRUE...
...BUT THE WILL IS SOMETIMES STRONGER THAN THE BODY.
AND INSTINCT IS SOMETIMES STRONGER THAN THOUGHT.
INSTINCTS THAT TELL HIM TO RUN.
INSTINCTS THAT HELP HIM TO ESCAPE.

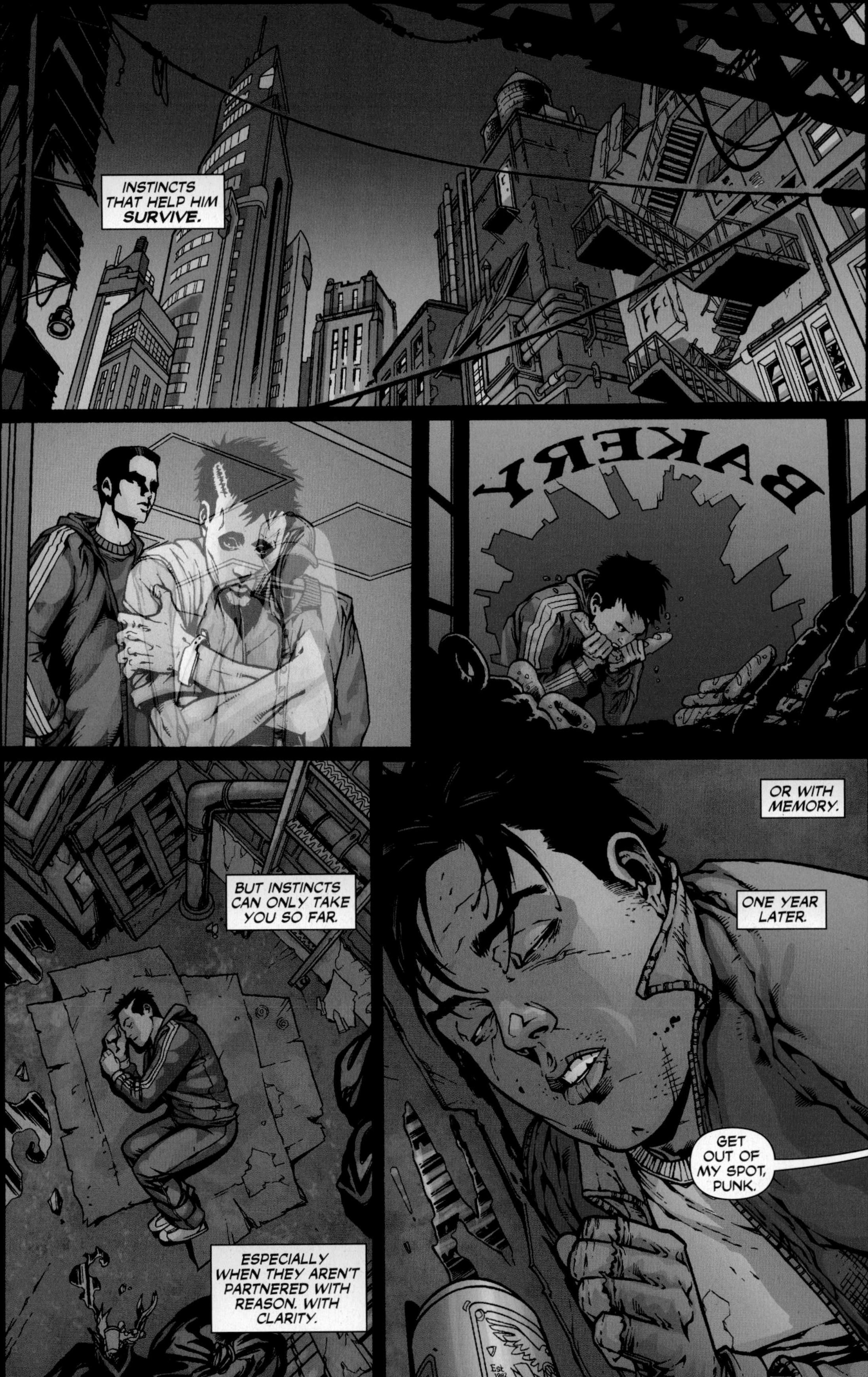

INSTINCTS THAT HELP HIM SURVIVE.
BAKERY
BUT INSTINCTS CAN ONLY TAKE YOU SO FAR.
ESPECIALLY WHEN THEY AREN'T PARTNERED WITH REASON. WITH CLARITY.
OR WITH MEMORY.
ONE YEAR LATER.
GET OUT OF MY SPOT, PUNK.

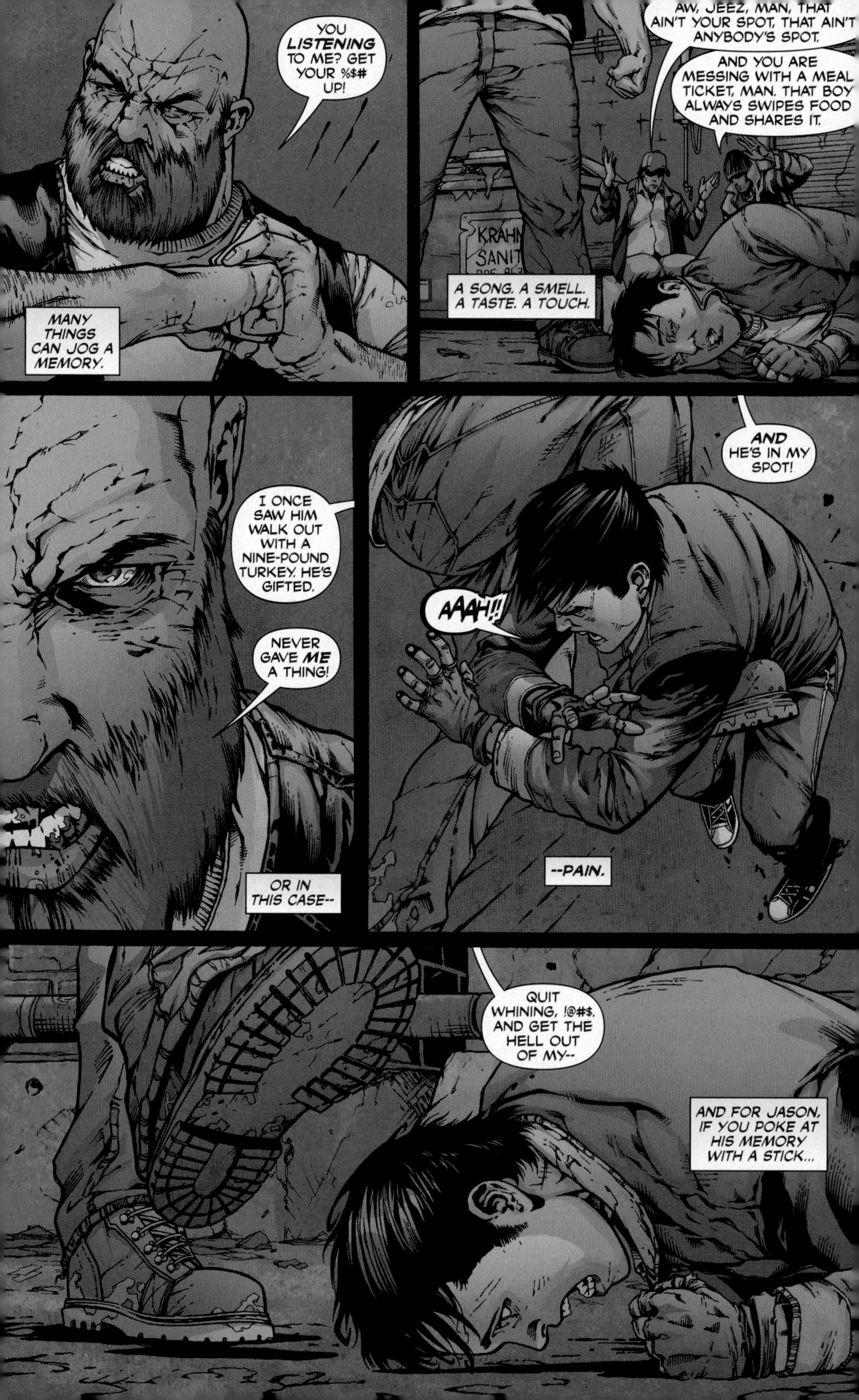
YOU LISTENING TO ME? GET YOUR %$# UP!
MANY THINGS CAN JOG A MEMORY.
AW, JEEZ, MAN, THAT AIN'T YOUR SPOT, THAT AIN'T ANYBODY'S SPOT.
AND YOU ARE MESSING WITH A MEAL TICKET, MAN. THAT BOY ALWAYS SWIPES FOOD AND SHARES IT.
A SONG. A SMELL. A TASTE. A TOUCH.
I ONCE SAW HIM WALK OUT WITH A NINE-POUND TURKEY. HE'S GIFTED.
NEVER GAVE ME A THING!
OR IN THIS CASE--
AND HE'S IN MY SPOT!
AAAH!!
--PAIN.
QUIT WHINING, !@#$, AND GET THE HELL OUT OF MY--
AND FOR JASON, IF YOU POKE AT HIS MEMORY WITH A STICK...

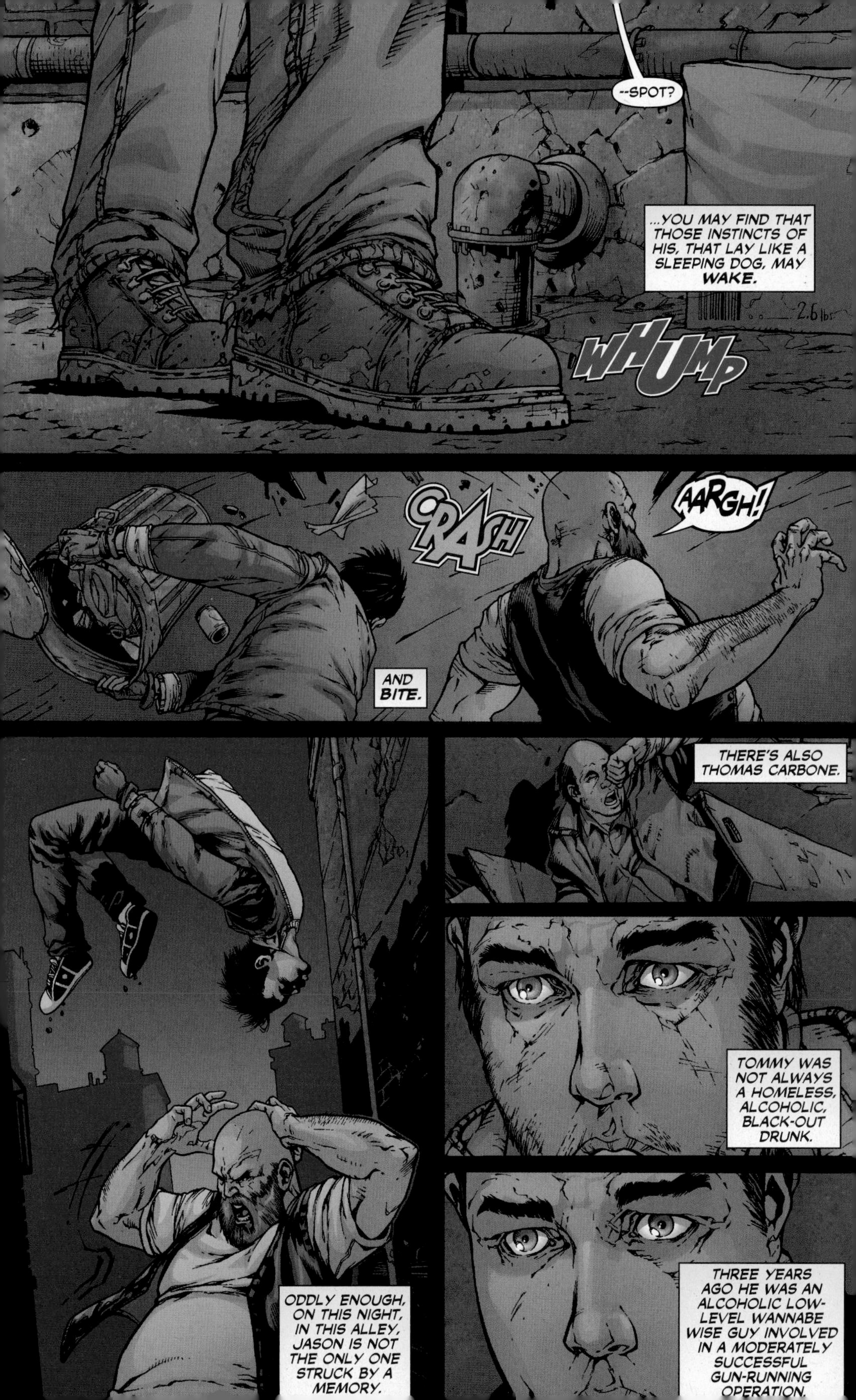
--SPOT?
...YOU MAY FIND THAT THOSE INSTINCTS OF HIS, THAT LAY LIKE A SLEEPING DOG, MAY WAKE.
2.6 lbs.
WHUMP
CRASH
AARGH!
AND BITE.
THERE'S ALSO THOMAS CARBONE.
TOMMY WAS NOT ALWAYS A HOMELESS, ALCOHOLIC, BLACK-OUT DRUNK.
ODDLY ENOUGH, ON THIS NIGHT, IN THIS ALLEY, JASON IS NOT THE ONLY ONE STRUCK BY A MEMORY.
THREE YEARS AGO HE WAS AN ALCOHOLIC LOW-LEVEL WANNABE WISE GUY INVOLVED IN A MODERATELY SUCCESSFUL GUN-RUNNING OPERATION.

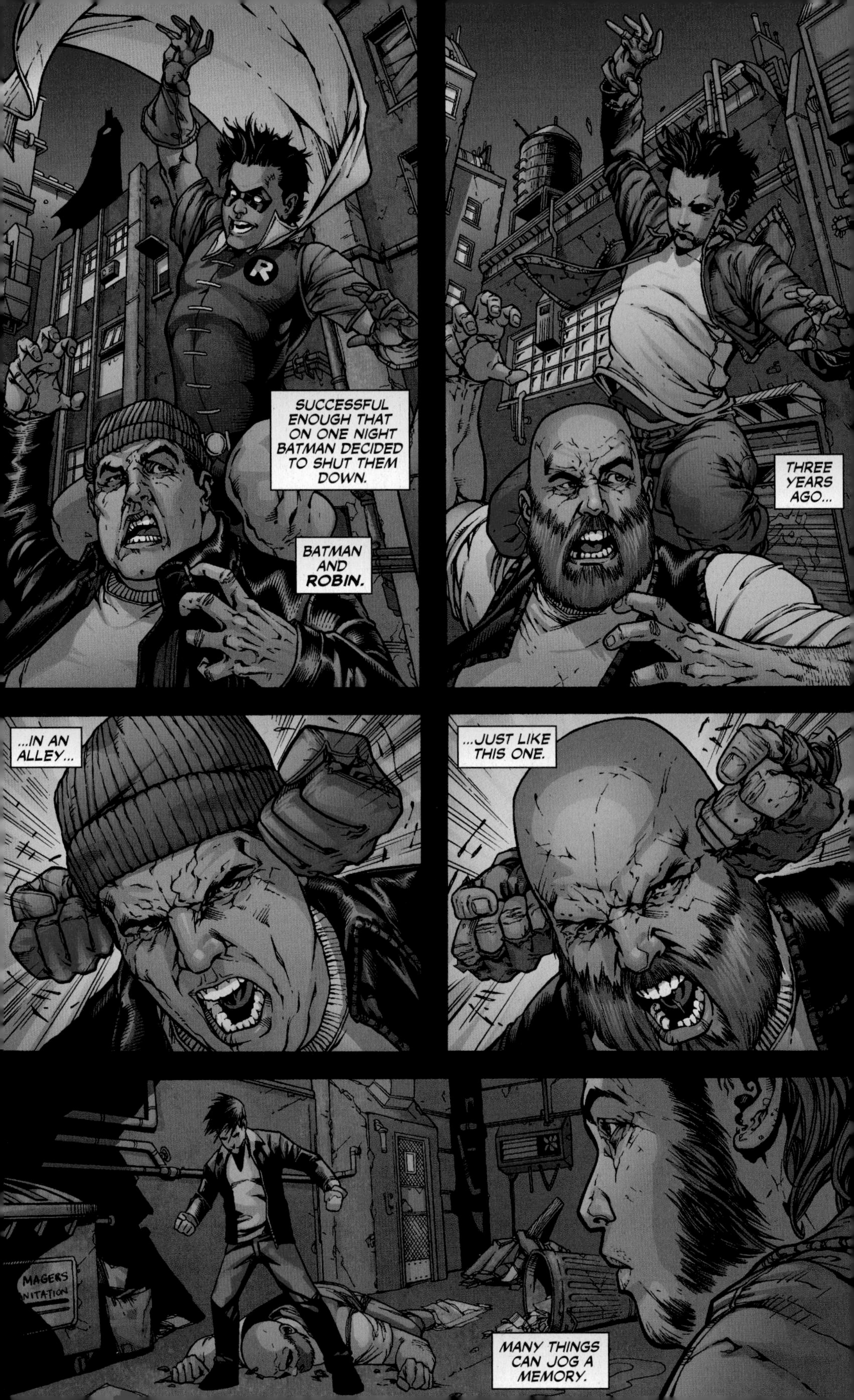
SUCCESSFUL ENOUGH THAT ON ONE NIGHT BATMAN DECIDED TO SHUT THEM DOWN.
BATMAN AND ROBIN.
THREE YEARS AGO...
...IN AN ALLEY...
...JUST LIKE THIS ONE.
MAGERS
NITATION
MANY THINGS CAN JOG A MEMORY.

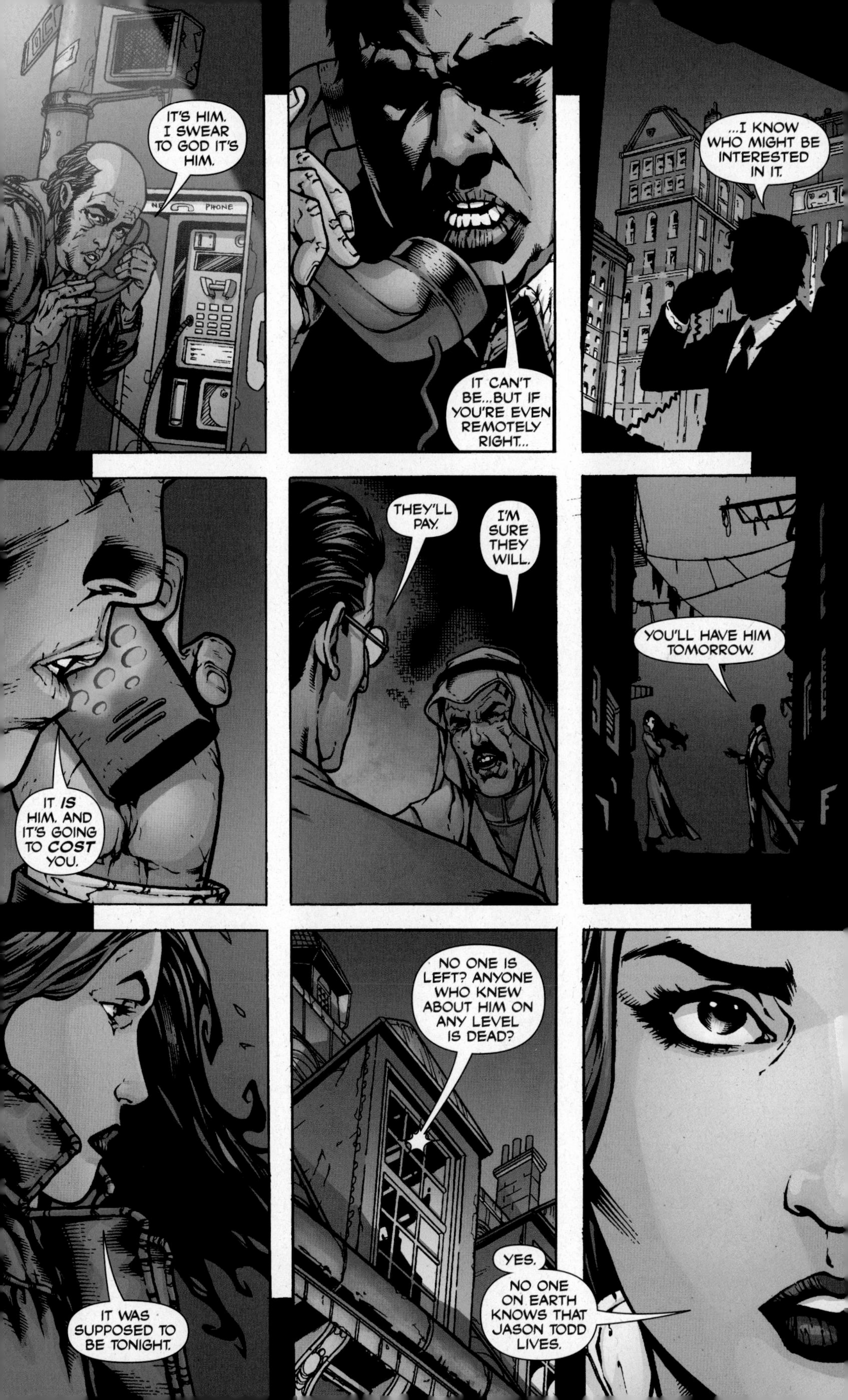
IT'S HIM. I SWEAR TO GOD IT'S HIM.
IT CAN'T BE...BUT IF YOU'RE EVEN REMOTELY RIGHT...
...I KNOW WHO MIGHT BE INTERESTED IN IT.
IT *IS* HIM. AND IT'S GOING TO ***COST*** YOU.
THEY'LL PAY.
I'M SURE THEY WILL.
YOU'LL HAVE HIM TOMORROW.
IT WAS SUPPOSED TO BE TONIGHT.
NO ONE IS LEFT? ANYONE WHO KNEW ABOUT HIM ON ANY LEVEL IS DEAD?
YES.
NO ONE ON EARTH KNOWS THAT JASON TODD LIVES.

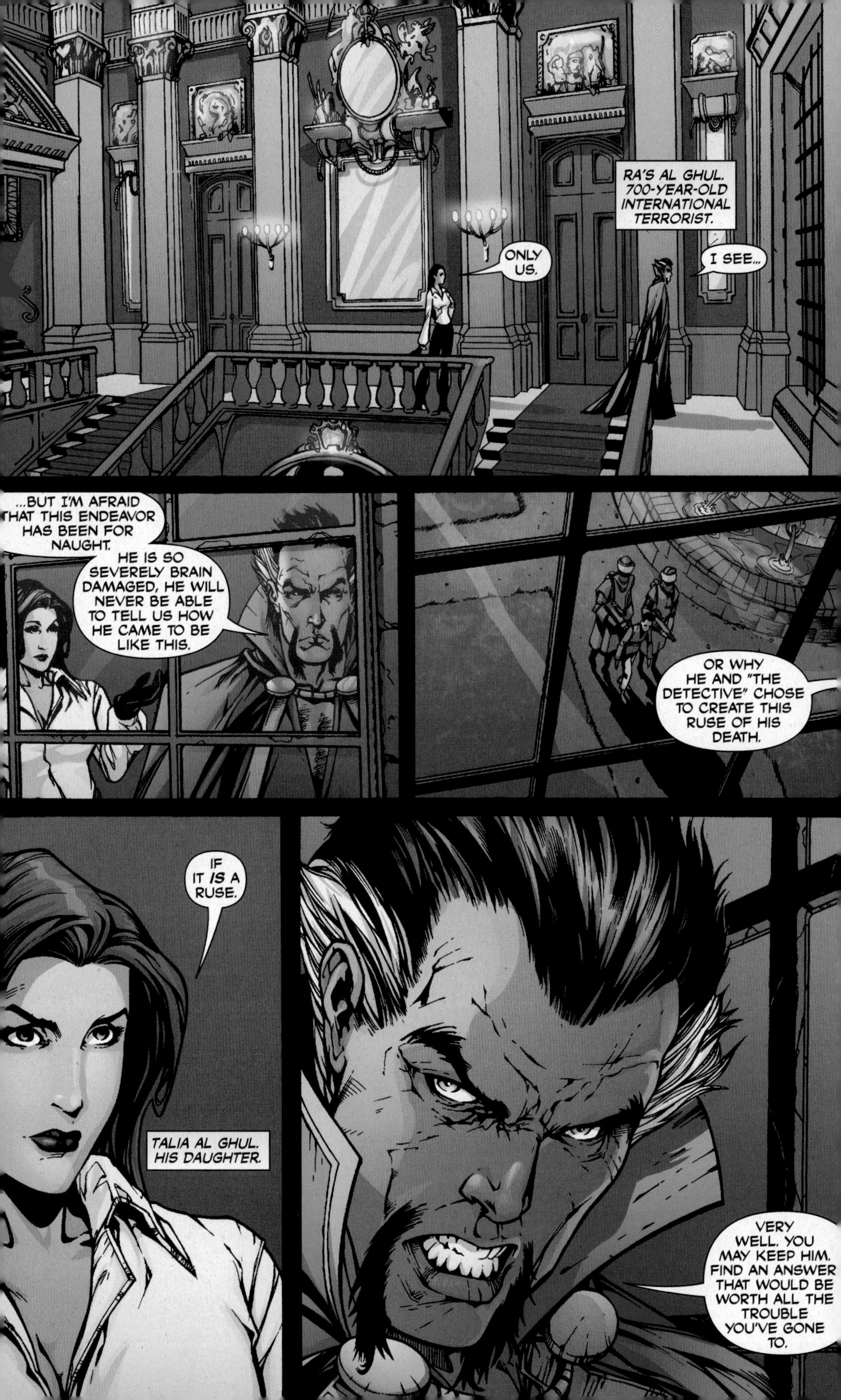
RA'S AL GHUL. 700-YEAR-OLD INTERNATIONAL TERRORIST.
ONLY US.
I SEE...
...BUT I'M AFRAID THAT THIS ENDEAVOR HAS BEEN FOR NAUGHT.
HE IS SO SEVERELY BRAIN DAMAGED, HE WILL NEVER BE ABLE TO TELL US HOW HE CAME TO BE LIKE THIS.
OR WHY HE AND "THE DETECTIVE" CHOSE TO CREATE THIS RUSE OF HIS DEATH.
IF IT IS A RUSE.
TALIA AL GHUL. HIS DAUGHTER.
VERY WELL. YOU MAY KEEP HIM. FIND AN ANSWER THAT WOULD BE WORTH ALL THE TROUBLE YOU'VE GONE TO.

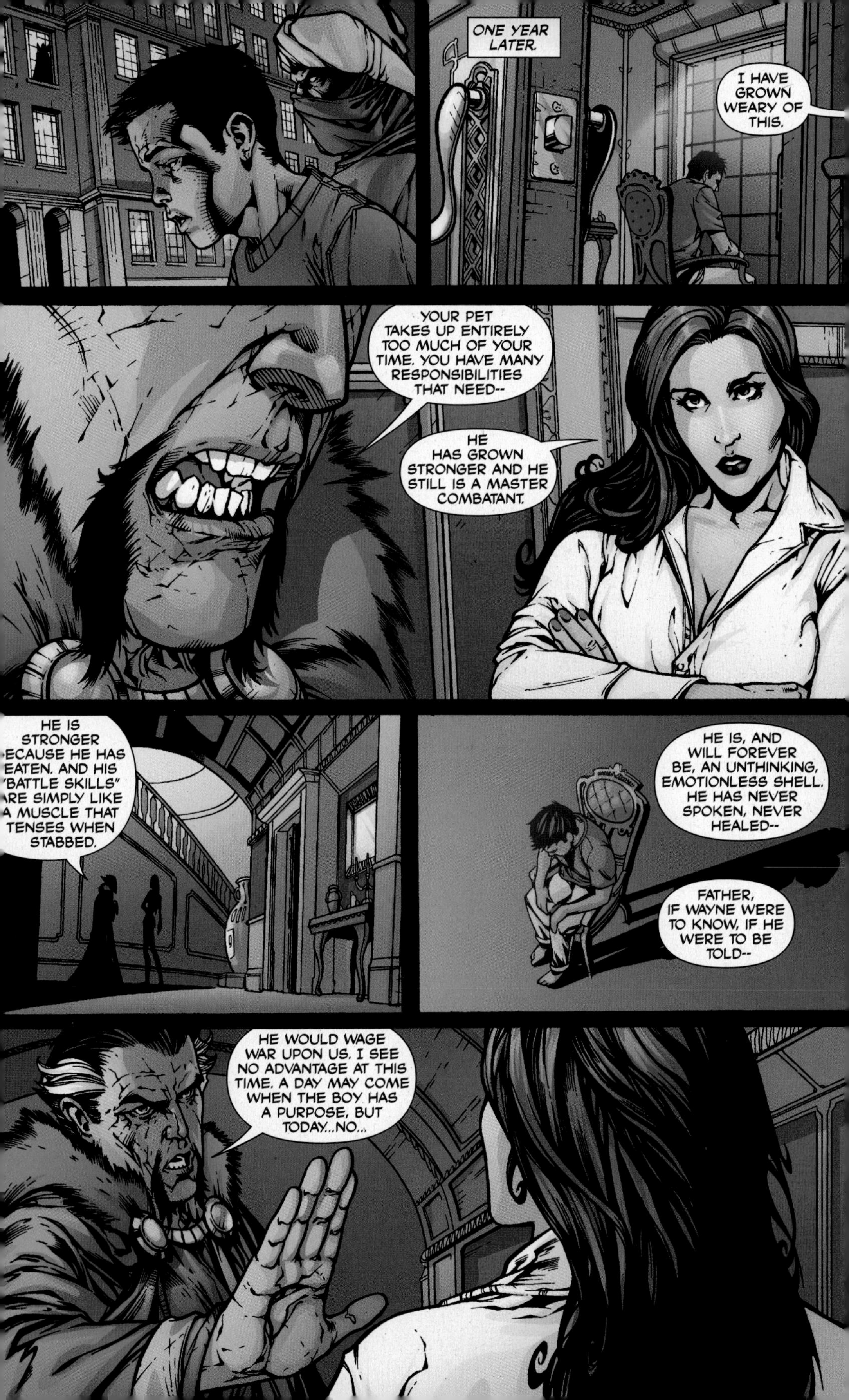
ONE YEAR LATER.
I HAVE GROWN WEARY OF THIS.
YOUR PET TAKES UP ENTIRELY TOO MUCH OF YOUR TIME. YOU HAVE MANY RESPONSIBILITIES THAT NEED--
HE HAS GROWN STRONGER AND HE STILL IS A MASTER COMBATANT.
HE IS STRONGER ECAUSE HE HAS EATEN. AND HIS "BATTLE SKILLS" RE SIMPLY LIKE A MUSCLE THAT TENSES WHEN STABBED.
HE IS, AND WILL FOREVER BE, AN UNTHINKING, EMOTIONLESS SHELL. HE HAS NEVER SPOKEN, NEVER HEALED--
FATHER, IF WAYNE WERE TO KNOW, IF HE WERE TO BE TOLD--
HE WOULD WAGE WAR UPON US. I SEE NO ADVANTAGE AT THIS TIME. A DAY MAY COME WHEN THE BOY HAS A PURPOSE, BUT TODAY...NO...

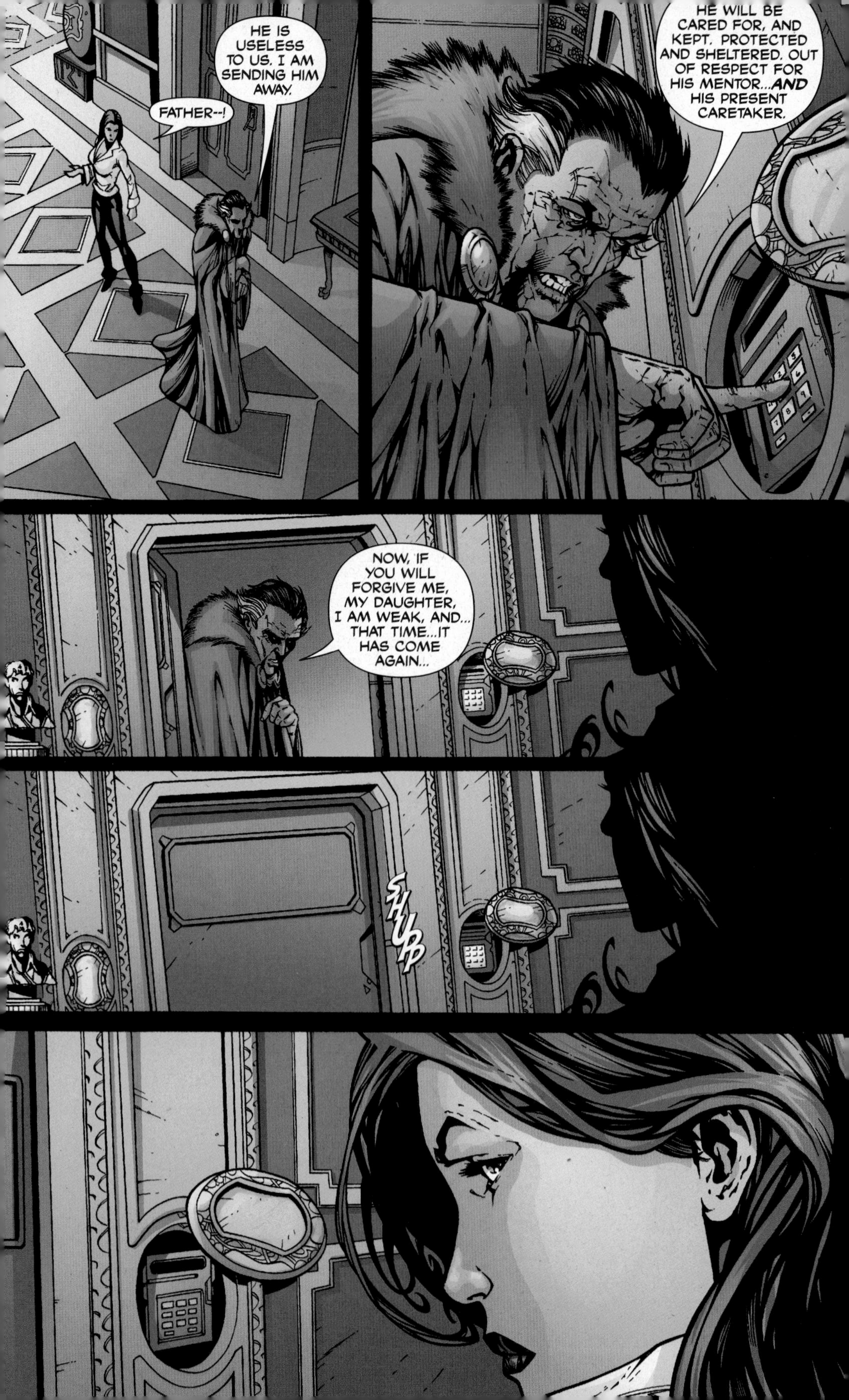
FATHER--!
HE IS USELESS TO US. I AM SENDING HIM AWAY.
HE WILL BE CARED FOR, AND KEPT. PROTECTED AND SHELTERED. OUT OF RESPECT FOR HIS MENTOR...AND HIS PRESENT CARETAKER.
NOW, IF YOU WILL FORGIVE ME, MY DAUGHTER, I AM WEAK, AND... THAT TIME...IT HAS COME AGAIN...
SHUP

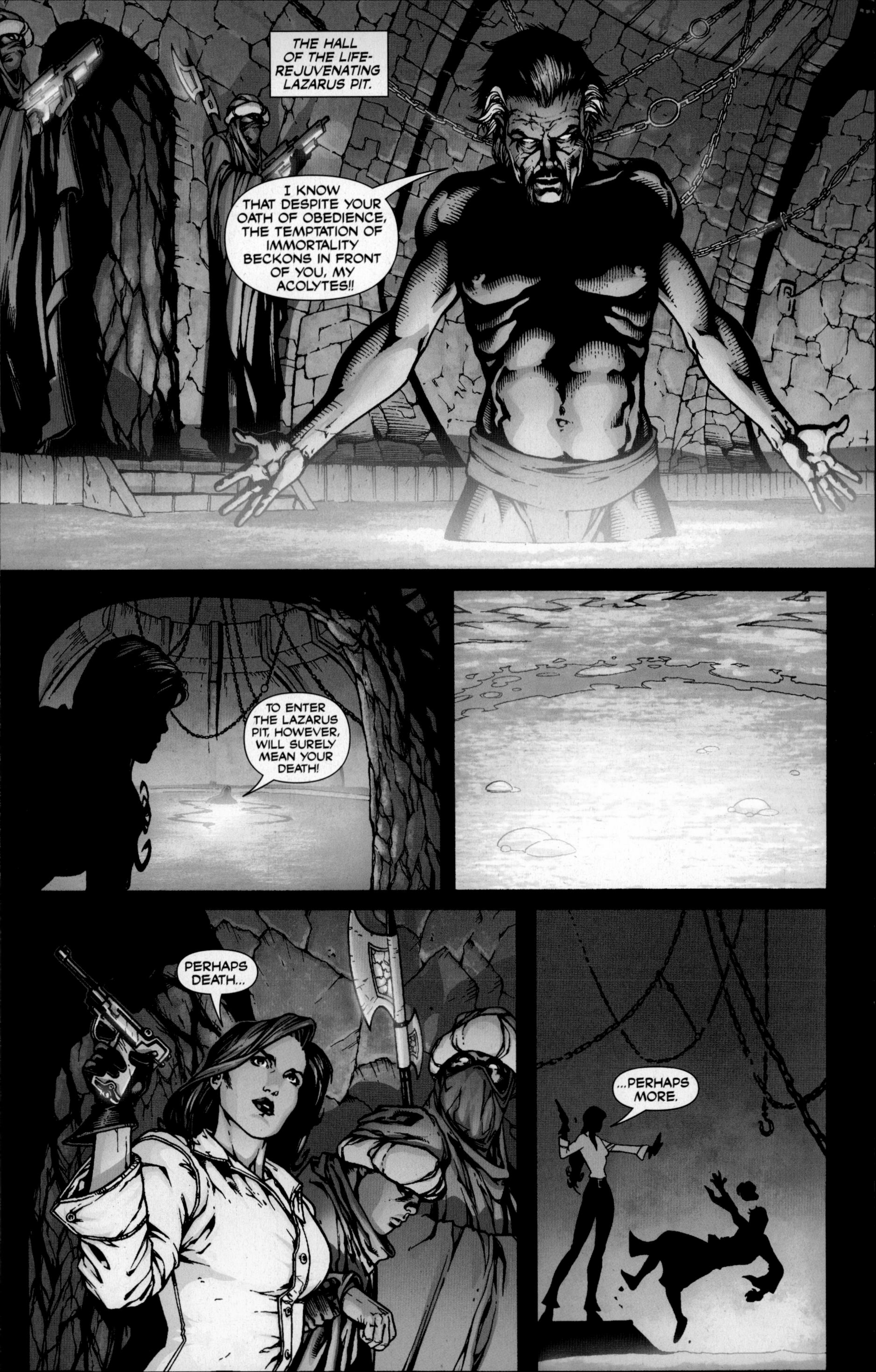
THE HALL OF THE LIFE-REJUVENATING LAZARUS PIT.
I KNOW THAT DESPITE YOUR OATH OF OBEDIENCE, THE TEMPTATION OF IMMORTALITY BECKONS IN FRONT OF YOU, MY ACOLYTES!!
TO ENTER THE LAZARUS PIT, HOWEVER, WILL SURELY MEAN YOUR DEATH!
PERHAPS DEATH...
...PERHAPS MORE.

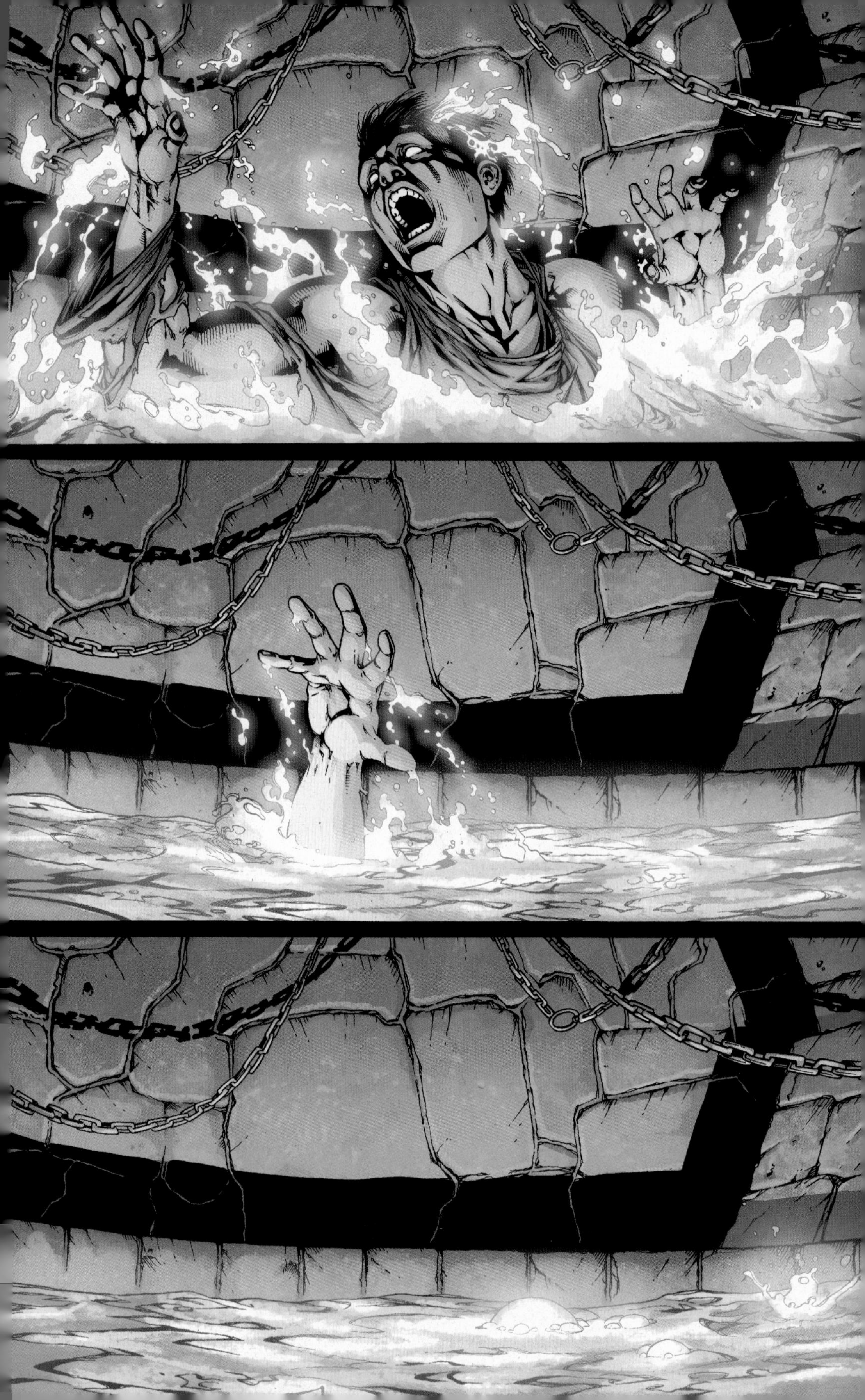

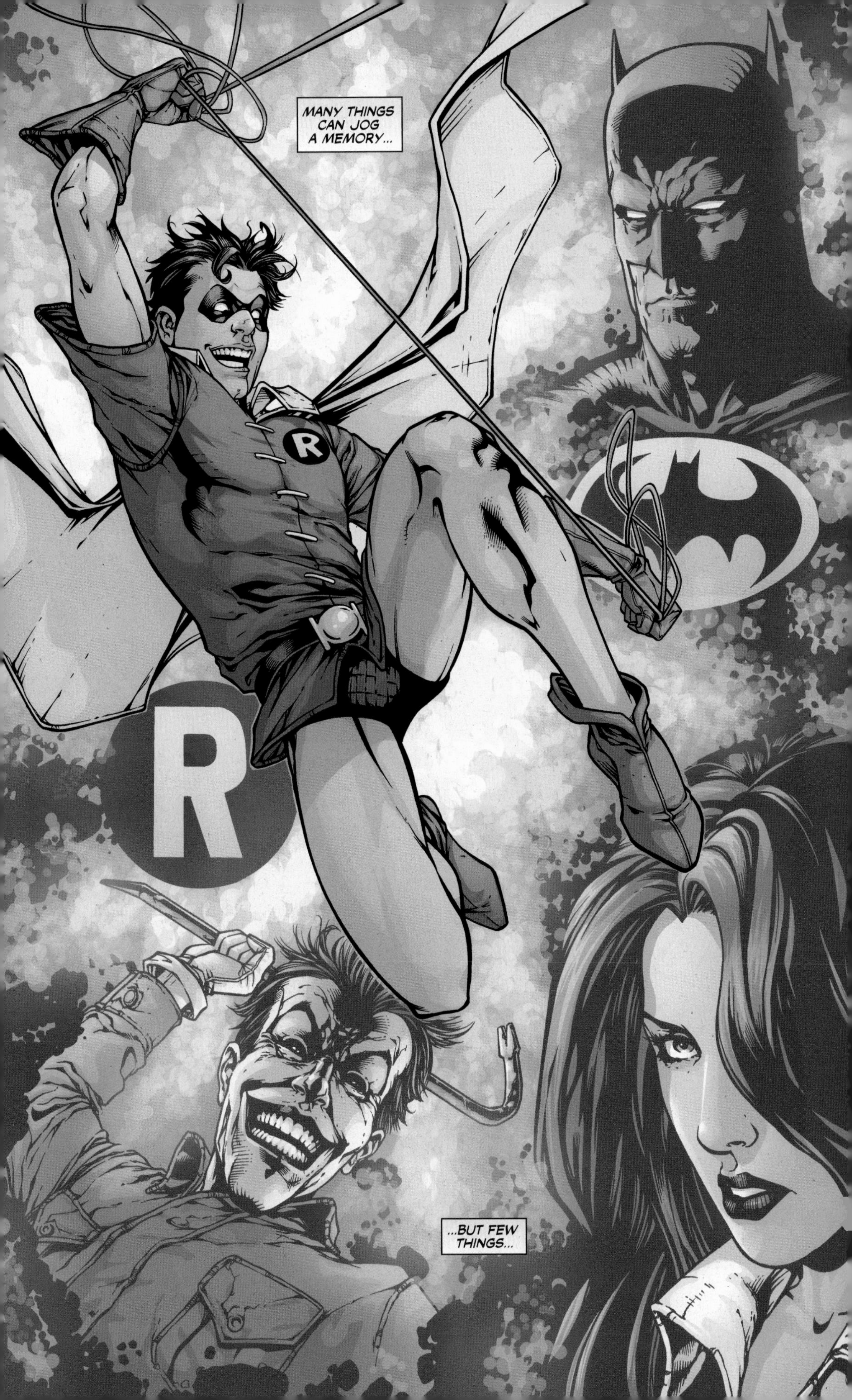
MANY THINGS CAN JOG A MEMORY...
...BUT FEW THINGS...

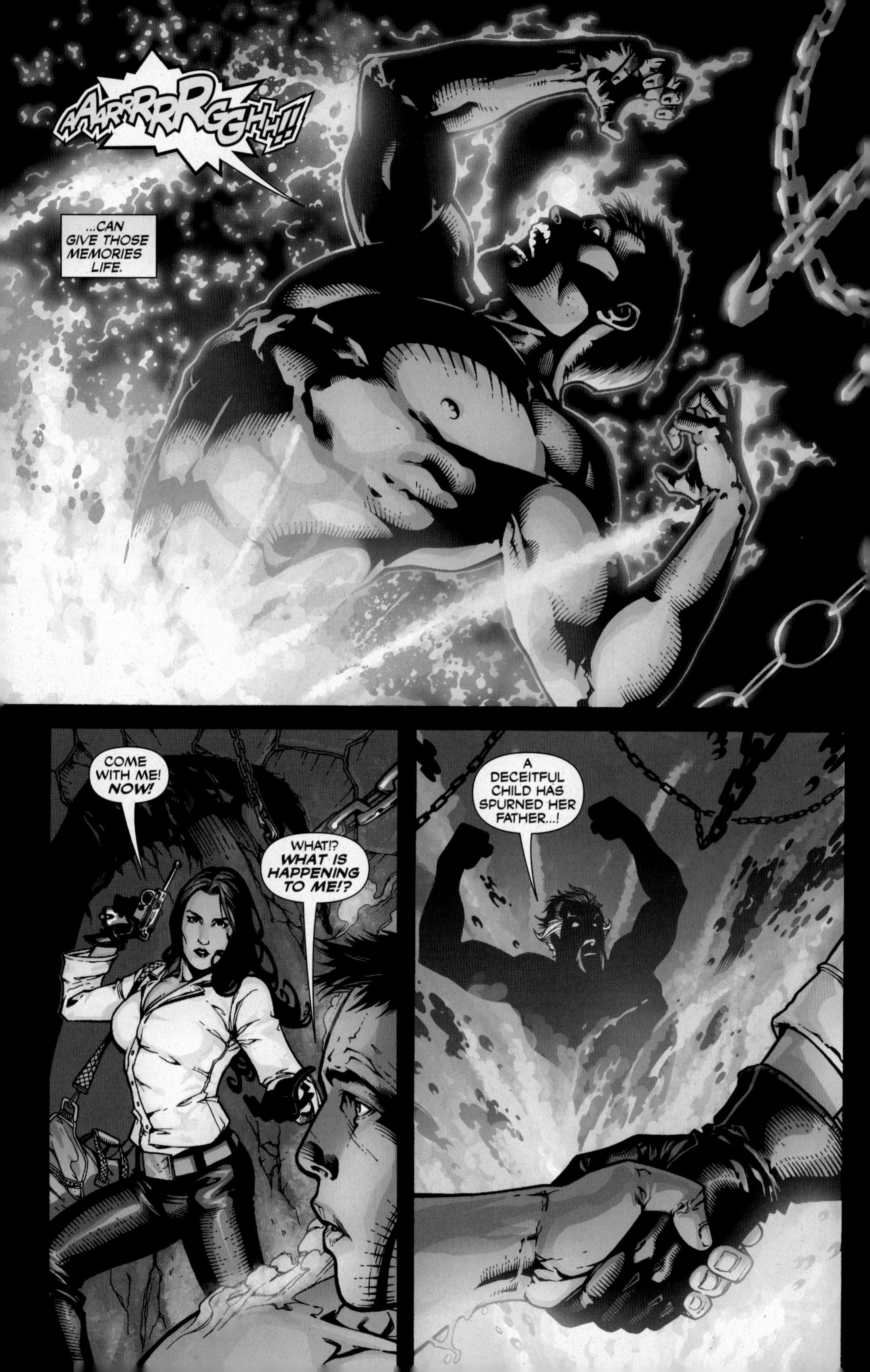

AAARRRRRGGHH!!!
...CAN GIVE THOSE MEMORIES LIFE.
COME WITH ME! NOW!
WHAT!? WHAT IS HAPPENING TO ME!?
A DECEITFUL CHILD HAS SPURNED HER FATHER...!

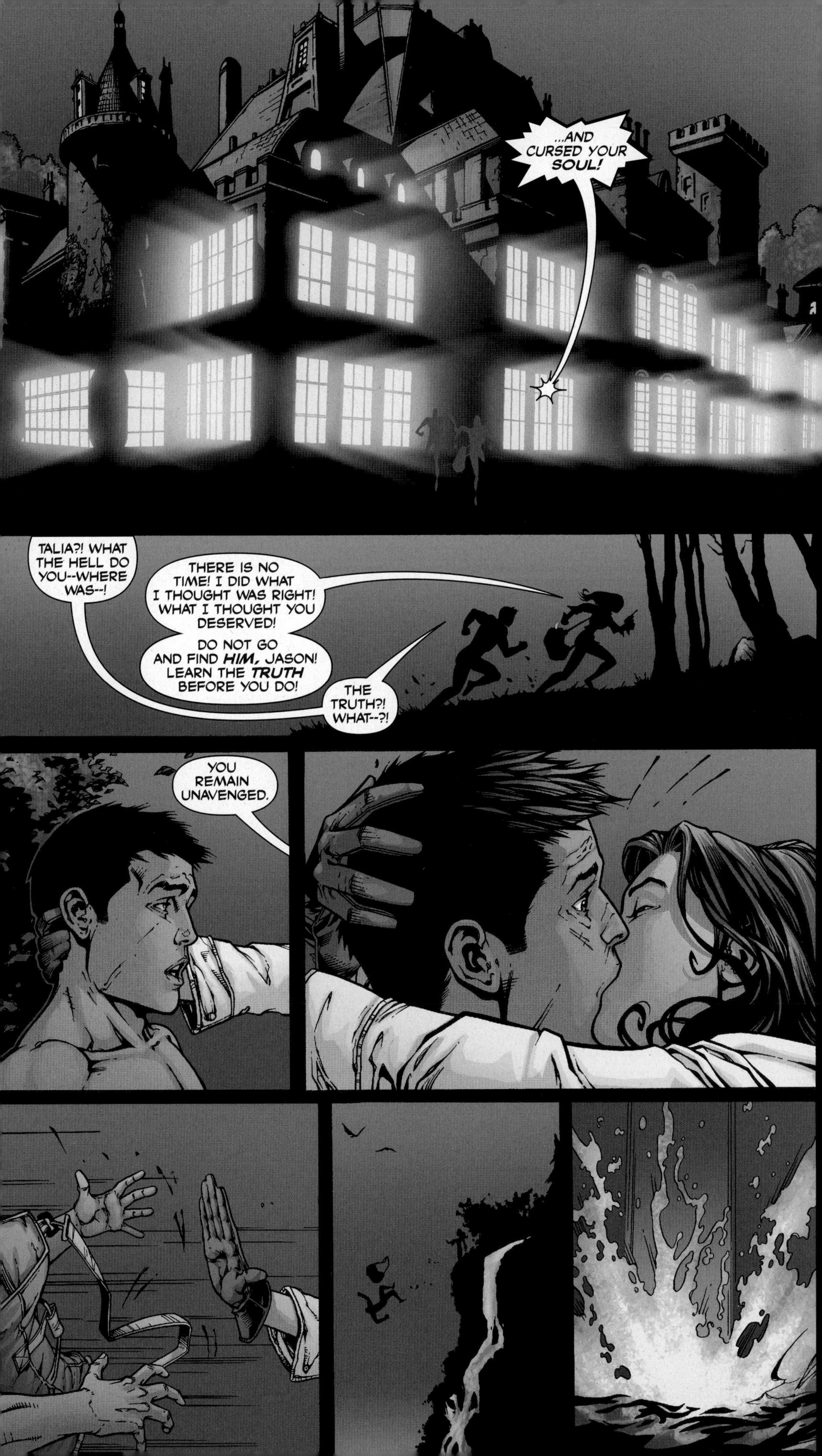
...AND CURSED YOUR SOUL!
TALIA?! WHAT THE HELL DO YOU--WHERE WAS--!
THERE IS NO TIME! I DID WHAT I THOUGHT WAS RIGHT! WHAT I THOUGHT YOU DESERVED!
DO NOT GO AND FIND HIM, JASON! LEARN THE TRUTH BEFORE YOU DO!
THE TRUTH?! WHAT--?!
YOU REMAIN UNAVENGED.

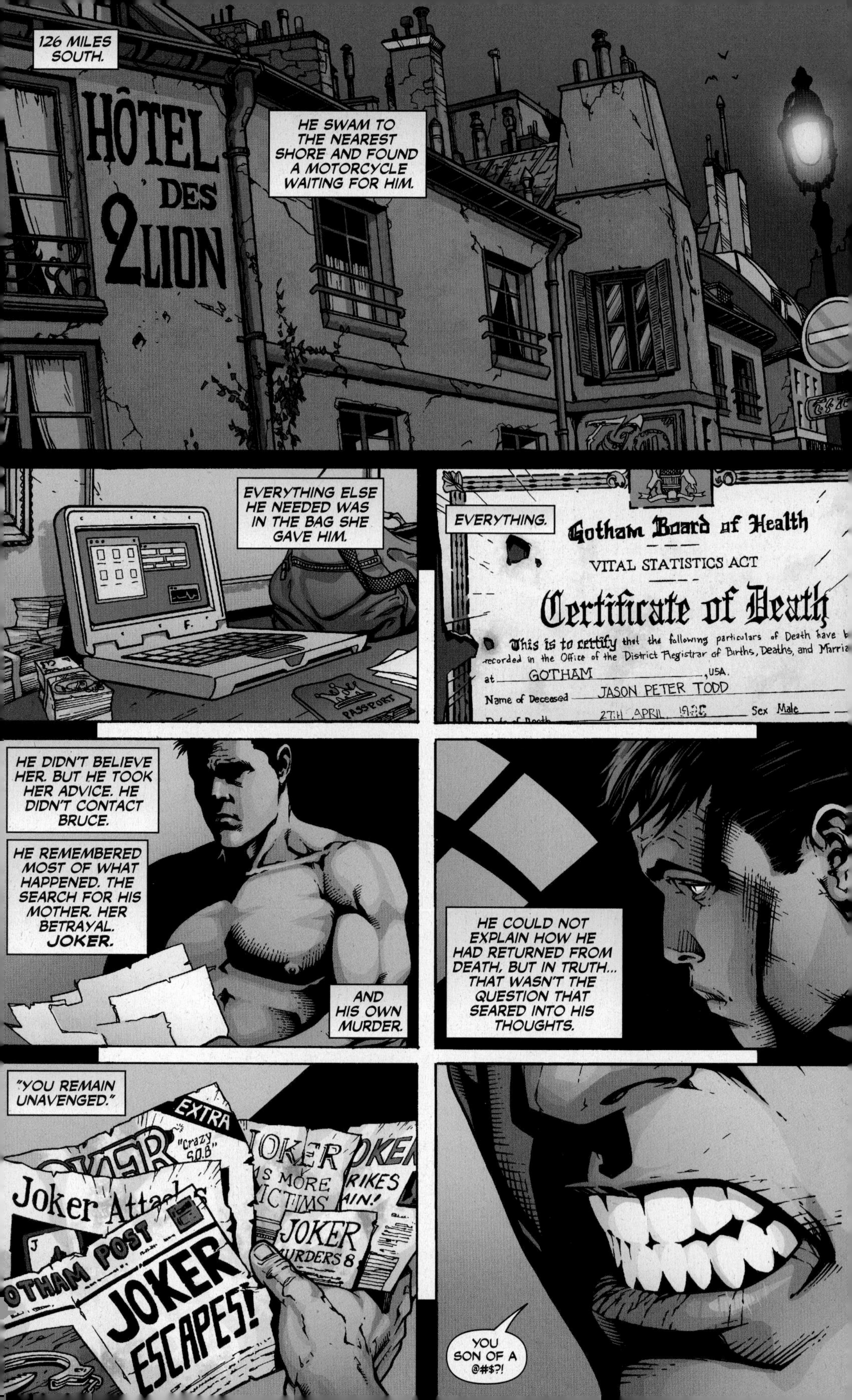
126 MILES SOUTH.
HÔTEL DES 2 LION
HE SWAM TO THE NEAREST SHORE AND FOUND A MOTORCYCLE WAITING FOR HIM.
EVERYTHING ELSE HE NEEDED WAS IN THE BAG SHE GAVE HIM.
PASSPORT
EVERYTHING.
Gotham Board of Health
VITAL STATISTICS ACT
Certificate of Death
This is to certify that the following particulars of Death have b
recorded in the Office of the District Registrar of Births, Deaths, and Marria
at GOTHAM , USA.
Name of Deceased JASON PETER TODD
Sex Male
HE DIDN'T BELIEVE HER. BUT HE TOOK HER ADVICE. HE DIDN'T CONTACT BRUCE.
HE REMEMBERED MOST OF WHAT HAPPENED. THE SEARCH FOR HIS MOTHER. HER BETRAYAL. JOKER.
AND HIS OWN MURDER.
HE COULD NOT EXPLAIN HOW HE HAD RETURNED FROM DEATH, BUT IN TRUTH... THAT WASN'T THE QUESTION THAT SEARED INTO HIS THOUGHTS.
"YOU REMAIN UNAVENGED."
EXTRA
"Crazy S.O.B"
Joker Attac
JOKER
MORE
ICTIMS
RIKES
AIN!
OTHAM POST
JOKER ESCAPES!
JOKER MURDERS 8
YOU SON OF A @#$?!

...OR WAS IT A MOST SURREAL TURN OF DISAPPOINTMENT.

THE QUESTION WILL BE FOREVER ASKED...WAS IT THE FIRES OF THE LAZARUS PIT, OR THE LIFE FORCE OF RA'S AL GHUL...

...OR PERHAPS THAT MORTAL FLESH CAN NEVER TRULY RETURN FROM THE GRAVE UNSULLIED...

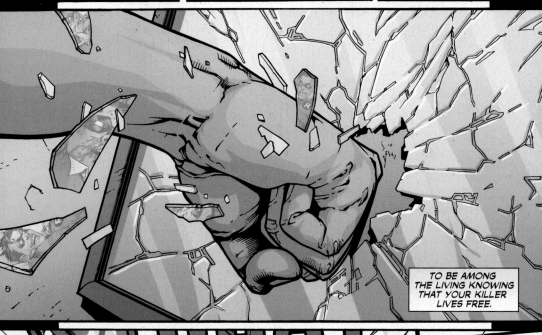

TO BE AMONG THE LIVING KNOWING THAT YOUR KILLER LIVES FREE.

AND KNOWING WHO IS TO BLAME FOR IT.

Batman Returns Joker
To Police Custody

By Todd Magers

Gotham City (AP)—
The Joker was returned to Arkham Asylum
last night by officers of the 18th Precinct
Police officials did confirm the Joker was
by Bat...

WAS IT THAT WHICH TURNED HIS HEART?

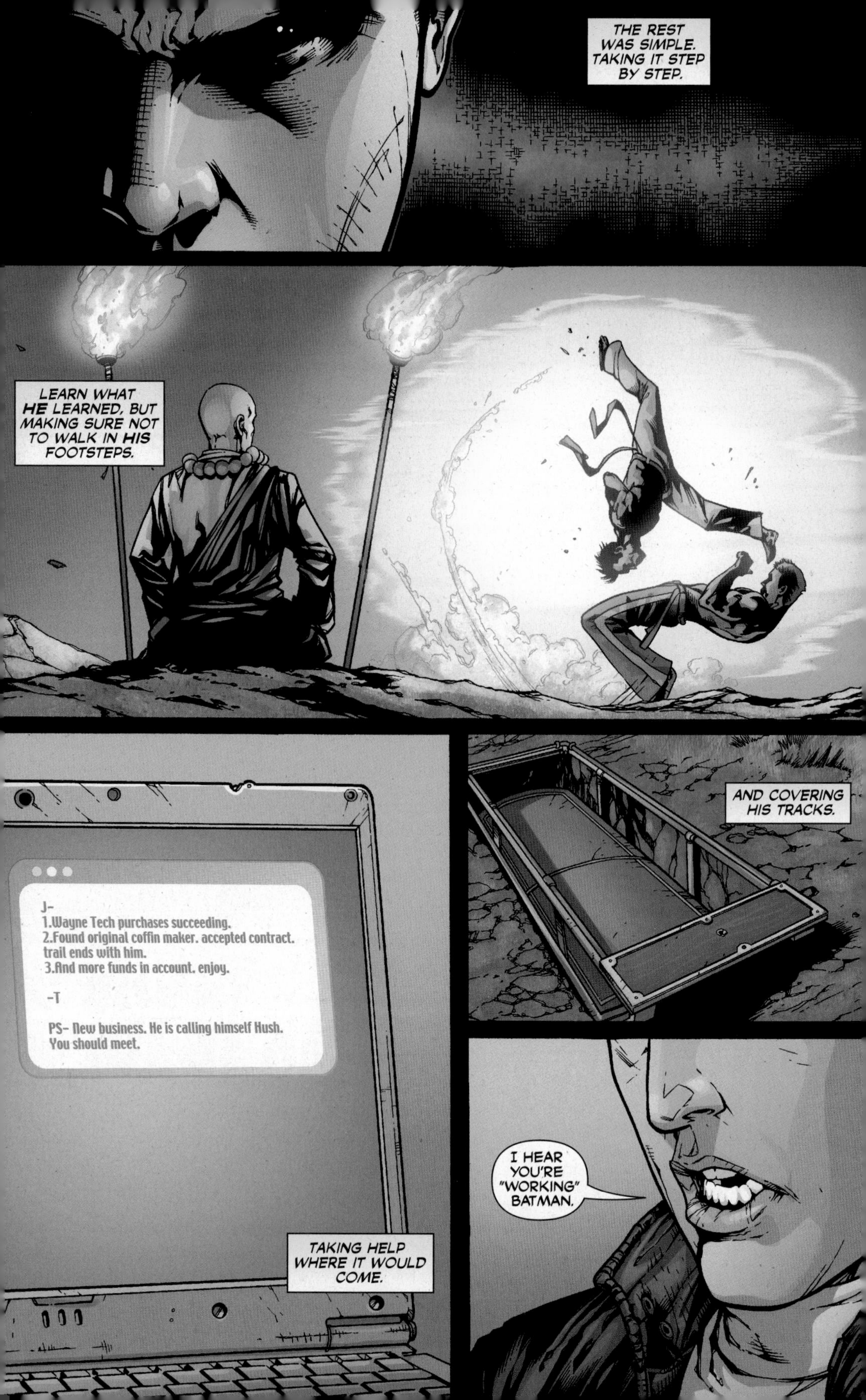
THE REST WAS SIMPLE. TAKING IT STEP BY STEP.
LEARN WHAT HE LEARNED, BUT MAKING SURE NOT TO WALK IN HIS FOOTSTEPS.
J-
1.Wayne Tech purchases succeeding.
2.Found original coffin maker. accepted contract. trail ends with him.
3.And more funds in account. enjoy.
-T
PS- New business. He is calling himself Hush. You should meet.
TAKING HELP WHERE IT WOULD COME.
AND COVERING HIS TRACKS.
I HEAR YOU'RE "WORKING" BATMAN.

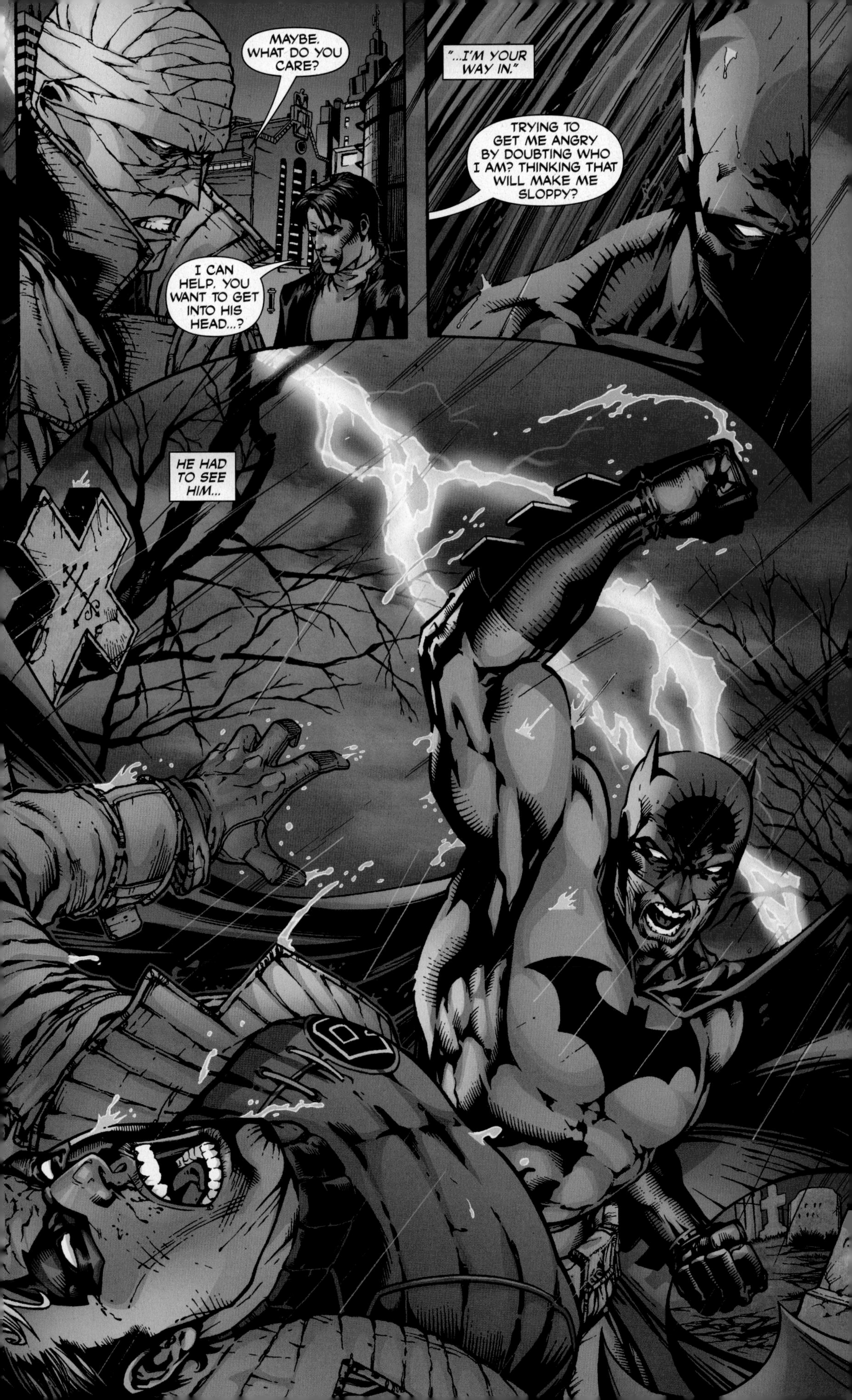
MAYBE. WHAT DO YOU CARE?
I CAN HELP. YOU WANT TO GET INTO HIS HEAD...?
"...I'M YOUR WAY IN."
TRYING TO GET ME ANGRY BY DOUBTING WHO I AM? THINKING THAT WILL MAKE ME SLOPPY?
HE HAD TO SEE HIM...

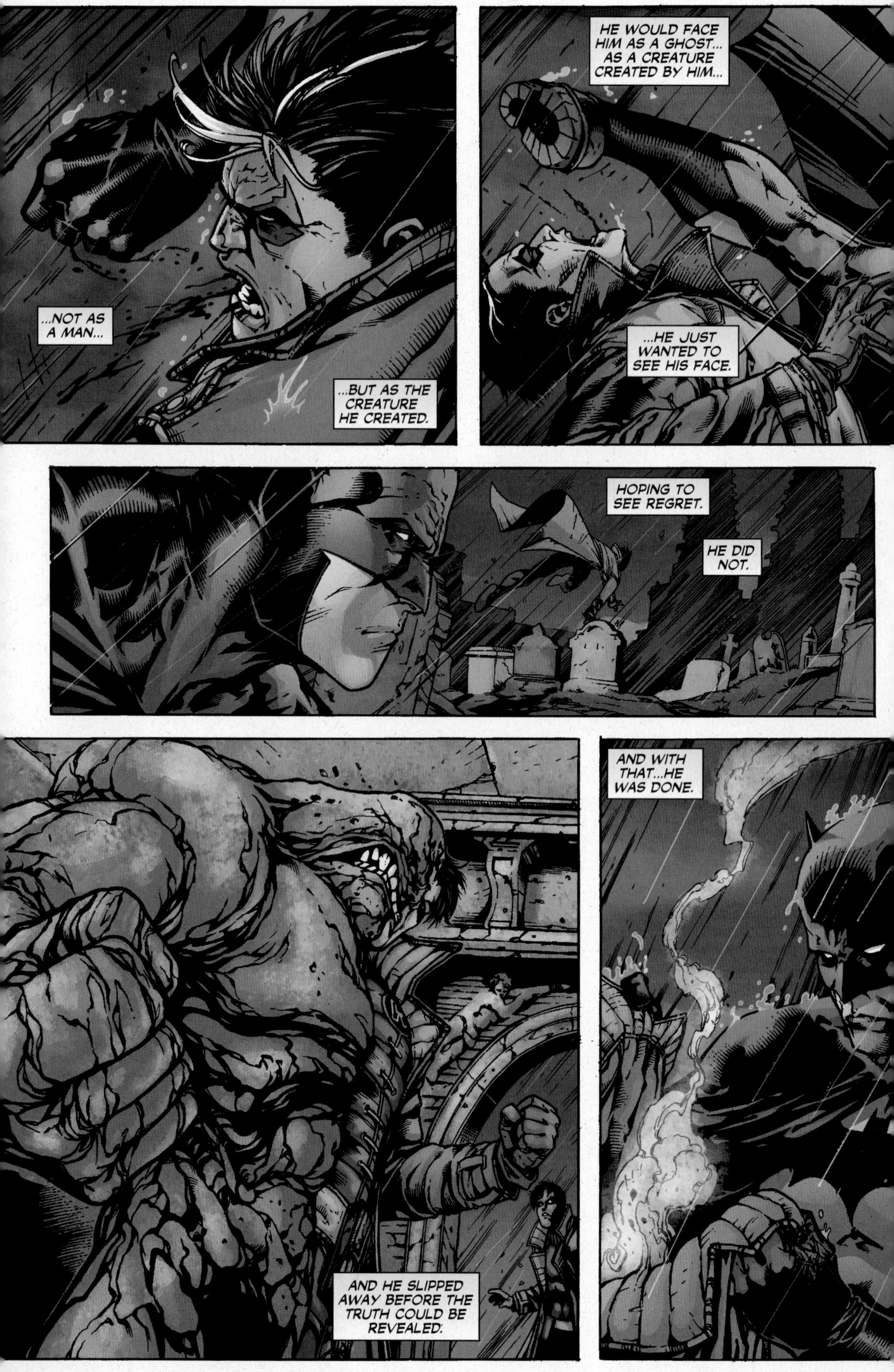
...NOT AS A MAN...
...BUT AS THE CREATURE HE CREATED.
HE WOULD FACE HIM AS A GHOST... AS A CREATURE CREATED BY HIM...
...HE JUST WANTED TO SEE HIS FACE.
HOPING TO SEE REGRET.
HE DID NOT.
AND HE SLIPPED AWAY BEFORE THE TRUTH COULD BE REVEALED.
AND WITH THAT...HE WAS DONE.

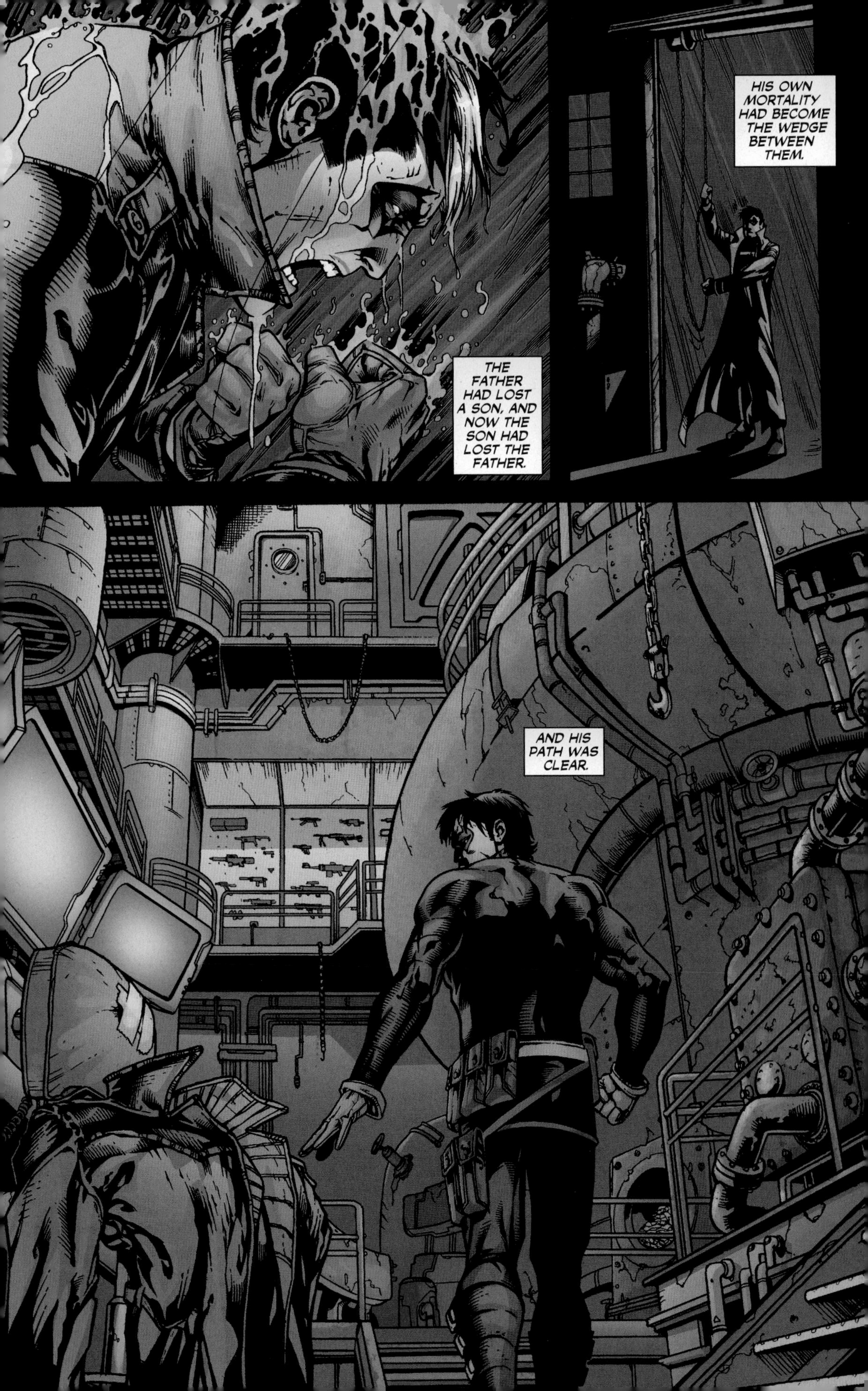
THE FATHER HAD LOST A SON, AND NOW THE SON HAD LOST THE FATHER.
HIS OWN MORTALITY HAD BECOME THE WEDGE BETWEEN THEM.
AND HIS PATH WAS CLEAR.

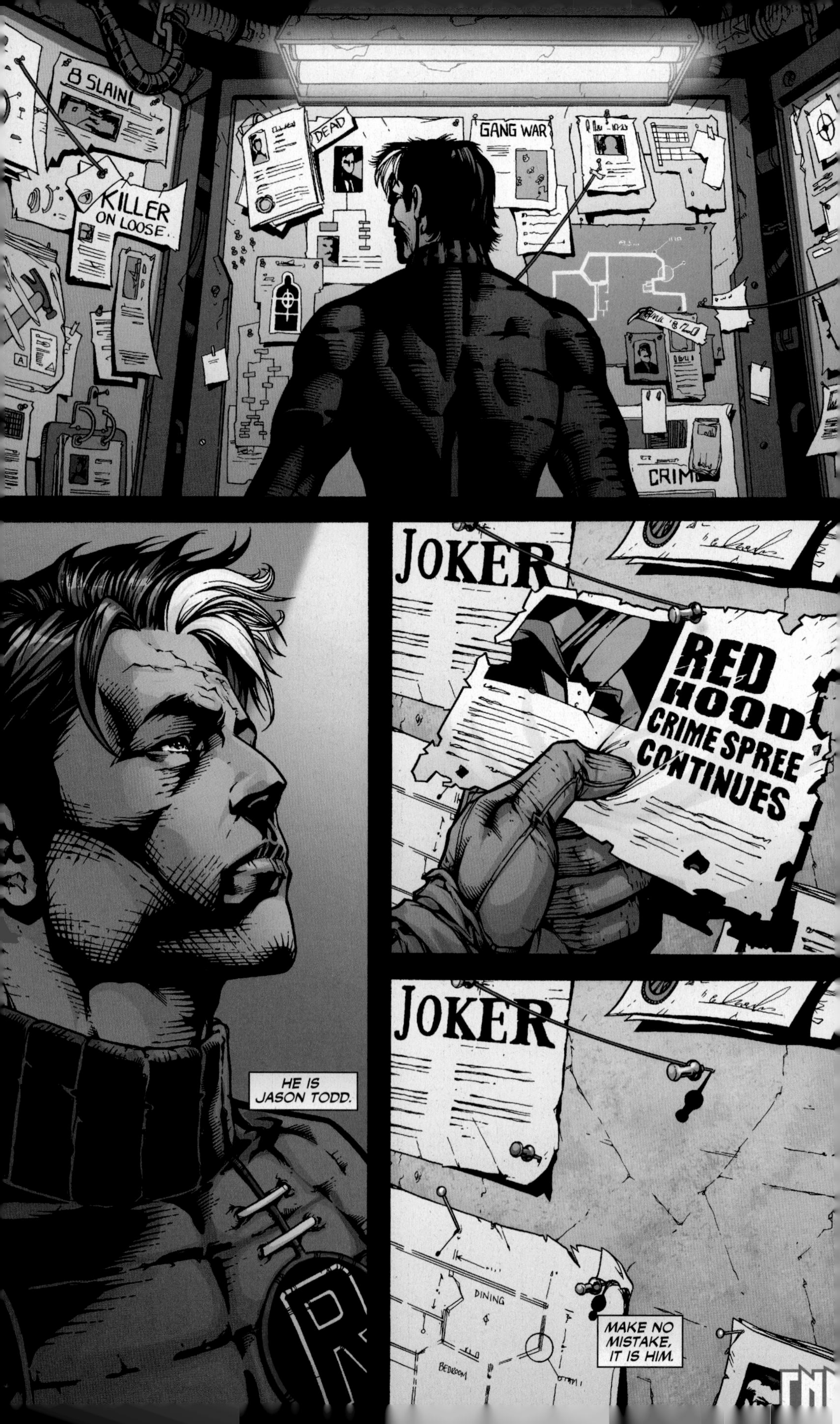
8 SLAIN
KILLER ON LOOSE
DEAD
GANG WAR
HE IS JASON TODD.
JOKER
RED HOOD CRIME SPREE CONTINUES
JOKER
DINING
BEDROOM
MAKE NO MISTAKE, IT IS HIM.

BATMAN 638 (Second Printing) Cover by Matt Wagner

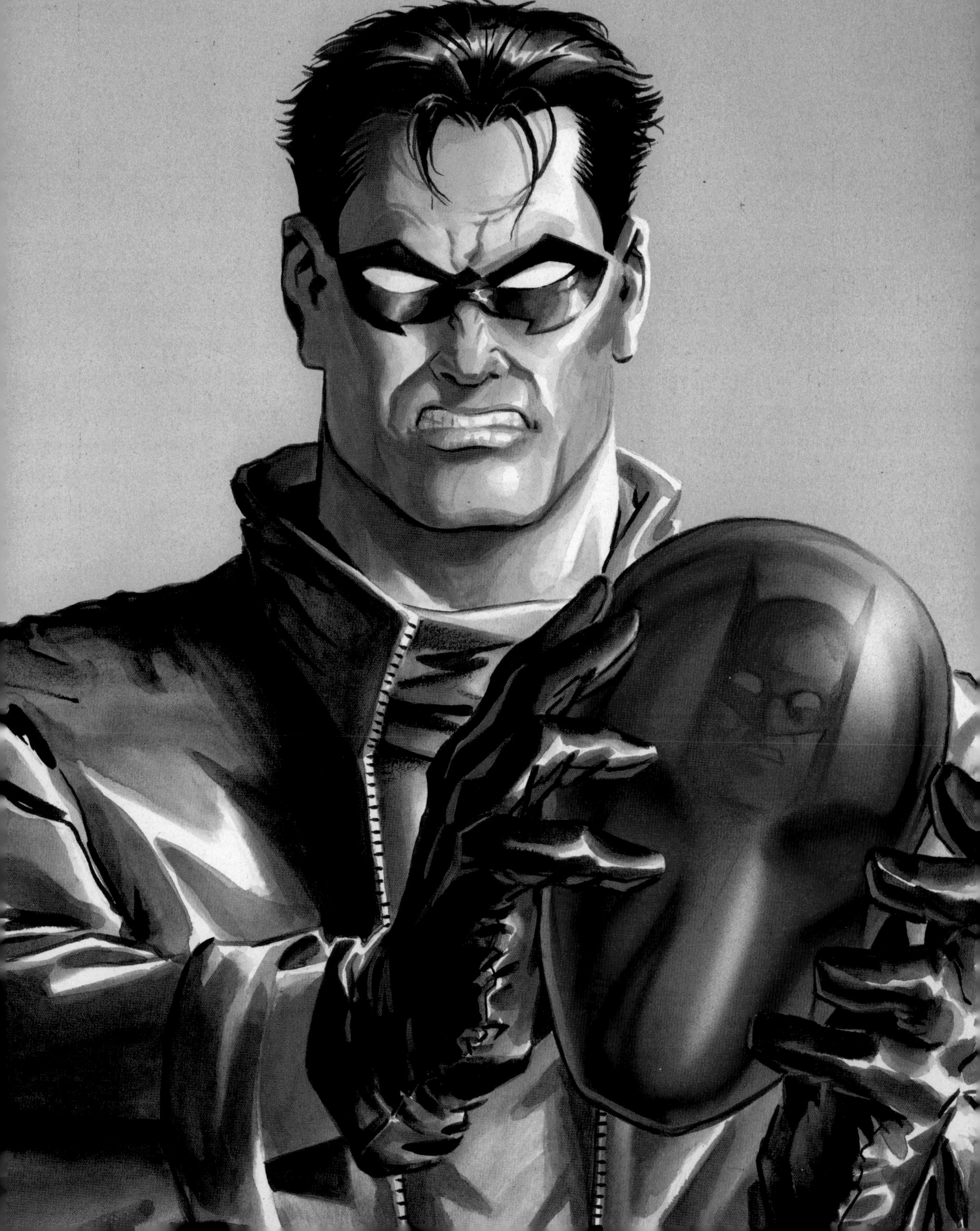

BATMAN ANNUAL 25 (Second Printing) Cover by Shane Davis

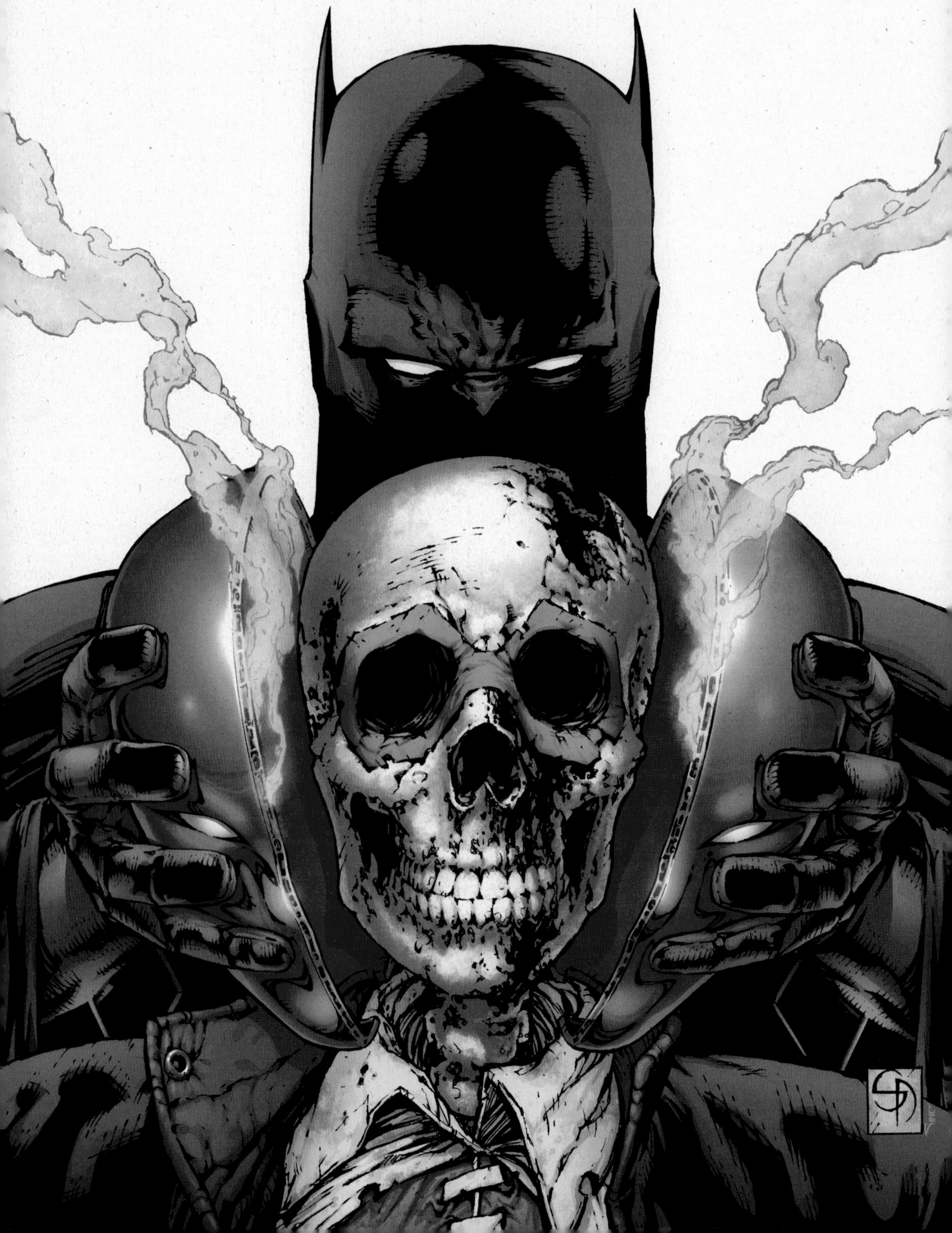

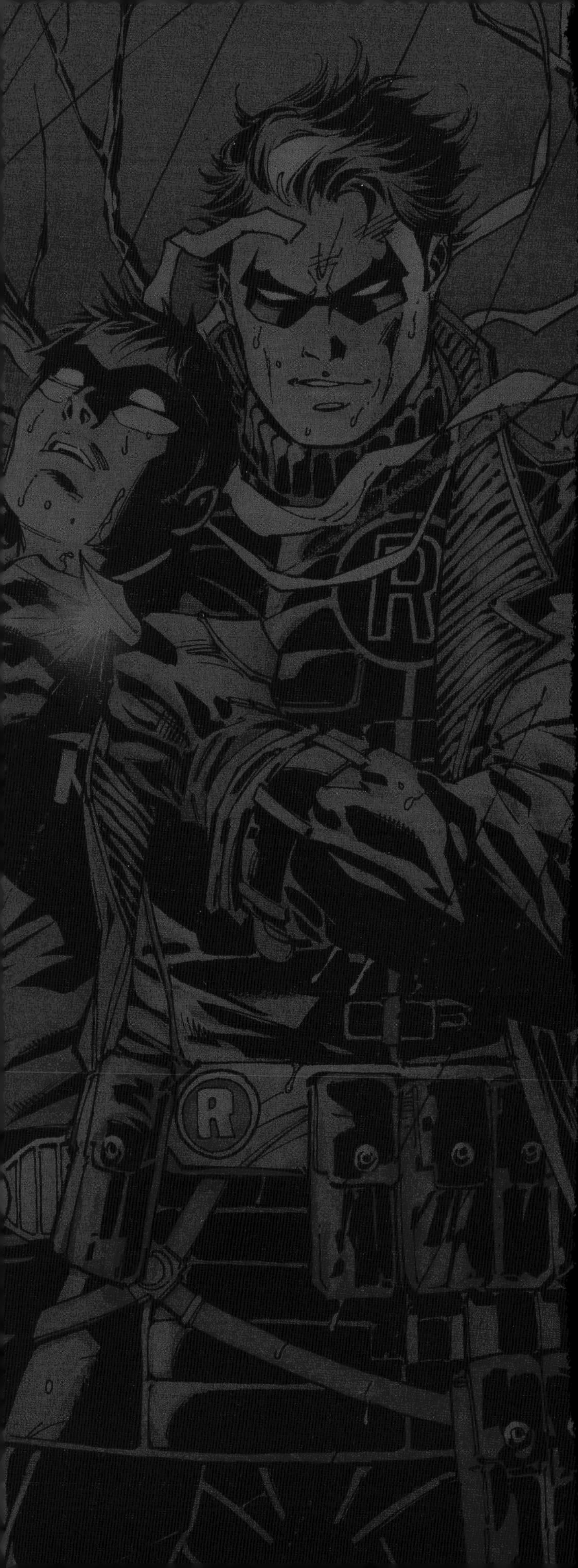

FIRST ENCOUNTER

Red Hood shook Batman's world when he revealed himself to be former Robin Jason Todd, miraculously returned to life, but this was not the first time since his resurrection that Jason had faced off with his former mentor.

The death of Robin at the Joker's hands was Batman's greatest defeat, and his adversaries know it. Revealing a resurrected Jason, even if Batman believed it to be a trick, would still be enough to torture the Caped Crusader with his own enduring feelings of guilt and regret over his failure to save his partner.

Reprinted from Jeph Loeb and Jim Lee's **BATMAN: HUSH**, the following pages show Batman's first encounter with the rogue former Robin: While on the hunt for the bandaged villain known as Hush, the Dynamic Duo and Catwoman are lured to a graveyard – the same graveyard where Jason's body was once buried...

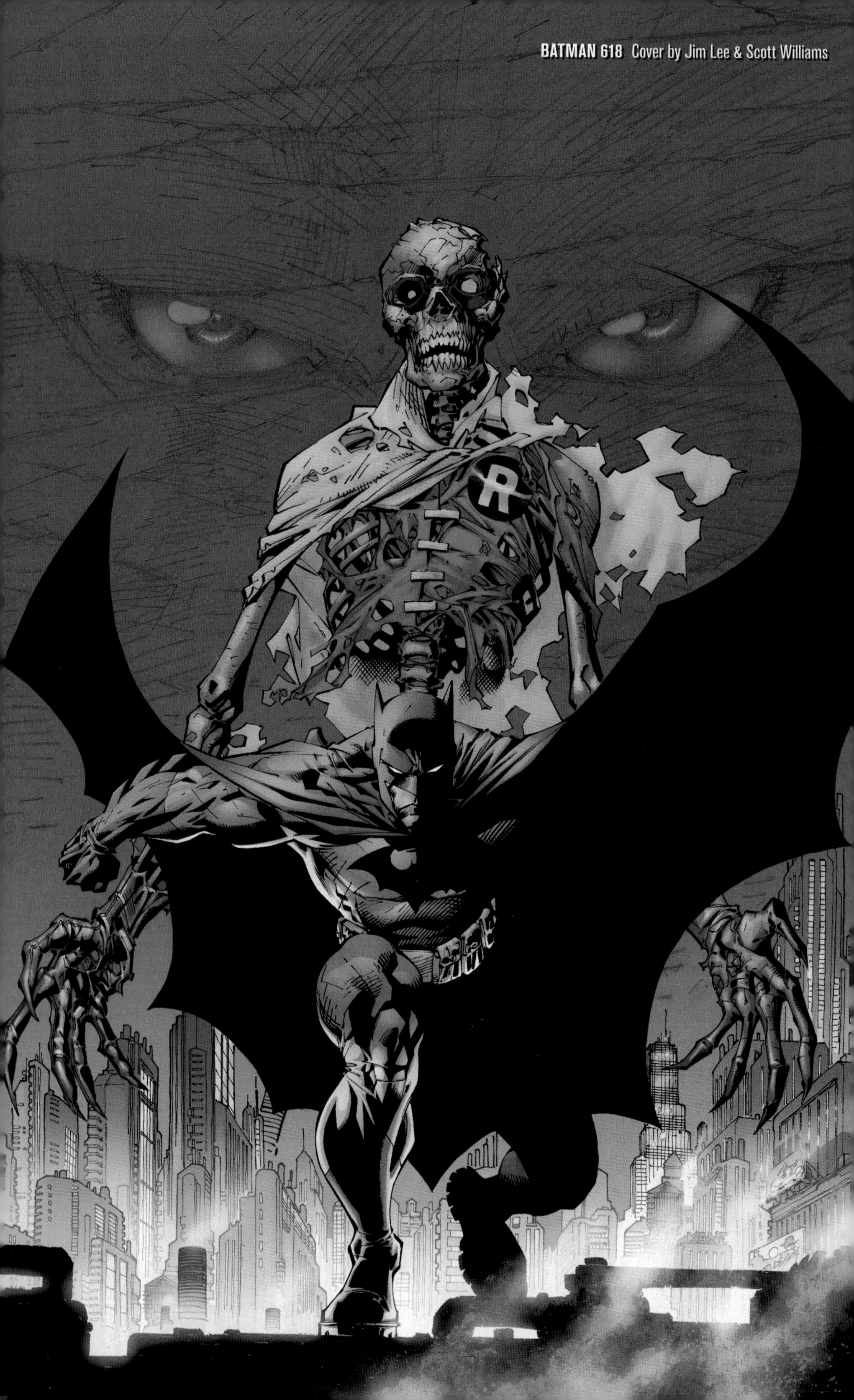
KANE

BATMAN 618 Cover by Jim Lee & Scott Williams

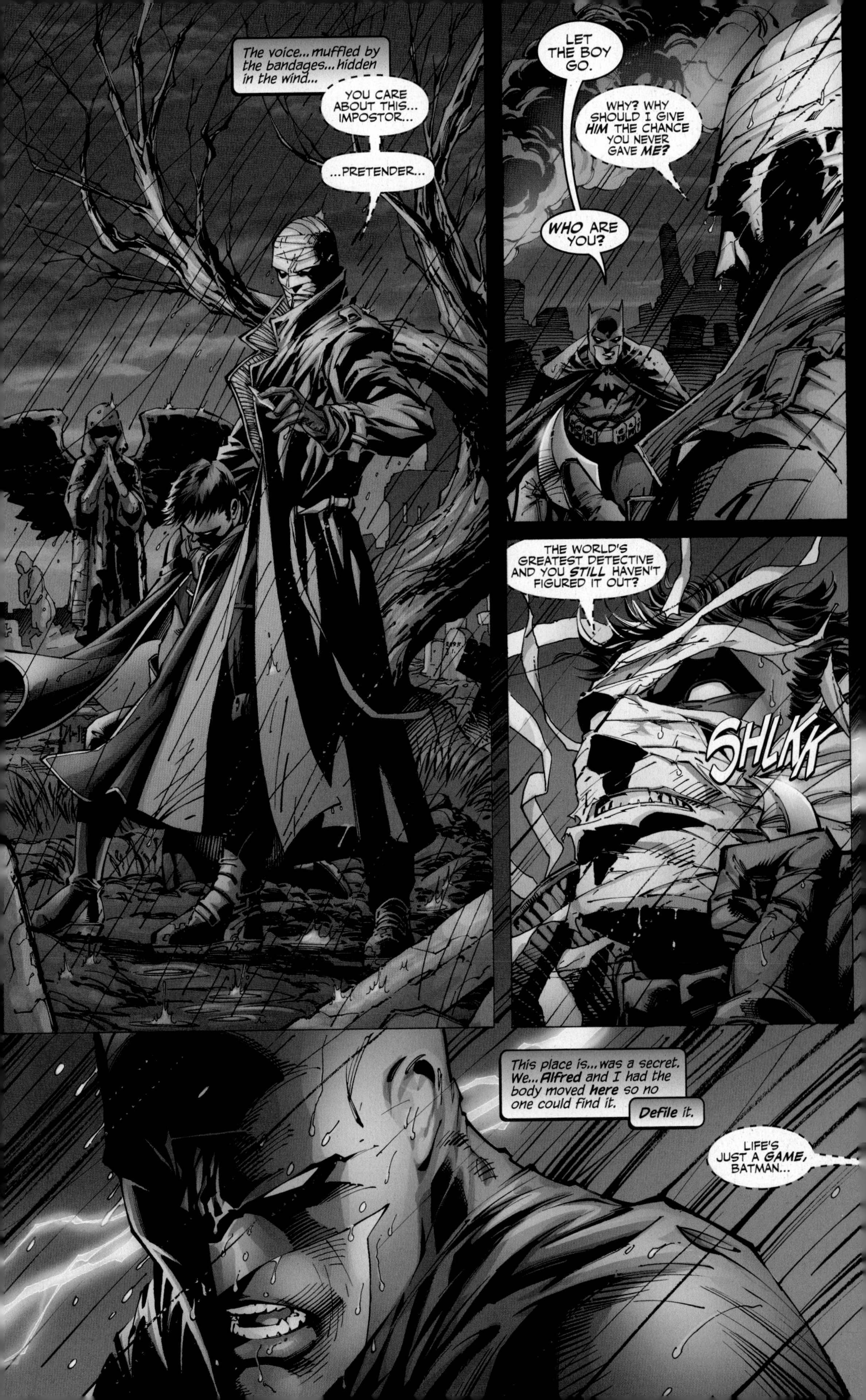
The voice... muffled by the bandages... hidden in the wind...
YOU CARE ABOUT THIS... IMPOSTOR...
...PRETENDER...
LET THE BOY GO.
WHY? WHY SHOULD I GIVE HIM THE CHANCE YOU NEVER GAVE ME?
WHO ARE YOU?
THE WORLD'S GREATEST DETECTIVE AND YOU STILL HAVEN'T FIGURED IT OUT?
SHLKK
This place is... was a secret. We... Alfred and I had the body moved here so no one could find it.
Defile it.
LIFE'S JUST A GAME, BATMAN...

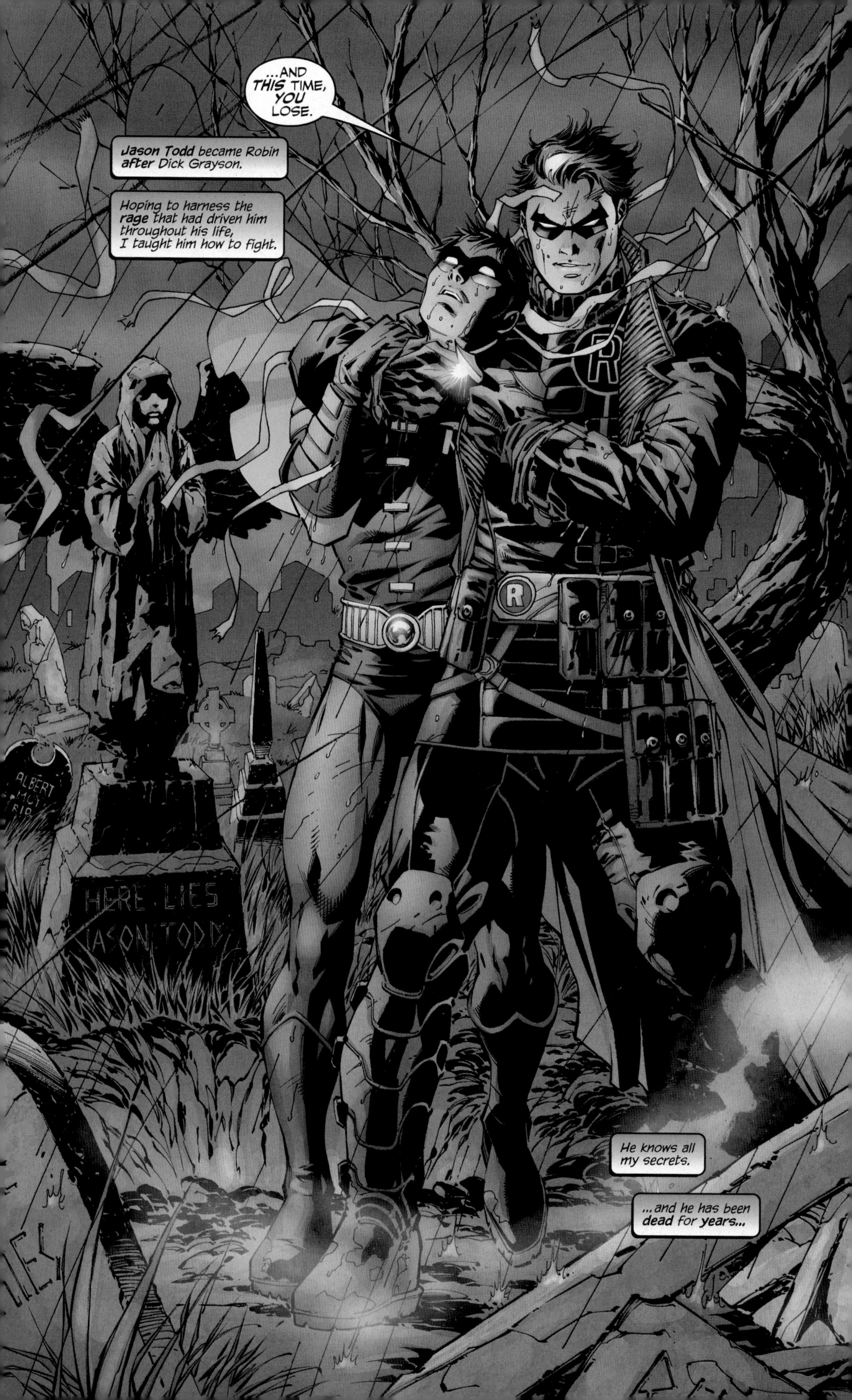
...AND THIS TIME, YOU LOSE.
Jason Todd became Robin after Dick Grayson.
Hoping to harness the rage that had driven him throughout his life, I taught him how to fight.
HERE LIES JASON TODD
He knows all my secrets.
...and he has been dead for years...

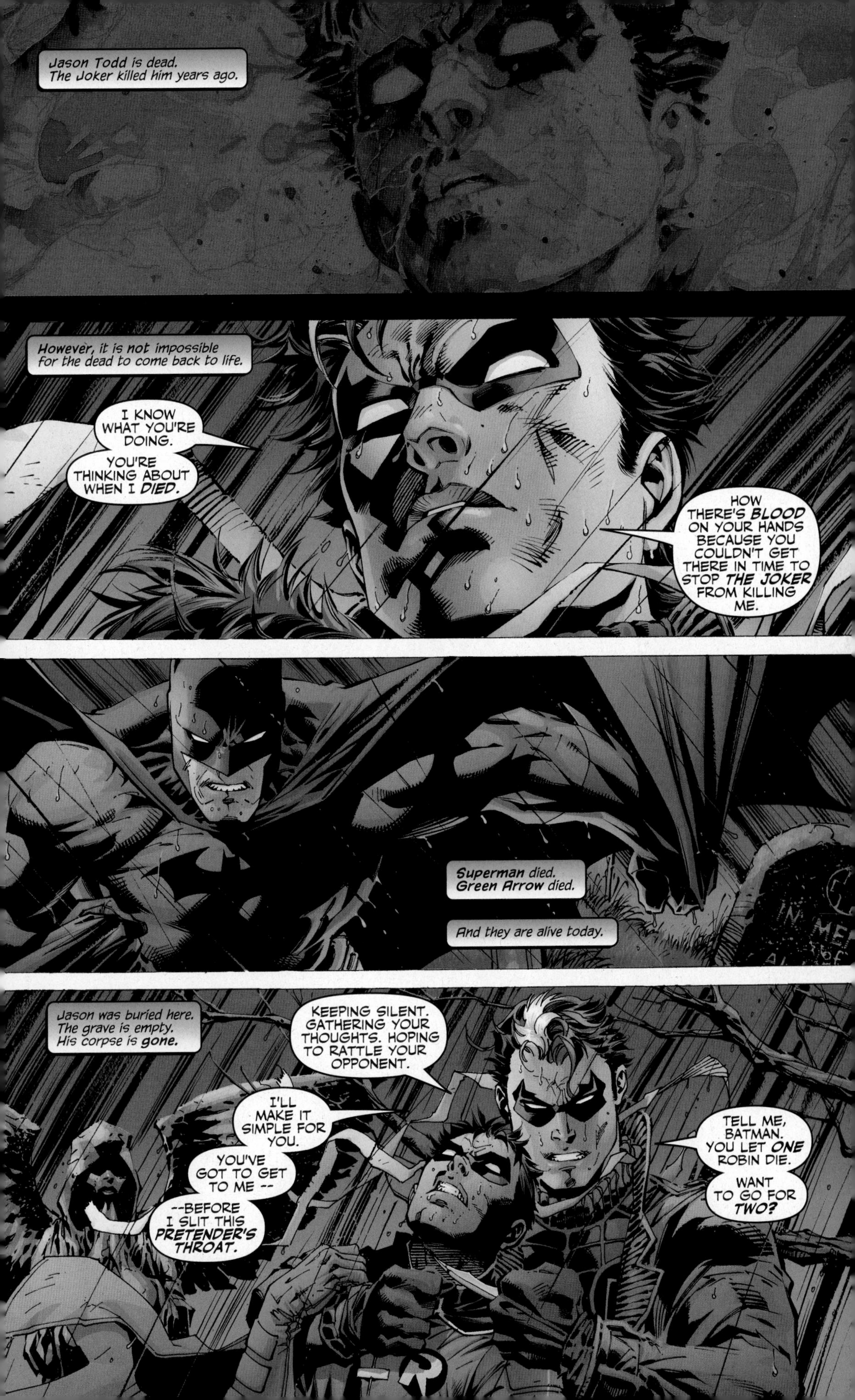
Jason Todd is dead.
The Joker killed him years ago.
However, it is not impossible for the dead to come back to life.
I KNOW WHAT YOU'RE DOING.
YOU'RE THINKING ABOUT WHEN I DIED.
HOW THERE'S BLOOD ON YOUR HANDS BECAUSE YOU COULDN'T GET THERE IN TIME TO STOP THE JOKER FROM KILLING ME.
Superman died.
Green Arrow died.
And they are alive today.
Jason was buried here.
The grave is empty.
His corpse is gone.
KEEPING SILENT. GATHERING YOUR THOUGHTS. HOPING TO RATTLE YOUR OPPONENT.
I'LL MAKE IT SIMPLE FOR YOU.
YOU'VE GOT TO GET TO ME --
--BEFORE I SLIT THIS PRETENDER'S THROAT.
TELL ME, BATMAN. YOU LET ONE ROBIN DIE.
WANT TO GO FOR TWO?

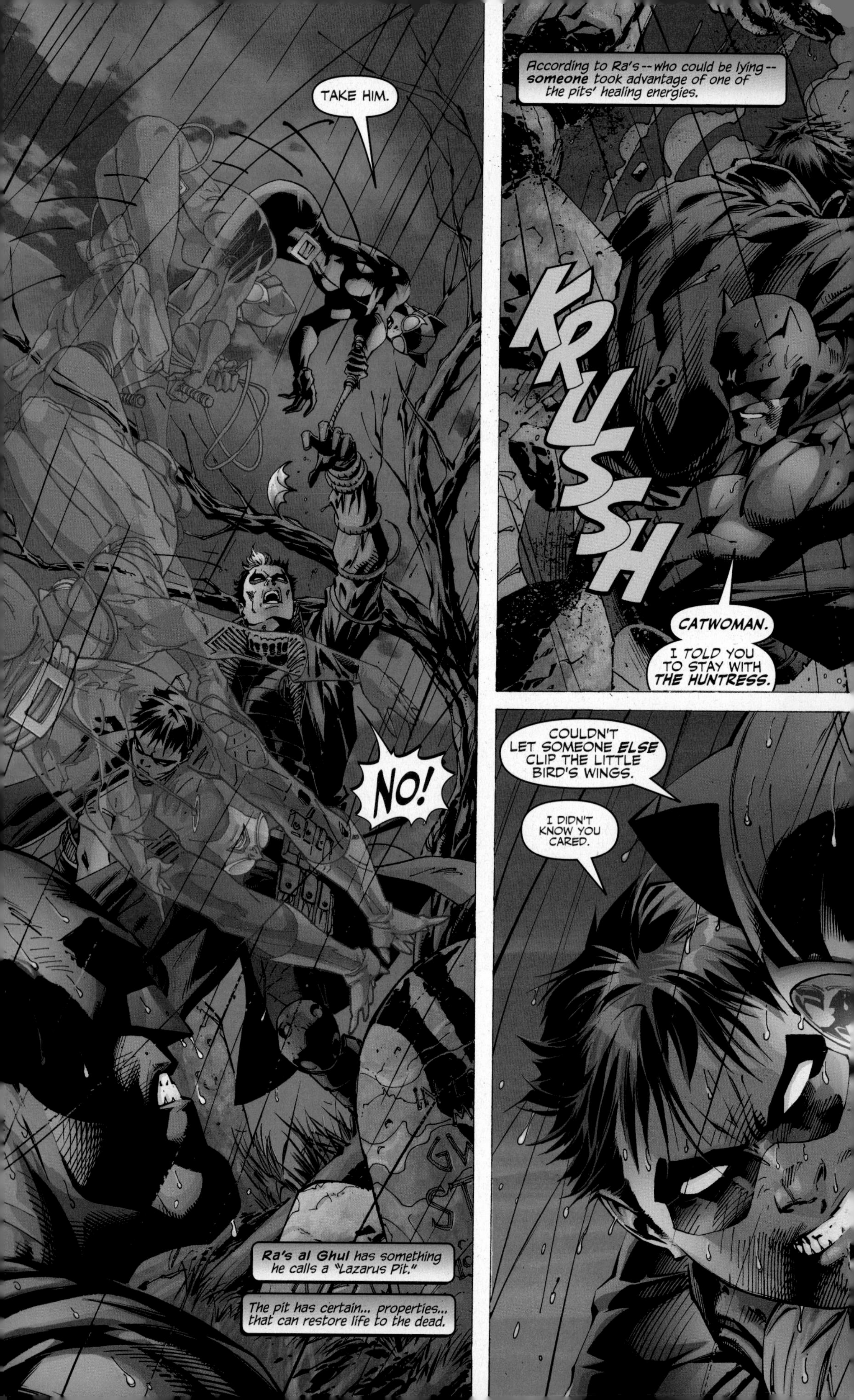
TAKE HIM.
NO!
Ra's al Ghul has something he calls a "Lazarus Pit."
The pit has certain... properties... that can restore life to the dead.
According to Ra's -- who could be lying -- someone took advantage of one of the pits' healing energies.
KRUSSH
CATWOMAN.
I TOLD YOU TO STAY WITH THE HUNTRESS.
COULDN'T LET SOMEONE ELSE CLIP THE LITTLE BIRD'S WINGS.
I DIDN'T KNOW YOU CARED.

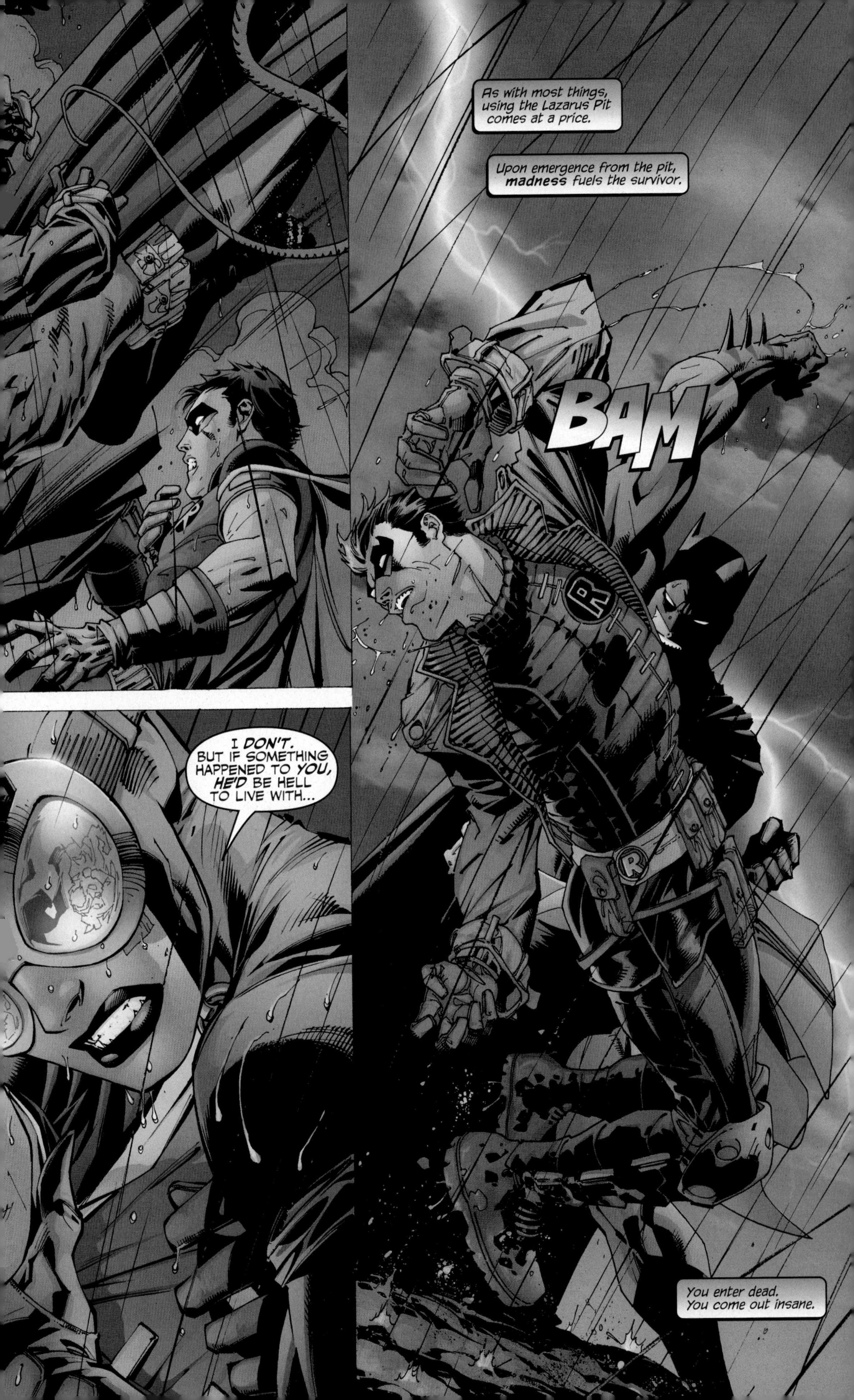
I DON'T. BUT IF SOMETHING HAPPENED TO YOU, HE'D BE HELL TO LIVE WITH...
As with most things, using the Lazarus Pit comes at a price.
Upon emergence from the pit, madness fuels the survivor.
BAM
You enter dead. You come out insane.

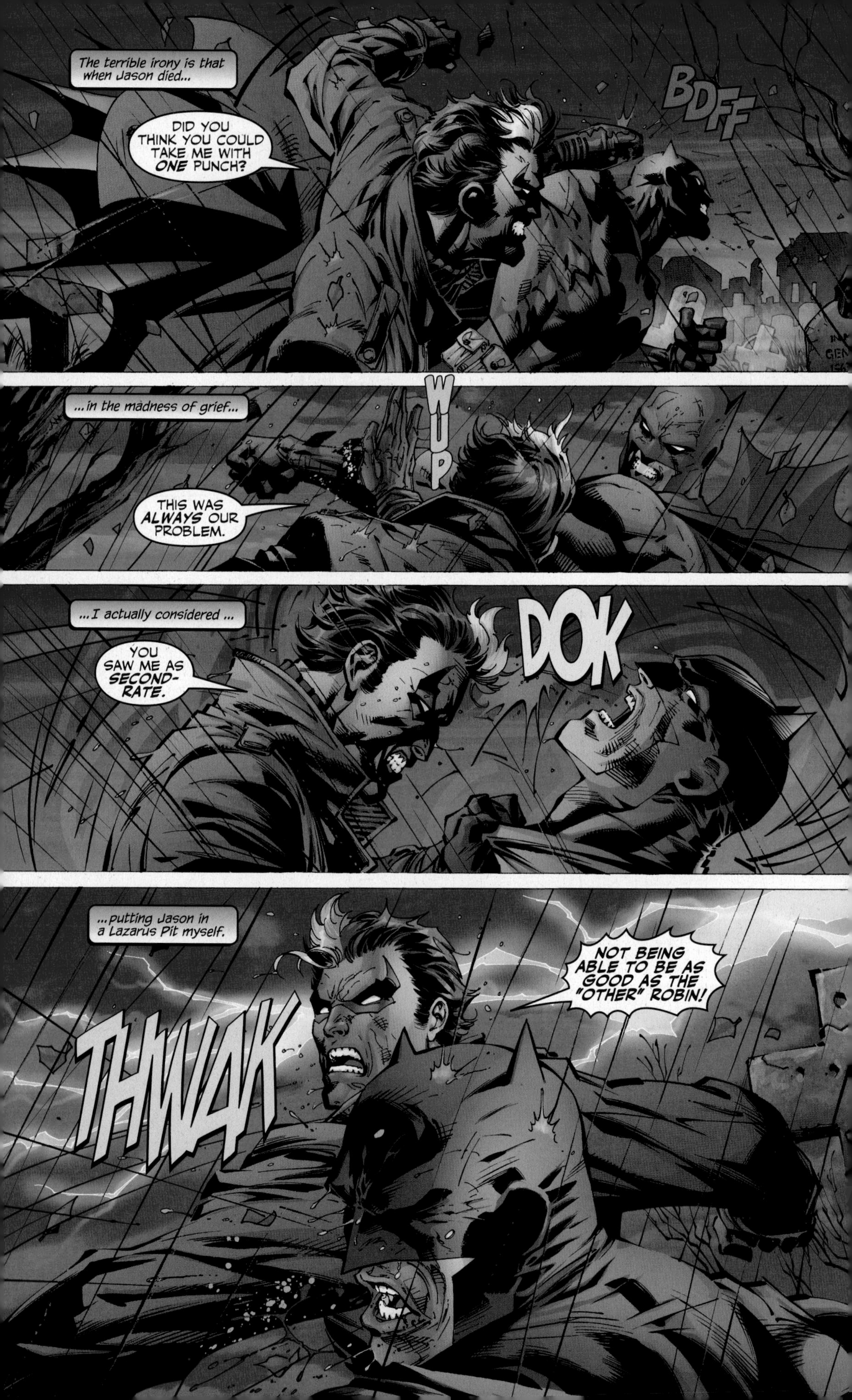

The terrible irony is that when Jason died...
DID YOU THINK YOU COULD TAKE ME WITH ONE PUNCH?
BDFF
...in the madness of grief...
WUP
THIS WAS ALWAYS OUR PROBLEM.
...I actually considered ...
YOU SAW ME AS SECOND-RATE.
DOK
...putting Jason in a Lazarus Pit myself.
NOT BEING ABLE TO BE AS GOOD AS THE "OTHER" ROBIN!
THWAK

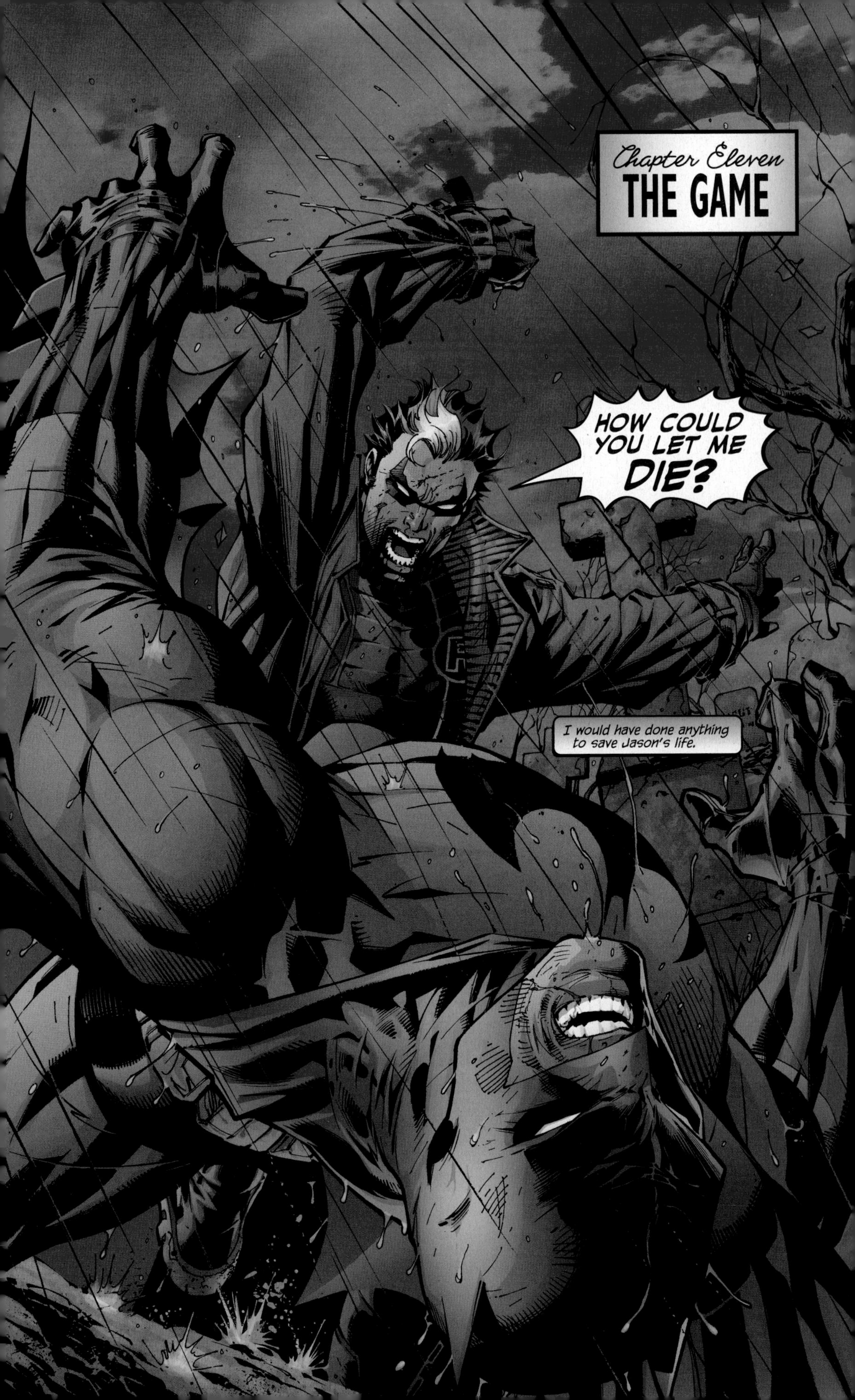
Chapter Eleven
THE GAME
HOW COULD YOU LET ME DIE?
I would have done anything to save Jason's life.

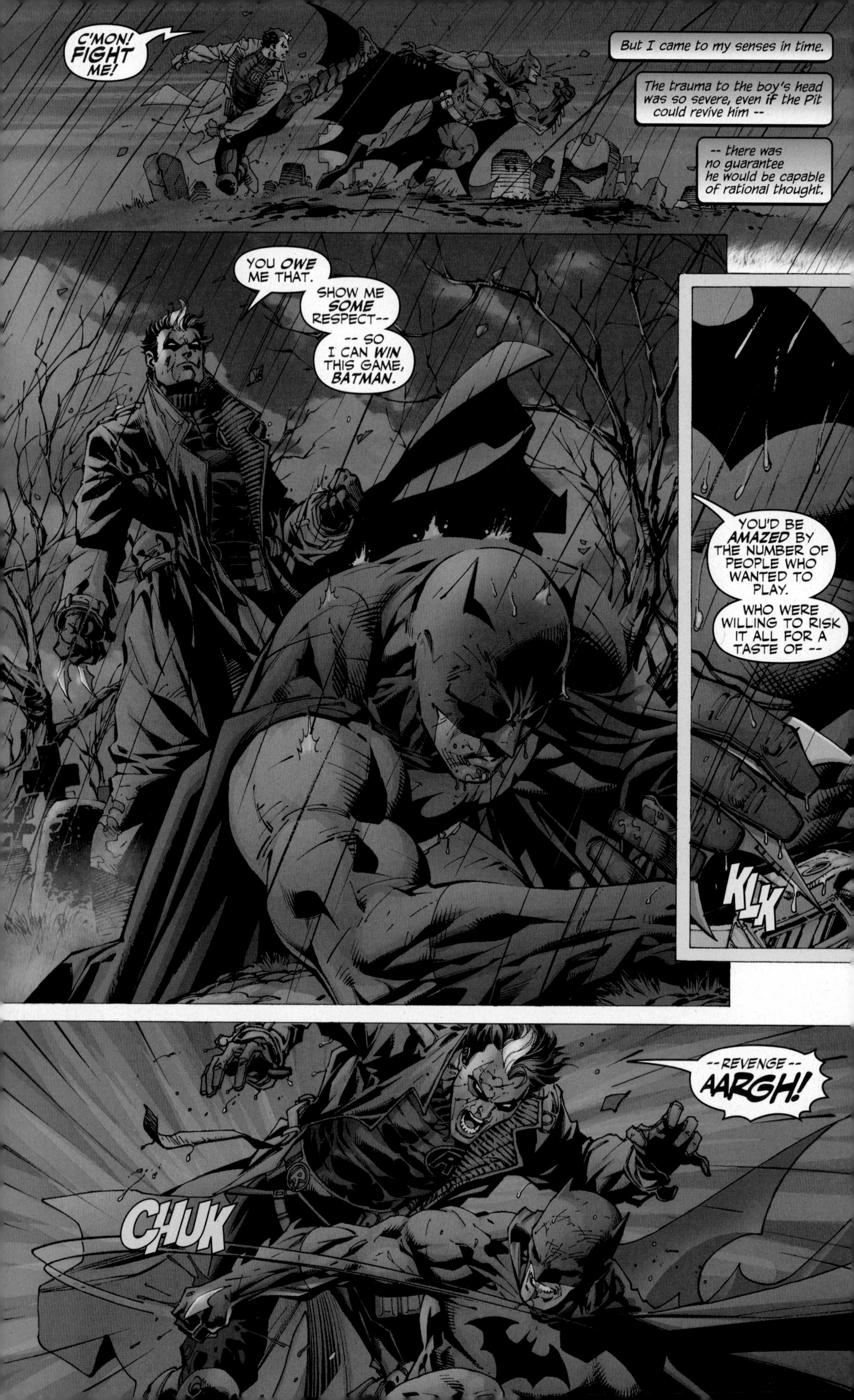

C'MON! FIGHT ME!
But I came to my senses in time.
The trauma to the boy's head was so severe, even if the Pit could revive him --
-- there was no guarantee he would be capable of rational thought.
YOU OWE ME THAT.
SHOW ME SOME RESPECT--
-- SO I CAN WIN THIS GAME, BATMAN.
YOU'D BE AMAZED BY THE NUMBER OF PEOPLE WHO WANTED TO PLAY.
WHO WERE WILLING TO RISK IT ALL FOR A TASTE OF --
KLIK
--REVENGE-- AARGH!
CHUK

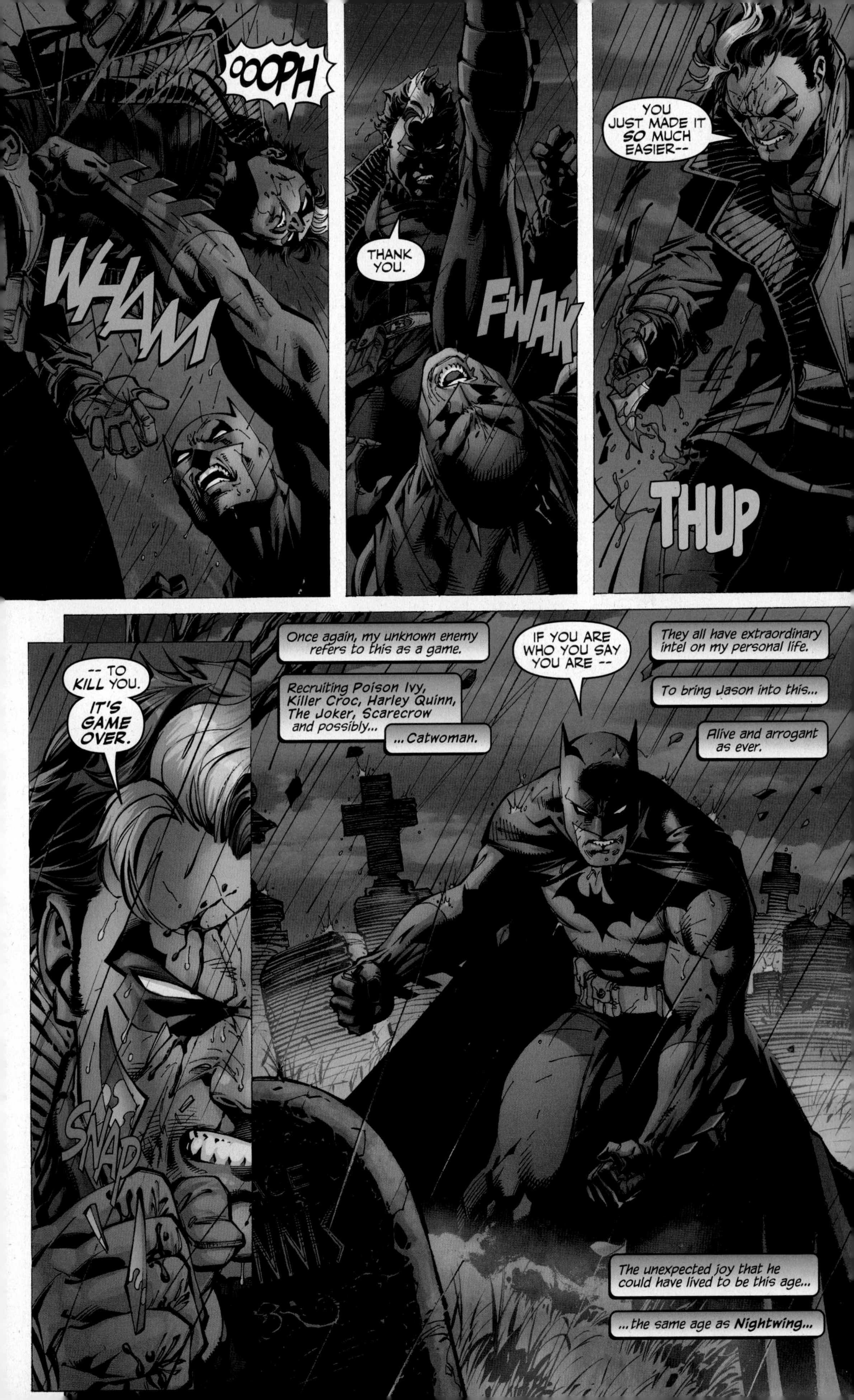
OOOPH
WHAM
THANK YOU.
FWAK
YOU JUST MADE IT SO MUCH EASIER--
THUP
-- TO KILL YOU.
IT'S GAME OVER.
SNAP
Once again, my unknown enemy refers to this as a game.
Recruiting Poison Ivy, Killer Croc, Harley Quinn, The Joker, Scarecrow and possibly...
...Catwoman.
IF YOU ARE WHO YOU SAY YOU ARE --
They all have extraordinary intel on my personal life.
To bring Jason into this...
Alive and arrogant as ever.
The unexpected joy that he could have lived to be this age...
...the same age as Nightwing...

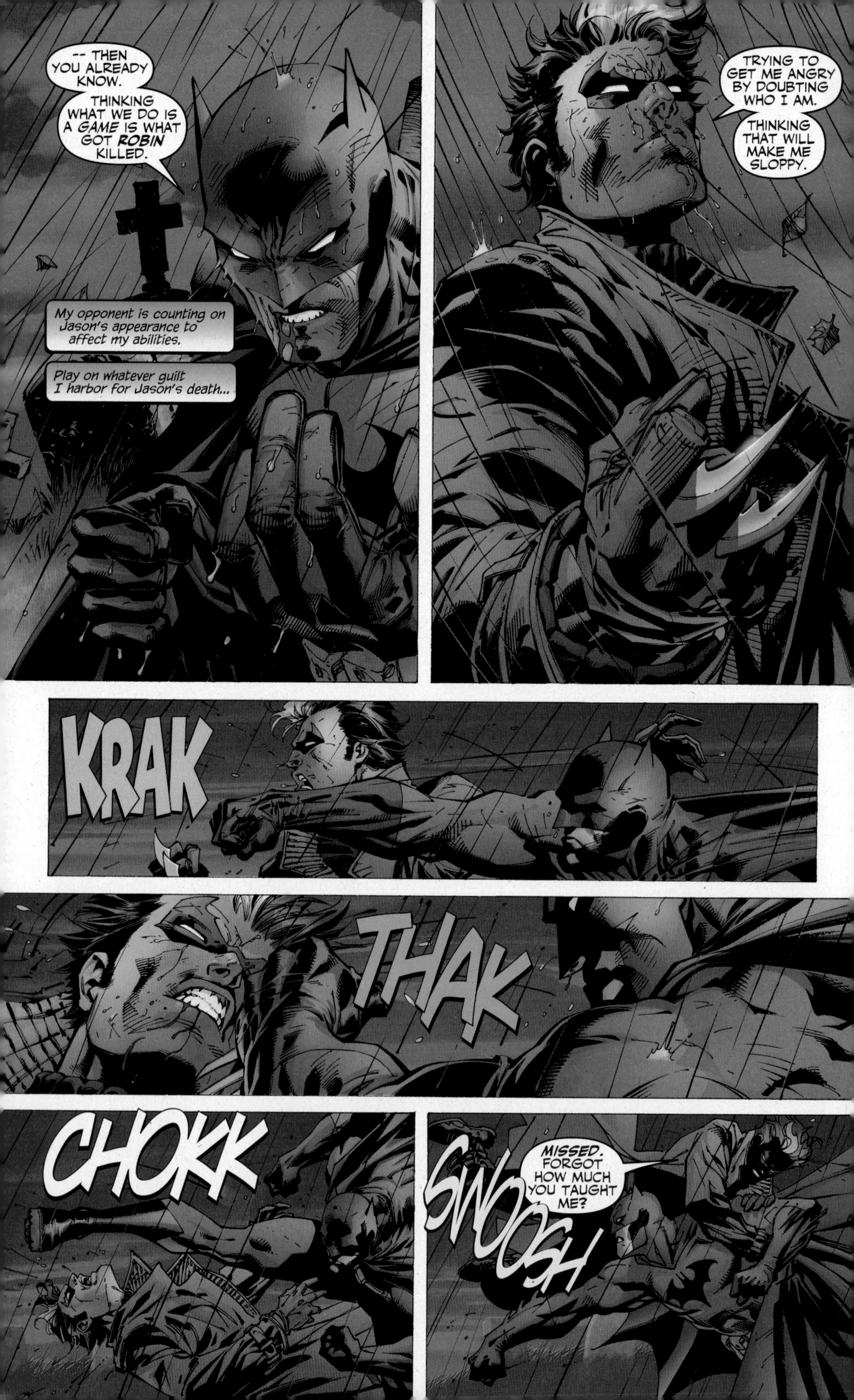
-- THEN YOU ALREADY KNOW.
THINKING WHAT WE DO IS A GAME IS WHAT GOT ROBIN KILLED.
My opponent is counting on Jason's appearance to affect my abilities.
Play on whatever guilt I harbor for Jason's death...
TRYING TO GET ME ANGRY BY DOUBTING WHO I AM.
THINKING THAT WILL MAKE ME SLOPPY.
KRAK
THAK
CHOKK
SWOOSH
MISSED. FORGOT HOW MUCH YOU TAUGHT ME?

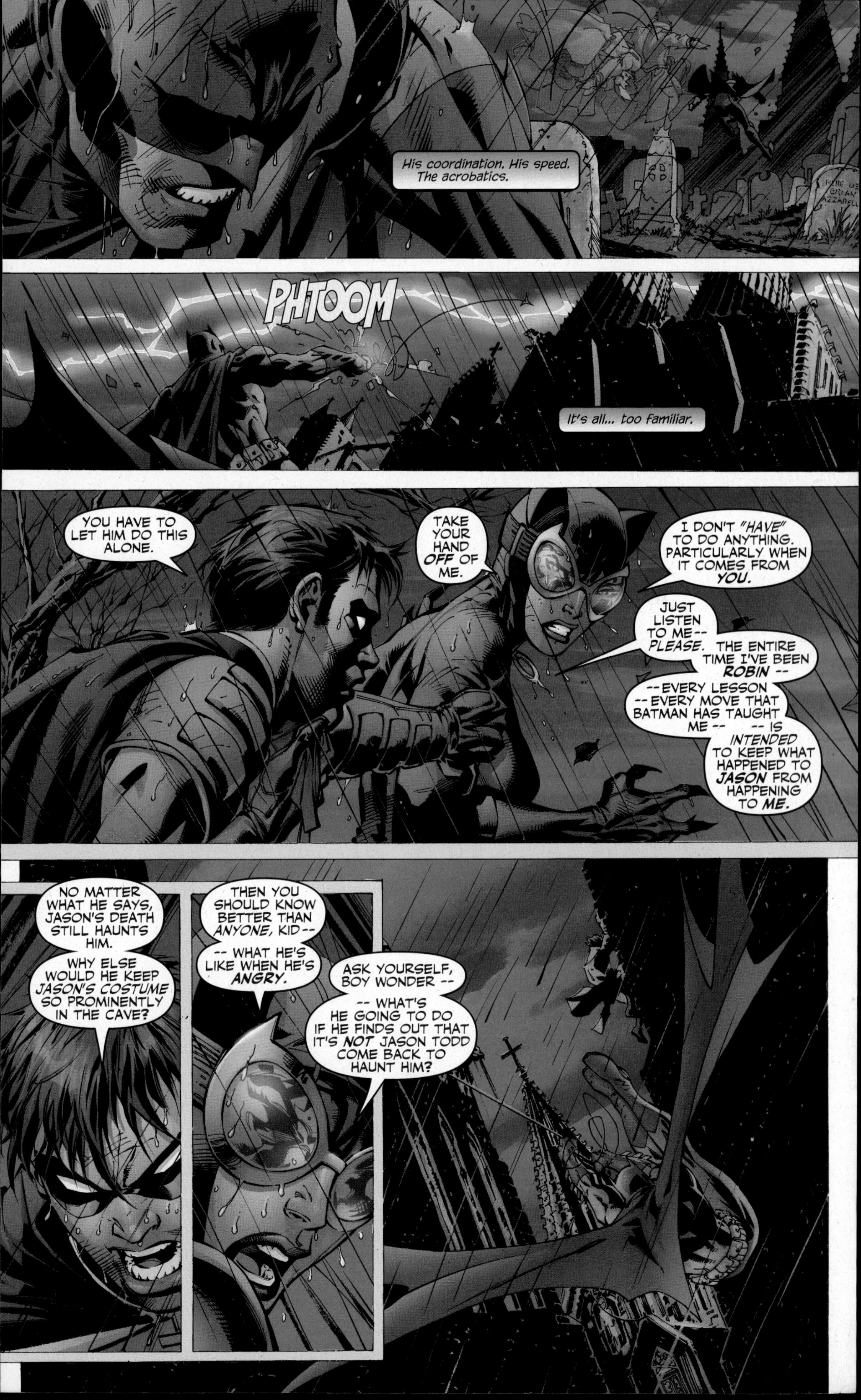
His coordination. His speed. The acrobatics.
PHTOOM
It's all... too familiar.
YOU HAVE TO LET HIM DO THIS ALONE.
TAKE YOUR HAND OFF OF ME.
I DON'T "HAVE" TO DO ANYTHING. PARTICULARLY WHEN IT COMES FROM YOU.
JUST LISTEN TO ME-- PLEASE. THE ENTIRE TIME I'VE BEEN ROBIN --
--EVERY LESSON --EVERY MOVE THAT BATMAN HAS TAUGHT ME -- -- IS INTENDED TO KEEP WHAT HAPPENED TO JASON FROM HAPPENING TO ME.
NO MATTER WHAT HE SAYS, JASON'S DEATH STILL HAUNTS HIM.
WHY ELSE WOULD HE KEEP JASON'S COSTUME SO PROMINENTLY IN THE CAVE?
THEN YOU SHOULD KNOW BETTER THAN ANYONE, KID --
-- WHAT HE'S LIKE WHEN HE'S ANGRY.
ASK YOURSELF, BOY WONDER --
-- WHAT'S HE GOING TO DO IF HE FINDS OUT THAT IT'S NOT JASON TODD COME BACK TO HAUNT HIM?

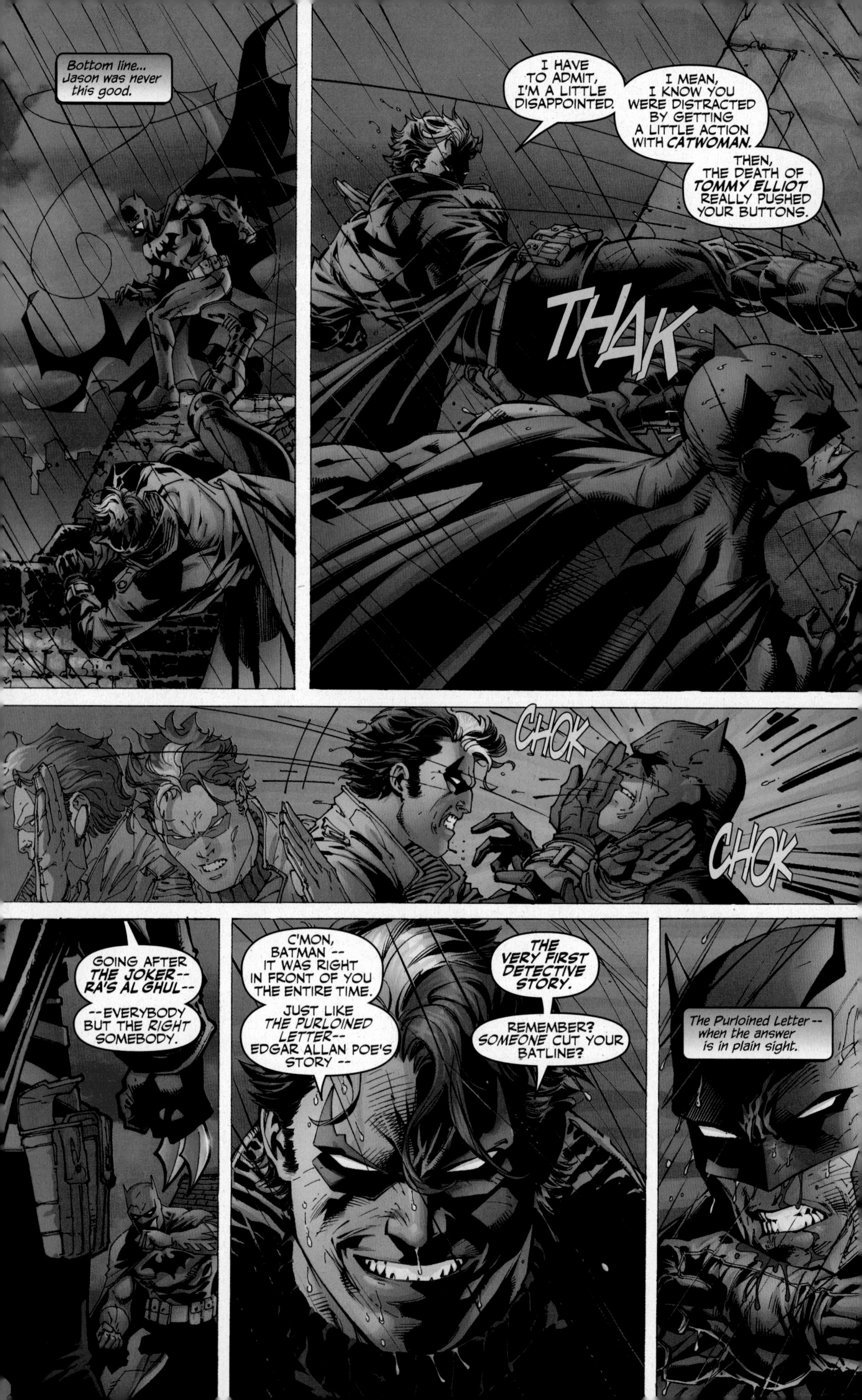
Bottom line... Jason was never this good.
I HAVE TO ADMIT, I'M A LITTLE DISAPPOINTED.
I MEAN, I KNOW YOU WERE DISTRACTED BY GETTING A LITTLE ACTION WITH CATWOMAN.
THEN, THE DEATH OF TOMMY ELLIOT REALLY PUSHED YOUR BUTTONS.
THAK
CHOK
CHOK
GOING AFTER THE JOKER-- RA'S AL GHUL--
--EVERYBODY BUT THE RIGHT SOMEBODY.
C'MON, BATMAN -- IT WAS RIGHT IN FRONT OF YOU THE ENTIRE TIME.
JUST LIKE THE PURLOINED LETTER-- EDGAR ALLAN POE'S STORY --
THE VERY FIRST DETECTIVE STORY.
REMEMBER? SOMEONE CUT YOUR BATLINE?
The Purloined Letter -- when the answer is in plain sight.

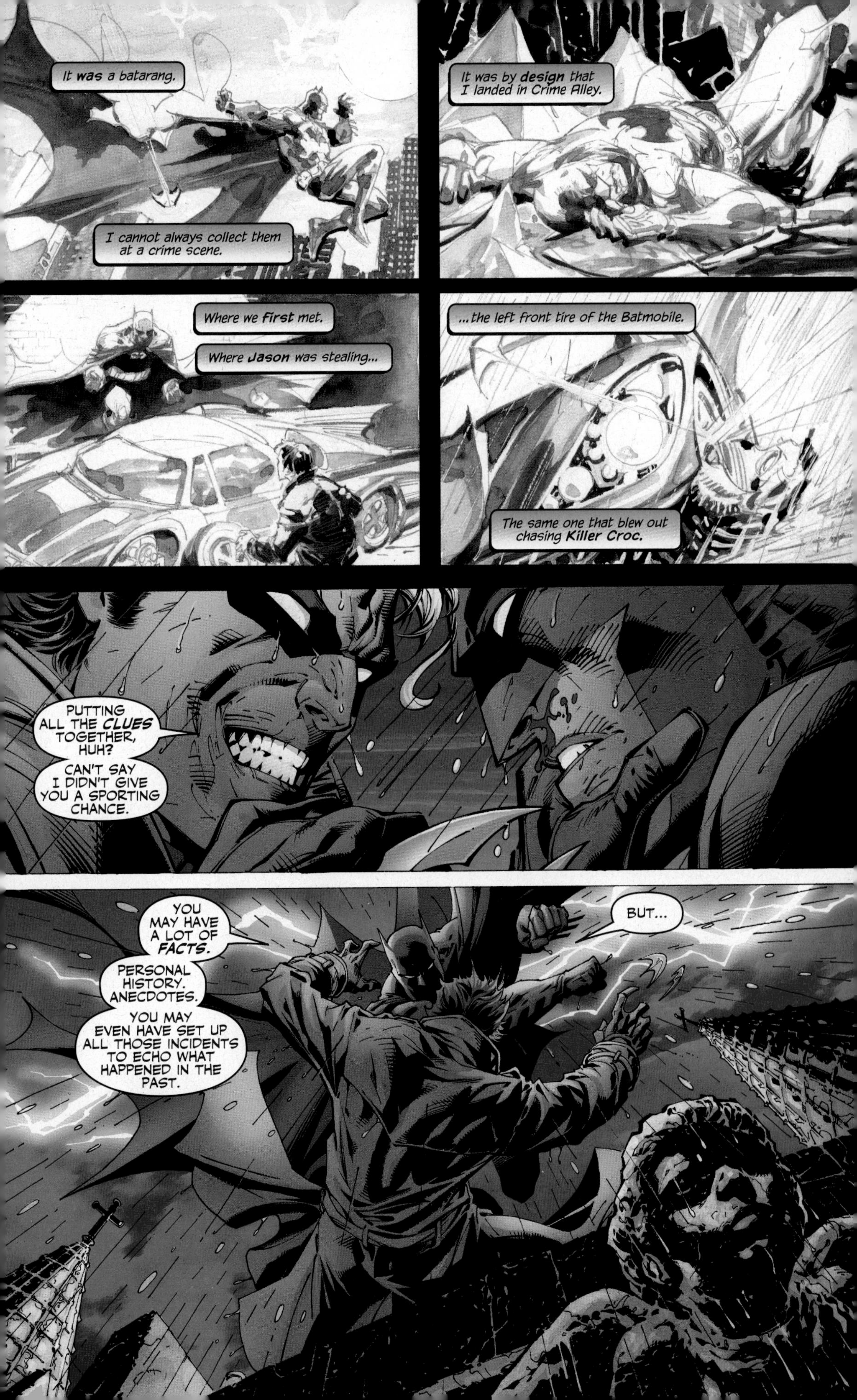
It was a batarang.
I cannot always collect them at a crime scene.
It was by design that I landed in Crime Alley.
Where we first met.
Where Jason was stealing...
...the left front tire of the Batmobile.
The same one that blew out chasing Killer Croc.
PUTTING ALL THE CLUES TOGETHER, HUH?
CAN'T SAY I DIDN'T GIVE YOU A SPORTING CHANCE.
YOU MAY HAVE A LOT OF FACTS.
PERSONAL HISTORY. ANECDOTES.
YOU MAY EVEN HAVE SET UP ALL THOSE INCIDENTS TO ECHO WHAT HAPPENED IN THE PAST.
BUT...

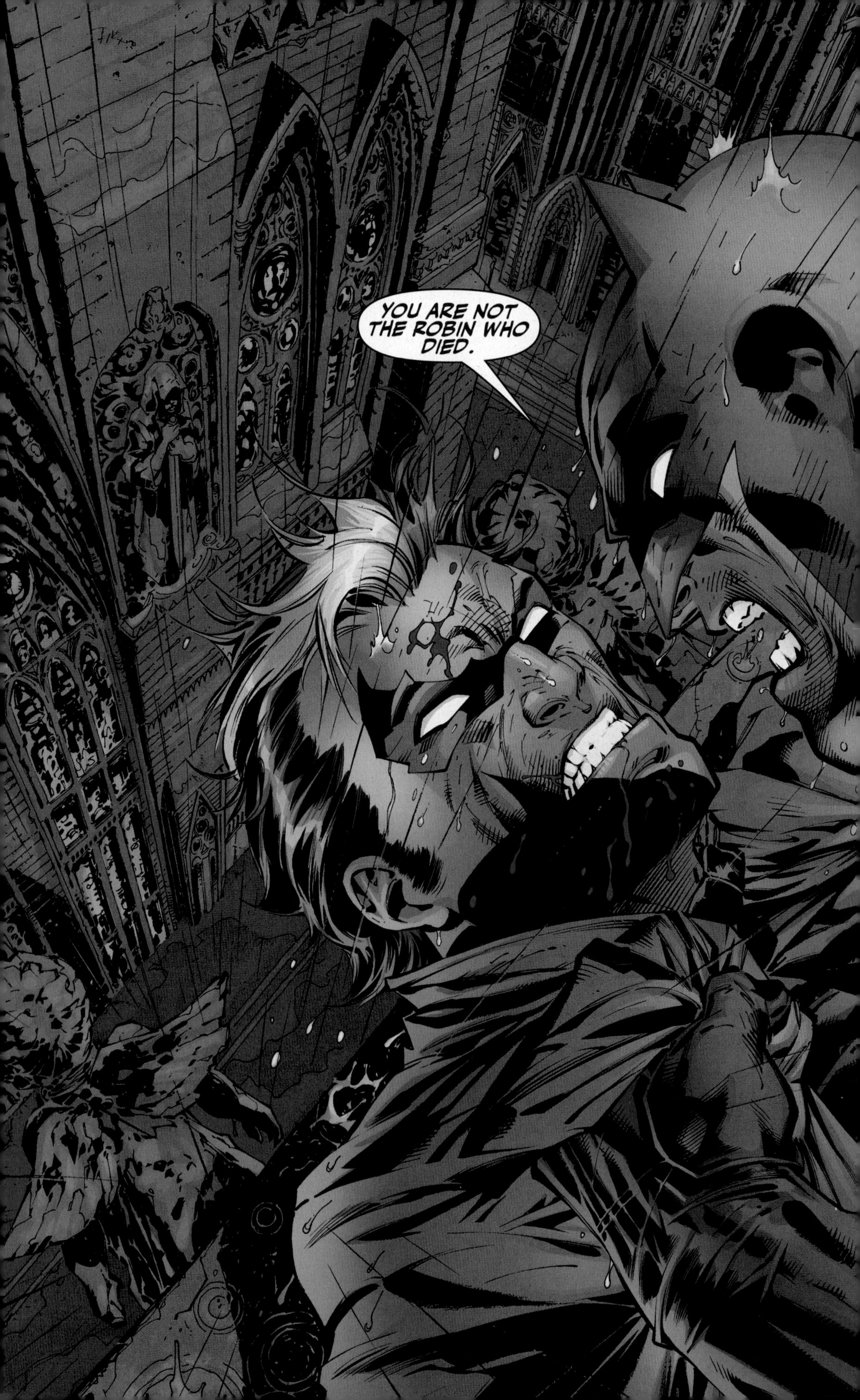
YOU ARE NOT THE ROBIN WHO DIED.

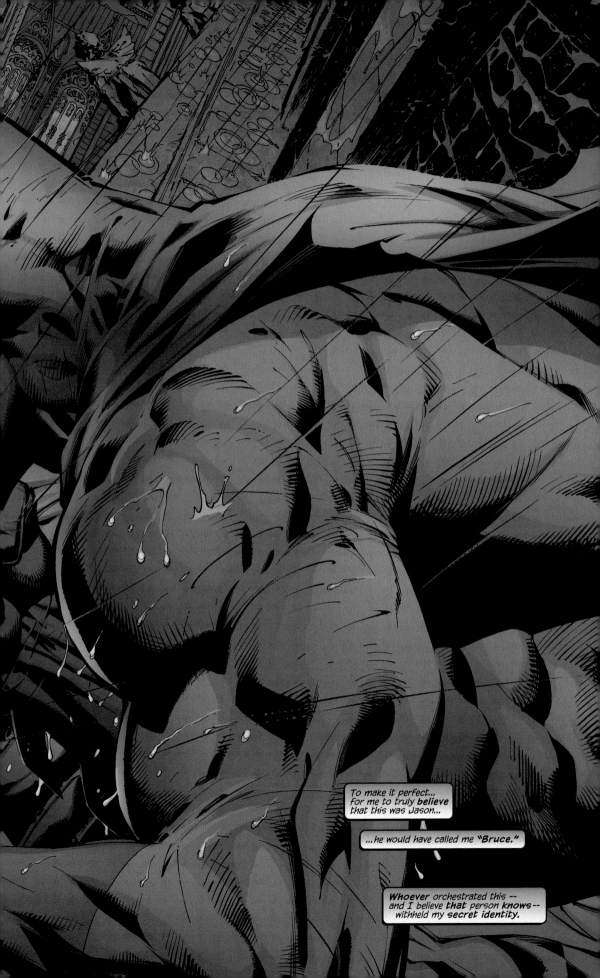

To make it perfect... for me to truly *believe* that this was Jason...

...he would have called me "*Bruce*."

Whoever orchestrated this -- and I believe *that* person *knows*-- withheld my *secret identity*.

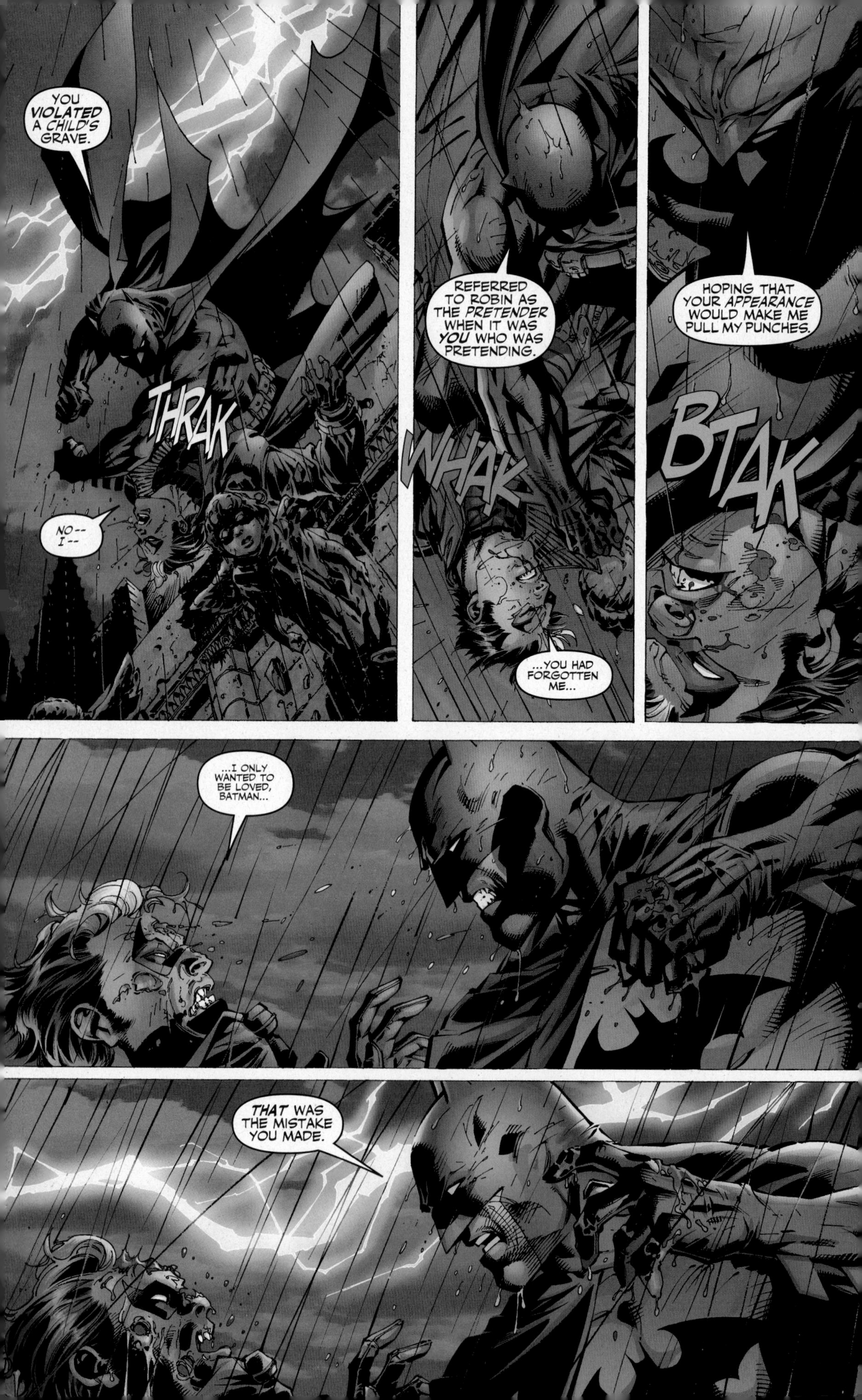
YOU VIOLATED A CHILD'S GRAVE.
THRAK
NO-- I--
REFERRED TO ROBIN AS THE PRETENDER WHEN IT WAS YOU WHO WAS PRETENDING.
WHAK
...YOU HAD FORGOTTEN ME...
HOPING THAT YOUR APPEARANCE WOULD MAKE ME PULL MY PUNCHES.
BTAK
...I ONLY WANTED TO BE LOVED, BATMAN...
THAT WAS THE MISTAKE YOU MADE.

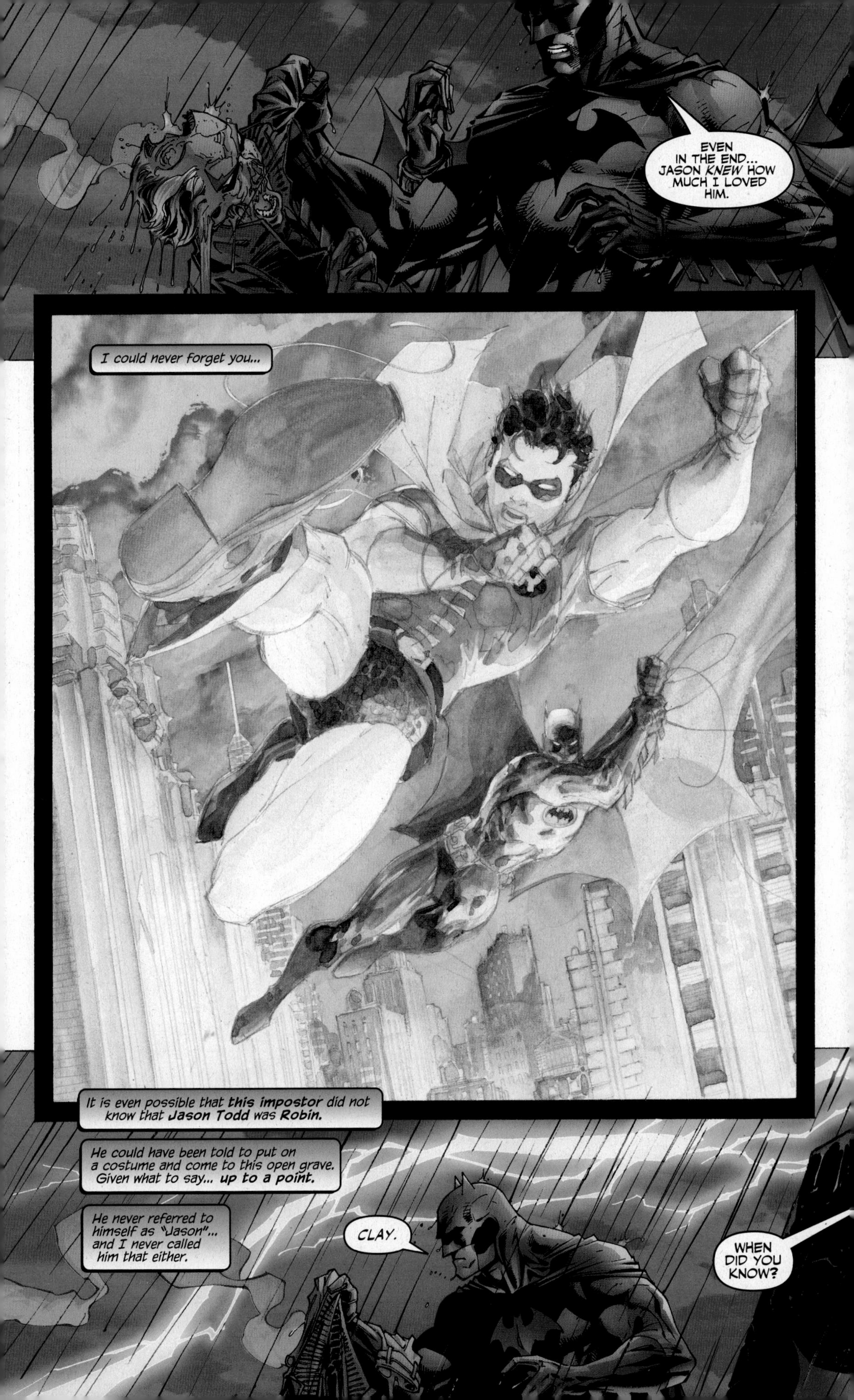
EVEN IN THE END... JASON KNEW HOW MUCH I LOVED HIM.
I could never forget you...
It is even possible that this impostor did not know that Jason Todd was Robin.
He could have been told to put on a costume and come to this open grave. Given what to say... up to a point.
He never referred to himself as "Jason"... and I never called him that either.
CLAY.
WHEN DID YOU KNOW?

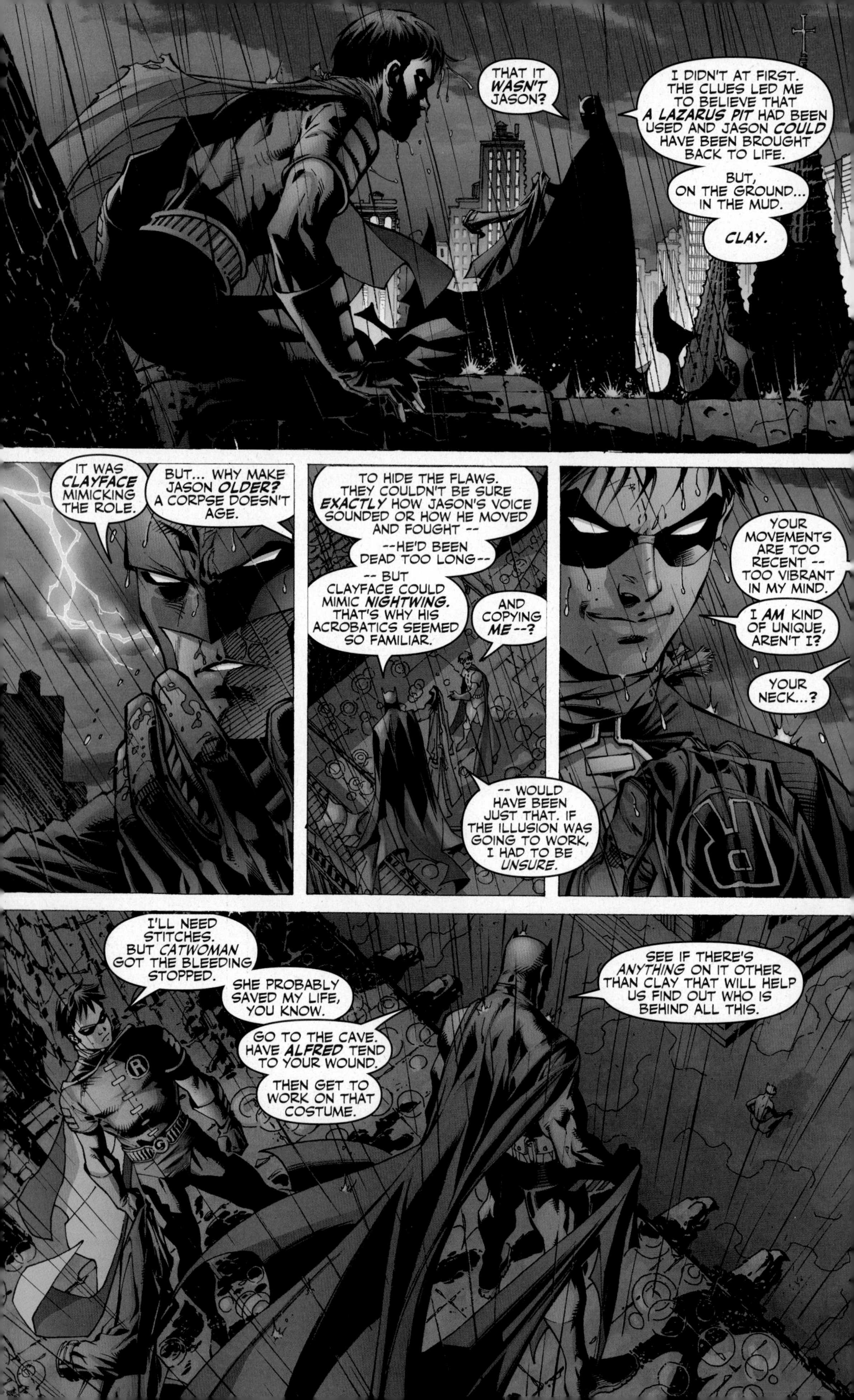
THAT IT WASN'T JASON?
I DIDN'T AT FIRST. THE CLUES LED ME TO BELIEVE THAT A LAZARUS PIT HAD BEEN USED AND JASON COULD HAVE BEEN BROUGHT BACK TO LIFE.
BUT, ON THE GROUND... IN THE MUD.
CLAY.
IT WAS CLAYFACE MIMICKING THE ROLE.
BUT... WHY MAKE JASON OLDER? A CORPSE DOESN'T AGE.
TO HIDE THE FLAWS. THEY COULDN'T BE SURE EXACTLY HOW JASON'S VOICE SOUNDED OR HOW HE MOVED AND FOUGHT --
--HE'D BEEN DEAD TOO LONG--
-- BUT CLAYFACE COULD MIMIC NIGHTWING. THAT'S WHY HIS ACROBATICS SEEMED SO FAMILIAR.
AND COPYING ME --?
-- WOULD HAVE BEEN JUST THAT. IF THE ILLUSION WAS GOING TO WORK, I HAD TO BE UNSURE.
YOUR MOVEMENTS ARE TOO RECENT -- TOO VIBRANT IN MY MIND.
I AM KIND OF UNIQUE, AREN'T I?
YOUR NECK...?
I'LL NEED STITCHES. BUT CATWOMAN GOT THE BLEEDING STOPPED.
SHE PROBABLY SAVED MY LIFE, YOU KNOW.
GO TO THE CAVE. HAVE ALFRED TEND TO YOUR WOUND.
THEN GET TO WORK ON THAT COSTUME.
SEE IF THERE'S ANYTHING ON IT OTHER THAN CLAY THAT WILL HELP US FIND OUT WHO IS BEHIND ALL THIS.

FROM THE WRITER OF
300 & SIN CITY

FRANK MILLER

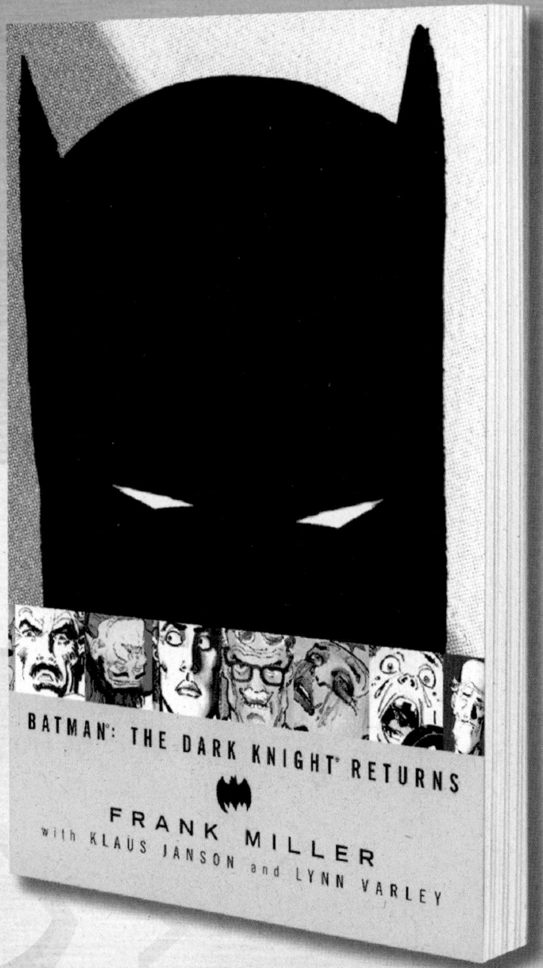
BATMAN: THE DARK KNIGHT RETURNS
FRANK MILLER
with KLAUS JANSON and LYNN VARLEY

Frank Miller's classic graphic novel features a Gotham City that has sunk into decadence and lawlessness ten years after an aging Batman retired. The Dark Knight returns in a blaze of glory when his city needs him most to end the threat of a brutal new generation of criminals while encountering the Joker, Two-Face and the Man of Steel for the final time.

"Groundbreaking."
– USA TODAY

"It's film noir in cartoon panels."
– VANITY FAIR

BATMAN:
THE DARK KNIGHT
STRIKES AGAIN

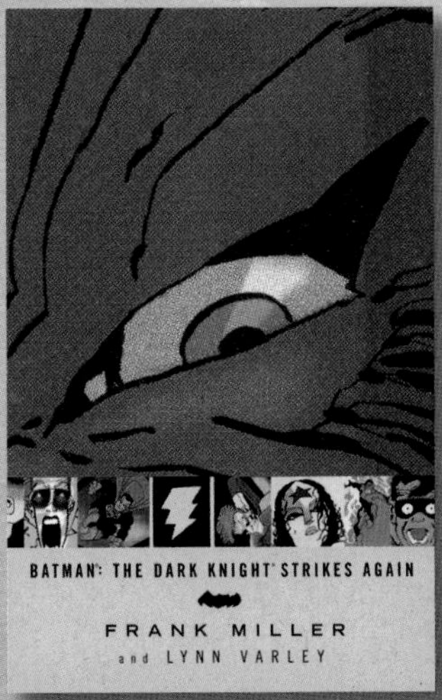
BATMAN: THE DARK KNIGHT STRIKES AGAIN
FRANK MILLER
and LYNN VARLEY

BATMAN: YEAR ONE

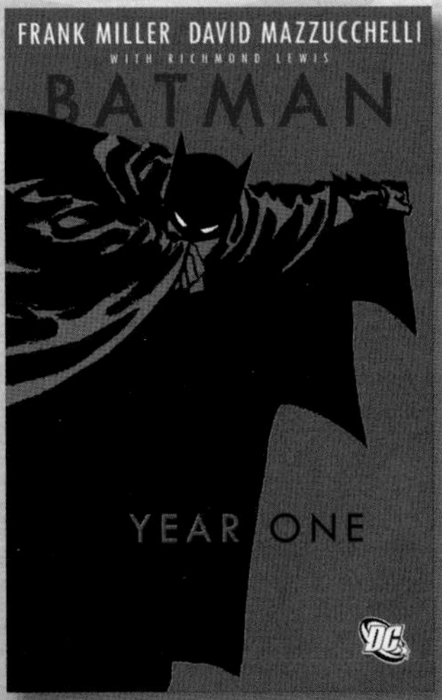
FRANK MILLER DAVID MAZZUCCHELLI
WITH RICHMOND LEWIS
BATMAN
YEAR ONE

with
DAVID MAZZUCCHELLI

ALL STAR BATMAN & ROBIN,
THE BOY WONDER VOL. 1

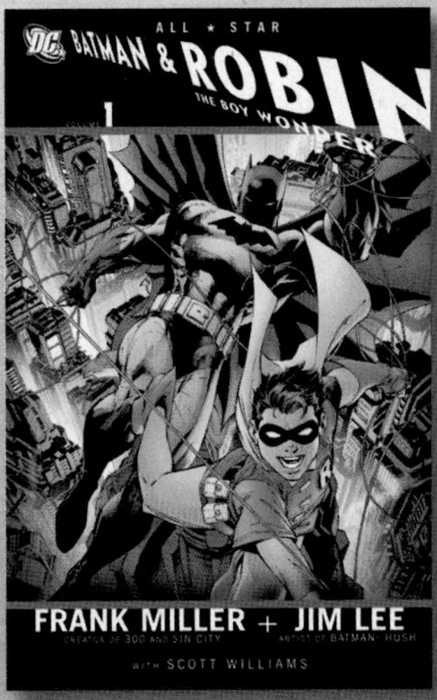
ALL STAR
BATMAN & ROBIN
THE BOY WONDER
1
FRANK MILLER + JIM LEE
WITH SCOTT WILLIAMS

with
JIM LEE

SEARCH THE GRAPHIC NOVELS SECTION OF
DCCOMICS.COM
FOR ART AND INFORMATION ON ALL OF OUR BOOKS!